LANDSCAPE
ARCHITECTURE
CONSTRUCTION

LANDSCAPE ARCHITECTURE CONSTRUCTION

Second Edition

Harlow C. Landphair
Fred Klatt, Jr.

Department of Landscape Architecture
Texas A&M University

ELSEVIER
New York • Amsterdam • London

Elsevier Science Publishing Co., Inc.
655 Avenue of the Americas, New York, New York 10010

Sole distributors outside the USA and Canada:

Elsevier Science Publishers B.V.
P.O. Box 211, 1000 AE Amsterdam, The Netherlands

Library of Congress Cataloging in Publication Data

Landphair, Harlow C.
    Landscape architecture construction.

    Bibliography: p.
    Includes index.
    1. Building 2. Landscape architecture. 3. Garden
structures. I. Klatt, Fred. II. Title.
TH153.L29 1987   624   87-15718
ISBN 0-444-01286-9

Current printing (last digit)
10 9 8 7 6 5 4 3

Manufactured in the United States of America

To: Wendie & Deborah

CONTENTS

SHAPING THE LANDSCAPE

LANDSCAPE STRUCTURES

SPECIAL SYSTEMS

PREFACE

Since the publication in 1979 of the first edition of *Landscape Architecture Construction,* technical advances, recent progress in the field, and our wish to correct and update the original text have all combined to urge a second edition. While the original has remained in use as a reference for both practitioners and instructors, unanticipated shifts of emphasis in the coverage of technical fundamentals have required the reorganization, revision, and reinterpretation of much of the previous work.

In this new edition, we sought to probe beyond corrections and reprintings of erroneous or outdated material; many of the changes we have incorporated are in direct response to questions from students using the book in class, and to comments from teaching colleagues at other institutions and practitioners on the jobsite. We have tried to simplify the presentation of the material, rewriting and reillustrating the text where necessary, and also to fill in the gaps in coverage of technical material previously omitted.

The material remains organized into four major subject areas: shaping the landscape (Chapters 2, 3, and 4), landscape structures (Chapters 5, 6, and 7), special systems (Chapters 8, 9, and 10), and the Landscape Construction Manual that appears at the end of the book.

The chapter on grading has been completely revised to illustrate the entire process of developing a grading plan. More time is spent on the development of a drainage strategy and the use of spot elevations, and less emphasis is placed on contour lines.

The drainage design chapter has been completely rewritten to place more emphasis on basic site hydraulics and hydrology. The new material will be of more use to the entry-level student and professional, since the profession is becoming increasingly involved in the planning decisions that revolve around drainage issues, and much less involved in the physical design of stormwater conveyance channels. The new chapter includes discussion of both the "Rational Method" and the revised Soil Conservation Service method (TR-55, Urban Hydrology for Small Watersheds, second edition June 1986) for site drainage analysis. Each of these methods is accompanied by illustrated problems and a discussion of their applications.

The chapters on structures (Chapters 5, 6, and 7) have been reorganized so that all the theory is included in the first chapter (Chapter 5). The remaining two chapters are devoted strictly to construction materials and detailing.

The chapter on irrigation design has been rewritten to provide a more comprehensive discussion of irrigation design and now includes information about drip irrigation.

The appendix from the first edition is now repositioned as Chapter 1, Landscape Architectural Construction. This reworking of the appendix material as Chapter 1 is in response to concerns students voiced in understanding the relationship between construction documents and the conceptual drawings (design development drawings). Chapter 1 is intended to help explain the relationship between the documents produced at various times during the development of a project, and the differences in the levels of information required. Included is a discussion of technical specifications intended to make the students aware of the relationship that exists between all of the construction documents required to take a project from conceptual drawings to a finished project. The assumption is made that this material will be expanded in another course using a more detailed text. The last part of Chapter 1 is devoted to a review of basic symbols and surveying and dimensioning conventions used in the day-to-day preparation of working drawings. For most students and professionals, this material will provide a brief review of the surveying information that gets rusty when it is not used on a regular basis.

ACKNOWLEDGMENTS

There are several individuals who have contributed time and thoughtful criticism to this second edition, to whom I wish to express my sincere thanks. First, I wish to recognize Charles Burger of North Carolina State University for his thoughtful, straightforward review. His comments, and sometimes pointed criticism, did much to focus the discussion and content. In addition to Charles' review, letters and comments from Jot Carpenter, Kurt Nathan, Robert Sykes, Cal Cumin, Jon B. Burley, Joanna Doughetry, and others, have done much to improve the quality and detail of this second effort.

I owe a very special note of thanks to both Ron Tuttle and Norman Miller of the U.S. Department of Agriculture, Soil Conservation Service, for their critical review and advice on the drainage chapter. Special thanks are also in order for Dan Pope of Rainbird and Delancey Carey of Toro, for their assistance in obtaining a review of the irrigation chapter and for the contribution of special graphic materials used in the chapter illustrations.

LANDSCAPE
ARCHITECTURAL
CONSTRUCTION

Introduction

Landscape architectural projects are a form of construction requiring a unique blend of technical skill and understanding. While much of the basic range of materials is the same as for architects and engineers, the landscape architect adds a unique understanding of plant materials and natural processes. The information presented in this text deals principally with the theory and fundamental construction skills required of the entry-level landscape architect. Much of what is presented is simplified and intended to provide a foundation for further study and development as an individual acquires experience and more practical, indepth knowledge of landscape architectural practice.

PROJECT DEVELOPMENT AND CONSTRUCTION

Landscape architectural projects go through several developmental cycles before they reach completion. For the average project, the actual time span between early design studies and completion of construction ranges between 18 months and 3 years. During this period, each project goes through four different phases: (1) preliminary design and feasibility, (2) design development, (3) contract documents, and (4) construction.

PRELIMINARY DESIGN AND FEASIBILITY

The preliminary design and feasibility portion of a project sets the stage for all of the work to follow. Work during this phase usually includes the development of an initial program of requirements, location of possible sites, development of preliminary budgets and estimates, time schedules, and an analysis of the return on investment. The landscape architect is not always involved in these preliminary studies, but many important decisions are made during this phase that affect the final form of the project. Few, if any, drawings are prepared at this time since most of the emphasis is placed on the need for the project, its potential market, and other financial considerations.

DESIGN DEVELOPMENT

In the design development phase, actual design concepts are developed to a more detailed stage to see if the budget, program, and general site criteria set down in the feasibility phase can be reached. The kinds of drawings prepared during the design development stage are very much like those done by students in the design studio. Typically, the design development package includes several different analysis drawings, rendered site plans and perspective sketches, palettes of plant and building materials, as well as refined programs and more detailed cost estimates.

1

CONTRACT DOCUMENTS

During the contract document phase, the actual construction drawings and technical specifications are prepared. The contract documents consist of two distinct sets of documents: the project manual and the construction drawings. The project manual contains the bid documents, general conditions of the contract between the owner and contractor, the technical specifications, and other contract forms. The construction drawings are the scale drawings and plans that describe and locate the work to be accomplished. These drawings are much different from the drawings developed during the design development stage of the project. Design development drawings communicate concepts and ideas while the construction drawings must communicate very specific and exact information. For this reason, construction drawings lack some of the eye appeal associated with design development drawings.

The information in this chapter provides an overview of the procedures, conventions, and skills required for the preparation of landscape architectural construction documents. The discussion is general and is intended to help the student understand the contextural relationship between design development drawings used to communicate design concepts, and the contract documents used to get a project built. The first part of the chapter is devoted to a discussion of the project manual that includes the bidding documents and the technical specifications. The material in this section is not designed to teach how to write specifications, but to make students aware of all the materials required to make up a complete package of construction documents. Next, a typical construction drawing package for a landscape architectural project is discussed with some basic conventions that apply to the preparation of these drawings, along with references to other chapters in the text that cover the subject matter in more detail. The final portion of the chapter reviews basic surveying and layout skills that are essential to the preparation of all construction drawings.

The Project Manual

With the exception of the construction drawings, all of the documents used to describe and direct a project are bound in a single document called *The Project Manual.* It is an almost universal practice to refer to this document as the "specs," meaning the technical specifications. This practice is somewhat misleading since the technical specifications are only one part of the project manual.

A typical project manual usually contains the following sections:

The Bidding Documents
    Advertisement or invitation to bid
    Addenda
    Instructions to bidders
    Bid forms
    Bid bond forms
Contract Forms
    The agreement form
    Performance bond form
    Materials and maintenance bond forms
    Insurance requirements and forms
Contract Conditions
    General conditions
    Supplementary conditions
The Technical Specifications

The technical specifications are most often arranged in 16 divisions that conform to the standard format of the Construction Specifications Institute (CSI).

These materials, together with the construction drawings, constitute a complete set of construction documents. By definition, the project manual is complementary to the construction drawings, and neither document takes precedence over the other. This in itself is an important concept because conflicts sometimes arise between the wording of the specifications and what appears on the plans. A popular misconception, when this happens, is that the written specifications govern. This notion is not in concert with the premise of complementary documents. When a discrepancy does occur between the written material and the drawings, decisions should be governed by the intent of the documents as a whole.

BIDDING DOCUMENTS

Invitation to Bid

Most project manuals include a complete set of bid documents in the first section of the project manual. The first document will be either the "Legal Advertisement" to bid or a "Letter of Invitation" to bid. These documents will have a brief description of the work to be accomplished, where the project is located, the time and place the bids will be received, and to whom the bids should be directed. If a full set of contract documents is not sent with the individual invitations, then the letter will give instructions on where copies of the construction documents can be obtained.

Instructions to Bidders

The "Instructions to Bidders" document usually provides a more detailed description of the scope of work to be performed under the contract and gives specific instructions for submitting a bid. Instructions usually cover how the bid forms are to be filled out. They outline the procedures for submitting alternatives for materials and/or specified brand names that may be called out in the specifications, along with any other special requirements that may affect the submission of a valid bid. Other topics that are also frequently included are: how the contract will be awarded, where and how bids will be opened, requirements to visit and inspect the site, and the owner's right to accept or reject bids. The amount of detail in the instructions to bidders is a function of the size and complexity of the project.

Addenda

An addendum is a document issued during the bidding period that formally modifies the plans and or specifications. It may be issued as the result of questions from prospective bidders which indicate that certain parts of the package are not clear, or an addendum may be necessary to correct errors in the drawings or specifications found during the bidding process.

Bid Forms

Bid forms are used so that each bidder presents a proposal for the work in the same format to allow an equitable comparison of each submission. The bid forms are tailored to each project and bids are taken in one of three forms: cost plus a fixed commission, unit price, or lump sum. A cost plus a fixed commission (Cost Plus) format means that the contractor will be paid for all material and labor costs involved in the project plus a fixed commission on the cost. This type of contract is most often done by negotiation rather than by the formal bidding process. The unit price format requires that the contractor bid each item in the contract on a fixed price for each unit. Some typical pricing units used are: 4 in concrete walk $/sq ft, asphalt pavement $/sq yd, turf area $/sq yd, or Live Oaks 6 in cal. $/each. The lump sum contract form simply asks for a total price to accomplish all the work covered by the plans and specifications. In an increasing number of cases, contracts are being put together combining both the lump sum and unit price formats. This often provides a much better means of evaluating the bids that are received.

Bid Bonds

Bid bonds are usually required on projects to ensure that the bidders are submitting valid bids and will not withdraw the bid once it has been formally submitted. The most common practice is to require the contractor to submit a cashier's check or a bid surity (insurance bond) in the amount of 1% to 10% of the total bid price. The percentage us usually a function of the estimated cost of the work. For example, a project with a million-dollar-plus budget will likely have a 1% to 2% bid bond requirement, while a 50 to 60 thousand dollar project will likely have an 8% to 10% bond requirement.

Even though the bid documents are only used in the process of obtaining bids on the project, they are always included in the project manual as a part of the permanent record of the project. This is done should any question arise over what the contractor or owner thought was included in the scope of the work at the time of bidding.

CONTRACT FORMS

The contract forms are placed behind the bidding documents or, sometimes, in the last section of the project manual. The first form is the "Agreement." The agreement form is the document that names the parties to the contract and lists the documents that describe the work to be accomplished. The agreement has five distinct parts: (1) parties to the contract, (2) statement of the work to be performed, (3) statement of consideration (how the work is to be paid for), (4) time of performance, and (5) signatures.

The parties to the contract must be accurately described. In most cases, large contracts are between corporate bodies and it is important that the parties be clearly identified.

The statement of work to be performed is usually a brief description of the scope of work and the location of the project. This statement is then followed by a list of all the contract documents, including all of the bid documents, the general and special conditions, the technical specifications, bond and insurance forms, and the working drawings.

The statement of consideration sets the payment schedule for the work. On projects with extended construction periods, payments for work are usually made on a monthly basis, called a "draw." The monthly draw is based on the percentage of work completed. The means of determining the percentage of completed work will usually be described in some detail, along with the procedures for submitting pay requests.

Time of performance is often a key factor in a project and there is often a penalty clause included that will allow the owner to deduct a substantial sum of money from the original contract amount if the work is not finished within the prescribed period. Penalty clauses must be used with caution since some states now require that if a penalty clause is included, the contractor has a right to extra compensation if the project is finished early.

The signatures on the contract indicate the official acceptance of terms by all parties. Since the agreement is the document that carries the signatures, it is often thought of as the contract, but it is not. All of the documents described in the statement of work are officially a part of the contract.

CONTRACT CONDITIONS

The next section in the project manual is usually the contract conditions section. The contract conditions set the legal ground rules that will govern the execution of the work. Most offices and agencies utilize a standard form of general conditions tailored to their specific kind of practice. The standard form of general conditions published by The American Institute of Architects (AIA) is probably the most popular with landscape architectural offices. These forms can be obtained from the AIA by requesting AIA Document A201. Although the AIA document is excellent, backed by years of use, it is still recommended that users have the documents reviewed by an attorney before using them.

The AIA general conditions cover 14 different topics that are important to the administration of almost any project regardless of its size. These are:

1. Contract documents (this is simply a list of all documents and drawings included in the contract)
2. Architect (administrative responsibilities)
3. Owner (rights and responsibilities)
4. Contractor (rights and responsibilities)
5. Subcontractors
6. Work by owner or by separate contractors
7. Miscellaneous provisions
8. Time
9. Payments and completion
10. Protection of persons and property
11. Insurance
12. Changes to the work
13. Uncovering and correction of work
14. Termination of the contract

The general conditions cover in much greater detail those contract conditions that are mentioned in the agreement form.

SUPPLEMENTARY CONDITIONS

The general conditions do not always cover every aspect of the contract, and it is sometimes necessary to revise or note exceptions to the standard form general conditions. If there is anything in the standard form general conditions that does not apply to the project at hand, the place to indicate the change is in the supplementary conditions.

TECHNICAL SPECIFICATIONS

The technical specifications provide detailed information about the general character of the work to be performed, the materials to be used, and how the materials are to be installed. For many years, the format of

technical specifications was a matter of professional preference; however, broad variation in form and language often results in errors and disagreements. To avoid this kind of confusion, most professional offices now use the CSI specification format for all of their work.

The CSI Format

The CSI Format is organized by "division" and "section." There are 16 divisions in the CSI Format that form the permanent, unchanging, framework for the technical specifications. Each division is then divided into sections. The sections separate the broad scope of each division into a basic unit of work. The 16 divisions of the CSI Format are as follows:

Division 1—General Requirements
Division 2—Site Work
Division 3—Concrete
Division 4—Masonry
Division 5—Metals
Division 6—Wood and Plastics
Division 7—Thermal and Moisture Protection
Division 8—Doors and Windows
Division 9—Finishes
Division 10—Specialties
Division 11—Equipment
Division 12—Furnishings
Division 13—Special Construction
Division 14—Conveying Systems
Division 15—Mechanical
Division 16—Electrical

Under each of the divisions there are a number of sections, called "broadscope" and "narrowscope." These are groups or "families of work." A broadscope section can be thought of as a family of work that may involve several subcontractors, while narrowscope sections are those that cover a very small unit of work likely to be accomplished by a single subcontractor.

Under the CSI Format, each of the sections is given a five-digit number. The first two digits are the division number, and the last three digits are the section designation. For example, Landscaping is Section Number 02800. The 02 designates Division 2—Site Work, 800 is the section designation. The first two digits of the section designation are used to indicate broadscope sections, and the last digit identifies a narrowscope section. Therefore, landscaping is considered a broadscope section. In general the broadscope section numbers will be the same for most specifications, but the narrowscope section numbers will change to suit the type of practice and the wishes of the specification writer. The most common broadscope section numbers under Division 2—Site Work are:

Division 2—Site Work
02010 Subsurface Exploration
02100 Clearing
02110 Demolition
02200 Earthwork
02250 Soil Treatment
02300 Pile Foundations
02350 Caissons
02400 Shoring
02500 Site Drainage
02550 Site Utilities
02600 Paving and Surfacing
02700 Site Improvements
02800 Landscaping
02850 Railroad Work
02900 Marine Work
02950 Tunneling

Some examples of narrowscope sections that might be used under the broadscope section "Landscaping" would be:

02800 Landscaping
02801 Digging and Storage of Existing Trees
02802 Planting
02803 Sodding
02804 Hydro-seeding
02805 Soil Fumigation

The narrowscope sections as illustrated here are not standardized as are the divisions and broadscope sections; they are at the discretion of the specification writer.

Writing Specifications

The task of writing specifications has almost always been accomplished using the "cut-and-paste method." The specification writer usually started with a set of specifications from a previous project and edited them to meet the conditions for the project at hand. The edited materials were then turned over to the typist who drafted the final project specifications. Now, with the availability of inexpensive word processing equipment, the task of specification writing is becoming more and more automated by using what is generally called a "master specification."

The AIA, CSI, and other independent organizations offer automated master specification packages. One of the most popular is the package offered by the AIA called *Master Spec*. Using a master specification form has a number of advantages. The standardized format helps readers understand what is required and avoids costly misinterpretation of the documents. There is also a marked saving in the time required to prepare the finished documents. The standardized specification is

not, however, a stand-alone document. It must be used and monitored by a trained professional who understands what is needed for each different project.

Construction Drawings

Construction drawings (or working drawings), are necessary to communicate the location, form, and arrangement of materials to be incorporated into a project. The key word in this description is **communicate**. All of the lines, titles, and symbols used should be directly related to communicating what is to be done or they should not be on the drawing. This is the primary difference between a construction drawing and other graphic presentations. This is sometimes difficult for students to accept since construction drawings are not necessarily visually exciting drawings. In most cases they will look either too simple (i.e., too much blank space) or they will appear too complicated. To illustrate this point, consider the drawings in Figure 1-1 and Figure 1-2. Figure 1-1 is a drawing that might be prepared to show a client how planting was to be handled for a project. Figure 1-2 is the actual planting plan for that project in the form of a construction drawing. It is important to remember that the only purpose of a construction drawing is to show what is to be done in the field. The information on the drawing should be complete and relate directly to the task, or group of tasks, being performed at a particular point in the construction project.

THE CONSTRUCTION DRAWING PACKAGE

The following list is an example of a typical landscape architectural construction drawing package.

Sheet 1 of 9—Clearing grubbing and demolition
Sheet 2 of 9—Site layout
Sheet 3 of 9—Grading and drainage
Sheet 4 of 9—Irrigation
Sheet 5 of 9—Planting
Sheet 6 of 9—Site lighting
Sheet 7 of 9—Details
Sheet 8 of 9—Details
Sheet 9 of 9—Details

Plan Drawings

The first six drawings shown in the example list are plan drawings and will usually be prepared on copies of a uniform base drawing. The clearing grubbing and demolition plan provides information on how to prepare the site for construction. It usually includes

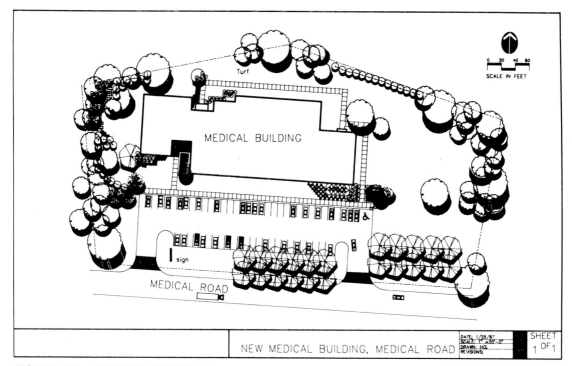

FIGURE 1.1 DESIGN DEVELOPMENT DRAWING

such information as trees, buildings, walks, streets, fences and other features that are to be removed or protected. It also gives instructions on how to prepare the initial grade so that construction can begin.

The site layout and plan carries information about the location of all major structures and pavements on the site. Depending on the scope of the project and the work to be accomplished, layout information is sometimes combined with demolition and grading on a single sheet. The site layout drawing is one of the most important drawings in the construction document package since it is the basis for establishing the spatial relationships of the project elements. Any errors in this drawing will usually result in serious, and sometimes costly, problems during the course of construction. For this reason, layout will be covered in more detail in the final section of this chapter.

Grading and drainage are most often combined on a single sheet since they are so closely related. The preparation of grading and drainage plans involves a great deal of technical skill and knowledge. An entire chapter of this text has been devoted to each subject; Chapter 2, on grading, and Chapter 4, on drainage.

Planting, irrigation, and lighting are usually also presented on separate sheets. The primary reason for the separation of these three onto different plans is that in most cases the work will be accomplished by a different subcontractor. Irrigation and lighting are each covered in individual chapters in the text; Chapter 8, on irrigation, and Chapter 9, on lighting.

Planting has not been included in this text since actual planting operations are affected by regional concerns and other factors that are in themselves worthy of an entire text. The fact that planting is not discussed does not mean that it is any less important to a successful landscape construction project; it is, in fact, one of the most important considerations.

Detail Drawings

The last three sheets of drawings shown in the example list are detailed drawings that supplement the information on the plans. The listing of three detail sheets is purely arbitrary. In some cases, all of the construction details can be included on the various plan sheets and, in the case of a very complicated project, there may be more than 50 sheets of details. The number of detail sheets is simply a function of the project.

The construction details are sections, elevations, and enlarged portions of the plan that are used to give more detailed information about individual parts of the project. All of the drawings on the detail sheets must be clearly referenced to the appropriate plan with proper notes or symbols. Figure 1-3 illustrates one of the most common methods used to key details from a plan to the appropriate detail sheet. Keep in mind that one detail may be used in a number of different places within the same project. It is important that sufficient keys be provided on the plans so that the contractor will know exactly which detail is to be used.

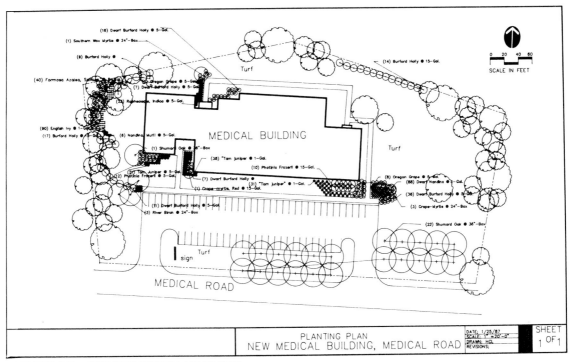

FIGURE 1.2 CONSTRUCTION DRAWING

Notice also that the order of the list of example drawings deliberately follows the general order of construction for a typical project. This same principle should also be followed when arranging the information on a construction drawing or a detail; "first things first." Arrange the information, insofar as possible, in the order that it will be used. For example, consider the wall detail in Figure 1-4. When recording dimensions on a construction detail, begin with the overall dimensions and place them where they will stand out from the more detailed information of the drawing. Then proceed to show the dimensions of the major parts—footing and cap, and end with the detail dimensions of small features.

In addition to the dimensional information shown on a construction detail, materials and finishes must also be shown. This is done in two ways: with symbols and labels. Clear, complete labels should be provided for each individual detail. Labels and dimensions should not be shared between two different drawings. The sharing of labels may seem to save work but it can lead to confusion in the field. Just because a material is labeled in one place does not excuse the need to label that same material again on another similar detail. Symbols are also used to help communicate the desired information, but the proper symbols must be used. Figure 1-5 shows a variety of map, material, and construction symbols that are the generally accepted standards. At times it is tempting to create different symbols for common materials just to be more expres-

sive, but this is a practice that can cause more confusion than it's worth. The creation of innovative symbols is best left to those materials and practices that do not already have a recognized standard. This is particularly true in electrical and mechanical work where the symbol vocabulary has been refined to the point where very few labels are required. In cases like this, the use of an improper symbol will achieve unwanted results.

Site Layout and Control

One of the most important parts of effectively communicating construction information is dimensional control of work in the field. Some of the most costly construction mistakes can be related directly to the lack of good horizontal and vertical control information. Incomplete or inaccurate dimensions often result in buildings or other structures being located in the wrong place horizontally or in the wrong vertical plane. When this happens, it is sometimes impossible to access utilities or make smooth transitions in grade. Improper location may also violate the setback and easement requirements of the city. These are costly mistakes and they are usually related to either faulty site survey and topographic data, or a lack of accurate or clear layout information on the working drawings. While these mistakes are not always the fault of the designer, the designer has an obligation to the client to make every effort to see that problems of this nature do not occur.

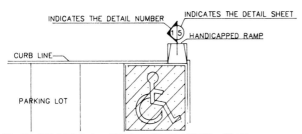

THE SECTION KEY INDICATES THE LOCATION AND DIRECTION OF THE SECTION. THE FIRST NUMBER IS THE NUMBER OF THE DETAIL AND THE SECOND, (BOTTOM), NUMBER IS THE SHEET NUMBER WHERE THE DETAIL WILL BE FOUND.

FIGURE 1.3 TYPICAL SECTION KEYS

The following discussion reviews the basic principles and tools of site surveying as they relate to the preparation of construction drawings that control the horizontal and vertical dimensions of the site. Three topics are addressed: horizontal measurement and control, vertical measurement and control, and site layout. Each part of the discussion concentrates on the information and knowledge necessary to prepare the working drawings for landscape construction projects. Surveying techniques and practices are limited to those simple procedures used in day-to-day construction drawing preparation.

HORIZONTAL MEASUREMENT AND CONTROL

To properly establish the location of a line in the field, it is necessary to define the line in three ways: its point of origin, its length, and its direction. The point of origin of a line should always be some existing point that can be located in the field. Common reference points used as points of origin are the intersection point of the center lines of existing streets, the center of sewer manhole covers, permanent benchmarks and right-of-way monuments, and permanent property line monuments. The length of a line is established by simple measurements made with a steel tape. Line direction is defined using angles and bearings.

Chaining

Field measurements are most often made with a 100-ft steel tape that is often called a "chain." The term chain comes from the old English system of land measure

related to the acre. The English surveyor's chain was 66 ft long, and the acre was any parcel that was 10 chains square, 43,560 sq ft. The true English chain is no longer used but the name still hangs on.

Chains and tapes are graduated in either feet and inches or feet and decimals of a foot. The use of decimals of a foot is common to most site work for field measurements of property boundaries and for road and highway work, and avoids the manipulation of cumbersome fractions. Dimensions for the layout and control of buildings, walks, parking, and smaller structures are, however, given in feet and inches.

The accuracy of horizontal measurements is dependent on the quality and accuracy of the chain used to make the measurements, and the precision of the work done in the field. The amount of precision (accuracy), required for most field construction is generally 1:5,000, or an allowable error of 1 ft in 5,000 ft. To obtain this

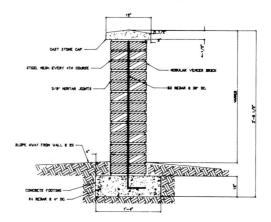

SECTION—BRICK VENEER WALL   SCALE 1/2″=1′-0″

NOTE THAT THE MOST IMPORTANT DIMENSIONS ARE PLACED TO THE OUTSIDE OF THE DRAWING. THESE ARE THE DIMENSIONS THAT WILL BE USED FIRST IN BUILDING THE WALL.

DETAILS SHOULD ALWAYS BE LABELED COMPLETELY AND THE PROPER SYMBOLS USED TO SHOW THE MATERIALS.

THE NUMBER USED TO DESIGNATE THE SECTION SHOULD BE THE SAME AS THAT USED IN THE SECTION KEY ON THE PLAN

FIGURE 1.4 ARRANGING INFORMATION ON CONSTRUCTION DETAILS

accuracy it is necessary to use the following procedure in making field measurements.

1. All measurements should be made in two directions and the results of the two measurements should be averaged. The reason for making measurements in two directions is to correct for any error induced by improper tape alignment. If the measurement is made along a line that is not absolutely straight, the net effect is a measurement longer than the actual distance.
2. Since all construction measurements are planar, measurements on a slope must be made in short runs, keeping the chain level at all times, as shown in Figure 1-6.
3. The chain length should be checked against a certified chain for length, and measurements should be corrected for differences. If the chain is short, the difference in length is subtracted for each 100 ft and if the chain is long the difference in length is added to the total for each 100 ft. For example, if a tape used to make site measurements is 0.25 ft long it is necessary to add 0.25 ft to each 100 ft measured. If a distance of 475.65 ft was made with such a chain, the actual dimension would be:

4.7565 100 ft x 0.25 ft /100 ft = 1.19 ft
475.65 ft + 1.19 ft = 476.84 ft

If the chain had been equally short, the 1.19 ft would have been subtracted from the total measurement.

This simple procedure is the basis for making all horizontal, straight line measurements in the field.

Turning Angles, and Establishing Direction

Angles in the field are measured using the horizontal plate on a surveying instrument. For most construction work, an instrument called a builder's transit-level is used. This instrument combines the features of both the engineer's transit and level into a single instrument, as shown in Figure 1-7. The difference between this instrument and those used by the engineer and surveyor is its precision capability. The engineer's transit will read angles to the nearest 20 seconds of angle, while the transit-level can only read angles to the nearest 5 minutes. This lack of precision is only a matter of concern if angles are being turned to run very long lines, such as in highway construction. For most site work, the precision afforded by reading angles to the nearest 5 minutes is satisfactory.

The direction of a line can be described in two ways: azimuth and bearing. Azimuth establishes the direction of a line with reference to either true north or magnetic north by angles from 0–359 degrees, 0 degrees being north, 90 degrees east, 180 degrees south, and 270 degrees west. While azimuth does establish the relative direction of a line from a point, it does not designate a direction of travel when in reference to a sequence of intersecting lines, such as the boundaries of a site. For this reason, the system of bearings rather than azimuths is used to establish field directions.

A bearing references a line by locating the line in either a northerly or southerly direction, and then establishes the actual direction of travel by designating an angle of so many degrees to either the east or the west. For example, consider line A, Figure 1-8.

To be sure that the proper bearing of a line is found, bearings should always be computed from azimuths using the following rules.

1. The bearing of a line in the southeast quadrant which is any line with an azimuth greater than 90 degrees but less than 180 degrees, such as the line in Figure 1-8, is found by subtracting the azimuth from 180°; e.g., a line with an azimuth of 125° has a bearing of

180°−125° = 55°
The bearing is S 55°00'00"E

2. The bearing of a line in the southwest quadrant, azimuths of more than 180 degrees but less than 270 degrees, are found by subtracting 180 degrees from the azimuth; e.g., the bearing for a line with an azimuth of 195 is:

195°−180° = 15°
The bearing is: S 15°00'00"W

3. The bearing of a line in the northwest quadrant, azimuths greater than 270 degrees but less than 360 degrees, are found by subtracting the azimuth of the line from 360 degrees; e.g., a line with an azimuth of 310° has a bearing of

360°−310° = 50°
The bearing is: N 50°00'00"W

The bearings of lines in the northeast quadrant are always equal to the azimuth; e.g., a line with an azimuth of 65° has a bearing of N 65°00'00"E.

To find the azimuth of a line simply reverse the procedures above.

The manipulation of angles given in degrees, minutes, and seconds is cumbersome at best, but by

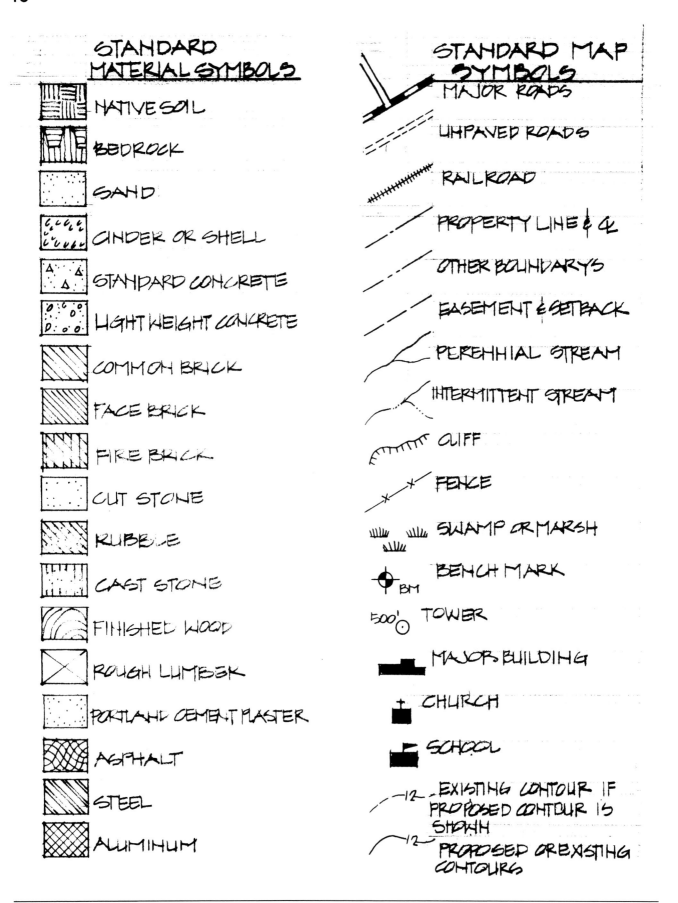

FIGURE 1.5 STANDARD SYMBOLS

PLUMBING & IRRIGATION SYMBOLS

⊙DF DRINKING FOUNTAIN

Ⓜ WATER METER

□ DRAIN INLET

TCO CLEAN OUT

Ⓜ MANHOLE

Ⓓ DRY WELL

⊠ CONTROLLER

⊕ REMOTE CONTROL VALVE

△VB VACUUM BREAKER

SPRINKLER IRRIGATION HEADS

ELBOW - 90°

TEE

CROSS

GATE VALVE

GLOBE VALVE

CHECK VALVE

DOUBLE CHECK VALVE

UNION

ELECTRICAL SYMBOLS

Oₐ OUTLET W/ FIXTURE DESCRIBE IN SPECS.

Ⓙ JUNCTION BOX

DUPLEX OUTLET

DUPLEX OUTLET, WEATHERPROOF

SPECIAL FIXTURE DESCRIBE IN SPECS

S SWITCH, SINGLE POLE

S₂ SWITCH, DOUBLE POLE

S₃ THREE WAY SWITCH

SCB CIRCUIT BREAKER

SWCB WEATHERPROOF BREAKER

SWP WEATHERPROOF SWITCH

SF FUSED SWITCH

LIGHTING PANEL

POWER PANEL

HOME RUN TO PANEL

BRANCH CIRCUIT, SLASHES SHOW NUMBER OF WIRES

Ⓜ MOTOR

Ⓣ TRANSFORMER

convention they are always given on drawings in this manner. To avoid making mistakes and to take full advantage of simple hand-held calculators, it is recommended that calculation of bearings be done using decimals of degrees rather than doing manual calculations. One of the features that should be included on a good scientific calculator is an automatic function key that converts degrees, minutes, and seconds to decimals of degrees and back to degrees, minutes, and seconds. If there is no function key to accomplish this task, then the procedure for converting degrees, minutes, and seconds to decimals of degrees is as follows:

Divide the minutes by 60 min/degree
Divide seconds by 3,600 sec/degree and add

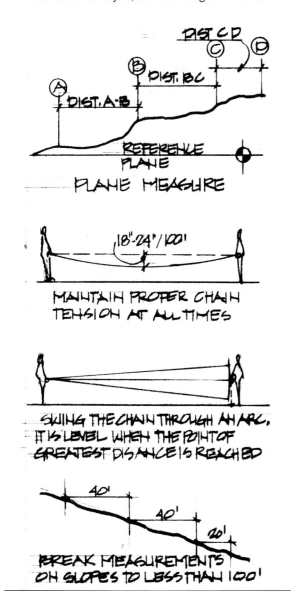

FIGURE 1.6 PRINCIPLES OF CHAINING AND PLANE MEASURE

For example, to convert 18°36'15" to decimals of a degree proceed as follows:

36' ÷ 60 min/degree = 0.60 degrees
15" ÷ 3,600 sec/degree = 0.0042 degrees

To convert a decimal back to minutes and seconds multiply the decimal by 60 min/degree. The whole number is minutes. Then multiply the remaining decimal by 60 sec/min. as follows:

0.6042 degrees x 60 min/degree = 36.2520
    or 36'

0.2520 minutes x 60 sec/min = 15.12
    or 15"

In the discussion of angles and bearings, decimals of degrees will be used in all calculations. Only the final result will be converted to the degree, minute, and second convention.

The process of turning angles and running lines in the field is called "traversing." To begin a traverse the surveying instrument is set up over some known point and leveled. The instrument is then sighted down a line of a known bearing or azimuth and the scales of the base plate are set to zero. Once the instrument is set and zeroed, the angles can be turned in either direction. It is important to note in which direction the angle is turned if several lines are to be run. In boundary surveys that have to close, the convention is to turn all angles to the right.

Seldom if ever will the landscape architect have occasion to do a boundary survey, so the actual field procedures for running a closed or open traverse are not covered here. The reason for this is not a lack of skill or knowledge but a matter of responsibility. Most contractual agreements between landscape architect and owner require that the topographic data and boundary survey be furnished by the client. The primary reason for this is that, by law, boundary surveys must be certified by a registered surveyor.

On the other hand, to ensure there is no problem during construction and to avoid any question of liability that could arise as a result of a faulty survey, the landscape architect should always check both boundary and topographic information.

Checking Boundary Surveys for Closure

If a survey of a property is accurate the boundaries should close mathematically. The method used to check a boundary survey for closure is called "Latitudes and Departures." The latitude of a line is the distance from a line's point of origin to its end point in a true

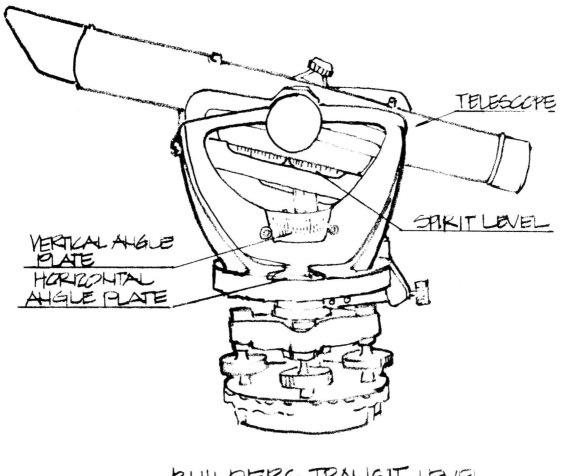

TELESCOPE

SPIRIT LEVEL

VERTICAL ANGLE PLATE

HORIZONTAL ANGLE PLATE

BUILDERS TRANSIT-LEVEL

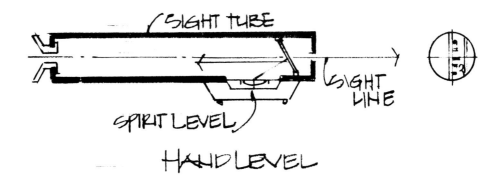

SIGHT TUBE

SIGHT LINE

SPIRIT LEVEL

HAND LEVEL

FIGURE 1.7 INSTRUMENTS FOR SURVEYING

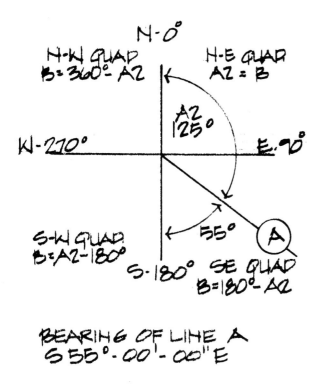

FIGURE 1.8 *PRINCIPLES OF BEARINGS*

north or south direction. The departure is the distance either east or west. The principles of latitudes and departures is illustrated in Figure 1-9. If a survey closes mathematically, the sum of the north latitudes is equal to the south latitudes, and the sum of the east departures is equal to the sum of the west departures.

The latitude of a line is found by multiplying the length of the line by the cosine of the bearing, and the departure is found by multiplying the length of the line by the sine of the bearing. To illustrate the checking of a boundary survey, consider the irregularly shaped tract in Figure 1-10. The information shown is typical of the information on a standard plat of record prepared by a surveyor. To check the survey, record the information from the plat in the form shown in Figure 1-11. Then simply multiply each line length by the cosine and sine of the bearings respectively. When beginning, it is best to fill out the work sheet and cross out the columns that will not be used, as shown in Figure 1-11. The direction of the latitude or departure corresponds to the directions of the bearing. Thus, if a bearing is N 12°15′20″ E the latitude will be a north latitude and the departure will be an east departure.

Figure 1-12 shows the completed latitude and departure sheet for the example, and the survey does close. It should be pointed out that no survey information gathered in the field will close regardless of the precision of the measurements or the accuracy of the survey equipment. The surveyor will always have to adjust the

measurements to make the survey close as the one in the example problem did. In the event that a survey is encountered that does not close, which is not at all uncommon, the surveyor of record should be contacted right away and informed of the mistake. The information in hand could be raw field data or just the wrong information.

Topographic information such as the locations of buildings and their dimensions, locations of utilities, trees, and other structures, should be spot checked in the field. If the information is ambiguous or does not seem right, call the surveyors; it is their responsibility to provide the information specified by the landscape architect and the client. Bad information will lead to trouble later.

VERTICAL MEASUREMENTS, LEVELING

Vertical measurements are made by a procedure called leveling. Leveling is done with an instrument called a level or with the builders transit-level mentioned earlier, and a rod. Another handy instrument that can be used is a hand level. This little instrument is hand-held and has a spirit level incorporated in the sight tube which can be seen in a mirror while sighting on a rod or tape. The accuracy is not sufficient for preparing final working drawings, but it is handy for doing preliminary field studies and making rough calculations prior to the completion of an accurate survey, Figure 1-7. A rod, like a chain, may be graduated in either feet and inches or in decimals of a foot. For most site work, a rod graduated in decimals of a foot will be used.

All vertical dimensions for a project are made in relation to a datum that is the reference elevation. The

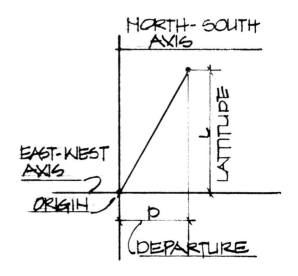

FIGURE 1.9 *PRINCIPLES OF LATITUDES AND DEPARTURES*

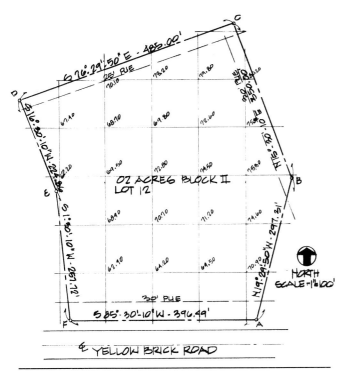

FIGURE 1.10   TYPICAL BOUNDARY SURVEY

usual datum for site work is mean sea level, but it may also be any other convenient, permanent reference point. The reference point for vertical dimensions is called a benchmark, and has a known or assumed elevation. It is important that the reference elevation for any topographic survey be known, and it should always be noted on the plan if it is other than the mean sea level standard. The use of assumed elevation benchmarks is much less common than it used to be because the development of electronic survey equipment makes it much easier to transfer and translate field information to the mean sea level standard. In fact, many governmental jurisdictions now require that all elevations be referenced to the sea level standard.

The procedure for making vertical measurements in the field has three steps: setting up the instrument, backsighting, and foresighting.

To set up a leveling instrument, try to find a place on the site that is about halfway between the high and low points of the site, and where most areas of the site are visible. This location will reduce the need to move the

COURSE	LENGTH	BEARING	LATITUDE COSINE N	S	DEPARTURE SINE E	W
A·B	297.31'	N 19.4972° W				
B·C	350.00'	N 15.5028 E				
C·D	485.00'	S 76.4972 E				
D·E	224.86	S 16.5028 W				
E·F	257.72	S 01.5028 W				
F·A	396.49	S 85.5028 W				

FIGURE 1.11   LATITUDE AND DEPARTURE WORKSHEET

COURSE	LENGTH	BEARING	LATITUDE COSINE N	S	DEPARTURE SINE E	W
A·B	297.31'	N 19.4972° W	280.27			99.24
B·C	350.00'	N 15.5028 E	337.27		93.54	
C·D	485.00'	S 76.4972 E		113.24	471.58	
D·E	224.86'	S 16.5028 W		215.59		63.87
E·F	257.72'	S 01.5028 W		257.63		6.76
F·A	396.49'	S 85.5028 W		31.08		395.26
TOTALS			617.54	617.54	565.12	565.12

FIGURE 1.12   CHECKING FOR CLOSURE

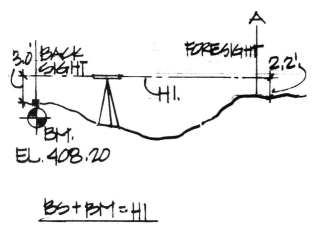

FIGURE 1.13 PRINCIPLES OF LEVELING

instrument to complete the leveling tasks. Once a likely place is found, the instrument is set up and leveled.

The backsight is a reading taken taken to the benchmark to establish the elevation of the instrument, called the HI, height of instrument. The HI is found by adding the rod reading to the known elevation of the benchmark.

Foresights are readings made at known points on the site, such as the tops of manholes, walks, curbs, or the floors of buildings. The reference points may also be a grid laid over the site for the purpose of obtaining the data for making a contour map. Foresight readings are subtracted from the HI to establish the elevation of the points read. Figure 1-13 illustrates the principles of leveling. This simple procedure is used to find and record the existing conditions of a site and to establish new grades in the field.

Topographic Interpolation

Surveys of existing conditions are usually made for the purpose of confirming the legal property boundaries, precisely locating existing structures, and to develop a topographic contour map.

All contour maps are made by interpolating even 1-, 2-, 5-, or 10-foot elevations between points of measured elevation on the ground. In most cases, contour maps are interpolated from 100-ft grids laid out on the site. In cases where more accuracy is necessary the grid may be 50 ft square or even smaller. To illustrate the interpolation procedure, consider the information shown in

Figure 1-14 where there are four adjacent grids with elevations at the intersection of each grid line. For the example, the even 1-ft elevations will be interpolated. To interpolate these points, find the vertical difference in elevation between any two points and then, using a scale, divide the line into equal increments corresponding to the difference in elevation.

To demonstrate this, start in the upper right hand corner of Figure 1-14 with the line between elevation 79.80 and 72.60. The difference in elevation is 7.20 ft. For this difference it is necessary to divide the line between the two elevations into 72 equal parts. This is done by laying the scale diagonally between the two horizontal lines of the grid until there are exactly 72 increments between the upper and lower line. Each of these increments represents a vertical elevation difference of 0.10 ft. Now, working from the lower elevation of 72.60, the even 1-ft elevation, 73.00, will be at a point represented by 4 increments on the scale, since each increment represents 0.10 ft. The next even 1-ft elevation, 74, is 10 increments from the 73.00 elevation, and so on. The procedure for this is enlarged to show the horizontal lines and the line between elevations 79.80 and 72.60 in Figure 1-15. This same procedure is followed until all the even 1 ft elevations are found on each line of the grid, as shown in Figure 1-16. When this is complete, all the points are connected with smooth dashed contour lines. Remember, existing contours are shown in dashed lines and proposed contours are shown in solid lines. The completed contours are shown in Figure 1-17.

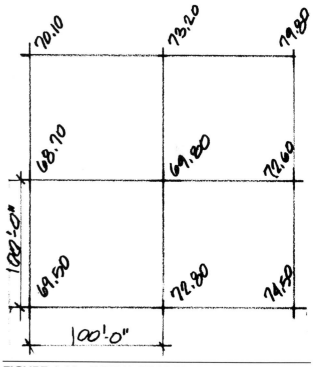

FIGURE 1.14 TYPICAL TOPOGRAPHIC SURVEY GRID

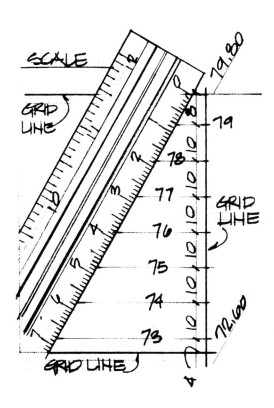

FIGURE 1.15 *INTERPOLATION PROCEDURE*

SITE LAYOUT

The landscape architect must be familiar with the procedures for laying out and controlling the horizontal and vertical dimensions of a project in the field in order to prepare accurate, legible working drawings. To produce a good layout drawing and grading plan, the landscape architect should acknowledge the order of work in the field by placing elevations and dimensions on the plans where they will be easy to locate and read. There is no best place for dimensions, nor are there any hard and fast rules about the form they should take. The principles that should be used to guide the preparation of the plans are: first things first, and be consistent.

Keeping First Things First

In most working drawing packages there two drawings that control the layout and dimensioning of the site. The first is the site layout plan that controls all the horizontal dimensions of the site. It will have all the new and existing buildings, all walks and paving, all parking, and all the streets and drives that connect the site with adjacent streets and roads. The second drawing is the grading and drainage plan. This drawing controls all the vertical dimensioning of the site. It will give the finished floor elevations of all buildings,

existing and new, the elevations of all drainage structures, and will give spot elevations at all critical points on the site. The procedures for developing a proper grading and drainage plan are given in detail in Chapters 2 and 4. The principle of "first things first" should guide the preparation of both of these sheets.

First things first means that the written dimensions and grades should be presented in a hierarchy that corresponds to the order of work on the site during construction. The general order of construction for most projects is as follows:

1. Clearing grubbing and demolition.
2. Horizontal and vertical layout of buildings and major new utility lines; i.e., sewers, underground power, water, gas, and communication lines. Roads, drives, and other pavements are in most cases limited to temporary access roads at this stage. All utility services, water, communications, power, and even sewer will also be temporary, in that only the main service lines that have to be under structures or future pavements will be laid at this time. Quite often these are installed in the early construction phases as open conduits or sleeves that will later be used to house the actual utility services.
3. Much later in the course of construction, usually after the buildings are well out of the ground and dried-in, the parking and primary roads to service the site will be laid out and installed. The order of pavement work is excavation and sub-base preparation, pavement base installation, curbs and drainage inlets, and finally the surfacing.

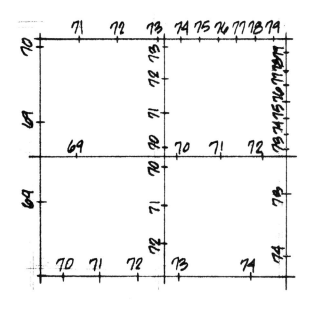

FIGURE 1.16 *EVEN ONE FOOT ELEVATIONS INTERPOLATED ON GRID*

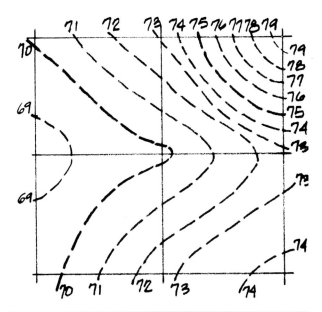

FIGURE 1.17 ONE FOOT CONTOUR LINES FROM INTERPOLATION

4. The final stage of construction involves setting the final utilities, running all the electrical services, water, communications, and gas. Then the various bases for fixtures are set. For example: footings for lights, transformer pads, telephone risers, fire protection hydrants, etc. Once these are in place and set to the proper elevation, final backfilling and grading will begin and the site is brought to a finished grade. Finished grade is still plus or minus a tenth of a foot. At this point, work begins on the final installation of walks and other light-duty paved surfaces, irrigation will be installed, and planting operations will begin.

5. Planting operations begin with the installation of all large trees, then the planting beds are prepared and planted, and finally the turf areas are fine graded and the turf is installed.

The order of construction presented here is important because it should guide the preparation of the dimensioned drawings. It allows the designer to organize the dimensioning of the drawing in units related to the construction operations in the order they will occur. The outline that follows translates the construction order into groups of dimensions in the order they will be used during the construction period, and the points of reference that should be used for the various dimensions. The notion of reference points is very important to the concept of a dimensioned drawing. Things must be referenced to objects that exist, or will exist at the time the work is laid out. The outline follows the illustrations in Figures 1-18–1-20.

1. **Building and Utility Location.** Buildings and major utility services such as storm lines, sanitary lines, power, and water are most often located from property corner references. Before construction begins the site will be staked by a registered surveyor to locate the property corners, required easements, and to verify the location and elevations of the primary utility services. At this time any errors in the property dimensions or utility locations will show up. Do not be surprised if some of the field dimensions do not match the assumed dimensions on the drawings; very often adjustments will have to be made in this initial stage of the work. If changes are required at this point, the designer must be sure that all dimensions are checked and adjusted or else there will be constant problems and adjustments during the course of the work. The means of locating a building and the major utilities is shown in Figure 1-18.

2. **Parking, Streets, and Connecting Utilities.** The next order of dimensioning is the parking and streets with the associated underground utility connections. These facilities are located in reference to the building and the existing streets and utilities. They should not be related to the property lines or other lines of reference, because the critical relationship is usually the building and the point of access to the street or an existing utility line. It is usually wise to establish the dimensions in such a way that a "flex zone" is provided. This is done by deciding ahead of time where any differences in the dimensions is to be absorbed. A "flex zone" is indicated on a plan by using a + − dimension, called a floating dimension. The layout of parking and streets is shown in Figure 1-19.

3. The final set of dimensions controls the location of walks, paved pedestrian areas, site furniture, and other finish work such as striping of parking stalls. These features are referenced to adjacent features such as parking lot curblines, building entrances, and stairs, or other features that will exist at the time of layout. Again, these should never be tied to property lines or references used to locate buildings, since these may have changed slightly during construction. These final dimensions should always show the critical relationship points as the points of reference. Likewise, avoid using redundant dimensions. Too much information is just as bad as not enough. If dimensions of a gridded pattern are the same, dimension one grid and indicate that it is typical. A finished layout is shown in Figure 1-20.

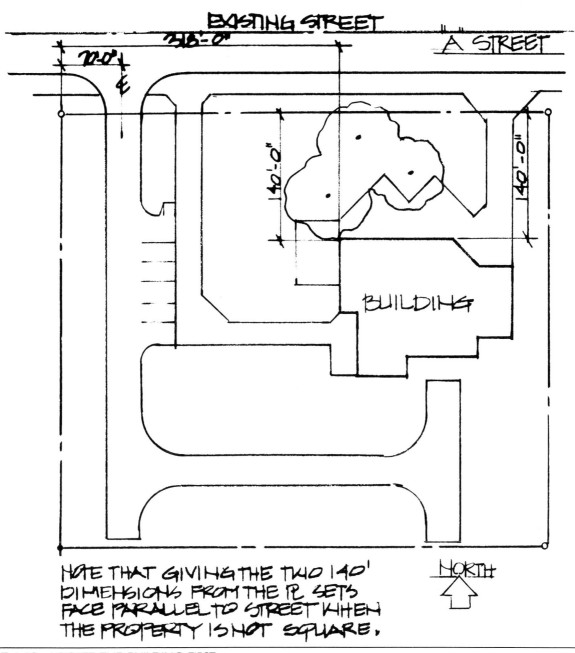

FIGURE 1.18 LOCATE THE BUILDING FIRST

Being Consistent

There are many different techniques and conventions
for indicating dimension data on drawings; some use
arrowheads, some use a combination of arrowheads
and dots, other systems, such as the illustrations here,
use slashes. Some dimensioning systems break the
dimension lines and write the dimensions in the line,
others write the dimensions above or below the dimension line. The technique that is used is not important,
but whatever system is adopted, it is important to be
consistent.

Some basic principles that will help achieve a
consistency and readability in the dimensioned drawing
are:

- Always adjust the line weights of the dimension lines
and reference lines so that they will not be confused
with the object lines of the drawing.
- Dimension reference lines should be continuous
from the corner of the object being referenced,
broken lines are very hard to read when there is a lot
of information on a sheet.

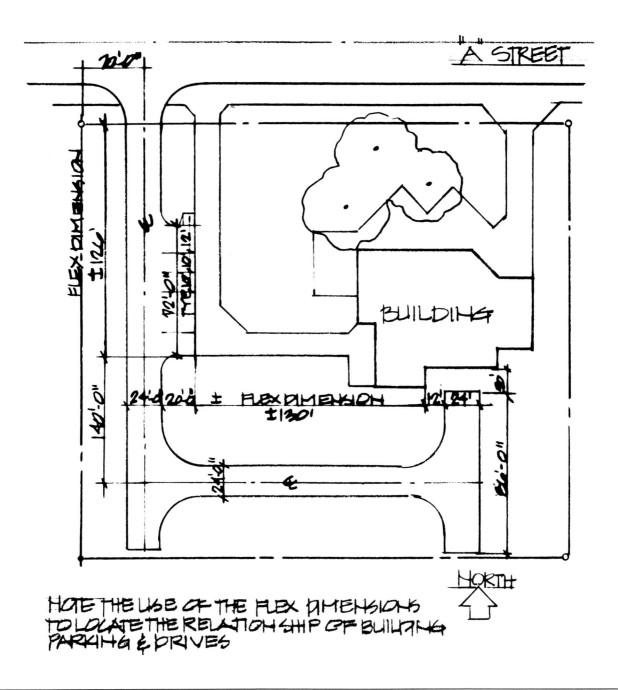

FIGURE 1.19 LOCATE DRIVES AND PARKING

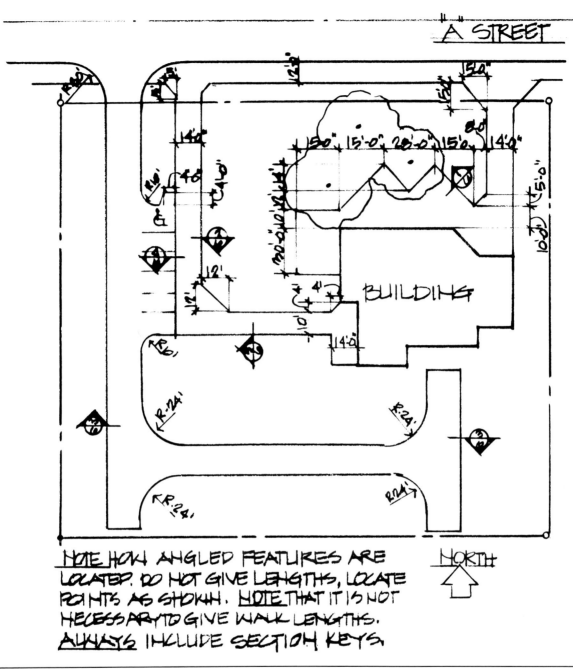

FIGURE 1.20 FINAL TIE OF WALKS AND OTHER FEATURES

- The written dimensions should parallel the dimension line so there will be no confusion about the relationship of the dimension and the reference.
- Arcs should always show the dimension of the radius. It is not necessary, however, to tie down the radius point for short radius connections for things like parking islands and curb returns. These are easily done in the field after the intersecting lines have been laid out.

Other Dimensional References

Remember that all of the dimensional references are not carried on the two dimensional plan drawings, they are supplemented by the detail drawings done in the form of sections. These supplemental details carry dimensional information that should not be recorded on the plan. For example, the width of curbs, walls, pole and post footings, and pavement grids are usually done in the form of larger scale details. The supplemental drawings are referenced on the dimensioned plans by means of section keys. The keys allow the field personnel to quickly reference the proper drawing to pick up any additional dimensions required to complete the work. The use of section keys is shown in Figure 1-20.

Supplemental Notes and Instructions

Final dimensioned drawings should always carry some supplemental notes and instructions to the contractor to clearly establish how the dimensioning was done, and to establish the contractor's responsibility in laying out the work. The following items are some common things covered in the notes.

1. The contractor should verify all dimensions on the plan. This simply means that the contractor should notify the landscape architect if the dimensions of the drawing do not meet field conditions.
2. The name and address of the surveyor of record should always be recorded in the notes on the plan along with the source of any utility data.
3. While it is usually customary to show pavement dimensions from back-of-curb to back-of-curb, it is wise to note this, along with any other dimensioning convention used; e.g., face-of-wall to face-of-wall, etc. This will avoid any confusion that might arise as a result of the scale of the drawing.
4. Vegetation and existing features such a fences and other site furniture that are to be saved and protected should be clearly spelled out in notes on the plans.
5. The responsibility for establishing dimensional controls, such as a permanent benchmark and the property lines, should be noted on the plan.

6. Finally, if there are any known or suspected hazards to the work, such as buried utilities, septic tanks or cisterns, old foundations, or pavement bases, this should be indicated clearly on the plans. This establishes the contractor's responsibility for taking these hazards into account in bidding the work and will serve to protect the client from additional expense for dealing with these problems.

STAKING PROCEDURES

A basic knowledge of the methods used to stake out construction work is also helpful in making decisions about how to prepare dimensioned drawings. There are four staking techniques used to control work in the field: hubs, offset stakes, grade stakes or blue-tops, and batter boards.

Hubs

Hubs are heavy 2 in × 2 in stakes used to mark the exact locations of corners and intersections. The stakes are set firmly in the ground and a tack is placed in the stake at the exact point of intersection. Hubs are usually set at the property corners at the beginning of construction if permanent pins or monuments are not in place or if they have been disturbed or destroyed. They are also used to establish any base line references and building corners (Figure 1-21).

Offset Stakes

Offset stakes are used to locate roads and parking structures that require base excavation and preparation. Offset stakes are so named because they are set back

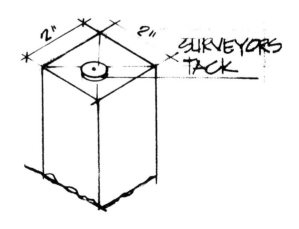

FIGURE 1.21 *LAYOUT HUB*

FIGURE 1.22 SURVEYOR'S OFFSET STAKE

some predetermined distance from the work to be accomplished, usually between 5 and 10 ft. This allows work to be accomplished on the structure without destroying the stakes. Offset stakes are usually set with standard 1 in × 2 in stakes at grade to mark the location of the line or corner of a structure. Then the stakes are marked with 3–4 ft pieces of ¼ in × 1½ in lath and flagged for visibility so they will not be destroyed during construction. The lath will usually be labeled to indicate the amount of offset, the station or edge that is marked (e.g., edge of parking lot), and may also be labled to indicate the approximate rough grading information (e.g., cut 3 ft). Figure 1-22 shows a typical offset stake marking.

Grade Stakes

Grade stakes are set after the rough grading has been accomplished. These stakes are set in the exact location that a particular grade is to be reached. The stakes will either be 1 in × 2 in or 2 in × 2 in with the top of the stake set at the exact finished elevation. Grade stakes are usually distinguished by coloring the top of the

stake blue with chalk or paint, and hence the name "blue-tops" or "blue-topping." A method that is now becoming very popular for marking grade stakes is a very tough plastic bristle material that comes in a variety of colors. The plastic bristles are clinched in a metal fastener that can be nailed to the top of a 2 in × 2 in grade stake. This adds to the stake's visibility and helps the equipment operators find stakes that will get covered during the course of a day's work.

Batter Boards

Batter boards are used to locate the corners of buildings. They combine the features of grade stakes and offset stakes. The batter boards are set 3 to 5 ft from the corner of the structure. Each set of batter boards consists of three heavy stakes, usually 2 in × 4 in, connected by two horizontal members, Figure 1-23. The horizontal boards are set so that the top surface of the board is at the finished floor elevation of the building. Then, nails are set in the boards for the purpose of attaching a string that is stretched to a nail in the opposite batter board, which marks the face of the foundation at the exact finished floor elevation. The point where the strings cross marks the corner of the structure. The batter boards allow work on the foundation to proceed and be checked without the need of destroying the stakes.

The preparation of good layout drawings is the first step to ensuring the success of a construction project. If the horizontal or vertical control is lost in the field it will lead to costly and sometimes unwanted changes in the final design product.

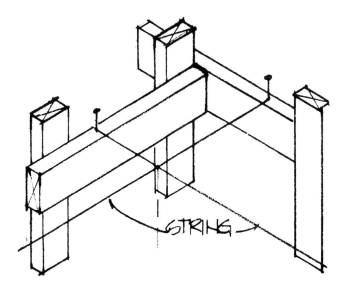

FIGURE 1.23 BATTER BOARDS

GRADING
AND
EARTHWORK

Introduction

Changing the land from an existing use to a new use requires that the surface of the land be changed or graded. Grading involves changing the elevations of the existing landscape to accommodate structures, parking, and circulation, and to facilitate the removal of storm water. Installation of subsurface structures for the distribution of water, gas, power, and communications services, and for the disposal of waste water and storm runoff is also taken into consideration in the grading process.

All construction projects, regardless of their size, involve some modification of the earth's surface. The manner and the extent to which the surface is changed will, to a large measure, determine the success or failure of the project. For example, failure to respect the natural drainage system can cause flooding, accelerate erosion, undermine foundations, and damage desirable vegetation. In essence, the grading plan for a project is the foundation that supports all other structures and connects them to their environment.

Grading, then, is the primary construction skill to be developed by the landscape architect, for if this fundamental skill is weak, no amount of expertise in design or management can make a project succeed. On the other hand, when grading is integrated into the design vocabulary and applied by a skilled, sensitive designer, it can reduce project and maintenance costs and improve the quality of the natural setting.

This chapter introduces the student to some of the parameters that affect developing a grading strategy for a site. The first part of the discussion is intended to develop skill in reading topography, both existing and proposed. This skill is an important part of developing confidence. The next part of the chapter introduces the grading process and presents some basic standards to help direct the development of workable grading solutions. Finally, the grading process is illustrated in a step-by-step example that shows how to use the process and evolve a grading plan from start to finish. All of the important steps, including cut and fill computations, are covered in relation to the grading process rather than as separate units. This was done to give the student a better feel of how all the information covered fits together and is applied.

Why Grade

Some contemporary environmentalists would have us believe that any modification of the natural environment is unnecessarily destructive. This is not, and need not be, true. While it must be acknowledged that a change in the natural system will affect the operation of that system, the effect need not be deleterious. On the contrary, many practicing ecologists have demonstrated that proper use and management of a natural system can in fact diversify the system further, and even increase its vitality. The key, of course, is proper management.

Unfortunately, grading decisions are often made apart from the overall design of a project. They may be relegated instead to the consulting engineer or draftsman who is faced with a "make it work" situation when in fact the design of the project should be changed. When this does occur, it is usually due to a lack of understanding on the part of the designer. Ignoring the character of the land to keep a road straight, siting a building on an unstable hillside for the view, removing the dune just to see the ocean, or filling in the drainage swales to increase lot size or build roads is rarely justified. Poor judgments such as these make development appear to be a growing cancer on the landscape, and indeed it will be if these practices continue. Destructive land development practices should not be condoned nor should they be justified by economic or functional arguments. Bad design is bad design. Designers must learn to grade in sympathy with the natural setting and have imagination enough to work within the natural constraints. This is the essence of creativity and leads to good design.

So what is the answer? Why grade? As a landscape architect or site planner, you have an ethical and professional obligation to do two things: Produce a design solution that will satisfy the client's needs within the budget and, at the same time, seek to enhance the quality of the natural environment. If a solution does not do both, the fee has not been earned.

It might appear from this discussion that a least-grading solution is always to be favored. Not so. Many projects may require extensive grade revision to meet the program needs and achieve a suitable environmental fit. The trick is knowing the difference; that is why grading skill is a must for the landscape architect.

Grading and the Soil

Grading requires the excavation and moving of soil, and sometimes rock; however, all soils are not created equal. A reasonable understanding of the soil on a construction site is a fundamental requirement before developing any grading plan.

Soils are produced by the weathering of rocks and decomposition of organic matter. Weathering occurs when rocks become exposed to water, air, and organisms that cause the rock or organic material to change its composition or break into smaller pieces. There two kinds of weathering process: chemical and mechanical.

Chemical weathering is the changing of the materials' atomic structure to produce a new material. Typically, chemical weathering is involved in the formation of the clay minerals in soils. The types of clay minerals that are formed are related to temperature and the availability of water. Mechanical weathering is the simple breaking-up of the parent material into smaller particles. Sands and gravels are typically the products of mechanical weathering processes. No soil, however, is the product of just one process, even though one may be dominant. In colder climates where frequent freezes and thaws occur, physical weathering processes tend to dominate, while chemical weathering tends to dominate in humid tropical areas and deserts.

Mature soils, common to forests and virgin prairie in temperate climates, are characterized by distinct layers called horizons. These horizons are designated A, B, and C. Together they form the soil profile, or regolith. Figure 2-1 illustrates the regolith and the characteristics of each horizon; however, all soils do not have these distinct layers. In very young soils, such as those found along streams or rivers or in areas that have been subjected to poor land management prac-

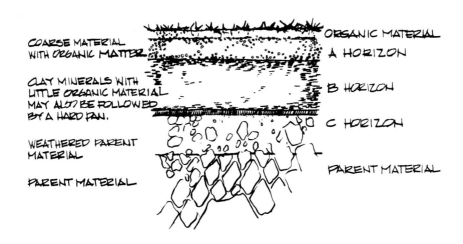

FIGURE 2.1 SCHEMATIC SOIL PROFILE

tices, the horizon characteristics may be poorly developed or absent altogether. Other soil profiles may simply be incomplete. One common example of where incomplete soil profiles are found is in soils that are weathered on steep slopes. These soils usually develop a very shallow A horizon but a B horizon is not formed since infiltration is very limited.

A general knowledge of how soils form and the characteristics of the various layers can provide many clues to problems that might be encountered in a development. The relative importance of these characteristics is a function of what use is intended for the site. For example, some parts of the site will require that the soil be dealt with as a growth medium, while other parts of the project will demand that issues of stability, strength, and plasticity be taken into account. In each of these situations the concern is with a different set of soil properties. The need to characterize a soil for different uses has led to the development of three soil classification systems.

SOIL CLASSIFICATION

Soils may be classified by geologic characteristics, engineering characteristics, or agricultural characteristics. The agricultural classification system is primarily concerned with the soil as a growth medium, the geological classification is concerned with the physical and morphological properties, and the engineering system is based on the mechanical and structural properties of the soil.

Agricultural soils are classified by a system similar to that used to classify plant and animal life. Classification begins with a grouping of the broadest worldwide characteristic, working toward more and more specific characteristics. The complete system has eight parts to the classification: order, suborder, great group, subgroup, family, series, type, and texture (A horizon).

The designer is most often concerned with the soil series, type, and texture. The series gives a broad understanding of the behavior of the soils of a region and their probable relationships to major land form types. It does not, however, provide enough information to make site-specific judgments. These judgments must be based on a knowledge of soil type and texture. Soil types carry the name of the place where a soil was first identified. Lakeland soils for example, were found and first described near Lakeland, Florida, but lakeland soils are found as far west as Texas.

Soil textures are based on the relative percentage of sand, silt, or clay particles in the soil. By definition, sand particles are from 2 mm to 0.50 mm, silt is from 0.50 mm to 0.002 mm and clay is less than 0.002 mm in size. The smallest sand particles, 0.05 mm, are barely visible to the naked eye. Silt particles are not visible individually, but can be felt when rubbed between the fingers. Clay particles are not visible and feel like powder or fine flour when dry. When wet, clay will be sticky and can be rolled into a ball. Typical soil texture designations are: silty clay (40-60% clay, 40-60% silt); sandy clay loam (20-35% clay, 0-25% silt, and 60-90% sand). Any soil that is 65% clay minerals or greater is classified a clay. A loam is a soil that has a percentage of all three particle sizes.

The Soil Conservation Service maps these soil types on aerial photographs and publishes soil surveys for individual counties or parishes throughout the country. These surveys provide information about the land suitability for various agricultural crops, susceptibility to erosion, moisture and drainage characteristics, potential flooding, slopes, and current land use. In the newer generation of soil reports, particularly those for urban counties, they have begun to include information about soil capability and hazards to various kinds of land uses other than agriculture. Along with this information, the report also includes some engineering soil data. This information is presented as soil groups under the United Soil Classification System, shown in Table 2-1. If there is a published soil survey for the county or parish where you live, it is recommended that you obtain a copy of that report and become familiar with it. Pay particular attention to the sections on land classification, since there will be a lot of useful information about site opportunities and constraints. Single copies of these survey reports are free from the local U.S.D.A. Soil Conservation Service office. You should also visit with the local agent to see what other information and services are available.

The geologic classification of soils is based on the mineral composition of the crustal material and how it was formed and deposited. This means that geologists' definition of soil is broader in the sense that any mass of unconsolidated surface material would be considered soil. In most cases, geologic soil classification is too coarse to be of any real use to the designer; however, some knowledge of the geologic processes that formed a landscape is very important to developing the ability to correctly interpret soil information.

The engineering soil classification is also based on the physical composition of a soil; however, the major concern is the structural characteristics of the soil. The engineering classification is divided into 15 groups based on their suitability as a foundation material for different kinds of construction. The 15 groups are shown in Table 2-1, along with their general structural characteristics. The classifications are useful in establishing some general guidelines for site design, but they must be used with caution. Often, in a large project, only a thorough geotechnical report should be used to guide the final decisions.

A quick glance at Table 2-1 shows that sands and gravels tend to be the best foundation soils. Non-plastic clays and silts, on the other hand, are troublesome soils for any kind of construction. This does not mean they should not be used, but it does mean that certain precautions must be taken to ensure the safety and longevity of the project.

Geotechnical reports are prepared by engineering geologists for any project that involves a major structure. Copies of these reports should be obtained and reviewed before beginning work on any job. The report is based on the analysis of test borings taken from the site. The cores are tested in a lab and interpreted by a soils engineer. In a typical report there will be information about the bearing capacity of the soil, plastic index, compaction rates, moisture contents, etc. This information will be followed by a recommendations section that will suggest such things as recommended compaction densities under pavements, soil treatments to stabilize poorly behaved soils, paving materials and thicknesses. All of this information should be in hand before any grading solution is begun.

Maps for Grading

The basic tool for recording and displaying land form information is the topographic map. Maps are an indispensable tool to the designer, but they are frequently the source of problems because the designer assumes the information is correct. The best way to check a map is to take it to the site and see if what is on the map is indeed what you see in the field. Other methods to verify the accuracy of the information are to note the publication date of the map, the scale, and the source of the data. In general, old maps should not be relied upon for site design.

The scale of a map is also a measure of the map's dimensional accuracy. In most cases, the horizontal accuracy is one one-hundredth of the the map scale, expressed in decimals of a foot. For example, a map scale of 1″ = 20 ft should be horizontally accurate to +/− 0.20 ft. This means that there is a possible cumulative error of 0.40 ft in any horizontal dimension. While this is not a critical range of error for all but the most exacting of tasks, consider the magnitude of error using a map with a scale of 1″ = 2,000 ft (1:24,000). In this case, the horizontal accuracy is +/− 20 ft or a potential cumulative error of 40 ft.

This particular example is used because the 1″ = 2,000 ft scale is the scale of the the United States Geological Survey (USGS) 7½-minute series maps, more commonly called "quad sheets." These maps are readily available and are very popular for doing planning studies and preliminary, large scale design. But, they cannot be photographically enlarged and used for site specific design decisions because the dimensional error is too great.

The map contour interval is the key to the vertical accuracy of the map. The contour interval is the vertical distance between the contour lines on the map. Contour lines connect points of the same elevation on the surface of the earth, so any point on a given contour is the same elevation. According to the USGS standard, a contour map is supposed to be accurate to +/− 0.20 of the contour interval. Thus, a map with a 1 ft contour interval should be accurate to +/− 0.20 ft or a potential cumulative error of 0.40 ft vertical. A map with a 10 ft contour interval would have a possible cumulative error of 4 ft. Again, this margin of error would not be acceptable for site work.

The data source of a map is also a primary consideration. Photointerpretation technology has developed to the point that most topographic maps published, or maps done for large sites, are compiled from aerial surveys. This technology is capable of producing maps of very high quality; however, the accuracy varies with the quality of the ground controls established, the weather, and the season. Whether to use a topographic map compiled from aerial data must be weighed against the margin of acceptable error for the project at hand. In most site-specific work it is still best to make all final decisions on conventional field survey information if the budget will permit.

AVAILABILITY OF MAPS

Topographic maps are available from many sources. Cities and other jurisdictions usually have topographic maps of the lands inside their political boundaries. Engineering and office supply houses often publish or carry maps or atlases of their trade areas. Another source of topographic maps is the United States Geological Survey. These maps are published and updated periodically and are usually available at libraries or supply houses for purchase. The scales of some common USGS map series are 1:12,000, 1:24,000, and 1:62,500. Before using a USGS map check the date of publication to be sure that the information is current. The state-level USGS office is the best source of current information.

Representation of Land Form

One of the most important design skills is the ability to visualize the two-dimensional graphic techniques used to represent three-dimensional land form. In the begin-

TABLE 2.1 CHARACTERISTICS OF SOIL GROUPS IN UNITED SOIL CLASSIFICATION SYSTEM[1]

Major Divisions	Group Symbol	Soil Description	Value as Foundation Material[2]	Value as Base Course Directly Under Bituminous Pavement	Value for Embankments
Coarse-grained soils *(less than 50 percent passing No. 200 sieve).*	GW	Well-graded gravels and gravel-sand mixtures: little or no fines.	Exellent	Good	Very stable; use in previous shells of dikes and dams.
Gravels and gravelly soils *(more than half of coarse traction retained on No. 4 sieve).*	GP	Poorly graded gravels and gravel-sand mixtures; little or no fines.	Good to excellent	Poor to fair	Reasonably stable; use in previous shells of dikes and dams.
	GM	Silty gravels and gravel-sand-silt mixtures.	Good	Poor to Good	Reasonably stable; not particularly suited to shells, but may be used for impervious cores or blankets.
	GC	Clayey gravels and gravel-sand-clay mixtures.	Good	Poor	Fairly stable; may be used for impervious core.
	SW	Well-graded sands and gravelly sands; little or no fines.	Good	Poor	Very stable; may be used in pervious sections; slope protection required.
	SP	Poorly graded sands and gravelly sands; little or no fines.	Fair to good	Poor to not suitable.	Reasonably stable; may be used in dike sections having flat slopes.
Sands and sandy soils *(more than half of coarse fraction passing No. 4 sieve).*	SM	Silty sands and sand-clay mixtures.	Fair to good	Same	Fairly stable; not particularly suited to shells, but may be used for impervious cores or dikes.
	SC	Clayey sands and sand-clay mixtures.	Fair to good	Not suitable	Fairly stable; use as impervious core for flood-control structures.
Fine-grained soils *(more than 50 percent passing No. 200 sieve):*	ML	Inorganic slits and very fine sands, rock flour, silty or clayey fine sands, and clayey silts of slight plasticity.	Fair to poor	Not suitable	Poor stability; may be used for embankments if properly controlled.
Silts and clays *(liquid limit of 50 or less).*	CL	Inorganic clays of low to medium plasticity, gravelly clays, sandy clays, silty clays, and lean clays.	Fair to poor	Not suitable	Stable; use in impervious cores and blankets.
	OL	Organic silts and organic clays having low plasticity.	Poor	Not suitable	Not suitable for embankments.

Compaction Characteristics and Recommended Equipment	Approximate Range in A.A.S.H.O. Maximum Dry Density[3]	Field (In-Place) CBR	Subgrade Modulus, K	Drainage Characteristics	Comparable Groups in A.A.S.H.O. Classification
	Lb/cu ft		*Lb/sq in/in*		
Good, use crawler-type tractor, pneumatic-tire roller, or steel-wheel roller.	125–135	60–80	300+	Excellent	A–1.
Same	115–125	25–60	300+	Excellent	A–1.
Good, but needs close control of moisture; use pneumatic-tire or sheepsfoot roller.	120–135	20–80	200–300+	Fair to practically impervious	A–1 or A–2.
Fair, use pneumatic-tire or sheepsfoot roller.	115–130	20–40	200–300	Poor to practically impervious	A–2.
Good; use crawler-type tractor or pneumatic-tire roller.	110–130	20–40	200–300	Excellent	A–1.
Same	100–120	10–25	200–300	Excellent	A–1, or A–3.
Good, but needs close control of moisture; use pneumatic-tire or sheepsfoot roller.	110–125	10–40	200–300	Fair to practically impervious	A–1, A–2, or A–4.
Fair use pneumatic-tire roller or sheepsfoot roller.	105–125	10–20	200–300	Poor to practically impervious	A–2, A–4, or A–6.
Good to poor, close control of moisture is essential, use pneumatic-tire or sheepsfoot roller.	95–120	5–15	100–200	Fair to poor	A–4, A–5, or A–6.
Fair to good, use pneumatic-tire or sheepsfoot roller.	95–120	5–15	100–200	Practically impervious	A–4, A–6, or A–7.
Fair to poor, use sheepsfoot roler.	80–100	4–8	100–200	Poor	A–4, A–5, A–6 A–7.

continued on the next page

TABLE 2.1   *(continued)*

Major Divisions	Group Symbol	Soil Description	Value as Foundation Material[2]	Value as Base Course Directly Under Bituminous Pavement	Value for Embankments
Silts and clays *(liquid limit of 50 or less).*	MH	Inorganic silts, micaceous or diatomaceous fine sandy or silty soils, and elastic silts.	Poor	Not suitable	Poor stability; use in core of hydraulic fill dam; not desirable in rolled fill construction.
	CH	Inorganic clays having high plasticity and fat clays.	Poor to very poor.	Not suitable	Fair stability on flat slopes; use in thin cores, blankets, and dike sections of dams.
Silts and clays *(liquid limit greater than 50)*	OH	Organic clays having medium to high plasticity and organic silts	Same	Not suitable	Not suitable for embankments
Highly organic soils	Pt	Peat and other highly organic soils	Not suitable	Not suitable	Not used

[1]Based on information in The Unified Soil Classification System, Technical Memorandum No. 3-357. Volumes 1, 2, and 3, Waterways Experiment Station, Corps of Engineers, 1953. Ratings and ranges in text values are for guidance only. Design should be based on field survey and test of samples from construction site.
[2]Ratings are for subgrades and subbases for flexible pavement.
[3]Determined in accordance with Designation T99–49 AASHO
[4]Pneumatic-tire rollers may be advisable, particularly when moisture content is higher than optimum.

ning some students find it difficult to interpret land form from two-dimensional drawings. This is understandable since they are expected to visualize reality in reduced scale with the vertical dimension removed. With a little practice, however, and by learning some common signatures, visualization of land form from a map will become second nature.

The oldest method for representing land form is called hachures. Hachures are evenly spaced lines drawn parallel to the lines of steepest slope, with breaks at equal increments of vertical change in elevation. Maps drawn with hachures, Figure 2-2(a) give an excellent feel for the shape of the land; however, because they cover the sheet so completely, recording other information is most difficult, to say nothing of the time required to prepare the map. The most practical use of hachures is for presentation drawings. They have little place in the preparation of analysis or construction drawings.

The most popular method of representing land form is the use of contour lines. Contour lines are the same elevation along their entire length and have the same vertical separation, as illustrated in Figure 2-2(b). In other words, the line in Figure 2-2(b) labeled 10 is 10

units above some known point of elevation called a datum, which is usually mean sea level. Any point on that line is exactly 10 units above that plane. This principle is very easy to visualize if we think of putting an object in water, as in Figure 2-3.

If water is added in one foot increments and a line is traced around the object at the water's surface, each point on the line will be the same elevation. Then, if the object is represented in plan, the lines show up as contour lines representing a vertical change in elevation of one foot between each pair of lines (Figure 2-4).

It is also possible to determine the elevation of any point between the contour lines by simple interpolation. For example, a point halfway between the 20 and 21 contour would be elevation 20.50. A point three-tenths of the distance between the 23 and 24 contour would be elevation 23.30.

Contours are the most popular and widely-used method of representing land form because they allow the display of other information on the same map. Along with this advantage, they also allow the designer to approximate the elevations of other points with relative accuracy and, with time and practice, contours provide a very good feel for land form.

Compaction Characteristics and Recommended Equipment	Approximate Range in A.A.S.H.O. Maximum Dry Density[3]	Field (In-Place) CBR	Subgrade Modulus, K	Drainage Characteristics	Comparable Groups in A.A.S.H.O. Classification
	Lb/cu ft		*Lb/sq in/in*		
Poor to very poor, use sheepsfoot roller[4].	70–95	4–8	100–200	Fair to poor	A-5 or A-7
Fair to poor, use sheepsfoot roller[4].	75–105	3–5	50–100	Practically impervious	A-7
Poor to very poor, use sheepsfoot roller[4].	65–100	3–5	50–100	Practically impervious	A-5 or A-7.
In embankments, dams or subgrades for pavements				Fair to poor	None

REPRESENTING LAND FORM IN SECTION

Contours are a handy tool for showing land form in relation to the horizontal plane, but they sometimes fall short in telling the whole story. Cross sections, usually called sections, are drawings that represent the vertical relationship of elements.

While grading information is usually displayed on a plan, much of the information recorded there was either generated or checked on some type of sectional drawing. Therefore, the importance of the section cannot be overemphasized.

A section is a two-dimensional plane taken perpendicular to the earth's surface along its entire length, but only on that line. There is no indication of what happens on either side of that plane. This is important, since a section taken at the wrong point may give a false picture of conditions. The use of sections and where they should be taken will be discussed in more detail with respect to their specific applications.

What is important here is the preparation of the sectional drawing and its relationship to the plan. The steps in preparing a section are outlined below and illustrated in Figure 2-5.

- The plane of the section should be clearly shown and labeled on the plan.
- The section sheet should have the vertical elevation increments labeled with reference lines on both sides of the sheet.
- The scale(s) should be clearly labeled on the drawing. It is sometimes desirable to exaggerate the vertical scale of a section, (this will be explained later). If this is done, be sure to note both the horizontal and vertical scale.
- As shown in Figure 2-5, the points where the plane of the section intersect the contour lines are projected onto the section sheet at the appropriate elevation line.
- The plotted points are then connected with a smooth, freehand line, in much the same way that a graph is drawn for a mathematics problem.

Contour Interpretation

To the landscape architect, the ability to interpret and visualize land form from contours is as essential as being able to read, write, or speak effectively. Skill in reading topography from a contour map can never be

(a)

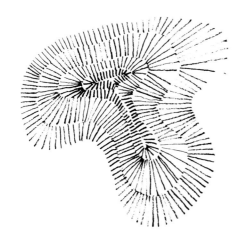

(b)

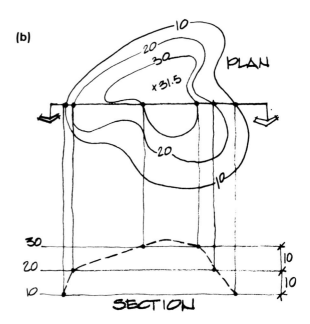

FIGURE 2.2 REPRESENTATION OF LAND FORM

substituted for actually visiting the site, but when the two are combined, the information that can be gathered and recorded is indispensable to the designer. Before actually beginning to study a contour map, several things should be checked to be sure of the proper interpretation.

Check the contour interval. This will be recorded somewhere in the legend or near the scale notation on the map. Common contour intervals are 1 ft, 2 ft, 5 ft, and 10 ft English, and vertical distance between each pair of contour lines is 1 ft, 2 ft, 5 ft, or 10 ft.

Check the horizontal scale of the map. This will be recorded graphically or by a notation of one inch equals so many feet or by a unit equivalent notation. The unit equivalent is always used in the metric system and simply means that for each unit of measure on the map it equals so many in the field. For example, a scale of 1:24000 means that each inch on the map equals 24,000 inches in the field or, for the same map, 1 mm equals 24000 mm. To convert this to a scale of so many feet per inch, divide by 12. Thus, a scale of 1:24000 converted to feet per inch is: 24000/12 = 2000 or 1 inch = 2000 ft.

Check the data source. This will usually be shown by a note or in the legend. Field surveys will usually be more accurate than maps interpreted from aerial photographs. Also note the date that the map was done to be sure the information is current.

These three things directly affect the accuracy of the map and thus the accuracy of your interpretation. Small-scale maps with 5-10 ft contour intervals are much less dependable than maps of larger scale.

In the beginning it is best to start the interpretation of a topographic map systematically. Later, with more practice, each individual will develop a personal system that is more comfortable. But until that proficiency is developed, the system presented here will help the student get started.

Orient the map with north to the top of the sheet. Then, identify focal points such as buildings, towers, power lines, or other man-made objects that will help you stay oriented. Observe the road and railroad patterns; they establish boundaries that are easily recognized, and major highways and railroads are most often located along or near the ridge lines.

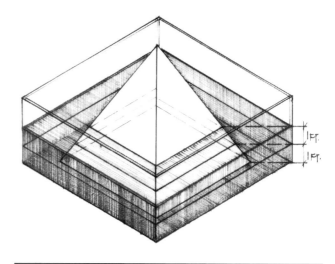

FIGURE 2.3 CONTOUR LINES

To effectively read topography, the student must develop a vocabulary of land form. This is much the same as learning a graphic alphabet that describes land form for, in fact, all similar land forms will be depicted the same way again and again. The contour pattern that describes a particular land form is referred to here as the contour signature. The objective is to develop a working vocabulary of contour signatures and the associated land form. Once this is mastered, the job of analysis becomes quite easy.

RIDGE AND VALLEY CONTOUR SIGNATURES

The contour signature for a ridge or valley is similar and easily identified. Both are repetitions of U-shaped lines as illustrated in Figure 2-6. If the bottom of the U-shape points to a contour of lower elevation, it is a

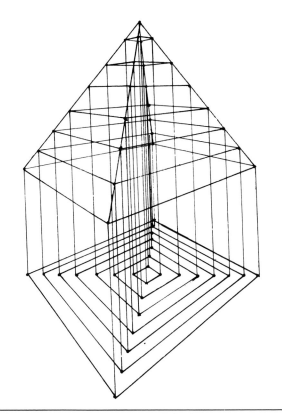

FIGURE 2.4   FROM 3-DIMENSIONS TO 2-DIMENSIONS

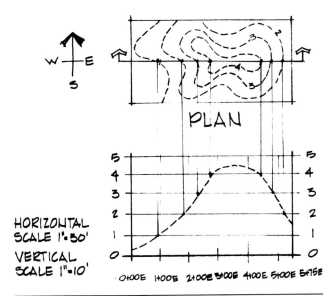

HORIZONTAL SCALE 1"=30'

VERTICAL SCALE 1"=10'

FIGURE 2.5   SECTION

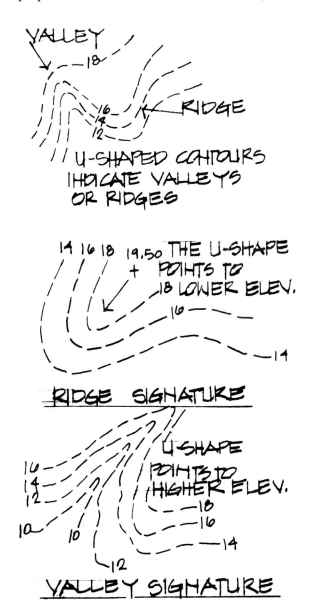

FIGURE 2.6   RIDGE AND VALLEY SIGNATURES

FIGURE 2.7 USGS MAP

ridge. On the other hand, if the bottom of a U-shaped contour points to a contour of higher elevation, it is a valley.

Usually ridge contours will be rounded, much less arrow-shaped than those of a valley. This is caused by the more intensive weathering and concentrated stream flow that occurs in a valley. The small section from a USGS map (Figure 2-7) illustrates this difference.

Once the ridge and valley lines have been identified, consider what is known about the site at this point. Notice that if you move away from the ridge line in any direction you will be going to a point of lower elevation. Likewise, if you move away from a valley line you are moving to a higher elevation. This all seems elementary, but it is important. A valley channel carries all the runoff from the land area upstream from any point between the ridge lines. What we have accomplished in this step is an identification of the natural drainage pattern as well as the high and low elevation points.

These ridge and valley associations are called watersheds. More specifically, a watershed is the total land area that contributes runoff to a stream or group of streams.

EXAMINING THE CHARACTER OF THE LAND FORM

Observe the spacing of the contours in Figure 2-8. Contours that are closely spaced indicate steep slopes while widely spaced contours indicate flat, gently sloped land.

Steep slopes should generally be avoided for development since extensive grading will probably be required. In addition, any modification of the surface vegetation will accelerate erosion and markedly increase runoff. Likewise, be suspicious of very flat terrain. Too little slope is just as bad as too much, because drainage will be sluggish and flooding becomes a distinct possibility.

Now observe how the contours are arranged in terms of spacing over a distance. This tells a lot about the overall character of the land itself. Contours closely spaced at the top of a slope and more widely spaced at the bottom are the signature of a concave slope, as can be seen in Figure 2-9. Contours spaced closely at the bottom of a slope and spread at the higher elevations, as in Figure 2-10, are the signature of a convex slope. Contours that are evenly spaced throughout are the signature of a uniform slope (see Figure 2-11). Contours that completely close within the limits of the map are the signatures of hills or depressions, as shown in Figure 2-12.

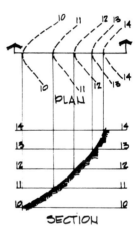

FIGURE 2.9 CONCAVE SLOPE

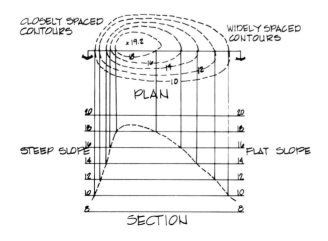

FIGURE 2.8 PLAN SECTION RELATIONSHIP

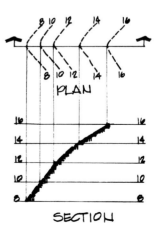

FIGURE 2.10 CONVEX SLOPE

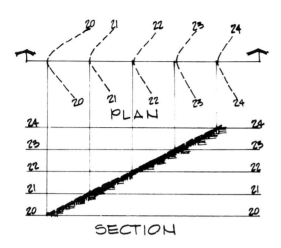

FIGURE 2.11 UNIFORM SLOPE

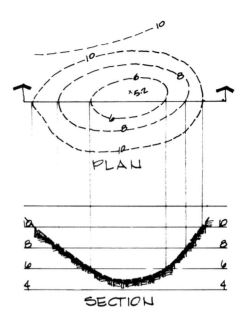

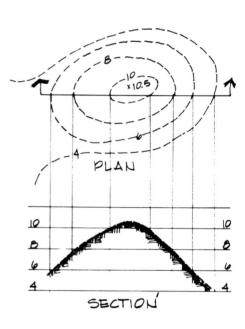

FIGURE 2.12 HILL AND DEPRESSION SIGNATURES

Now we can take this basic information a step further and begin to develop a catalog of land forms that will place these groups of contour signatures in a more meaningful vocabulary. These terms are not new; in fact, they are rather old-fashioned, and for some reason they seem to have been lost to our more contemporary engineering-conditioned vocabularies.

Classifying the Land Form

In this step we think about the contour pattern in terms of the visual image it presents. The following is a vocabulary that describes and characterizes the various shapes.

TERMS ASSOCIATED WITH LAND AREAS BOUNDED BY RIDGE LINES

Valleys

Glen or Dale. A small narrow valley usually bounded by gently sloped concave sides (Figure 2-13).

Ravine. A deep valley bounded by steep slopes with little flat land at the base, usually only a stream bed (Figure 2-14).

Flood Plain. A broad, flat to gently rolling land area bounded by distant distinct ridge lines (Figure 2-15).

Types of Hills and Ridge Lines

Hogs Back. A long distinct ridge line, characterized by concave slopes at the sides (Figure 2-16).

Knoll. A hill usually round to oval-shaped with convex slopes (Figure 2-17).

FIGURE 2.13 GLEN

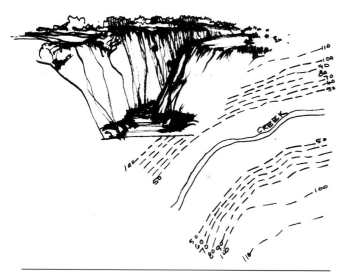

FIGURE 2.14 RAVINE

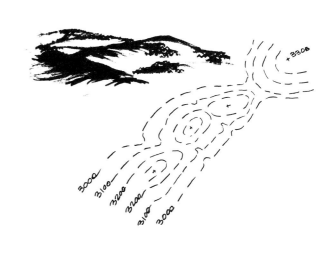

FIGURE 2.16 HOGS BACK RIDGE

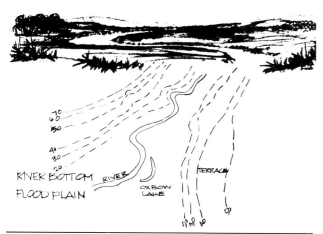

FIGURE 2.15 RIVER BOTTOM

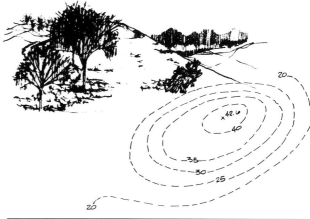

FIGURE 2.17 KNOLL

Knob. An abrupt hill with concave slopes and a rounded top (Figure 2-18).

Camel Back Ridge. Paired knolls of near equal size that occur along a ridge line (Figure 2-19).

Butte. A steep-sided formation with a nearly flat top. These are usually igneous rock intrusions that have been exposed by the forces of erosion (Figure 2-20).

General Terms

These general terms describe topographic features that occur as points or as complete landscape units:

Bay and Promontory, or Headland. A bay is shaped by a ridge line, and the promontory is the dominant upland feature that shapes the bay (Figure 2-21).

Meadow or Terrace. A flat to gently rolling plain that occurs on a hillside or along a ridge line (Figure 2-22).

Swale. A shallow lineal depression with a parabolic cross section and gently sloped sides (Figure 2-23).

Fan (Alluvial Fan). A nearly flat deposition of water-transported soil at the base of a watershed. The fan will usually be dissected by several water courses rather than a single stream as shown (Figure 2-24).

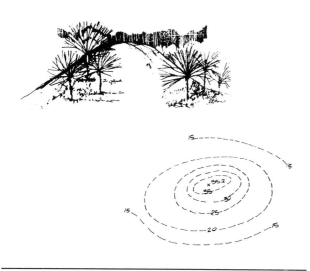

FIGURE 2.18 KNOB

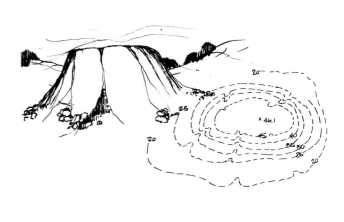

FIGURE 2.20 BUTTE

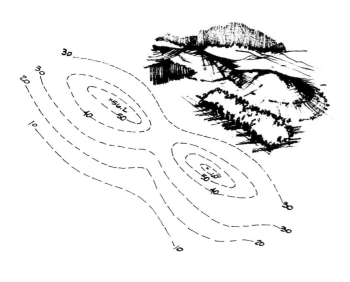

FIGURE 2.19 CAMEL BACK RIDGE

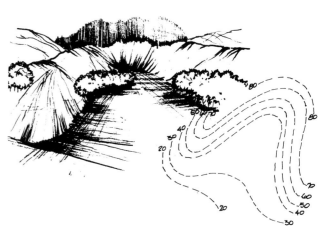

FIGURE 2.21 BAY AND PROMONTORY

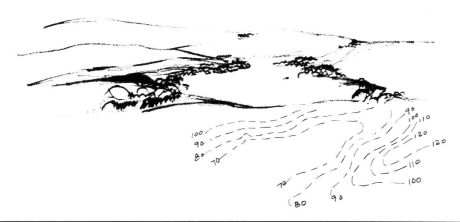

FIGURE 2.22 MEADOW

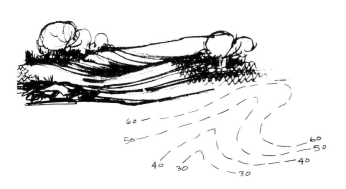

FIGURE 2.23 SWALE

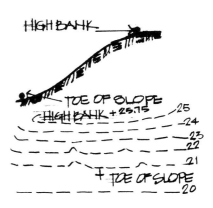

FIGURE 2.25 SLOPE REFERENCE

FIGURE 2.24 FAN

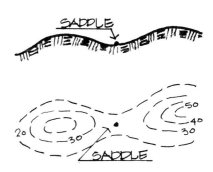

FIGURE 2.26 THE SADDLE

Toe (of the Slope). The toe is the point where the slope of a hill changes from its steep downward face to more gently sloped terrain. Where a structure is involved, it may refer to the base of the cut or fill (Figure 2-25).

Saddle. The low point between two domes or knolls along a ridge line. This feature is sometimes referred to as a pass as well (Figure 2-26).

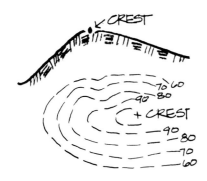

FIGURE 2.27 CREST OF HILL

Crest. The point of highest elevation on a hill. This point is usually marked on a topographic map by a spot elevation (Figure 2-27).

Military Crest. The point on the slope of a hill that will not allow any person or object to be silhouetted against the horizon and also allows full view of the slope below (Figure 2-28).

This list is by no means all-inclusive, nor is it meant to be; however, it can be most beneficial to beginning students to have a basic vocabulary of land form that

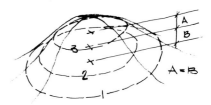

FIGURE 2.31

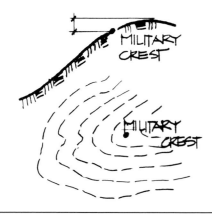

FIGURE 2.28 MILITARY CREST

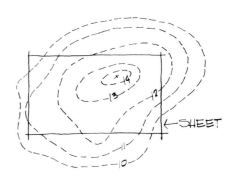

FIGURE 2.32

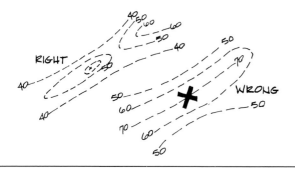

FIGURE 2.29

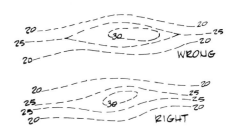

FIGURE 2.33

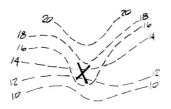

FIGURE 2.30

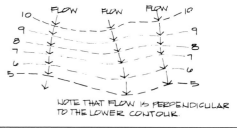

NOTE THAT FLOW IS PERPENDICULAR TO THE LOWER CONTOUR.

FIGURE 2.34

helps associate contour signature with a mental image. Use of this vocabulary and a little practice will have you on your way to reading contour maps with little difficulty.

The Six Cardinal Laws of Contours

The following six contour characteristics are called laws because any deviation from them is not possible. Any time a plan indicates something contrary to these laws, it is wrong.

- **Contours always occur in pairs.** Contours that indicate a ridge will always close; therefore, on a map if you cross a 50 ft contour moving uphill, you must cross another 50 ft contour in making the transition to a downhill direction, as shown in Figure 2-29.
- **Contours never cross.** Contour lines never cross each other unless an overhanging ledge is indicated. The situation shown in Figure 2-30 will sometimes occur on USGS maps, but if it should occur on a site plan it is suspect.
- **Contours have equal vertical separation.** Contour lines always indicate equal change in vertical measure. In some unusual cases maps are made with intermediate contours, but these are carefully marked and should be noted in the map legend. The principle of equal separation is shown in Figure 2-31.
- **All contour lines close on themselves.** All contour lines will close someplace on the face of the earth, even though they may not appear to on an individual map. This principle is illustrated in Figure 2-32. The 13 and 14 close, but the 12 ft contour appears to end at the edge of the sheet when, in fact, it closes, as do the 11 ft and 10 ft contour lines.
- **Contours do not merge, nor split.** Since contours must always occur in pairs they cannot merge as shown at the top of Figure 2-33. Contours must always be continuous and close on themselves.
- **The steepest slope is a line perpendicular to the contour.** This principle is illustrated in Figure 2-34. This point is important because water will always flow along the line of steepest slope.

Revised Contour Signatures

Just as natural land forms have distinctive signatures, land that has been graded for some specific use such as a road, building pad, slab, drainage swale, parking lot, etc., will have an equally distinctive signature. A thorough knowledge of these patterns is a very useful tool. First, it allows you to spot land areas that have at one time been used or graded, even though there may be no other surface manifestations. More important

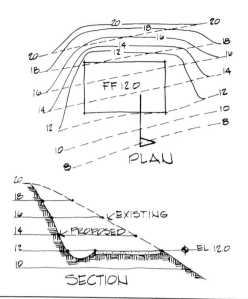

FIGURE 2.35 GRADING BY CUTTING

than this, however, is that a good understanding of these revised patterns will help you quickly visualize a grading solution and help you avoid errors. In this section there are numerous examples of conditions common to practically any type of site development. These conditions occur time and time again. In each sketch there is a plan that shows a revised contour signature along with a section or sections that explain the vertical relationship. You should become familiar with each of these patterns and the situations where they occur. For each example, there will be a brief discussion of some of the design considerations involved in selecting one solution over the other. To help you catalog this information better, the examples are grouped into three categories: grading around buildings, parking and roads, and drainage ways.

GRADING AROUND BUILDINGS

The floor of a building is a level plane and the land must be sloped in such a way that surface water flows away from the structure, positively in all directions. There are four ways to accomplish this: cutting, filling, cutting and filling, or by elevating the slab (floor).

Placing the Slab On Cut

Placing a slab on cut is most common where access to an existing road or parking facility makes it necessary to lower the grade. It could also be necessitated by having to remove highly organic soils, i.e., peat or muck. Figure 2-35 illustrates the signature generated by cutting. The new contours (solid lines) are located uphill of the existing contours (dashed lines). Note that the finished floor elevation (FF) is the same as the first

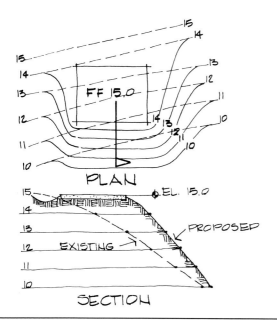

FIGURE 2.36 *GRADING BY FILLING*

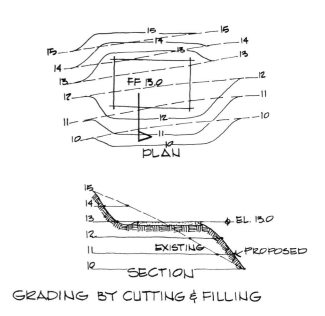

FIGURE 2.37 *GRADING BY CUTTING AND FILLING*

existing downhill contour. This provides for a shallow swale (drainage channel) to intercept the water flowing downhill and divert it around the building as shown in the section.

Placing the Slab on Fill

Placing a building on fill is usually done for two reasons. In low lying areas a slab may be raised to ensure proper drainage away from the building and avoid flooding. Very plastic or expansive soils may also make it desirable to place an entire structure on fill. Figure 2-36 illustrates a slab entirely on fill. Notice that the finished floor elevation (FF) is set equal to the first existing uphill contour. This provides a shallow swale to collect the water from up the hill and transport it around the building, as shown in the section.

Placing the Slab on Cut and Fill

Placing a structure on cut and fill is the most common and desirable situation since it does not require the import or export of material from the site. In this case the revised contours are relocated in such a way that half have been moved uphill and half in a downhill direction. The finished floor elevation is set equal to the first revised contour uphill to provide a shallow swale to collect and divert surface water away from the slab, Figure 2-37.

Elevating the Slab

The fourth way to handle the placement of a structure on a site is to elevate the slab or floor above the existing grade using retaining walls, as in Figure 2-38, or by placing the structure on piers. This solution is

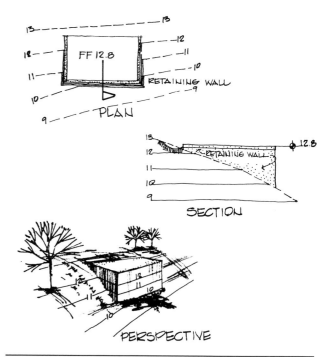

FIGURE 2.38 *ELEVATING THE SLAB*

frequently employed in situations where limited site disturbance is essential or where steep grades and soil conditions make cutting and filling undesirable. The example shown in Figure 2-38 uses retaining walls to contain the fill material to level the building pad, limiting the grade revision to the area immediately under the slab. Once again, notice that the finished floor elevation was set so that a swale would intercept the water flowing toward the slab (section Figure 2-38).

Steps

Accessing an elevated slab or terraced level will usually require the use of steps. Steps are sometimes hard to visualize since in plan the contour lines appear to end at the cheek walls of the steps. Figure 2-39 illustrates how the contour lines actually follow around the face of the steps.

GRADING OF PARKING AND ROADS

Parking lots and roads are essentially large slabs or planes that are uniformly sloped to move water off the surface. Since the surfaces are sloped, contour lines will cross them in distinctive patterns depending on the slope. There are four basic patterns that revised

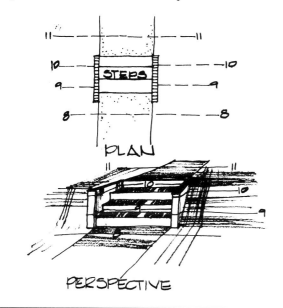

FIGURE 2.39 STEP SIGNATURE

contours will take: sheet flow with a single slope, sheet flow with a double slope, a valley section, or a crowned section. Each of these conditions is illustrated and the design considerations are noted for each case.

Sheet Drainage, Single Slope

Sheet drainage means that water flowing on the surface stays in a thin layer (sheet) uniformly covering the entire area, as opposed to being collected in a swale or gutter. The designation "single slope" means that the surface is sloped uniformly along only one axis. This is illustrated by the longitudinal and cross section in Figure 2-40. When a surface has a uniform slope in only one direction, the revised contours are evenly spaced and usually parallel to the longitudinal axis of the slab. Note in the example that a small swale is used to divert water away from the slab. This is usually a good idea unless, as in the case of many streets and parking lots, the surface is being used as a part of the surface drainage strategy. Sheet flow with a single slope is usually used where it is desirable to keep one edge of a plane level over its entire length; for example, terraces, walks, or parking lots that parallel the face of a building.

Sheet Drainage, Double Slope

Double slope means that the surface is sloped along both axes, as shown in the sections in Figure 2-41. In this situation the revised contour lines will cross the

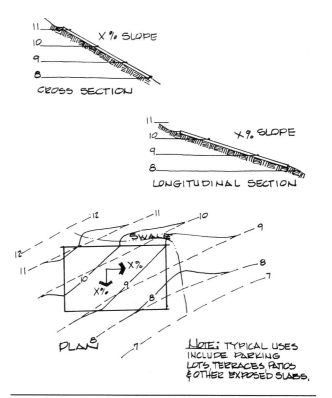

FIGURE 2.41 SHEET DRAINAGE DOUBLE SLOPE

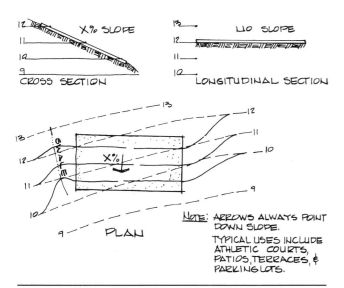

FIGURE 2.40 SHEET DRAINAGE SINGLE SLOPE

slab in a diagonal pattern. This particular situation is very common to parking lots, service drives and access roads, terraces, and other exposed slabs. In practice, a combination of double and single slopes will be used to meet the site conditions.

Valley Drainage

Valley drainage collects the water, usually along the center line of the pavement as illustrated in Figure 2-42. This pattern is quickly recognized by the distinctive repetition of the "V" shape. The most common use of this pattern is in flexible pavements (asphalt) such as parking lots, service drives, alleys, or service areas. When electing to use this pattern, the designer should always be aware of any pedestrian traffic that might have to cross the water flowing along the valley to access a building.

Crowned Drainage

Crowned drainage is most often used on streets and roads. It raises the pavement along the center line to direct the water to the edge of the road. You will notice in Figure 2-43 that the cross section is curved rather than coming to a peak. This is done to provide a smooth transition from one side of the pavement to the

other. This rounded form is also reflected in the contour signature which has a more rounded shape. Figure 2-43 is a typical urban street with a curb, Figures 2-44 and 2-45 illustrate the crowned section for typical rural section streets.

High Points and Low Points

Figures 2-46 and 2-47 illustrate the signature of a low point in a road and a high point in a road, respectively. At a low point, the contours bend toward the low point forming an hourglass shape. At the high point they face away from the peak. Learning to recognize the patterns will help you quickly spot breaks in the drainage pattern.

GRADING FOR DRAINAGE

Drainage ways take the form of either ditches or swales. As you can see in Figures 2-48, 2-49, and 2-50, the difference in the contour signatures is subtle. The primary difference is in depth and shape of the cross section. Chapter 3 deals with the subject of size, shape, and depth in much greater detail; here you should only be concerned with being able to identify a ditch or swale by its signature.

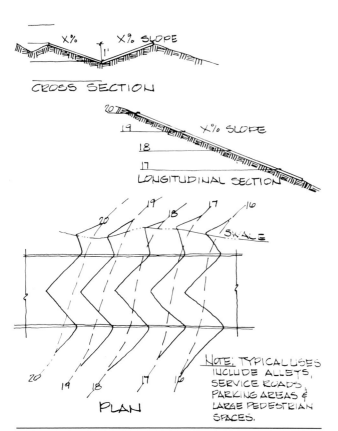

FIGURE 2.42 VALLEY DRAINAGE SIGNATURE

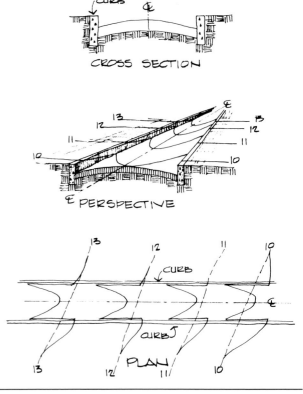

FIGURE 2.43 CURB AND GUTTER STREET SIGNATURE

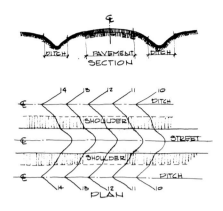

FIGURE 2.44 STREET W/DITCH DRAINAGE

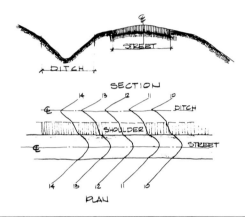

FIGURE 2.45 STREET ON A SIDE SLOPE

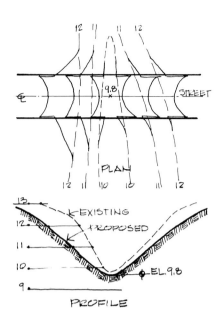

FIGURE 2.46 LOW POINT SIGNATURE

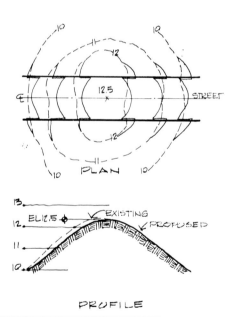

FIGURE 2.47 HIGH POINT SIGNATURE

Drainage Ditches

A drainage ditch is much deeper than a swale in proportion to its width; therefore, the revised contour will cross several of the original contour lines. Each of the existing contour lines crossed by the new contour line represents 1 ft of depth if the map has a 1 ft contour interval. Figure 2-48 illustrates a ditch 2 ft deep.

Drainage Swales

Drainage swales are very shallow in proportion to their depth and generally have a parabolic shaped cross section. Figure 2-49 illustrates a 1 ft deep swale. Notice that the revised contours are very flat compared to those of the ditch. Figure 2-50 shows the pattern made by a curving swale that is about 1½ ft deep. Swales of the kind illustrated in these figures show up distinctly on a plan or in sections; however, these same features are hardly noticeable on site, due to the proportion of depth to width. Figure 2-51 illustrates the signature of swales as they are frequently seen around a building slab or foundation.

Drainage Culverts

Drainage culverts are pipes that carry water under roads or pavements. They have a distinct signature that sometimes confuses the beginning student since the contours are hidden by the road. Figure 2-52 illustrates this point. Notice that the 14 contour appears to be broken by the street. It actually continues under the road on the wall of the pipe.

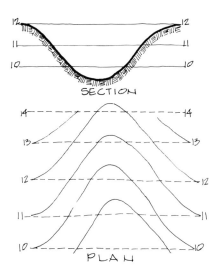

FIGURE 2.48 DRAINAGE DITCH SIGNATURE

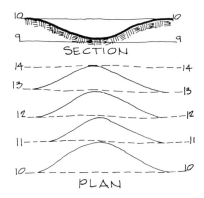

FIGURE 2.49 DRAINAGE SWALE SIGNATURE

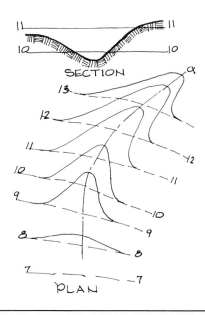

FIGURE 2.50 CURVED SWALE SIGNATURE

The Grading Process

Until this point, the discussion has been limited to recognizing existing and revised land form by contour pattern. This is an important and useful skill that should be cultivated and practiced. This section moves from pattern recognition into the actual process of evolving and refining a grading plan. First, an overview of the process is presented, followed by grading standards, grading computations, and an example problem that illustrates how a grading plan is evolved and refined, including the estimating of cut and fill.

The grading process has six distinct steps:

- Analyzing the site plan for existing drainage, soil types and fixed conditions
- Developing a new grading strategy
- Establishing preliminary grades and zones
- Evolving the solution
- Refining the solution
- Preparing the grading plan

These six steps are very important to developing an accurate and workable solution to any grading problem. If they are followed as illustrated in this section, students will find that grading will not be difficult; however, if you move from one step to the next without completing or understanding a step, you will most likely have problems.

The first step in the process is a careful examination of the existing topography and the proposed site development to be sure you have all the information you need and to identify the existing conditions that must not be changed. This step draws on the topographic interpretation skills presented earlier. The second step involves the development of a new grading strategy for the site. This is a very important step since it is the conceptual base for the entire grading plan. If this step is done carefully, the other steps in the process are basically mechanical.

Step four involves setting some trial elevations to work from. These are trial and error probes that are likely to change as the plan is evolved. As the solution is evolved in step four, spot elevations are computed for critical points on the site and the revised contours are constructed. Once this is completed, the solution is evaluated (step five) for the character and quality of the resulting land form, and to be sure that the amount of earth work required is reasonable. The last step is the preparation of the final grading plan.

GRADING STANDARDS

Good grading practice is based on many considerations. Probably the most important are: climate, character of the existing topography, soil, and substrate properties and visual context. These four criteria will largely establish the upper and lower limits of an acceptable solution. For example, it is usually desirable to set the slope on residential streets at 8% or less. But in difficult hilly or mountainous terrain it is not uncommon to set slopes in excess of 14%. The final decision as to what constitutes an acceptable solution must rest with the judgment of the individual designer.

Tables 2-2 through 2-5 provide some guidelines for maximum and minimum slopes for the most common site zones: around structures, open space, streets and parking, and drainage ways.

Please keep in mind that these are suggested standards and in no way cover all possible situations. Beginning students are often puzzled and very unsure about what is too steep and what is too flat. These questions are almost impossible to answer, but some general observations may be of use. The question of "too steep" is usually one of either access or of slope stability. With good footing, a person in good health can negotiate slopes of 30% or more. Automobiles can climb sustained grades of about 18% in low gear, and even trucks are capable of climbing slopes of up to 17% in low gear. The handicapped standard, however, is 8.33%, (12:1). If slope stability is the governing factor this decision should be based on a thorough geotechnical investigation of the site. Acceptable slopes may range from almost flat in silty soils to vertical cuts which are possible in stable geological materials.

The question of "too flat" is usually related to drainage considerations. Most finished surfaces, concrete, asphalt, fine turf, will require a slope of 1% or more to allow the material itself to be finished evenly. Slopes less than 1% always have small shallow depressions that will hold water. These are sometimes referred to as "bird baths." Drainage channels, on the other hand, are often set at slopes less than ½%.

GRADING COMPUTATIONS

Natural contour signatures are the result of geologic weathering processes. Like anything else created by nature, each feature is unique. The shapes of revised contours, however, are the result of deliberate and predetermined values for either the slope, the horizontal distance, or the vertical difference in elevation. These variables have an exact mathematical relationship represented by the algebraic expression: $D = G \times L$, where:

D = The vertical difference in elevation
L = The horizontal distance
G = The gradient

This is illustrated in Figure 2-53 on page 49.

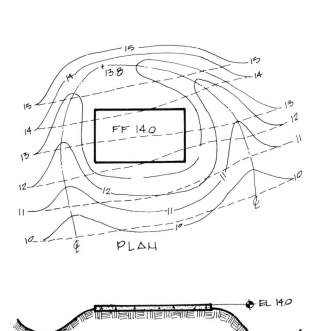

FIGURE 2.51 SWALE TRANSITION AROUND A SLAB

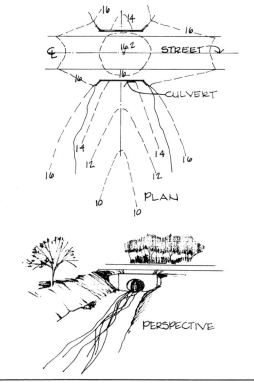

FIGURE 2.52 CULVERT SIGNATURE

TABLE 2.2 STANDARDS FOR GRADING AROUND STRUCTURES

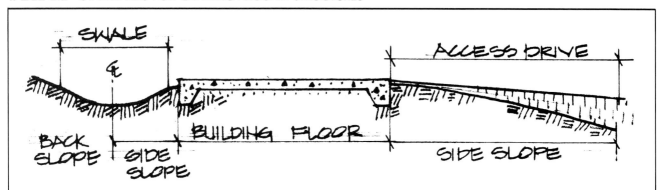

Condition	Maximum		Minimum		Range Preferred
Side slopes with vehicular access	10%	10:1	0.5%	200:1	1–3%
Back slopes with vehicular access	15%	6.66:1	0.5%	200:1	1–5%
Side slopes without vehicular access	15%	6.66:1	0.5%	200:1	1–10%
Back slopes without vehicular access	20%	5:1	0.5%	200:1	1–10%

Note: Upper limits should be avoided where icing is frequent. Flat slopes should also be avoided in wet climates.

TABLE 2.3 STANDARDS FOR GRADING ADJACENT LANDS

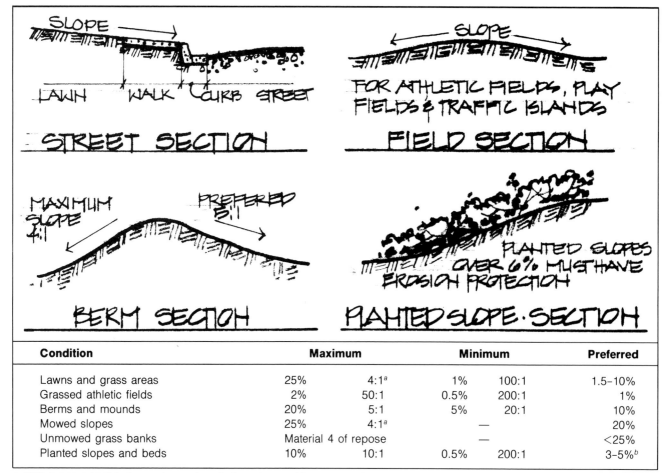

Condition	Maximum		Minimum		Preferred
Lawns and grass areas	25%	4:1[a]	1%	100:1	1.5–10%
Grassed athletic fields	2%	50:1	0.5%	200:1	1%
Berms and mounds	20%	5:1	5%	20:1	10%
Mowed slopes	25%	4:1[a]	—		20%
Unmowed grass banks	Material 4 of repose		—		<25%
Planted slopes and beds	10%	10:1	0.5%	200:1	3–5%[b]

a: 25% is approximately the maximum slope that mowing machinery can work.
b: Slopes covered only by shrub material will tend to erode above 10%.

TABLE 2.4 STANDARDS FOR GRADING STREETS AND WAYS

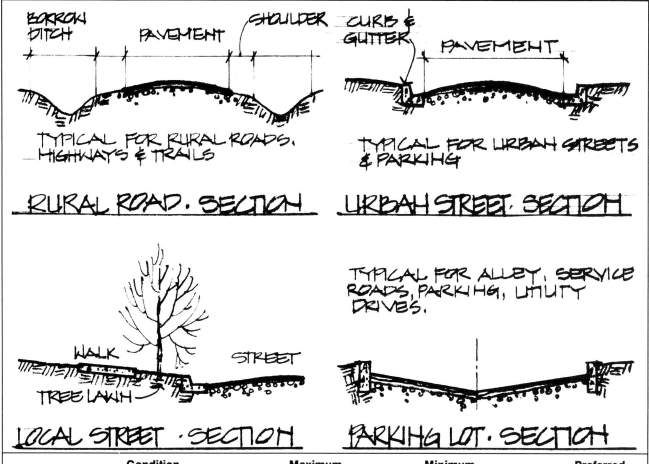

Condition	Maximum		Minimum		Preferred
Crown of improved streets	3%	33⅓:1	1%	100:1	2%
Crown of unimproved roads	3%	33⅓:1	2%	50:1	2.5%
Slide slope on walks	4%	25:1	1%	100:1	1–2%
Tree lawns	20%	5:1	1%	100:1	2–3%
Slope of shoulders	15%	66⅔:1	1%	100:1	2–3%
Longitudinal slope of streets	20%	5:1	0.5%	200-1	1–10%
Longitudinal slope of driveways	20%	5:1	0.25%	400:1	1–10%
Longitudinal slope of parking areas	5%	20:1	0.25%	400:1	2–3%
Longitudinal slope of sidewalks	10%	10:1	0.5%	200:1	1–5%
Longitudinal slope of valleyed section	5%	25:1	0.5%	200:1	2–3%

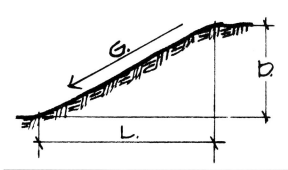

L = HORIZONTAL DISTANCE
D = VERTICAL DIFFERENCE
G = THE GRADIENT

FIGURE 2.53 GRADING EQUATION TERMS

TABLE 2.5 STANDARDS FOR DRAINAGE CHANNELS

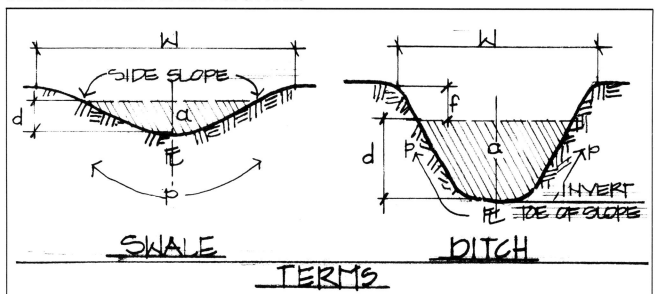

SWALE DITCH

TERMS

W . WIDTH OF CROSS SECTION
d. - DEPTH OF CROSS SECTION
a. - AREA OF CROSS SECTION
p - WETTED PERIMETER
f - FREEBOARD
FL - FLOW LINE, BOTTOM OF THE CHANNEL
INVERT - THE ELEVATION AT THE BOTTOM OF THE
   CHANNEL AT A GIVEN POINT.
TOE OF SLOPE - WHERE THE SIDE SLOPE MEETS THE
   INVERT OF THE CHANNEL

Condition	Maximum		Minimum		Preferred
Swale side slopes	10%	10:1	1%	100:1	2%
Longitudinal slope of swales					
a) grass invert (bottom)	8%	12.5:1	1%	100:1	1.5–2%
b) paved invert (bottom)	12%	8.33:1	0.5%	100:1	4–6%
Ditch side slopes	> of repose		—		20–25%
a) grass invert (bottom)	8%	13:1	1%	100:1	10–20%
b) paved invert (bottom)	—		—		20–30%

As with any three-term algebraic relationship, when any two terms in the expression are known, the other can be found. Thus, if $D = G \times L$, then:

$G = D \div L$
$L = D \div G$

This basic equation is an indispensable tool in the grading process and must be committed to memory because it will be used time and time again. It is strongly recommended that you practice on several basic exercises, learning to do the computations mentally rather than relying on a calculator. The calculator takes time and, more importantly, takes your concentration away from the overall problem at hand. Table 2-6 has some handy information about contour spacing at common slopes. If some of these relationships are committed to memory, now it will help develop speed and reduce the amount of calculation time.

TABLE 2.6 SLOPE AND DISTANCE RELATIONSHIPS

Slope %	Horizontal Distance For 1 ft Vertical	
½	200	ft
1	100	ft
2	50	ft
2.5	40	ft
3	33.33	ft
4	25	ft
5	20	ft
6	16.67	ft
7	14.28	ft
8	12.50	ft
8.33*	12.00	ft
9	11.11	ft
10	10.00	ft
20	5.00	ft
33.33	3.00	ft
50	2.00	ft

*8.33% is the maximum slope for a handicapped ramp if the vertical difference in elevation is over 0.5 ft. Other handicapped standards may vary from state to state, and city to city. Codes and local standards are usually available from the local planning departments.

Using Decimals of Feet

Grading computations, spot elevations, and site survey dimensions are expressed in feet and decimals of a foot. This is most convenient since it removes the need to manipulate cumbersome fractions. Spot elevations are elevations, existing or proposed, referenced to some point of known elevation called a benchmark. Most benchmarks have elevations referenced to mean sea level. Site dimensions that are usually referenced in decimals of feet are property lines and center line data for roads and streets. Other site dimensions, however, are commonly given in feet and inches. Table 2-7 provides a quick reference for conversion from inches to decimals of a foot.

Expressions of Slope

In practice there are four ways that slope may be expressed as a gradient, a percent, a ratio, or as a degree of slope. The gradient is the decimal form and expresses rise and fall in ft/ft. For example if a gradient (G) is given as 0.03, the rise or fall in a line of slope is 0.03 ft for every horizontal foot of run. When the slope is expressed as a percent (%) it is the rise or fall in feet/100 ft. In other words a 3% slope is a rise or fall of 3 ft for every 100 ft of horizontal run. A slope expressed as a ratio, such as 1:0.03, gives the vertical rise or fall in ft per lineal foot. The way it is written here is the correct

mathematical relationship; however, in practice you will most often see it expressed as a 0.03:1, meaning a .03 ft rise or fall for each foot of horizontal run. Sometimes slopes are also expressed as degree of slope, such as a 15-degree slope. This indicates a slope with a 15-degree angle between the face of the slope and horizontal. Most of the time the degree of slope designation will be encounterd in geologic and soil reports, but it is seldom used in grading and site work.

Application of the Basic Grading Equation

To illustrate the various situations that require basic computations, consider the parking bay illustrated in Figure 2-54. To provide an evenly sloped, usable area, the surface will have to be revised. But to minimize the amount of earth work it would make sense to set the slope of the new surface about the same slope as that of the existing surface. The first task, then, is to find the existing slope of the land.

The elevation in the street, point A, is 126.50, and the elevation at the end of the bay is 124.00. The difference in elevation is:

$$\begin{array}{r} 126.50 \\ -124.00 \\ \hline 2.50 \text{ ft} \end{array}$$

The horizontal distance from point A to point B is 140 ft. The existing gradient is:

$D = 2.50$ ft
$L = 140$ ft
$G = 2.50 \div 140 = 0.0179$ or 1.79%

TABLE 2.7 DECIMALS OF A FOOT

Ft/in	Decimal
⅛ in	0.0104 ft
¼ in	0.0208 ft
1 in	0.0833 ft
2 in	0.1667 ft
3 in	0.2500 ft
4 in	0.3333 ft
5 in	0.4167 ft
6 in	0.5000 ft
7 in	0.5833 ft
8 in	0.6667 ft
9 in	0.7500 ft
10 in	0.8333 ft
11 in	0.9167 ft
12 in	1.0000 ft

This is close to 2% so a 2% longitudinal slope is selected for the center line of the parking bay. Now points of even one-foot elevation need to be located along the center line of the parking bay. Working along the center line from point A the first even one-foot elevation will be 126.00. The difference in elevation between point A, 126.50 and 126.00 is 0.50 ft and the gradient is .02, so find L:

$L = D \div G$
$L = 0.50$ ft $\div 0.02 = 25$ ft

This means that the even 126.00 elevation lies 25 ft downhill from point A as shown. The next points of even one-foot elevation will be evenly spaced and represent a vertical difference in elevation of 1 ft at a slope of 2%. So find L for:

$G = 0.02$
$D = 1.00$ ft
$L = 1.00$ ft $\div 0.02 = 50.00$ ft

This means all other even one-foot elevations are spaced 50 ft apart as shown in Figure 2-54.

Assume now that we have elected to use a valley cross section with the low point being the center line of the parking bay. This means that the edges of the parking bay are higher than the center line and, in this case, assume a cross slope of 1%. To locate the new elevations along the upper edge of the parking bay, first find the elevation on the center line opposite the upper left corner, point A, Figure 2-55. Point A is 10 ft from the 126.50 elevation and the slope of the center line is 2%, so the vertical difference in elevation is:

$D = G \times L$
$D = 0.02 \times 10$ ft $= 0.20$ ft

The elevation at point A is:

126.50 ft
−   0.20 ft
──────────
126.30 ft

Since the cross slope is 1% and the distance from point A to point B is 30 ft, the vertical difference in elevation is:

$D = G \times L$
$D = 0.01 \times 30$ ft $= 0.30$ ft

The elevation at point B is:

126.30 ft
+   0.30 ft
──────────
126.60 ft

The first point of even one-foot elevation, point C, is found by computing L where:

$D = 0.60$ ft
$G = 0.02$

Note: *This is the the longitudinal gradient of the parking bay.*

$L = D \div G$
$L = 0.60 \div 0.02 = 30.00$ ft

The even one-foot elevation 126.00 lies 30 ft downhill of point B. Next find L for a vertical difference in elevation of 1 ft for a 2% slope to find the remaining points of even one-foot elevation as follows:

$L = D \div G$
$L = 1.00$ ft $\div 0.02 = 50.00$ ft

These points are plotted as shown in Figure 2-55.

Since the cross section of the pavement is uniform, the points of even one-foot elevation are the same along the opposite edge of the parking bay. These points have also been plotted in Figure 2-55.

Notice that there is a curb indicated around the parking bay. Standard curb height is 6 in (0.50 ft). This means that the elevation on the curb directly above the even elevation 126.00 is 126.50. So the even one-foot elevation 126.00 is located by:

$D = 0.05$ ft
$G = 0.02$
$L = D \div G$
$L = 0.50$ ft $\div 0.02 = 25$ ft

Once again, since the parking bay cross section is uniform, all other points are the same, as shown in Figure 2-55.

Plotting the revised contours is now a simple matter of connecting the points with a line. When the contour lines are on a paved surface they are straight, mechanical lines. When they are on grade they are drawn freehand as shown in Figure 2-56.

This simple example illustrates the application of the basic grading equation. The math is very simple addition, subtraction, multiplication, and division, and with a little practice will not require a calculator. Practice is the key word.

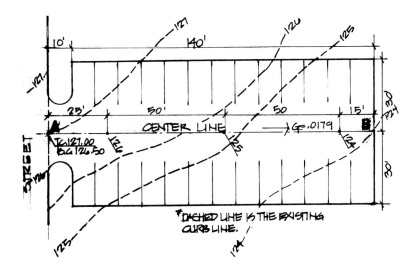

FIGURE 2.54   USING THE GRADING EQUATION

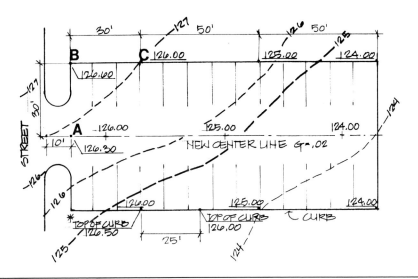

FIGURE 2.55   USING THE GRADING EQUATION

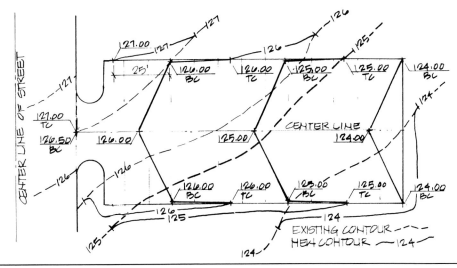

FIGURE 2.56   USING THE GRADING EQUATION

APPLYING THE GRADING PROCESS

To illustrate the entire grading process and how it is applied to a typical project, consider the site plan for High-Tech Inc., Figure 2-57. It is a single-level office building located on a corner lot, with a parking lot and service area to the north of the building. The streets, Sunset Drive and South Street, are existing, and there are two 30-in oak trees that should be saved. The existing topography is shown at a 1 ft contour interval.

The main entrance to the building is to the northwest, and there is a service entry at the northeast corner with a 4 ft elevated loading dock. The small rectangular structure on the walk at the main entrance is a pylon for a sign.

Step One: Analyzing the Site Plan for Existing Drainage and Fixed Conditions

Figure 2-58 is an analysis diagram of the existing drainage pattern and the fixed conditions that will influence the grading solution. The numbered notes on the diagram indicate specific information of importance typical of many, if not most, projects of this type.

1. Except in very special circumstances, the grades cannot be changed at the property line; therefore, you should usually consider the property line a fixed condition.
2. The entire site is draining into a broad swale at the east property line. This channel will have to remain relatively unchanged since it carries water from other adjoining parcels.
3. The grade at the existing oak tree is 93.90 and this becomes a fixed point. This elevation was estimated visually since the information was not on the survey base.
4. The grades along Sunset Drive are fixed; existing streets cannot be changed. This means that the intersection of the street and the parking lot is fixed by the existing grade of the street.
5. The arrows indicate the existing surface drainage pattern. The solid dashed line notes a ridge that marks a break in the flow. The dashed and dotted line indicates the flow line (FL) of existing drainage ways. Notice that where the building is located there is quite a bit of water flowing toward the building. This condition will have to be corrected in the grading solution.
6. The * at note 6 is the point where all of the runoff water is collecting and being discharged from the site. This is considered a fixed condition as well.
7. This is the other existing oak tree with an elevation of 91.90. As in the previous case, this constitutes a fixed point.
8. South Street is also existing, so the elevations along the south of the property may not be changed.

Step Two: Developing a New Grading Strategy

The second step involves making important decisions about how the grading is going to be done. Most of the decisions are, in fact, design decisions that have a lot to do with the details of how everything is going to fit together. It must be pointed out that in the example there are any number of different decisions that could have been made regarding how the grading is handled. A lengthy discussion of all the various alternatives is not presented here. In most cases, however, reasons will be given for why a certain decision was made. With practice, students will come to recognize alternative approaches and their merits.

Figure 2-59 is the new grading and drainage strategy for the site. Again, numbered notes are keyed to the plan to indicate important decisions or information.

1. Since the parking lot was situated to follow the center line of the existing swale to the north, it was decided to drain each parking bay to the center median and release the water through curb cuts across the east drive to the main drainage channel along the east property line. This solution will keep the main driving aisles of the parking lot dry during wet periods and pedestrians will not have to cross the water flowing along the face of the median curb.
2. The dark dashed line across the entrances to the parking lot indicates that the pavement should be raised slightly to keep the water flowing down the street from entering the parking lot. This should be done both to keep water in the street and to keep water in the parking lot from flowing into the street.
3. This shows that the bay to the south will be handled in the same way that the bay to the north was handled, (note 1).
4. The dashed and dotted line along the east of the property indicates that the grading solution will maintain the existing swale.
5. The broken line indicates the approximate drip line of the existing oak tree. If possible, this zone should not be disturbed.
6. The heavy dashed lines near the main entrance indicate new break points in the surface flow of water. The break to the west recognizes the main entry walk and will keep the water off this important area. The break at the service area is necessary because the service drive will be depressed to accommodate the loading dock.
7. The zone along the west side of the building will be regraded to provide a new swale to transport water around the building to the outlet point at the east. This is essential since the existing grade in this part of the site was draining toward the building.

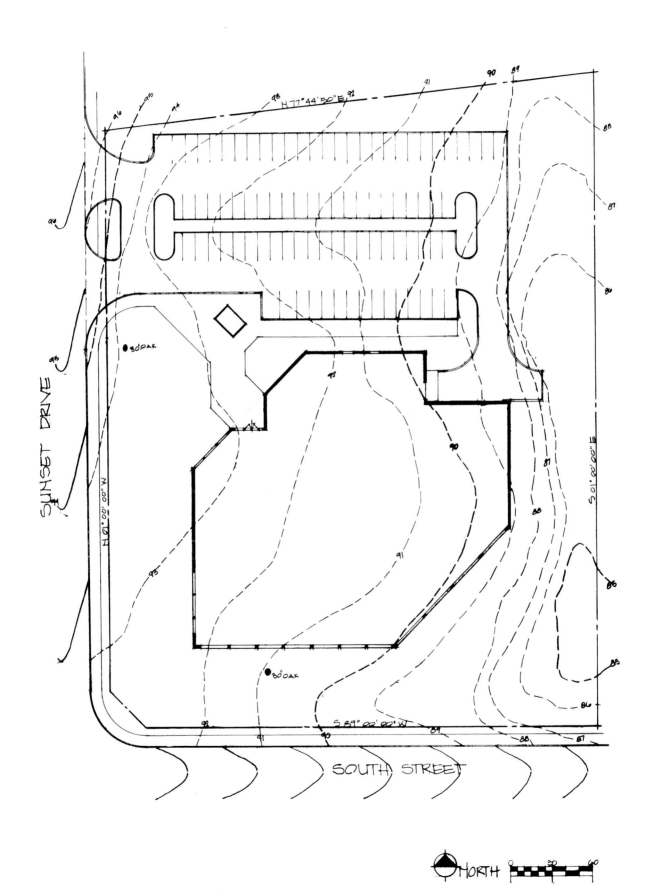

FIGURE 2.57 HIGH-TECH INC.

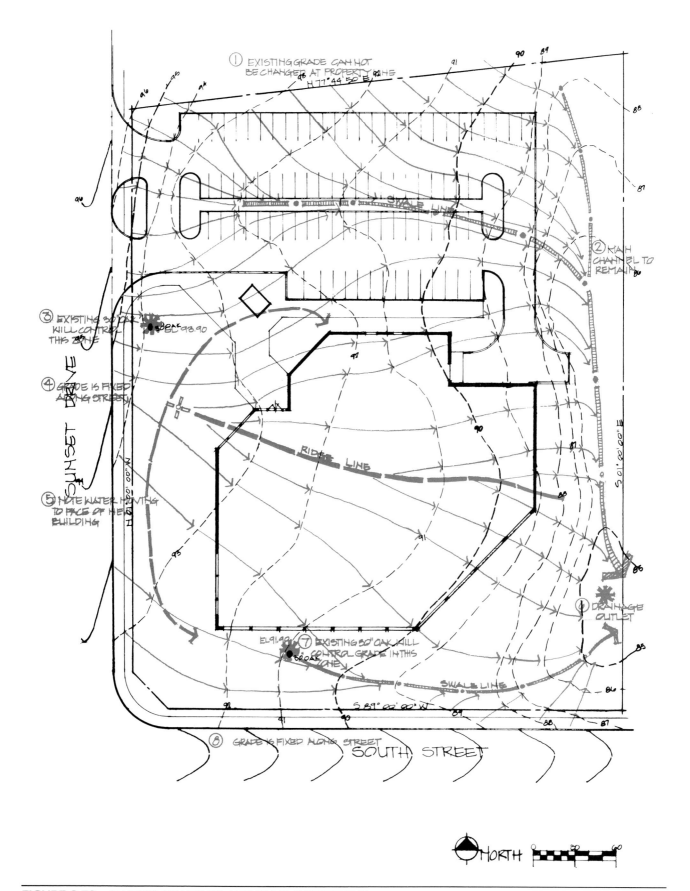

① EXISTING GRADE CAN NOT BE CHANGED AT PROPERTY LINE

② MAIN CHANNEL TO REMAIN

③ EXISTING 30" OAK KILL CONTROL THIS ZONE

④ GRADE IS FIXED ALONG STREET

⑤ NOTE WATER MOVING TO FACE OF THE BUILDING

⑥ DRAINAGE OUTLET

⑦ EXISTING 30" OAK KILL CONTROL GRADE IN THIS AREA

⑧ GRADE IS FIXED ALONG STREET

SWALE LINE

RIDGE LINE

SUNSET DRIVE

SOUTH STREET

NORTH

FIGURE 2.58 ANALYSIS DRAINAGE AND FIXED CONDITIONS

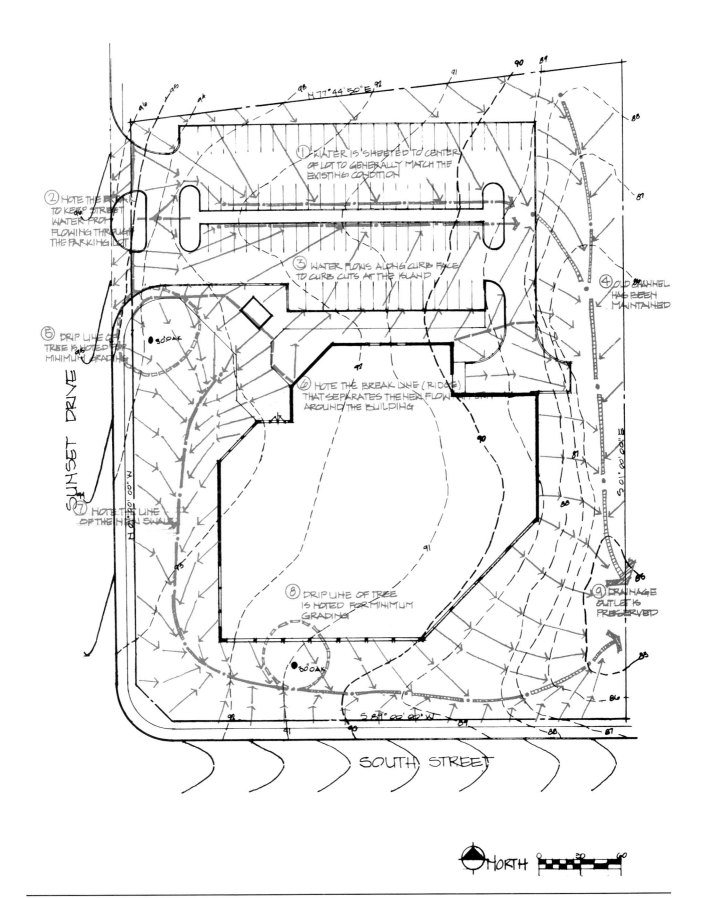

FIGURE 2.59 NEW GRADING AND DRAIN STRATEGY

8. The drip line of the existing tree is noted for minimum grading. Notice that the building is in fact located inside the drip line. This is a problem, and if the client is serious about saving the tree, the building should be moved farther north.
9. The main drainage outlet is to be left unchanged.

Now look at the pattern made by the arrows noting surface flow. These arrows are almost like hachures denoting a network of sloping planes. The ability to visualize this pattern is very important to the beginning student, and it is the key to really understanding the grading process. It is recommended that even experienced designers do a rough strategy diagram, and students are encouraged to do neat, very detailed diagrams.

Step Three: Establishing Preliminary Grades and Zones

This next step requires setting some preliminary numbers and lines of slope in order to find a set of conditions that will allow all the parts to fit. The first numbers, as you will see, seldom work out. This point is emphasized because students are frequently stumped since they just do not want to change the numbers that are already on the paper. It is very important to realize that the first efforts are a trial-and-error process.

The other question is: Where to start? There is not a pat answer to this, but it is usually possible to find one or two fixed conditions that are reasonably close together. Once identified, these fixed conditions provide a good beginning point. In the example problem, the only direct connection between fixed conditions and the new development is the intersection of the street and the parking lot, so this is where work will begin.

The average slope of the existing land was estimated first to determine an appropriate slope for the parking lot. If we take the elevation at the street to be 96.00 and the end of the upper parking bay to be about 89.00, there is a 7 ft difference in elevation. The length of the lot is 290 ft so the existing gradient is:

$G = D \div L$
$G = 7.00 \text{ ft} \div 290.00 \text{ ft} = 0.024$, about a 2½% slope.

In these early probing efforts it is neither necessary nor desirable to be very precise in your numbers. Estimating grades to 0.50 ft is close enough.

Since the existing slope is about 2½%, it was decided to use this as the longitudinal slope of the parking lot. Beginning at the street in the upper bay, 96.00 was set to provide a slight high point at the entrance. Next, points of even one-foot elevation were marked off at 2½%. The contour spacing for a 2½% slope is:

$D = 1.00 \text{ ft}$
$G = 0.025$
$L = D \div G$
$L = 1.00 \text{ ft} \div 0.025 = 40.00 \text{ ft}$

Figure 2-60 shows these points plotted along the center line of the upper bay. The same procedure was followed in the lower bay. First, the high-point elevation was set by estimating the grade in the gutter of the existing street (+95.05). Then the high-point elevation of 95.40 was set. Next, the average slope of the existing surface was calculated and found to be about 3%. See the note in Figure 2-60. Then, the even one-foot elevation, 95.00 was plotted as follows:

$D = 0.40 \text{ ft}$
$G = 0.03$
$L = D \div G$
$L = 0.40 \text{ ft} \div 0.03 = 13.33 \text{ ft}$

This was plotted as shown. The remaining even one-foot elevations were then laid off. For a 3% slope the even one-foot elevations are 33.33 ft apart.

$L = D \div G$
$D = 1.00 \text{ ft}$
$G = 0.03$
$L = 1.00 \text{ ft} \div 0.03 = 33.33 \text{ ft}$

Next, consider the broken line around an area labeled "Flex Zone." This is the area that must take up the elevation differences between the parking and the building. In this example problem, the flex zone was rather limited because the building was very close to the edge of the parking lot along its northernmost wall. This is a very common problem and will be seen often. At this point this was just an observation; there was still not enough information to indicate whether it would be a problem, so the initial probe was continued.

The next step was to establish a finished floor elevation. The existing ground sloped 4 ft from 93.0, to 89.0. In this case, the building was a slab on grade so it was best to select a finished floor elevation that would help balance the cut and fill. It appeared that an elevation of 92.00 would provide a reasonable balance. As soon as the finished floor was set the grades at entrances and grades on the ground around the structure could be set.

In this example, the elevation at the front door was set 0.10 ft lower than the finished floor, (91.90). The grades on the entry walk were set at 2% away from the door in both directions. Keep in mind that the area in front of a door, and at steps, should always be level. Slope the pavement only beyond these lines.

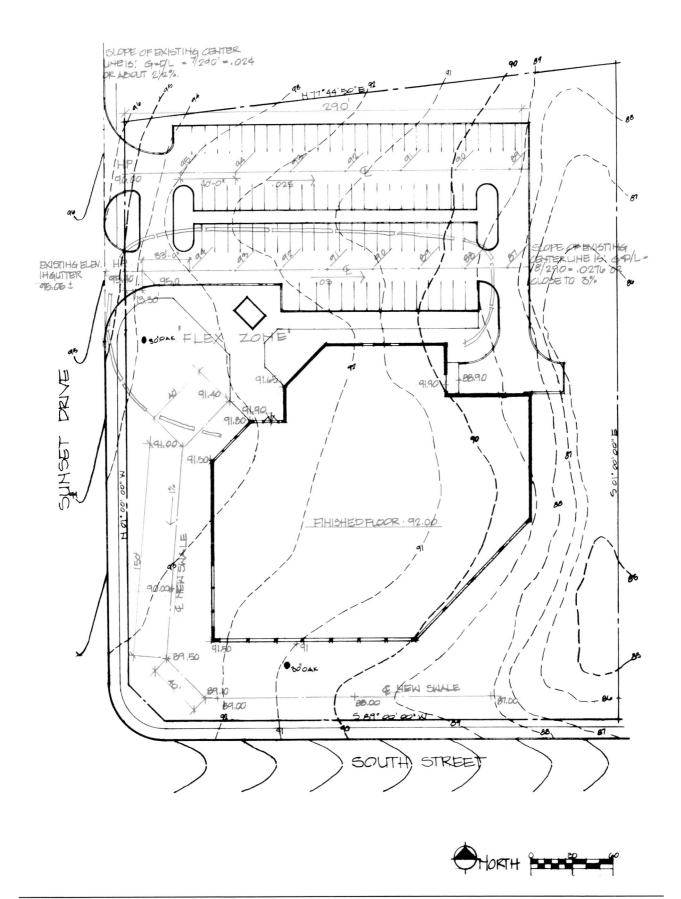

FIGURE 2.60 ESTABLISHING PRELIMINARY GRADES

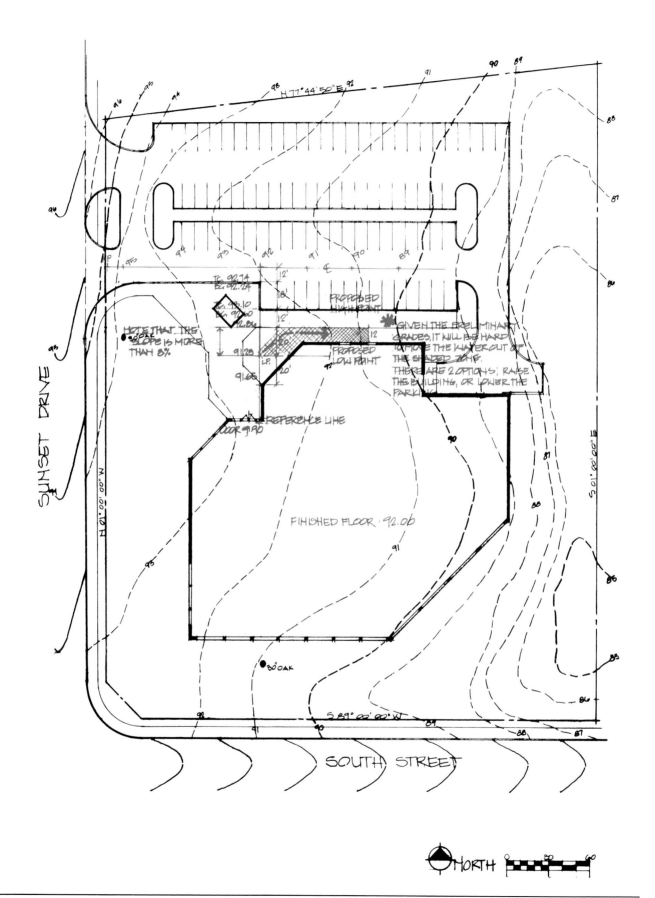

FIGURE 2.61   EVALUATE FOR PROBLEM ZONES

The ground elevations along the west wall of the building were set 0.50 ft below the finished floor. This is a common minimum value for slab on grade buildings, due to dampness and the potential for termite infestation; however, if the building has a suspended slab, a basement, or other conditions that require air circulation under the slab, 0.50 ft may not be sufficient. On the south wall of the building the grade will have to fall off to the 91.00 elevation if there is any hope of saving the tree.

The other spot elevations that had to be set at the building were at the loading area on the east. Once again, 91.90 was set at the door. Then the elevation at the bottom of the loading dock was set 4 ft lower, as required.

The final task was to lay out the center line of the swale, beginning at the entry walk, following around the building to the south and east. This is shown in Figure 2-60. The center line is moved away from the building as it moves downhill. If this is not done, the slope away from the building will become increasingly steep as the swale moves downhill.

Finally the critical spot elevations were set along the swale. The 91.40 elevation at the top of the swale, near the entrance, represents a 2% slope away from the door. The remaining elevations are based on the 1% slope selected for the drainage swale. With this done we move to the next step in the grading process.

Step Four: Evolving the Solution

This step is where the connections between zones, building to parking, parking to property line, etc., are worked out. It is a simple trial-and-error process of fitting the pieces together. Most of the time it will be necessary to revise some of the preliminary decisions about slopes and grading details. In many cases it may involve changes in the actual design of the project itself. As we continue working through the example, many recurring situations will be pointed out.

Remember, when the grades were being set along the center line of the parking lot, it was pointed out that the flex zone between the building and the parking was probably going to be a limiting factor. Since this was the only major area of concern apparent at the time, it is the logical place to begin evolving the grading plan. Every project and every site is going to be different, so it is not possible to make any suggestions about precisely where to start this step. With time and practice you will learn to spot the problem areas quickly.

To begin working out the connection between the building and the parking, a reference line was struck from the proposed 92.00 elevation in the parking lot, parallel to the short north-south wall near the main entrance, Figure 2-61. A 2% slope was selected as the cross sectional slope for the parking, walks, and ground. The 2% slope is an excellent working slope because it provides positive drainage on most any surface, and hard surfaces can be finished with few "bird baths." Computation of the spot elevations on the reference line are as follows:

From the proposed 92.00 to the base of the curb.

L = 12.00 ft
G = 0.02
$D = G \times L$
$D = 0.02 \times 12.00$ ft = 0.24 ft

The bottom of curb elevation (BC) is

  92.00 ft
+ 0.24 ft
———
  92.24 ft

The elevation at the top of curb (TC) is 0.50 ft higher, 6″ is the standard curb height.

  92.24 ft
+ 0.50 ft
———
  92.74 ft

From the edge of the drive to the curb line at the parking stall.

L = 18 ft
G = 0.02
$D = G \times L$
$D = 0.02 \times 18$ ft = 0.36 ft

The BC elevation is:

  92.24 (the BC elevation at the line of the drive)
+ 0.36 ft
———
  92.60 ft

The TC elevation is:

  92.60 ft
+ 0.50 ft
———
  93.10 ft

From the top of curb to the back of the walk.

L = 12 ft
G = 0.02
$D = G \times L$
$D = 12 \times 0.02$ = 0.24 ft

The elevation at the back of the walk is:

  93.10 ft
− 0.24 ft
———
  92.86 ft

Note: Since the 93.10 curb elevation was higher than the finished floor it was judged best to warp the walk down rather than pitching it to the parking, which is usually the case.

Working north from the corner of the building, the lowest point occurs in the planting area 20 ft north of the proposed 91.65 elevation set at the corner of the building.

L = 20 ft
G = 0.02
$D = G \times L$
D = 20 ft × 0.02 = 0.40 ft

The low point elevation is:

$$\begin{array}{r} 91.65 \text{ ft} \\ -\ 0.40 \text{ ft} \\ \hline 91.25 \text{ ft} \end{array}$$

The slope from the proposed 92.86 to the proposed low point elevation of 91.25.

L = 20 ft
$$D = \begin{array}{r} 92.86 \text{ ft} \\ -91.25 \text{ ft} \\ \hline 1.61 \text{ ft} \end{array}$$

$G = D \div L$
G = 1.61 ft ÷ 20 ft
G = 0.0805 slightly over 8%

Two important things need to be considered here: First, note that the slope in the shaded zone on the plan will have to be very flat to keep the edge of the walk from being too high in reference to the building wall. This means that water movement in this zone is going to be rather sluggish. Likewise, the 8% slope noted on the reference line will also be on the walk immediately to the left. While this slope is acceptable in terms of handicapped standards, it will appear visually steep in reference to the other grades around it.

What has been learned from this probe is that the building is too low in reference to the parking; something has to change. In this case there are two choices: lower the parking or raise the building.

The decision made was to lower the parking to avoid placing more fill under the building. To accomplish this, the entrances to the parking were sloped down at 5%, then the grade was decreased to a 2½% slope for the remaining length. Changing the slopes along a drive or parking lot is quite common where there is a need to connect several different site elements. New spot elevations were then calculated along the center lines of the two parking bays as shown in Figure 2-62. The

following computations are referenced to the numbered notes in Figure 2-62.

1. The upper parking was sloped down at 5% for the first 40.00 ft of run, then leveled out to 2½%. The distance between points of even one-foot elevation at a 5% slope is:

   D = 1.00 ft
   G = 0.05
   $L = D \div G$
   L = 1.00 ft ÷ 0.05
   L = 20.00 ft

   The 95.00 and 94.00 are plotted as shown from the even 96.00 elevation previously set as the high point.
   For a 2½% slope, points of even one-foot elevation are spaced by finding L where:

   D = 1.00 ft
   G = 0.025
   $L = D \div G$
   L = 1.00 ft ÷ 0.025 =
   L = 40.00 ft

   The remaining points were plotted as shown in Figure 2-62.

2. In the lower parking bay the entry was sloped down at 5% for the first 80 ft to provide a more favorable building-to-parking lot relationship in grade. Then the slope was reduced to the 2½% slope as before. The only difference in the computations here is the location of the first point of even one-foot elevation (95.00). It was computed as follows:

   The high point elevation, 95.35, was reduced 0.05 ft from the original 93.40 to avoid too sharp a break in the grade transition. The elevation difference to the even one-foot 95.00 is 0.35 ft. Find L for:

   D = 0.35 ft
   G = 0.05
   $L = D \div G$
   L = 0.35 ft ÷ 0.05 =
   L = 7.00 ft

   The 95.00 point was plotted and the other points laid off as shown in Figure 2-62.

3. The last revision from the early probe was to pitch the main entrance walk entirely to the west, toward the swale that runs along Sunset Drive. Instead of sloping the entry walk along the short north-south wall as before, the grade is set the same as at the entrance. Then the walk slopes down at 1½% to the

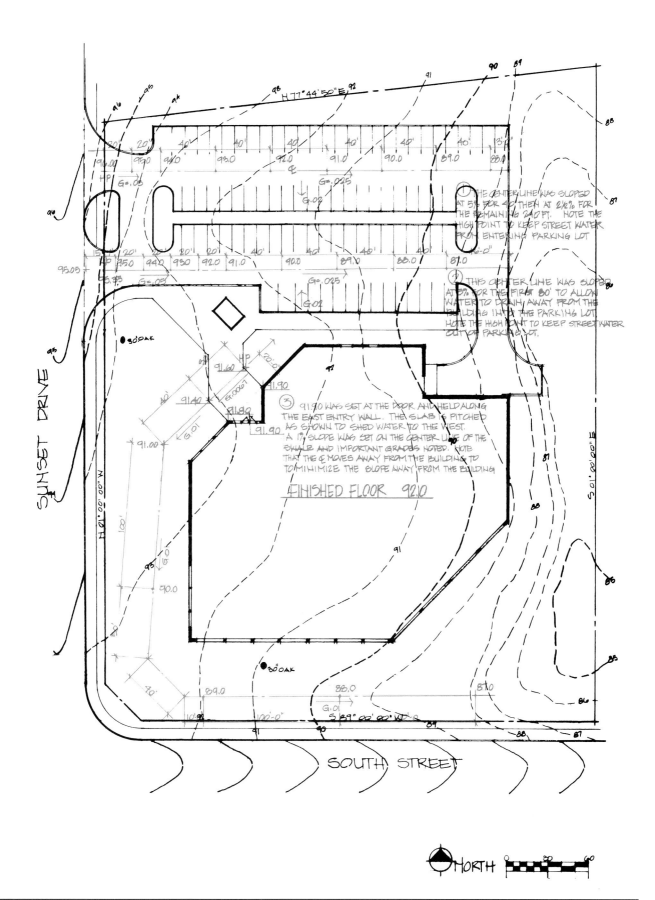

FIGURE 2.62 ESTABLISHING CENTER LINE GRADES

NORTH

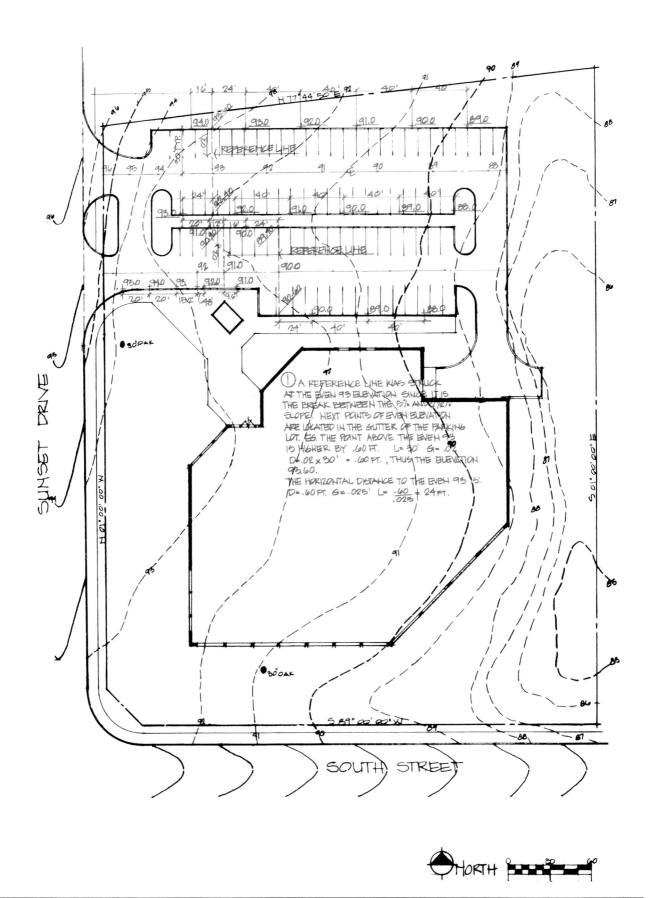

FIGURE 2.63 ESTABLISHING ELEVATIONS ALONG THE GUTTER

91.60 elevation designated as the high point (HP). The 91.40 elevation is a function of sloping 2% away from the 91.80 elevation set to the left of the door. The cross slope in the entrance walk, based on these grades is:

D = 91.60 (the HP elevation)
 91.40 (the left edge of the walk)
 ‾‾‾‾‾‾
 0.20 ft
$G = D \div L$
G = 0.20 ft ÷ 30 ft (the width of the walk)
G = 0.0067 or ⅔%

Although this is flat, it is essentially the longitudinal slope of a drainage way and the slopes perpendicular to this line will cause the water to move positively in the desired direction.

The swale has been plotted on this sheet again, but it is unchanged.

At this point, most of the major decisions have been made and the rest of the work is a matter of plotting points of even one-foot elevation difference in preparation to draw the revised contours. This process was initiated by plotting the points of even one-foot elevation along the gutter lines of the parking, as shown in Figure 2-63.

In the upper bay, a reference line was struck perpendicular to the center line through the even 93.00 elevation. This point was selected because it is the first symmetrical contour line that will cross this bay. First, the elevation in the north gutter was computed opposite the 93.00 elevation. Remember a 2% cross slope was selected for the parking. The computations are as follows:

Find D for:

G = 0.02 (the cross-slope)
L = 30 ft
$D = G \times L$
D = 0.02 × 30.00 ft =
D = 0.60 ft

 93.00 ft
+ 0.60 ft
‾‾‾‾‾‾‾
 93.60 ft

The even 93.00 elevation lies downhill of this point, at a slope of 2½%. Find L for:

D = 0.60 ft
G = 0.025 (the longitudinal slope)
$L = D \div G$
L = 0.60 ft ÷ 0.025 =
L = 24.00 ft

The even one-foot elevation 94.00 lies uphill of this point, at a slope of 2½%. Compute L for:

D = 0.40 ft
G = 0.025
$L = D \div G$
L = 0.40 ft ÷ 0.025 =
L = 16 ft

The remaining points in the north gutter are plotted 40 ft apart. This is the distance computed earlier for a 1 ft vertical difference at a 2½% slope. Next the elevation south of the 93.00 was computed and the points of even one-foot elevation were plotted along the south gutter as follows:
Find D for:

G = 0.02
L = 30.00 ft
$D = G \times L$
D = 0.02 × 30.00 ft =
D = 0.60 ft

The elevation at the curb is:

 93.00 ft
− 0.60 (remember the lot is sloping to the median)
‾‾‾‾‾‾‾
 92.40 ft

The even 93.00 lies uphill so find L for:

D = 0.60 ft
G = 0.025
$L = D \div G$
L = 0.60 ft ÷ 0.025 =
L = 24 ft

Next find the distance to the even 92.00 by finding L for:

D = 0.40 ft
G = 0.025
$L = D \div G$
L = 0.04 ft ÷ 0.025 =
L = 16 ft

Once again the even foot elevation is plotted and the other points are laid off in equal increments, as shown in Figure 2-63.

In the lower parking bay another reference was struck through the 90.00 elevation. The numbers uphill and downhill of this line are the same as in the upper bay, so the points were plotted as shown. A second reference line was struck through the 91.00 to plot the points in the drive and parking bay where the longitudinal slope is 5%. Remember from the last

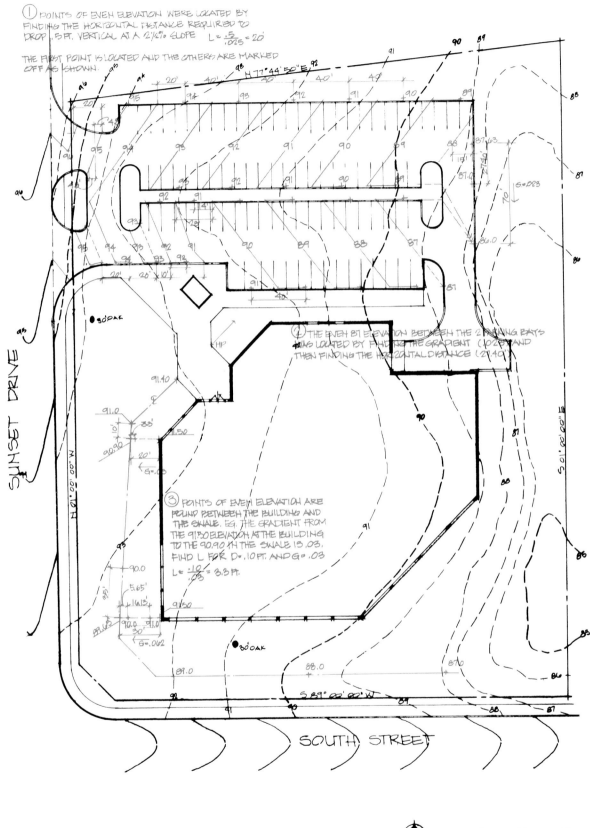

① POINTS OF EVEN ELEVATION WERE LOCATED BY FINDING THE HORIZONTAL DISTANCE REQUIRED TO DROP .5 FT. VERTICAL AT A 2½% SLOPE $L = \frac{.5}{.025} = 20'$

THE FIRST POINT IS LOCATED AND THE OTHERS ARE MARKED OFF AS SHOWN.

② THE EVEN 87 ELEVATION BETWEEN THE 2 PARKING BAYS WAS LOCATED BY FINDING THE GRADIENT (.025) AND THEN FINDING THE HORIZONTAL DISTANCE (27.40')

③ POINTS OF EVEN ELEVATION ARE FOUND BETWEEN THE BUILDING AND THE SWALE. EG. THE GRADIENT FROM THE 91.50 ELEVATION AT THE BUILDING TO THE 90.90 IN THE SWALE IS .03, FIND L FOR D=.10 FT. AND G=.03 $L = \frac{.10}{.03} = 3.3$ FT.

SUNSET DRIVE

SOUTH STREET

NORTH

FIGURE 2.64 BEGINNING THE REVISED CONTOURS

computations that the difference in elevation for a 2% cross slope and a run of 30 ft is 0.60 ft. Thus, the elevation in the north gutter opposite the 91.00 is:

$$
\begin{array}{r}
91.00 \text{ ft} \\
-\ 0.60 \text{ ft} \\
\hline
90.40 \text{ ft}
\end{array}
$$

The even 91.00 lies uphill so compute L for:

$D = 0.60$ ft
$G = 0.05$
$L = D \div G$
$L = 0.60$ ft $\div\ 0.05\ =$
$L = 12$ ft

The even 90.00 lies downhill of the 90.40, but notice that to the right of the reference line the slope has changed to 2½%. Now find L for:

$D = 0.40$ ft
$G = 0.025$
$L = D \div G$
$L = 0.40$ ft $\div\ 0.025\ =$
$L = 16$ ft

This point is plotted and the other points are located as shown in Figure 2-63.

The points along the curb of the south entrance were located from a reference line struck through the even 92.00 on the center line. This was done for illustration purposes since the dimensions and numbers might run together. From the center line of the drive to the south curb is 12 ft. The 2% cross slope is still maintained on the drive, so compute D for:

$G = 0.02$
$L = 12$ ft
$D = G \times L$
$D = 0.02 \times 12$ ft $=$
$D = 0.24$ ft

The elevation at the curb is 92.24, the even 92.00 lies downhill so find L for:

$D = 0.24$ ft
$G = 0.05$
$L = D \div G$
$L = 0.24$ ft $\div\ 0.05\ =$
$L = 4.80$ ft

The 93.00 is uphill so find L for:

$D = 0.76$ ft
$G = 0.05$
$L = D \div G$
$L = 0.76$ ft $\div\ 0.05\ =$
$L = 15.20$ ft

These points have been plotted in Figure 2-63.

From the information plotted in Figure 2-63, the first segments of the revised contour lines can be drawn in the parking lot, as shown in Figure 2-64. Notice that the 94.00 contour has been constructed parallel to the 93.00 in the upper bay and extended until it intersected the 94.00 contour in the lower bay. The geometric construction and extension of lines such as this is quick and mathematically accurate.

1. After the first contour segments were drawn in the parking lot, the points of even one-foot elevation were plotted on the curb lines. The computations for these points are as follows:
   Find L for:

   $D = 0.50$ ft (remember a standard curb is
   $\qquad\qquad 6'' \div 0.50$ ft)
   $G = 0.025$ (the longitudinal slope of the lot)
   $L = D \div G$
   $L = 0.50$ ft $\div\ 0.025\ =$
   $L = 20$ ft

   The contour line follows along the face of the curb for a distance of 20 ft. The remaining points of even one-foot elevation can now be plotted on the 2½% sloped sections by simply laying off 40 ft increments along the curb as shown in Figure 2-63.
   The 95.00 was constructed by finding D for:

   $L = 12$ ft (half the width of the drive)
   $G = 0.02$ (the cross sectional slope)
   $D = G \times L$
   $D = 12$ ft $\times\ 0.02\ =$
   $D = 0.24$ ft

   Since the upper gutter line is higher, the even 95.00 is downhill, find L for:

   $D = 0.24$ ft
   $G = 0.05$ (the longitudinal slope)
   $L = D \div G$
   $L = 0.24$ ft $\div\ 0.05\ =$
   $L = 4.8$ ft

   Because the slope is constant, the even 95.00 lies 4.8 ft uphill in the lower gutter as shown in Figure 2-64. The even 96.00 in the upper gutter is 20 ft uphill from the 95.00, so the 96.00 contour is plotted by connecting the proposed HP 96.00 with the existing 96.00 in the gutter line of Sunset Drive and then to the 96.00 elevation plotted in the upper gutter.
   In the drive of the lower bay the even 95.00 and 93.00 points on the curb were located by first finding L for:

D = 0.50 ft (the height of the curb)
G = 0.05 (the longitudinal slope)
$L = D \div G$
L = 0.50 ft $\div$ 0.05 =
L = 10 ft

The elevations at the top of the south curb were then plotted as shown. The points of even one-foot elevation on the curved sections of curb (contours 95.00 and 93.00) can be located by simply projecting a line from the point plotted on the south curb, parallel to the contour line, until it intersects the opposite curb. This is shown by the dashed reference lines, Figure 2-63.

2. At the east end of the parking lot the 87.00 contour line was simply plotted parallel to the 88.00, extending the line until it intersected either curb, as shown. A low point of 86.00 was set at the intersection of the center line of the south bay and east curb, where water will be released into the main drainage swale through a curb cut. Then the even 87.00 elevation in the gutter of the east drive was located as follows:

Working from the even 88 elevation in the upper bay find D for:

L = 15 ft
G = 0.025
$D = G \times L$
D = 15 ft $\times$ 0.025 =
D = 0.37 ft

The elevation where the center line of the upper bay intersects the east curb line is:

88.00 ft
$-$ 0.37 ft
87.63 ft

Then the slope between the 87.63 and the proposed 86.00 was found by:

L = 70 ft (the distance between center lines)
D = 1.63 ft (87.63 $-$ 86.00)
$G = D \div L$
G = 1.63 ft $\div$ 70 ft =
G = 0.023 or 2.3%

Next find L for:

D = 0.63 ft
G = 0.023
$L = D \div G$
L = 0.63 ft $\div$ 0.023 =
L = 27.40 ft

The 87.00 was plotted as shown Figure 2-64.

In the service drive, the even 87.00 was plotted by simply extending the 87 contour until it intersected the curb line of the drive as shown. The other dashed lines indicate the flow pattern of water from the proposed curb cuts in the median island to the proposed curb cut in the drive.

3. The elevations along the swale on the west side of the building were plotted in the previous figure. Now the points of even one-foot elevation are found between the building and the center line of the swale. The first point, directly opposite the 91.50 elevation at the northwest corner of the building, lies 10 ft south of the 91.00. The elevation on the center line of the swale is found by computing D for:

L = 10 ft
G = 0.01 (the slope set on the swale)
$D = G \times L$
D = 0.01 $\times$ 10 ft =
D = 0.10 ft

The elevation is:

91.00 ft
$-$ 0.10 ft
90.90 ft

Locate the 91.00 between the building and the swale by finding the slope from the corner of the building to the swale at this point as follows:

D = 0.60 ft
L = 20 ft
$G = D \div L$
G = 0.60 ft $\div$ 20 ft =
G = 0.03 or 3%

Next find L for:

D = 0.10 ft
G = 0.03
$L = D \div G$
L = 0.10 ft $\div$ 0.03 =
L = 3.3 ft

The procedure was followed to locate the 90.00 and 91.00 points at the southwest corner of the building (Figure 2-64). Now look at Figure 2-65. The first segments of the 90 and 91 contour lines have been drawn in and the connections have been made for the contour lines that cross the median in the parking lot. In all of the foregoing discussion the computations for each individual point have been shown. But, by now these basic computations should be quite clear. So, for

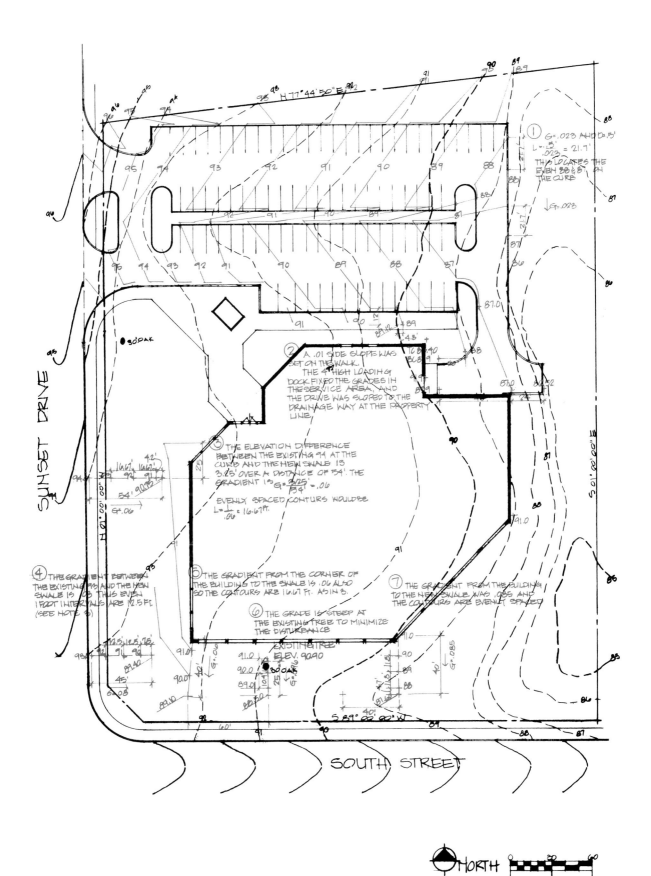

FIGURE 2.65 REVISED CONTOURS CONTINUED (1)

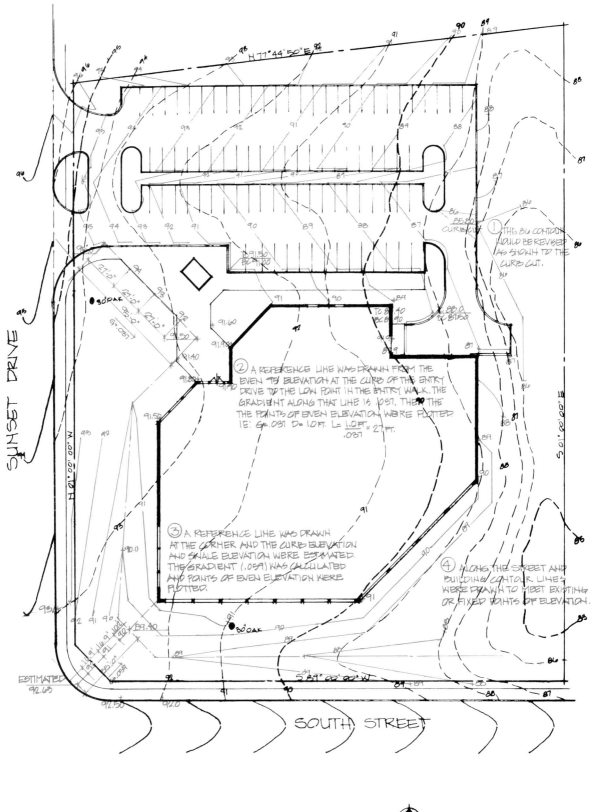

① THE 86 CONTOUR WOULD BE REVISED AS SHOWN TO THE CURB CUT.

② A REFERENCE LINE WAS DRAWN FROM THE EVEN 92 ELEVATION AT THE CURB OF THE ENTRY DRIVE TO THE LOW POINT IN THE ENTRY WALK. THE GRADIENT ALONG THAT LINE IS .037, THEN THE THE POINTS OF EVEN ELEVATION WERE PLOTTED IE: G=.037 D=1.0FT. L=1.0FT = 27 FT.
.037

③ A REFERENCE LINE WAS DRAWN AT THE CORNER AND THE CURB ELEVATION AND SWALE ELEVATION WERE ESTIMATED. THE GRADIENT (.059) WAS CALCULATED AND POINTS OF EVEN ELEVATION WERE PLOTTED.

④ ALONG THE STREET AND BUILDING CONTOUR LINES WERE DRAWN TO MEET EXISTING OR FIXED POINTS OF ELEVATION.

SUNSET DRIVE

SOUTH STREET

NORTH

FIGURE 2.66   REVISED CONTOURS CONTINUED (2)

the remaining discussion on this part of the process, the text will simply reference the notes on the plan with a brief explanation, omitting the detailed calculations.

1. Note 1, Figure 2-65, shows the location and plot ting of the even one-foot points, 87 and 88.
2. Note 2, Figure 2-65, shows the location of points of even one-foot elevation along the back edge of the 12 ft-wide walk. Walks should always be set with a side slope of between 1 and 2%, and they are usually pitched to the street or parking lot. They should not be pitched toward a building if at all possible.

    The grades were also set in the service area to the east. All of the grades in this area were set using a 2% slope to the east. Remember, the grades at the door and at the bottom of the loading dock are a function of the finished floor elevation.
3. Notes 3-7, Figure 2-65, deal with plotting the contours of the the new swale. In note 6 the slope must be steep to avoid disturbing the tree as much as possible.

Figure 2-66 completes the plotting of the revised contours. All of the points plotted in previous figures have been connected with lines, and the revised contour pattern is becoming very clear.

1. In note 1, Figure 2-66, the gutter elevation was lowered an additional 0.20 ft to illustrate the pattern that would be made by a contour at a curb cut.
2. Note 2 shows how the points of even one-foot elevation were plotted on the front entry walk. The gradient between two previously fixed points was computed and the the points of even one-foot elevation were plotted as shown.
3. Note 3 shows how the 90, 91, and 92 elevations were found as they move around the corner of the building.
4. Note 4 makes reference to the freehand connection of contour lines back to existing condition, illustrated by the 88 contour connection at the northeast corner of the building.

The new grading is now substantially complete. The revised contours have been plotted and most of the important spot elevations have been noted for control. Once this picture is in front of you, it needs to be carefully evaluated to see if there are areas that, while technically correct, could be improved to either make the solution work better or simplify the construction detailing. This leads to step five of the grading process: refining the solution.

Step Five: Refining the Solution

Turn now to Figure 2-67. All of the revised contours have been plotted and joined to the existing contours. Refining the solution requires that the designer look very closely at the solution to be sure that it is practical, reasonably economic, functional, safe, and attractive. It requires a critical eye. Glossing over this step leads to poor work and, more often than not, serious problems during and after construction.

The numbered notes on the plan reference needed refinements or show additional information that is needed to complete the work in the field.

1. First, a paved swale was indicated to carry the water through the curb of the island of the parking lot. Then the spot elevations were calculated for both ends. To calculate these spots, use the information on the plan. The slope of the parking bay is 2½% and the distance from the point where the 89 contour touches the curb can be scaled off. Find the difference in elevation and subtract from 89. To illustrate the procedure, the figures are shown here for the first curb cut. The distance from the 89 elevation in the gutter scales 38 ft and the slope is 2½%. Find D for:

    $L = 38$ ft
    $G = 0.025$
    $D = G \times L$
    $D = 0.025 \times 38$ ft $=$
    $D = 0.95$ ft

    The elevation at the entrance to the paved swale is:

    $$\begin{array}{r} 89.00 \text{ ft} \\ -\ \ 0.95 \text{ ft} \\ \hline 88.05 \text{ ft} \end{array}$$

2. A curb cut needs to be added in the service drive corner that would trap water. The contour lines show this, and earlier there had been no provision made to release this water even though all the grades were set to pitch the water in that direction.
3. At the main entrance, spot elevations were set on every corner of the walk. Arrows have been added in the illustration to show how the water will be flowing. The current grading solution forces the water to make about a 180 degree turn and it all happens at the front door. This is cause for some concern because heavy rains and wind could, in some cases, drive water into the door. The solution to this problem involves changing the design to include steps. This will be explained more in the next figure.

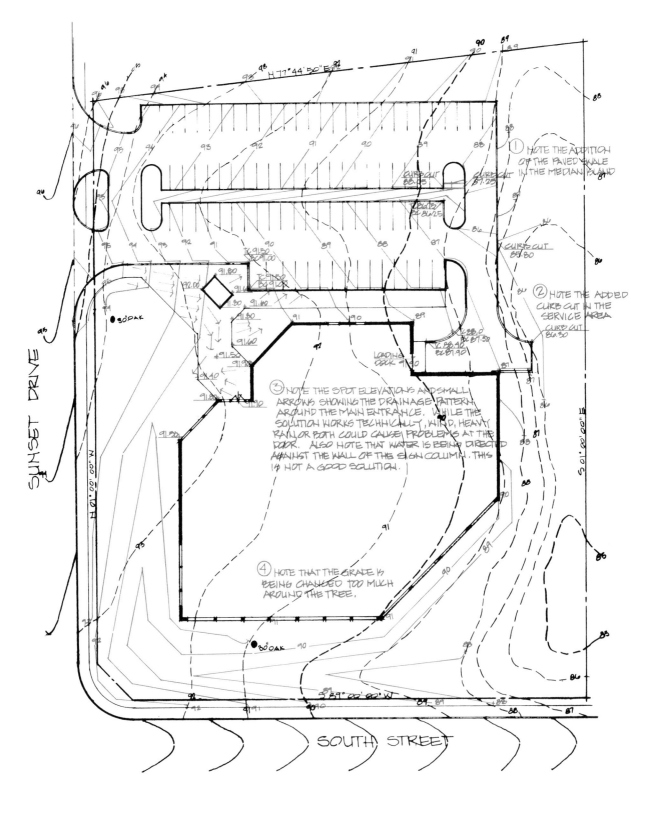

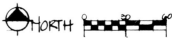

FIGURE 2.67 BEGIN REFINING THE SOLUTION

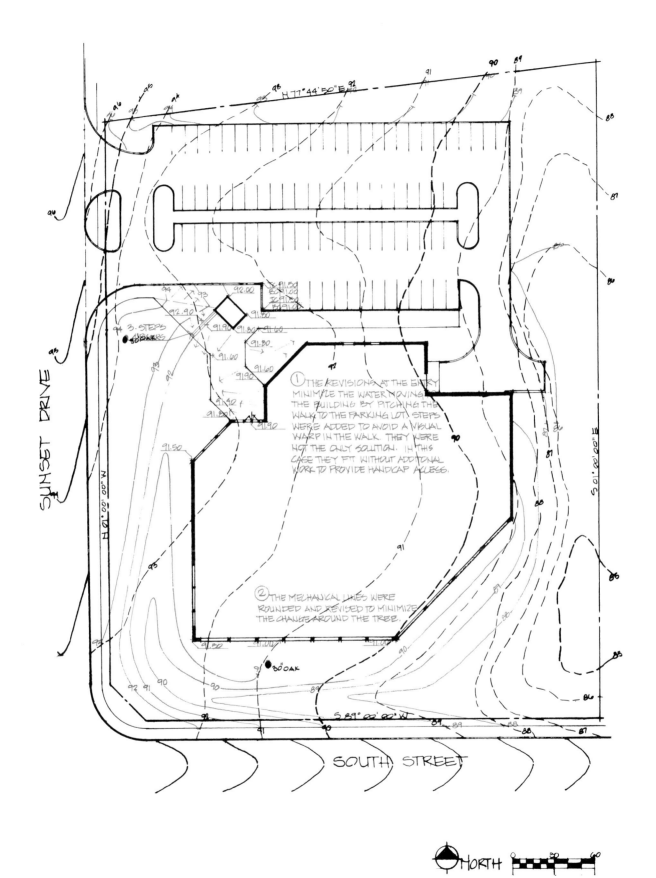

① THE REVISIONS AT THE ENTRY MINIMIZE THE WATER MOVING TO THE BUILDING BY PITCHING THE WALK TO THE PARKING LOT. STEPS WERE ADDED TO AVOID A VISUAL WARP IN THE WALK. THEY WERE NOT THE ONLY SOLUTION. IN THIS CASE THEY FIT WITHOUT ADDITIONAL WORK TO PROVIDE HANDICAP ACCESS.

② THE MECHANICAL LINES WERE ROUNDED AND REVISED TO MINIMIZE THE CHANGE AROUND THE TREE.

SUNSET DRIVE

SOUTH STREET

NORTH

FIGURE 2.68   REFINED SOLUTION

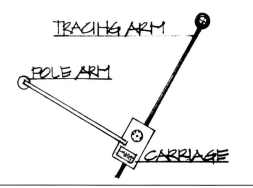

FIGURE 2.69 COMPENSATING POLAR PLANIMETER

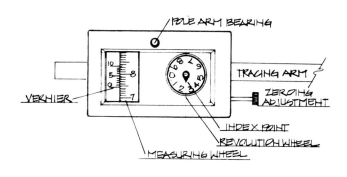

FIGURE 2.70 PLANIMETER CARRIAGE

4. Based on the mechanically constructed contours, the grade around the oak tree is being changed much more than is necessary. This can be changed by visually adjusting the contour pattern in this area. Likewise, the contour of the swale is very rigid and, in fact, could not be done like this unless the swale was paved. These lines should all be redrawn with a smooth freehand line.

Figure 2-68 highlights the revisions that were needed from the review of the grading solution in Figure 2-67. Each of the changes has been referenced by a numbered note on the plan.

1. It was noted that the drainage around the main entrance to the building needed to be looked at for a better solution. Much of the problem was caused by water being routed down the walk to the swale west of the building. The preferred solution is to have the water moving across a walk to one edge. This means that one side of the walk would always be drier.

    If steps are added to the entry area as shown, that will allow just such a solution. Notice the arrows in the illustration are now all moving to the edge of the walk and toward the swale. The proposed sign pylon provides an excellent point to break the grade and all the cross slopes can be held to 2%.

One word of caution about adding steps: Do not forget the legal requirement to provide handicapped access. In most projects used by the general public, the decision to use steps may also necessitate the installation of a ramp, making the step solution very expensive. In this case, a ramp was not necessary since unencumbered access is available to the right of the sign pylon.

2. The other refinement was to change the mechanically constructed contour lines to smooth, freehand lines. This was done for the swale as well as along the north edge of the parking lot, and along the east next to the drainage swale.

There still remains one very important part to the refinement of the grading process: estimating the cut and fill. In most texts, including the first edition of this book, cut and fill computation was treated as a separate topic; however, it is an integral part of doing a good grading solution. So the discussion of cut and fill is included here to clearly show how a grading plan should be refined.

Estimating Cut and Fill

There are two methods that can be used to estimate earth quantities for site work: *the average end area method,* and the *plan planimeter method.* The cut and fill quantities will be computed using both methods for the example problem.

Both methods require the use of an instrument called a *compensating polar planimeter,* or just planimeter. This instrument measures the area of irregular shapes by simply tracing the outline. Technology is changing so rapidly at this time that it is hard to generalize what form planimeters may take. They have already entered the computer age with digital readouts and direct computer interfaces, but the principle of operation and use is still the same as the manual instrument shown in Figure 2-69. The instrument has two parts: the pole arm, and the tracing arm, which is attached to the planimeter carriage. The planimeter carriage houses the measuring mechanism that, regardless of the type of instrument—electronic or mechanical—is very fragile. The carriage should be kept clean and should never be tampered with. The carriage is illustrated in Figure 2-70. On the face of the carriage there are three scales that read out the measurements. The revolution wheel is the tens place of an instrument calibrated in sq in. The measuring wheel, the scale to the left of the revolution wheel, is the ones' place and tenths place. The scale to the far left is the vernier, which reads the hundredths of inches. To read the planimeter begin with the revolution wheel, the measuring wheel, and then the vernier. For example, the reading of the planimeter shown in Figure 2-70 is: 27.47.

When operating the planimeter, the table surface should be level and free of dirt and other materials. Place the pole arm outside the figure to be measured and rest the pole arm in the pole arm bearing on the carriage. Move the tracing arm around the figure to be sure that the position of the instrument will not overextend the arm. Then move the pin or sight glass to a starting point and zero the scales. If the instrument does not have a zeroing device, write down the starting reading and subtract this from the end reading. Always trace in a clockwise direction. If the instrument is moved counterclockwise it will show the wrong reading.

A planimeter reads the actual area measured on a drawing in square inches. This "raw information" must be converted to obtain the equivalent area for the scale of the drawing being measured. For example, if the reading of 27.47 sq in from the example above had been made on a drawing with a horizontal scale of 1″ = 40 ft, then the reading must be multiplied by 1,600 sq ft/sq in to find the equivalent area on the drawing.

One final word about the planimeter. A good instrument is very accurate, but the user must use care to get accurate results. A reading error of 0.10 in at a scale of 1″ = 100 ft is an error of 1,000 sq ft

Estimating Cut and Fill with the Average End Area Method

The average end area method estimates earth volume by taking the arithmatic average of the areas of adjacent sections and then multiplying by the distance between the sections to obtain a volume. By averaging the areas of two adjacent sections, the differences in depths of cut or fill between the two sections are recognized; then, multiplying by the horizontal distance between the sections provides a volume (see Figure 2-71). At the point where the grading ends there is a conform line or a line of no cut, no fill. This is usually at the edge of the property or along a street or some other natural boundary. The volume of earth work between this line and the first section is found by simply dividing the area of the first section by 2 and multiplying by the distance between the no cut/no fill line and the adjacent section. In Figure 2-71 the no cut/no fill line is designated by the number 0. To obtain the volume between that line and section number 1, the area of section 1 would be divided by 2, giving the average sectional area, and then multiplying by the horizontal distance between 0 and section 1.

Quite often the horizontal distance between the last section and the no cut/no fill line will be different from the distance between the other sections. When this occurs, be sure that the proper multiplier is used for the

horizontal distance between those sections. This point will be illustrated in the example problem.

The accuracy of the average end method depends on the horizontal distance between the sections. In other words, an estimate of earth work volume made by taking sections at a 10 ft interval would be more accurate than an estimate made with sections taken at a 100 ft interval. For most site work, sections taken at 50 ft intervals will provide sufficient accuracy.

For the example problem, sections were taken at 50 ft intervals beginning 50 ft from the south property line. The sections are numbered on the plan (Figure 2-68) and the numbers correspond to the numbers of the sections in Figures 2-72 and 2-73. No section is cut at the property line because there is no change of grade at this point. Near the north property line another reference line was drawn that represents another line of no cut/no fill. It lies 38 ft from the plane of section 8.

In most cases such as the problem at hand, it is desirable to exaggerate the vertical scale of the section to obtain more accuracy. This is very important for relatively flat sites where the thickness of an ink or pencil line can introduce a substantial error. For sections that have exaggerated scale, the conversion factor used to convert the planimeter reading from sq in to area in sq ft is the product of the horizontal scale times the vertical scale. In the sections drawn for the example problem, the horizontal scale was 1″ = 30 ft and the vertical scale was 1″ = 2 ft, so the conversion factor is: 30 ft × 2 ft = 60 sq ft. The planimeter readings for each section are multiplied by 60 sq ft/sq in to find the actual area of the section.

The areas between the dashed and solid lines of the sections in Figures 2-72 and 2-73 represent areas of cut or fill. Each of these areas was measured with a planimeter and recorded. As in the illustration, it is

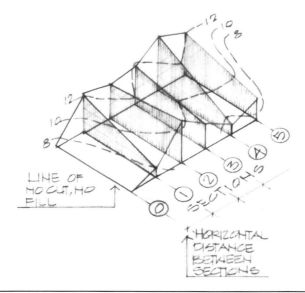

FIGURE 2.71 *AVERAGE END AREA METHOD*

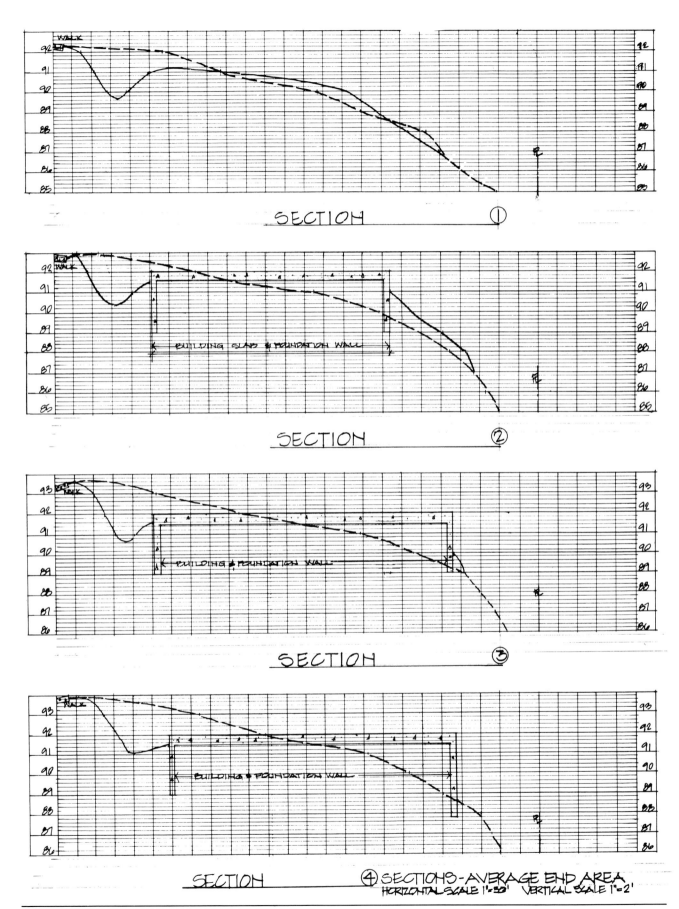

FIGURE 2.72 SECTIONS AVERAGE END AREA (1–4)

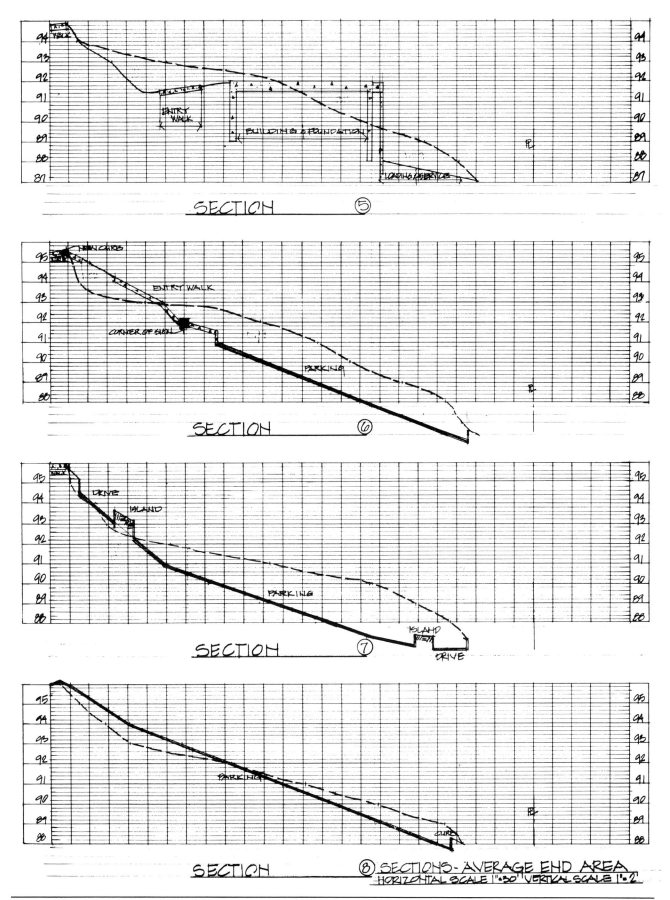

FIGURE 2.73 SECTIONS AVERAGE END AREA (5–8)

recommended that the numbers be referenced separately by section. This will make errors less likely to occur; if they do, they will be much easier to find.

Table 2-8 lists the planimeter readings for each of the sections and areas of cut and fill for each section. The left columns are the planimeter readings in sq in. The columns to the right show the readings converted from sq in to sq ft. The volumes for the cut or fill for each section are calculated as follows.

$$\text{Volume} = 50 \text{ ft} \times \left(\frac{A1}{2}\right) +$$

$$50 \text{ ft} \times \left(\frac{A1 + A2}{2}\right) +$$

$$50 \text{ ft} \times \left(\frac{A2 + A3}{2}\right) +$$

$$50 \text{ ft} \times \left(\frac{A3 + A4}{2}\right) +$$

$$50 \text{ ft} \times \left(\frac{A4 + A5}{2}\right) +$$

$$50 \text{ ft} \times \left(\frac{A5 + A6}{2}\right) +$$

$$50 \text{ ft} \times \left(\frac{A6 + A7}{2}\right) +$$

$$50 \text{ ft} \times \left(\frac{A7 + A8}{2}\right) +$$

$$38 \text{ ft} \times \left(\frac{A8}{2}\right)$$

Plugging the numbers into the expression above, find the volume of cut and the volume of fill as follows:

$$\text{Volume, Cut} = 50 \text{ ft} \times \left(\frac{144.60}{2}\right) +$$

$$50 \text{ ft} \times \left(\frac{144.60 + 112.20}{2}\right) +$$

$$50 \text{ ft} \times \left(\frac{112.20 + 127.20}{2}\right) +$$

$$50 \text{ ft} \times \left(\frac{127.20 + 208.80}{2}\right) +$$

$$50 \text{ ft} \times \left(\frac{208.80 + 231.00}{2}\right) +$$

$$50 \text{ ft} \times \left(\frac{231.00 + 237.20}{2}\right) +$$

$$50 \text{ ft} \times \left(\frac{237.20 + 455.40}{2}\right) +$$

$$50 \text{ ft} \times \left(\frac{455.40 + 94.80}{2}\right) +$$

$$38 \text{ ft} \times \left(\frac{94.80}{2}\right) =$$

Vc = 79,991.20 cu ft. To convert to cubic yards divide by 27.

79,991.20 ÷ 27 = 2,962.64 cu yd

TABLE 2.8 AREAS OF CUT AND FILL— AVERAGE END AREA METHOD

| | Measured Area in sq in | | Actual Area in sq ft | |
Section	Cut	Fill	Cut	Fill
1	1.98,0.43	0.96	144.60	57.60
2	1.87	2.66	112.20	159.60
3	2.12	1.96	127.20	117.60
4	3.48	1.84	208.80	110.40
5	2.26,1.59	0.88	231.00	52.80
6	5.62	1.02	337.20	61.20
7	7.59	0.29,0.51	455.40	48.00
8	1.58	1.69	94.80	101.40

The volume of fill would be found as follows:

$$\text{Volume, Fill} = 50 \text{ ft} \times \left(\frac{57.60}{2}\right) +$$

$$50 \text{ ft} \times \left(\frac{57.60 + 159.60}{2}\right) +$$

$$50 \text{ ft} \times \left(\frac{159.60 + 117.60}{2}\right) +$$

$$50 \text{ ft} \times \left(\frac{117.60 + 110.40}{2}\right) +$$

$$50 \text{ ft} \times \left(\frac{110.40 + 52.80}{2}\right) +$$

$$50 \text{ ft} \times \left(\frac{52.80 + 61.20}{2}\right) +$$

$$50 \text{ ft} \times \left(\frac{61.20 + 48.00}{2}\right) +$$

$$50 \text{ ft} \times \left(\frac{48.00 + 101.40}{2}\right) +$$

$$38 \text{ ft} \times \left(\frac{101.40}{2}\right) =$$

Vf = 34,821.60 cu ft. To convert to cu yd divide by 27:

34,821.60 ÷ 27 = 1,289.69 cu yd

The difference in cut and fill is:

Vc 2,962.64 cu yd
−Vf 1,289.69 cu yd
1,672.95 cu yd excess cut.

The Plan Planimeter Method for Estimating Cut and Fill

This method is generally preferred in office practice since it does not require the drawing of sections. Also, the estimates of volumes is slightly more conservative, in that the volumes are usually somewhat larger or

TABLE 2.9 *AREAS OF CUT AND FILL—PLAN PLANIMETER METHOD*

Contour Elevation	Measured Area in sq in Cut	Fill	Area sq ft[1] Cut	Fill
96	0.37	0.43	333.00	387.00
95	0	2.22	0	1,998.00
94	0.18	2.45	162.00	2,205.00
93	10.53	3.78	9,477.00	3,402.00
92	0.45,19.02	0.93,16.15[2]	17,523.00	15,372.00
91	8.75, 6.84	15.09	14,031.00	13,581.00
90	11.40, 3.44	7.69	13,356.00	6,921.00
89	12.31, 2.70	2.37	13,509.00	2,133.00
88	10.81, 2.13	1.02	11,646.00	918.00
87	4.19	0	3,771.00	0
86	1.14	0	1,026.00	0

[1] Note that since the contour interval is 1 ft the areas read in sq ft are also equal to the volume in cubic feet since the area is multiplied by the contour interval.

[2] The area of fill under the building must be reduced to account for the volume of concrete in the slab. In this case allowance was made for a 6″ slab thickness so the 16.15 sq in represents ½ of the actual measured area.

overestimated. Keep in mind that regardless of the method the volume is an estimate, not an exact quantity. There are only varying degrees of accuracy and accuracy is related more to the scale of the drawing and the precision of the information takeoff.

Preparation for estimating cut and fill by the plan planimeter method requires only a copy of the revised grading plan, showing both the existing and proposed contours. For reference purposes, the areas of cut and fill (represented by the areas on the plan that lie between the existing contour and the proposed contour) are shaded as shown in Figure 2-74. In this case, areas of cut are hatched with vertical lines; areas of fill have horizontal lines. Using color is usually faster and less time consuming than the way it is illustrated here.

To compute the volume of cut and fill with the plan planimeter method, the areas between the existing and proposed contours are measured with a planimeter. The planimeter measurements are then converted to an actual area based on the scale of the drawing. For the example problem, the original drawing scale was 1″ = 30 ft so the conversion factor is 30 ft × 30 ft = 900 sq ft. To obtain a volume, the areas between the old and new contour lines are multiplied by the contour interval. In the example problem, the contour interval is 1 ft, so each of the areas is multiplied by 1 to obtain the volume in cu ft.

The planimeter readings in sq in and the areas in sq ft are shown in Table 2-9.

The total volume of cut is:

V_c = 84,834.00 cu ft or 3,142.00 cu yd
V_f = 46,917.67 cu ft or 1,737.67 cu yd

The volume of excess material is:

    3,142.00 cu yd
  −1,737.67 cu yd
    1,404.33 cu yd

As indicated earlier, the plan planimeter method usually yields a slightly more conservative estimate. Using the two different methods, the amounts of excess cut differ by 267.67 cu yd, which is about 4% of the total earth work volume. This amount of error is not a concern since it could easily be a function of drawing scale and or planimeter accuracy.

It should be noted here that microcomputers are beginning to take a lot of the labor out of doing cut and fill computations. It is recommended that students and professionals alike take the time to become familiar with some of these systems, and see how they can help in the day-to-day office work. A longer discussion of computer applications has been avoided here since the technology is evolving at such a pace that any attempt to discuss their use would be quickly dated.

Balancing Cut and Fill

Having calculated the cut and fill for the problem at hand, and finding that the solution yields 1400-1500 cu yd of excess, the question must be asked: Is this reasonable? The answer is a matter of design judgment, economics, and soil type. Economics will always favor a balance of cut and fill, with a minimum of earth work, i.e., the solution requiring the least amount of earth movement.

Soil type, however, may dictate that the soil under the building pads and other structures be removed and replaced with select (engineered) fill to achieve the necessary compaction. This will usually be required in soils with a high plastic index, or in highly organic soils. Soil "bulking factor" may also be a consideration if large earth quantities are involved. Bulking factor refers to the tendency of a soil to increase in relative volume when it is disturbed, due to loss of compaction. Some soils may expand as much a two times their original volume.

Decisions regarding soil and bedrock conditions should always be made on the basis of a thorough geotechnical investigation of the particular site. Some

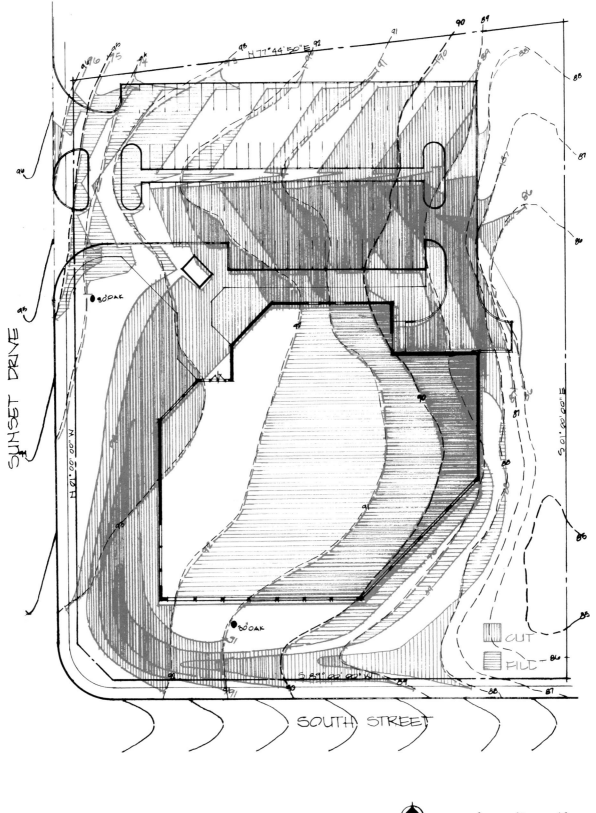

FIGURE 2.74 CUT AND FILL PLAN PLANIMETER METHOD

prior knowledge of the geology of a region will allow the designer to make some preliminary judgments, but the final decision must be based on good engineering information.

The question must be asked: Is the solution at hand warranted based on the overall design concept for the project? If it is, then the removal of the excess fill material can be justified; if not, then a more balanced solution should be sought.

Using the illustrated sample, assume that the soil immediately below the surface is an acceptable foundation and fill material. Then consider the fact that it was necessary to add steps at the main entrance to make the surface drainage work better. Given these two general considerations, the economics of the situation would suggest that a solution which more closely balanced the cut and fill is warranted.

Looking at Figure 2-74, it is easy to see that the majority of the cut material is being generated in the east end of the parking lot, and from the new swale to the west of the building. Therefore, to reduce the volume of cut, the elevations in these areas need to be raised. Having already done a complete solution, a change of this kind is accomplished easily by simply changing to a flatter slope in the lower end of the parking lot, thus reducing the depth of cut. To reduce the cut volume in the new swale somewhat, the finished floor elevation of the building can be raised 0.50 ft. This change also allows the entrance to the building to be handled without the need for steps. The final adjustments made in the plan were as follows:

1. Reduce the slope in the east end of the parking lot from the original 2½% to 2%. The slopes in the upper end of the lot were not changed so that the relationship of the entrance drive and the building entrance would remain approximately the same.
2. Raise the finished floor of the building 0.50 ft to get more positive drainage and remove the need for the steps.

Based on these criteria, the contours were quickly revised and a new cut and fill sheet was prepared to estimate the volumes, Figure 2-75. The method and procedure for doing the revised contours is the same as for earlier examples. If you look at Figures 2-74 and 2-75, you can see that the pattern of the revised contour signatures is the same. They are just spread farther apart in the revised solution. This is why being familiar with the patterns that contour lines take in various situations is a very handy tool in doing grading studies.

Having revised the plan, a new estimate of cut and fill was done as follows, Table 2-10.

TABLE 2.10 REVISED CUT AND FILL

Contour Elevation	Measured Area in sq in Cut	Fill	Area sq ft[1] Cut	Fill
96	0.25	0.44	225.00	396.00
95	1.60	0.39	1,440.00	351.00
94	3.51	0	3,159.00	0
93	3.90	17.20	3,510.00	15,480.00
92	1.00,16.81*	0.46,3.59, 5.84	16,029.00	8,901.00
91	14.92	7.47,2.70	13,428.00	9,153.00
90	8.44	6.52,1.31	7,596.00	7,047.00
89	3.05, 0.29	5.73,0.77	3,006.00	5,850.00
88	0.94, 0.19	3.93	1,017.00	3,537.00
87	0.87	0	783.00	0
86	1.44	0	1,296.00	0

*There is still a deduction of about 0.50 ft of depth under the building slab to account for concrete and sand backfill material.

The revised volumes of cut and fill are:

Vf = 51,489 cu ft or 1,907 cu yd

Vc = 50,715 cu ft or 1,878 cu yd

$$\begin{array}{r} Vf\ 1,907\ \text{cu yd} \\ -Vc\ 1,878\ \text{cu yd} \\ \hline 29\ \text{cu yd additional fill required.} \end{array}$$

This figure of only 29 cu yd difference is an unusually close balance. Usually a difference in volumes of about 10% of the total earth work volume is considered a good balance. It should also be noted that in these figures there was no adjustment made for the required excavation under the parking lot and walks, nor has any allowance been made for the stripping and replacement of topsoil. These adjustments at this point in the grading process are not necessary to know that a reasonable balance has been reached. However, if a detailed estimate was being done for price or construction contract, these quantities would have to be taken into account.

Step Six: Preparing the Grading Plan

Figure 2-76 is the final grading plan prepared for the example problem. There are several things that have been added to this plan that have not shown up on other plans. Rather than discuss the specifics of this particular plan, this final discussion is prepared in the form of a check list that will apply to any grading plan in general. In presenting the check list, specific information will be related to the example problem to be sure each point is clear.

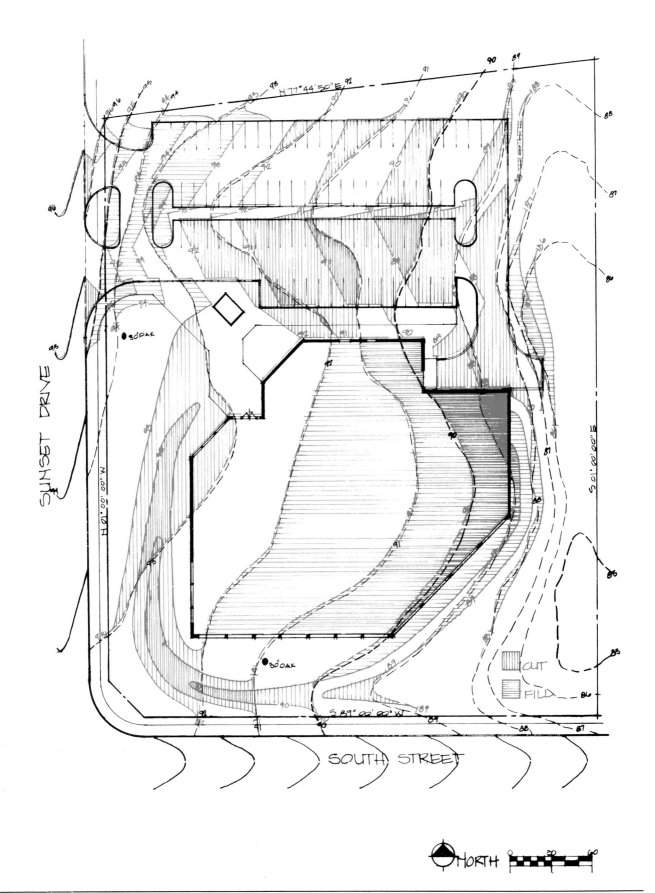

FIGURE 2.75 REVISED CUT AND FILL

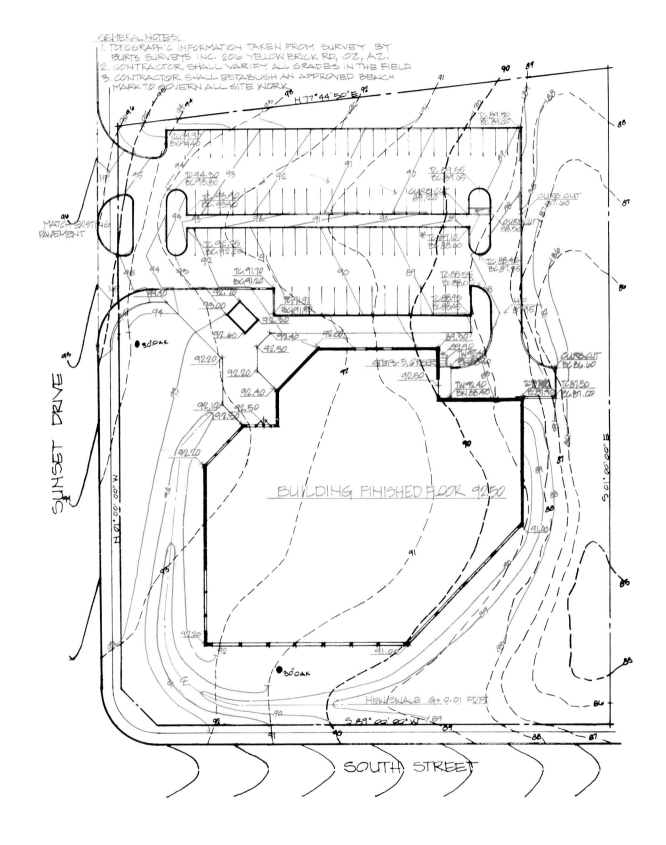

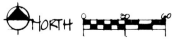

FIGURE 2.76 GRADING PLAN

Grading Plan Check List

- **North arrow and scale.** These should be placed on the plan and not in the title block of the drawing. It is all right to note the scale in the title block, but it should also be on the plan. North arrows should never be placed in a title block. It is usually a good idea to use a graphic scale when there is a chance that the plan may be photographically reduced.
- **Title block.** Every construction drawing should have a title block that carries all the reference information about the drawing. Included should be: the project title, the owner, the consultant(s), the date that the drawing was issued, the dates of revisions, initials of the draftsman, appropriate approvals, and a drawing number. The drawing number should always be in the extreme lower left corner of the sheet to provide ready reference.
- **Drawing Title.** The drawing should be titled appropriately. In most cases grading information and drainage information are combined on the same sheet. In the case of the example, it is only a grading plan because all the drainage has not been addressed at this point.
- **Finished floor elevation.** The finished floor elevation should be given for every building on a site, existing or proposed. This is one of the most important references on the whole plan and the single most important spot elevation.
- **Existing and proposed contours.** Existing and proposed contours are always shown on a grading plan. Contours are important on a plan because they help establish the intent of the plan and make the solution easy to visualize. Also remember that having the existing and proposed contours together is essential to estimating the cut and fill.
- **Appropriate spot elevations.** Spot elevations should be placed at all building corners, the corners of all walks and paved surfaces, all corners in parking lots, at high and low points, at the entrance to any drainage structure, or any point important to the final solution.

When large open areas such as play fields must be regraded, a grid will be placed over the area to be graded with spot elevations at the grid intersection points. The contours and spot elevations on the plan almost always note the finished ground elevation. Contractors are aware of this and they will use the construction details that show pavement thickness, foundation depths, pipe depths, etc., to establish the rough grade of the site. There is such a thing as too much information. Do not overload the plan with extraneous data.

- **Construction notes.** When preparing a grading plan, always note the name of the surveyor and the date of the survey that was used as the base information. The plan should also require that the contractor verify the information in the field and report any discrepancy to the designer. Mistakes in dimensions and layout are not uncommon and must be resolved quickly to avoid costly errors. The contractor should also be required to set a common benchmark to establish a point of common vertical control during construction. Other notes include labeling existing trees, drainage structures, existing structures, and other field conditions that have to be met.
- **Flow lines/center lines of drainage ways.** The flow lines of swales should be clearly marked, and the slope or gradient noted. It cannot be assumed that the contractor will be able to interpret the intent of the contour pattern.
- **Slope arrows.** Sometimes it is desirable to put small slope arrows on the plan to indicate the direction of slope or water flow. These arrows always point down the slope.

The development of skill in doing grading is a matter of practice. The process presented here is a method that works and will help you develop the needed skill quickly. In the learning stages each step should be accomplished in order and in complete detail. Later, as speed and skill are developed, individual shortcuts will be found.

CIRCULATION

DESIGN

Introduction

The system of roads, streets, paths, walks, and parking facilities is one of the most expensive elements of any site development, with the exception of major buildings. While these facilities are functionally essential, they are potentially costly in terms of environmental and visual quality. The purpose of this chapter is to teach the principles of circulation design in a way that will allow the landscape architect to make sound judgments about the location, design, and character of this important site system.

If the aesthetic implications of a street and parking lot system are considered for a moment, it is apparent that this system is one of the most dominant visual parts of any site. The roads, in fact, control the way a development is seen from vehicles by dictating the path, and therefore the sequence, of viewing points. Walks have a similar influence on the pedestrian, but at lower speeds. Once the pattern of streets is fixed, the buildings of the site are oriented directly to the street. The walk and utility systems will most often follow the streets. Since so much of the final form of a site is related to the circulation system, designers must understand how it works, what its limitations are, and how to deal with it responsibly and creatively.

This chapter explores circulation design from a comprehensive point of view and covers both vehicular circulation and pedestrian circulation, with a brief, final section on bicycle ways.

Throughout the discussion of each circulation type it should be remembered that circulation systems are linear spaces that should be scaled to meet the expectations and needs of the users. They are not merely utilitarian space to transport goods, people, and vehicles. Much of our daily experience is related directly to circulation systems: roads, streets, drives, parking lots, walks, paths, etc; therefore, their design is worthy of great attention to planning and detail.

Vehicular Circulation

Vehicular systems are a major force in shaping the visual landscape of a place. Regardless of the kind or order of the vehicle hierarchy, people tend to relate their experience of city spaces in terms of the vehicular circulation pattern. For example, people do not relate the location of an activity center by giving a block number; it is usually given by the street location. Kevin Lynche's work in *The Image Of The City* demonstrates this very clearly by noting how people draw maps of a city. For this reason, the designer must realize that the layout of the street pattern within a project is not just a matter of functional criteria and cost. Design image is also important; good design should help people understand where they are and how to use the system to get where they want to go safely. If the system is functional, it will probably provide a pleasant experience as well. Secondary vehicular circulation systems for bicycles, offroad vehicles, motorcycles, and other specialized vehicles, are usually less dominant form-giving elements at the city scale, but they are no less important. When possible, separate circulation systems for different kinds of vehicles are desirable. Aside from the safety benefits of traffic separation, the scale of the lineal space is much different. This scale difference is a major contributor to the uneasiness experienced by pedestrians or bicyclists on major thoroughfares.

PLANNING HIGHWAY SYSTEMS

Highway systems or networks are almost universally discussed in a hierarchy of six classes. These classes are based on maintenance requirements, traffic volumes, speed, and general design requirements. The most frequently used terms for these six classes are freeway, expressway, arterial, collector, local street, and cul-de-sac.

The freeway is characterized by the interstate highway system. It is a limited-access highway with grade separated interchanges. Its primary function is to move vehicles between cities and across urban areas.

The expressway is usually a multilane divided highway with controlled access. Not all interchanges are grade separated, and some direct property access is provided. The usual means of controlling access to the expressway is by a boundary or frontage road that collects traffic at the side and moves it to selected access points.

Arterial streets are major intracity streets. They provide direct property access at their boundaries, but on-street parking is usually not permitted. Traffic control is usually accomplished by signalized intersections. Traffic speed and volume is less than for a freeway or expressway, but higher than for a collector.

Collector streets are interneighborhood streets. They pick up the traffic from local streets and transfer it to arterial streets. Traffic control is usually provided by stop signs on the side streets and on-street parking may be permitted.

Local streets are short streets that discourage through traffic. They provide direct access to residential properties and permit on-street parking.

The cul-de-sac, or any of its variations, is a short dead-end street with a turnaround provided at the end.

Street Location

Traffic planners and engineers determine street classification by traffic volume estimates. The most widely used measure of traffic volume is ADT, average daily traffic. This is the 24-hour traffic volume average for a 1-year period. Another measure frequently used is DHV, design hourly volume. This is an estimated value based on a projection system or traffic model. The actual method of projection varies from area to area and much estimation is based on an educated guess.

The DHV is usually given as total number of vehicles and accompanied by a T factor, which is the number of trucks in the traffic stream, expressed as a percent. For example, for a DHV of 8000 and a T of .10, we would expect 7200 automobiles and 800 trucks.

Most landscape architects do not become involved with traffic volume projections, so methodology is not a concern; however most municipalities will have an official street map or transportation plan that will be based on some type of traffic study, and any new project will have to conform to the official map.

Once a street is officially classified, the location is governed by two basic criteria: access and topography. Each of these basic criteria have far-reaching implications that the designer must understand. As we have already pointed out, the street corridor provides not only a vehicular channel, but is also the location of other utility services as well. Beyond the mechanical considerations, street corridors also carry with them visual and environmental concerns. In most cases, if the two basic criteria are handled properly, all the problems created by a street can be solved economically.

First and foremost, each part of the circulation network must perform its function. For example, a freeway should provide access to expressways and arterial streets; collector and local streets should provide direct access to adjacent properties. Figure 3-1 illustrates recommendations for the spacing and location of the various street classifications provided by the American Association of State Highway and Transportation Officials.

In addition to providing access for the general public, access must be convenient for service and emergency vehicles. This is why most codes and ordinances will specify maximum block lengths and

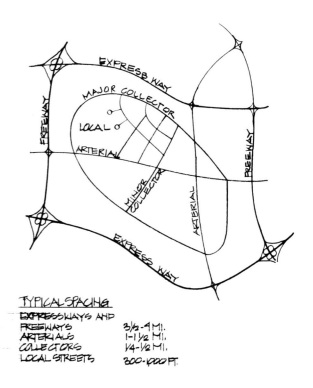

TYPICAL SPACING
EXPRESSWAYS AND
FREEWAYS   3½-4 MI.
ARTERIALS   1-1½ MI.
COLLECTORS   ¼-½ MI.
LOCAL STREETS   300-1000 FT.

FIGURE 3.1 *TYPICAL SPACING OF STREETS BY CLASSIFICATION*

permissible lengths for cul-de-sacs. The gridiron pattern of our older cities usually provided blocks 250 ft to 300 ft long. This arrangement provided excellent accessibility to adjacent properties and land parcels that were easily marketed. As development costs for streets and other utilities increased, it became desirable to reduce the street frontage to save money. This led to what is usually called the "super block" concept. In some cases blocks were as long as 3000 ft between cross streets. Blocks this long have proved unacceptable for emergency vehicle access. The general rule of thumb today is block lengths that are limited to no more than 1000 ft and cul-de-sacs are usually limited to 500 ft depths. Local development codes are usually very specific about these requirements.

One of the most frequently overlooked elements of accessibility is the visual coherence of a street pattern. The gridiron pattern is probably the most visually coherent because it is so easy to catalog mentally, but it can also be visually sterile. It is, therefore, incumbent on the designer to reach some balance between mental image and visual quality in the development of a street pattern, Figure 3-2.

Accessibility criteria must also be balanced with the topography of the site. As the topography becomes more severe, the location and alignment of streets will be more and more influenced by the land form. The reason for this is largely economics. Road construction costs will rise proportionately to the amount of cut and fill necessary to complete the job. Steep cuts or fills also decrease the accessibility of the adjacent property, which in turn decreases the value of the land. The actual topographic placement of streets depends on their classification.

Freeways, expressways, and arterial streets are best located along major ridge lines. A quick look at any large-scale topographic map will confirm this. The major reason for this is that the ridge has the least overall variation in vertical elevation. This minimizes the grading required to fit the road to the landscape. It also minimizes the need for bridges and other major drainage structures.

Collector streets, local streets, and cul-de-sacs, on the other hand, are best located along the lines of natural drainage ways. This is because these streets usually make up an integral part of the surface drainage system. The streets themselves will collect water from abutting properties and transfer it to collection points along the way.

The final location is a balance of functional, visual, and environmental concerns. As we have already mentioned, if the access and topographic considerations have been properly handled, the other problems should fall within the realm of economic feasibility. The importance of these criteria should not be taken

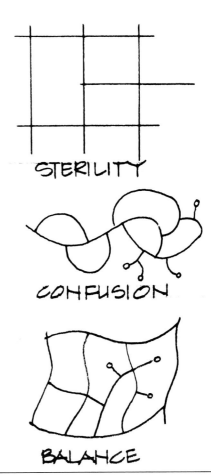

FIGURE 3.2 STREET PATTERN

lightly. There are literally volumes of information dealing with just the visual and environmental problems of streets. Many of these problems are regional or political concerns and cannot be dealt with effectively in the scope of this text.

Design Standards for Streets

To be functional, streets must meet some very basic design criteria. As with grading standards and other rules of thumb, the materials presented here are not absolute; they are general guidelines. Most local governments will have a similar set of guidelines for the development of streets within their jurisdiction.

A street, in plan, is essentially a geometric line composed of arcs (parts of circles) and tangents (straight lines) with a predetermined cross section. Before the actual configuration of the line and cross section can be fixed, however, several things must be considered. It is important to remember that the street is a circulation path for machines that have limitations. Thus, we are designing not only for human performance, but for the performance of the machine as well. The basic criteria that must be determined are outlined below.

TABLE 3.1 MINIMUM RECOMMENDED DESIGN SPEEDS BY HIGHWAY CLASSIFICATION

Highway Type	Design Speed mph
Freeway	70 >
Expressway	60 >
Arterial	45–60
Collector, major	45–60
Collector, minor	40–50
Local	30–45
Cul-de-sac	30 <

Adapted from information in AASHO, A Policy on the Geometric Design Highways and Streets, 1984

Design Speed

The design speed is the maximum safe speed at which an average vehicle and driver can be expected to negotiate the curves and grade of the street. At low design speeds, the curves can be sharper and the gradients steeper. As operating speeds increase, the curves must be longer and slopes decreased. Design speed is usually determined by the road classification; for example, expressway, arterial, or local. The minimum recommended design speeds for the various classifications are given in Table 3-1. The design speed is then used to establish the minimum standards for horizontal and vertical alignment of the street. Horizontal alignment refers to the location and configuration of the street in plan, and the vertical alignment is the configuration of the street in section.

Maximum Gradient

The maximum gradient is the steepest gradient that the vehicles utilizing the street can be expected to negotiate in a normal operating mode. The application of this standard requires some design judgment, because a great deal depends on properly estimating the types of vehicles and understanding weather limitations. For example, the gradients on streets subject to frequent icing will have to be flatter than those in a subtropical climate. Table 3-2 summarizes the operating capabilities of the various classes of vehicles for dry pavement conditions.

Sight Distances

Sight distance is measured from a point 4 in above the pavement to a point 4.5 ft above the pavement. The critical points occur at either a transition to an upgrade or a downgrade. At first glance, a downgrade would not seem critical since the cone of vision includes the uphill portion of the road as shown in Figure 3-3. However, at night the headlights of a vehicle would not reach the uphill portion of the road.

Table 3-3 summarizes the various design criteria in relation to design speed. Keep in mind that the criteria given as minimum are just that. Most frequently it will be desirable to exceed these minimum values. For example, the minimum curve radius for a design speed of 20 mph is 100 ft. While a curve with a radius of 100 ft can be negotiated at 20 mph, it is not, in most cases, visually pleasant or comfortable. Thus, when it is possible, a longer radius should be considered.

Street Widths

Street width varies with the type of traffic, the estimated DHV, the street classification, and the local restrictions. Highways in the freeway and expressway classification are usually multilane divided pavements. Streets in the arterial class are not usually divided, but may be multilane. Collectors, local streets and cul-de-sacs are usually two-lane, undivided pavements, with parking lanes as required. Table 3-4 summarizes and illustrates the cross-sectional dimensions of streets by classification.

Design of the Cross Section

Plans and longitudinal profiles of streets must be supplemented by a cross section of the facility before the design can be built. All too frequently the cross

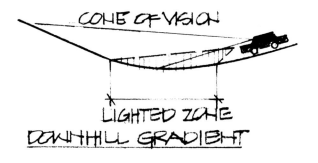

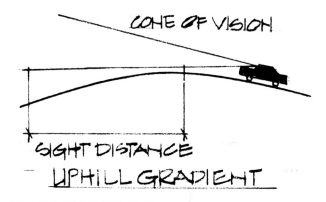

FIGURE 3.3 SIGHT DISTANCES

TABLE 3.2 MAXIMUM GRADIENTS FOR VEHICLES, DRY PAVEMENTS

Vehicle Type	Maximum Gradient In High Gear[a]	Maximum Gradient In Low Gear[b]
Heavy Trucks	3%—33.33:1	5%—20:1
Medium Trucks	3%—33.33:1	7%—14:1
Light Trucks	4%—25:1	17%—6:1
Automobiles	7%—14:1	25%—4:1

[a] The maximum gradient considered safe for operation in iced conditions is 5% for all vehicles.
[b] Gradients of as much as 32% are encountered on local streets in mountainous areas. These cannot be considered all-weather roads.

TABLE 3.3 ROAD DESIGN CRITERIA AS A FUNCTION OF DESIGN SPEED

Design Speed	Degree of Curve		Minimum Radius	Minimum Sight Dist. No Passing	Minimum Sight Dist. Passing	Minimum Vertical Curve L Each 1% Difference	Maximum Gradient
mph	Degrees	R=ft	ft	ft	ft	ft	G
20	57	100.53	100	150	500	10	0.15
30	22	260.45	250	200	600	20	0.12
40	12	477.50	450	275	1,100	35	0.08
50	7	818.57	750	350	1,600	70	0.06
60	5	1,146.00	1,100	475	2,300	150	0.05
70	3	1,910.00	1,600	600	3,200	200	0.03

TABLE 3.4 CROSS-SECTIONAL DIMENSIONS OF STREETS BY CLASSIFICATION

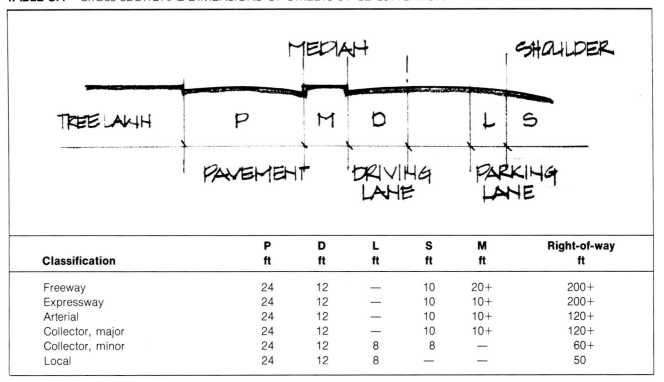

Classification	P ft	D ft	L ft	S ft	M ft	Right-of-way ft
Freeway	24	12	—	10	20+	200+
Expressway	24	12	—	10	10+	200+
Arterial	24	12	—	10	10+	120+
Collector, major	24	12	—	10	10+	120+
Collector, minor	24	12	8	8	—	60+
Local	24	12	8	—	—	50

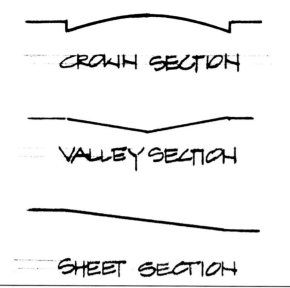

FIGURE 3.4 TYPICAL PAVEMENT CROSS-SECTIONS

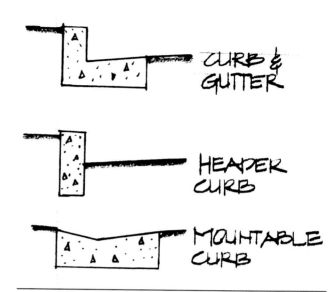

FIGURE 3.5 TYPES OF CURBS

section is thought of only in terms of the actual pavement cross section. This kind of thinking can lead to some rough problems in construction, such as steep intersection slopes and inaccessible lots. The cross section should include the normal pavement data, as well as some reasonable standards for how the transition is to be made to the right-of-way line and then to the adjacent properties. There are three basic cross sections used for street and parking lot pavements: the crowned section, the valleyed section, and the sheet section. These are illustrated in Figure 3-4.

The crowned section is a parabolic curve, which means the slope becomes progressively steeper as the edge of the pavement is reached. The crowned section is used for street and driveway pavements of all types. It is most efficient in keeping the pavement dry without producing the uncomfortable tilting feeling that would result from an even-sided slope.

The valleyed section is most frequently used for parking lots, minor interior streets, and service alleys. It allows the use of single drainage inlets along the center line rather than requiring two inlets as the crowned section does. Valleyed sections should not be used with flexible asphaltic pavements because of the possible damage to the base caused by standing water in the low spots along the center line.

The sheet section is also used for minor service roads and parking lots, because it has the advantage of directing water to single drainage inlets. It can be used with flexible asphaltic pavements, since there is little danger of standing water on the paved surface.

Handling of pavement edges can vary from no treatment at all to very elaborate curb and gutter details. The type of treatment used at the edge of a street depends a great deal on the type of pavement, the drainage system,

and the purpose of the street. Typical curbs are shown in Figure 3-5.

Concrete is a rigid material and as such does not require a great deal of treatment at the edge of the pavement. Usually a slight thickening of the edge of the slab and backfill that will prevent undermining of the pavement are sufficient. Flexible pavements such as asphalt will require more attention to prevent moisture penetration at the edges, which may cause the material to sluff off. Rural roads often rely only on a well-stabilized shoulder that will carry the water away. On urban streets this is not a satisfactory solution, due to the volume of traffic moving over the edge of the pavement. The only satisfactory solution to this problem is to finish the edge with some type of curb structure. The curb can be anything from a flush concrete header or stone to an extruded asphalt curb.

The type of curb used on a street depends upon the drainage system and the adjacent land use. If an underground storm sewer system is used to carry storm runoff, a vertical curb of some type will be used to channel the water in the street to a collection point. If drainage ditches are used to collect storm water, then a flush header will be used for asphalt pavements, or no curb at all for concrete pavements. Vertical curbs are classified in two ways: mountable curbs and nonmountable curbs. Mountable curbs are preferred in residential subdivisions where frequent driveway cuts would be required. This allows access to all properties without the need to break out and rework the existing curb. Nonmountable curbs are used for most commercial, collector, and arterial streets to provide a barrier as well as a more positive drainage channel. The height of nonmountable curbs may run as high as 10 in for extreme cases, but heights over 6 in are seldom justified.

Between the edge of the pavement and the right-of-way (property) line, several things must be taken into account. This zone is usually occupied by utility lines, sidewalks, trees, and light fixtures, plus any access drives that connect adjacent properties. For most situations, any back slope greater than 10% in this area will cause problems. Automobiles "bottom-out" turning into driveways, sidewalk installation is difficult, and erosion becomes a problem; however, most of these problems can be avoided if the differences between existing and proposed grades are well balanced on the profile sheets. Figure 3-5 shows some typical highway sections.

Pavement Design

The types and numbers of vehicles using a road will determine the pavement design. Large volumes of heavy trucks will require much heavier pavements than automobile traffic, and such volumes will also modify the criteria used in conjunction with design speed.

The treatment of the base and the type of pavement to be used in any situation should be based on good geotechnical data for the site. These data will result in recommendations about the preparation and compaction of the sub-base, the material and thickness to be used for the road base, and the type and thickness of the pavement to be used. Actual pavement mixes are usually specified in relation to the standard state highway specification. Each state publishes a standard specification for the construction of roads and bridges; this reference is the best source of technical information on road construction for any region. Within these standard specifications, regional differences in climate, soil type, and geologic structure will be taken into account.

Intersections

To this point, streets have only been considered as lineal corridors moving between two points. We have not as yet considered how access to a street is handled. The at-grade intersection is the cheapest, most practical solution for most local and collector streets; but as volumes of traffic increase, the intersection design becomes more complex. The lowest level of traffic control utilizes the at-grade intersection with some type of control device, such as stop signs or traffic signals. Some of the control systems used for major at-grade intersections are quite sophisticated, utilizing metal sensing devices and computers for operation of the traffic signals.

The next level is the channelized intersection that provides separate lanes for through traffic and lanes for right- and left-turning movements, Figure 3-6.

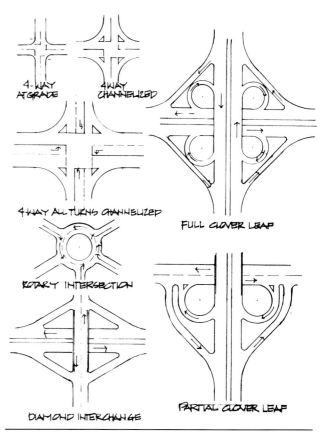

FIGURE 3.6 TYPICAL INTERSECTIONS

A variation of the channelized intersection is the rotary, or traffic circle. This type of intersection has been widely used in European countries, but has not been popularized in this country. Perhaps the reason it is not more widely used is that the average driver is probably not familiar with it and does not use it properly. Since we have had the technological ability to build grade-separated interchanges, rotaries have never been popular.

The grade-separated intersection removes the turning conflicts generated by an at-grade intersection. This type of intersection represents the highest level of control. Grade separations are efficient but very expensive. Because of the high expense factor, grade-separated interchanges are used only on streets with extremely high design volumes, usually expressways and freeways. Figure 3-8 illustrates some typical intersections.

Factors that must be taken into account in the design of an intersection are the ease of turning movements, and safety. The ease of the turning movement depends on the vehicle type and the radius of the corner. The maneuvering characteristics of vehicles and recommended turning radii for intersections are discussed later in the chapter. The safety of an intersection is primarily a function of visibility. If all parts of the intersection are visible, the intersection should be safe. Criteria that will help ensure visibility are outlined in Figure 3-7. For all but the most demanding situations, these criteria should be considered minimum requirements.

Parking and Service Facilities

A street does not terminate at the right-of-way line. Like any utility, it is connected to adjacent properties by means of access drives, parking lots, or service areas. These facilities also have some very specific design criteria that must be met if they are to function successfully.

The design of a parking or service facility is governed by the characteristics of the vehicles that will use it. There are four types of vehicles that must be considered: automobiles, automobile and trailer combinations, long wheelbase trucks and buses, and tractor-trailer rigs.

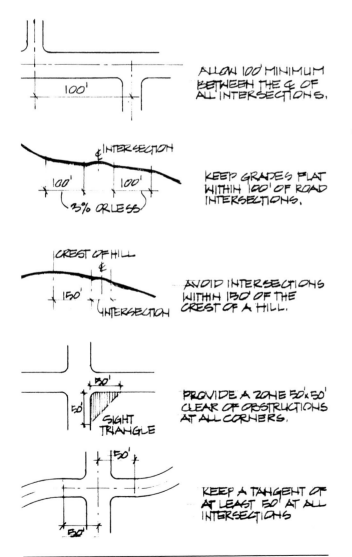

FIGURE 3.7 RULES FOR INTERSECTIONS

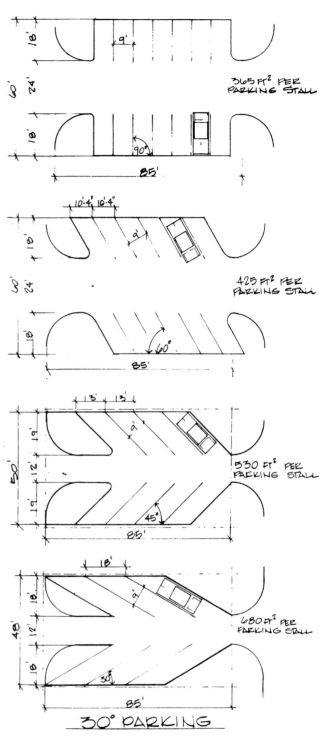

FIGURE 3.8 PARKING LOT LAYOUTS

The design standards for turning radii, land width, maneuvering space, and vertical clearance should always be determined by the largest vehicle that requires access to the space. The vehicles that require the least maneuvering space are automobiles. Long-wheelbase vehicles like buses require the greatest area for maneuvering.

When designing for large vehicles, tractor-trailers, and buses, the best practice is to avoid situations that require backing movements. This is particularly true in the case of boat trailers and recreational vehicles. Backing movements in these vehicles require skill levels that the average driver may not have. Even if the driver does have the skill necessary, these vehicles do not have good rearward visibility, and the lack of visibility can contribute to accidents. When backing movements are required of trailers, be liberal with the maneuvering area and, if possible, avoid backing movements of more than 100 ft.

Since there is so much variation in the performance of vehicles, and because the actual performance depends on the skill of the operator, it is impossible to design for all possible combinations of circumstances. The standards presented here will cover a majority of the common situations, but there is never a substitute for checking the actual conditions.

Parking bays are classified by the angle between the curb and the parking stalls. The angles used are; 90, 60, 45, and 30 degrees. The decision as to which angle is best depends on the available space for parking and the number of vehicles that will require storage. Figure 3-8 illustrates the four basic parking arrangements.

Parking schemes of 30 and 45 degrees are most frequently used when the width of the parking area is restricted. Stalls on both sides of the drive with 30-degree parking can be accomplished comfortably in a space as narrow as 46 ft; 45-degree parking requires a 50-ft width. The circulation in the 30- and 45-degree parking layouts is usually one way, visibility to the rear is good, and the stalls are easy to maneuver into and out of. The disadvantage of these solutions is that they require more paved area for each parking stall: 430–520 sq ft per vehicle.

Probably the most popular scheme is the 60-degree layout, for several reasons. It lends itself to either one-way or two-way traffic, maneuvering in and out of spaces is easier than for 90-degree stalls, visibility for backing is good, and it has a reasonable pavement-to-vehicle-stored ratio: 350–425 sq ft per vehicle.

Ninety-degree parking is usually selected when the number of spaces per square foot of pavement is the critical consideration. From this standpoint it is the most efficient. It should always be designed with two-way traffic because the aisle widths must be a minimum of 20 ft wide for the backing movement.

Some general guidelines for parking design are illustrated in Figure 3-9. Table 3-5 summarizes the recommended turning radii for various street intersections and parking lots.

Horizontal Alignment

The term horizontal alignment refers to the configuration of a roadway in the horizontal plane, or the plan. The alignment is controlled by a desired operating speed (design speed) that, in turn, controls other minimum criteria. These minimum standards are given in Table 3-3. As noted earlier, the plan configuration of a street is made up of straight lines (tangents) and arcs (portions of circular curves). For reasons of safety and visual continuity, not all combinations of arcs and tangents are acceptable, even if they are of the minimum recommended dimensions. For example, two curves in the same direction connected by a tangent is called a broken back curve. A broken back curve is visually awkward and, if design speeds are greater than 30 mph, it can be a safety problem too. If the tangent between the two arcs is short, motorists may fail to straighten their wheels, causing the vehicle to run off the road on the inside of the curve or cross the center line into oncoming traffic. In the event that a broken back curve is necessary, it must be separated by a tangent length of at least 150 ft. Figure 3-10 shows some of the common curve combinations and restrictions for their use.

HORIZONTAL CONTROL

Straight lines are relatively easy to lay out in the field, but circles are quite another matter. The layout of curves requires that some precise information be provided on the plan to ensure that the road will be located correctly. The layout information given for a road or street is always referenced to the center line, (CL). The width of the pavement and treatment of the right-of-way is controlled by typical cross section.

Since the center line will be composed of both straight and curved lines, conventional straight-line dimensioning systems will not always work for streets. Dimensional data for streets are given by a system called "stationing." A station designation is simply a lineal measurement along a center line from some

TABLE 3.5 *RECOMMENDED TURNING RADII*

	ft
Expressway intersections (at grade)	50
Arterial intersections	40
Collector intersections	35
Local intersections	24
Residential driveways	12
Public drives and parking lot entrances with bus and truck traffic	30
Public drives and parking	24
90 degree parking aisles	20
60 degree parking aisles	15
30 and 45 degree parking aisles	12

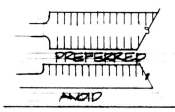

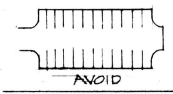

PROVIDE PARKING STALLS
ON BOTH SIDES OF DRIVING
AISLE

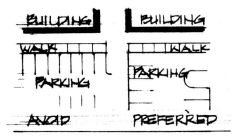

AVOID THE USE OF DEAD-
HEAD LOTS. IF USED LIMIT
TO 12 CAR MAX.

KEEP THE DRIVING AISLES
PERPENDICULAR TO THE
BUILDING IF POSSIBLE

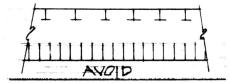

DO NOT MIX PARALLEL
PARKING WITH OTHER
PARKING

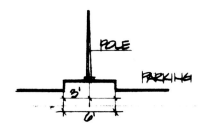

PROTECT STRUCTURES AND
POLES WITH NON-MOUNTABLE
CURBS.

FIGURE 3.9 NOTES ON PARKING

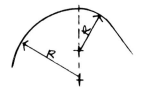

COMPOUND CURVE
SHOULD NEVER BE USED
WHEN DESIGN SPEED IS
MORE THAN 20 MPH.

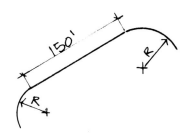

BROKEN-BACK CURVE
THESE CURVES ARE VISUALLY
AWKWARD. IF USED SEPARATE
WITH MINIMUM TANGENT OF
130' AND USE LONG RADIUS

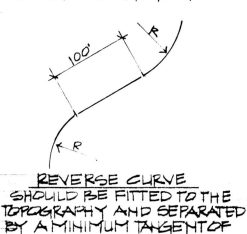

REVERSE CURVE
SHOULD BE FITTED TO THE
TOPOGRAPHY AND SEPARATED
BY A MINIMUM TANGENT OF
100'

FIGURE 3.10 HORIZONTAL CURVES

known point. It is standard practice to place a plus sign (+), between the hundreds place and the tens place. For example, a dimension of 1,250 ft would be written as 12 + 50. This practice stems from the use of a 100-ft-long steel tape, (chain), for doing field layout. So, to a surveyor, the station designation says to go 12 chains and 50 ft. The beginning point in a stationing sequence is designated as 0 + 00. This point is always referenced to an object that can be found in the field. All of the horizontal data are referenced to this point of beginning by angles, bearings, linear dimensions, curve lengths, and curve radii. All of this information must be on the plan if the street is to be properly located.

GEOMETRY OF CIRCULAR CURVES

The geometric terms and symbols used in the computations and recording of circular curve data are shown in Figure 3-11. Also shown are the formulas for solving for each part. The formulas given are machine formulas to make the computations quicker using a small scientific calculator. The symbols and terms are defined as follows:

Arc, (L). L or Arc are the terms used to note the length of a circular curve. Its dimension is given in lineal ft, to the nearest 0.00 ft.

Delta (Δ). The Greek letter delta is used to designate the angle subtended by the circular arc and is shown in degrees, minutes and seconds.

Tangent, (T). The tangent is the distance from the beginning of the circular arc, (point of curvature), the point of intersection between the two lines being joined.

Radius, (R). The length of the radius given in ft to the nearest 0.00 ft.

Point of Curvature, (PC). The point where the arc begins.

Point of Tangency, (PT). The point where the arc becomes tangent with the departing line. Point of curvature and point of tangency are given by station number.

Point of Intersection, (PI). The point where the two connected tangent lines intersect.

Chord, (C). The chord is a line drawn from PC to PT.

Deflection Angle. The angle between the chord and the tangent. The deflection angle is always one-half of the angle subtended by the arc.

Degree of Curve. The angle required for a curve of a given radius to subtend an arc of 100.00 ft, Figure 3-12.

LAYING OUT THE STREET

In the initial phases of design streets are laid out with a freehand line to explore and fit the road to the land form. Every effort should be made to preserve significant trees and natural features. Once this is done, the roads can be drafted mechanically on a plan or on a sheet of plan-profile paper. Plan-profile paper has a blank area at the top of the sheet for drawing the plan and a gridded section at the bottom of the sheet for drawing a section of the street. To construct the street mechanically requires a T-square, triangles, and a compass—preferably a good beam compass. First, draw a series of connected tangent lines that generally describe the freehand line of the study. Use long unbroken lines, not a series of short tangents. Next, the bearings and line lengths should be determined. When this is complete some initial design decisions should be made about the street.

In most cases the street geometry and controls will be influenced by the governmental jurisdiction over the site. Most cities have subdivision ordinances that specify pavement width, right-of-way width, design speeds, minimum curve radii, minimum tangent lengths between curves, etc. These standards vary widely from region to region and should be researched carefully before developing any final documents.

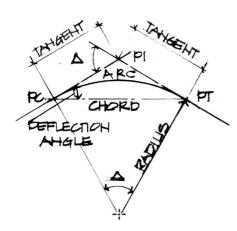

$$T = R \, TAN \, \frac{\Delta}{2} \qquad L = \frac{\Delta R}{57.3}$$

$$C = 2R \, SIN \, \frac{\Delta}{2} \qquad \Delta = \frac{57.3 \, L}{R}$$

$$R = \frac{57.3 \, L}{\Delta} \qquad \Delta^\circ = \frac{5730}{R}$$

FIGURE 3.11 GEOMETRY OF THE CIRCULAR CURVE

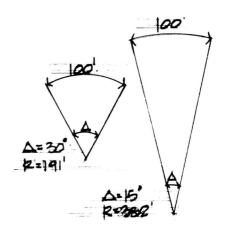

FIGURE 3.12 DEGREE OF CURVE

Once the geometric requirements are known, proceed to construct the curves using a compass to draw the arcs between the tangent lines constructed earlier. To illustrate the procedure for laying out a street, an example problem will be worked through in detail. For the example we will assume a location in Tucson, Arizona. The street will be a small local street in a residential subdivision. Tucson requires a minimum right-of-way for local streets of 50 ft; the minimum curve radius is 300 ft for local streets, with a minimum intervening tangent of 100 ft between curves. Figure 3-13 shows the freehand study for the proposed street. Notice that a number of things controlled the fitting of the new road to the site. It was necessary to parallel the Pima county drainage canal to the north of the site and still have a reasonable lot depth. In addition, it was necessary to align the road with the existing segments of Rosemary Road. While it is not true in all cases, most cities will require that new streets align with existing streets and carry the same name.

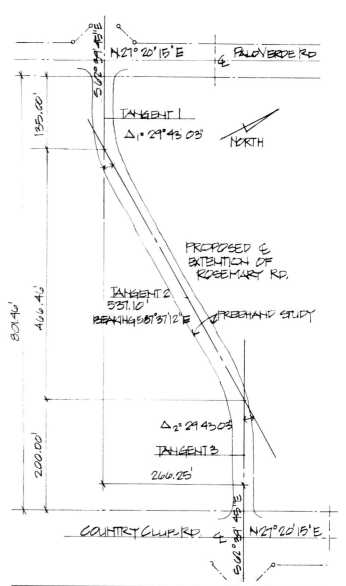

FIGURE 3.14 *FINDING ANGLES, BEARINGS, AND STRAIGHT LINE DIMENSIONS*

The first step is to construct the tangent lines that conformed reasonably to the freehand layout and compute the lengths and bearings of the tangent lines. In this case the lengths of tangents 1 and 3 were scaled off the drawing and recorded. Since the lengths of tangents 1 and 3 are scaled from the drawing, it will be necessary to compute the length of tangent 2 to be sure that the layout of the road will close in the field. The length of tangent 2 is computed using the survey data given on the drawing. The distance between the right-of-way lines of Palo Verde Rd. and Country Club Rd. is 801.46 ft. Notice that the two roads are parallel to each other (the bearings are the same). The length of the line taken perpendicular to the two roads between the two points of intersection is 466.46 ft, Figure 3-14.

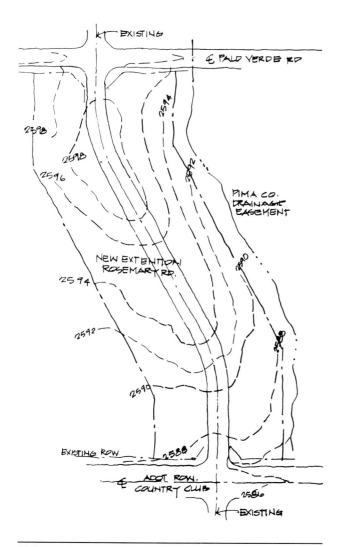

FIGURE 3.13 *FREEHAND STUDY*

Tangent 1 135.00 ft
+Tangent 3 200.00 ft
335.00 ft

801.46 ft
−335.00 ft
466.46 ft

The surveyed distance between the two intersections is 266.25 ft so the length of tangent 2 can be found by computing the hypotenuse of a right triangle:

(466.46 ft^2 + 266.25 ft^2)$^{.5}$
The length of tangent 2 = 537.10 ft

Next find the bearings of the lines. Beginning at Palo Verde Rd., bearing N 27°20′15″E, tangent 1 is 90 degrees to that line so the azimuth (the direction of a line referenced to true or magnetic north) of tangent 1 is:

27°20′15″
+ 90°00′00″
117°20′15″

Since the azimuth is between 90 and 180 degrees, the bearing is in the southeast quadrant, so subtract from 180 degrees as follows:

179°59′60″   (180 degrees is written this way to
−117°20′15″   allow the subtraction function)
S 62°39′45″E

The next task is to find the angle delta.

$$\text{Sine } A = \frac{\text{the distance between intersections}}{\text{tangent 2 (the hypotenuse)}}$$

$$\text{Sine } A = \frac{266.25 \text{ ft}}{537.10 \text{ ft}}$$

Sine A = 0.4957
A = 29°43′02″

The bearing of tangent 2 is:

Azimuth tangent 1 =   179°59′60″
−   62°39′45″
117°20′15″

Since this angle was turned to the left, the angle is subtracted from the azimuth as follows:

Azimuth of tangent 1 =   117°20′15″
−Δ 1 29°43′03″
87°37′12″

The azimuth is in the northeast quadrant so the bearing is:

N 87°37′12″E

Tangent 3 is parallel to tangent 1, therefore Delta 2 and the bearing of tangent 3 are the same as tangent 1 and Delta 1.

The city required a 300-ft minimum radius on all curves, so the 300-ft minimum was elected as the radius. In this case it was appropriate since a larger radius would leave a tangent of less than 50 ft at the intersection of Palo Verde Rd. A tangent of 50 ft is generally considered the minimum for connecting adjacent arcs. This is the zone where the driver must straighten the wheels of the vehicle and then set them again as the next curve is entered.

Figure 3-15 shows the radius points, curves, and straight-line dimensions for the center line of Rosemary Road. Since the radius length was selected, the radius points were plotted by constructing a parallel line 300 ft from each tangent. The point where these lines intersect is the radius point. The arcs were then drawn as shown. Then the tangent lengths were calculated as follows:

$$T = R \text{ Tan } \frac{\Delta}{2}$$

$$T = 300 \text{ ft Tan } \frac{29°43′03″}{2}$$

$$T = 300 \times 0.2653$$
$$T = 79.59 \text{ ft}$$

The tangent length is the same for both curves, so the dimensions for each remaining straight line tangent were computed by subtracting the tangent length of the arc. Then the arc lengths were calculated as follows:

$$L = \frac{\Delta R}{57.3}$$

$$L = \frac{29°43′03″ \times 300 \text{ ft}}{57.3}$$

$$L = \frac{29.7172° \times 300 \text{ ft*}}{57.3}$$

$$L = 155.59 \text{ ft}$$

*Remember when using these machine formulas that degrees must always be used as a decimal rather than as degrees, minutes, seconds. Most good scientific calculators have a function that converts decimals of degrees so no longhand conversion is necessary.

Figure 3-16 shows the new center line of Rosemary Rd. plotted with all of the appropriate information for layout. The locations of the PCs and PTs are given by station number, and all of the other even 100-ft stations are noted. The curve data is displayed to the inside of each curve. Some drawings will show the curve data in a legend, but locating the information near the curve is preferred. The horizontal alignment data is now complete. Figure 3-17 shows a typical plan layout for a local street, with all the stations, curve data, lot lines, and other required information.

Vertical Alignment

Establishing the horizontal alignment is only half the job. To build the street, finished elevations must also be set along the center line. The term vertical alignment refers to the location of the street in the vertical plane.

Vertical alignment is similar to horizontal alignment in that it is a series of tangent lines connected with curve segments. In the horizontal alignment, circular curves were used but in vertical alignment a parabolic curve is used. The parabola differs from a circular curve starting very shallow and becoming steeper as it approaches its middle ordinate. The gradual increas ing and decreas-

ing of slope characteristic of the parabolic curve provides a very smooth transition in vertical grades.

Consider, for a moment, what would happen if no thought were given to vertical transitions. The average automobile will drag the ground if the total grade difference is 9% or more, Figure 3-18. If an abrupt grade difference occurs at the top of a hill, the tendency is for a rapidly moving vehicle to become airborne. Needless to say, each of these conditions is dangerous, and care must be taken to provide a proper transition.

To avoid rough transitions in roads and drives it is recommended that a vertical curve transition be provided any time the difference in two intersecting lines of slope is 3% or greater. The minimum curve length required is based on the algebraic difference in the two intersecting lines of slope. For example, if a street has two intersecting lines of slope, one +5% and the second at −4%, the difference is 9%. If the design speed is 40 mph, find from Table 3-3 that a minimum curve length of 35 ft per each 1% of difference is recommended. Thus 9 × 35 = 135 ft. Keep in mind this is a recommended minimum value and where possible more generous allowances are recommended.

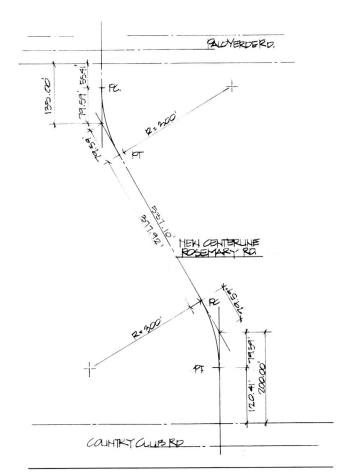

FIGURE 3.15 CONSTRUCTED CURVES AND STRAIGHT LINE DIMENSIONS

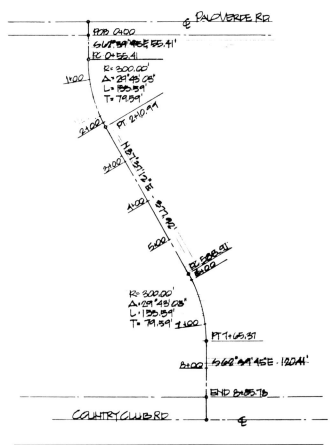

FIGURE 3.16 COMPLETE ALIGNMENT DATA, ROSEMARY ROAD

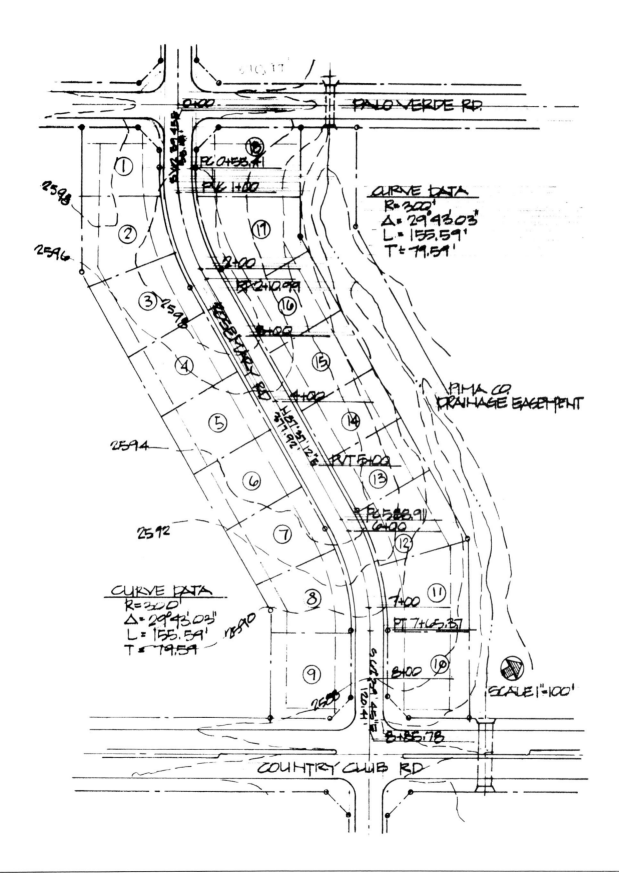

FIGURE 3.17 PLAN, ROSEMARY ROAD

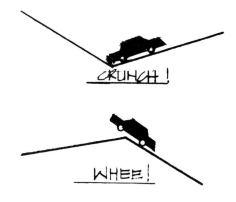

FIGURE 3.18 VERTICAL TRANSITION

GEOMETRY OF THE VERTICAL CURVE

Figure 3-19 illustrates the geometry of the parabolic curve and the associated terms. A curve such as the one shown is actually composed of two different parabolic sections. This is usually the case and is the result of differing lines of slope. In terms of the basic geometry, there are two important things to notice: First, the middle ordinate of the curve lies halfway between the elevation of the PVI (point of vertical intersection) and the middle ordinate of the chord. Second, the middle ordinate of the chord lies halfway between the elevation of PVC (point of vertical curvature), and PVT (point of vertical tangency), unless the curve is symmetrical. In this case, the chord is a level line and PVC, PVT, and the middle ordinate of the chord are all the same elevation.

To lay out a parabolic curve, first construct the two intersecting vertical tangents and drop a perpendicular line through PVI; then lay out half the curve length to either side of this line. Remember, horizontal distances are strictly horizontal (plane) measure, not distances along the sloping lines. Next, project the lines up to their points of intersection with the slope lines, Figure 3-21. After the curve is laid out, points of elevation must be computed along the curve. To illustrate the procedure for computing the vertical curve we will continue with the same example used earlier to illustrate horizontal alignment.

The first step was to plot a profile of the center line of Rosemary Rd., as shown in Figure 3-20. Since a street profile is a section taken along a curved line, it is necessary to use a tick sheet or dividers to transfer the dimensions from the plan to the profile. A tick sheet is simply a piece of scrap paper with a straight edge that is used to mark distances and elevations along the center line of the street. The sheet is rotated in very short tangent sections using tick marks to note the point of each rotation, Figure 3-21. This is a handy tool

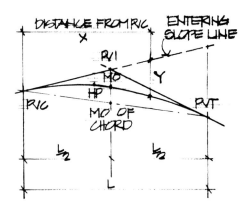

L · LENGTH OF CURVE
Mo · MIDDLE ORDINATE OF CURVE
PVC · POINT OF VERTICAL CURVATURE
PVT · POINT OF VERTICAL TANGENCY
PVI · POINT OF VERTICAL INTERSECTION
X · DISTANCE FROM PVC
Y · OFFSET FROM ENTERING SLOPE
LINE TO CURVE
d · DIFFERENCE IN SLOPE
$$Y = \frac{X^2 d}{2L}$$

FIGURE 3.19 GEOMETRY OF THE PARABOLA

since the tick sheet can be taped down below the profile sheet and the information projected directly onto the profile paper.

When the profile is completed, the new vertical alignment is generalized by constructing a series of intersecting vertical tangent lines, as shown in Figure 3-20. It can be seen from the profile that there will be a reasonable balance in cut and fill, and that the deepest cut or fill will be about 2 ft. You will also note that the area to the right of station 3 + 00 was generalized to a single grade line rather than two or three tangents. This is preferred since several short changes in slope will not be visually pleasant or comfortable to drive on.

Once the vertical tangent lines are drawn the gradient of each line is determined.

Vertical Tangent 1
from station 0+00 to station 3+00

L = 300 ft
D =   2600.40 ft
    $-$2597.40 ft
        3.00 ft

$$G = \frac{D}{L}$$

$$G = \frac{3.00 \text{ ft}}{300 \text{ ft}}$$

$$G = 0.01$$

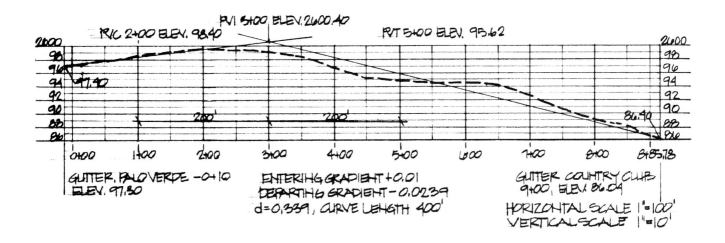

FIGURE 3.20 PROFILE, ROSEMARY ROAD

Vertical Tangent 2
from station 3+00 to station 8+85.78

L = 585.78 ft

$$D = \begin{array}{r} 2600.40 \text{ ft} \\ -2586.40 \text{ ft} \\ \hline 14.00 \text{ ft} \end{array}$$

$$G = \frac{D}{L}$$

$$G = \frac{14.00 \text{ ft}}{585.78 \text{ ft}}$$

$$G = -0.0239$$

(the minus designation indicates a downhill gradient)

Now find the algebraic difference between the two intersecting vertical tangents:

$$(+0.01) - (-0.0239) = 0.339$$

If a design speed of 40 mph is assumed, from Table 3-3 we find that 35 ft of curve are recommended for each 1% difference; thus, 35 ft × 3.39 = 189.65 ft of curve is the minimum. As noted earlier, however, these are minimums; so, for the example, a 400-ft curve was elected. This provides a much smoother transition.

The formulas for computing the offsets from the extended entering slope line to the vertical curve are given in Figure 3-20, but since so many different computations are required to plot several points on a curve, it is handy to use a computation sheet such as the one shown in Figure 3-22. This sheet orders all the data and makes it very easy to check for errors. In most cases, elevations for vertical curves are plotted at 50-ft intervals along the curve. So the 400-ft curve would be laid out as shown in Figure 3-20, and elevations

computed at 50-ft intervals beginning at station 1+00. The completed vertical curve data sheet for the example problem is shown in Figure 3-23.

Once the data sheet is complete the curve can be plotted as shown in Figure 3-24. Notice that the offsets computed using this method *are all measured from the entering slope line!* In this case, the vertical curve occurs at a crest so the offsets are subtracted from the elevations of the entering slope line. If it had been a sag curve, a curve that changes from a downhill slope to an uphill slope, then the offsets would be added to the grades of the entering slope line.

The final step is to note the station of the high point or low point on the curve. This is important since it does not fall at the middle ordinate on a curve that is

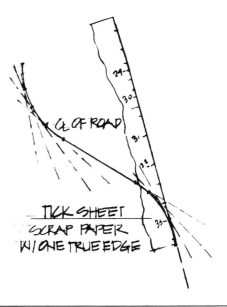

FIGURE 3.21 THE TICK SHEET

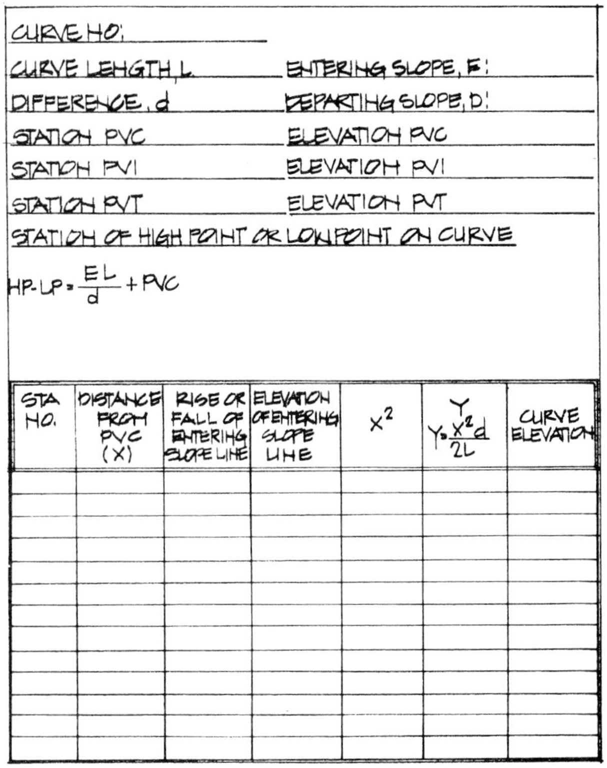

Figure 3.22 (blank data sheet):

CURVE NO:
CURVE LENGTH L _____   ENTERING SLOPE, E: _____
DIFFERENCE, d _____   DEPARTING SLOPE, D: _____
STATION PVC _____   ELEVATION PVC _____
STATION PVI _____   ELEVATION PVI _____
STATION PVT _____   ELEVATION PVT _____
STATION OF HIGH POINT OR LOW POINT ON CURVE

$$HP\text{-}LP = \frac{EL}{d} + PVC$$

STA NO.	DISTANCE FROM PVC (X)	RISE OR FALL OF ENTERING SLOPE LINE	ELEVATION OF ENTERING SLOPE LINE	X^2	$Y = \frac{X^2 d}{2L}$	CURVE ELEVATION

FIGURE 3.22 VERTICAL CURVE DATA SHEET

Figure 3.23 (data sheet for Rosemary Road):

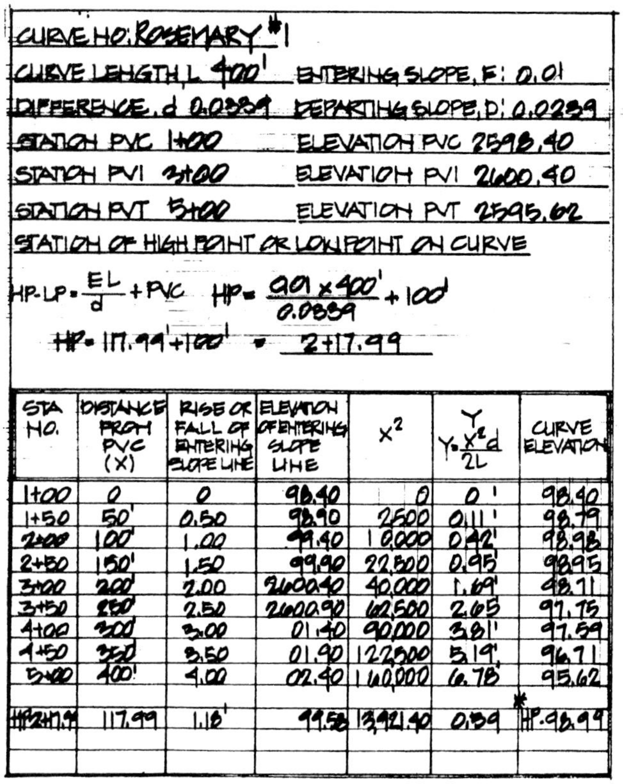

CURVE NO: ROSEMARY #1
CURVE LENGTH L 400'   ENTERING SLOPE, E: 0.01
DIFFERENCE, d 0.0339   DEPARTING SLOPE, D: 0.0239
STATION PVC 1+00   ELEVATION PVC 2598.40
STATION PVI 3+00   ELEVATION PVI 2600.40
STATION PVT 5+00   ELEVATION PVT 2595.62
STATION OF HIGH POINT OR LOW POINT ON CURVE

$$HP\text{-}LP = \frac{EL}{d} + PVC \qquad HP = \frac{0.01 \times 400'}{0.0339} + 100'$$
$$HP = 117.99' + 100' = 2+17.99$$

STA NO.	DISTANCE FROM PVC (X)	RISE OR FALL OF ENTERING SLOPE LINE	ELEVATION OF ENTERING SLOPE LINE	X^2	$Y = \frac{X^2 d}{2L}$	CURVE ELEVATION
1+00	0	0	98.40	0	0	98.40
1+50	50'	0.50	98.90	2500	0.11	98.79
2+00	100'	1.00	99.40	10,000	0.42	98.98
2+50	150'	1.50	99.90	22,500	0.95	98.95
3+00	200'	2.00	2600.40	40,000	1.69	98.71
3+50	250'	2.50	2600.90	62,500	2.65	97.75
4+00	300'	3.00	01.40	90,000	3.81	97.59
4+50	350'	3.50	01.90	122,500	5.19	96.71
5+00	400'	4.00	02.40	160,000	6.78	95.62
HP 2+17.99	117.99	1.18	99.58	13,921.40	0.39	HP 98.99

FIGURE 3.23 VERTICAL CURVE DATA SHEET FOR ROSEMARY ROAD

not symmetrical. For the example problem, the station of the high point of the curve is:

$$HP = \frac{EL}{d} + PVC$$

$$HP = \frac{0.01 \times 400}{0.0339} + 100 \text{ ft}$$

$$HP = 117.99 \text{ ft} + 100.00 \text{ ft}$$

The station of HP is $2 + 17.99$

In most cases the station of the high point of a curve is not nearly as important as the low point in a sag curve, since some provision will usually be necessary to handle storm water at the low point.

The need for vertical curves is not limited only to streets. Drives, access ramps, and parking lots should also be laid out with vertical transitions in mind. In fact, this is where the landscape architect will most frequently encounter the need to use the vertical curve.

SUPERELEVATION

Superelevation is the rotation of the pavement surface around the center line to counteract the centrifugal force of a moving vehicle turning a curve. Supereleva-

tion is seldom needed at low design speeds, but is often used on long access drives, such as those associated with bus access for schools, or on park roads. The accepted standard for finding the maximum superelevation required is:

$$e = \frac{V^2}{15R} - f$$

Where:

e = superelevation in ft/ft
f = the side friction factor (the ability of the vehicle to hold the pavement at an average speed and pavement condition)
V = the speed in mph
R = the radius of the curve

The value of the side friction factor is a function of the design speed of the curve. The maximum value of e, the superelevation, is a function of climatic conditions, and development adjacent to the street that might limit speed. The values of f and the maximum recommended values of e are given in Table 3-6.

To illustrate the application of superelevation, consider the park road in Figure 3-25. The road makes

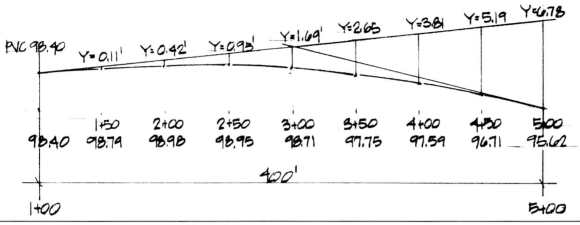

FIGURE 3.24 PLOTTING THE VERTICAL CURVE

a sharp turn with a relatively short radius. This is a place where superelevation is appropriate. To find the value of *e* for this case write as follows:

$$e = \frac{V^2}{15R} - f$$

Assume a design speed of 40 mph and, from Table 3-6, find that *f* has a value of 0.15; thus:

$$e + 0.15 = \frac{40 \text{ mph}^2}{15 \times 477.5 \text{ ft}}$$
$$e + 0.15 = 0.2234$$
$$e = 0.2234 - 0.15$$
$$e = 0.07 \text{ ft/ft}$$

Notice in Table 3-6 that the maximum recommended value is 0.10 and the minimum is 0.06. The minimum value would be used where there was development or climatic conditions, such as ice and snow, that would reduce the relative friction factor or pose some hazard. In this case there is no such hazard so the computed value is valid.

TABLE 3.6 SUPERELEVATION VALUES FOR SELECTED SPEEDS AND SELECTED VALUES OF F

Design Speed mph	e ft/ft	f ft/ft	e + f ft/ft
40	0.06	0.15	0.21
max	0.10	0.15	0.25
50	0.06	0.14	0.20
max	0.10	0.14	0.24
60	0.06	0.13	0.19
max	0.10	0.13	0.23

Adapted from AASHO, *A Policy on Geometric Design of Highways and Streets*, 1984.

When laying out the superelevation, the transition is made in the straight road sections leading to the curve, called runoff zones. Full superelevation is reached at the PC and maintained to PT and then the transition is repeated. Figure 3-25 illustrates the layout of superelevation.

Pedestrian Ways

Just as the vehicular system is the force that shapes the cityscape, the pedestrian circulation system is a major force in shaping the landscape at the project scale. The way a site or group of buildings is perceived is largely a

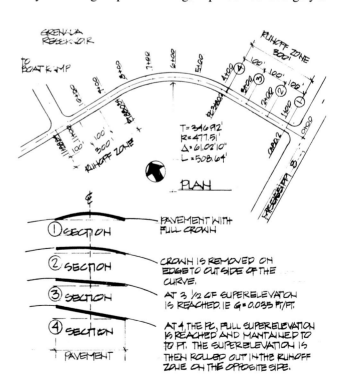

FIGURE 3.25 LAYOUT OF SUPERELEVATION

function of the position of the viewers as they move along a circulation system.

The scale of pedestrian spaces is much smaller than that of the vehicular circulation system and, because movement through them is much slower, detail becomes increasingly important. Much more attention is required in the definition of the movement corridors, views, transition spaces, and access points. Mechanical considerations are no less important with respect to steepness of slopes, transition grades with ramps and steps, intersections, and the materials used in construction.

The design and layout of pedestrian circulation systems is much less exacting but no less important than the street. Stop and consider for a moment that most all projects are experienced by people on foot. The impressions of a park, a group of buildings, a campus, or a shopping center is largely a matter of how it is seen from the eye level of a pedestrian. If the access is obstructed or circuitous, if the walks are steep and steps are uncomfortable, the experience of the place is not going to be pleasant. On the other hand, if the system of access is well done, with attention to detail, the experience of arriving can be pleasant and exciting.

Another very important part of the pedestrian circulation system in any project is the provision of barrier-free access. The law requires that all new construction be free of architectural barriers to the disabled. A detailed discussion of barrier-free design is beyond the scope of this text; however, meeting these barrier-free design requirements is the responsibility of the site designer. During the course of this discussion several of the more important and common requirements will be noted.

The most important design criterion for pedestrian ways is the slope of the walking surface. A discussion of various types of walks and steps follows.

Longitudinal Slopes. The most comfortable slopes for walks lie between 1% and 5%. Above 5%, most pedestrians will begin to feel the slope if it is carried over any distance. For short distances slopes of up to 10% can be used so long as there is no need for handicapped access. Where ice and snow are common, 6% is the recommended maximum, Figure 3-26.

Handicapped Slopes. Handicapped ramps that have a rise of 6 in or less can have a slope of 10%. For vertical changes of greater than 6 in the maximum slope is 8.33%, (12:1), Figure 3-27. If the vertical change is greater than 3 ft then the ramp must be broken with landings, generally one landing for each vertical change of 3 ft. Ramps must be 4 ft wide and have railings on both sides.

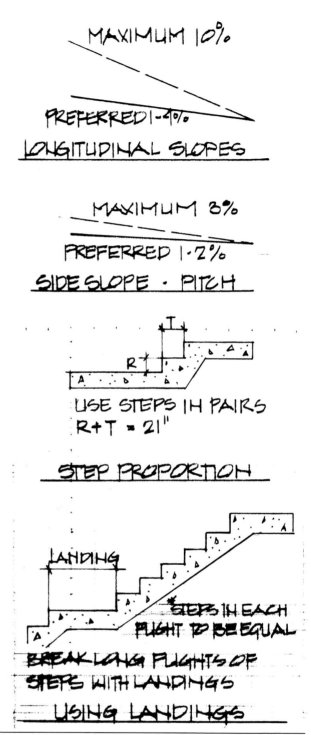

FIGURE 3.26 WALKS AND STEPS

Side Slope. The side slope, or pitch, on walks should be between 1% and 3%. Side slopes greater than 3% become noticeable and are very uncomfortable.

Steps. Outdoor steps are proportioned differently than for interior steps. In general, lower risers of 4 in to

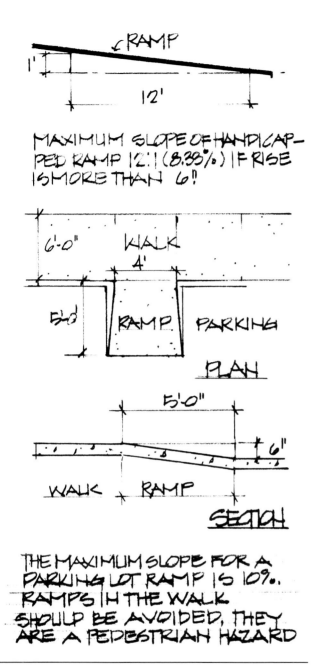

MAXIMUM SLOPE OF HANDICAP-
PED RAMP 12:1 (8.33%) IF RISE
IS MORE THAN 6"

PLAN

SECTION

THE MAXIMUM SLOPE FOR A
PARKING LOT RAMP IS 10%.
RAMPS IN THE WALK
SHOULD BE AVOIDED, THEY
ARE A PEDESTRIAN HAZARD

FIGURE 3.27 HANDICAPPED RAMPS

Materials. The materials used on pedestrian surfaces outdoors should be considered carefully. No slick or polished finishes should ever be used. This includes materials like ceramic tile, steel trowel finished concrete, terrazzo, and polished stones. Even small amounts of moisture on these surfaces can make footing treacherous. Always try to select materials and finishes that will provide positive footing in all weather conditions.

Material texture is also another important consideration. Any material used on a walk should be relatively smooth. The aggregate size used in exposed aggregate pavements should be reasonably small, on the order of ¼ to ⅜ in. Larger rock makes a very uncomfortable surface. Sharp aggregates should also be avoided.

Bicycle Ways

The bicycle has become very popular as a means of transportation and recreation. Unfortunately, the bicycle is not a vehicle that mixes well with motorized vehicles or with pedestrians. The motorized vehicle is a hazard to the cyclist, and the cyclist poses a hazard to the pedestrian. The obvious solution to the problem, of course, is to provide totally separate paths for the three different types of traffic but, in most cases, the cost is prohibitive; however, on new projects the relative cost as a percentage of the overall development cost can be quite low in comparison to the amenity value, if the bicycle is considered early in the planning stages.

Many of the publications that deal with standards for bicycle paths and systems deal with the problems by marking paths along streets, providing special signage, and other markings. For the most part, these have proved to be stop-gap measures at best, and in some cases unworkable. The current trend seems to be to take the bicycles off the streets in urban areas and put them on the walk system adjacent to the streets. The thinking now seems to be that less serious injuries occur from bicycle-pedestrian incidents than from bicycle-motor vehicle incidents. The other considerations that seem to be prompting this move is that the design criteria for bicycles is more compatible with those of pedestrian ways. Some of the general design considerations for bicycles are outlined below.

Longitudinal Slopes. Long runs with gradients in excess of 5% should be avoided if possible. Any gradient greater than 3% is going to be noticeable to the average cyclist. This does not mean that slopes should be avoided, since many people use bicycles for exercise.

5 in are preferred. The proportion of rise to run should be that the rise plus the run equals 21 in. Thus, a step with a 5 in riser would have a tread length of 16 in. This particular proportion is one of the most comfortable.

For safety reasons, steps should always have a minimum of two risers. A single riser may not be seen and might cause people to fall. Likewise, long runs of steps should be broken by landings. A good rule of thumb is that any time the number of risers exceeds a total of 12, a landing should be provided if at all possible, Figure 3-26.

Also, some change in topography adds variety and character to a bikeway.

Side Slopes.   The pitch of a bike path should be 2%. This will get the water off the surface without any noticeable effect on bicycle performance. If possible, a crowned section is preferred, similar to a road.

Width of Lanes.   About 3 ft of width should be provided for each lane of bicycle traffic. A width of 7 ft is preferred for a path with two-way traffic.

Materials.   The material for bicycle paths should be some type of cemented material: concrete, asphalt, or synthetic material. Loose materials such as gravel or clay do not provide a stable riding surface, and are difficult to maintain.

The joints and seams in materials must always be perpendicular to the direction of traffic and as narrow as practical, since bicycle tires have a tendency to follow these grooves and cause spills. Other structures like meter boxes, drain inlets, or manhole covers should be located outside the path if possible. If they must be in the path they should be set level with tight, smooth surface covers. In the case of drainage inlets, the slots in the cover should be narrow and perpendicular to the flow of traffic.

STORMWATER
MANAGEMENT AND
DRAINAGE DESIGN

Introduction

Site designers must consider all the water moving onto and through a site at or below the surface. Water may enter a site as precipitation, surface runoff, or as subsurface flow. Each of these water sources must be taken into account as a design solution is developed. Site hydrology is very important to the site designer because it will usually affect the final spatial form of a project.

To deal effectively with site drainage issues it is necessary that the landscape architect have some general knowledge about hydrology and hydraulics. The sciences of hydraulics and hydrology are highly specialized areas of study that deal with fluid mechanics, and the hydrologic cycle. A basic knowledge of hydraulic principles is important to understanding how water behaves as it flows over the surface, in pipes, and in other open channels, a general knowledge of hydrologic principles is essential to understanding how water is cycled and the relationships between land form, soils, geology, and water.

This chapter provides a simplified approach to the application of both hydraulic and hydrologic principles as they affect the traditional practice of landscape architectural design. It begins with an overview of some of the contemporary stormwater management issues and problems that affect the decision-making process of site design. Then, two generally accepted methods of doing hydrologic and hydraulic analysis are introduced along with appropriate examples of their application. The final part of

the chapter is devoted to some general discussion of drainage materials and structures. All of the material presented is intended to give the reader a general background in the principles, vocabulary, and application of drainage design and stormwater management technology. Much of what is presented is very general, however, and for this reason students are encouraged to consult other reference materials cited in the bibliography for more information and detailed explanations of principles and methods used in this text.

Contemporary Issues in Stormwater Management

Design decisions about site drainage must be made with a broad understanding of the hydrologic system of the region. In this discussion, some of the more important regional issues will be addressed to provide a general background and help the student appreciate the need to master the technical material that follows.

DRAINAGE PROBLEMS: CAUSE AND EFFECT RELATIONSHIP

Site drainage poses a set of five interrelated problems: flooding, soil erosion, sedimentation, pollution, and interference with groundwater recharge. In our urban centers, the occurrence of most of these problems is most often related to new construction. The net effect of a construction project is to change the variables in the existing hydrologic system, which in turn results in some modification to the operation of that system. Some common cause/effect relationships that are important to the discussion at hand are outlined here.

Changes in Infiltration

Infiltration is the movement of water from the soil surface into the soil. The infiltration rate or infiltration capacity of the soil is the maximum rate at which water will enter the soil, measured in inches per hour. Infiltration capacity depends on a number of different variables but, for the most part, it is related to the composition and permeability of the ground surface. Construction projects almost invariably reduce the surface permeability by the addition of paved surfaces: streets, buildings, parking facilities, and other impermeable materials. The net result is a decrease in infiltration and an increase in surface runoff. Loss of infiltration will usually contribute to an increase in downstream flooding, and a direct decrease in on-site groundwater recharge.

Changes in Hydrologic and Hydraulic Character

The addition of structures, or any change to the existing surface, results in a change of the hydrologic and hydraulic characteristics of the site. More simply put, changes at the surface change the way water flows on, and through, the site. Most construction has the net effect of increasing the hydraulic efficiency of the surface. This means that water is transported across the site faster, which can further exacerbate any problems of downstream flooding and on-site groundwater recharge. The concentration and increased velocity of surface flow can also increase the potential for surface erosion, which is directly related to problems of pollution and sedimentation. The most severe erosion and sedimentation problems are usually encountered during the construction period of a project, but designers must also be alert to potential long-term hazards such as steep slopes or existing, unlined drainage channels that may require additional treatment.

Increased Pollution Potential

The increased pollution potential is the result of numerous variables. Initial construction is almost unavoidably going to contribute to some increased erosion and sedimentation, unless special measures such as siltation ponds, grading, and concurrent revegetation are taken. Simply making a site accessible increases the pollution potential. Vehicles contribute gas, oil, and other chemical pollutants. Buildings bring

with them the potential of further pollution from the generation of simple household waste and trash to more complex chemical wastes that might be associated with building maintenance or manufacturing processes.

GOALS AND OBJECTIVES OF STORMWATER MANAGEMENT PROGRAMS

The current interest and commitment to the control of urban stormwater problems is mostly related to amendments passed to the Federal Water Pollution Control Act in 1972, followed by passage of the Federal Flood Disaster Protection Act of 1973. The Flood Disaster Protection Act provided for the National Flood Insurance Program, which is administered by the Federal Emergency Management Agency. Under this act, real property located in designated flood hazard areas cannot qualify for federally insured financing or federal grants unless the property is covered by flood insurance. The requirement to have flood insurance is also an effective means of alerting prospective buyers to the potential flood hazard.

In addition to the Federal Emergency Management Agency, three other federal agencies play a major role in stormwater management: U.S. Army Corps of Engineers, Soil Conservation Service, and U.S. Environmental Protection Agency.

The Army Corps of Engineers is primarily responsible for the construction and maintenance of major flood control structures, and the identification and designation of floodplains along major rivers and their tributaries. Until recently, federal policy prevented the Corps from using federal funds for the development of nonstructural flood control projects, such as the aquisition of floodplain. Now Congress has authorized the Corps, and other federal agencies, to pay up to 80% of the cost of nonstructural flood control projects.

The policies of the U.S. Department of Agriculture Soil Conservation Service (SCS) have also shifted away from the traditional cost-shared projects to a more comprehensive technical assistance policy on land treatment watersheds. The major shift in policy is the extension of SCS programs and funding activities into urban fringe areas. The primary difference between the activities of the Corps of Engineers and the SCS is the scope and size of their projects, and the level of funding and control. The Corps of Engineers owns and operates all of its projects, while the SCS limits its activities to technical services in planning, design, and construction, and limited funding participation. Of the federal agencies the nature and flexibility of the SCS programs makes them the most responsive to the management needs of local governments.

The primary role of the Environmental Protection Agency (EPA) is to monitor, restore, and maintain the quality of the country's water resources. The policies of the EPA are usually administered by an agency of the state government with the sanction and under the direction of EPA.

Even though there is a great deal of involvment and interest in stormwater management at the federal level, the ultimate responsibility for most stormwater management programs falls to the city and county governmental units. For the most part, they are responsible for identifying the needs unique to the local environment and developing programs that will satisfy those needs.

The primary goal of any stormwater management program is the control and mitigation of flooding and associated problems. The better and more successful programs approach the problems in a comprehensive manner that is based on the premise that floodplains are easements prescribed by natural, rather than statute, law. They also take into account that management measures must recognize the total watershed, not just the political boundaries.

In working toward the goal of flood control, other problems of pollution, erosion, sedimentation, and groundwater protection can be corrected. This does not mean that flood control alone solves the other problems; it means that the methods used to solve the flooding problems can, and should, address the other issues as well. The following are some examples of how these measures are complementary.

Runoff control structures can, if properly located and designed, act as groundwater recharge basins to help make up for the infiltration lost to construction. Properly placed and managed, stormwater detention structures can also be used as siltation structures to reduce sedimentation. There are also construction techniques that can be used to trap and filter pollutants out of stormwater by passive means before it is returned to natural channels. Some of this technology is well developed and of proven benefit, yet there is still a need to develop a better understanding of the problems and the means of dealing with them. Students of landscape architecture should be particularly alert to any new developments in the area of stormwater management, pollution control, groundwater recharge, or wastewater management because they are so important to the long-range success and utility of the project environment.

The American Public Works Association cites nine objectives for a stormwater management program. These objectives are cited here because they clearly describe what stormwater management is all about, and establish an ethical base for the professionals charged with the design and development of the land.

1. Retain non-urbanized floodplains in a condition that minimizes interference with floodwater conveyance, floodwater storage, special important aquatic and terrestrial ecosystems, and the ground/surface water interface.
2. Reduce the exposure of people and property to flood hazards.
3. Systematically reduce the existing level of flood damages.
4. Ensure that corrective works are consistent with the overall goals and objectives of the region.
5. Minimize soil erosion and sedimentation problems.
6. Protect environmental quality and social well-being.
7. Improve the usefulness of floodplains by developing them as active and passive recreational areas, compatible with protection and preservation of flora and fauna.
8. View stormwater as a resource that may be useful in many situations.
9. Minimize receiving water pollution from stormwater runoff.

STORMWATER MANAGEMENT TOOLS

The means of achieving stormwater management objectives usually takes the form of a coordinated, comprehensive program of public works and regulations that addresses unique local problems. While it is not possible to discuss all of the measures that can be adopted, some of the more common tools employed in stormwater management programs are noted.

Designation and Regulation of Floodplains

Before a community is eligible to participate in the Federal Flood Insurance Program, there must be an approved floodplain management ordinance and an official floodplain map. In general, the floodplain regulations restrict development in the designated floodplain to those uses that will not impede or increase the water depth of the intermediate regional flood. Figure 4-1 illustrates the cross section of a floodplain. The zone designated the intermediate regional flood is the area inundated by a flood having an average frequency of occurrence approximately once in 100 years. The standard project flood is the zone that would be inundated by the most severe combination of meteorological and hydrological conditions that are considered reasonably characteristic of the geographical area in which the drainage basin is located, excluding extremely rare combinations. The floodway is the minimum area of a floodplain required to convey a flood peak of a selected magnitude, usually the intermediate regional flood.

To minimize the chance of severe flood damage, most cities restrict construction in the floodplain to types of development that would not be destroyed by

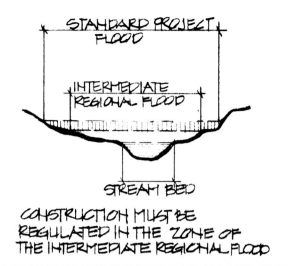

FIGURE 4.1 FLOODPLAIN ZONES

floodwaters, such as parks and golf courses. In some cases, regulations allow construction at the edges of the floodplain if the finished floors of the buildings are at least one foot above the predicted flood elevation, and if it can be demonstrated that the development will not raise or obstruct the passage of floodwater. This provision usually means that substantial modifications will have to be made to the existing channel.

Some other ways communities prevent construction in the floodplains is to purchase the land outright, or to refuse the extension of utility service into the flood zone. The expense of fee-simple aquisition is often prohibitive, even in more affluent communities, while the refusal of utility service has proved most effective.

Construction of Flood Control Works

Flood control works are large citywide or regional projects that are designed to store or convey stormwater in such a way that flooding and the attendant problems are minimized. The more common structures are: flood control reservoirs along rivers and their tributaries, storm sewers, and stream channelization. These large-scale measures are very expensive and usually fall under the jurisdiction of the Army Corps of Engineers, depending on the location and scope of the work and the ownership of the land involved. In most of these projects the environmental costs are considered quite high, so the benefits of these projects must be weighed against those costs.

Site-Based Stormwater Management Measures

Site-based management tools are the most important to the landscape architect, since a majority of all cities now has some runoff control measures in their land

development regulations. The intent of these measures is to prevent stormwater runoff, associated with development, from causing increased downstream flooding. In general there are two ways this can be accomplished: stormwater detention or retention. Stormwater detention captures and regulates the release of runoff from a site at a rate that will not exceed the capacity of the existing drainage channels downstream. Stormwater retention is the capture and holding of all excess runoff water on site.

Detention of stormwater is most often accomplished by collecting the water in a surface storage basin and then metering the water into a drainage way or storm sewer at at fixed rate. It can also be accomplished using large pipes or drainage channels that can store and meter the flow of stormwater. Surface detention structures may be depressed turf areas with earth dams to catch the excess runoff with a pipe that restricts the discharge rate to an accepted level, Figure 4-2. Parking lots can also be used as retention structures quite effecively. Water is allowed to pond on the surface of the parking lot at a depth of 2–6 in, and it is metered by designing the storm drainage inlets to restrict flow to the rate desired.

On sites that have limited space for surface detention basins, underground structures can be employed to store and meter excess runoff. Underground structures are usually large concrete or metal pipes set below parking areas or green spaces. Water enters these underground storage areas through surface inlets and, if there is suffcient difference in elevation, the water is metered off just as it is for surface structures. On very flat sites, metering may have to be accomplished by pumping water out of the storage structure. The cost of meeting the detention requirements with underground structures is much greater than for surface structures.

On-site retention of stormwater does not differ in form so much as in principle. Retention requires that excess stormwater be held and disposed of on the site. The requirement to retain stormwater on site will most often be encountered in very flat terrain, common to

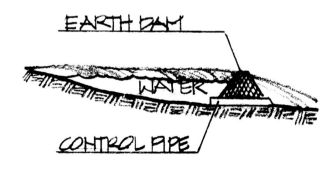

FIGURE 4.2 DETENTION BASIN

river valleys and coastal zones. In these areas the natural dissipation of stormwater is often a matter of infiltration rather than surface flow, and the topography is so flat or so near sea level that it is not possible to develop additional channels to move the water away from development. This makes it necessary to provide additional storage for stormwater in the form of large regional infiltration basins or small scale on-site retention basins.

The means of collecting excess stormwater are essentially the same as for detention; however, the water must either be held in the collection structure until it evaporates or until it can be percolated into the groundwater reservoir. The most common method of disposing of retained water is the dry-well, Figure 4-3. Dry-wells are drilled just like a water well. They are usually 6 in or larger in diameter and drilled deep enough to penetrate a very permeable substrate. The problem with dry-wells is that, over time, they may become clogged with silt and clay particles that reduce their efficiency. They are also a potential pollution hazard if they are drilled into an aquifer layer because any pollutants that are introduced at the surface will be transmitted directly to the aquifer below.

Another retention technique that is used in dry climates is collection of water on roofs. This solution is good where only limited retention volumes are required and the structure can be designed to carry the additional weight.

The need to provide stormwater detention or retention as a part of a project must be taken into account early in the design process, since it often requires that a large land area be left open. The total area required for retention need not be contiguous, however, and this opens the door for some very creative site design. The need to provide basins for stormwater collection presents a whole host of opportunities to sculpture and reform the land. Sometimes the need to build a dam will allow the designer to capture and maintain water on the site as an additional feature in the landscape. It is important that the designer look at the stormwater management requirements as a design opportunity and not simply a functional requirement of the site.

PLANNING METHODS FOR STORMWATER MANAGEMENT

The methods of planning and designing for stormwater management presented in this discussion are the most common and widely used methods of stormwater analysis in day-to-day practice. But, stormwater management is by no means an exact science, as any review of the literature will quickly reveal. In practice you will doubtless encounter different methodologies

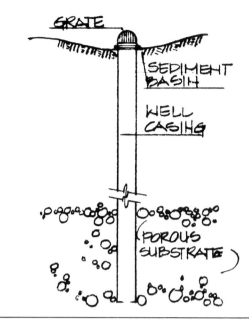

FIGURE 4.3 DRY WELL

and requirements for doing retention volume estimates, discharge volume estimates, and runoff volume estimates. This in no way detracts from the information presented, since any methodology can at best give an estimate of what is likely to occur for a specified rainfall-runoff event at a given place and time. Estimate is the key word. It must be remembered that you are dealing with random occurrences that cannot be predicted in absolute terms. This fact naturally leaves the door open to argument about the best method for modeling these events, and the subsequent promulgation of numerous theories. Decisions about what method to use must be made with a knowledge of the local characteristics of rainfall, local policy and practice, and the objectives of the local stormwater management program.

The designer must also be aware that the on-site stormwater management actions are not going to solve all downstream flooding problems. There is a great deal of evidence that detention and retention solutions that have gained so much acceptance in the past decade do not necessarily cure down-stream flooding, since there is no way to predict the uniformity of the rainfall over the entire watershed. This is pointed out here so that the student understands that good stormwater management decisions must be made in reference to the entire drainage basin and not on a site-by-site basis.

By studying the material presented here, the student will become familar with the vocabulary and the theory of site hydraulics. This knowledge will allow the student to understand and deal with the logic of other methodologies.

Principles of Site Hydrology

Site hydrology is the study of the water delivered to a site by precipitation, and the subsequent transport of the water over and through the site.

STORM CHARACTERISTICS

Storms are random events. This means that it is not possible to predict when a storm will occur, how long it will last, or how much precipitation will be generated by a single event. Yet the concepts of storm frequency, duration, intensity, and volume are very important to the discussion of site drainage.

Rainfall frequency refers to the statistical probability of a storm of a given volume, duration, and intensity being equalled or exceeded in a given year. This is most often given as a storm return period in years, such as a 100-year storm. This expression of frequency is often misinterpreted. People often think that if a storm of the 100-year frequency occurs then it will be 99 years before a similar storm will occur. This, of course, is not the case. A storm designated as a 100-year storm has a statistical probability of 0.01 (1%) of occurring in any given year. The 50-year storm has a 2% probability, the 25 year storm has a 4% probability, the 10-year storm has a 10% probability, and the 2-year storm has a 50% probability.

Storm duration is the length of time a precipitation event lasts. This characteristic is important to making estimates of the volume of water that will be available for runoff over a given time period. Closely related to storm duration is the concept of precipitation intensity, which is a ratio of precipitation volume to time, usually given in in/hr. The notion of intensity is very important to making prediction of peak runoff discharge. It has been demonstrated that there is a direct relationship between storm duration and rainfall intensity. Storms of short duration are usually of greater intensity than storms of longer duration. For example, a storm that produced a total of 2 in of rain during a 1-hour period has a rainfall intensity of 2 in/hr. A 15-minute storm may produce only 1 in of rainfall, but if the storm had continued for a full hour at the same intensity it would have produced a total of 4 in of rainfall. In other words, in this example, the 15-minute storm is twice as intense as the 1 hour storm. Figure 4-4 illustrates the relative relationship between storm duration and precipitation intensity.

The total volume of precipitation produced by a storm is important to making estimates of retention and detention basin volumes, as well as studying the effects of runoff on downstream channels. Total precipitation volume should not be confused with precipitation intensity. Precipitation volume is

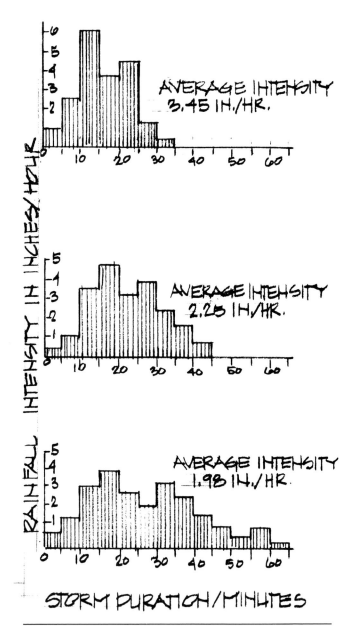

FIGURE 4.4   RELATIONSHIP OF STORM DURATION TO AVERAGE RAINFALL INTENSITY

expressed in inches of depth, and intensity is expressed as a ratio of volume to time (in/hr).

Rainstorms for a given geographic region have similar volume, intensity, frequency, and duration characteristics that can be modeled to provide the profile of a typical storm event. Information about rainfall intensity is most often presented as an "isohyetal map." An isohyetal map shows contours (isohyets) that connect points of equal precipitation for storms of a specified frequency amd duration, Figure 4-5. Isohyetal maps are based on the statistical analysis of hundreds of recorded rainfall events over long periods of time.

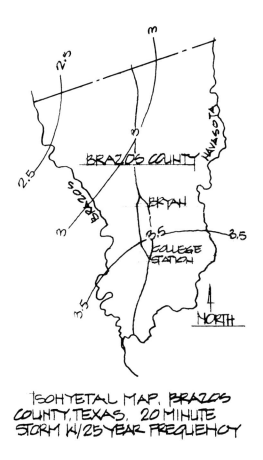

FIGURE 4.5 *ISOHYETAL MAP*

watershed to another is particularly important when making estimates of peak discharge. There are two different time concepts that should be understood and evaluated in any analysis of a drainage problem: travel time (t_t), and time of concentration (t_c).

Travel time is the time it takes water to flow through any designated portion or segment of the watershed with similar characteristics. In most cases travel times will be figured for such conditions as sheet flow over pavement, sheet flow over grass, shallow concentrated flows, and for flows in open pipes and channels.

Time of concentration is the time it takes water to travel from the hydrologically most distant point of the watershed to a specified outlet; thus, the time of concentration may be composed of one or more travel-time segments.

The time of concentration is most important when selecting the "design storm" for a project. The design storm is the typical storm, described by its frequency, duration, and intensity characteristics, that will be used as a basis for making all drainage design decisions. For example, if a drainage study is being done for a small watershed where the water will only take 10 minutes to travel from the most distant point of the site to a culvert under a road, the design should be based on a storm with no more than a 10-minute duration since a longer storm will not be as intense.

RAINFALL TO RUNOFF RELATIONSHIPS

Once precipitation reaches the ground, four things can happen to the water: It can be evaporated back to the atmosphere; it can be captured in depressions, on structures or vegetation; it can infiltrate into the ground; or it can travel across the surface as runoff, Figure 4-6. All methods of estimating runoff volume take these possibilities into account; thus, the actual anticipated runoff is always the total precipitation (P) less some volume loss due to evaporation, depression storage, or infiltration. The degree of rigor applied to making these estimates of volume loss has a direct effect on the accuracy of any method to make reasonable estimates of runoff volume and peak discharge.

TRAVEL TIME AND TIME OF CONCENTRATION

In addition to accounting for water loss, understanding how long it takes water to travel from one point in the

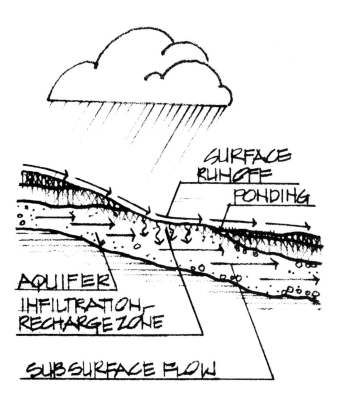

FIGURE 4.6 *RAINFALL TO RUNOFF RELATIONSHIP*

SELECTING A DESIGN STORM CONDITION

In most cases, selection of a design storm is a matter of professional judgment based on the likelihood of property damage or loss of life. For example, in most projects it would not be a problem to have streets and lawn areas inundated for short periods of time as a result of a 10- or 25-year storm, as long as there was no danger of obstructing access of emergency vehicles. However, it would not be acceptable to have buildings flooded by the 10- to 25-year storm. For this reason, the design of on-site drainage will usually be sized to accommodate the 10- to 25-year storms, allowing lawn and street areas to be flooded for short periods of time during the 50- and 100-year storm events. Major drainage channels that serve large areas of the city are most often designed to carry the 100-year storm. Only in the most extreme circumstances will designs be based on storms with rainfall volumes greater than the typical 100-year storm, since the costs are usually prohibitive and the risk does not justify the cost.

RAINFALL DATA

Rainfall data can be taken directly from the National Oceanographic and Atmospheric Administration's rainfall atlas, or by using a rainfall characteristic model. For illustration purposes, maps for rainfall volumes from 24-hour duration storms of 2- to 100-year frequency for states east of the 100th meridian have been included in the text.

A second method that can be used to determine rainfall intensity for the same return frequencies is the Steel formula. This method is primarily used to estimate the rainfall intensity in in/hr for storms with a duration of less than one hour. The formula uses two rainfall coefficients, designated k and b, which are statistical constants that model the rainfall characteristics for storms that occur in a given region. The map in Figure 4-7, shows the rainfall regions for use with the Steel formula, and Table 4-1 gives the values for k and b for storms of various return frequencies. In light of recent research data, the rainfall values obtained from the Steel formula in the western states should be viewed with some suspicion.

To illustrate the use of the Steel formula, assume that the rainfall intensity is needed for a 25-year-frequency storm in Baton Rouge, Louisiana, for a site that has a t_t of 20 minutes. The Steel Formula is:

$$i = \frac{k}{t_t + b}$$

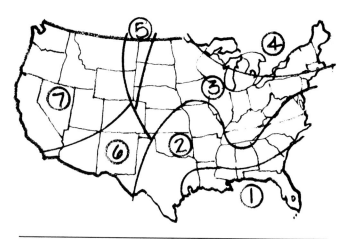

FIGURE 4.7 RAINFALL REGIONS FOR STEEL FORMULA

From Figure 4-7 it can be seen that Baton Rouge is in rainfall region 1, and for a storm of a 25-year frequency the values of k and b are 327 and 33, respectively. Substituting these values in the formula find i as follows:

$$i = \frac{327}{20 \text{ min} + 33}$$

$$i = 6.17 \text{in/hr}$$

Do not confuse the values obtained using the Steel formula with data obtained from the NOAA weather atlas maps included in this chapter. The maps are only for storms with a 24-hour duration at a specified return frequency. The values of i obtained from the Steel formula are for a storm with a duration equal to the time of concentration of the watershed or, in the case of the example, a storm with a return frequency of 25 years and a duration of 20 minutes. The NOAA weather atlases will have more accurate rainfall intensity data for storms of all durations if they are available.

FINDING THE TIME OF CONCENTRATION

There is no real consensus in the scientific or engineering community about the best way to determine the time of concentration of a watershed. This is pointed out because the student will likely encounter a variety of state and local regulations that require the use of procedures different from those presented here. But regardless of the specific procedure, the objective remains the same: to determine the time required for water to travel from the hydraulically most distant point in the watershed to a point of interest, Figure 4-8. With this in mind this text will use the procedures

TABLE 4.1 REGIONAL VALUES OF k AND b FOR THE STEEL FORMULA

Design Storm Frequency	Rainfall Constants	Region (See Figure 4-7)						
		1	2	3	4	5	6	7
2	k	206	140	106	70	70	68	32
	b	30	21	17	13	16	14	11
5	k	247	190	131	97	81	75	48
	b	29	25	19	16	13	12	12
10	k	300	230	170	111	111	122	60
	b	36	29	23	16	17	23	13
25	k	327	260	230	170	130	155	67
	b	33	32	30	27	17	26	10
50	k	315	350	250	187	187	160	65
	b	28	38	27	24	25	21	8
100	k	367	375	290	220	240	210	77
	b	33	36	31	28	29	26	10

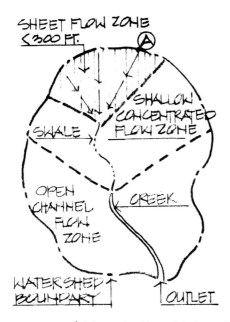

SHEET FLOW ZONE <300 FT.

POINT 'A' IS THE HYDRAULICALLY MOST DISTANT POINT OF THE WATERSHED

TIME OF CONCENTRATION (T_c) IS THE SUM OF THE TRAVEL TIMES (T_t) FOR EACH OF THE FLOW ZONES OF THE WATERSHED.

WATERSHED SCHEMATIC

FIGURE 4.8 TRAVEL TIMES AND TIME OF CONCENTRATION

recommended by the Soil Conservation Service in the revised edition of *Technical Release Number 55, Second Edition,* June 1986 (TR-55). This document presents one of the most widely accepted procedures for doing hydrologic analysis of small urban watersheds.

TR-55 divides surface drainage into three different types of flow to estimate time of concentration: overland sheet flow, shallow concentrated flow, and open channel flow. The sum of the travel times (t_t), for each of these types of flow are used to determine the t_t for any specified watershed. The determination of time of concentration is presented first since it is applicable to both methods of hydrologic analysis covered in this text.

Travel Time for Sheet Flow

Sheet flow is water moving in a thin film, <0.10 ft over a plane surface. For flows of this type up to 300 ft in length, SCS uses the Manning kinematic solution:

$$t_t = \frac{0.007 \, (nL)^{0.8}}{(P_2)^{0.5} s^{0.4}}$$

Where:

t_t = travel time in hours
n = Manning's roughness coefficient from Table 4-2
L = the horizontal flow length in feet
P_2 = the 2-year, 24-hour rainfall in inches
s = average slope of the hydraulic (land) surface in ft/ft

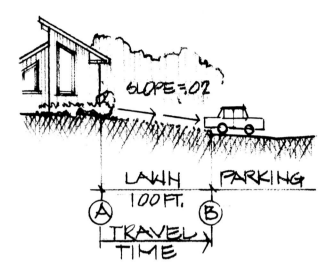

FIGURE 4.9 TRAVEL TIME—SHEET FLOW

To illustrate the use of this equation, assume sheet flow over a bluegrass lawn area to a parking lot for a run of 100 ft, with an average slope of 0.02 ft/ft located in Lexington, Kentucky, Figure 4-9. From Table 4-2, find that the roughness coefficient (*n*) for dense clump grasses is 0.24, and from the the 24-hour, 2-year rainfall map that Lexington will have about 3 in of rain for the typical 2-year storm.

TABLE 4.2 FRICTION FACTORS (MANNING'S n) FOR SHEET FLOWS SCS TR-55 Sheet Flow Method

Type of Surface	Value of n[1]
Smooth surfaces (concrete, asphalt, gravel, or bare soil)	0.011
Fallow land (no residue)	0.050
Cultivated ground ≤ 20% residue cover	0.060
Cultivated ground > 20% residue cover	0.170
Grass	
Short grass prairie	0.150
Dense grasses[2]	0.240
Bermudagrass	0.410
Range (natural)	0.130
Woods[3]	
Light underbrush	0.400
Dense underbrush	0.800

[1]The n values are a composite of information compiled by Engman (1986).
[2]Includes species such as weeping lovegrass, bluegrass, buffalo grass, blue grama grass, and native grass mixtures.
[3]When selecting n, consider cover to a height of about 0.1 ft. This is the only part of the plant cover that will obstruct sheet flow.
From TR-55 Second Ed., June 1986

Substituting into the equation write:

$$t_t = \frac{0.007 \, (0.24 \times 100 \text{ ft})^{0.8}}{3\text{in}^{0.5} \times 0.02^{0.4}}$$

$$t_t = \frac{0.089}{0.3622}$$

$$t_t = .25 \text{ hr}$$

Travel Time for Shallow Concentrated Flows

After a maximum of 300 ft, sheet flow will become a shallow concentrated flow. The average velocity of shallow concentrated flows can be read directly from Figure 4-10, based on either a paved or unpaved surface. Shallow concentrated flows will usually not exceed runs of more than 800 to 1000 ft before they enter a well-defined channel such as a creek or storm sewer. It is also important to measure the length of flow in the direction of actual travel rather than measure the line of steepest slope. For example, a site such as the one in Figures 4-9 and 4-11 may slope in the direction of the abutting street. Yet the parking lot will intercept the water and carry it to a grass swale that carries the water to an adjoining creek, Figure 4-11.

The water entering the parking lot will become a shallow concentrated flow along the center line. The greatest distance the water has to travel is 400 ft from the upper edge until it reaches the swale to the east. The travel time for this segment would be found as follows:

From Figure 4-10 find that the average velocity of flow for a paved surface and slope of .008 ft/ft is 1.8 ft/sec. The travel time in hours is equal to:

$$t_t = \frac{L}{3600 \, V}$$

Where:

t_t = travel time in hours
L = the flow length in feet
V = the average velocity of flow in ft/sec
3600 = the conversion constant from seconds to hours

Thus, for the example:

$$t_t = \frac{400 \text{ ft}}{3600 \times 1.8 \text{ ft/sec}} =$$

$$t_t = 0.06 \text{ hr}$$

Travel Time for Open Channel Flows

Open channels are any form of drainage conveyance open to the atmosphere such as ditches, swales, pipes or concrete-lined channels. Any time water flows at a

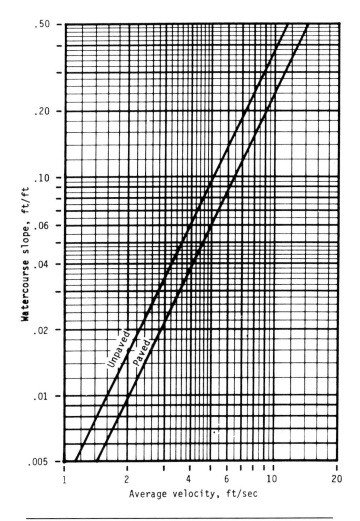

FIGURE 4.10   AVERAGE VELOCITIES FOR ESTIMATING TRAVEL TIME FOR SHALLOW CONCENTRATED FLOW, SCS TR-55, Second Ed., June 1986

The term n, the roughness coefficient, accounts for the channel's resistance to flow. The rougher the surface of the channel the more resistance to flow there will be. Slope, the third term, accounts for the influence of gravity on the water stream.

The Manning equation is usually applied on the assumption that the channel is flowing full. This means that it is necessary to have field information that will allow the cross-sectional area of the channel to be computed. Figure 4-13 is a quick reference for computing the hydraulic properties of common drainage sections.

To illustrate the application of the Manning equation, consider the drainage swale in Figure 4-11. The swale runs back to the north along the east side of the property for a length of 600 ft at a slope of 0.006 ft/ft, and the cross section is reasonably uniform for the entire

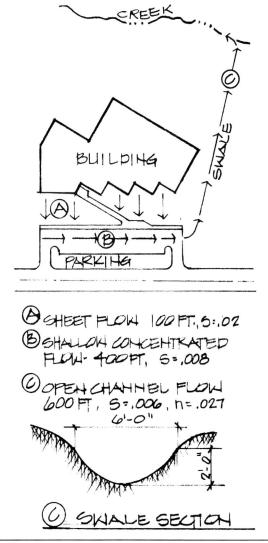

FIGURE 4.11   TRAVEL TIME FOR SHALLOW CONCENTRATED AND OPEN CHANNEL FLOWS

depth of 6 in or greater, it should probably be considered open channel flow. The most widely accepted method of determining the flow velocity in an open channel is the Manning formula:

$$V = \left(\frac{1.486}{n}\right) r^{2/3} s^{1/2}$$

Where:

V = the velocity of flow in ft/sec
n = Manning's roughness coefficient from Table 4-3
r = the hydraulic radius
s = the slope of the channel in ft/ft

The term r, the hydraulic radius, is the ratio of the cross-sectional area of the drainage channel to the wetted perimeter of the channel, Figure 4-12.

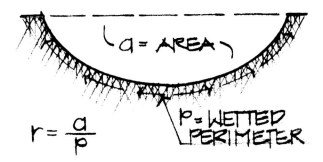

FIGURE 4.12 *HYDRAULIC RADIUS*

run. The length of the channel should always be measured as the exact distance of flow in the channel, not just a straight line distance. Likewise the channel should be broken into segments if the cross section is not generally uniform along the entire run.

The first step in applying the Manning equation is to compute the area of the cross section and the wetted perimeter. In this case the channel has a parabolic cross section, 6 ft wide and 2 ft deep, Figure 4-11. From Figure 4-13, find that the formula for the area of a parabolic section is:

$$a = 0.67 \; Wd$$
$$a = 0.67 \times 6 \text{ ft} \times 2 \text{ ft} =$$
$$a = 8.04 \text{ sq ft}$$

The formula for the wetted perimeter, also from Figure 4-13 is:

$$P = W + \left(\frac{8d^2}{3W}\right)$$
$$P = 6 \text{ ft} + \frac{(8 \times 2 \text{ ft})^2}{3 \text{ ft} \times 6 \text{ ft}}$$
$$P = 7.78 \text{ ft}$$

The hydraulic radius is:

$$r = \frac{a}{P}$$
$$r = \frac{8.04 \text{ sq ft}}{7.78 \text{ ft}}$$
$$r = 1.03 \text{ ft}$$

The value of *n* is found in Table 4-3. For an unlined channel with short grass and few weeds, the value of *n* is 0.027. Now, substituting into the Manning equation, write:

$$V = \left(\frac{1.486}{0.027}\right) \times 1.03^{2/3} \times 0.006^{1/2}$$
$$V = 55.03 \times 1.02 \times .08$$
$$V = 4.49 \text{ ft/sec}$$

Next find the travel time for the swale segment as follows:

$$t_t = \frac{L}{3600 \; V}$$
$$t_t = \frac{600 \text{ ft}}{3600 \times 4.49 \text{ ft/sec}}$$
$$t_t = 0.04 \text{ hr}$$

The time of concentration for the example problem is simply the sum of the travel times for each of the three different types of flow: sheet flow 0.25 hr, shallow concentrated flow 0.06 hr, and open channel flow 0.04 hr, a total of .35 hr. Therefore, it will be 0.35 hr or 21 min, before the area at the southwest corner of the building in Figure 4-11 will begin contributing water to the creek and the northeast corner of the property. At this time, the entire building site will be contributing runoff to that outlet and the peak flow will begin. If the rainfall remains constant after this time, peak flow will be maintained until the storm begins to subside, then the flow will begin to decrease.

THE RATIONAL METHOD FOR ESTIMATING PEAK RUNOFF

Surface runoff resulting from any single storm event begins at a point when all of the depressions and other storage capacity of a site has been filled, and the infiltration capacity of the soil has been exceeded. The

TABLE 4.3 *FRICTION FACTORS (MANNING'S n)*
FOR SELECTED CHANNEL SURFACES AND MATERIALS.
(Use with Manning Equation)

Type of Surface	Value of n[1]
Smooth Surface Pipe:	
Cast iron pipe	0.012
Concrete pipe	0.015
Clay pipe	0.014
Cement grout surfaces	0.013
Corrugated steel pipe	0.032
Unlined Channels	
Excavated soil, uniform	
Clean, no vegetation	0.022
Short grass few weeds	0.027
Dense weeds to flow depth	0.080
Dense brush, high stage	0.100
Rock Channels	
Smooth and uniform	0.033
Rough and irregular	0.040

[1]Values compiled from the National Corrugated Steel Pipe Association, the Clay Products Institute, *SCS National Engineering Handbook*, and Seelye, *Design: Data Book for Civil Engineers.*

SECTION OF CHANNEL	FORMULAS FOR AREA AND WETTED PERIMETER
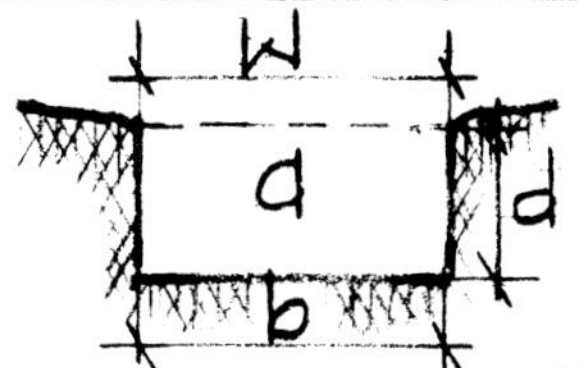 RECTANGULAR	$a = Wd$ $p = W + 2d$
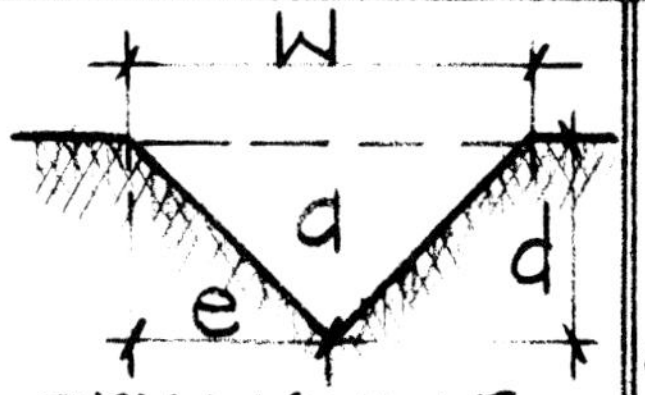 TRIANGULAR	$a = \dfrac{W}{2}d$ $p = 2\sqrt{e^2 + d^2}$
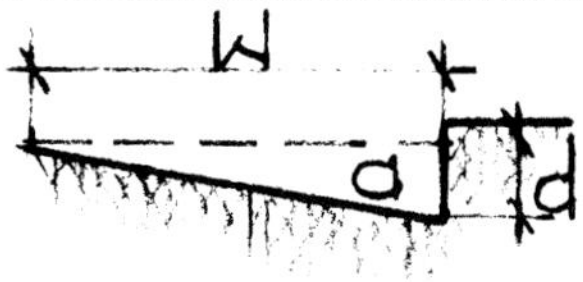 TYPICAL CURB & GUTTER	$a = \dfrac{W}{2}d$ $p = d + \sqrt{e^2 + d^2}$
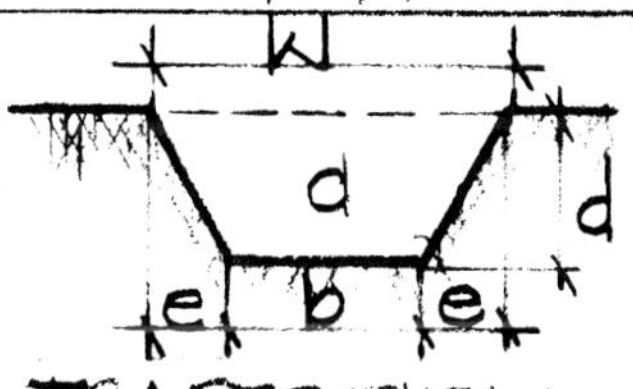 TRAPEZOIDAL	$a = \dfrac{W+b}{2}d$ $p = b + 2\sqrt{e^2 + d^2}$
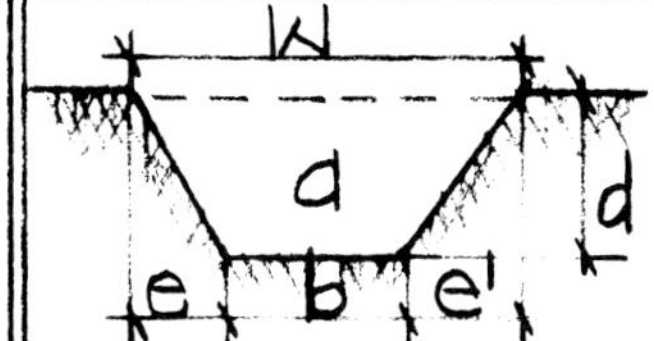 TRAPEZOID UNEVEN SIDES	$a = d\left(b + \dfrac{e + e'}{2}\right)$ $p = b + \sqrt{e^2 + d^2} + \sqrt{e'^2 + d^2}$
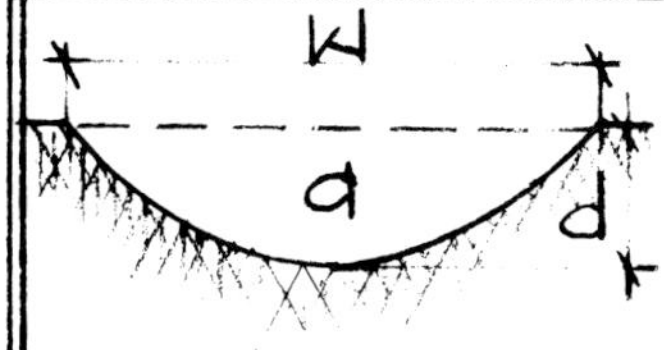 PARABOLIC	$a = 0.67 Wd$ $p = W + \left(\dfrac{8d^2}{3W}\right)$

FIGURE 4.13 HYDRAULIC PROPERTIES OF TYPICAL DRAINAGE CHANNEL SECTIONS

peak runoff volume will occur at the point when all areas of the watershed begin contributing runoff to the specified outlet.

The rational equation relates these variables in the algebraic expression:

$$Q_f = C\, i_f\, A$$

Where:

Q_f = the runoff in cubic feet per second (cfs) generated by a storm of a designated frequency of return, (design storm) e.g., a 50-year storm

C = the ratio of surface runoff to rainfall, expressed as a decimal, often called the runoff coefficient

A = the area of the watershed contributing to the outlet point in acres

i_f = the average rainfall intensity in in/hr for a period of time equal to the watersheds time of concentration, (t_c) for storm of a designated return frequency, (design storm)

t_c = time of concentration; the average time in minutes required for water to flow from the hydraulically most distant point of the watershed to the outlet

Table 4-4 provides average values for the runoff coefficient for use in the rational formula. Notice that there is a wide range of values for each land use and surface type. For example, downtown areas have a runoff coef-

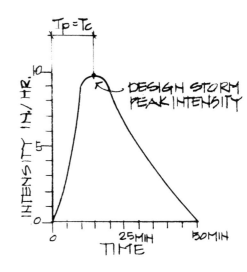

THE RATIONAL FORMULA REQUIRES THAT THE TIME TO PEAK (Tp) OF THE DESIGN STORM BE EQUAL TO THE TIME OF CONCENTRATION OF THE DRAINAGE AREA.

FIGURE 4.14 RELATIONSHIP OF TIME OF CONCENTRATION AND TIME TO PEAK ASSUMED BY THE RATIONAL FORMULA

TABLE 4.4 VALUES OF C FOR USE WITH THE RATIONAL FORMUAL

Surface Condition	Value of C	
	Low	High
Roofs	0.95	1.00
Pavements, asphalt and concrete	0.90	1.00
Roads, clay and gravel	0.30	0.90
Bare soil		
Sand	0.20	0.40
Clay	0.30	0.75
Grassed surfaces		
Sandy soil	0.05	0.40
Clayey soil	0.15	0.60
Developed areas		
Commercial zones 85%	0.60	
impervious	0.75	
High density residential		
65% impervious	0.55	0.65
Low density residential		
20-25% impervious	0.30	0.55
Parks and open space		
(developed turf)	0.20	0.40

Adapted from *Design: Data Book for Civil Engineers*, Seelye.

ficient range of 0.70 to 0.95. Use of the upper or lower limit of the range will yield substantially different values of Q_f. The reason the range is so wide is that the designer is expected to take into account several other variables when selecting the runoff coefficient. Some of the major considerations are:

- Slope: The steeper the slope the greater the runoff coefficient.
- Soil type: Heavy clay soils would suggest a higher value of C while sandy soils would suggest a lower value.
- Surface condition: Rough surfaces will tend to retard the flow of runoff while smooth, unbroken surfaces will increase the runoff velocity.

Because the runoff coefficient accounts for a number of different variables, it is usually best to develop a composite value for C. This will be illustrated in the example problem.

Determining the value of i_f requires that the time of concentration (t_c) of the drainage area be estimated. Time of concentration is critical to the proper application of the rational formula due to the increased rainfall intensity in storms of short duration. The rational formula is based on the assumption that the point at

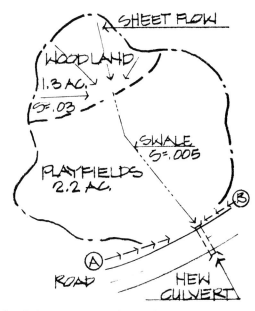

DRAINAGE DATA
WOODLAND:
  AREA: 1.3 ACRES
  SLOPE: 0.03 FT./FT
  L = 250 FT.
  n = 0.40
SWALE:
  DRAINAGE AREA: 2.2 ACRES
  SLOPE: 0.005 FT./FT.
  L = 800 FT.
  n = 0.027
OFFSITE CONTRIBUTION TO CULVERT

Ⓐ 4 CFS
Ⓑ 6 CFS   W = 12'

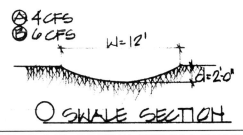

SWALE SECTION

FIGURE 4.15 RATIONAL FORMULA EXAMPLE

which the storm event reaches its peak intensity is equal to the time of concentration of the watershed, Figure 4-14. The procedure for finding the time of concentration was explained earlier. Once time of concentration is known, the value of i_i can be computed using the Steel formula.

The most frequent and appropriate use of the rational method is in estimating peak runoff rates from small drainage areas of a site for the purpose of determining approximate pipe and drainage channel sizes. To illustrate a typical application, consider the diagram in Figure 4-15. Assume that the site is located in Manhattan, Kansas, and will be a developed park area. The upper part of the drainage area will be a wooded

picnic area of 1.3 acres and has an average slope of 0.03 ft/ft. The lower area will be open, turf playfields, and has an area of 2.2 acres. The turf area is bisected by a turf swale 12 ft wide and 2 ft deep. The task is to determine the approximate size of the culvert required to carry the runoff from this area under the new road at the lower end of the drainage area.

The first step is to determine the time of concentration of the watershed using the procedure explained earlier. In this case there are two flow segments. The wooded area constitutes a sheet flow of about 250 ft; then the water is picked up in the drainage swale, which is an open channel.

Travel time for the wooded section is found by the Manning kinematic solution as follows:

$$t_t = \frac{0.007\,(nL)^{0.8}}{(P_2)^{0.5}\,s^{0.4}}$$

$$t_t = \frac{0.007\,(0.4 \times 250\text{ ft})^{0.8}}{(3.5\text{in}^*)^{.5} \times (0.03)^{0.4}}$$

$$t_t = \frac{0.279}{0.460}$$

$$t_t = 0.61\text{ hr}$$

0.61 hr × 60 min/hr = 36.60 min or 37 min

*The 3.5 in was read from the 2-year frequency, 24-hour rainfall map at the end of the chapter.

The travel time for the grass swale through the playfields is found using the Manning formula as follows:

First compute the hydraulic radius from the information in Figure 4-13.

The area of a parabolic cross section is:

$a = 0.67\,Wd$
$a = 0.67 \times 12\text{ ft} \times 2\text{ ft}$
$a = 16\text{ sq ft}$

The wetted perimeter is

$$P = W + \left(\frac{8d^2}{3W}\right)$$

$$p = 12\text{ ft} + \frac{(8 \times 2\text{ ft}^2)}{3 \times 12\text{ ft}}$$

$$p = 12.89\text{ ft}$$

The hydraulic radius is:

$$r = \frac{a}{p}$$

$$r = \frac{16\text{ sq ft}}{12.89\text{ ft}}$$

$$r = 1.24\text{ ft}$$

Now substituting into the Manning equation:

$$V = \left(\frac{1.486}{n}\right) r^{2/3} s^{1/2}$$

$$V = \left(\frac{1.486}{0.027}\right) \times 1.24^{0.67} \times 0.005^{0.5}$$

$$V = 55.03 \times 1.155 \times 0.07$$

$$V = 4.45 \text{ ft/sec}$$

The travel time for the segment in minutes is:

$$t_t = \frac{L}{60 \text{ sec/min} \times 4.45 \text{ ft/sec}}$$

$$t_t = \frac{800 \text{ ft}}{60 \text{ sec/min} \times 4.45 \text{ ft/sec}}$$

$$t_t = 2.96 \text{ min (use 3 min)}$$

The time of concentration t_t is:

```
  37 min, the travel time for the wooded section
+  3 min, the travel time in the swale
  40 min
```

With the time of concentration known, the Steel formula is used to find the value of i for an appropriate design storm frequency. Since the road is a public road, it is advisable to use the 100-year frequency storm. If the road had been a minor park service road the 50-year storm may have been a better choice. Now from Table 4-1 and Figure 4-7, find the appropriate values of the Steel coefficients k and b. Manhattan is in zone 2, and the values of k and b, respectively, are 375 and 36. Substituting these values into the formula, find i as follows:

$$i = \frac{k}{t_t + b}$$

$$i = \frac{375}{40 + 36}$$

$$i = 4.93 \text{ in/hr}$$

Next, it is necessary to determine the value of the runoff coefficient C. While in a simple situation such as the one at hand, the value of C could probably be assumed to be reasonably uniform; however, for the sake of illustration a composite value of C will be computed.

In the wooded picnic area, assume that the ground is covered with dense grass and underbrush with a deep sandy loam. In a case like this, the value of C would trend toward the lower values on the scale so a value of 0.15 will be used. In the turf areas, a slightly higher value of 0.30 will be used, based on the assumption that there will be more compaction of the surface from mowing machinery and a relatively short turf.

To develop a composite value of C simply multiply each value of C by the total acreage in that zone and divide by the total area, as follows:

$$1.3 \text{ acres} \times 0.15 = 0.195$$

$$2.2 \text{ acres} \times 0.30 = \frac{0.660}{0.855}$$

$$\frac{0.855}{3.5 \text{ acres}} = 0.24$$

Therefore, the appropriate value of C for the problem at hand is 0.24.

Now that all the values have been established, substitute into the the rational formula as follows:

$$Q = C_t i_t A$$
$$Q = 0.24 \times 4.93 \text{ in/hr} \times 3.5 \text{ acres}$$
$$Q = 4.14 \text{ cfs}$$

ESTIMATING PIPE SIZE

With the runoff rate known, it is usually necessary to estimate the size of the pipe or channel required to carry the volume to the next point of transfer. In the example here, the water is being transported under the road in a pipe culvert. A quick way of estimating the appropriate pipe size is by combining an equation known as the continuity formula with the Manning equation. The continuity formula is:

$$Q = Va$$

Where:

Q = the discharge from a pipe or channel in cubic feet per second
V = the velocity of flow in feet per second
a = the cross-sectional area of the drainage channel or pipe in square feet

Since the Manning equation is equal to the value of V, the continuity formula can be written as:

$$Q = \left(\frac{1.486}{n}\right) r^{2/3} s^{1/2} a$$

Given this relationship, it is possible to estimate the pipe or channel size by trial and error. To illustrate, continue with the example problem in Figure 4-15. It was determined that the area in the diagram contributed 4.14 cfs to the culvert. There is also a drainage ditch along the road that will contribute additional water to the culvert under the road. Assume for this example that these rates have already been estimated and that another 10 cfs is being contributed to the culvert by the drainage ditch, see Figure 4-15, for a total of 14.14 cfs. For the first trial, assume the culvert will be reinforced concrete pipe, with an *n* value of 0.015, Table 4-3, and that the slope of the culvert will be 0.006.

First compute the hydraulic radius of the pipe.

$a = \pi r^2$
$a = 3.14 \times 0.5 \text{ ft}^2$
$a = 0.78 \text{ sq ft}$

The wetted perimeter of a circular section flowing full is:

$p = \pi d$
$p = 3.14 \times 1.0 \text{ ft}$
$p = 3.14 \text{ ft}$

The hydraulic radius is:

$r = \dfrac{a}{p}$

$r = \dfrac{0.78}{3.14}$

$r = 0.25$

Now substituting into the revised form of the continuity formula write:

$Q = \left(\dfrac{1.486}{0.015}\right) \times 0.25^{0.67} \times .006^{0.5} \times 0.78 \text{ sq ft}$

$Q = 99.07 \times 0.395 \times 0.077 \times 0.78$

$Q = 2.35 \text{ cfs}$

This quite obviously will not do the job, since it is less than 14.14 cfs. For the second trial assume a 24-in pipe.

First find the hydraulic radius:

$a = 3.14 \times 1 \text{ ft}^2$
$a = 3.14 \text{ sq ft}$

$p = 3.14 \times 2 \text{ ft}$
$p = 6.28 \text{ ft}$

$r = \dfrac{3.14 \text{ sq ft}}{6.28 \text{ ft}}$

$r = 0.5 \text{ ft}$

Substituting into the equation write:

$Q = \left(\dfrac{1.486}{0.015}\right) \times 0.5^{0.67} \times .006^{0.5} \times 3.14 \text{ sq ft}$

$Q = 99.07 \times 0.6285 \times 0.078 \times 3.14 \text{ sq ft}$

$Q = 15.25 \text{ cfs}$

Thus, the 24-in round reinforced concrete pipe will carry the required 14.14 cfs at a slope of 0.006 ft/ft.

This same procedure can be used to estimate the size of an open grass channel or a lined channel, but there are some important limitations to this method. First, the continuity formula assumes that there is uniform flow along the length of the channel. In other words, the water is flowing at a uniform depth at the same velocity. It makes no allowance for a change in velocity or depth of flow as the water enters or leaves the pipe or specified channel. And, finally, the assumption is made that the entrance and downstream opening of the drainage way or pipe are not submerged. If any of these assumptions are not valid, the resulting computations will not be accurate. For most small-scale site developments, the use of this method is acceptable since there will usually be no backwater condition, and the increased velocity that occurs due to acceleration of flow in the pipe has the net effect of increasing the capacity of the pipe somewhat. In cases where there are a number of combined flows, however, long runs of pipe, a need for specialized inlet structures, or flows that exceed the capacity of a 36-in pipe, a more detailed analysis method is in order. There are a number of good references available that provide very clear explanations of open channel design. These are noted in the reference bibliography.

The SCS TR-55 Method Of Hydrologic Analysis

The Soil Conservation Service's publication; *Urban Hydrology for Small Water Sheds, Technical Release No. 55,* is a very comprehensive methodology for doing hydrologic studies of small watersheds. It is of particular use to landscape architects who are becoming more and more involved in land development projects that demand on-site management of storm runoff. The fact that most municipal agencies now require that stormwater management be addressed in order to obtain approval of preliminary development plans makes it absolutely essential that design professionals understand basic site hydrology and the methods of doing hydrologic analysis. While the final development plans will, in most cases, require the services of a professional engineer, the landscape architect must be able to do the preliminary studies necessary to allocate land parcels for detention and retention structures as well as making estimates of runoff volume, discharge rates, and channel sizes. Failure to deal with these issues properly will render the design solutions useless.

The TR-55 provides the most comprehensive means of doing site scale hydrologic analysis without the necessity of having access to complex computer technology or a sophisticated knowledge of hydraulics. On the other hand, it does have to be used with a knowledge of its limitations and assumptions. These limitations will be pointed out during the course of this discussion, along with recommendations for further study.

TR-55 sets forth manual procedures for estimating peak runoff rate, total runoff volume, and required detention volumes. The procedures for making these estimates use a computer-based hydrologic analysis model developed by the SCS, known as TR-20. The TR-55 methods were developed by making numerous runs of the TR-20 model to develop the results of the manual procedures.

TR-55; THE BASIC RAINFALL-RUNOFF MODEL

In order to apply the TR-55 methods properly, it is important to understand the theory of the SCS rainfall-runoff model. The development of the SCS model began with an analysis of rainfall frequency data taken from the NOAA rainfall frequency atlases for areas of less than 400 square miles, at frequencies of 1 to 100 years, and for storm durations of up to 24 hours. Detailed analyses of these rainfall events have indicated that there are four different regions of rainfall distribution which have been designated as Type I, Type IA, Type II, and Type III. Figure 4-16 shows the location and types of rainfall distribution, and the curves for each type. The primary differences in the rainfall distribution are the most intense precipitation and the time when the most intense precipitation occurs within a 24-hour period. In other words, an area with a Type IA rainfall distribution will experience a distinct increase in rainfall intensity around the eighth hour, while an area with a Type II distribution will not experience an increased intensity until around the twelfth hour. The procedure used to derive these distribution results in the rainfall intensities of shorter duration storms being included within the intensities of storms of longer duration. Since all the critical storm intensities are within the storm distribution, they are appropriate for the analysis of both large and small watershed areas.

The SCS uses the rainfall-to-runoff relationship illustrated in Figure 4-17. The model divides the volume of precipitation into three parts designated by the terms I_a, F, and Q. I_a is called the "initial abstraction" which is used to account for the volume of total precipitation that is captured by interception, infiltration, depression storage, or lost to evaporation before runoff begins. The term F accounts for the water lost to infiltration after runoff begins. Note that infiltration is assumed to decrease in relation to time. Q is that

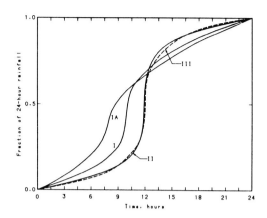

SCS 24-hour rainfall distributions.

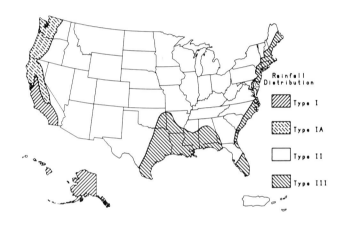

FIGURE 4.16 SCS 24-HOUR RAINFALL DISTRIBUTIONS TR-55, Second Ed., June 1986

portion of the precipitation that appears as direct runoff. Based on this model, the SCS assumes the following rainfall-runoff relationship:

$$\frac{F}{S} = \frac{Q}{P - I_a}$$

Where:

P = the total precipitation in inches
Q = the total runoff in inches
F = the volume of infiltration (actual retention in inches) after runoff begins
I_a = the initial abstraction (interception, and other surface storage)
S = the potential maximum retention of a site

Since the terms S and I_a are both affected by the character of the land cover and soil condition, and since it can be demonstrated that there is a direct

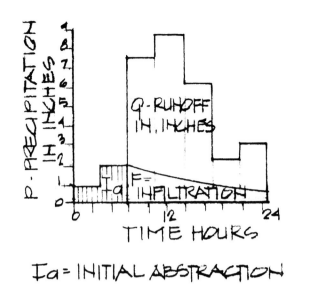

I_a = INITIAL ABSTRACTION

FIGURE 4.17   SCS ASSUMED RAINFALL TO RUNOFF
RELATIONSHIP
TR-55, Second Ed., June 1986

relationship between I_a and S, the following runoff
equation has been suggested:

$$Q = \frac{(P-0.2S)^2}{P + 0.8\,S}$$

Where:

$$I_a = 0.2\,S$$

Since S, the potential maximum retention, is a function of such variables as soil, plant cover, and the amount of impervious area, a detailed analysis was made to model these effects for various soil types and land cover complexes. This resulted in a series of rainfall-runoff curves that have been designated as runoff curve numbers (CN). The CN for a given set of surface cover and soil conditions allows the designer to estimate the value of S for substituting into the equation above. The value of S is found by:

$$S = \frac{1000 - 10}{CN}$$

A much more detailed explanation of these relationships is given in the *SCS National Engineering Handbook,* Section 4, *Hydrology,* if further explanation is desired. The important part of what is presented here is that the student understands that the initial abstraction (I_a) and the maximum potential retention (S) are a function of soil and cover complex, and the runoff curve number is the means by which these variables are taken into account.

THE SCS CURVE NUMBER METHOD FOR ESTIMATING RUNOFF

The first step in selecting the appropriate curve number is to determine the hydrologic soil group(s) of the soil(s) on the site. Hydrologic soil groups are designated by the letters A-D, and can be determined from the SCS master list of hydrologic soil groups. The 1986 revision of TR-55 has a copy of the master list of hydrologic soil groups by soil name.

The second step in estimating the CN is the determination of the cover complex classification. The cover complex considers three variables: land use, agricultural treatment or practice, and hydrologic condition. These variables can be interpreted directly from soil reports, aerial photographs, and topographic maps, and the CN can be read from Table 4-5.

Table 4-5 is a compilation of the CN tables from the 1986 TR-55 revision. Figures 4-18 and 4-19 are for use in making adjustments to the CNs in Table 4-5 when the assumptions made in the table do not meet the field conditions.

The term "connected impervious areas" means roads, rooks, parking, and paved areas connected directly to the channels of the drainage system. "Unconnected impervious areas" are those impervious surfaces from which runoff flows on to permeable open spaces, such as lawns, playfields, pastures or cultivated lands as sheet flow. The logic diagram in Figure 4-20 should be used to determine the appropriate means of establishing the curve number value.

To illustrate a situation where an adjustment should be made, assume that a parking lot is releasing water onto a turf area as sheet flow along one edge, Figure 4-21. The building and parking constitute only 20% of the total site area, and the pervious area CN from Table 4-5 is 70. Enter Figure 4-19 at the right side at 20% and read up to the line where the ratio of unconnected pervious area to total impervious area is 1.0, then read left to CN 70 and down to read the composite curve number of 72.

Another case, in Table 4-5, indicates the assumption that ¼-acre lots have 38% connected impervious area. But assume that the project estimates indicate there is really about 50% connected impervious area due to large driveways and swimming pools. Assuming soil group C with a pervious CN of 90, go to Figure 4-18 and enter the bottom at 50% impervious area and read up to CN 90, then left to read a composite CN of 94.

For doing runoff analysis of complex sites such as sites with soils of different hydrologic soil groups and different types of land cover and use, it is recommended that a composite CN be developed for the site. In the revised edition of TR-55, the SCS provides worksheets to help develop composite CNs and the example problem will utilize the SCS worksheet.

TABLE 4.5a   RUNOFF CURVE NUMBERS FOR URBAN AREAS[1]

Cover Description		Curve Numbers for Hydrologic Soil Group—			
Cover Type and Hydrologic Condition	Average Percent Impervious Area[2]	A	B	C	D
Fully developed urban areas (vegetation established)					
Open space (lawns, parks, golf courses, cemeteries, etc.)[3]:					
Poor condition (grass cover < 50%).............		68	79	86	89
Fair condition (grass cover 50% to 75%).........		49	69	79	84
Good conditon (grass cover > 75%)		39	61	74	80
Impervious areas:					
Paved parking lots, roofs, driveways, etc. (excluding right-of-ways)......................		98	98	98	98
Streets and roads:					
Paved; curbs and storm sewers (excluding right-of-way).............................		98	98	98	98
Paved; open ditches (including right-of-way)		83	89	92	98
Gravel (including right-of-way)..................		76	85	89	91
Dirt (including right-of-way).....................		72	82	87	89
Western desert urban areas:					
Natural desert landscaping (pervious areas only)[4]..		63	77	85	88
Artificial desert landscaping (impervious weed barrier, desert shrub with 1- to 2-inch sand or gravel mulch and basin borders)............................		96	96	96	96
Urban districts:					
Commercial and business	85	89	92	94	95
Industrial..	72	81	88	91	93
Residential districts by average lot size:					
⅛ acre or less (town houses).....................	65	77	85	90	92
¼ acre	38	61	75	83	87
⅓ acre	30	57	72	81	86
½ acre	25	54	70	80	85
1 acre	20	51	68	79	84
2 acres	12	46	65	77	82
Developing urban areas					
Newly graded areas (pervious areas only, no vegetation)[5]......................................		77	86	91	94
Idle lands (CN's are determined using cover types similar to those in table 4-5c).					

[1]Average runoff condition, and $I_a = 0.2S$.
[2]The average percent impervious area shown was used to develop the composite CN's. Other assumptions are as follows: impervious areas are directly connected to the drainage system, impervious areas have a CN of 98, and pervious areas are considered equivalent to open space in good hydrologic condition. CN's for other combinations of conditions may be computed using Figure 4-18 or 4-19.
[3]CN's shown are equivalent to those of pasture. Compostie CN's may be computed for other combinations of open space cover type.
[4]Composite CN's for natural desert landscaping should be compted using Figures 4-18 or 4-19 based on the impervious area percentage (CN = 98) and the pervious area CN. The pervious area CN's are assumed equivalent to desert shrub in poor hydrologic condition.
[5]Composite CN's to use for the design of temporary measures during grading and construction should be computed using Figure 4-18 or 4-19, based on the degree of development (impervious area percentage) and the CN's for the newly graded pervious areas.
TR-55, Second Ed., June 1986

TABLE 4.5b RUNOFF CURVE NUMBERS FOR CULTIVATED AGRICULTURAL LANDS[1]

Cover Description			Curve Numbers for Hydrologic Soil Group—			
Cover Type	Treatment[2]	Hydrologic Condition[3]	A	B	C	D
Fallow	Bare soil	—	77	86	91	94
	Crop residue cover (CR)	Poor	76	85	90	93
		Good	74	83	88	90
Row crops	Straight row (SR)	Poor	72	81	88	91
		Good	67	78	85	89
	SR + CR	Poor	71	80	87	90
		Good	64	75	82	85
	Contoured(C)	Poor	70	79	84	88
		Good	65	75	82	86
	C + CR	Poor	69	78	83	87
		Good	64	74	81	85
	Contoured & terraced (C&T)	Poor	66	74	80	82
		Good	62	71	78	81
	C&T + CR	Poor	65	73	79	81
		Good	61	70	77	80
Small Grain	SR	Poor	65	76	84	88
		Good	63	75	83	87
	SR + CR	Poor	64	75	83	86
		Good	60	72	80	84
	C	Poor	63	74	82	85
		Good	61	73	81	84
	C + CR	Poor	62	73	81	84
		Good	60	72	80	83
	C&T	Poor	61	72	79	82
		Good	59	70	78	81
	C&T + CR	Poor	60	71	78	81
		Good	58	69	77	80
Close-seeded or broadcast legumes or rotation meadow	SR	Poor	66	77	85	89
		Good	58	72	81	85
	C	Poor	64	75	83	85
		Good	55	69	78	83
	C&T	Poor	63	73	80	83
		Good	51	67	76	80

[1]Average runoff condition, and I_a = 0.2S.

[2]*Crop residue cover* applies only if residue is on at least 5% of the surface throughout the year.

[3]Hydrologic condition is based on combination of factors that affect infiltration and runoff, including (a) density and canopy of vegetative areas, (b) amount of year-round cover, (c) amount of grass or close-seeded legumes in rotations, (d) percent of residue cover on the land surface (good ≥ 20%), and (e) degree of surface roughness.

Poor: Factors impair infiltration and tend to increase runoff.

Good: Factors encourage average and better than average infiltration and tend to decrease runoff.

TR-55, Second Ed., June 1986

TABLE 4.5c *RUNOFF CURVE NUMBERS FOR OTHER AGRICULTURAL LANDS*[1]

Cover Description		Curve Numbers for Hydrologic Soil Group—			
Cover Type	Hydrologic Condition	A	B	C	D
Pasture, grassland, or range—continuous forage for grazing.[2]	Poor	68	79	86	80
	Fair	49	69	79	84
	Good	39	61	74	80
Meadow—continuous grass, protected from grazing and generally mowed for hay.	—	30	58	71	78
Brush—brush-weed-grass mixture with brush the major element.[3]	Poor	48	67	77	83
	Fair	35	56	70	77
	Good	[4]30	48	65	73
Woods—grass combination (orchard or tree farm).[5]	Poor	57	73	82	86
	Fair	43	65	76	82
	Good	32	58	72	79
Woods.[6]	Poor	45	66	77	83
	Fair	36	60	73	79
	Good	[4]30	55	70	77
Farmsteads—buildings, lanes, driveways, and surrounding lots.	—	59	74	82	86

[1]Average runoff condition, and $I_a = 0.2S$.

[2]*Poor:* <50% ground cover or heavily grazed with no mulch.
Fair: 50 to 75% ground cover and not heavily grazed.
Good: >75% ground cover and lightly or only occasionally grazed.

[3]*Poor:* <50% ground cover.
Fair: 50 to 75% ground cover.
Good: >75% ground cover.

[4]Actual curve number is less than 30 for runoff computations.

[5]CN's shown were computed for areas with 50% woods and 50% grass (pasture) cover. Other combinations of condiions may be computed from the CN's for woods and pasture.

[6]Poor: Forest litter, small trees, and brush are destroyed by heavy grazing or regular burning.
Fair: Woods are grazed but not burned, and some forest litter covers the soil.
Good: Woods are protected from grazing, and litter and brush adequately cover the soil.
TR-55, Second Ed., June 1986

TABLE 4.5d RUNOFF CURVE NUMBERS FOR ARID AND SEMIARID RANGELANDS[1]

Cover Description		Curve Numbers for Hydrologic Soil Group—			
Cover Type	Hydrologic Condition[2]	A[3]	B	C	D
Herbaceous—mixture of grass, weeds, and low-growing brush, with brush the minor element.	Poor		80	87	93
	Fair		71	81	89
	Good		62	74	85
Oak-aspen—mountain brush mixture of oak brush, aspen, mountain mahogany, bitter brush, maple, and other brush.	Poor		66	74	79
	Fair		48	57	63
	Good		30	41	48
Pinyon-juniper—pinyon, juniper, or both; grass understory.	Poor		75	85	89
	Fair		58	73	80
	Good		41	61	71
Sagebrush with grass understory.	Poor		67	80	85
	Fair		51	63	70
	Good		35	47	55
Desert shrub—major plants include saltbush, greasewood, creosotebush, blackbrush, bursage, palo verde, mesquite, and cactus.	Poor	63	77	85	88
	Fair	55	72	81	86
	Good	49	68	79	84

[1]Average runoff condition, and I_a = 0.2S. For range in humid regions, use Table 4-5c.

[2]*Poor:* <30% ground cover (litter, grass, and brush overstory).
Fair: 30 to 70% ground cover.
Good: >70% ground cover.

[3]Curve numbers for group A have been developed only for desert shrub.
TR-55, Second Ed., June 1986

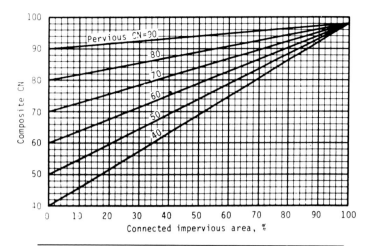

FIGURE 4.18 COMPOSITE CN WITH CONNECTED IMPERVIOUS AREA
TR-55, Second Ed., June 1986

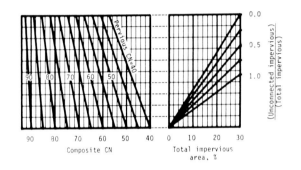

FIGURE 4.19 COMPOSITE CN WITH UNCON SCS TYPE I RAINFALL DISTRIBUTION
TR-55, Second Ed., June 1986

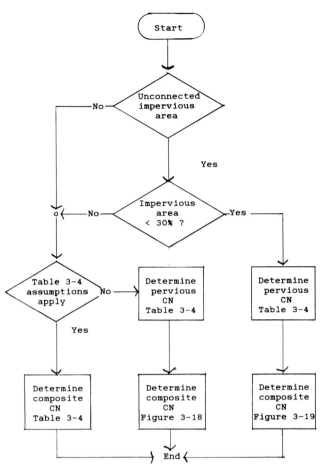

FIGURE 4.20 LOGIC DIAGRAM

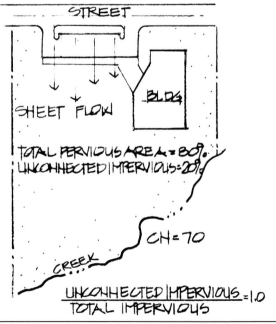

FIGURE 4.21 ADJUSTING CN FOR LESS THAN 30% UNCONNECTED IMPERVIOUS AREA

To illustrate the development of a composite CN, consider the site shown in Figure 4-22. The land is a 20-acre parcel located in Columbus, Ohio. The land has two different hydrologic soil types, B and C, and four different types of surface cover. Eight acres of the site are devoted to grazing, five acres are open with good stands of forage grass, with soils in group B. The other three acres are partially wooded with good grass cover, and group C soils. Another eight acres of the site are heavily wooded lowlands with lots of underbrush but very little litter cover, so the hydrologic condition is considered fair. The soils in this area are hydrologic group C. At the northeast corner of the site there is a four-acre tract used for feed grain production. The grain is planted in straight rows, and there is usually a good stand, or thatch cover. The hydrologic soil type in the cultivated zone is B.

The information from this description is shown on the SCS worksheet, Figure 4-23. The CN values were found in Table 4-5. A weighted CN is developed by multiplying the CN for each area by the acreage and

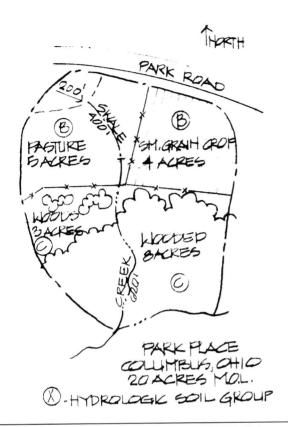

FIGURE 4.22 FINDING THE COMPOSITE CN

dividing that by the total acreage. In this case, the average CN was 69.05 so CN 70 will be used. The higher CN was used here since the majority of the site had CNs above 70.

Next, the precipitation volumes were found for the 2-, 25-, and 100-year storms for the region from the maps at the end of the chapter. Runoff volume in inches can be estimated for each of these storms using Table 4-6, the graph in Figure 4-24, or the runoff equation. To illustrate all three, the table will be used for the 2-year storm, the graph for the 25-year storm, and the equation for the 100-year storm.

Using Table 4-6, find 2.5 inches in the left column and move right to find 0.46 inches in the column under CN 70. Using the graph, Figure 4-24, read right along the bottom line, rainfall (P) in inches, to 4 in. Then read up the CN 70, then left to 1.3 in.

To use the equation method, the first step is to solve for S as follows:

$$S = \frac{(1000)}{CN} - 10$$

$$S = \frac{(1000)}{70} - 10$$

$$S = 14.2857 - 10$$

$$S = 4.2857$$

Then find Q as:

$$Q = \frac{(P - 0.2S)^2}{P + 0.8S}$$

$$Q = \frac{(5 \text{ in} - .2 \times 4.2857)^2}{5 \text{ in} + 0.8 \times 4.2857}$$

$$Q = \frac{(5 \text{ in} - 0.8571)^2}{5 \text{ in} + 3.4286}$$

$$Q = \frac{17.1633}{8.4286}$$

$$Q = 2.04 \text{ in}$$

A quick look at Figure 4-24, or Table 4-6, will show the same results.

The value of Q given by the SCS equation should not be confused with the value Qf given by the rational formula. The value of Q given using the SCS CN formula is the total runoff anticipated for a 24-hour period over a specific area in inches. The relationship in the formula has no expression for storm duration or rainfall intensity, so it cannot be used to recreate the features of a specific short-duration storm. Likewise, this method only estimates direct surface runoff,

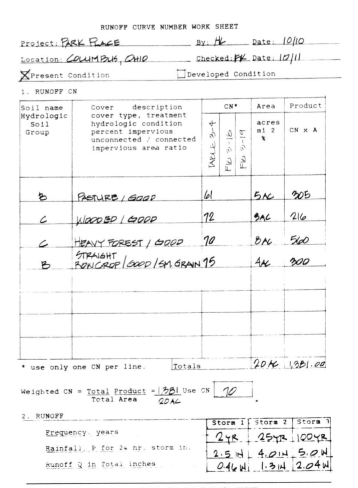

FIGURE 4.23 RUNOFF CN WORKSHEET

making no allowance for subsurface flows. Usually groundwater tables, in small watersheds, contribute very little to total runoff. The possibility of subsurface flow contributing to the total runoff is high in soils of the hydrologic soil group A, and good judgment must be used in selecting the CN values in these cases.

The CN method should only be used when the time of concentration of the area is greater than 0.1 hr (6 min), and where the weighted CN is greater than 40. SCS also notes additional limitations that should be taken into account.

1. CNs describe average conditions that are useful for design purposes. If the rainfall event used is a historical storm the modeling accuracy decreases.
2. Use the runoff curve number equation with caution when recreating specific features of an actual storm. The equation does not contain an expression for time and, therefore, does not account for rainfall duration or intensity.
3. The user should understand the assumption reflected in the initial abstraction term (I_a) and should ascertain that the assumption applies to the situation. I_a, which consists of interception, initial infiltration, surface depression storage, evapotranspiration, and other factors, was generalized as $0.2S$ based on data from *agricultural watersheds* (S is the potential maximum retention *after runoff begins*). This approximation can be especially important in an urban application because the combination of impervious areas

with pervious areas can imply a significant initial loss that may not take place. The opposite effect, a greater initial loss, can occur if the impervious areas have surface depressions that store some runoff. To use a relationship other than $I_a = 0.2S$, one must redevelop equation 2-3, Figure 2-1, Table 1-1 and Table 2-2 (2nd edition, TR-55, June 1986) by using the original rainfall-runoff data to establish new S or CN relationships for each cover and hydrologic soil group.

4. Runoff from snowmelt or rain on frozen ground cannot be estimated using these procedures.
5. The CN procedure is less accurate when runoff is less than 0.5 inch. As a check use another procedure to determine runoff.
6. The SCS runoff procedures apply only to direct surface runoff: do not overlook large sources of subsurface flow or high groundwater levels that contribute runoff. These conditions are often related to HSG A soils and forest areas that have been assigned relatively low CNs in Table 4-5. Good judgment and experience based on stream gage records are needed to adjust CNs as conditions warrant.

THE SCS GRAPHICAL METHOD OF ESTIMATING PEAK DISCHARGE

The graphical method is an alternative to using the rational formula for estimating peak discharge. The

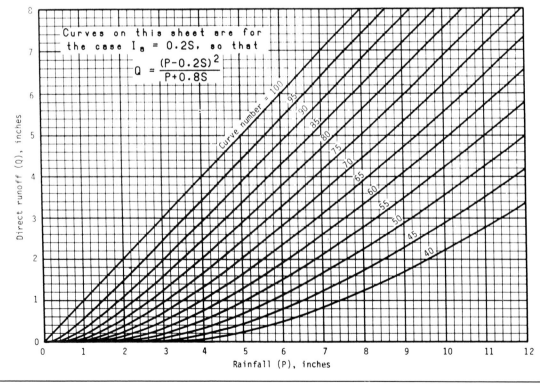

FIGURE 4.24 GRAPHICAL SOLUTIONS OF SCS RUNOFF EQUATION
TR-55, Second Ed., June 1986

TABLE 4.6 RUNOFF DEPTH FOR SELECTED CN'S AND RAINFALL AMOUNTS[1]

Rainfall	Runoff Depth for Curve Number of—												
	40	45	50	55	60	65	70	75	80	85	90	95	98
	inches												
1.0	0.00	0.00	0.00	0.00	0.00	0.00	0.00	0.03	0.08	0.17	0.32	0.56	0.79
1.2	.00	.00	.00	.00	.00	.00	.03	.07	.15	.27	.46	.74	.99
1.4	.00	.00	.00	.00	.00	.02	.06	.13	.24	.39	.61	92	1.18
1.6	.00	.00	.00	.00	.01	.05	.11	.20	.34	52	76	1.11	1.38
1.8	.00	.00	.00	.00	.03	.09	.17	.29	.44	.65	.93	1.29	1.58
2.0	.00	.00	.00	.02	.06	.14	.24	.38	.56	.80	1.09	1.48	1.77
2.5	.00	.00	.02	.08	.17	.30	.46	.65	.89	1.18	1.53	1.96	2.27
3.0	.00	.02	.09	.19	.33	.51	.71	.96	1.25	1.59	1.98	2.45	2.77
3.5	.02	.08	.20	.35	.53	.75	1.01	1.30	1.64	2.02	2.45	2.94	3.27
4.0	.06	.18	.33	.53	.76	1.03	1.33	1.67	2.04	2.46	2.92	3.43	3.77
4.5	.14	.30	.50	.74	1.02	1.33	1.67	2.05	2.46	2.91	3.40	3.92	4.26
5.0	.24	.44	.69	.98	1.30	1.65	2.04	2.45	2.89	3.37	3.88	4.42	4.76
6.0	.50	.80	1.14	1.52	1.92	2.35	2.81	3.28	3.78	4.30	4.85	5.41	5.76
7.0	.84	1.24	1.68	2.12	2.60	3.10	3.62	4.15	4.69	5.25	5.82	6.41	6.76
8.0	1.25	1.74	2.25	2.78	3.33	3.89	4.46	5.04	5.63	6.21	6.81	7.40	7.76
9.0	1.71	2.29	2.88	3.49	4.10	4.72	5.33	5.95	6.57	7.18	7.79	8.40	8.76
10.0	2.23	2.89	3.56	4.23	4.90	5.56	6.22	6.88	7.52	8.16	8.78	9.40	9.76
11.0	2.78	3.52	4.26	5.00	5.72	6.43	7.13	7.81	8.48	9.13	9.77	10.39	10.76
12.0	3.38	4.19	5.00	5.79	6.56	7.32	8.05	8.76	9.45	10.11	10.76	11.39	11.76
13.0	4.00	4.89	5.76	6.61	7.42	8.21	8.98	9.71	10.42	11.10	11.76	12.39	12.76
14.0	4.65	5.62	6.55	7.44	8.30	9.12	9.91	10.67	11.39	12.08	12.75	13.39	13.76
15.0	5.33	6.36	7.35	8.29	9.19	10.04	10.85	11.63	12.37	13.07	13.74	14.39	14.76

[1]Interpolate the values shown to obtain for CN's or rainfall amounts not shown.
TR-55, Second Ed., June 1986.

graphical method is used for small homogeneous watersheds that can be characterized by a single CN value. The information required to use the graphical method is: t_t in hr, the drainage area in sq mi, the SCS rainfall distribution type, the 24-hr rainfall in inches, and the SCS CN. In addition to these data, if ponds or swampy areas are present in the watershed, it is necessary to make an adjustment for these.

The formula for peak discharge is:

$$q_p = q_u \, A_m \, Q \, F_p$$

Where:

q_p = peak discharge in cfs (The same as Q_t in the rational formula)

q_u = unit peak discharge in cubic feet per second per square mile per inch of runoff (csm/in)

A_m = area of the watershed in sq mi

Q = the runoff in inches

F_p = pond and swamp adjustment factor as required

To illustrate the graphical method of estimating peak discharge we will use the same problem used to illustrate the rational method. This will allow the results of the two different methods to be compared.

The first step was to determine the appropriate CN for the site following the same procedures outlined earlier. The weighted CN for the 3.5 acre site was 65, based on the cover complex of dense woods and good turf, with soils of hydrologic soil group B and C, see Figure 4-29.

The 50-year, 24-hr rainfall for the Manhattan, Kansas, area was read from the maps at the end of the chapter as 7 in, and the total runoff Q, was 3.10 in read from Table 4-6. The time of concentration was computed earlier to be 40 min. All of this information is summarized in the SCS worksheet, Figure 4-30.

Next, step 4 in the SCS worksheet, read the value of I_a for a CN of 65 from Table 4-7 to be 1.077, and compute the I_a/P ratio as follows:

I_a = 1.077
P = 7.00 in
I_a/P = 0.15

From Figure 4-27 read q_u to be 425 csm/in.

With the value of q_u known, substitute into the equation as follows:

$q_p = q_u \, A_m \, Q \, F_p$
q_p = 425 csm/in × 0.0055 sq mi × 3.10 in × 1
q_p = 7.25 cfs

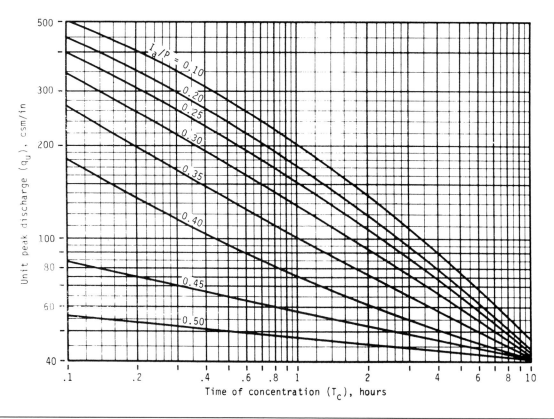

FIGURE 4.25 UNIT PEAK DISCHARGE FOR SCS TYPE I RAINFALL DISTRIBUTION
TR-55, Second Ed., June 1986

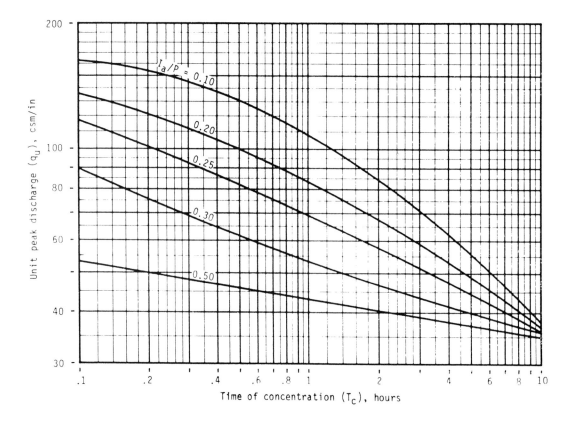

FIGURE 4.26 UNIT PEAK DISCHARGE FOR SCS TYPE IA RAINFALL DISTRIBUTION
TR-55, Second Ed., June 1986

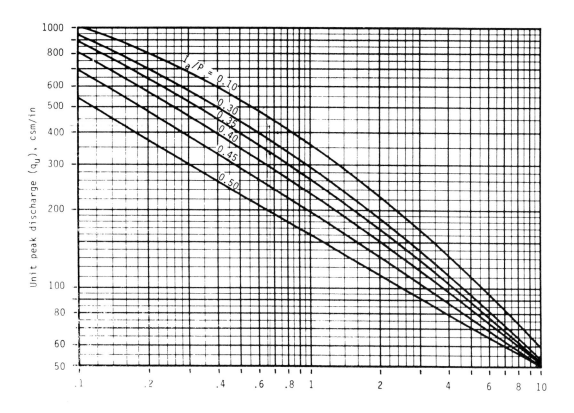

FIGURE 4.27 UNIT PEAK DISCHARGE FOR SCS TYPE II RAINFALL DISTRIBUTION
TR-55, Second Ed., June 1986

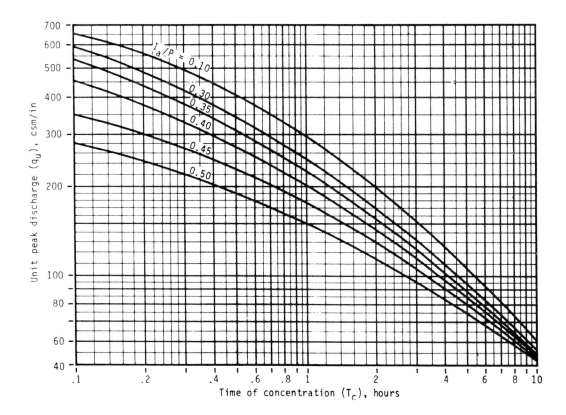

FIGURE 4.28 UNIT PEAK DISCHARGE FOR SCS TYPE III RAINFALL DISTRIBUTION
TR-55, Second Ed., June 1986

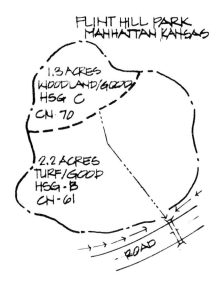

FLINT HILL PARK
MANHATTAN KANSAS

1.3 ACRES
WOODLAND/GOOD
HSG C
CN 70

2.2 ACRES
TURF/GOOD
HSG B
CN 61

ROAD

DRAINAGE DATA
LOCATION: MANHATTAN, KANSAS
P= 7", 50 YR 2 HR
TYPE II DISTRIBUTION
Tc = 40 MIN OR 0.67 HR.
TOTAL AREA 3.5 ACRES OR .0055 MI²

WEIGHTED CN = 65

FIGURE 4.29 *GRAPHICAL PEAK DISCHARGE*

Note that the ponding factor is set at 1, since there was no adjustment needed in the example.

The SCS graphical peak discharge method yields a runoff rate of 7.25 cfs while the estimate made with the rational method yielded an estimated volume of 4.14 cfs for the similar conditions. This is a difference of 3.11 cfs, which is substantial considering the small area of the watershed. The reason for the difference is in the selection of the value of C, (the runoff coefficient), in the rational method. Had a slightly higher value been used, say 0.40 instead of the 0.24, the rational formula would have yielded an estimate of 6.90 cfs, making the results much closer. This comparison is noted here to emphasize the need for good judgment in selecting the variables used in any equation.

The SCS notes several limitations to the graphical method.

- The graphical method provides a determination of peak discharge only. If a hydrograph is needed or watershed subdivision is required, use the Tabular Hydrograph method. Use TR-20 if the watershed is very complex or a higher degree of accuracy is required.

- The watershed must be hydrologically homogeneous, that is, describable by one CN. Land use, soils, and cover are distributed uniformly throughout the watershed.
- The watershed may have only one main stream or, if more than one, the branches must have nearly equal t_ts.
- The method cannot perform valley or reservoir routing.
- The F_p factor can be applied only for ponds or swamps that are not in the t_t flow path.
- Accuracy of peak discharge estimated by this method will be reduced if I_a/P values are used that are outside the range given in Figures 4-25 to 4-28 of this text. The limiting I_a/P values are recommended for use.
- This method should only be used if the weighted CN is greater than 40.
- When this method is used to develop estimates of peak discharge for both present and developed conditions of a watershed, use the same procedure for estimating t_t.
- t_t values with this method may range from 0.1 to 10 hours.

SCS TABULAR HYDROGRAPH METHOD FOR ESTIMATING PEAK RUNOFF

A hydrograph is the flow in cfs measured at a selected point in a stream or drainage channel plotted against time, Figure 4-31. The rational formula and the SCS graphical methods of estimating peak runoff rates can only be used for small homogeneous drainage areas. (To be homogeneous the watershed should have similar slopes, relatively uniform landcover and surface characteristics.) The tabular method is used when as hydrograph is required and the watershed is not hydrologically homogeneous.

The TR-55 tabular hydrograph procedure is particularly useful for making estimates of the effects of development on peak discharge characteristics since it closely approximates the Soil Conservation Service's TR-20 computer model for doing detailed hydrologic analysis. It has gained widespread popularity in many parts of the country and has been adopted by many governmental agencies as the required method for doing estimates of increased runoff caused by development. The information required to use the tabular method is as follows:

1. A map of the watershed subdivided into generally homogeneous subareas by land cover and soil type. Each subarea can have only one main drainage channel.
2. The area of each subarea in square miles.

GRAPHICAL PEAK DISCHARGE METHOD

Project: FLINT HILL PARK   By: HL   Date: 10/10

Location: MANHATTAN, KANSAS   Checked: DA   Date: 10/11

☐ Present Condition   ☒ Developed Condition

1. Data

Drainage area	A_m = .0055	mi2 (acres/640)
Runoff curve number	CN = 65	(use CN worksheet)
Time of Concentration	T_c = .07	in hours
Rainfall distribution	= II	(I, IA, II, III)
Pond and swamp areas	= 0	percent of total area

		Storm 1	Storm 2	Storm 3
2.	Frequency, year	50		
3.	Rainfall, P (24 hour period)	7.0 IN		
4.	Initial abstraction, Ia (use CN with Table 4-7)	1.077		
5.	Compute Ia/P	0.15		
6.	Unit peak discharge, qu (use Tc and Ia/P with Figure 4-25, 4-26, 4-27, 4-28)	425 CSM/IN		
7.	Runoff, Q (from CN worksheet)	3.10 IN		
8.	Pond and swamp adjustment factor, Fp (Use precent pond and swamp area with the table included below. Factor is 1.0 for areas with no ponds or swamps.)	1		
9.	Peak discharge, qp (where $q_p = q_u A_m Q F_p$)	7.25 CFS		

q_p = 425 CSM/IN × .0055 sq mi × 3.10 IN = 7.25 CFS

Pond and Swamp Adjustment Percentage of pond and swamp areas	Fp
0	1.00
0.2	0.97
1.0	0.87
3.0	0.75
5.0	0.72

FIGURE 4.30 GRAPHICAL PEAK DISCHARGE WORKSHEET

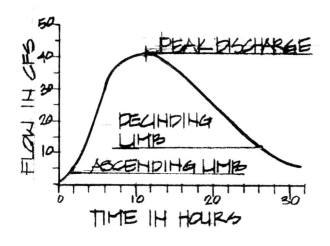

FIGURE 4.31 STREAM HYDROGRAPH

3. The time of concentration for each subarea, and the travel time through the subarea for any runoff contributed by subareas upstream.
4. Weighted CN's for each of the subareas.
5. The rainfall distribution type for the region; e.g., Type II.
6. The 24-hour rainfall in inches for the storm(s) of a specified return frequency.
7. The total runoff volume, Q, in inches computed using the CN.
8. The value of I_a from Table 4-7.

9. The ratio of I_a to P for each of the subareas. If the I_a to P ratio is greater than 0.50 or less than 0.10 the closest value should be used. For example, if the computed value of I_a/P is 0.008 use 0.10.

To illustrate the application of the tabular hydrograph method, consider the watershed diagram and summary data in Figure 4-32, a & b. The watershed has a total area of 523 acres, and is located in Alachua County, Florida. The land is to be developed from its current state into a mixed-use land subdivision. The task is to determine the net increase in runoff that will result from the development so that on-site stormwater detention structures can be provided in the preliminary land plan. Since the watershed is not hydrologically homogenous, and has more than a single drainage channel, it will be necessary to break the area down into subareas and use the tabular hydrograph method to determine the peak discharge for both the developed and undeveloped conditions.

The preliminary data were developed to determine the weighted CNs, the time of concentration, and travel times through the lower reaches. The rainfall data were taken from the maps at the end of the chapter, and the values of I_a were read directly from Table 4-7. All of the preliminary data are summarized on the SCS worksheets in Figures 4-33 and 4-34.

In the basic watershed data worksheet, notice that the travel time through the subarea and the travel time

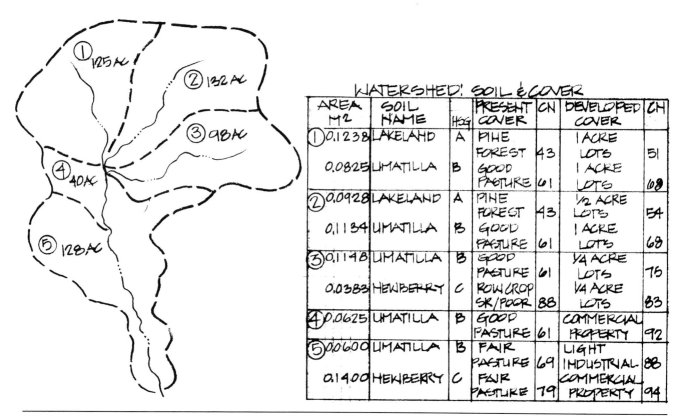

AREA M²	SOIL NAME	HSG	PRESENT COVER	CN	DEVELOPED COVER	CN
① 0.1238	LAKELAND	A	PINE FOREST	43	1 ACRE LOTS	51
0.0825	UMATILLA	B	GOOD PASTURE	61	1 ACRE LOTS	68
② 0.0928	LAKELAND	A	PINE FOREST	43	½ ACRE LOTS	54
0.1134	UMATILLA	B	GOOD PASTURE	61	1 ACRE LOTS	68
③ 0.1148	UMATILLA	B	GOOD PASTURE	61	¼ ACRE LOTS	75
0.0383	NEWBERRY	C	ROW CROP SR/POOR	88	¼ ACRE LOTS	83
④ 0.0625	UMATILLA	B	GOOD PASTURE	61	COMMERCIAL PROPERTY	92
⑤ 0.0600	UMATILLA	B	FAIR PASTURE	69	LIGHT INDUSTRIAL	88
0.1400	NEWBERRY	C	FAIR PASTURE	79	COMMERCIAL PROPERTY	94

WATERSHED: SOIL & COVER

TABLE 4.32a WATERSHED DIAGRAM GAINE'S WOOD SUBDIVISION

SHEET FLOW DATA

DRAINAGE SUBAREA	FLOW LENGTH	'n' PRESENT	'n' DEVELOPED	AVERAGE SLOPE, FT/FT
①	250 FT.	0.24	0.41	.025
②	220 FT	0.24	0.41	.020
③	275 FT.	0.24	0.05	.023
④	100 FT	0.24	0.011	.010
⑤	300 FT	0.24	0.05	.015

SHALLOW CONCENTRATED FLOW DATA

DRAINAGE SUBAREA	FLOW LENGTH	SURFACE PRESENT	SURFACE DEVELOPED	AVERAGE SLOPE FT/FT
①	1,200 FT	UNPAVED	PAVED	.015
②	750 FT	UNPAVED	PAVED	.010
③	850 FT	UNPAVED	PAVED	.015
④	650 FT	UNPAVED	PAVED	.010
⑤	940 FT	UNPAVED	PAVED	.015

OPEN CHANNEL FLOW DATA

	FLOW LENGTH	SLOPE FT/FT	'n'	CHANNEL AREA	WETTED PERIMETER	'r'	SECTION AT OUTLET
①	1,400'	.004	.027	32 FT²	15.31'	2.09	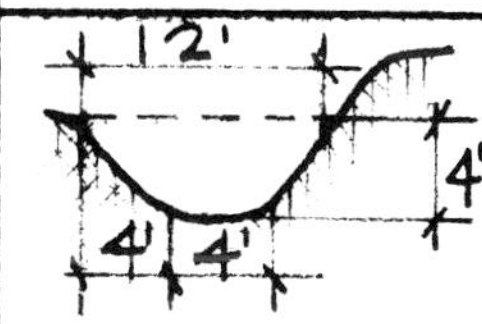
②	1,900'	.003	.027	48.24 FT²	19.37'	2.49	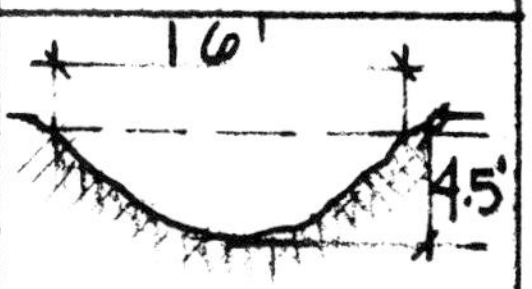
③	2,300'	.004	.027	42 FT²	20.04'	2.10	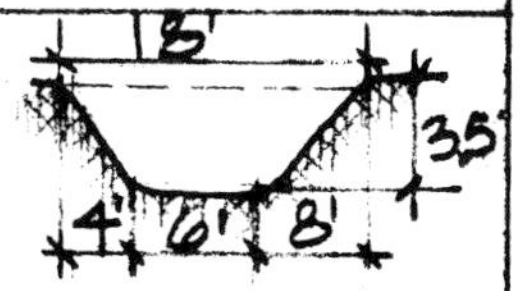
④	1,200 / 1,500*	.003	.027	64 FT²	24.42'	2.62	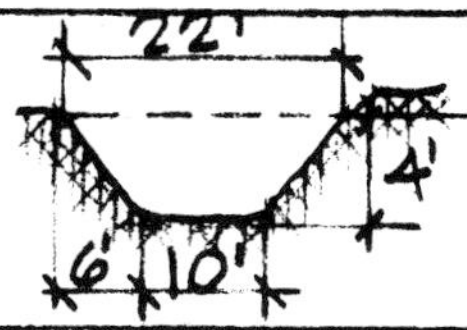
⑤	2,800' / 3,100'*	.003	.027	100 FT²	32.36'	3.09	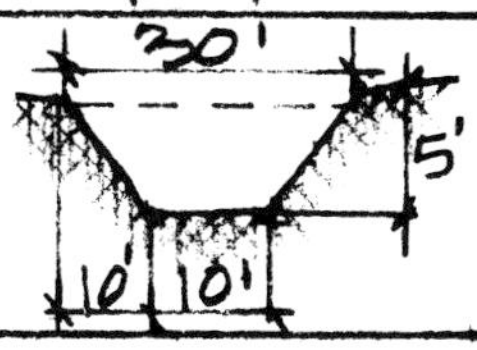

* LENGTH OF CHANNEL FOR TRAVEL TIME

FIGURE 4.32b SUMMARY OF FLOW DATA: GAINE'S WOOD SUBDIVISION

BASIC WATERSHED DATA WORKSHEET

Project: GAINE'S WOOD   Location: ALACHUA COUNTY   By: HL   Date: 10/20

☒ Present Condition   ☐ Developed Condition   Checked By: DA   Date: 10/20

Sub area No.	Area sq.mi Am	Tc hr.	Travel time hr.	Down stream sub area Nos.	Time to outlet hr.	24 hr rain fall P	Runoff CN	Runoff Q in	Am x Q sq.mi. & in.	Ia in.	Ia/P
1	.21	.62/.75	∅	4,5	.18/.10	10"	50	3.56	.75	2.00	.20/.10
2	21	.60/.75	∅	4,5	.18/.10	"	53	3.96	.83	1.774	.18/.10
3	.15	.60/.75	∅	4,5	.18/.10	"	68	5.96	.89	0.941	.09/.10
4	.06	.43/.40	.06	5	.12/.10	"	61	5.03	.30	1.279	.13/.10
5	.20	.80/.75	.12	—	∅/∅	"	76	7.01	1.40	0.632	.06/.10

◹ — COMPUTED VALUE
◿ — TABLE VALUE USED

FIGURE 4.33   BASIC WATERSHED DATA WORKSHEET: GAINE'S WOOD, PRESENT

BASIC WATERSHED DATA WORKSHEET

Project: GAINE'S WOOD   Location: ALACHUA COUNTY   By: HL   Date: 10/20

☐ Present Condition   ☒ Developed Condition   Checked By: DA   Date: 10/20

Sub area No.	Area sq.mi Am	Tc hr.	Travel time hr.	Down stream sub area Nos.	Time to outlet hr.	24 hr rain fall P	Runoff CN	Runoff Q in	Am x Q sq.mi. & in.	Ia in.	Ia/P
1	.21	.58/.75	—	4,5	.20/.10	10"	58	4.63	0.97	1.448	.14/.10
2	.21	.57/.50	—	4,5	.20/.20	"	62	5.17	1.09	1.226	.12/.10
3	.15	.63/.75	—	4,5	.20/.10	"	77	7.14	1.07	0.597	.06/.10
4	.06	.41/.40	.07	5	.13/.10	"	92	9.03	0.54	0.174	.02/.10
5	.20	.77/.75	.13	—	∅/∅	"	92	9.03	1.80	0.174	.02/.10

FIGURE 4.34   BASIC WATERSHED DATA WORKSHEET: GAINE'S WOOD, DEVELOPED

to the outlet are independent of the time of concentration. The travel time through the subarea is the time it will take water entering the the subarea from upstream to travel through the area. The travel time to the outlet for a subarea is the sum of all the subarea travel times that the water will pass through. Notice in Figure 4-32 that subareas 1, 2, and 3 all come together at the upper edge of subarea 4. This means that the water leaving each of these first three subareas passes through subarea 4 and subarea 5. The travel time for the creek segment of subarea 4 is 0.05 hr and the travel time for the creek segment of subarea 5 is 0.12 hr in the present condition. The total time to the outlet for the first three subareas is 0.18 hr. Water leaving subarea 4 travels only through subarea 5 to reach the outlet so it has a time to the outlet of 0.12 hr.

Once the basic watershed data worksheet is complete, a portion of the discharge hydrograph can be developed for the appropriate rainfall distribution using the tabular hydrograph discharge summary

TABLE 4.7 I_a VALUES FOR RUNOFF CURVE NUMBERS[1]

Curve Number	I_a (in)	Curve Number	I_a (in)
40	3.000	70	0.857
41	2.878	71	0.817
42	2.762	72	0.778
43	2.651	73	0.740
44	2.545	74	0.703
45	2.444	75	0.667
46	2.384	76	0.632
47	2.255	77	0.597
48	2.167	78	0.564
49	2.082	79	0.532
50	2.000	80	0.500
51	1.922	81	0.469
52	1.846	82	0.439
53	1.774	83	0.410
54	1.704	84	0.381
55	1.636	85	0.353
56	1.571	86	0.326
57	1.509	87	0.299
58	1.448	88	0.273
59	1.390	89	0.247
60	1.333	90	0.222
61	1.279	91	0.198
62	1.226	92	0.174
63	1.175	93	0.151
64	1.125	94	0.128
65	1.077	95	0.105
66	1.030	96	0.083
67	0.985	97	0.062
68	0.941	98	0.041
69	0.899		

[1]TR-55 Second Ed., June 1986

TABLE 4.8 SCS ROUNDING METHOD FOR VALUES OF t_c and t_t

Computed Values		Rounding Strategy		
		a	b	c
t_c	0.62	0.50	0.75	0.50
t_t	0.18	0.20	0.10	0.20
Total	0.80	0.70	0.85*	0.70

*Value closest to sum of computed values

worksheet and the tabular hydrograph unit discharge tables at the end of the chapter. The discharge rates shown in the tables should not be interpolated for values of t_t and t_t that do not match. Instead, the SCS recommends that three different rounding strategies be employed to decide which of the table values for t_t and t_t should be used.

a. Round t_t and t_t separately to the nearest table value and add them together.
b. Round t_t up and t_t down to the nearest table value and add them together.
c. Round t_t down and t_t up to the nearest table value and add them together.

The total closest to the the sum of the computed values of t_t and t_t should be the table values used. For example, the values of t_t and t_t computed for subarea 1 of the example problem, for the present condition, are 0.62 hr and 0.18 hr, respectively. The rounding procedure is shown in Table 4-8.

Option b gives the sum closest to the sum of the computed values so the table values of 0.75 for t_t and 0.10 for t_t will be used to develop the composite flood hydrograph. Notice in the basic watershed data worksheets, and on the tabular hydrograph worksheets, the table value used is noted next to the computed value.

The values for the I_a/P ratio can be rounded to the nearest value in the tables or the values can be interpolated. In cases where interpolation would be desirable for reasons of additional accuracy, the computation time can be reduced by obtaining a copy of the TR-55 computer program from SCS. The program is very simple and will run on any IBM PC compatible machine.

In the example the I_a/P ratio was simply rounded to the nearest table value. Figures 4-35 and 4-36 are the tabular hydrograph summary worksheets for the present and developed conditions of the example problem. The basic watershed data was taken from the appropriate worksheet, Figures 4-33 and 4-34. The computed values of t_t, time to outlet, and I_a/P are shown to the left of the slash and the table value used in the computation is shown to the right of the slash.

TABULAR HYDROGRAPH WORKSHEET

Project: GAINE'S WOOD Location: ALACHUA COUNTY By: HL Date: 10/20

[X] Present Condition [ ] Developed Condition Checked By: DA Date: 10/20

Rainfall Distrubution: II Storm Frequency: 100 YR

Subarea No.	Basic Watershed Data Used: sub area Tc	Time to outlet	Ia/P	Am x Q	Discharges at selected times, cfs: 12.1	12.2	12.3	12.4	12.5	12.6	12.7	12.8	13.0	13.2	13.4	13.6
1	.67/.75	.18/.10	.20/.10	.75	44	72	121	187	252	296	303	285	209	143	101	75
2	.60/.75	.18/.10	.18/.10	.83	49	80	134	207	279	327	336	316	231	158	112	83
3	.66/.75	.18/.10	.09/.10	.89	52	86	144	222	299	351	360	339	248	169	120	89
4	.43/.40	.12/.10	.13/.10	.30	65	115	156	167	141	107	78	58	35	25	20	17
5	.80/.75	0/0	.06/.10	1.40	95	161	271	411	532	593	574	516	352	240	172	130
Composite hydrograph at outlet					305	514	826	1194	1503	1674	1,651	1514	1075	735	525	394

Select and enter hydrograph times from appropriate table at the end of the chapter.

FIGURE 4.35 TABULAR HYDROGRAPH WORKSHEET: GAINE'S WOOD, PRESENT

TABULAR HYDROGRAPH WORKSHEET

Project: GAINE'S WOOD Location: ALACHUA COUNTY By: HL Date: 10/20

[ ] Present Condition [X] Developed Condition Checked By: DA Date: 10/20

Rainfall Distrubution: II Storm Frequency: 100 YR

Subarea No.	Basic Watershed Data Used: sub area Tc	Time to outlet	Ia/P	Am x Q	Discharges at selected times, cfs: 12.1	12.2	12.3	12.4	12.5	12.6	12.7	12.8	13.0	13.2	13.4	13.6
1	.58/.75	.20/.10	.14/.10	0.97	57	94	157	242	326	383	392	369	270	185	130	97
2	.57/.50	.20/.20	.12/.10	1.09	75	126	225	361	473	519	489	412	259	162	110	83
3	.63/.75	.20/.10	.06/.10	1.07	63	103	173	267	360	422	433	407	298	204	144	107
4	.41/.40	.13/.10	.02/.10	0.54	118	207	282	300	255	192	142	105	64	45	36	30
5	.77/.75	0/0	.02/.10	1.80	122	207	349	529	684	763	738	664	453	309	221	167
Composite hydrograph at outlet					435	737	1186	1699	2098	2279	2194	1957	1344	905	641	484

Select and enter hydrograph times from appropriate table at the end of the chapter.

FIGURE 4.36 TABULAR HYDROGRAPH WORKSHEET: GAINE'S WOOD, DEVELOPED

The composite hydrograph is developed by going to the appropriate set of tables for the rainfall distribution type and selecting the time range that will include the peak discharges of all the subareas of the watershed. Then, for each subarea, find the table with the appropriate t_t value at the proper I_a/P ratio. Select the row with the proper time to outlet value and multiply the discharge shown in the table for each of the selected time periods by the A_mQ value for the subarea. This is done for each subarea and then the values for each time period selected are totaled for the composite hydrograph.

To illustrate the process, look at subarea 1, for the present condition, Figure 4-35. The rounded table values used are:

$$t_c = 0.75$$
$$t_t = 0.10$$
$$I_a/P = 0.10$$

Go to the tables at the end of the chapter for Type II rainfall distribution, and find the table for $t_c = 0.75$ with $I_a/P = 0.10$. The appropriate unit discharge rates are read from the line where $t_t = 0.10$. The first hydrograph point is 12.1 hours and the discharge rate shown in the table is 59 cfs. This value is multiplied by the A_mQ value of 0.75, as follows:

$$59 \text{ cfs} \times 0.75 = 44 \text{ cfs}$$

This is repeated for each of the hydrograph times until all the subarea hydrographs are computed. The total of the subarea hydrographs provide a composite hydrograph for the entire drainage basin. In the example problem, the peak discharge occurs at 12.6 hours into a 24-hour storm event for both the present and the developed condition. The estimated undeveloped peak discharge is 1,674 cfs, Figure 4-35, and the estimated developed peak discharge is 2,279 cfs, Figure 4-36, an increase of 605 cfs.

SCS lists some specific limitations to the use of the tabular hydrograph method:

The tabular method is used to determine peak flows and hydrographs within a watershed. However, its accuracy decreases as the complexity of the watershed increases. If you want to compare present and developed conditions of a watershed, use the same procedures for estimating t_t for both conditions.

Use the TR-20 computer program (SCS 1983) instead of the Tabular method in any of the following applies:

- t_t is greater than 3 hours (largest t_t in hydrograph tables).
- t_c is greater than 2 hours (largest t_t in hydrograph tables).

- Drainage areas of individual subareas differ by a factor of 5 or more.
- The entire composite flood hydrograph or entire runoff volume is required for detailed flood routings. The hydrograph based on extrapolation is only an approximation of the entire hydrograph.
- The time of peak discharge must be more accurate than that obtained through the tabular method.

ESTIMATING DETENTION BASIN VOLUME

On-site detention of stormwater has become the most common means of affecting a reduction in downstream flooding that often results from new development. Provision of stormwater detention basins requires that some land be set aside in the early stages of design. TR-55 provides a simple method for making preliminary estimates of detention basin volumes once the peak discharges from a site are known.

To estimate the approximate volume of storage that will be needed for a project the following information is required:

1. The total runoff volume (V_r)
2. The maximum allowable outflow from the detention basin
3. The maximum inflow into the detention basin, (q_i)

For making detention volume estimates, V_r is usually expressed in acre-ft. An acre-foot of water is 1 acre covered by 1 ft of water or a total of 43,560 cu ft of water. V_r in acre-ft is found by the following:

$$V_r = 53.33 \ Q \ A_m$$

Where:

V_r = the runoff volume in acre-ft
Q = runoff in inches
A_m = the drainage area in square miles
53.33 = the conversion constant for in/sq mi to acre-ft

In most cases, the allowable outflow (q_o) is set at the predevelopment peak discharge for a selected storm frequency or frequencies. In most urban areas that require stormwater detention it is becoming common to require detention of more than a single storm. The reason for this is that if a detention basin outlet is designed for only the 100-year storm frequency, the control structure will allow the the water from a lesser storm to be discharged with little or no detention.

When detention design is based on more than one storm frequency, there will usually be two different

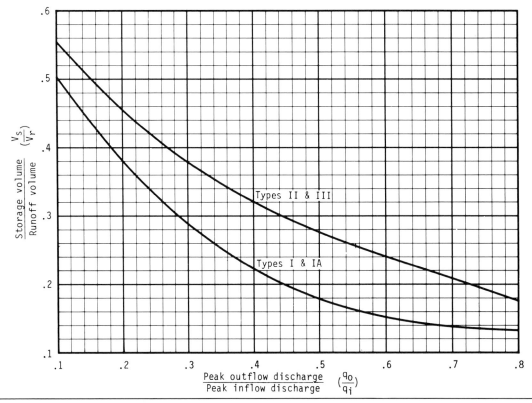

FIGURE 4.37 APPROXIMATE DETENTION BASIN ROUTING FOR RAINFALL TYPES I, IA, II, III

values for q_o and there will be more than one outlet structure used to control the discharge from the basin. Regardless of the design requirements for single or multiple discharge stages, however, the largest volume of detention required will be based on the greatest storm frequency and the maximum allowable discharge for that storm.

The maximum inflow (q_i) is simply the peak discharge based on either the graphical or tabular hydrograph method. SCS suggests that the greatest accuracy in estimating the detention volume is achieved using the tabular hydrograph method for estimating q_i.

To illustrate the procedure for estimating the required volume of detention, the information generated for the previous example problem will be used.

Step 1. Determine the value of q_o and q_i. For the example, assume that the design requirements are to limit the peak discharge from the site to the undeveloped 100-year peak discharge. In Figure 4-35 this was estimated to be 1,674 cfs. From Figure 4-36, the value of q_i was estimated as 2,279 cfs.

Step 2. Compute the ratio of q_o/q_i as follows:

$$q_o/q_i = \frac{1,674 \text{ cfs}}{2,279 \text{ cfs}}$$

$$q_o/q_i = 0.73$$

Use the graph in Figure 4-37 and enter on the bottom line at $q_o/q_i = .73$ and read up to the rainfall Type II & III line, then left to find $V_s/V_r = 0.20$.

Step 3. Find the total runoff in in/sq mi from Figure 4-36 by adding the A_mQ values for each of the subareas as follows:

1. 0.97
2. 1.09
3. 1.07
4. 0.54
5. 1.80
   $\overline{5.47}$ in/sq mi

Inches per sq mi are now converted to acre-feet as follows:

$V_r = 53.33 \ Q \ A_m$
$V_r = 53.33 \times 5.47$
$V_r = 291.72$ acre-ft

Step 4. Solve for V_s as follows:

$$V_s = V_r \left(\frac{(V_s)}{V_r}\right)$$

$V_s = 291.72$ acre-ft $\times 0.20$

$V_s = 58.34$ acre-ft

The 58.34 acre-ft represents the total detention volume required for the 100-year storm frequency. A quick way to get some idea of the area that will be required to hold this volume of water is to assume a square basin and an average depth in ft. Divide the required detention volume by the assumed depth and multiply by 43,560 sq ft/acre and take the square root to find the approximate surface dimensions of the detention basin.

For example, assume an average depth of 10 ft for the detention basin and divide:

58.34 acre ft ÷ 10 ft = 5.83 acres

5.83 acres × 43,560 sq ft/acre = 253,954 sq ft

$253,954^{0.5}$ = 503 ft

Thus, a square detention basin 503 ft × 503 ft and an average depth of 10 ft would be required to store the required 58.34 acre-ft of water. This example makes no provision of extra volume to adjust for siltation of the detention basin during construction and assumes that an average depth of 10 ft is possible and practical. In most situations it is advisable to increase the volume of the detention basin to account for siltation that will occur over time and during the initial construction period. It is also advisable to check the local regulations for any restrictions that might be placed on the cross-sectional shape and depth of detention basins.

Keep in mind that a five-acre tract is a sizable land commitment for stormwater management. Quite often it will be desirable to break up the total detention requirement into smaller basins located upstream of the primary outlet. This can be accomplished by designing retention basins for each of the subareas or in some combination of the subareas. Exploring the alternatives is relatively simple if the tabular hydrograph method is used to develop the peak discharge data.

The SCS points out that the margin of error in using this method for estimating detention volumes can be as high as 25%, but the graph in Figure 4-37 has a bias so that basins will be oversized rather than undersized. Students are also cautioned that this method for estimating detention volume can only be used with the SCS methods of determining peak discharge. Peak discharges developed with the rational formula cannot be used.

The material presented in this section has been developed to give students and professionals a practical introduction to the subject of site hydraulics. All of the materials and procedures presented can be used to make preliminary estimates of runoff volumes, pipe sizes, and retention volumes. However, final design of a drainage system will require a more detailed understanding of hydraulics. It is suggested that some of the references listed in the bibliography be consulted for further study.

Drainage Structures

There are several kinds of common drainage structures that enter into a completed storm drainage system. Each structure is designed to perform a specific task and is just as important as the pipes or surface channels of the system.

HEADWALLS AND ENDWALLS

A headwall is used where a surface channel enters a closed conduit. Typically headwalls will occur at the entrance to culverts that carry drainage water under roads or other surface structures. The headwall is designed to make the transition of the water flowing in the open channel as smooth as possible and to prevent the water from backing up beyond a specified backwater elevation.

Endwalls are used at the discharge at the downstream ends of culverts and storm sewers to transition the flow from a pipe to an open channel. At the discharge end of a culvert or storm sewer, the water velocities are typically high due to the pressure generated by the elevation of water upstream and the hydraulic efficiency of the smoother pipe surface. Therefore, endwalls are usually designed to reduce the velocity of flow in the transition zone and to reduce the possibility of erosion, Figure 4-38.

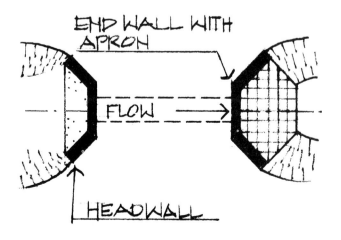

FIGURE 4.38 TYPICAL CULVERT WITH HEADWALL AND ENDWALL

SURFACE INLET STRUCTURES

There are two types of inlet structures used to collect water from the surface and transition it to a subsurface conduit: the drop inlet, and the catch basin. The names of the structures have to do with how the water is transferred to the pipe. It is not related to the configuration of the surface inlet.

Drop inlets collect water at the surface and transfer it directly to the pipe below. The shape of the bottom of the structure is smooth to maintain self-cleaning velocities and to minimize the turbulence generated as the water changes directions.

The catch basin is designed with a sediment basin at the bottom of the structure. The sediment basin is used to catch trash and heavy sediment that might become lodged in the pipe downstream. Catch basins should only be used where there is a need to protect the storm system from large volumes of trash or silt, and where proper maintenance can be provided. It should also be kept in mind that a catch basin holds water for some

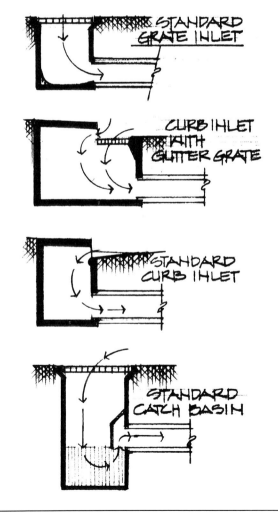

FIGURE 4.39 COMMON DRAINAGE INLETS

time after a storm, which can serve as a breeding ground for mosquitos.

The shape and configuration of the opening to a surface structure varies with local practice and the drainage problem at hand. Some of the more typical opening configurations are shown in Figure 4-39. The size and shape of the surface opening is very important to ensure that the water flowing along a gutter or a turf channel will enter the structure.

If a curb inlet is used, the formula for determining the volume of water that will enter the opening is:

$$Q = 0.7L (a + y)^{1.5}$$

Where:

Q = inlet rate in cfs
L = the length of the curb opening in ft
a = the depression of the curb inlet below the existing gutter line in ft
y = the depth of flow at the inlet in ft

In most cases the depth of flow at the inlet is taken to be the height of the curb, which is usually 6 in or 0.5 ft.

To estimate the volume of flow for a flush-mounted grate for flow depths of up to 0.4 ft the formula is:

$$Q = 3Py^{1.5}$$

Where:

Q = flow through the inlet in cfs
P = the perimeter of the grate surface in ft, no allowance is made for the bars in the grate
y = the depth of flow over the grate in ft. This can be estimated from the cross section of the swale, but can not exceed 0.4 ft

These formulas will provide a good initial estimate of the the flow through either type of opening. There are a number of engineering references that have graphic solutions to these and other equations used to estimate flows into openings of different shapes and sizes. Several of the more useful graphic solutions have been included in the material at the end of the chapter. Before using any of the graphic solution figures, be sure it is appropriate to the specific application.

ACCESS STRUCTURES

Access structures are provided in a drainage system to facilitate periodic maintenance.

Access to small diameter pipes such as those used to drain small turf areas, pool decks, or other small surface areas is usually provided by a cleanout.

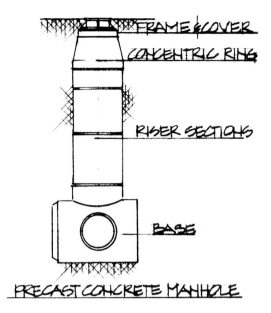

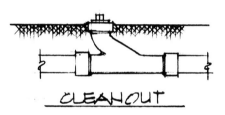

FIGURE 4.40 ACCESS STRUCTURES

Cleanouts are "Y" shaped fittings usually set at the upper end of the pipe. The Y is set so that a cable tool can be inserted in the pipe from the surface to clean out any trash that becomes lodged in the line.

Maintenance access to large sewer and storm drain lines is provided by manholes. Manholes are large structures that are made of bricks or precast concrete sections, Figure 4-40.

Pipe and Drainage Materials

There are a variety of materials used for site drainage systems. Some of the more common materials and applications are noted here.

CLAY PIPE

Common clay pipe, often called agricultural tile, is made in 2-ft lengths and is usually available in 4-in and 6-in diameter. Its most common application is for drain fields and subsurface drainage applications. With the improvements and general acceptance of plastic pipe, common clay pipe is not used as much as in the past.

REINFORCED CONCRETE PIPE

Reinforced concrete pipe (RCP), is one of the most common of all pipe materials used for storm drainage applications. It is stronger than most pipes and is usually preferred where the pipe will be subject to heavy wheel loads. Some concrete pipe is manufactured with reinforced walls so that traffic loads can be carried by the pipe. Ordinary concrete pipe is usually set with a minimum of 2 ft of soil over the top of the pipe. Concrete pipe is usually available in sizes from 12 in diameter up to 6 ft diameter.

The primary disadvantages of concrete pipe are the expense and the weight.

CORRUGATED METAL PIPE

Corrugated metal pipe, (CMP), is a very popular material for use in culverts. It is much lighter than concrete pipe and less expensive as well. It comes in a wide range of shapes and sizes for almost any application. Its primary disadvantage is its longevity. Depending on the metal alloy used, corrugated metal pipe will be shorter lived than concrete, particularly if the soils have either a high or low pH. In these situations, corrugated pipe should only be used if it is coated with a material that will protect the metal from the soil.

PLASTIC PIPE

Plastic has become the most common material used for site drainage work. Plastic is not only used to manufacture pipe, but also for fabrication of drainage inlet structures, valve boxes and other fittings. Manufacturers of plastic site drainage systems usually offer a complete line of inlet types, pipe and fittings to satisfy most site-scale drainage needs.

SUBSURFACE DRAINAGE

Runoff is not just a surface phenomenon. Part of the water that falls to the surface infiltrates the soil and becomes groundwater. The movement of this water below the surface is called subsurface runoff. Subsurface runoff moves much slower than surface runoff and is much less predictable in the unsaturated soil near the surface. There are a number of site problems associated with near-surface groundwater that sometimes require the installation of subsurface drainage systems. Some of the more notable problems associated with groundwater are:

a. Frost heave: Frost heave is the result of ice crystal growth in the soil profile that can damage pavements and building foundations.
b. Basement flooding: High groundwater tables are frequently responsible for damage to basements and other building rooms that extend below grade.
c. Soil swelling and shrinkage: Plastic soils are very sensitive to changes in soil moisture content. When water is available the soils will swell and they can damage pavements and foundations just like frost heave.

The primary tool available for controlling high groundwater conditions is the installation of a subdrainage system. A subdrain is simply a trench, porous backfill, and an open conduit. The water traveling in the soil is captured in the porous material and conveyed to the open pipe and then carried to a point of disposal, as shown in Figure 4-41.

The depth of a subdrain is determined by two factors: (1) The pipe must be set deep enough so the free moisture in the soil will be forced into the porous material in the trench. (2) It must be set deep enough to drop the water table to the desired elevation. For example, if the subdrain is being installed to prevent frost heave, the pipe should be set just below the frost line. The line will then intercept the capillary water moving up through the soil. If the subdrain is installed to control the soil moisture in expansive soils, it should be set just below the level of the foundation or pavement to be protected. Deeper drains are generally more effective because there is more head (pressure) available to move water down through the soil and into the pipe.

The horizontal spacing of drainage lines is affected by the depth and the soil type. Coarse, sandy soils will allow a wider spacing, while finer soils will require that lines be spaced closer together to overcome the adhesive force of the soil. The information in Table 4-9 can be used as a general guide for determining trench depth and spacing for most applications. Additional information about subdrainage design is usually available from the County Agent or the local Soil Conservation Service office.

The layout pattern used for a subdrainage system is a matter of site condition and the available outlet point. Like any drainage system, a subdrain must be connected to an outlet. This can be an existing creek or surface drainage channel or a storm sewer. Figure 4-42 illustrates some of the typical layout patterns used.

The material used for subdrainage systems is most often perforated PVC pipe, or flexible polyethelene pipe. These materials are manufactured specifically for these applications and are readily available.

When backfilling a subdrainage system, a filter material should always be placed between the native soil backfill and the the trench. The filter material will prevent fine soil particles from clogging the pore space of the gravel, which can drastically reduce the effectiveness of the subdrainage system.

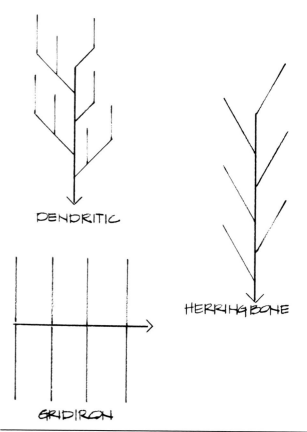

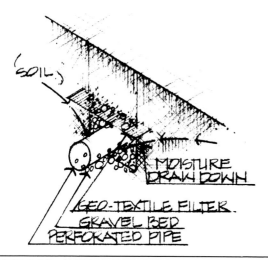

FIGURE 4.41 TYPICAL SUBDRAIN

FIGURE 4.42 TYPICAL SUBDRAINAGE LAYOUTS

TABLE 4.9 RECOMMENDED DEPTH AND SPACING OF SUBDRAINS BY SOIL TYPE

Soil Character	Silt	Clay	Depth ft	Spacing o.c. ft
Sand with >20% fine gravel and sand	0-15% < 20% silt	0-10% and clay	5	200
Sandy loam with >20% fine gravel and sand	10-35% silt and >20%	5-15% clay <50%	4	120
Fine sandy loam with <20% fine gravel and sand	10-25% silt and >20%	— clay <50%	3.5	100
Loam	0-55% silt and >50%	15-25% clay	4	75
Clay loam	25-50% silt and >50%	25-35% clay	3	45
Clay	— silt and >60%	35-100% clay	3	25

Pages 150 to 186 contain information from TR-55, Second Ed., June 1986.

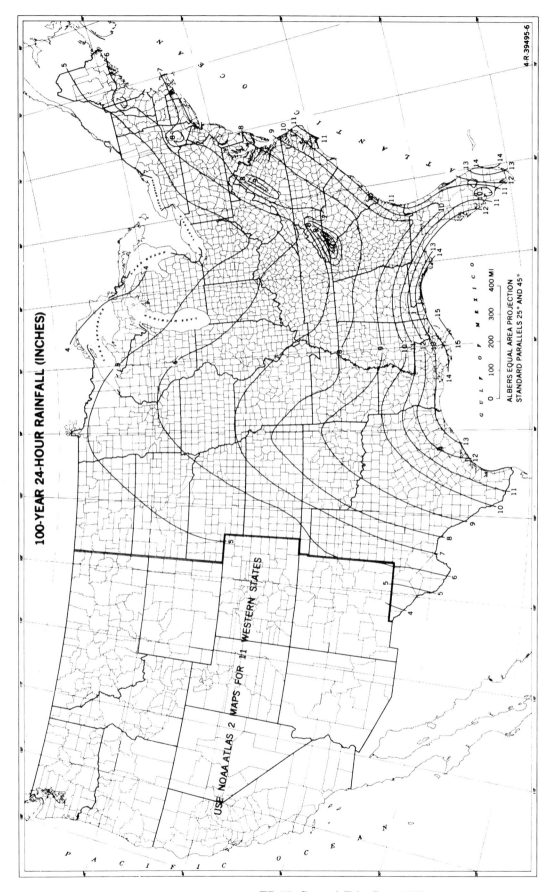

TR-55, Second Ed., June 1986

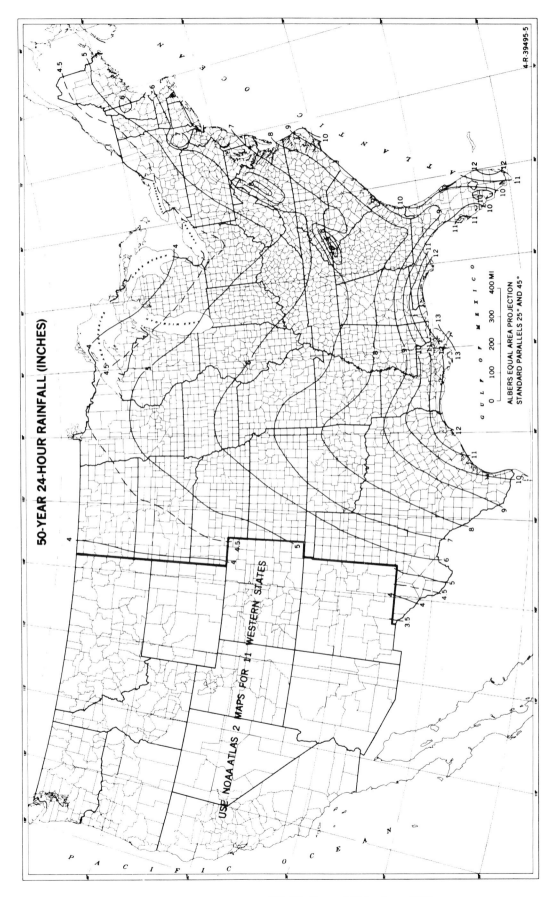

50-YEAR 24-HOUR RAINFALL (INCHES)

ALBERS EQUAL AREA PROJECTION
STANDARD PARALLELS 25° AND 45°

0   100   200   300   400 MI

USE NOAA ATLAS 2 MAPS FOR 11 WESTERN STATES

TR-55, Second Ed., June 1986

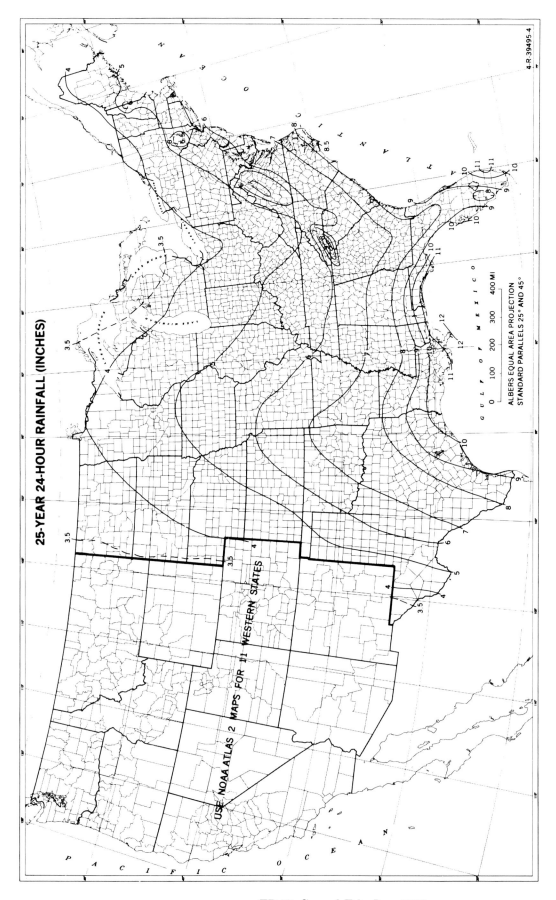

25-YEAR 24-HOUR RAINFALL (INCHES)

USE NOAA ATLAS 2 MAPS FOR 11 WESTERN STATES

ALBERS EQUAL AREA PROJECTION
STANDARD PARALLELS 25° AND 45°

0 100 200 300 400 MI

4-R-39495-4

TR-55, Second Ed., June 1986

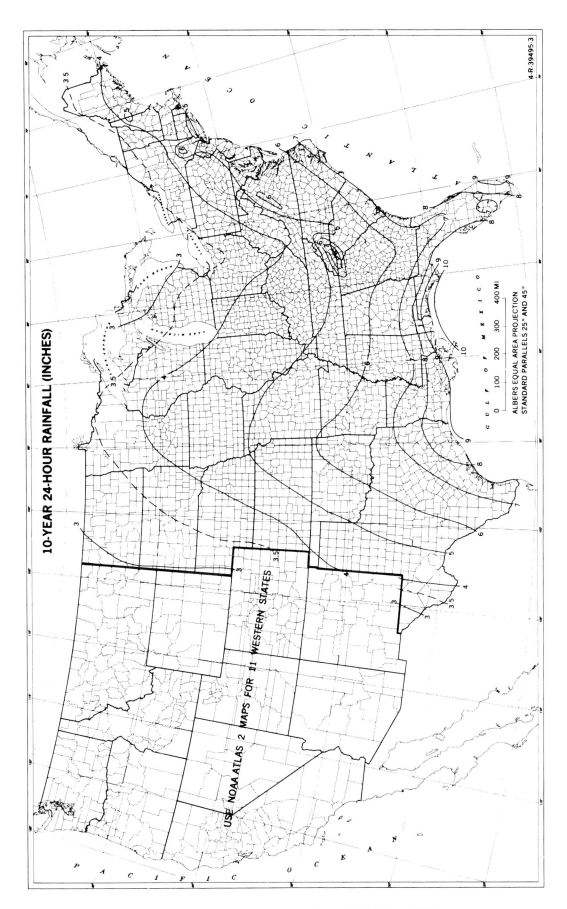

10-YEAR 24-HOUR RAINFALL (INCHES)

USE NOAA ATLAS 2 MAPS FOR 11 WESTERN STATES

ALBERS EQUAL AREA PROJECTION
STANDARD PARALLELS 25° AND 45°

0   100   200   300   400 MI

TR-55, Second Ed., June 1986

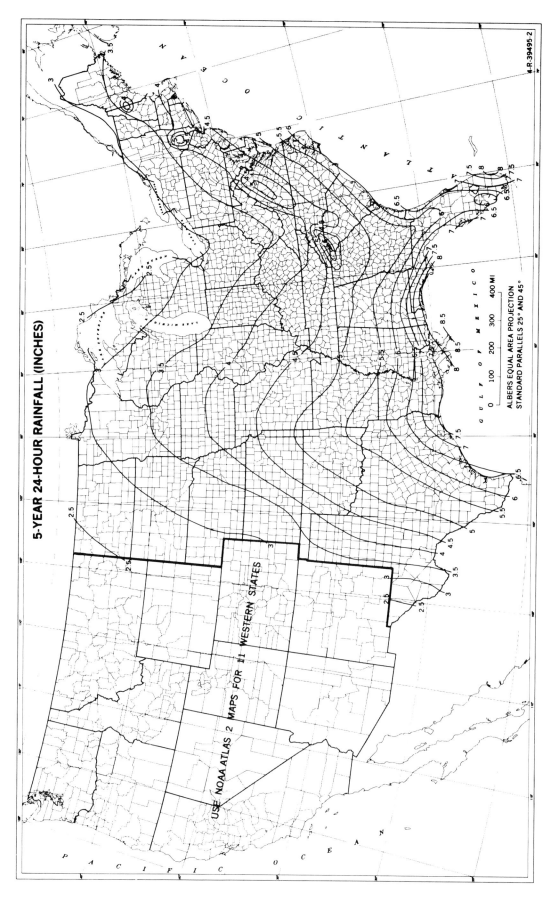

5-YEAR 24-HOUR RAINFALL (INCHES)

TR-55, Second Ed., June 1986

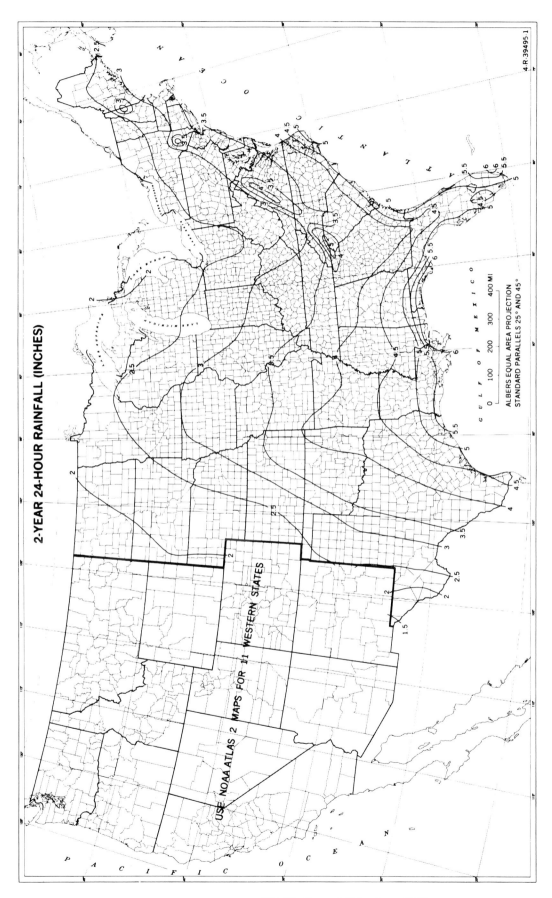

2-YEAR 24-HOUR RAINFALL (INCHES)

USE NOAA ATLAS 2 MAPS FOR 11 WESTERN STATES

ALBERS EQUAL AREA PROJECTION
STANDARD PARALLELS 25° AND 45°

0   100   200   300   400 MI

4-R-39495-1

Tabular hydrograph unit discharges (csm/in) for type II rainfall distribution

RAINFALL TYPE = II

Hydrograph time (hours) column headers: 11.0, 11.3, 11.6, 11.9, 12.0, 12.1, 12.2, 12.3, 12.4, 12.5, 12.6, 12.7, 12.8, 13.0, 13.2, 13.4, 13.6, 13.8, 14.0, 14.3, 14.6, 15.0, 15.5, 16.0, 16.5, 17.0, 17.5, 18.0, 19.0, 20.0, 22.0, 26.0

IA/P = 0.10, TC = 2.0 HR

TRVL TIME (HR)	11.0	11.3	11.6	11.9	12.0	12.1	12.2	12.3	12.4	12.5	12.6	12.7	12.8	13.0	13.2	13.4	13.6	13.8	14.0	14.3	14.6	15.0	15.5	16.0	16.5	17.0	17.5	18.0	19.0	20.0	22.0	26.0
0.0	7	9	12	16	18	21	27	36	49	64	82	104	127	171	201	226	208	193	171	132	105	79	58	45	36	30	26	23	20	17	13	3
.10	6	8	10	15	15	17	20	25	33	43	57	74	94	139	179	204	218	205	188	150	118	88	63	48	38	32	27	24	20	17	13	4
.20	6	8	10	14	14	16	19	23	29	39	51	66	84	128	169	198	213	207	192	157	123	91	65	49	39	33	28	24	20	17	13	4
.30	6	7	9	14	14	13	18	21	27	35	45	59	76	117	159	191	208	196	196	163	128	95	68	51	40	33	28	25	20	18	13	4
.40	5	6	8	11	12	13	15	17	20	24	31	41	53	87	128	167	197	209	205	180	145	106	75	55	43	35	30	26	21	18	14	5
.50	5	6	7	10	11	13	14	16	18	22	28	37	48	78	118	158	191	208	202	185	151	111	77	57	44	36	30	26	22	18	14	5
.75	4	6	7	9	10	11	12	13	15	18	22	27	35	58	91	129	164	191	202	194	167	125	87	63	48	38	32	27	22	18	14	6
1.0	4	4	6	7	8	8	9	10	11	12	16	18	26	28	46	74	110	147	178	201	178	156	108	76	56	45	35	30	23	19	14	8
1.5	2	3	5	5	5	5	6	6	7	8	8	9	10	12	16	23	36	57	86	137	178	195	160	113	79	58	44	36	26	21	16	11
2.0	1	2	3	4	3	4	4	4	5	5	6	6	7	8	10	12	16	23	35	57	86	169	190	154	110	78	57	44	30	23	17	11
2.5	0	1	3	2	2	2	3	3	3	4	4	4	5	6	7	8	9	12	16	28	52	105	170	185	149	107	76	56	38	27	19	12
3.0	0	0	1	1	1	1	1	2	2	2	2	3	3	3	4	5	6	7	8	12	18	41	99	161	180	152	112	80	45	30	28	28

IA/P = 0.30, TC = 2.0 HR

TRVL TIME (HR)	11.0	11.3	11.6	11.9	12.0	12.1	12.2	12.3	12.4	12.5	12.6	12.7	12.8	13.0	13.2	13.4	13.6	13.8	14.0	14.3	14.6	15.0	15.5	16.0	16.5	17.0	17.5	18.0	19.0	20.0	22.0	26.0
0.0	2	3	5	5	5	5	8	9	15	25	38	54	74	115	148	168	185	170	159	131	110	89	70	57	49	45	42	38	34	29	26	20
.10	2	2	4	4	3	3	6	7	12	21	32	47	68	85	114	153	168	180	168	145	124	96	75	60	51	46	42	39	35	30	26	20
.20	1	2	3	3	2	2	5	5	10	17	21	41	62	75	85	114	165	175	170	149	124	99	76	62	52	45	41	38	35	30	27	21
.30	0	1	2	2	2	2	4	4	7	14	23	36	49	49	86	122	151	170	174	160	128	107	82	66	54	47	41	37	31	31	27	21
.40	0	0	1	1	1	1	2	3	6	11	19	43	43	77	113	144	165	173	170	144	113	85	57	45	37	34	32	29	27	26	22	17
.50	0	0	1	0	0	0	1	2	5	10	16	37	37	68	104	136	160	171	168	153	124	96	62	48	42	38	35	32	26	26	22	17
.75	0	0	0	0	0	0	1	1	3	8	14	34	34	62	96	127	152	167	174	160	124	99	65	52	45	41	38	34	27	27	23	18
1.0	0	0	0	0	0	0	1	1	2	5	13	23	24	49	79	111	151	166	174	166	136	107	82	66	58	49	43	40	34	31	29	19
1.5	0	0	0	0	0	0	0	0	0	1	3	8	10	24	45	88	130	161	161	122	148	89	115	88	57	48	37	34	31	24	17	17
2.0	0	0	0	0	0	0	0	0	0	1	0	4	4	16	32	68	113	145	122	157	143	122	68	60	62	56	42	34	26	21	18	18
2.5	0	0	0	0	0	0	0	0	0	0	0	1	1	4	16	38	79	114	116	51	144	114	95	102	77	52	45	27	22	19	
3.0	0	0	0	0	0	0	0	0	0	0	0	0	0	3	7	18	48	79	140	118	150	118	99	95	83	73	57	42	29	19	19	

IA/P = 0.50, TC = 2.0 HR

TRVL TIME (HR)	11.0	11.3	11.6	11.9	12.0	12.1	12.2	12.3	12.4	12.5	12.6	12.7	12.8	13.0	13.2	13.4	13.6	13.8	14.0	14.3	14.6	15.0	15.5	16.0	16.5	17.0	17.5	18.0	19.0	20.0	22.0	26.0
0.0	0	0	0	0	0	1	4	8	13	20	28	51	73	92	104	110	111	112	106	97	86	75	66	60	54	49	46	42	41	37	30	7
.10	0	0	0	0	0	1	3	6	11	17	24	45	68	87	101	107	109	112	107	98	88	76	67	60	55	50	46	46	37	30	30	8
.20	0	0	0	0	0	1	2	5	9	14	21	40	62	82	98	104	107	111	108	104	89	77	68	61	55	50	47	47	37	30	28	8
.30	0	0	0	0	0	0	2	4	7	12	18	26	46	67	86	100	108	108	111	108	93	80	70	63	57	52	48	48	38	30	28	10
.40	0	0	0	0	0	0	1	3	6	10	22	41	62	81	96	105	110	106	105	94	81	71	63	57	52	48	46	42	38	30	34	11
.50	0	0	0	0	0	0	1	2	5	8	17	27	46	67	85	99	107	99	108	98	85	74	66	59	54	50	47	43	39	31	36	13
.75	0	0	0	0	0	0	0	1	3	5	14	21	40	52	71	88	104	102	104	104	89	77	68	61	55	50	45	44	39	32	38	15
1.0	0	0	0	0	0	0	0	1	2	2	4	12	26	46	67	84	100	108	108	87	97	84	73	65	59	53	52	48	41	32	40	20
1.5	0	0	0	0	0	0	0	0	0	1	3	6	10	22	41	48	95	96	106	105	94	81	71	63	57	52	48	46	42	38	34	25
2.0	0	0	0	0	0	0	0	0	0	1	1	2	5	13	27	46	85	99	104	108	98	85	74	66	59	54	50	46	45	45	36	27
2.5	0	0	0	0	0	0	0	0	0	0	0	1	2	7	18	33	71	88	102	104	89	77	68	61	55	50	47	47	49	49	38	28
3.0	0	0	0	0	0	0	0	0	0	0	0	0	1	5	13	25	43	62	87	103	108	97	84	73	65	59	53	53	52	52	40	28

Tabular hydrograph unit discharges (csm/in) for type II rainfall distribution

Tabular hydrograph unit discharges (csm/in) for type II rainfall distribution

RAINFALL TYPE = II   SHEET 8 OF 10

TRVL TIME (HR) — HYDROGRAPH TIME (HOURS)

IA/P = 0.10, * * * TC = 1.25 HR * * *

TRVL TIME	11.0	11.3	11.6	11.9	12.0	12.1	12.2	12.3	12.4	12.5	12.6	12.7	12.8	13.0	13.2	13.4	13.6	13.8	14.0	14.3	14.6	15.0	15.5	16.0	16.5	17.0	17.5	18.0	19.0	20.0	22.0	26.0
0.0	10	13	18	25	29	38	54	81	118	163	213	256	284	311	266	212	163	129	104	78	61	47	37	31	27	24	22	20	18	16	12	1
.10	10	13	17	23	27	34	47	69	102	143	189	234	267	297	274	226	175	138	111	82	64	48	38	31	27	24	22	20	18	16	12	1
.20	9	11	15	20	22	26	31	42	60	88	124	168	212	280	292	261	212	166	131	95	72	53	40	33	28	25	23	21	18	17	13	1
.30	8	11	14	21	21	24	29	38	53	76	108	148	190	263	288	268	224	177	140	101	76	55	41	34	29	26	25	23	21	18	16	2
.40	8	10	13	18	20	23	27	34	46	66	94	130	170	245	282	273	235	188	149	107	80	58	42	34	29	26	25	25	22	19	17	3
.50	7	9	12	16	17	19	22	25	31	41	58	82	127	212	279	262	222	178	127	93	65	46	36	31	27	24	23	23	20	17	5
.75	6	8	10	14	15	17	22	31	41	56	78	139	208	254	245	208	152	110	75	54	41	33	28	25	22	20	17	6
1.0	5	6	8	10	11	13	14	17	19	22	26	33	60	109	173	230	261	255	208	153	100	64	46	36	30	27	24	21	18	10
1.5	3	4	5	7	7	8	9	9	10	11	12	15	19	27	45	79	130	186	247	239	180	108	68	48	37	31	27	22	19	14	15
2.0	2	3	3	4	4	6	7	7	8	11	13	16	22	35	59	98	171	236	163	156	95	62	44	35	27	24	23	20	15	11	13
2.5	1	2	2	3	3	4	5	5	6	7	8	10	14	19	28	58	114	197	226	102	65	46	32	28	26	25	21	16	11	18
3.0	1	1	1	2	2	3	4	4	5	6	7	9	10	13	35	88	184	218	169	109	70	49	34	30	27	24	18	12	18

IA/P = 0.30, * * * TC = 1.25 HR * * *

TRVL TIME	11.0	11.3	11.6	11.9	12.0	12.1	12.2	12.3	12.4	12.5	12.6	12.7	12.8	13.0	13.2	13.4	13.6	13.8	14.0	14.3	14.6	15.0	15.5	16.0	16.5	17.0	17.5	18.0	19.0	20.0	22.0	26.0
0.0	0	0	0	0	0	2	9	25	50	86	130	174	208	253	235	201	164	136	115	92	76	61	51	44	39	35	32	30	27	24	19	1
.10	0	0	0	0	0	1	7	19	40	71	110	153	191	247	227	191	157	131	103	84	66	53	46	41	36	33	31	28	24	19	2
.20	0	0	0	0	0	1	4	14	31	58	93	133	202	239	231	199	165	138	108	87	68	55	47	41	37	33	31	28	25	20	3
.30	0	0	0	0	0	1	3	10	24	46	77	152	236	222	210	190	158	122	97	74	58	49	43	38	34	32	28	25	20	3
.40	0	0	0	0	2	8	19	37	64	134	196	232	225	205	166	127	101	77	59	50	43	38	35	32	28	25	20	3
.50	0	0	0	0	1	2	6	14	30	82	151	206	228	217	189	146	113	85	64	52	45	40	36	33	29	26	21	5
.75	0	0	0	0	1	2	7	15	49	105	164	205	218	205	166	129	95	69	55	47	41	37	33	29	26	20	6
1.0	0	0	0	0	1	9	32	77	134	185	214	203	166	120	83	52	45	39	35	30	27	21	10
1.5	0	0	0	0	2	11	33	72	121	184	203	171	117	82	62	51	44	39	35	32	29	22	15
2.0	0	0	0	0	1	7	21	67	132	194	174	174	164	123	86	64	52	45	35	31	24	13
2.5	0	0	0	0	2	13	46	121	187	166	119	84	63	54	39	32	25	18
3.0	0	0	0	0	3	11	35	72	129	160	116	83	44	8	18

IA/P = 0.50, * * * TC = 1.25 HR * * *

TRVL TIME	11.0	11.3	11.6	11.9	12.0	12.1	12.2	12.3	12.4	12.5	12.6	12.7	12.8	13.0	13.2	13.4	13.6	13.8	14.0	14.3	14.6	15.0	15.5	16.0	16.5	17.0	17.5	18.0	19.0	20.0	22.0	26.0
0.0	0	0	0	0	0	1	5	13	26	44	68	91	125	142	142	128	117	107	94	83	72	63	57	52	47	44	42	38	34	29	2
.10	0	0	0	0	0	0	3	10	20	36	57	100	140	136	125	114	100	88	76	65	59	54	49	45	43	39	35	29	3
.20	0	0	0	0	0	0	2	7	16	30	48	90	122	139	127	117	102	90	77	66	60	54	49	45	43	39	36	29	3
.30	0	0	0	0	0	0	2	5	12	24	59	98	126	137	134	121	103	84	71	62	56	51	46	44	40	30	4
.40	0	0	0	0	1	4	10	19	51	89	112	127	136	119	98	83	70	62	56	51	47	44	40	36	29	5
.50	0	0	0	0	1	3	7	15	43	79	114	135	130	112	95	76	63	57	52	49	45	42	37	29	6
.75	0	0	0	0	1	3	11	39	71	102	123	125	111	94	78	67	60	54	49	46	41	30	9
1.0	0	0	0	0	1	4	17	40	71	101	121	121	103	84	71	62	56	51	47	42	38	30	13
1.5	0	0	0	0	3	10	26	51	92	119	125	105	86	72	63	57	52	44	40	32	23
2.0	0	0	0	0	1	3	11	35	72	112	102	103	85	71	63	56	47	42	34	26
2.5	0	0	0	0	1	5	39	71	94	119	111	101	71	62	51	46	38	27
3.0	0	0	0	0	1	7	17	40	103	121	116	110	84	23	4	1	103	27

TR-55, Second Ed., June 1986

Tabular hydrograph unit discharges (csm/in) for type II rainfall distribution

RAINFALL TYPE = II   SHEET 7 OF 10   TC = 1.0 HR

IA/P = 0.10

TRVL TIME (HR)	11.0	11.3	11.6	11.9	12.0	12.1	12.2	12.3	12.4	12.5	12.6	12.7	12.8	13.0	13.2	13.4	13.6	13.8	14.0	14.3	14.6	15.0	15.5	16.0	16.5	17.0	17.5	18.0	19.0	20.0	22.0	26.0
0.0	11	15	20	29	35	47	72	112	168	231	289	329	357	313	239	175	133	103	83	63	50	40	33	29	26	23	21	20	17	15	12	0
.10	10	13	17	24	27	33	42	62	95	144	202	260	306	340	293	222	165	126	98	72	56	43	35	30	27	24	22	20	18	15	12	0
.20	10	13	17	23	26	30	38	54	82	123	176	232	281	332	303	238	179	136	105	76	59	45	35	30	27	24	22	20	18	16	13	1
.30	9	12	16	22	24	28	35	48	70	105	152	205	256	323	310	254	193	146	113	81	61	46	36	31	27	24	22	20	18	16	12	1
.40	8	11	14	19	21	23	27	32	42	61	91	132	181	276	318	294	237	181	138	95	70	51	39	32	28	25	23	21	18	16	12	1
.50	7	10	13	18	20	22	25	30	38	53	78	114	159	253	311	300	251	195	149	102	74	53	40	33	29	25	23	21	18	16	13	1
.75	5	7	8	11	12	14	16	21	25	30	38	53	76	146	228	284	293	256	208	143	99	66	46	36	31	27	24	22	19	17	13	2
1.0	5	8	11	12	14	13	14	16	17	19	22	25	31	57	111	188	256	286	272	208	144	90	56	41	33	29	26	23	20	17	13	4
1.5	6	5	8	8	8	9	10	11	12	13	14	15	17	22	33	59	107	171	231	268	235	157	88	56	41	33	29	25	21	18	14	8
2.0	4	4	5	5	5	6	6	7	8	8	9	10	12	12	15	19	27	44	78	157	231	252	167	96	59	43	34	29	23	20	15	11
2.5	1	2	2	3	4	4	5	5	6	6	7	7	8	8	10	12	15	19	27	58	120	214	241	159	94	59	42	34	26	21	16	11
3.0	0	1	1	2	2	3	3	3	4	4	6	5	6	6	7	8	10	12	14	22	44	113	214	231	152	91	58	42	29	23	17	12

IA/P = 0.30

TRVL TIME (HR)	11.0	11.3	11.6	11.9	12.0	12.1	12.2	12.3	12.4	12.5	12.6	12.7	12.8	13.0	13.2	13.4	13.6	13.8	14.0	14.3	14.6	15.0	15.5	16.0	16.5	17.0	17.5	18.0	19.0	20.0	22.0	26.0
0.0	0	0	0	0	1	4	16	42	83	137	195	243	271	292	260	227	178	143	117	98	79	66	55	47	42	38	34	30	27	23	19	0
.10	0	0	0	0	0	0	1	12	32	66	113	168	218	279	277	225	180	136	113	79	72	59	49	43	39	35	34	30	27	24	19	1
.20	0	0	0	2	0	0	0	3	12	52	93	143	193	271	271	225	180	145	92	88	75	60	50	44	40	35	32	30	27	24	19	1
.30	0	0	0	1	0	0	0	6	18	41	75	120	169	246	264	234	191	153	96	78	62	51	44	40	36	33	34	31	27	26	18	1
.40	0	0	0	0	0	0	4	1	4	14	32	61	100	190	251	259	222	181	146	109	86	67	53	46	41	37	35	31	28	25	19	2
.50	0	0	0	0	0	0	3	1	3	10	24	49	83	168	237	254	230	191	155	115	90	69	54	47	42	37	34	31	28	25	19	4
.75	0	0	0	0	0	0	2	0	0	1	4	12	25	76	150	213	239	228	198	149	112	82	61	50	44	39	35	32	29	26	20	7
1.0	0	0	0	1	1	0	1	0	0	0	0	1	15	15	51	113	182	226	234	197	150	104	72	56	47	42	38	34	30	27	20	7
1.5	0	0	0	0	0	0	0	0	0	0	0	0	0	0	4	18	51	104	162	220	210	158	102	71	56	47	42	37	31	28	22	13
2.0	0	0	0	0	0	0	0	0	0	0	0	0	0	0	0	1	5	20	49	121	187	209	152	100	70	55	47	41	34	29	23	17
2.5	0	0	0	0	0	0	0	0	0	0	0	0	0	0	0	0	0	0	7	32	87	171	199	146	98	69	54	46	37	31	24	18
3.0	0	0	0	0	0	0	0	0	0	0	0	0	0	0	0	0	0	0	2	2	10	34	84	158	192	151	103	73	62	41	26	18

IA/P = 0.50

TRVL TIME (HR)	11.0	11.3	11.6	11.9	12.0	12.1	12.2	12.3	12.4	12.5	12.6	12.7	12.8	13.0	13.2	13.4	13.6	13.8	14.0	14.3	14.6	15.0	15.5	16.0	16.5	17.0	17.5	18.0	19.0	20.0	22.0	26.0
0.0	0	0	0	0	0	0	0	7	21	42	71	101	126	160	154	138	123	110	100	87	77	67	60	55	50	46	43	41	38	34	28	1
.10	0	0	0	0	0	0	0	1	5	15	33	58	87	134	156	149	120	108	93	82	71	62	57	52	47	44	42	38	34	28	1	1
.20	0	0	0	0	0	0	0	0	4	12	26	48	74	123	134	137	123	111	95	84	72	63	57	56	52	47	44	42	38	34	28	1
.30	0	0	0	0	0	0	0	0	3	9	20	38	62	111	140	143	150	127	114	98	84	73	63	58	53	48	45	42	39	35	28	1
.40	0	0	0	0	0	0	0	2	6	16	31	75	120	137	145	148	137	123	91	77	66	59	54	50	46	43	39	35	29	2		
.50	0	0	0	0	0	0	1	5	12	25	64	109	139	146	139	127	123	106	94	84	79	70	67	62	56	55	51	47	44	40	36	3
.75	0	0	0	0	0	0	2	5	12	25	39	78	101	123	134	140	136	127	117	101	84	70	62	56	51	47	44	40	36	4		
1.0	0	0	0	0	0	0	0	1	7	26	59	96	117	133	133	139	133	117	97	78	66	56	49	46	41	8						
1.5	0	0	0	0	2	2	7	26	54	86	119	133	123	95	77	66	59	54	49	45	43	39	31	17								
2.0	0	0	0	0	2	9	26	54	104	129	116	104	94	79	70	62	56	53	50	46	41	33	24									
2.5	0	0	0	0	3	10	25	84	125	117	96	84	78	66	59	53	49	43	35	24												
3.0	0	0	0	0	0	0	6	32	89	122	114	94	77	66	54	45	39	27														

Exhibit 5-II, continued: Tabular hydrograph unit discharges (csm/in) for type II rainfall distribution

RAINFALL TYPE = II

HYDROGRAPH TIME (HOURS)

IA/P = 0.10   * * TC = 0.75 HR * * *

TRVL TIME (HR)	11.0	11.3	11.6	11.9	12.0	12.1	12.2	12.3	12.4	12.5	12.6	12.7	12.8	13.0	13.2	13.4	13.6	13.8	14.0	14.3	14.6	15.0	15.5	16.0	16.5	17.0	17.5	18.0	19.0	20.0	22.0	26.0
0.0	13	18	24	36	46	68	115	194	294	380	424	410	369	252	172	123	93	74	61	49	41	35	31	27	24	22	20	19	17	15	12	0
.10	13	17	23	34	42	59	97	162	250	337	395	405	381	279	191	135	100	79	65	51	42	36	31	28	25	22	21	19	17	15	12	0
.20	11	15	20	28	32	39	52	82	135	211	295	362	391	351	255	178	127	95	75	57	46	38	32	29	26	23	21	20	17	15	12	0
.30	11	14	19	26	30	36	47	70	113	179	256	326	379	360	277	196	140	103	80	60	48	38	33	29	26	23	21	20	18	15	12	0
.40	10	12	16	22	25	28	33	42	61	96	151	221	291	367	336	255	182	131	98	69	54	42	34	30	27	24	22	20	18	16	12	0
.50	9	12	16	21	24	27	31	39	53	82	128	190	258	358	343	274	200	144	106	74	56	43	35	30	27	24	22	18	16	16	12	0
.75	8	10	13	17	18	21	23	26	31	39	55	82	122	230	281	329	217	161	104	72	51	38	33	29	26	23	21	20	16	12	1	
1.0	6	8	10	15	14	15	17	19	21	23	27	32	42	89	272	303	249	161	163	105	66	45	36	31	27	24	22	17	13	3	
1.5	4	6	7	9	10	12	15	16	18	20	27	46	90	163	241	275	204	119	66	45	35	31	27	24	20	18	13	7	
2.0	3	4	5	6	7	9	10	11	12	13	16	28	48	89	151	245	274	213	115	65	44	30	22	19	16	14	10	
2.5	1	2	3	4	5	7	7	8	9	11	17	24	37	170	260	219	127	71	47	36	31	20	16	11	
3.0	1	1	2	3	3	4	5	5	5	6	7	8	10	14	17	30	64	157	247	205	122	70	46	36	31	22	17	12	

IA/P = 0.30   * * TC = 0.75 HR * * *

TRVL TIME (HR)	11.0	11.3	11.6	11.9	12.0	12.1	12.2	12.3	12.4	12.5	12.6	12.7	12.8	13.0	13.2	13.4	13.6	13.8	14.0	14.3	14.6	15.0	15.5	16.0	16.5	17.0	17.5	18.0	19.0	20.0	22.0	26.0
0.0	0	0	0	0	1	6	30	86	174	266	326	348	328	246	181	138	110	92	79	66	57	49	44	40	36	32	31	29	26	23	19	0
.10	0	0	0	0	0	1	4	22	65	137	223	292	305	303	228	170	131	106	89	73	61	52	46	41	37	33	31	29	26	23	19	0
.20	0	0	0	0	0	0	3	15	48	108	185	256	321	321	260	184	141	112	93	75	63	53	47	42	38	34	31	30	26	23	19	0
.30	0	0	0	0	0	0	2	11	36	84	151	221	277	308	277	199	152	120	98	78	65	54	47	42	38	34	31	30	27	23	19	1
.40	0	0	0	0	0	0	0	1	8	27	65	122	188	301	301	243	187	144	114	87	66	57	48	43	39	35	32	30	27	24	19	1
.50	0	0	0	0	0	0	0	0	6	20	50	98	158	263	292	254	200	155	122	91	73	61	49	44	40	35	34	30	27	24	20	2
.75	0	0	0	0	0	1	1	0	2	8	23	51	140	231	269	253	211	167	119	75	53	46	42	37	34	30	29	24	20	5	
1.0	0	0	0	0	0	0	0	1	0	2	8	23	96	186	231	249	169	120	84	61	50	44	40	36	33	29	26	20	
1.5	0	0	0	0	0	0	0	0	0	1	8	34	91	163	220	241	197	131	83	50	44	40	35	31	27	21	12	
2.0	0	0	0	0	0	0	0	0	0	11	36	85	174	226	200	127	82	60	49	44	39	32	29	22	17	
2.5	0	0	0	0	0	0	0	0	0	1	6	37	105	196	214	135	87	62	51	44	31	24	18	
3.0	0	0	0	0	0	0	0	0	0	8	37	105	196	214	135	189	130	85	62	24	96	46	34	26	18	

IA/P = 0.50   * * TC = 0.75 HR * * *

TRVL TIME (HR)	11.0	11.3	11.6	11.9	12.0	12.1	12.2	12.3	12.4	12.5	12.6	12.7	12.8	13.0	13.2	13.4	13.6	13.8	14.0	14.3	14.6	15.0	15.5	16.0	16.5	17.0	17.5	18.0	19.0	20.0	22.0	26.0
0.0	0	0	0	0	0	0	2	16	45	92	137	166	185	170	146	125	110	98	89	79	70	63	58	53	48	44	42	41	37	33	28	0
.10	0	0	0	0	0	0	0	1	11	34	115	180	149	163	141	122	107	96	84	75	66	59	54	50	45	43	38	33	28	0
.20	0	0	0	0	0	0	0	1	8	25	57	96	131	173	166	126	111	99	86	80	66	59	55	50	46	43	41	38	34	29	
.30	0	0	0	0	0	0	2	1	5	18	44	79	143	170	160	141	122	108	92	81	69	61	56	52	47	44	42	38	37	29	
.40	0	0	0	0	0	0	0	0	14	34	66	127	166	162	145	123	111	95	82	70	62	57	52	47	44	42	38	34	28	1
.50	0	0	0	0	0	0	0	0	2	10	26	115	138	157	162	140	123	103	88	75	64	58	53	49	45	43	39	35	28	2
.75	0	0	0	0	0	0	1	1	1	4	12	47	126	154	148	139	113	98	80	67	60	55	50	46	43	39	36	29	3	
1.0	0	0	0	0	0	0	0	0	1	10	73	119	141	134	113	91	74	63	58	53	48	45	42	37	29	7	
1.5	0	0	0	0	0	0	0	0	14	30	66	105	143	143	117	90	73	63	57	52	48	42	39	30	18	
2.0	0	0	0	0	0	0	0	2	11	30	77	121	137	114	88	72	63	57	53	44	40	32	25	
2.5	0	0	0	0	0	0	1	3	10	55	111	132	111	87	71	62	56	47	43	36	27	
3.0	0	0	0	0	0	1	2	12	51	112	128	108	86	71	62	51	45	41	37	27	

Tabular hydrograph unit discharges (csm/in) for type II rainfall distribution

HYDROGRAPH TIME (HOURS)

TC = 0.5 HR

TRVL TIME (HR)	11.0	11.3	11.6	11.9	12.0	12.1	12.2	12.3	12.4	12.5	12.6	12.7	12.8	13.0	13.2	13.4	13.6	13.8	14.0	14.3	14.6	15.0	15.5	16.0	16.5	17.0	17.5	18.0	19.0	20.0	22.0	26.0

IA/P = 0.10

TRVL	11.0	11.3	11.6	11.9	12.0	12.1	12.2	12.3	12.4	12.5	12.6	12.7	12.8	13.0	13.2	13.4	13.6	13.8	14.0	14.3	14.6	15.0	15.5	16.0	16.5	17.0	17.5	18.0	19.0	20.0	22.0	26.0
0.00	17	23	32	57	94	170	308	467	529	507	402	297	226	140	96	74	61	53	47	41	36	32	29	26	23	21	20	19	16	14	12	0
.10	16	22	30	51	80	140	252	395	499	434	343	265	162	108	80	65	55	49	42	36	33	30	26	23	21	20	19	16	14	12	0	0
.20	14	19	25	38	47	116	207	332	434	477	449	378	238	149	101	77	62	53	45	39	34	31	27	24	22	20	19	17	14	12	0	0
.30	13	18	24	35	43	97	170	278	382	446	448	401	270	171	114	83	66	56	46	40	34	32	28	24	23	20	19	17	15	12	0	0
.40	12	15	21	29	33	53	141	233	332	408	361	243	157	107	79	64	51	43	36	32	29	26	23	20	17	15	12					
.50	11	15	20	28	31	48	83	194	286	367	378	271	178	119	86	68	55	44	37	32	29	25	22	19	17	15	12					
.75	9	11	14	19	21	37	71	141	194	286	328	374	312	169	117	76	53	43	35	31	26	20	17	15	12					
1.0	7	9	12	16	17	19	24	37	49	76	172	245	309	359	188	102	68	49	38	33	31	26	21	16	12					
1.5	5	7	11	12	13	14	15	17	19	21	23	27	43	89	175	269	322	309	225	140	77	49	38	32	29	25	23	20	17	13	11	5
2.0	3	4	8	9	9	10	11	10	11	12	14	15	18	23	35	65	123	202	280	297	181	88	52	39	33	29	26	19	16	11	11
2.5	3	3	5	6	6	7	7	7	8	8	10	12	15	18	24	136	66	244	278	171	87	52	39	33	29	20	15	11	11
3.0	1	2	3	4	4	4	5	6	6	7	8	11	13	16	20	188	198	263	182	96	56	40	33	16	11	11

IA/P = 0.30

TRVL	11.0	11.3	11.6	11.9	12.0	12.1	12.2	12.3	12.4	12.5	12.6	12.7	12.8	13.0	13.2	13.4	13.6	13.8	14.0	14.3	14.6	15.0	15.5	16.0	16.5	17.0	17.5	18.0	19.0	20.0	22.0	26.0
0.00	1	9	53	157	314	433	439	379	299	237	159	118	95	81	71	65	56	50	42	38	34	32	29	28	25	22	19	19	0	0	0
.10	1	1	6	37	157	314	416	391	330	218	150	113	92	70	60	54	47	43	39	35	33	30	29	26	22	19	19	0	0	0
.20	1	0	4	22	87	248	382	388	244	167	122	97	72	64	57	48	44	40	35	32	30	27	24	22	19	19	0	0	0
.30	0	0	0	3	26	194	259	341	372	223	156	117	94	80	67	58	53	46	41	36	34	31	28	25	23	19	19	2			
.40	0	0	0	0	0	0	0	0	5	30	95	183	249	265	217	152	96	66	53	46	41	37	34	30	26	20	8			
.50	0	0	0	0	0	0	0	0	3	16	59	125	221	245	174	105	69	54	47	42	38	35	32	28	22	16			
.75	0	0	0	0	0	0	0	0	0	0	5	21	84	174	230	212	103	69	54	46	42	39	35	31	29	23	18			
1.0	0	0	0	0	0	0	0	0	0	0	0	5	16	56	157	217	163	101	53	31	25	23	18			
1.5																													20	13	0	0
2.0																																
2.5																																
3.0																																

IA/P = 0.50

TRVL	11.0	11.3	11.6	11.9	12.0	12.1	12.2	12.3	12.4	12.5	12.6	12.7	12.8	13.0	13.2	13.4	13.6	13.8	14.0	14.3	14.6	15.0	15.5	16.0	16.5	17.0	17.5	18.0	19.0	20.0	22.0	26.0
0.00	2	26	89	170	217	229	200	179	144	119	104	93	85	78	70	64	59	55	51	46	43	41	40	36	32	28	0	0	0
.10	1	7	18	65	135	190	216	205	178	137	115	101	91	83	74	67	61	56	52	47	44	42	40	36	32	28	0	0	0
.20	0	1	12	47	106	162	198	203	178	145	121	105	94	85	76	68	62	57	52	48	44	42	37	33	28	0	0	0
.30	0	0	1	8	34	82	135	177	194	168	139	117	102	92	80	71	63	58	54	49	45	43	41	37	33	28	2		
.40	0	0	0	0	6	25	63	111	155	189	174	146	128	106	94	85	73	64	58	54	50	45	41	37	33	0	0	0
.50	0	0	0	0	4	18	48	90	133	177	169	144	110	97	84	74	65	59	56	51	47	44	42	38	34	28	0	0	0
.75	0	0	0	0	1	0	7	22	47	108	142	164	166	112	91	79	68	61	57	54	49	45	39	35	28	0	0	2
1.0	0	0	0	0	0	0	0	1	3	11	51	112	155	166	134	109	91	76	65	58	54	49	45	43	39	35			
1.5											16	50	136	154	145	121	95	75	64	58	45	41	37	29	10
2.0					18	47	134	146	125	94	75	64	49	42	39	31	21
2.5					3	11	44	95	127	77	65	54	41	45	41	33	26
3.0					0	1	7	29	86	122	95	76	65	58	49	43	35	27

* * * HR * * *

TR-55, Second Ed., June 1986

Exhibit 5-II, continued: Tabular hydrograph unit discharges (csm/in) for type II rainfall distribution

HYDROGRAPH TIME (HOURS)

IA/P = 0.10 * * * TC = 0.4 HR * * *

TRVL TIME (HR)	11.0	11.3	11.6	11.9	12.0	12.1	12.2	12.3	12.4	12.5	12.6	12.7	12.8	13.0	13.2	13.4	13.6	13.8	14.0	14.3	14.6	15.0	15.5	16.0	16.5	17.0	17.5	18.0	19.0	20.0	22.0	26.0
0.0	18	25	36	77	141	271	468	592	574	431	298	216	163	104	77	63	55	49	44	38	34	31	28	25	22	21	20	18	16	14	12	0
.10	18	24	34	67	116	219	385	557	523	473	357	263	196	119	84	67	57	51	46	39	35	32	29	25	22	21	20	19	16	14	12	0
.20	15	20	28	44	59	97	179	316	454	523	489	401	309	178	112	81	65	56	49	42	37	33	30	26	23	21	20	17	14	14	12	0
.30	15	20	27	41	53	82	147	260	389	478	486	429	349	129	89	69	58	51	43	38	33	30	27	24	24	21	20	19	17	14	12	0
.40	13	17	23	33	38	48	71	121	214	331	429	467	442	308	189	120	85	66	56	47	41	35	31	28	24	22	20	19	17	15	12	0
.50	12	16	22	31	36	44	62	102	176	266	379	438	440	339	218	137	94	71	59	49	42	35	31	28	26	23	20	19	17	15	12	1
.75	10	13	17	26	30	30	45	65	106	170	251	326	341	245	164	112	81	59	48	44	39	33	30	26	23	21	20	18	15	15	12	1
1.0	8	10	13	21	19	24	27	31	37	37	50	75	118	251	376	292	205	138	83	60	45	36	32	28	22	22	21	16	16	12	11	1
1.5	6	7	9	12	13	15	17	19	21	23	26	31	31	56	121	333	311	224	192	115	66	45	36	31	28	25	22	19	17	13	4	
2.0	4	5	6	8	8	9	10	11	12	14	15	16	20	27	43	85	159	306	264	154	74	47	37	32	29	25	22	21	18	14	9	
2.5	2	3	4	5	6	7	8	9	10	11	13	10	16	13	20	27	46	85	184	285	262	147	74	47	39	32	30	28	23	22	16	11
3.0	1	2	2	3	4	4	5	6	7	8	10	7	8	10	12	14	17	23	47	109	227	268	160	83	50	38	32	31	25	21	16	11

IA/P = 0.30 * * * TC = 0.4 HR * * *

TRVL TIME (HR)	11.0	11.3	11.6	11.9	12.0	12.1	12.2	12.3	12.4	12.5	12.6	12.7	12.8	13.0	13.2	13.4	13.6	13.8	14.0	14.3	14.6	15.0	15.5	16.0	16.5	17.0	17.5	18.0	19.0	20.0	22.0	26.0
0.0	0	0	4	26	113	296	480	495	413	306	234	186	127	100	84	74	67	61	54	49	45	41	37	37	33	31	29	28	25	22	19	0
.10	0	0	0	18	81	224	395	462	430	347	272	172	121	96	73	66	59	51	45	42	38	37	34	38	31	31	28	25	22	19	0
.20	0	0	2	13	59	169	320	414	424	373	305	196	134	103	85	75	67	59	52	47	43	39	34	39	30	32	29	26	22	19	0
.30	0	0	1	9	42	127	255	361	403	383	274	181	127	99	83	73	63	55	51	48	44	40	36	40	33	30	30	23	19	0
.40	0	0	1	6	30	94	202	308	372	379	298	203	141	106	87	76	65	56	49	44	40	36	31	31	29	29	26	20	6
.50	0	0	0	0	4	21	70	158	258	334	364	270	187	133	102	85	70	60	51	46	41	37	30	30	27	21	15
.75	0	0	0	0	2	8	30	76	145	219	305	321	241	177	130	102	78	65	55	47	43	38	30	30	24	23	18
1.0	0	0	0	1	0	0	0	0	1	42	150	267	308	272	209	154	103	79	62	51	45	41	37	33	31	31	28	25	20	13
1.5	0	0	0	0	0	0	0	0	0	0	0	10	51	136	226	263	195	131	85	62	51	45	41	36	33	29	26	20	15
2.0	0	0	0	0	0	0	0	0	0	0	0	0	0	86	162	252	239	162	64	52	45	41	37	31	28	21	18
2.5	0	0	0	0	0	0	0	0	0	0	0	0	0	6	0	33	112	202	235	155	92	64	52	41	33	29	23
3.0	0	0	0	0	0	0	0	0	0	0	0	0	0	1	0	0	21	76	182	221	148	90	63	51	45	36	31	24

IA/P = 0.50 * * * TC = 0.4 HR * * *

TRVL TIME (HR)	11.0	11.3	11.6	11.9	12.0	12.1	12.2	12.3	12.4	12.5	12.6	12.7	12.8	13.0	13.2	13.4	13.6	13.8	14.0	14.3	14.6	15.0	15.5	16.0	16.5	17.0	17.5	18.0	19.0	20.0	22.0	26.0
0.0	0	0	0	7	59	168	245	257	213	186	163	128	109	96	88	81	75	67	62	58	54	50	45	43	41	39	35	31	29	28	0
.10	0	0	0	0	5	125	205	240	222	163	123	106	94	86	79	71	64	60	58	56	51	46	43	42	40	36	32	28	28	0
.20	0	0	0	0	3	28	168	216	220	205	164	131	110	97	88	81	72	65	60	56	51	46	43	43	40	36	32	28	28	0
.30	0	0	0	0	2	20	135	189	209	192	155	126	107	95	86	77	69	62	57	53	48	44	44	41	37	33	28	28	0
.40	0	0	0	1	14	50	106	161	193	202	163	133	112	98	89	78	70	62	58	53	48	44	42	41	37	33	28	0
.50	0	0	0	0	0	37	83	135	174	177	154	117	102	91	79	71	63	56	51	47	45	43	42	38	34	28	1
.75	0	0	0	0	0	3	1	40	76	147	131	124	107	80	68	60	56	51	45	47	43	42	39	35	28
1.0	0	0	0	0	0	0	0	7	21	78	146	167	125	101	86	73	63	58	53	48	45	42	39	29
1.5	0	0	0	0	0	0	0	0	0	0	5	26	71	121	153	159	139	113	89	72	63	57	53	48	44	40	37	29	7
2.0	0	0	0	0	0	0	0	0	0	0	0	16	45	86	138	150	125	93	74	64	58	53	48	42	39	31	20
2.5	0	0	0	0	0	0	0	0	0	0	0	4	17	59	112	143	121	91	73	64	56	51	45	40	32	26
3.0	0	0	0	0	0	0	0	0	0	0	0	1	0	11	40	101	138	117	90	73	63	57	48	42	34	27

RAINFALL TYPE = II

SHEET 4 OF 10

Tabular hydrograph unit discharges (csm/in) for type II rainfall distribution

HYDROGRAPH TIME (HOURS)

IA/P = 0.10 * * * TC = 0.3 HR * * *

TRVL TIME (HR)	11.0	11.3	11.6	11.9	12.0	12.1	12.2	12.3	12.4	12.5	12.6	12.7	12.8	13.0	13.2	13.4	13.6	13.8	14.0	14.3	14.6	15.0	15.5	16.0	16.5	17.0	17.5	18.0	19.0	20.0	22.0	26.0
0.0	20	28	41	118	235	447	676	676	459	283	196	146	114	80	66	57	51	46	42	37	33	31	28	24	22	20	19	18	16	13	12	0
.10	19	26	39	99	189	361	676	641	520	362	251	181	136	89	70	60	53	48	43	37	34	31	28	25	22	21	19	18	16	14	12	0
.20	17	23	32	53	83	154	520	587	478	422	308	223	127	86	68	58	52	46	46	35	32	29	26	26	23	21	20	19	16	14	12	0
.30	16	22	30	49	72	127	237	398	524	536	460	359	268	151	97	73	61	53	48	41	36	32	29	26	23	21	20	19	16	14	12	0
.40	14	19	25	37	45	63	105	193	330	459	510	477	398	237	139	92	70	59	52	44	38	34	30	27	24	21	20	19	17	14	12	0
.50	13	18	24	35	42	56	89	158	272	397	472	475	424	274	163	104	76	62	54	46	39	34	30	27	24	22	20	19	17	15	12	0
.75	11	14	19	26	30	34	42	95	159	250	339	417	398	299	196	128	89	69	54	45	32	29	26	23	22	20	17	17	15	15	12	0
1.0	9	11	14	19	21	24	27	30	36	46	68	109	174	328	346	248	163	109	70	54	43	35	31	28	25	23	21	20	13	12	12	1
1.5	6	8	10	13	14	15	17	19	21	23	26	31	38	77	169	282	347	330	264	158	94	58	42	35	31	27	24	22	19	17	13	3
2.0	4	5	7	8	9	10	11	12	14	15	16	18	23	32	57	116	205	285	264	205	128	64	44	36	31	28	25	22	20	18	14	9
2.5	2	4	5	6	6	7	8	10	10	10	11	12	15	18	23	33	60	89	196	245	223	125	65	44	35	31	27	22	22	19	15	11
3.0	1	2	3	4	4	4	5	7	7	6	7	8	9	11	13	16	20	27	61	138	246	275	246	139	72	46	36	31	25	21	16	11

IA/P = 0.30 * * * TC = 0.3 HR * * *

TRVL TIME (HR)	11.0	11.3	11.6	11.9	12.0	12.1	12.2	12.3	12.4	12.5	12.6	12.7	12.8	13.0	13.2	13.4	13.6	13.8	14.0	14.3	14.6	15.0	15.5	16.0	16.5	17.0	17.5	18.0	19.0	20.0	22.0	26.0
0.0	0	11	64	251	525	574	454	303	221	173	140	104	88	77	70	64	58	51	47	44	40	36	32	29	28	24	21	28	21	21	19	0
.10	0	0	7	45	183	520	476	360	268	205	173	133	101	85	77	69	62	55	47	45	41	37	33	31	30	25	22	28	25	21	19	0
.20	0	0	5	32	132	411	520	396	310	240	188	109	90	78	70	64	56	52	46	42	38	33	31	28	28	26	23	28	22	21	19	0
.30	0	0	3	22	96	318	452	440	383	344	217	142	105	87	76	69	60	53	49	44	40	35	32	30	29	26	24	29	24	22	19	0
.40	0	2	2	16	69	186	317	399	407	365	246	160	115	92	79	71	61	54	51	43	39	35	32	30	29	26	30	29	26	22	19	1
.50	0	0	0	2	11	50	140	258	352	389	327	223	149	110	89	77	66	57	50	45	41	36	33	31	31	31	31	31	28	23	19	1
.75	0	0	0	1	4	20	63	135	219	290	335	281	205	146	110	89	72	62	52	46	40	34	31	30	30	30	33	40	29	23	19	1
1.0	0	0	0	0	0	2	9	32	78	243	216	320	306	243	176	128	90	72	59	49	44	36	33	31	31	33	36	45	31	24	19	1
1.5	0	0	0	0	0	0	0	0	20	84	185	264	281	246	168	112	77	58	49	44	40	36	32	29	28	32	36	40	26	20	5	5
2.0	0	0	0	7	0	0	0	0	0	1	12	50	121	200	257	224	141	83	61	50	44	36	33	31	31	36	40	44	28	21	14	14
2.5	0	0	0	5	0	0	0	0	0	0	0	0	16	51	145	239	223	137	82	62	52	46	34	31	33	40	50	51	29	22	17	17
3.0	0	0	0	3	0	0	0	0	0	0	0	0	0	19	74	138	184	224	90	72	59	49	44	40	36	46	63	51	31	24	18	18

IA/P = 0.50 * * * TC = 0.3 HR * * *

TRVL TIME (HR)	11.0	11.3	11.6	11.9	12.0	12.1	12.2	12.3	12.4	12.5	12.6	12.7	12.8	13.0	13.2	13.4	13.6	13.8	14.0	14.3	14.6	15.0	15.5	16.0	16.5	17.0	17.5	18.0	19.0	20.0	22.0	26.0
0.0	0	1	25	151	299	277	219	187	162	141	113	100	90	84	78	72	65	58	53	48	44	41	39	35	31	28	39	35	31	28	0	0
.10	0	1	17	106	235	263	234	202	175	152	120	104	93	85	79	73	66	59	54	49	44	41	39	35	31	28	39	35	31	28	0	0
.20	0	0	12	75	182	235	234	213	188	173	144	116	101	91	84	78	70	63	55	50	45	43	40	36	31	28	40	36	31	28	0	0
.30	0	0	8	52	138	205	224	217	197	154	123	105	94	86	79	71	64	59	51	46	43	42	36	32	28	42	36	32	28	0	0	0
.40	0	0	0	5	37	105	170	206	213	164	131	110	97	88	81	72	65	56	46	43	40	41	37	32	42	40	42	40	32	0	0	0
.50	0	0	0	0	4	26	78	140	184	155	126	107	95	86	79	73	69	48	45	44	41	45	44	43	41	47	42	41	33	0	0	0
.75	0	0	0	0	1	10	34	73	117	173	146	122	105	82	64	61	58	54	49	45	44	49	52	57	45	51	51	42	35	0	0	0
1.0	0	0	0	0	0	0	4	17	42	114	178	159	134	114	82	70	61	57	47	46	44	57	61	68	55	60	55	46	36	0	0	0
1.5	0	0	0	0	0	0	0	0	0	10	44	98	144	163	130	84	69	56	52	47	44	56	61	69	52	44	40	44	36	29	6	6
2.0	0	0	0	0	0	0	0	0	0	0	2	14	44	127	141	87	61	53	48	45	48	57	69	82	56	47	42	47	38	30	17	17
2.5	0	0	0	0	0	0	0	0	0	0	0	4	16	97	138	110	82	54	49	52	58	64	73	105	60	51	43	51	40	32	25	25
3.0	0	0	0	0	0	0	0	0	0	0	0	0	1	27	71	127	139	114	94	73	61	70	81	105	68	55	44	55	41	33	27	27

RAINFALL TYPE = II SHEET 3 OF 10

Exhibit 5-II, continued: Tabular hydrograph unit discharges (csm/in) for type II rainfall distribution

HYDROGRAPH TIME (HOURS)

IA/P = 0.10   * * * TC = 0.2 HR * * *

TRVL TIME (HR)	11.0	11.3	11.6	11.9	12.0	12.1	12.2	12.3	12.4	12.5	12.6	12.7	12.8	13.0	13.2	13.4	13.6	13.8	14.0	14.3	14.6	15.0	15.5	16.0	16.5	17.0	17.5	18.0	19.0	20.0	22.0	26.0
0.0	23	31	47	209	403	739	800	481	250	166	128	102	86	70	61	54	49	44	40	35	33	30	27	24	21	20	19	18	16	13	12	0
.10	19	26	39	86	168	325	601	733	565	355	229	161	122	83	69	59	53	47	43	37	34	31	28	25	22	21	19	18	16	14	12	0
.20	17	23	32	49	74	136	262	488	601	594	435	298	207	115	81	67	58	51	46	40	35	32	29	26	23	21	20	19	16	14	12	0
.30	16	22	30	46	64	112	212	396	566	585	485	360	258	139	90	71	60	53	48	41	36	32	29	26	23	21	20	19	16	14	12	0
.40	14	19	25	37	43	57	94	173	322	485	551	507	409	227	129	87	68	58	52	44	38	33	30	27	24	21	19	19	17	14	12	0
.50	13	18	24	35	40	52	80	142	262	410	504	506	441	269	153	98	73	61	53	45	39	34	30	27	25	22	20	19	17	15	12	0
.75	10	13	17	23	26	30	34	40	86	150	247	349	438	438	240	151	101	75	57	47	33	29	26	23	20	18	18	15	13	12	0
1.0	9	11	14	19	21	24	26	30	35	44	62	101	167	337	353	245	157	104	75	68	53	42	35	31	28	24	22	20	18	16	12	0

IA/P = 0.30   * * * TC = 0.2 HR * * *

TRVL TIME (HR)	11.0	11.3	11.6	11.9	12.0	12.1	12.2	12.3	12.4	12.5	12.6	12.7	12.8	13.0	13.2	13.4	13.6	13.8	14.0	14.3	14.6	15.0	15.5	16.0	16.5	17.0	17.5	18.0	19.0	20.0	22.0	26.0
1.5	6	8	10	13	14	15	17	19	21	23	26	30	37	73	166	288	356	337	264	154	91	57	42	35	30	27	24	22	19	17	13	3
2.0	4	5	7	8	9	10	11	11	14	15	16	18	23	31	55	114	206	291	324	239	125	63	44	35	31	28	21	20	18	14	9	9
2.5	3	4	5	6	6	7	8	8	9	9	10	12	15	18	22	32	58	111	227	298	246	122	63	43	35	31	28	22	19	15	11	11
3.0	1	2	3	4	4	4	5	5	6	6	7	7	8	11	13	16	19	27	59	138	280	248	137	70	46	36	31	28	19	16	11	11

IA/P = 0.30   * * * TC = 0.2 HR * * *

TRVL TIME (HR)	11.0	11.3	11.6	11.9	12.0	12.1	12.2	12.3	12.4	12.5	12.6	12.7	12.8	13.0	13.2	13.4	13.6	13.8	14.0	14.3	14.6	15.0	15.5	16.0	16.5	17.0	17.5	18.0	19.0	20.0	22.0	26.0
0.0	0	0	39	180	545	697	497	276	198	158	130	93	81	67	61	56	46	43	39	35	32	30	27	24	21	19	0	0	0	0	0	0
.10	0	0	0	2	27	129	407	600	532	361	252	190	108	79	65	59	44	41	36	34	32	30	28	25	21	19	0	0	0	0	0	0
.20	0	0	2	19	92	302	501	521	415	306	228	176	119	95	67	61	48	45	37	33	31	28	25	21	19	0	0	0	0	0	0	0
.30	0	0	1	13	66	223	408	484	438	350	269	163	114	93	72	65	51	46	38	35	31	28	25	22	19	0	0	0	0	0	0	0
.40	0	0	9	47	164	327	431	436	379	306	189	127	98	83	74	67	52	47	43	38	34	31	30	25	22	19	0	0	5	0	0	0
.50	0	0	6	31	120	258	374	415	391	271	173	121	95	81	72	53	48	44	40	35	32	30	26	22	19	0	0	13	0	0	0	0
.75	0	0	2	13	50	126	221	302	348	323	240	167	96	81	68	59	50	45	41	37	33	31	29	26	22	19	17	0	0	0	0	0
1.0	0	0	0	6	24	69	139	221	285	331	280	204	145	109	72	68	56	48	43	39	35	30	27	24	19	18	0	0	0	0	0	0

IA/P = 0.50   * * * TC = 0.2 HR * * *

TRVL TIME (HR)	11.0	11.3	11.6	11.9	12.0	12.1	12.2	12.3	12.4	12.5	12.6	12.7	12.8	13.0	13.2	13.4	13.6	13.8	14.0	14.3	14.6	15.0	15.5	16.0	16.5	17.0	17.5	18.0	19.0	20.0	22.0	26.0
1.5	0	0	0	1	16	79	186	271	288	247	165	110	76	49	58	44	40	38	35	32	29	26	20	5	0	0	0	0	0	0	0	0
2.0	0	0	0	0	3	24	80	163	235	262	202	123	76	58	49	41	39	35	30	27	21	13	0	0	0	0	0	0	0	0	0	0
2.5	0	0	0	0	1	6	28	77	179	242	207	120	80	57	48	43	32	29	22	17	0	0	0	0	0	0	0	0	0	0	0	0
3.0	0	0	0	0	0	0	6	30	101	227	207	130	59	49	44	30	24	18	0	0	0	0	0	0	0	0	0	0	0	0	0	0

IA/P = 0.50   * * * TC = 0.2 HR * * *

TRVL TIME (HR)	11.0	11.3	11.6	11.9	12.0	12.1	12.2	12.3	12.4	12.5	12.6	12.7	12.8	13.0	13.2	13.4	13.6	13.8	14.0	14.3	14.6	15.0	15.5	16.0	16.5	17.0	17.5	18.0	19.0	20.0	22.0	26.0
0.0	0	0	0	7	98	371	322	221	182	158	137	104	94	80	74	69	62	60	57	52	47	44	42	40	39	39	35	30	28	0	0	0
.10	0	0	0	4	67	270	305	249	204	174	149	108	97	82	76	71	64	60	57	53	48	44	42	39	39	38	35	28	0	0	0	0
.20	0	0	0	0	3	45	195	268	255	221	189	125	106	87	80	75	67	62	58	54	49	45	43	37	31	28	0	0	0	0	0	0
.30	0	0	0	2	31	140	226	245	229	203	134	111	89	82	76	68	62	59	55	50	46	43	36	31	28	0	0	0	0	0	0	0
.40	0	0	1	21	101	184	225	228	211	183	144	117	91	84	78	69	63	59	55	50	45	43	41	40	36	28	0	0	0	0	0	0
.50	0	0	0	1	14	72	146	199	213	175	137	113	99	89	82	73	66	60	56	52	47	41	38	32	0	0	0	0	0	0	0	0
.75	0	0	0	0	5	28	71	121	162	186	161	133	98	88	70	62	57	53	48	43	37	33	28	0	0	0	0	0	0	0	0	0
1.0	0	0	0	0	2	13	38	77	122	154	186	147	105	78	74	66	60	56	51	46	42	34	0	0	0	0	0	0	0	0	0	0

TRVL TIME (HR)	11.0	11.3	11.6	11.9	12.0	12.1	12.2	12.3	12.4	12.5	12.6	12.7	12.8	13.0	13.2	13.4	13.6	13.8	14.0	14.3	14.6	15.0	15.5	16.0	16.5	17.0	17.5	18.0	19.0	20.0	22.0	26.0
1.5	0	0	0	0	0	0	2	22	71	129	163	168	120	98	90	80	67	60	55	51	46	43	40	36	28	4						
2.0	0	0	0	0	0	0	0	5	25	146	157	134	103	54	55	50	46	41	38	28	14											
2.5	0	0	0	0	0	0	0	0	26	66	136	101	79	66	57	50	43	39	31	24												
3.0	0	0	0	0	0	0	0	2	40	90	142	130	99	78	54	45	41	34	33	26												

RAINFALL TYPE = II

SHEET 2 OF 10

Tabular hydrograph unit discharges (csm/in) for type II rainfall distribution

RAINFALL TYPE = II

IA/P = 0.10 — TC = 0.1 HR

TRVL TIME (HR)	11.0	11.3	11.6	11.9	12.0	12.1	12.2	12.3	12.4	12.5	12.6	12.7	12.8	13.0	13.2	13.4	13.6	13.8	14.0	14.3	14.6	15.0	15.5	16.0	16.5	17.0	17.5	18.0	19.0	20.0	22.0	26.0
.0	24	34	53	334	647	1010	623	217	147	123	104	86	76	66	57	51	46	42	38	34	32	29	26	23	21	20	19	18	15	13	12	0
.10	21	29	43	134	267	520	701	378	224	157	122	98	75	64	56	50	45	41	36	33	30	27	24	21	20	19	16	15	13	12	12	0
.20	18	25	35	61	110	215	418	702	312	209	151	94	73	54	49	45	41	38	33	31	28	25	22	22	20	19	18	17	15	12	12	0
.30	17	23	33	56	92	174	337	582	545	269	190	79	65	56	50	45	39	35	32	29	25	24	22	21	20	18	16	14	12	12	12	0
.40	15	20	28	41	51	78	142	272	478	601	563	447	328	172	104	76	63	55	49	42	37	33	29	26	23	21	20	19	17	14	12	0
.50	14	19	26	39	47	68	117	220	392	531	553	482	380	209	121	84	67	57	51	43	38	33	30	27	24	22	19	17	14	13	12	0
.75	12	15	21	29	33	33	49	73	126	224	343	432	464	385	252	156	103	76	62	50	43	36	31	28	25	22	19	17	15	14	12	0
1.0	9	12	15	21	23	26	29	33	40	55	86	148	238	406	434	317	205	130	89	62	50	41	34	30	27	24	20	18	16	12	12	0
1.5	7	8	10	14	15	16	18	20	22	25	29	34	45	101	220	339	373	320	234	131	80	53	40	34	30	27	24	21	19	17	12	2
2.0	4	6	7	9	9	10	11	12	13	15	16	18	20	25	37	72	150	252	336	312	216	109	58	42	34	30	27	24	20	18	13	8
2.5	3	4	5	6	6	7	8	9	10	11	12	13	16	19	25	39	75	142	262	303	229	108	58	41	34	30	28	22	16	11	11	11
3.0	1	2	3	4	4	5	6	6	7	7	8	10	12	14	17	22	31	75	131	169	288	236	122	64	43	35	30	24	16	11	11	11

IA/P = 0.30 — TC = 0.1 HR

TRVL TIME (HR)	11.0	11.3	11.6	11.9	12.0	12.1	12.2	12.3	12.4	12.5	12.6	12.7	12.8	13.0	13.2	13.4	13.6	13.8	14.0	14.3	14.6	15.0	15.5	16.0	16.5	17.0	17.5	18.0	19.0	20.0	22.0	26.0
.0	0	0	0	0	0	154	568	936	524	217	172	149	126	107	97	86	76	69	63	58	53	48	42	38	34	31	30	28	27	24	20	0
.10	0	0	0	0	0	19	109	415	762	603	346	230	176	143	119	96	84	74	68	62	57	50	44	40	37	32	29	29	27	24	21	0
.20	0	0	0	0	0	10	13	77	302	609	432	605	297	217	167	115	94	81	73	66	60	53	48	45	41	33	31	29	28	26	0	
.30	0	0	0	0	0	8	54	219	479	563	476	357	263	199	129	99	85	75	68	62	54	49	47	45	41	35	33	31	30	24	0	
.40	0	0	0	0	6	38	159	372	500	484	399	309	183	123	96	82	73	66	58	51	46	42	38	34	31	30	29	28	25	20	4	
.50	0	0	0	0	4	27	115	287	429	465	346	346	213	138	103	86	76	68	59	52	47	43	39	35	32	31	30	29	27	21	11	
.75	0	0	0	0	0	0	10	46	132	246	338	421	341	243	165	94	80	67	58	50	45	41	37	33	30	31	33	32	28	24	17	17
1.0	0	0	0	0	0	0	1	4	22	69	149	246	357	331	246	170	122	96	76	64	54	47	42	37	34	35	38	42	43	24	18	
1.5	0	0	0	0	0	0	0	0	0	0	0	0	0	41	142	255	285	224	142	97	71	55	47	43	39	35	32	29	25	20	17	
2.0	0	0	0	0	0	0	0	0	0	0	0	0	0	10	49	221	279	255	182	108	76	58	49	42	38	34	30	27	22	20	17	
2.5	0	0	0	0	0	0	0	0	0	0	0	0	0	2	14	52	224	256	193	107	70	55	47	42	38	33	30	28	23	21	17	
3.0	0	0	0	0	0	0	0	0	0	0	0	0	0	0	0	22	119	141	240	199	117	74	56	48	43	35	30	24	18	

IA/P = 0.50 — TC = 0.1 HR

TRVL TIME (HR)	11.0	11.3	11.6	11.9	12.0	12.1	12.2	12.3	12.4	12.5	12.6	12.7	12.8	13.0	13.2	13.4	13.6	13.8	14.0	14.3	14.6	15.0	15.5	16.0	16.5	17.0	17.5	18.0	19.0	20.0	22.0	26.0
.0	0	0	0	0	70	539	377	196	154	134	117	108	99	89	83	77	72	67	58	56	51	46	43	42	40	38	36	34	31	28	0	
.10	0	0	0	0	47	375	376	256	169	146	126	114	102	92	85	79	73	68	59	56	52	47	43	42	40	38	36	34	32	29	0	
.20	0	0	0	0	31	260	338	289	199	189	161	112	99	90	83	77	72	65	57	54	50	47	44	43	41	39	37	35	33	31	0	
.30	0	0	0	0	0	208	285	284	246	208	176	131	110	97	88	82	76	62	59	55	50	46	43	41	39	36	34	31	26			
.40	0	0	0	0	14	125	232	266	223	192	142	115	100	91	77	69	63	59	55	50	45	43	41	40	36	31						
.50	0	0	0	0	9	86	183	239	248	205	154	122	104	93	79	71	65	59	55	49	46	43	41	40	36	32						
.75	0	0	0	0	3	31	87	147	190	211	184	147	121	103	84	75	67	57	52	47	44	41	37	32								
1.0	0	0	0	0	0	8	1	13	45	92	141	165	134	112	98	84	75	55	50	46	43	41	38	28								
1.5	0	0	0	0	0	0	0	0	0	0	0	9	51	118	167	183	143	111	92	77	65	59	54	45	43	35	28	2	
2.0	0	0	0	0	0	0	0	0	0	0	0	2	15	103	170	156	127	96	76	65	58	49	45	37	29	12	
2.5	0	0	0	0	0	0	0	0	0	0	0	0	31	148	131	159	78	66	54	50	43	39	31	24	
3.0	0	0	0	0	0	0	0	0	0	0	0	0	0	0	69	101	134	99	77	59	54	45	41	34	26	

SHEET 1 OF 10

TR-55 CURVE NUMBER COMPUTATION **VERSION 1.11**

```
Project : GAINES' WOOD                    User: HCL      Date: 10/16/86
County  : ALACHUA          State: FL   Checked: ____     Date: _____
Subtitle: PRESENT CONDITION
Subarea : 1
-----------------------------------------------------------------------
                                              Hydrologic Soil Group
        COVER DESCRIPTION                 A       B       C       D
                                               Sq miles (CN)
-----------------------------------------------------------------------
OTHER AGRICULTURAL LANDS
Pasture, grassland or range    good       -   .083(61)    -       -

Woods - grass combination      fair   .124(43)    -       -       -



Total Area (by Hydrologic Soil Group)    .124    .083
                                         ====    ====



-----------------------------------------------------------------------
SUBAREA: 1     TOTAL DRAINAGE AREA: .207 Sq miles   WEIGHTED CURVE NUMBER:50
-----------------------------------------------------------------------
```

TR-55 CURVE NUMBER COMPUTATION **VERSION 1.11**

```
Project : GAINES' WOOD                    User: HCL      Date: 10/16/86
County  : ALACHUA          State: FL   Checked: ____     Date: _____
Subtitle: PRESENT CONDITION
Subarea : 2
-----------------------------------------------------------------------
                                              Hydrologic Soil Group
        COVER DESCRIPTION                 A       B       C       D
                                               Sq miles (CN)
-----------------------------------------------------------------------
OTHER AGRICULTURAL LANDS
Pasture, grassland or range    good       -   .113(61)    -       -

Woods - grass combination      fair   .093(43)    -       -       -



Total Area (by Hydrologic Soil Group)    .093    .113
                                         ====    ====



-----------------------------------------------------------------------
SUBAREA: 2     TOTAL DRAINAGE AREA: .206 Sq miles   WEIGHTED CURVE NUMBER:53
-----------------------------------------------------------------------
```

TR-55 CURVE NUMBER COMPUTATION   **VERSION 1.11**

```
Project : GAINES' WOOD                    User: HCL      Date: 10/16/86
County  : ALACHUA          State: FL      Checked: ____   Date: _____
Subtitle: PRESENT CONDITION
Subarea : 3
```

| COVER DESCRIPTION | | Hydrologic Soil Group | | | |
| | A | B | C | D |
		Sq miles (CN)		
CULTIVATED AGRICULTURAL LANDS				
Row crops Straight row (SR) poor	-	-	.038(88)	-
OTHER AGRICULTURAL LANDS				
Pasture, grassland or range good	-	.115(61)	-	-
Total Area (by Hydrologic Soil Group)		.115	.038	
		====	====	

```
SUBAREA: 3      TOTAL DRAINAGE AREA: .153 Sq miles   WEIGHTED CURVE NUMBER:68
```

TR-55 CURVE NUMBER COMPUTATION   **VERSION 1.11**

```
Project : GAINES' WOOD                    User: HCL      Date: 10/16/86
County  : ALACHUA          State: FL      Checked: ____   Date: _____
Subtitle: PRESENT CONDITION
Subarea : 4
```

| COVER DESCRIPTION | | Hydrologic Soil Group | | | |
| | A | B | C | D |
		Sq miles (CN)		
OTHER AGRICULTURAL LANDS				
Pasture, grassland or range good	-	.063(61)	-	-
Total Area (by Hydrologic Soil Group)		.063		
		====		

```
SUBAREA: 4      TOTAL DRAINAGE AREA: .063 Sq miles   WEIGHTED CURVE NUMBER:61
```

```
            TR-55 CURVE NUMBER COMPUTATION              VERSION 1.11


Project : GAINES' WOOD                 User: HCL       Date: 10/16/86
County  : ALACHUA          State: FL   Checked: ____    Date: _____
Subtitle: PRESENT CONDITION
Subarea : 5
-----------------------------------------------------------------------
                                         Hydrologic Soil Group
          COVER DESCRIPTION            A     B       C       D
                                            Sq miles (CN)
-----------------------------------------------------------------------
OTHER AGRICULTURAL LANDS
Pasture, grassland or range    fair    -  .06(69) .14(79)     -


Total Area (by Hydrologic Soil Group)     .06     .14
                                         ====    ====


-----------------------------------------------------------------------
SUBAREA: 5     TOTAL DRAINAGE AREA: .2 Sq miles   WEIGHTED CURVE NUMBER:76
-----------------------------------------------------------------------
```

TR-55 Tc and Tt THRU SUBAREA COMPUTATION   VERSION 1.11

Project : GAINES' WOOD   User: HCL   Date: 10/16/86
County : ALACHUA   State: FL   Checked: _____   Date: _____
Subtitle: PRESENT CONDITION

---------------------------------- Subarea #1 - 1 ----------------------------------

Flow Type	2 year rain	Length (ft)	Slope (ft/ft)	Surface code	n	Area (sq/ft)	Wp (ft)	Velocity (ft/sec)	Time (hr)
Sheet	4.5	250	.025	f				0.382
Shallow Concent'd		1200	.015	u				0.169
Open Channel		1400	.004		.02732	15.3		0.068

Time of Concentration = 0.62*
                        =====

---------------------------------- Subarea #2 - 2 ----------------------------------

Flow Type	2 year rain	Length (ft)	Slope (ft/ft)	Surface code	n	Area (sq/ft)	Wp (ft)	Velocity (ft/sec)	Time (hr)
Sheet	4.5	220	.02	f				0.377
Shallow Concent'd		750	.01	u				0.129
Open Channel		1900	.003		.02748.2	19.3		0.095

Time of Concentration = 0.60*
                        =====

---------------------------------- Subarea #3 - 3 ----------------------------------

Flow Type	2 year rain	Length (ft)	Slope (ft/ft)	Surface code	n	Area (sq/ft)	Wp (ft)	Velocity (ft/sec)	Time (hr)
Sheet	4.5	275	.023	f				0.426
Shallow Concent'd		850	.015	u				0.119
Open Channel		2300	.004		.02742	20.0		0.112

Time of Concentration = 0.66*
                        =====

---------------------------------- Subarea #4 - 4 ----------------------------------

Flow Type	2 year rain	Length (ft)	Slope (ft/ft)	Surface code	n	Area (sq/ft)	Wp (ft)	Velocity (ft/sec)	Time (hr)
Sheet	4.5	100	.01	f				0.265
Shallow Concent'd		650	.01	u				0.112
Open Channel		1200	.003		.02764	24.4		0.058

Time of Concentration = 0.43*
                        =====

Flow Type	2 year rain	Length (ft)	Slope (ft/ft)	Surface code	n	Area (sq/ft)	Wp (ft)	Velocity (ft/sec)	Time (hr)
Open Channel		1200	.003		.02764	24.4		0.058

Travel Time = 0.06*
              =====

* - Generated for use by TABULAR method

TR-55 Tc and Tt THRU SUBAREA COMPUTATION   **VERSION 1.11**

```
Project : GAINES' WOOD                 User: HCL      Date: 10/16/86
County  : ALACHUA        State: FL     Checked: ____  Date: _____
Subtitle: PRESENT CONDITION
```

```
------------------------------ Subarea #5 - 5 ------------------------------
Flow Type   2 year   Length   Slope  Surface   n     Area    Wp   Velocity  Time
            rain      (ft)    (ft/ft)  code          (sq/ft)  (ft) (ft/sec)  (hr)
----------------------------------------------------------------------------
Sheet         4.5      300    .015     f                                    0.542
Shallow Concent'd      940    .015     u                                    0.132
Open Channel          2800    .003           .027100  32.3                  0.121
                                         Time of Concentration = 0.80*
                                                                  =====

Open Channel          2800    .003           .027100  32.3                  0.121
                                              Travel Time = 0.12*
                                                           =====
```

```
        --- Sheet Flow Surface Codes ---
    A Smooth Surface          F Grass, Dense    --- Shallow Concentrated ---
    B Fallow (No Res.)        G Grass, Burmuda  ---    Surface Codes    ---
    C Cultivated < 20 % Res.  H Woods, Light        P Paved
    D Cultivated > 20 % Res.  I Woods, Dense        U Unpaved
    E Grass-Range, Short
```

* - Generated for use by TABULAR method

TR-55 CURVE NUMBER COMPUTATION   **VERSION 1.11**

```
Project : GAIN'S WOOD                      User: HCL     Date: 10/18/86
County  : ALACHUA          State: FL    Checked: ____    Date: _____
Subtitle: DEVELOPED
Subarea : 1
```

```
                                                 Hydrologic Soil Group
          COVER DESCRIPTION                  A      B      C      D
                                                 Sq miles (CN)
```

```
FULLY DEVELOPED URBAN AREAS (Veg Estab.)
Residential districts     Avg % imperv
  (by average lot size)
    1 acre                    20          .124(51) .083(68)   -      -



Total Area (by Hydrologic Soil Group)        .124   .083
                                             ====   ====
```

```
SUBAREA: 1     TOTAL DRAINAGE AREA: .207 Sq miles   WEIGHTED CURVE NUMBER:58
```

TR-55 CURVE NUMBER COMPUTATION   **VERSION 1.11**

```
Project : GAIN'S WOOD                      User: HCL     Date: 10/18/86
County  : ALACHUA          State: FL    Checked: ____    Date: _____
Subtitle: DEVELOPED
Subarea : 2
```

```
                                                 Hydrologic Soil Group
          COVER DESCRIPTION                  A      B      C      D
                                                 Sq miles (CN)
```

```
FULLY DEVELOPED URBAN AREAS (Veg Estab.)
Residential districts     Avg % imperv
  (by average lot size)
    1/2 acre                 25          .093(54)   -      -      -
      1 acre                 20             -     .113(68)  -      -



Total Area (by Hydrologic Soil Group)        .093   .113
                                             ====   ====
```

```
SUBAREA: 2     TOTAL DRAINAGE AREA: .206 Sq miles   WEIGHTED CURVE NUMBER:62
```

TR-55 CURVE NUMBER COMPUTATION   **VERSION 1.11**

```
Project : GAIN'S WOOD                    User: HCL    Date: 10/18/86
County  : ALACHUA         State: FL   Checked: ____   Date: _____
Subtitle: DEVELOPED
Subarea : 3
------------------------------------------------------------------------
                                         Hydrologic Soil Group
            COVER DESCRIPTION            A       B       C        D
                                              Sq miles (CN)
------------------------------------------------------------------------
FULLY DEVELOPED URBAN AREAS (Veg Estab.)
Residential districts    Avg % imperv
  (by average lot size)
  1/4 acre                    38         -   .115(75) .038(83)    -


Total Area (by Hydrologic Soil Group)        .115     .038
                                             ====     ====



------------------------------------------------------------------------
SUBAREA: 3     TOTAL DRAINAGE AREA: .153 Sq miles   WEIGHTED CURVE NUMBER:77
------------------------------------------------------------------------
```

TR-55 CURVE NUMBER COMPUTATION   **VERSION 1.11**

```
Project : GAIN'S WOOD                    User: HCL    Date: 10/18/86
County  : ALACHUA         State: FL   Checked: ____   Date: _____
Subtitle: DEVELOPED
Subarea : 4
------------------------------------------------------------------------
                                         Hydrologic Soil Group
            COVER DESCRIPTION            A       B       C        D
                                              Sq miles (CN)
------------------------------------------------------------------------
FULLY DEVELOPED URBAN AREAS (Veg Estab.)
Urban Districts          Avg % imperv
  Commercial & business       85         -   .063(92)    -        -


Total Area (by Hydrologic Soil Group)        .063
                                             ====



------------------------------------------------------------------------
SUBAREA: 4     TOTAL DRAINAGE AREA: .063 Sq miles   WEIGHTED CURVE NUMBER:92
------------------------------------------------------------------------
```

TR-55 CURVE NUMBER COMPUTATION   VERSION 1.11

```
Project : GAIN'S WOOD               User: HCL      Date: 10/18/86
County  : ALACHUA      State: FL    Checked: ____   Date: _____
Subtitle: DEVELOPED
Subarea : 5
```

		Hydrologic Soil Group		
COVER DESCRIPTION	A	B	C	D
		Sq miles (CN)		

```
FULLY DEVELOPED URBAN AREAS (Veg Estab.)
Urban Districts          Avg % imperv
   Commercial & business      85          -        -    .14(94)    -
   Industrial                 72          -   .06(88)      -       -


Total Area (by Hydrologic Soil Group)              .06      .14
                                                  ====     ====
```

```
SUBAREA: 5      TOTAL DRAINAGE AREA: .2 Sq miles   WEIGHTED CURVE NUMBER: 92
```

TR-55 Tc and Tt THRU SUBAREA COMPUTATION   **VERSION 1.11**

Project : GAIN'S WOOD   User: HCL   Date: 10/18/86
County : ALACHUA   State: FL   Checked: ____   Date: _____
Subtitle: DEVELOPED

------------------------------------ Subarea #1 - 1 ------------------------------------

Flow Type	2 year rain	Length (ft)	Slope (ft/ft)	Surface code	n	Area (sq/ft)	Wp (ft)	Velocity (ft/sec)	Time (hr)
Sheet	4.5	250	.025	f					0.382
Shallow Concent'd		1200	.015	P					0.134
Open Channel		1400	.004			.02732	15.3		0.068

Time of Concentration = 0.58*
=====

------------------------------------ Subarea #2 - 2 ------------------------------------

Flow Type	2 year rain	Length (ft)	Slope (ft/ft)	Surface code	n	Area (sq/ft)	Wp (ft)	Velocity (ft/sec)	Time (hr)
Sheet	4.5	220	.02	f					0.377
Shallow Concent'd		750	.01	P					0.102
Open Channel		1900	.003			.02748.2	19.3		0.095

Time of Concentration = 0.57*
=====

------------------------------------ Subarea #3 - 3 ------------------------------------

Flow Type	2 year rain	Length (ft)	Slope (ft/ft)	Surface code	n	Area (sq/ft)	Wp (ft)	Velocity (ft/sec)	Time (hr)
Sheet	4.5	275	.023	f					0.426
Shallow Concent'd		850	.015	P					0.095
Open Channel		2300	.004			.02742	20.0		0.112

Time of Concentration = 0.63*
=====

------------------------------------ Subarea #4 - 4 ------------------------------------

Flow Type	2 year rain	Length (ft)	Slope (ft/ft)	Surface code	n	Area (sq/ft)	Wp (ft)	Velocity (ft/sec)	Time (hr)
Sheet	4.5	100	.01	f					0.265
Shallow Concent'd		650	.01	P					0.089
Open Channel		1200	.003			.02764	24.4		0.058

Time of Concentration = 0.41*
=====

| Open Channel | | 1500 | .003 | | | .02764 | 24.4 | | 0.072 |

Travel Time = 0.07*
=====

* - Generated for use by TABULAR method

TR-55 Tc and Tt THRU SUBAREA COMPUTATION   **VERSION 1.11**

Project : GAIN'S WOOD   User: HCL   Date: 10/18/86
County : ALACHUA   State: FL   Checked: ____   Date: _____
Subtitle: DEVELOPED

----------------------------- Subarea #5 - 5 -----------------------------

Flow Type	2 year rain	Length (ft)	Slope (ft/ft)	Surface code	n	Area (sq/ft)	Wp (ft)	Velocity (ft/sec)	Time (hr)
Sheet	4.5	300	.015	f					0.542
Shallow Concent'd		940	.015	P					0.105
Open Channel		2800	.003			.027100	32.3		0.121

Time of Concentration = 0.77*
=====

Open Channel		3100	.003			.027100	32.3		0.134

Travel Time = 0.13*
=====

        --- Sheet Flow Surface Codes ---
   A Smooth Surface   F Grass, Dense   --- Shallow Concentrated ---
   B Fallow (No Res.)   G Grass, Burmuda   ---   Surface Codes   ---
   C Cultivated < 20 % Res.   H Woods, Light   P Paved
   D Cultivated > 20 % Res.   I Woods, Dense   U Unpaved
   E Grass-Range, Short

* - Generated for use by TABULAR method

TABULAR HYDROGRAPH WORKSHEET

Project:_____Location:_____By:_____Date:_____

☐ Present Condition   ☐ Developed Condition   Checked By:_____Date:_____

Rainfall Distrubution:_____Storm Frequency:_____

Subarea No.	Basic Watershed Data Used				Select and enter hydrograph times from appropriate table at the end of the chapter.												
	sub area Tc	Time to outlet	Ia/P	Am x Q	Discharges at selected times cfs												
Composite hydrograph at outlet																	

BASIC WATERSHED DATA WORKSHEET

Project:_____ Location:_____ By:_____ Date:_____

☐Present Condition   ☐Developed Condition   Checked By:_____ Date:_____

Sub area No.	Area sq.mi Am	Tc hr.	Travel time hr.	Down stream sub area Nos.	Time to outlet hr.	24 hr rain fall P	Runoff CN	Runoff Q in	Am x Q sq.mi. & in.	Ia in.	Ia/P

RUNOFF CURVE NUMBER WORK SHEET

Project: _____ By: _____ Date: _____

Location: _____ Checked: _____ Date: _____

☐ Present Condition   ☐ Developed Condition

1. RUNOFF CN

Soil name Hydrologic Soil Group	Cover description cover type, treatment hydrologic condition percent impervious unconnected / connected impervious area ratio	CN* TABLE 3-4	CN* FIG 3-18	CN* FIG 3-19	Area acres mi 2 %	Product CN x A
* use only one CN per line.		Totals				

Weighted CN = $\dfrac{\text{Total Product}}{\text{Total Area}}$ = _____ Use CN [   ]

2. RUNOFF

	Storm 1	Storm 2	Storm 3
Frequency, years			
Rainfall, P for 24 hr. storm in.			
Runoff Q in Total inches			

GRAPHICAL PEAK DISCHARGE METHOD

Project: _____ By: _____ Date: _____

Location: _____ Checked: _____ Date: _____

☐ Present Condition   ☐ Developed Condition

1. Data

Drainage area	A_m =	mi2 (acres/640)
Runoff curve number	CN =	(use CN worksheet)
Time of Concentration	T_c =	in hours
Rainfall distribution	=	(I, IA, II, III)
Pond and swamp areas	=	percent of total area

	Storm 1	Storm 2	Storm 3
2. Frequency, year			
3. Rainfall, P (24 hour period)			
4. Initial abstraction, Ia (use CN with Table 3-6)			
5. Compute Ia/P			
6. Unit peak discharge, qu (use Tc and Ia/P with Figure 3-25, 3-26, 3-27, 3-28)			
7. Runoff, Q (from CN worksheet)			
8. Pond and swamp adjustment factor, Fp (Use precent pond and swamp area with the table included below. Factor is 1.0 for areas with no ponds or swamps.)			
9. Peak discharge, qp (where $q_p = q_u A_m Q F_p$)			

Pond and Swamp Adjustment Percentage of pond and swamp areas	Fp
0	1.00
0.2	0.97
1.0	0.87
3.0	0.75
5.0	0.72

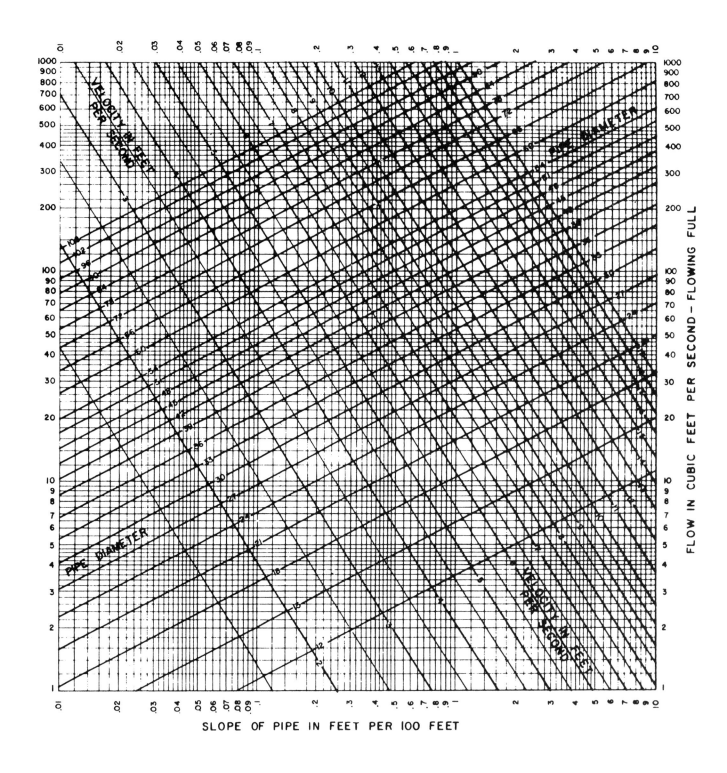

SLOPE OF PIPE IN FEET PER 100 FEET

CAPACITY OF CIRCULAR
PIPES FLOWING FULL

A GRAPHICAL SOLUTION
OF
MANNING'S EQUATION

$$V = \frac{1.486}{n} R^{2/3} S^{1/2}$$

$$n = 0.013$$

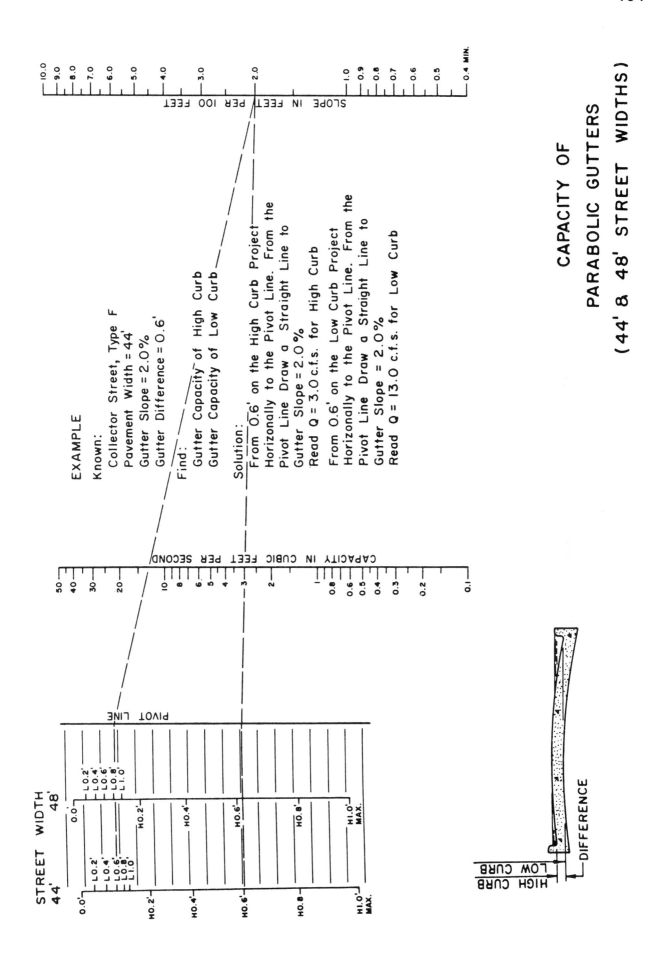

CAPACITY OF
PARABOLIC GUTTERS
(44' & 48' STREET WIDTHS)

EXAMPLE

Known:
    Major Thoroughfare, Type C
    Pavement Width = 33'
    Gutter Slope = 1.0 %
    Pavement Cross Slope = 1/4"/1'
    Depth of Gutter Flow = .5'

Find:
    Gutter Capacity

Solution:
    Enter Graph at .5'
    Intersect Cross Slope = 1/4"/1'
    Intersect Gutter Slope = 1.0%
    Read Gutter Capacity = 22 c.f.s.

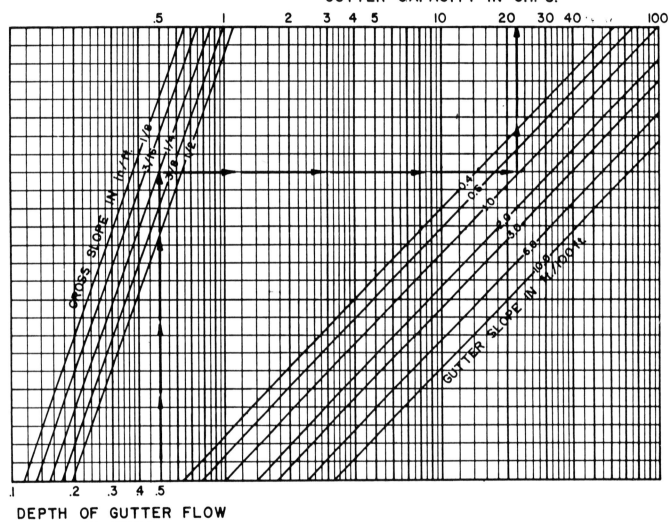

GUTTER CAPACITY IN C.F.S.

DEPTH OF GUTTER FLOW
IN FEET

CAPACITY OF
TRIANGULAR GUTTERS

(Roughess Coefficient n = .0175)

EXAMPLE

Known:

    Quantity of Flow = 4.3 c.f.s.
    Maximum Depth of Flow Desired
    at Low Point = 0.3'

Find:

    Inlet Required

Solution:

    Enter Graph at 4.3 c.f.s.
    Intersect 3 - Grate at 0.23'
    Intersect 2 - Grate at 0.51'
    Use 3 - Grate

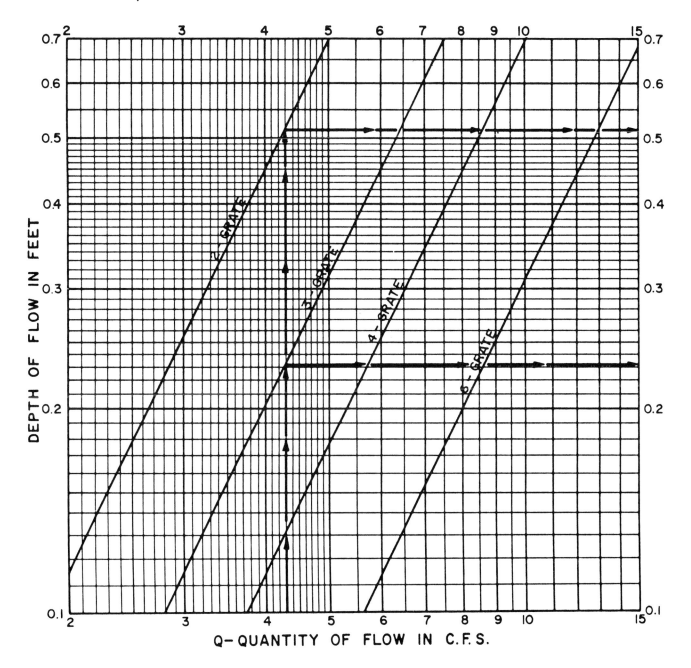

GRATE INLET
CAPACITY CURVES
AT LOW POINT

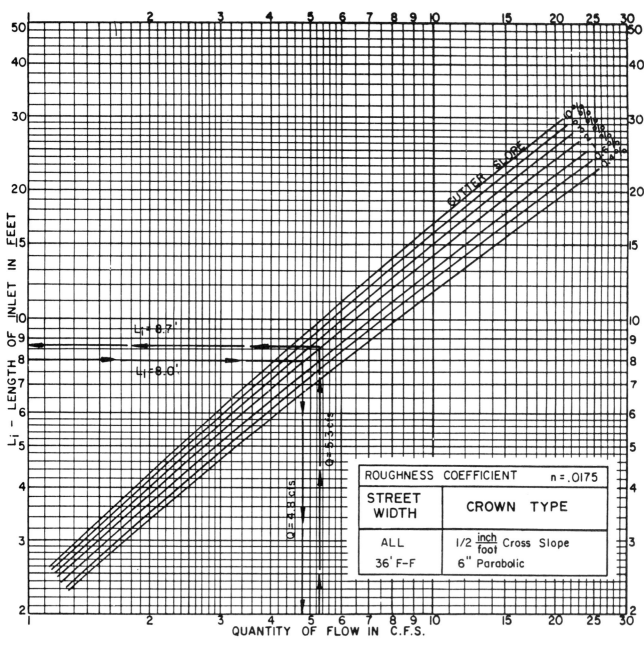

EXAMPLE

Known:
Pavement Width = 36'
Gutter Slope = 2%
6" Parabolic Crown
Gutter Flow = 5.3 cfs

Find:
Length of Inlet Required (L$_I$)

Solution:
Enter Graph at 5.3 cfs
Intersect Slope = 2%
Read L$_I$ = 8.7'

Decision:
1. Use 10' Inlet
   No Flow Remains In Gutter
2. Use 8' Inlet
   Intercept Only Part of Flow
Use 8' Inlet
Enter Graph at L$_I$ = 8'
Intersect Slope = 2%
Read Q = 4.8 cfs
Remaining Gutter Flow =
5.3 cfs − 4.8 cfs = 0.5 cfs

RECESSED AND STANDARD
CURB OPENING INLET
CAPACITY CURVES
ON GRADE

EXAMPLE

Known:

    Quantity of Flow = 16.0 c.f.s.

    Maximum Depth of Flow Desired
    in Gutter At Low Point (y_o) = 0.4'

Find:

    Length of Inlet Required (L_i)

Solution:

    Enter Graph at 16.0 c.f.s.

    Intersect y_o = 0.4'

    Read L_i = 9.2'

    Use 10' Inlet

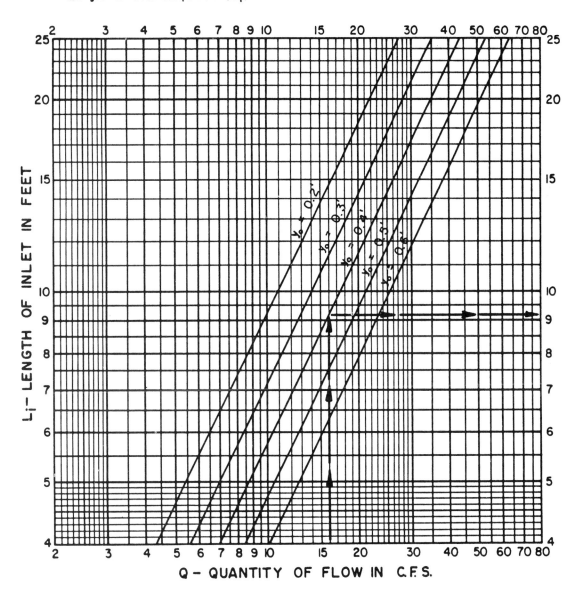

ROUGHNESS COEFFICIENT	n = .0175
STREET WIDTH	CROWN TYPE
ALL	Straight and Parabolic

**RECESSED AND STANDARD
CURB OPENING INLET
CAPACITY CURVES
AT LOW POINT**

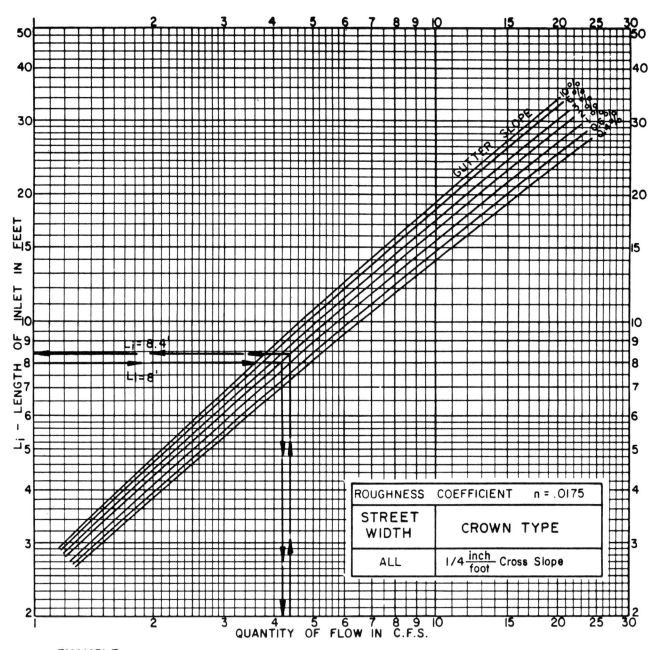

ROUGHNESS COEFFICIENT n = .0175

STREET WIDTH	CROWN TYPE
ALL	$1/4 \frac{inch}{foot}$ Cross Slope

QUANTITY OF FLOW IN C.F.S.

L_i — LENGTH OF INLET IN FEET

GUTTER SLOPE

EXAMPLE

Known:
  Pavement Width = 24'
  Gutter Slope = 2.0 %
  Pavement Cross Slope = 1/4"/1'
  Gutter Flow = 4.4 cfs

Find:
  Length of Inlet Required (L_i)

Solution:
  Enter Graph at 4.4 cfs
  Intersect Slope = 2.0 %
  Read L_i = 8.4'

Decision:
  1. Use 10' Inlet
    No Flow Remains In Gutter
  2. Use 8' Inlet
    Intercept Only Part of Flow
Use 8' Inlet
Enter Graph at L_i = 8'
Intersect Slope = 2.0 %
Read Q = 4.2 cfs
Remaining Gutter Flow =
4.4 cfs—4.2 cfs = 0.2 cfs

RECESSED AND STANDARD CURB OPENING INLET CAPACITY CURVES ON GRADE

PRINCIPLES OF STATICS AND MECHANICS

Introduction

During the **design** of a project, the landscape architect must make numerous decisions about materials, size, weight, and support system of the structures being designed. These decisions must be made with some fundamental knowledge of the principles of structural design and the strength of materials. It is not necessary to have the knowledge and expertise of a structural engineer, but it is essential that the designer be familiar with the language and principles of structural design so that the intent of the project can be communicated to this consultant.

The purpose of this chapter is to introduce the student to the basic principles of statics and mechanics as they apply to simple structures common to the practice of landscape architecture. Of necessity, much of what is presented in this chapter is simplified to direct application, with little discussion of theory. The chapter begins with some fundamental definitions of terms and basic principles, then progresses to direct applications for simple landscape structures. Students should take the time to master the material presented here before moving on to the chapters on carpentry, concrete, and masonry, since the information here helps explain why things are put together the way they are.

The science of mechanics studies the actions and transfer of forces through a structural system. Mechanics is divided into two branches of study: statics and dynamics. Statics studies stationary systems while dynamics studies systems in motion.

Force and Stress

FORCE

Force is any outside influence acting on a structure or structural member that tends to cause motion. For example, if you push on a piece of furniture that is not secured to the floor it will move once the friction between the floor and the object is overcome. The action of pushing is a force. Stress is the direct result of a force being applied to a material. For example, if an egg is squeezed, the eggshell will initially resist the force caused by squeezing. The internal reaction that resists failure by the shell is called stress. If the pressure on the shell is continuously increased, the stress in the shell continues to increase until the shell fails.

TYPES OF FORCE

A force is described by three characteristics: line, direction, and magnitude, as shown in Figure 5-1. Line is a reference of position, i.e., vertical, lateral, upward, etc. Direction refers to whether the force is moving toward the object or away from the object, pushing or pulling. Magnitude is measured as weight, usually in pounds.

Depending on the direction of a force, it is either compressive or tensile. A force that acts toward the center of mass is a compressive force. A compressive force shortens the material that it is acting on. A tensile force acts away from the center of the mass and causes

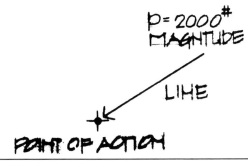

FIGURE 5.1 PROPERTIES OF A FORCE

the material to lengthen. As will be seen later, the amount of lengthening or shortening, called deformation, is very small but it does occur.

MEASURES OF FORCE AND STRESS

The magnitude of a force can be expressed in two ways: as a direct force in pounds or as a unit force in pounds-per-square-foot or pounds-per-square-inch. Stress is always measured as weight-per-unit area. The basic formula that expresses the relationship of force or stress per unit area is:

$$f = \frac{P}{A}$$

Where:

f = the unit force or stress in lbs/sq ft or lbs/sq in
P = the magnitude of direct force in lbs
A = the area over which the force is distributed

The lower-case letter f, with a subscript notation such as f_c refers to a specific force or stress. The term f_c, for example, means compressive force or stress. The mathematical term W is also frequently used to note the

magnitude of a force instead of P. P is usually used to designate a direct or concentrated load, while W is a composite load or total weight. The lower-case letter w is used to note a unit force for an evenly distributed load, i.e., lbs/lf (pounds per linear foot).

The concept of transfer of direct loads, through a structural system is the basic building block of the theory of mechanics. To illustrate the principle, consider the post in Figure 5-2. A direct force of 2,000 lbs is acting downward on the post; thus, the force is compressive. The compressive stress set up in the post would be:

$$f_c = \frac{P}{A}$$

$$f_c = \frac{2,000 \text{ lbs}}{4 \text{ in} \times 4 \text{ in}}$$

$$f_c = \frac{2,000 \text{ lbs}}{16 \text{ sq in}}$$

$$f_c = 125 \text{ lbs/sq in}$$

The stress in the post is 125 lbs/sq in and the load transferred to the ground at the base of the post is also 125 lbs/sq in.

The Principle of Moments

The second building block of structural theory is the principle of moments. Moment is defined as the tendency of a force to cause rotation about a point, and is described by the product of a direct force and a distance. For example, if a force is applied to a board resting on a dowel as shown in Figure 5-3, the tendency is for the board to rotate around the dowel. The point of rotation, the dowel, is referred to as the center of moments. The distance from the center of moments to the point where the force is acting is called the lever arm. For the conditions in Figure 5-3 the moment would be:

$$M = 500 \text{ lbs} \times 4 \text{ ft} = 2,000 \text{ ft lbs}$$

Equilibrium

For a structure to be stable it must be in equilibrium. The law of equilibrium is: The sum of the moments acting about a point are equal to zero or, stated another way, the actions must equal the reactions. For any structure to be stable, this relationship must be true. To illustrate this principle, consider the diagram in Figure 5-4. A simple beam is carrying a concentrated load of 500 lbs at the center of the span; each of the supports carries half of the load, or 250 lbs each. The right support

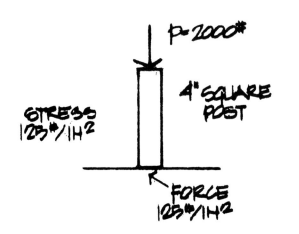

FIGURE 5.2 PRINCIPLE OF UNIT STRESS

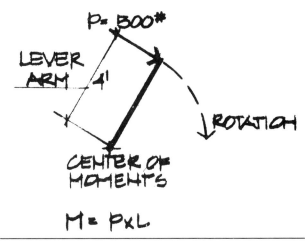

FIGURE 5.3   PRINCIPLE OF MOMENTS

is designated as the center of moments, and all clockwise rotation as positive moments and counterclockwise rotations as negative moments. The equation of moments is a follows:

$$(250 \text{ lbs} \times 10 \text{ ft}) = 2,500 \text{ ft lbs } (500 \text{ lbs} \times 5 \text{ ft}) = 2,500 \text{ ft lbs}$$

$$2,500 \text{ ft lbs} - 2,500 \text{ ft lbs} = 0$$

Thus the sum of the moments acting around R_2 is zero.

Finding Reaction with Moments

When a structural member is acted on by a force, it must have an opposite but equal reaction to be in equilibrium. In the previous example, the reactions of the supports were equal because the beam was symmetrically loaded; however, if a beam is loaded unevenly, the reaction required at the support will not be equal. To illustrate, consider the the condition shown in Figure 5-5.

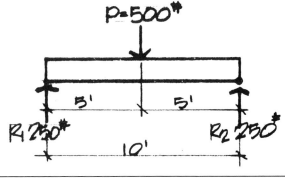

FIGURE 5.4   BEAM WITH CONCENTRATED LOAD

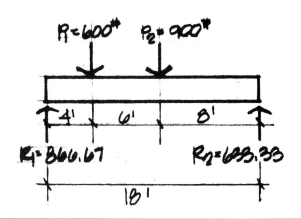

FIGURE 5.5   BEAM WITH TWO CONCENTRATED LOADS

A simple beam is loaded with two unequal forces that are 4 ft and 6 ft from the left support. $P_1 = 600$ lbs, $P_2 = 900$ lbs. Using the law of equilibrium, the sum of the moments must equal zero; therefore, it is possible to determine the reactions by writing an equation of moments for each reaction. Once again, clockwise rotation will be given positive values and counterclockwise rotation will be negative values.

To find R_1 designate R_1 as the center of moments and write as follows:

$$0 = (14 \text{ ft} \times 600 \text{ lbs}) + (8 \text{ ft} \times 900 \text{ lbs}) - (18 \text{ ft} \times R_1)$$

$$0 = (8,400 \text{ ft lbs}) + (7,200 \text{ ft lbs}) - (18 \text{ ft} \times R_1)$$

$$18 \text{ ft} \times R_1 = 15,600 \text{ ft lbs}$$

$$R_1 = \frac{15,600 \text{ ft lbs}}{18 \text{ ft}}$$

$$R_1 = 866.67 \text{ lbs}$$

Next designate R_1 as the center of moments and solve for R_2 as follows:

$$0 = (4 \text{ ft} \times 600 \text{ lbs}) + (10 \text{ ft} \times 900 \text{ lbs}) - (18 \text{ ft} \times R_2)$$

$$18 \text{ ft} \times R_2 = 2,400 \text{ ft lbs} + 9,000 \text{ ft lbs}$$

$$R_2 = \frac{11,400 \text{ ft lbs}}{18 \text{ ft}}$$

$$R_2 = 633.33 \text{ lbs}$$

It is wise to develop an intuitive feel for what the reactions are likely to be. By looking at the diagram, it is apparent that the load is more to the left support and thus the reaction to the left will have to be greater,

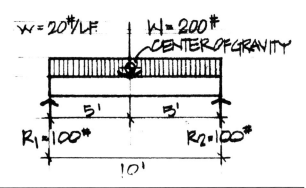

FIGURE 5.6 BEAM WITH EVENLY DISTRIBUTED LOAD

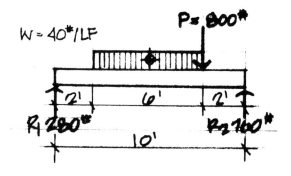

FIGURE 5.8 BEAM WITH COMPOUND LOAD

which is the case. However, students often reverse the center of moments in writing the equations and thus reverse the reactions.

REACTIONS FOR EVENLY DISTRIBUTED LOADS

An evenly distributed load is assumed to be the same as a concentrated load acting through the center of gravity of the mass. For example, in Figure 5-6 a simple 10-ft beam has an evenly distributed load of 20 lbs per linear foot over the entire beam. The total load (W), is 200 lbs and is assumed to be the same as a 200-lb load acting at the center of the span as shown. This principle applies if there is an evenly distributed load over only a portion of the beam as shown in Figure 5-7. In this case it would be treated as a concentrated load of 1,200 lbs acting at a point 7 ft from the left support.

FINDING REACTIONS WITH COMBINED LOADS

Quite often the total load acting on a structure is the result of a combination of individual forces. Reactions

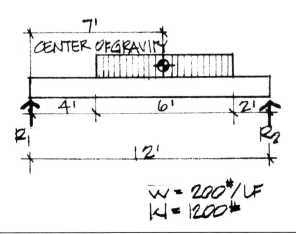

FIGURE 5.7 BEAM WITH EVENLY DISTRIBUTED LOAD OVER A PORTION OF THE SPAN

can also be determined for combined loads using moments. To illustrate, consider the beam in Figure 5-8. In this example, a simple beam has an evenly distributed load of 40 lbs/lf centered 2 ft from each support, and a concentrated load of 800 lbs acting 8 ft from the left support. The evenly distributed load is taken as a concentrated load of 240 lbs acting at the center of the span. Now designate R_2 as the center of moments and solve for R_1 as follows:

$$0 = (2 \text{ ft} \times 800 \text{ lbs}) + (5 \text{ ft} \times 240 \text{ lbs}) - (10 \text{ ft} \times R_1)$$

$$10 \text{ ft} \times R_1 = (1{,}600 \text{ ft lbs} + 1{,}200 \text{ ft lbs})$$

$$R_1 = \frac{2{,}800 \text{ ft lbs}}{10 \text{ ft}}$$

$$R_1 = 280 \text{ lbs}$$

Designate R_1 as the center of moments and solve for R_2

$$0 = (5 \text{ ft} \times 240 \text{ lbs}) + (8 \text{ ft} \times 800 \text{ lbs}) - (10 \text{ ft} \times R_2)$$

$$10 \text{ ft} \times R_2 = 1{,}200 \text{ ft lbs} + 6{,}400 \text{ ft lbs}$$

$$R_2 = \frac{7{,}600 \text{ ft lbs}}{10 \text{ ft}}$$

$$R_2 = 760 \text{ lbs}$$

REACTIONS FOR OVERHANGING BEAMS

An overhanging beam is a beam that extends past its supports as shown in Figure 5-9. In this situation the lever arm of R_1 and R_2 remains constant and the loads on the overhanging portion of the beam must be considered in relation to each axis. In this example all the moments caused by the loads acting around R_1 will be counterclockwise and negative, but around point R_2, the rotation caused by the 400-lb concentrated load would be clockwise-positive. This will be seen in the computations. Begin by solving for R_1 with R_2 as the center of moments.

$$0 = (10 \text{ ft} \times 300 \text{ lbs}) + (5 \text{ ft} \times 400 \text{ lbs}) - (3 \text{ ft} \times 400 \text{ lbs}) - (12 \text{ ft} \times R_1)$$

$$12 \text{ ft} \times R_1 = (3,000 \text{ ft lbs} + 2,000 \text{ ft lbs} - 1,200 \text{ ft lbs})$$

$$R_1 = \frac{3,800 \text{ ft lbs}}{12 \text{ ft}}$$

$$R_2 = 316.67 \text{ lbs}$$

Next designate R_1 as the center of moments and solve for R_2

$$0 = (2 \text{ ft} \times 300 \text{ lbs}) + (7 \text{ ft} \times 400 \text{ lbs}) + (15 \text{ ft} \times 400 \text{ lbs}) - (12 \text{ ft} \times 2)$$

$$12 \text{ ft} \times R_2 = (600 \text{ ft lbs} + 2,800 \text{ ft lbs} + 6,000 \text{ ft lbs})$$

$$R_2 = \frac{9,400 \text{ ft lbs}}{12 \text{ ft}}$$

$$R_2 = 783.33 \text{ lbs}$$

To check the work, subtract the sum of the reactions from the sum of the loads; the total should be zero. This is in accordance with the law that the sum of the actions must equal the sum of the reactions. For the problem just completed write:

$$[300 \text{ lbs} + (10 \text{ ft} \times 40 \text{ lbs/lf}) + 400 \text{ lbs}] - (316.67 + 783.33)$$

$$1,100 \text{ lbs} - 1,100 \text{ lbs} = 0$$

Students should work through several extra problems to be sure that the principles of using moments to find reactions is completely understood before going further in the chapter. Much of the material that is presented in succeeding sections requires the use of moments.

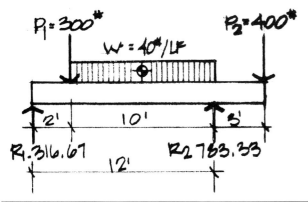

FIGURE 5.9 OVERHANGING BEAM WITH COMPOUND LOAD

Structural Properties of Materials

To this point, we have assumed that the materials in the force systems being discussed were strong enough to resist the loads placed on them. This, of course, cannot be assumed since the stability of any structural system depends on the strength of the materials incorporated in that system.

In the earlier discussion, the term stress was introduced, meaning an internal reaction to an outside force. This reaction takes place in the material itself, as a result of the external loads and reactions of the supports. The term "unit stress" was also introduced to describe the magnitude of the stress related to the sectional area of the material. These general concepts are very important to understanding material strength.

STRENGTH OF MATERIALS

The strength of a material is measured against the material's ability to maintain its structural integrity, under specific types of stress, for a particular cross-sectional configuration.

Direct stress

There are four types of direct stress: compression, tension, shear, and torque. Compressive stress and tensile stress are the direct result of a force acting along the axis of a material. Compression acts toward the center of the mass, while tension acts away from the center of the mass. Torque stress is the result of a non-axial load that tends to cause the material to twist or rotate around its axis. Shear stress is the result of multiple loads acting in different directions along different lines. In shear, the fibers of the material tend to slide past each other in a plane. Shear is further described as either horizontal or vertical, depending on the direction of the plane of slippage in reference to the axis of the material. Figure 5-10 illustrates the four types of direct stress.

Because the kinds of structures that landscape architects are usually charged with designing are extremely lightweight and usually supported by wood or simple metal frames, our discussion will not consider torque, which only becomes a major consideration in large structures or dynamic systems, such as an automobile engine. Likewise, shear will not be considered except as it relates to bending stress.

Deformation

When a force acts on a material, the material reacts by a corresponding change in shape or dimension. For example, if a weight is placed on a wood block, a

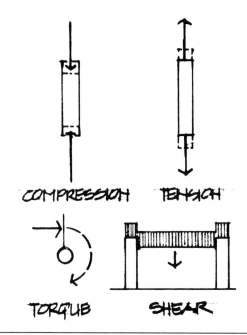

FIGURE 5.10 TYPES OF STRESS

compressive load, the wood block will become shorter. The actual dimensional change may not be visible but there will be a change. In physics there is a principle called Hooke's law that states that deformations of a material are directly proportional to the stress. While this theory has since been disproved, it does hold true for relatively light structural loads and does serve as a basic assumption for most structural theory.

Modulus of Elasticity

Modulus of elasticity is a measure of material stiffness. For example, if a steel bar is placed in a vise and a pressure of 1,000 lb is applied to the bar, it will become shorter, although it may require very sensitive instruments to measure. Now if a piece of wood with the same overall dimensions is placed in the same conditions, it would have a much greater deformation. The relative stiffness of a material is represented by the modulus of elasticity, which is defined as the ratio of unit stress to unit deformation. The average value for the modulus of elasticity for some common materials are shown in Table 5-1.

Bending

Bending is a form of what might be called indirect or compound stress. Like shear, it occurs when multiple forces are acting in opposite directions along different lines. In bending, the structural member deflects or bows along its axis. An example of bending is shown in Figure 5-11. Here a beam has a concentrated load at the center of its span. In this case the fibers in the upper portion of the beam are actually in compression and

the fibers in the bottom surface are in tension. Since bending and shear both result from the same loading conditions, there is a direct relationship between the two, as will be seen later.

Extreme Fiber Stress in Bending

All materials can be visualized as being composed of layers of continuous fibers. In the case of wood, the fibers are visible to the naked eye. When a structural member is subjected to bending, the magnitude of the stress increases in both directions from the neutral surface. The neutral surface is a plane that passes through the centroid (center of gravity) of the section as illustrated in Figure 5-12.

Ultimate Strength

Ultimate strength is the stress value measured in a material at the point of failure. For reasons of safety, and to account for variations in material quality and composition, ultimate strength is a value used only in testing materials.

Working Stress

Working stress is the design stress value considered safe for a given material. Table 5-1 shows working stress values for various building materials used in landscape construction. It should be noted that the recommended working stress values are changed from time to time by the various materials standards associations. For this reason, the values shown in the table should only be used as examples and to support the examples in this text. Copies of current values can be obtained at nominal cost from the appropriate materials organization.

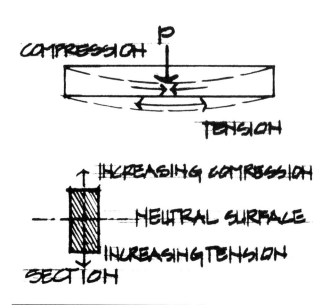

FIGURE 5.11 BENDING

TABLE 5.1 BUIDLING MATERIALS: AVERAGE WORKING STRESS VALUES

Material	Compression psi	Tension psi	Shear psi	Extreme Fiber Stress in Bending f_b/psi	Modulus of Elasticity (E)	Weight per cu ft
Concrete	625	—	70	—	3,000,000	150
Brick/CMU Masonry	100–250	—	—	—	—	120
Stone Masonry	200–400	—	—	—	—	145
Cast Iron	9,000	—	—	—	12,000,000	450
Wrought Iron	12,000	12,000	8,000	12,000	28,000,000	485
Steel	—	22,000	14,000	24,000	29,000,000	490
Aluminum	—	15,000	—	12,000	10,000,000	170
Parallel wood to grain	1,000	1,200	100 horizontal	1,200	1,200,000	40
perpendicular to grain	300		400 vertical			

These are average values for structural class materials. Values will differ for wood species, and structural grades, metal alloy types, and concrete mixture, and cement.

Properties of Sections

The strength of a material is not only dependent on the physical properties of the material but on its proportion and shape of the cross section. There are two mathematical relationships used to describe these sectional characteristics: moment of inertia, and section modulus. While it is not important that you understand the mathematics of the definition, it is important to understand their principles as they relate to the strength of building materials, and how they are related.

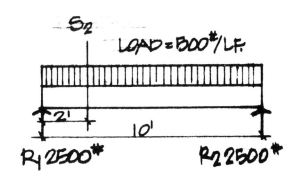

FIGURE 5.12 CALCULATING SHEAR

Moment of Inertia

The moment of inertia is defined as the sum of all infinitely small areas times the square of their distance from the neutral axis. This produces an abstract number in inches to the fourth power because an area is multiplied by a distance squared.

Section Modulus

The section modulus (S) is found by dividing the moment of inertia by the distance from the neutral axis to the most remote fiber of the section. Since a value to the fourth power is being divided by a distance in inches, the value of the section modulus is in inches³.

The significance of moment of inertia and section modulus lies in the fact that stress increases in any bending member as you move away from the neutral axis. Now if the cross section is small, the resulting stress must be distributed over a very small area, whereas a larger section has more area and the relative stress will be less. This fact is what led to the development of the I-beam as a structural form. The neutral surface of a beam is just that—neutral, no stress—while the greatest magnitude of stress will be at the extreme edge of the beam. The I-beam takes advantage of this

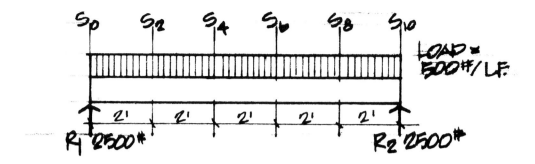

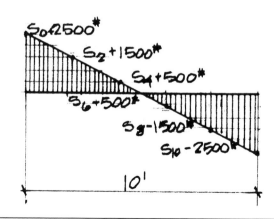

FIGURE 5.13 SHEAR COMPUTATIONS

by using a web at the center of the beam to separate the two stress-carrying flanges.

Shear and Bending Diagrams

It was noted earlier that there is a direct relationship between shear and bending. The best way to visualize this relationship is by constructing diagrams that graphically display the magnitude of the shear or bending stress at any point in a beam.

The magnitude of the shear stress at any point in a beam is equal to the sum of the loads on either side of the section. For example, consider the simple beam in Figure 5-12. There is an evenly distributed load of 500 lb/lf and since the load is uniform, R_1 and R_2 are 2,500 lb. Section S_2 is taken 2 ft from the right support. To find the shear stress at this point, let all the upward forces (reactions), be positive and all of the downward acting forces (loads), be negative, and write as follows:

$$S_2 = 2,500 \text{ lb} - (2 \text{ ft} \times 500 \text{ lb/lf})$$
$$S_2 = 2,500 \text{ lb} - 1,000 \text{ lb}$$
$$S_2 = +1,500 \text{ lb}$$

To construct a shear diagram, several points along the beam are calcualted and then plotted in graph form. Figure 5-13 shows sections being taken at 2 ft intervals along the beam, and the computations for shear are shown for each section. Remember, upward acting loads have been designated as positive and downward acting loads are to be negative, and computations are always to the left of the section.

To construct a shear diagram, let the horizontal axis (x-x) be scaled in feet, and points on the vertical axis (y-y) be scaled in pounds. The shear diagram would be plotted as shown in Figure 5-14.

The point where the shear passes through the x-x axis is called the inflection point, and shear stress is 0.00. The shear diagram in Figure 5-14 is for a simple beam with an evenly distributed load, and will be proportionally the same for any simple beam with an evenly distributed load.

The shear diagram for a simple beam with a concentrated load acting at the center of the span is different. To demonstrate this difference compute the shear stress for a 10-ft simple beam with a concentrated load of 5,000 lb acting at the center of the span. The computa-

FIGURE 5.14 SHEAR DIAGRAM EVENLY DISTRIBUTED LOAD

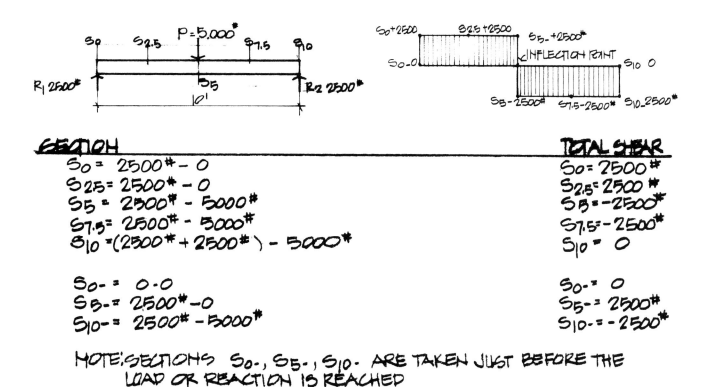

SECTION

$S_0 = 2500^\# - 0$
$S_{2.5} = 2500^\# - 0$
$S_5 = 2500^\# - 5000^\#$
$S_{7.5} = 2500^\# - 5000^\#$
$S_{10} = (2500^\# + 2500^\#) - 5000^\#$

$S_{0-} = 0 - 0$
$S_{5-} = 2500^\# - 0$
$S_{10-} = 2500^\# - 5000^\#$

TOTAL SHEAR

$S_0 = 2500^\#$
$S_{2.5} = 2500^\#$
$S_5 = -2500^\#$
$S_{7.5} = -2500^\#$
$S_{10} = 0$

$S_{0-} = 0$
$S_{5-} = 2500^\#$
$S_{10-} = -2500^\#$

NOTE: SECTIONS S_{0-}, S_{5-}, S_{10-} ARE TAKEN JUST BEFORE THE LOAD OR REACTION IS REACHED

FIGURE 5.15   SHEAR DIAGRAM, CONCENTRATED LOAD

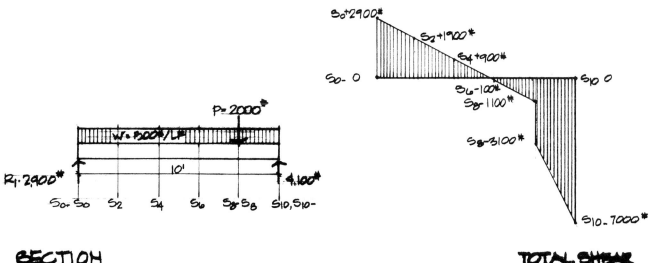

SECTION

S_{0-}	$0 - 0$	
S_0	$2900^\# - 0$	
S_2	$2900^\# - (2_{FT.} \times 500^\#/LF)$	
S_4	$2900^\# - (4_{FT.} \times 500^\#/LF)$	
S_6	$2900^\# - (6_{FT.} \times 500^\#/LF)$	
S_8-	$2900^\# - (8_{FT.} \times 500^\#/LF)$	
S_8	$2900^\# - (8_{FT.} \times 500^\#/LF + 2000^\#)$	
S_{10-}	$2900^\# - (10_{FT.} \times 500^\#/LF + 2000^\#)$	
S_{10}	$(2900^\# + 4100^\#) - (10_{FT.} \times 500^\#/LF + 2000^\#)$	

TOTAL SHEAR

S_{0-}	0
S_0	$+2900^\#$
S_2	$+1900^\#$
S_4	$+900^\#$
S_6	$+100^\#$
S_8	$-1100^\#$
S_8	$-3100^\#$
S_{10-}	$-7,000^\#$
S_{10}	0

FIGURE 5.16   SHEAR DIAGRAM, COMPOUND LOAD

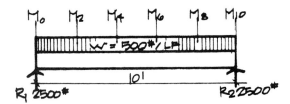

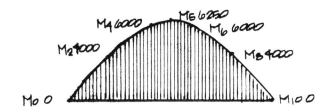

NOTE: SECTION M5, THE CENTER OF THE SPAN, IS THE POINT OF GREATEST BENDING.

$M_5 = (2500\# \times 5 FT) - (5 FT \times 500\#/LF \times 2.5 FT) = 6250 FT\#$

SECTION		TOTAL MOMENT	
M_0	$(2500\# \times 0) - 0$	M_0	0
M_2	$(2500\# \times 2 FT.) - (2 FT \times 500\#/LF \times 1 FT.)$	M_2	$4000 FT\#$
M_4	$(2500\# \times 4 FT.) - (4 FT \times 500\#/LF \times 2 FT.)$	M_4	$6000 FT\#$
M_6	$(2500\# \times 6 FT.) - (6 FT \times 500\#/LF \times 3 FT.)$	M_6	$6000 FT\#$
M_8	$(2500\# \times 8 FT.) - (8 FT \times 500\#/LF \times 4 FT.)$	M_8	$4000 FT\#$
M_{10}	$(2500\# \times 10 FT.) - (10 FT \times 500\#/LF \times 5 FT.)$	M_{10}	0

FIGURE 5.17   BENDING MOMENT DIAGRAM, EVENLY DISTRIBUTED LOAD

tions and resulting shear diagram are shown in Figure 5-15. In this case a section, S_5, has been taken at the point where the concentrated load acts, and the other sections are spaced at even 2.5-ft intervals. Once again, the upward acting loads are positive and the downward acting loads are negative.

In the computations section there are three sections noted as: S_0-, S_5-, $S_{10}-$. S_0- is taken at a point just to the left of where R_1 is acting. At this point there is no load and no reaction, so shear is equal to 0.00. S_5- is taken at a point just to the left of where the concentrated load (P), is acting; the 5,000-lb load is not yet a consideration, so shear at this point is still +2,500 lb. $S_{10}-$ is taken at a point immediately to the left of R_2, so shear at that point is still −2,500 lb. These points just before the point where a load or reaction is acting are important, particularly where multiple loads are involved.

To complete the discussion of shear, consider the beam in Figure 5-16. There is a 10-ft simple beam with an evenly distributed load of 500 lb/lf and a concentrated load of 2,000 lb acting 2 ft from the right side of the beam. The reactions have already been calculated and are shown by writing an equation of moments. Sections were taken at 2-ft intervals, and an extra section is taken before each load or reaction as noted.

In the shear diagram, note that the shear increases from a −1,000 to −3,100 lbs at the point where the 2,000-lb concentrated load is acting, then increases to a maximum of −7,000 lbs at the left support.

Bending Moment Diagrams

Bending moment at any point in a member is equal to the sum of the moments on either side of a section. To compute bending moments the upward acting forces will be designated positive, the downward acting forces will be designated negative, and moments will always be taken to the left of the section. Bending moment diagrams and the accompanying computations are shown for each of the examples used to illustrate shear computations, Figures 5-17 through 5-19. Notice that for simple beams with either an evenly distributed load over the entire span, or a concentrated load acting at the center of the span, the greatest bending stress occurs at the center of the span, and shear equals 0.00. This is a very important concept, since there is always a point of maximum bending stress at any point where shear is equal to 0.00. Now, look at the shear diagram for the compound load in Figure 5-16. Notice that the inflection point occurs just to the left of section S_6. This point is where the maximum bending will occur for this beam. Since the load is known and shear is equal to 0.00, we can find the exact location of the inflection point by writing:

0 (the value of shear) = 2,900 lb −
(X ft × 500 lb/lf)

X ft = 2,900 lb/500 lb/lf =
X ft = 5.80 ft

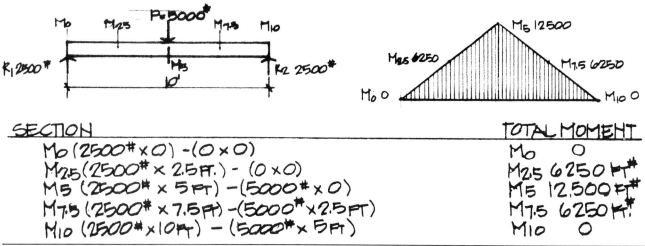

SECTION

$M_0 \ (2500^{\#} \times 0) - (0 \times 0)$
$M_{2.5} \ (2500^{\#} \times 2.5 \text{ ft.}) - (0 \times 0)$
$M_5 \ (2500^{\#} \times 5 \text{ ft}) - (5000^{\#} \times 0)$
$M_{7.5} \ (2500^{\#} \times 7.5 \text{ ft}) - (5000^{\#} \times 2.5 \text{ ft})$
$M_{10} \ (2500^{\#} \times 10 \text{ ft}) - (5000^{\#} \times 5 \text{ ft})$

TOTAL MOMENT

$M_0 \qquad 0$
$M_{2.5} \quad 6250 \ \text{ft}^{\#}$
$M_5 \quad 12,500 \ \text{ft}^{\#}$
$M_{7.5} \quad 6250 \ \text{ft.}^{\#}$
$M_{10} \qquad 0$

FIGURE 5.18 BENDING MOMENT DIAGRAM, CONCENTRATED LOAD

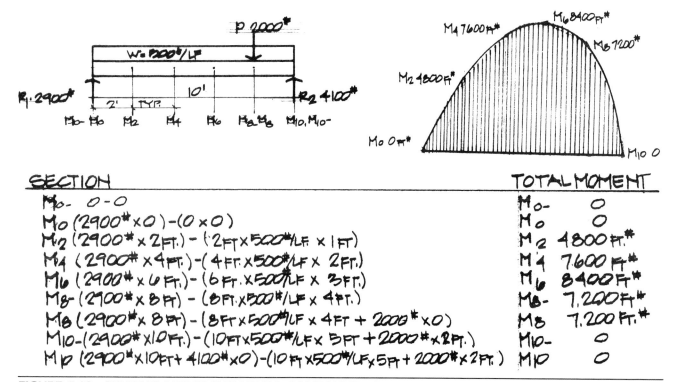

SECTION

$M_{0-} \quad 0 - 0$
$M_0 \ (2900^{\#} \times 0) - (0 \times 0)$
$M_2 \ (2900^{\#} \times 2 \text{ ft.}) - (2 \text{ ft} \times 500^{\#}/\text{LF} \times 1 \text{ ft})$
$M_4 \ (2900^{\#} \times 4 \text{ ft.}) - (4 \text{ ft} \times 500^{\#}/\text{LF} \times 2 \text{ ft.})$
$M_6 \ (2900^{\#} \times 6 \text{ ft.}) - (6 \text{ ft} \times 500^{\#}/\text{LF} \times 3 \text{ ft.})$
$M_{8-} \ (2900^{\#} \times 8 \text{ ft}) - (8 \text{ ft} \times 500^{\#}/\text{LF} \times 4 \text{ ft.})$
$M_8 \ (2900^{\#} \times 8 \text{ ft}) - (8 \text{ ft} \times 500^{\#}/\text{LF} \times 4 \text{ ft} + 2000^{\#} \times 0)$
$M_{10-} (2900^{\#} \times 10 \text{ ft.}) - (10 \text{ ft} \times 500^{\#}/\text{LF} \times 5 \text{ ft} + 2000^{\#} \times 2 \text{ ft.})$
$M_{10} \ (2900^{\#} \times 10 \text{ ft} + 4100^{\#} \times 0) - (10 \text{ ft} \times 500^{\#}/\text{LF} \times 5 \text{ ft} + 2000^{\#} \times 2 \text{ ft.})$

TOTAL MOMENT

$M_{0-} \qquad 0$
$M_0 \qquad 0$
$M_2 \quad 4800 \ \text{ft.}^{\#}$
$M_4 \quad 7600 \ \text{ft}^{\#}$
$M_6 \quad 8400 \ \text{ft}^{\#}$
$M_{8-} \quad 7,200 \ \text{ft}^{\#}$
$M_8 \quad 7,200 \ \text{ft.}^{\#}$
$M_{10-} \qquad 0$
$M_{10} \qquad 0$

FIGURE 5.19 BENDING MOMENT DIAGRAM, COMPOUND LOAD

Thus, the point of greatest bending will occur at a point 5.80 ft from the left support. Now compute the bending moment for a section 5.80 ft from the left support as follows:

$$M_{5.8} = (2,900 \text{ lb} \times 5.80 \text{ ft}) - (5.80 \text{ ft} \times 500 \text{ lb/lf} \times 2.90 \text{ ft})$$
$$M_{5.8} = 16,820 \text{ ft lb} - 8,410 \text{ ft lb}$$
$$M_{5.8} = 8,410 \text{ ft lb}$$

The fact that the point of maximum bending can be found by using the shear diagram is important when there are compound loads on a beam, or where a beam overhangs its supports and carries multiple loads. Otherwise, maximum bending can be computed by the formulas in Figure 5-20.

Sizing Beams and Other Horizontal Members

Beams and joists are common parts of all frame structures that are subject to bending. In light structures such as frame decks, shelters, and small bridges, the

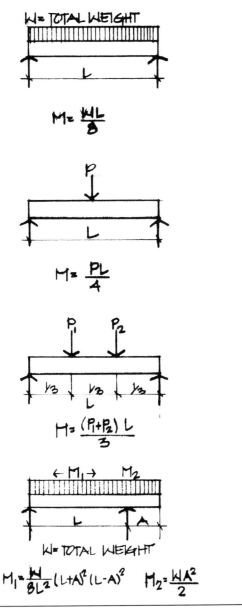

FIGURE 5.20 MAXIMUM BENDING MOMENT FOR TYPICAL BEAM CONDITIONS

primary structural consideration in selecting the size of these members is their ability to resist the bending stress. The maximum allowable bending stress for any beam can be found by the "flexure formula":

$$S = \frac{M}{f_b}$$

Where:

- S = The section modulus in in³
- M = The maximum bending moment of the design condition
- f_b = The maximum allowable value for extreme fiber stress in bending for the material to be used

You will recall that the section modulus and moment of inertia are sectional properties that characterize the distribution of stress over the cross section of a structural member, and that section modulus is the moment of inertia divided by the distance of the most remote fiber from the neutral surface.

Moment of inertia and section modulus for any rectangular cross section can be found by the following equations:

Moment of inertia $M = \dfrac{bd^3}{12}$

Section modulus $S = \dfrac{bd^2}{6}$

By using the flexure formula, the minimum required modulus can be determined for any beam or joist in the structure. Then, by trial and error, the size of the member can be determined. To illustrate the procedure, consider the beam in Figure 5-21. To use the flexure formula, the maximum bending moment must be calculated. From our previous discussion of shear and bending, you will remember that for an evenly distributed load on a simple beam the maximum bending stress occurs at the center of the span. Therefore, there are two ways to find the maximum moment: by computing the bending moment at point M6, or by using the equation from Figure 5-20. Figure 5-21 shows the computations for both methods.

The next task is to look up the value for extreme fiber stress in bending for the material being proposed for the beam. Table 5-2 gives working stress values for some of the more common lumber grades and species.

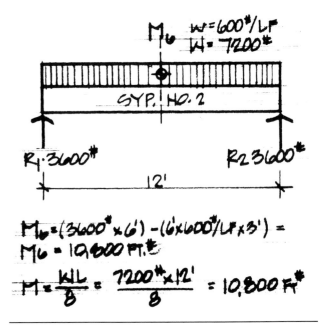

FIGURE 5.21 FINDING MAXIMUM BENDING

TABLE 5.2 WORKING STRESS VALUES FOR COMMON GRADES AND SPECIES

Grade	Thickness Inches	Extreme Fiber Stress in Bending f_b <lbs/sq in	Compression Prependicular to Grain lbs/sq in	Compression Parallel to Grain lbs/sq in	Modulus of Elasticity E
Southern Yellow Pine					
No.1	2	1,600	405	1,150	1,800,000
No. 2	2	1,350	405	1,000	1,600,000
No. 3	2	650	335	475	1,300,000
No. 1 SR KD	2/4	1,700	405	1,600	1,900,000
No. 2 SR KD	2/4	1,500	405	1,150	1,700,000
Douglas Fir - Larch					
Dense No. 1	2+	2,050	455	1,450	1,900,00
Dense No. 2	2+	1,700	455	1,150	1,700,000
Western White Pine - Idaho White Pine					
No. 1	2/4	1,150	190	800	1,100,000
No. 2	2/4	925	190	600	1,000,000
No. 3	2/4	525	190	375	900,000
Redwood					
Clear heart	2+	1,950	305	1,600	1,240,000
Select heart	2+	1,750	305	1,250	1,240,000
Construction	2+	1,450	305	1,050	1,240,000
Western Cedar					
Select Str.	2	1,100	265	925	1,000,000
No. 1	2	875	265	800	1,000,000

SR-Stress rated   KD-Kiln Dried

For the problem at hand, assume that southern yellow pine No.2 is being used. From Table 5-2 find that f_b is 1,350 lb/sq in, and compute the section modulus required as follows:

$$S = \frac{M}{f_b}$$

$$S = \frac{10,800 \text{ ft lb} \times 12 \text{ in/ft}}{1,350 \text{ lb/sq in}}$$

$$S = \frac{129,600 \text{ in lb}}{1,350 \text{ lb/sq in}}$$

$$S = 96.00 \text{ in}^3$$

Notice that it was necessary to convert ft lb to in lb by multiplying by 12 in/ft in order to keep the units of measurement alike. The section modulus value of 96.00^3 in means that the beam used will have to have a cross section with a minimum section modulus of 96.00^3 in.

Next, by trial and error we can determine the appropriate size beam. For this example we will begin by finding the section modulus for a standard 2 × 12. Remember, lumber is designated by its rough dimension before it is finished. A 2 × 12 has a finished dimen-

sion of 1½″ × 11¼″. Using the formula for section modulus of a rectangular section, write:

$$S = \frac{bd^2}{6}$$

$$S = \frac{1.5'' \times 11.25''^2}{6}$$

$$S = \frac{189.84}{6}$$

$$S = 31.64 \text{ in}^3$$

Since the required section modulus computed was 96.00, a 2 × 12 is far too small. So try a 6 × 12 timber, finished dimensions; 5½″ × 11½″.

$$S = \frac{5.5 \text{ in} \times 11.5 \text{ in}^2}{6}$$

$$S = \frac{727.38}{6}$$

$$S = 121.23 \text{ in}^3$$

This size will work but the question is: Does it have to be this big? This could be checked again using a

TABLE 5.3 PROPERTIES OF SECTIONS

PROPERTIES OF SECTIONS

Nominal Size Inches b d	Actual Size Inches b d	Area In.^{2}	AXIS XX S In.^{3}	AXIS XX I In.^{4}	AXIS YY S In.^{3}	AXIS YY I In.^{4}	Board Measure per Lineal Foot	Weight per Lineal Foot Lbs.
2 x 2	1-1/2 x 1-1/2	2.25	.56	.42	.56	.42	.33	.63
3	2-1/2	3.75	1.56	1.95	.94	.70	.50	1.05
4	3-1/2	5.25	3.06	5.36	1.31	.99	.67	1.46
2 x 5	1-1/2 x 4-1/2	6.75	5.06	11.39	1.69	1.27	.83	1.87
6	5-1/2	8.25	7.56	20.80	2.06	1.55	1.00	2.29
8	7-1/4	10.88	13.14	47.63	2.72	2.06	1.33	2.98
10	9-1/4	13.88	21.39	98.93	3.57	2.62	1.67	3.87
12	11-1/4	16.88	31.64	177.98	4.23	3.18	2.00	4.68
14	13-1/4	19.88	43.89	290.77	4.97	3.75	2.33	5.50
3 x 3	2-1/2 x 2-1/2	6.25	2.61	3.25	2.6	3.24	.75	1.73
4	3-1/2	8.75	5.10	8.93	3.64	4.56	1.00	2.43
6	5-1/2	13.75	12.60	34.66	5.73	7.16	1.50	3.82
8	7-1/4	18.13	21.90	79.39	7.56	9.53	2.00	5.03
10	9-1/4	23.13	35.65	164.88	9.63	12.16	2.50	6.44
12	11-1/4	28.13	52.73	296.63	11.75	14.79	3.00	7.83
14	13-1/4	33.13	73.15	484.63	14.91	17.34	3.50	9.18
4 x 4	3-1/2 x 3-1/2	12.25	7.15	12.50	7.14	12.52	1.33	3.39
6	5-1/2	19.25	17.65	48.53	11.23	19.64	2.00	5.34
8	7-1/4	25.38	30.66	111.15	14.82	26.15	2.67	7.05
10	9-1/4	32.38	49.91	230.84	18.97	33.23	3.33	8.98
12	11-1/4	39.38	73.82	415.28	23.03	40.30	4.00	10.91
14	13-1/4	46.38	102.41	678.48	27.07	47.59	4.67	12.90
★ 6 x 6	5-1/2 x 5-1/2	30.25	27.73	76.25	27.73	76.25	3	8.40
8	7-1/2	41.25	51.56	193.35	37.81	103.98	4	11.46
10	9-1/2	52.25	82.73	392.96	47.89	131.71	5	14.51
12	11-1/2	63.25	121.23	697.07	57.98	159.44	6	17.57
14	13-1/2	74.25	167.06	1127.67	68.06	187.17	7	20.62
★ 8 x 8	7-1/2 x 7-1/2	56.25	70.31	263.67	70.31	263.67	5.33	15.62
10	9-1/2	71.25	112.81	535.86	89.06	333.98	6.67	19.79
12	11-1/2	86.25	165.31	950.55	107.81	404.30	8	23.96
14	13-1/2	101.25	227.81	1537.73	126.56	474.61	9.33	28.12
★ 10 x 10	9-1/2 x 9-1/2	90.25	142.89	678.75	142.89	678.75	8.33	25.07
12	11-1/2	109.25	209.39	1204.03	172.98	821.65	10	30.35
14	13-1/2	128.25	288.56	1947.80	203.06	964.25	11.67	35.62
★ 12 x 12	11-1/2 x 11-1/2	132.25	253.48	1457.51	253.48	1457.51	12	36.74
14	13-1/2	155.25	349.31	2357.86	297.56	1710.98	14	43.12
★ 14 x 14	13-1/2 x 13-1/2	182.25	410.06	2767.92	410.06	2767.92	16.33	50.62

Source: Southern Yellow Pine; Southern Forest Products Association.
Note: Properties are based on minimum green size which is ½ inch off nominal in both b and d dimensions.

smaller beam size; however, it is much easier to make the size comparisons by using the sectional properties in Table 5-3. First, look in the table for the values of the section modulus for the 2 × 12, and the 6 × 12 just computed using the formula. Beams are always loaded perpendicular to the x-x axis. You will note that the values computed are exactly the same as those in the table. Further study of the table will indicate that the closest we could get to the 96.00³ in value computed would be a 4 × 14 with a section modulus of 102.14 in.³

One other way that the required section modulus could be achieved is by using more than a single piece of lumber to make a composite beam. In this case, for example, we might elect to use two 4 × 10s. A single 4 × 10 has a section modulus of 49.91 in³; two would have an equivalent section modulus of 99.82 in³ (49.91 × 2). This would also accomplish the job at hand. At the end of this chapter we will work through an entire problem to demonstrate how this information ties together.

Sizing Vertical Members

Vertical structural members are designated as columns, posts, piers, or pilings. These members transfer loads vertically in the structure from joists and rafters to beams and from beams to footings and then to the ground. In simple structures like shelters and decks, the loads carried by columns are considered to act along the longitudinal axis of the member as shown in Figure 5-22.

COLUMN FAILURE

Columns are subject to two kinds of failure: crushing and buckling. Crushing is the result of exceeding the material's compressive strength. In the case of wood columns, they are usually cut from the saw log in such a way that compressive loads are carried parallel to the wood grain. This is important when looking up the

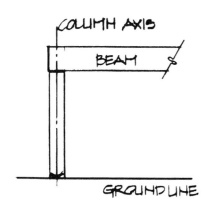

FIGURE 5.22 COLUMN LOADING

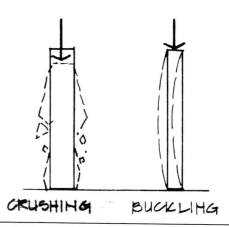

FIGURE 5.23 COLUMN FAILURE

working stress values in Table 5-2. Buckling is a form of bending stress. When a load is placed on a column there is a tendency for the column to bow or deflect from the vertical. If the column is relatively thin in relationship to its length it may fail by buckling, Figure 5-23.

CHECKING A COLUMN FOR CRUSHING

Checking columns for crushing is a relatively simple procedure. First compute the unit stress on the column, and then check that against the recommended working stress value in Table 5-2. To illustrate the procedure, consider the situation in Figure 5-24. A 6 ft tall, 4 × 4 nominal western red cedar column is to carry a 4,000-lb load. The unit stress in the column is found by:

$$f = \frac{P}{A}$$

$$f = \frac{4,000 \text{ lbs}}{3.5 \text{ in} \times 3.5 \text{ in}} \text{ (finished dimension)}$$

$$f = \frac{4,000 \text{ lbs}}{12.25 \text{ sq in}}$$

$$f = 326.53 \text{ lbs/sq in}$$

From Table 5-2, find that the allowable compressive stress parallel to the grain is 800 lb/sq in. Therefore, the column would not be in danger of crushing. In most cases you will find that crushing is of little significance, but it cannot be ignored.

CHECKING A COLUMN FOR BUCKLING

Buckling is a unique form of bending that is directly related to the unsupported length of the column and

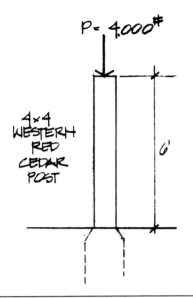

FIGURE 5.24 CHECKING FOR COMPRESSION STRESS

the shape of the cross section. This relationship can be characterized by the term "slenderness ratio," which is the ratio between the length of the column and the smallest dimension of the cross section.

$$R = \frac{l}{d}$$

Where:

l = the column's unsupported length in inches
d = the least dimension of the column's cross section in inches

The slenderness ratio of the column in Figure 5-23 would be:

$$R = \frac{12 \text{ in/ft} \times 6 \text{ ft}}{3.5 \text{ in}}$$

$$R = 20.57$$

Based on slenderness ratio and modulus of elasticity, a standard formula has been developed to estimate the maximum compressive stress allowable in a column before it would be in danger of buckling. It is recommended that this method not be used if the slenderness ratio of the column in question is greater than 30.00. The standard buckling formula is:

$$f_c = \frac{0.3E}{\left(\frac{l^2}{d}\right)}$$

Where:

f_c = the maximum allowable compressive stress in the column
0.03 = a conversion constant
l = the unsupported length of the column in inches
d = the least dimension of the column's cross section in inches

To illustrate the application of the formula, calculate the maximum allowable compressive stress for the column in Figure 5-24. The column has an unsupported length of 6 ft, the column is square with a least dimension of 3.5", and western red cedar has a modulus of elasticity of 1,000,000.

$$f_c = \frac{0.3 \times 1,000,000}{\dfrac{(12 \text{ in/ft} \times 6 \text{ ft})^2}{3.5 \text{ in}}}$$

$$f_c = \frac{300,000}{\left(\dfrac{5,184 \text{ sq in}}{3.5 \text{ in}}\right)}$$

$$f_c = \frac{300,000}{1,481.14}$$

$$f_c = 202.55 \text{ lbs/sq in}$$

The compressive stress for this column previously calculated was 326.53 lbs/sq in, and the maximum allowable in bending is 202.55 lbs/sq in, so this column would not be satisfactory. To correct the problem, either increase the column to a 6 × 6 or change wood species to one with a higher modulus of elasticity value.

Structural Investigation of Simple Structures

To demonstrate how all of these principles work together in the design of simple frame structures, consider the small deck in Figure 5-25. The L-shaped deck is supported by five simple beams resting on eight posts. The joists to support the decking are spaced 16 in on center, and the decking overhangs 6 in uniformly around the frame.

DESIGN LOAD

The first decision the designer has to make involves an estimate of how much weight the structure will be required to carry. This is the design load. Design load has two components: live load and dead load.

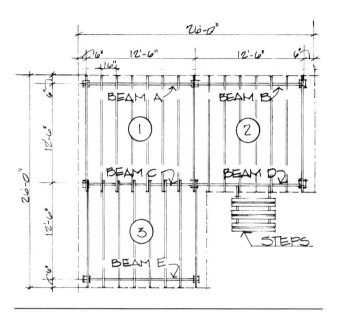

FIGURE 5.25 DECK FRAMING PLAN

The live load is the load composed of furniture, fixtures, and people that will be placed on or move over the structure. These loads are difficult to predict with any degree of accuracy since you can never be absolutely sure what is likely to take place once a structure is finished. For this reason, live loads are estimated as a unit weight per area for the entire structure. In most cases it will be taken as 20 lbs/sq ft, 30 lbs/sq ft, or 40 lbs/sq ft. The light load of 20 lbs/sq ft would be used for very light-duty structures, decks, arbors, and shelters used in residential work where no heavy vegetation would be supported by the structure and there would be no chance of winter snow or ice load. The 30-40 lbs/sq ft loads would be used for other classes of work where there would be heavy vegetation loads, large groups of people, as well as heavy winter snow and ice loads. Most building codes will require outdoor structures to be designed for 40 lbs/sq ft loads in public or semipublic places. The final judgment, responsibility, and liability rests with the designer.

Dead load is the weight of the structure itself. The weight of all of the structural components of the deck, for example, should be taken into account when estimating the load carried by the columns. This component of structural load is very important in large buildings with several floors, but for very simple structures such as the ones that are discussed here, dead load can be accounted for in the selection of the design live load.

To determine the design load for the problem at hand, we will assume a residential application in Athens, Ga., where there is some limited potential winter ice and snow load; so, a design value of 30 lbs/sq ft will be used and it will be taken to include the dead load of the structure.

DIAGRAMMING AND LOAD TRANSFER

The next step is to analyze the transfer of loads through the structure and to prepare diagrams of the members similar to those that were used in our earlier discussion. To begin, compute the total live load on the surface of the deck. The deck has been divided into three sections, designated 1, 2, 3. The areas of each section are found as follows:

Section 1: 13 ft × 13 ft   = 169.00 sq ft
Section 2: 13 ft × 13.5 ft = 175.50 sq ft
Section 3: 13 ft × 13.5 ft = 175.50 sq ft
                Total Area = 520.00 sq ft

The total load generated by the deck is:

520.00 sq ft × 30 lbs/sq ft = 15,600 lbs

The first point of load transfer in the structure is from the decking material to the joists. All of the joists have a span of 12 ft 6 in between supports. The joists in sections 1 and 3 overhang at one end and the joists in section 2 overhang at both ends. Thus the longest joists are those in section 2, 13.5 ft. These joists will carry a load equivalent to an area 16 in wide by 13.5 ft long; therefore, the load carried by a joist is:

13.5 ft × 1.33 ft × 30 lbs/sq ft = 538.65 lbs

This is an evenly distributed load, so the 538.65 lbs is distributed evenly over the 13.5 ft length and could be diagrammed as shown in Figure 5-26.

Next, the beams are diagrammed. Look at Figure 5-25 and notice that beam C will have to carry half the load from section 1, and half of the load from section 2. None of the other beams will carry any greater load, so

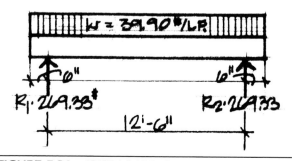

FIGURE 5.26 JOIST LOADING DIAGRAM

this beam will be the one upon which design calculations are based.

The load carried by beam C is equal to half the load of section 1, and half the load of section 3.

Section 1:
$$\frac{169.00 \text{ sq ft} \times 30 \text{ lbs/sq ft}}{2} = 2{,}535.00 \text{ lbs}$$

Section 3:
$$\frac{175.50 \text{ sq ft} \times 30 \text{ lbs/sq ft}}{2} = 2{,}632.50 \text{ lbs}$$

$$\text{Total load} = 5{,}167.50 \text{ lbs}$$

Again, the load is evenly distributed, so the beam is diagrammed as shown in Figure 5-27.

The columns that support the interior portion of the deck between sections 1 and 2 carry loads from the beams on either side. From Figure 5-27 we can see that beam C is transferring 5,167.50 lbs. Each of the two columns carries half of this or 2,583.75 lbs. Find the contribution from B as follows:

Half the load of section 2 is:

$$\frac{175.50 \text{ sq ft} \times 30 \text{ lbs/sq ft}}{2} = 2{,}632.50 \text{ lbs}$$

The beam will transfer half of this load to the column so:

$$\frac{2{,}632.50 \text{ lbs}}{2} = 1{,}316.25 \text{ lbs}$$

The total load carried by the column is:

2,583.75 lbs. The contribution from beam C
1,316.25 lbs. The contribution from beam D
3,900.00 lbs. Total carried by column

The column is diagrammed in Figure 5-28. The unsupported length of the column will be about 3.5 ft as noted.

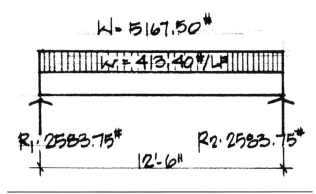

FIGURE 5.27 LOAD DIAGRAM BEAM C

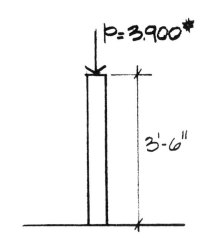

FIGURE 5.28 COLUMN LOADING DIAGRAM

This completes the design analysis portion and the various structural members can be sized once the proposed materials have been selected. Students should not attempt to go further in this discussion until they understand how each of the diagrams for the various structural members was derived.

SIZING THE MEMBERS

We will assume for the example that the framing of the deck will be of southern yellow pine, (SYP), No.2 grade. The first member to be sized is the joist. The joists in this case are the same as an overhanging beam, which means that it would not be appropriate to use one of the formulas to find the maximum bending moment, and a shear diagram should be constructed. The shear computations and the resulting shear diagram are shown in Figure 5-29. Notice that there are three inflection points in the shear diagram, indicating that there are three points where bending stress peaks. One point occurs in the center of the span between the two supports and one point over each support. This pattern will be the same for any symmetrically supported overhanging beam with an evenly distributed load over its entire length. The question is, which is the point of maximum bending stress? To answer this, the bending moment is computed for $M_{0.5}$ and $M_{6.75}$ as follows:

$M_{0.5}$ = (269.33 lb × 0.5 ft) − (.5 ft × 39.90 lb/lf × .25 ft)

$M_{0.5}$ = 129.68 ft lb

$M_{6.75}$ = (269.33 lb × 6.5 ft) − (6.75 ft × 39.90 lb/lf × 3.375 ft)

$M_{6.75}$ = 841.67 ft lb

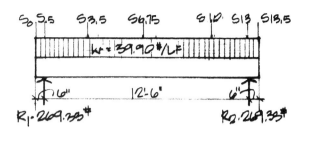

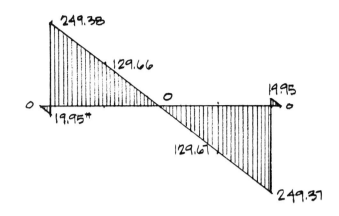

SECTION

So	0.0
S.5-	0 - (.5FT × 39.90#/LF) =
S.5	269.33# - (.5FT × 39.90#/LF) =
S3.5	269.33# - (3.5FT × 39.90#/LF) =
S6.75	269.33# - (6.75FT × 39.90#/LF) =
S10	269.33# - (10 FT × 39.90#/LF) =
S13-	269.33# - (13 FT. × 39.90#/LF) =
S13	(269.33# + 269.33#) - (13FT × 39.90#/LF) =
S13.5	(269.33# + 269.33#) - (13.5FT × 39.90#/LF) =

TOTAL SHEAR

So	0
S.5-	-19.95#
S.5	+249.38#
S3.5	+129.66#
S6.75	0
S10	-129.67#
S13-	-249.37
S13	+19.96#
S13.5	0

FIGURE 5.29 SHEAR DIAGRAM, JOISTS

The maximum moment is 841.67 ft lb and occurs at the center of the span, between the supports. This will usually be the case for very short overhangs and it will not usually be necessary to compute the moment at both points. The entire procedure is illustrated in the example.

After finding the maximum bending moment, the flexure formula is used to find the required section modulus. From Table 5-2, find that the f_b value for SYP No.2 is 1,350.

$$S = \frac{M}{f_b}$$

$$S = \frac{841.67 \times 12 \text{ in/ft}}{1,350}$$

$$S = 7.48 \text{ in}^3$$

Looking in Table 5-3, find that a 2 × 6 has a section modulus of 7.56 in³ which will satisfy the 7.48 in³ required; however, if a different lumber species were used with an f_b value of less than the 1,350, the joist size should be increased to a 2 × 8. Likewise, if the joists were spread to 24-in centers, it would also mean going to the larger joist size. This is pointed out because a lot of framing is done automatically using 2 × 6 joists on 16 in centers regardless of the lumber species, grade, or the anticipated design load. In most cases, the structures

work just fine, but that is because the peak load of 30 lbs/sq ft is probably never reached, and because there is a liberal safety factor built into the recommended working stress values published by the forest products associations. Landscape architects are cautioned about this sort of design by rule of thumb because, if a structure should fail, it will be the designer and not the contractor who will have the liability.

The beams that support the deck are simple beams with an evenly distributed load, so the maximum bending moment can be determined by using the formula from Figure 5-20 as follows:

$$M = \frac{WL}{8}$$

$$M = \frac{5,167.50 \text{ lb} \times 12.5 \text{ ft}}{8}$$

$$M = 8,074.22 \text{ ft lb}$$

Next, the required section modulus is found.

$$S = \frac{M}{f_b}$$

$$S = \frac{8,074.22 \text{ ft lb} \times 12 \text{ in/ft}}{1,350}$$

$$S = 71.77 \text{ in}^3$$

Again, looking in Table 5-3, find that a 4 × 12 meets the requirement with a section modulus of 73.82 in.³ It might be tempting to substitute two 2 × 12s for the single 4 × 12, but this would not be advisable since that would only have a section modulus of 63.28 in.³ If 2 × 12s are substituted, three pieces will be required.

The final step is to select the column size and check it for crushing and buckling. First compute the unit stress carried by the column, which will be a SYP No.2, 4 × 4.

$$f = \frac{P}{A}$$

$$f = \frac{3,900 \text{ lbs}}{3.5 \text{ in} \times 3.5 \text{ in}}$$

$$f = \frac{3,900 \text{ lbs}}{12.25 \text{ sq in}}$$

$$f = 318.36 \text{ lbs/sq in}$$

From Table 5-2, find that SYP No.2 has a working compressive stress value of 1,000 lbs/sq in, so the column is in no danger of crushing.

Last, compute the maximum allowable compressive stress for the column in buckling. From Table 5-2, find the modulus of elasticity value for SYP No.2 to be 1,600,000.

$$f_c = \frac{0.3E}{\left(\dfrac{l^2}{d}\right)}$$

$$f_c = \frac{0.3 \times 1,600,000}{\left(\dfrac{12 \text{ in/ft} \times 3.5 \text{ ft}^2}{3.5 \text{ in}}\right)}$$

$$f_c = \frac{480,000}{\left(\dfrac{1,764.00 \text{ in}}{3.5 \text{ in}}\right)}$$

$$f_c = 952.38 \text{ lbs/sq in}$$

Again, since No. 2 SYP has an f_c value of 1,000 lbs/sq in, the column proposed is more than adequate for the job at hand.

The Mechanics of Freestanding Walls

Fences and walls are structures found in most landscape projects of any size. The detail and structural design of fences and walls will be examined in more detail in Chapters 6 and 7. The purpose of this section is to discuss the stability of walls, assuming that the structural design of the wall is sound. Walls, unlike

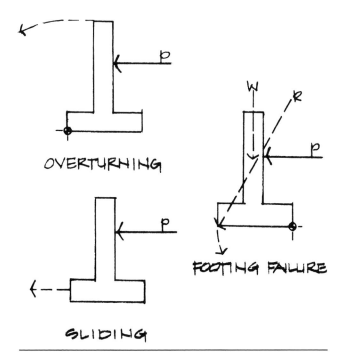

FIGURE 5.30 WALL STABILITY FAILURES

the structures considered in previous sections, are influenced by lateral loads caused by wind. A wall or a fence with a totally opaque surface may be subject to wind loads of as much as 50 lbs/sq ft of surface. Depending on the soil type and the weight of the wall, this kind of pressure can cause the wall to blow over.

KINDS OF WALL STABILITY FAILURE

Figure 5-30 shows the three types of stability failure that occur for walls.

Overturning failures are the direct result of a lateral load that pushes the wall over so that it rotates around the edge of the footing, in a direction away from the force.

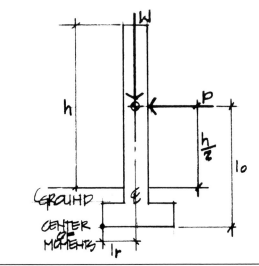

FIGURE 5.31 PRINCIPLE OF MOMENTS, WALL STABILITY

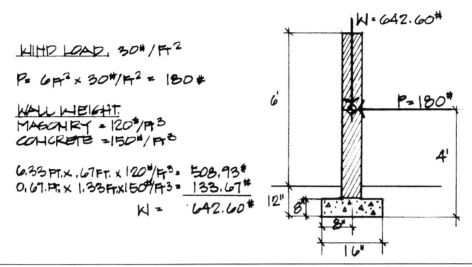

WIND LOAD, 30#/FT²

P = 6FT² × 30#/FT² = 180#

WALL WEIGHT.
MASONRY = 120#/FT³
CONCRETE = 150#/FT³

6.33 FT. × .67 FT. × 120#/FT³ = 508.93#
0.67 FT. × 1.33 FT. × 150#/FT³ = 133.67#
W = 642.60#

W = 642.60#

P = 180#

FIGURE 5.32 CHECKING WALLS FOR OVERTURNING

Footing failure is caused by the eccentric transfer of loads to the ground. In these cases the pressure on the edge of the footing away from the force becomes so great that the soil under the footing fails, and the wall will rotate forward around the edge of the footing closest to the force.

Sliding failures result when the lateral pressure is sufficient to exceed the horizontal shear strength of the soil in front of the wall and the plane of friction between the wall and the ground is broken, allowing the wall to slide forward.

WALLS AND THE PRINCIPLE OF MOMENTS

The wind pressure that acts on a wall constitutes an evenly distributed load acting at the center of gravity of the exposed stem of the wall. The distance from the base of the footing to the center of gravity of the exposed stem of the wall constitutes the lever arm of what is termed the overturning moment. The lateral wind load is designated by the letter P, and the lever arm for the overturning moment is designated l_o, Figure 5-31.

The system of force that has to counteract the overturning tendency is composed of the weight of the wall, W, and its corresponding lever arm, designated l_r, which is measured from the face of the footing to the centroid of the cross section, Figure 5-31.

To illustrate how to check a wall for overturning using moments, consider Figure 5-32. This is a typical 6-ft high, brick masonry wall, with a 12-in embedment. For this situation it is assumed that the wall is located in Champaign-Urbana, Ill. As shown in Figure 5-33, the recommended design wind load for this zone is 30 lbs/sq ft. For the purpose of design, take a typical 1-ft

long section of the wall and develop the values for P and W based on that section. Figure 5-32 shows the computations. Note the values for the weight of masonry and concrete are found in Table 5-1.

The computations of the overturning moment, M_o, and the righting moment, M_r, are as follows:

M_o = 180 lbs × 4 ft
M_o = 720 ft lbs
M_r = 642.60 lbs × 0.67 ft
M_r = 430.54 ft lbs

According to these numbers, a wall of this design with a direct wind load of 30 lbs/sq ft could blow over; yet there are any number of walls just like this one in Champaign-Urbana and in other cities all over the

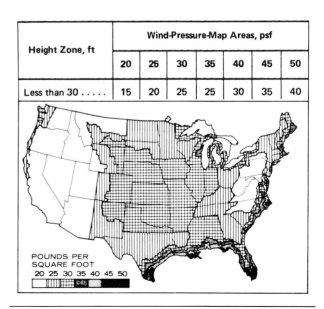

Height Zone, ft	Wind-Pressure-Map Areas, psf						
	20	25	30	35	40	45	50
Less than 30	15	20	25	25	30	35	40

POUNDS PER SQUARE FOOT
20 25 30 35 40 50

FIGURE 5.33 WIND PRESSURE MAP

country. Why? These computations assume that there are no intervening supports in the form of walls at right angles, buildings, or piers with deeper embedment to better resist the overturning moment. As this example illustrates, walls are basically unstable structures and must have some form of lateral support.

LATERAL SUPPORT OF WALLS

The spacing of lateral supports in walls is determined by the design wind load and the length to thickness ratio of the wall, length being the lateral distance between supports. This is logical since these are the components of the righting and overturning moments. Table 5-4 provides the maximum length to thickness, (L/T), ratios recommended for selected design wind pressures.

To find the recommended support spacing for the wall in Figure 5-32, use the values from Table 5-4 and solve for L as follows:

L/T for a 30 lb/sq ft wind load is 14

The wall thickness is 8 in or 0.67 ft (normal width of a brick masonry wall).

$$14 = \frac{L}{0.67 \text{ ft}}$$

$$L = .67 \text{ ft} \times 14$$

$$L = 9.38 \text{ ft}$$

Thus, the wall in Figure 5-32 should have supports every 9.38 ft or about 9 ft 4 in on center. Depending on the design intent it may be desirable to use a closer spacing module but the 9 ft 4 in spacing should not be exceeded.

Principles of Eccentric Loading of Walls

Eccentric loading is the primary cause of footing failure. Eccentric loading occurs when the force acting downward does not act through the center of gravity of the footing. This condition can be caused in two ways. First the vertical stem of the wall can be placed off-center on the footing, which shifts the weight toward one edge of the footing. If this happens the load will be greater on the edge closest to the stem of the wall. The second cause of eccentric loading is the result of lateral loads acting on the wall. When two forces are acting in different directions along different lines, a new force is generated, called a resultant, with a new line and direction. Figure 5-34.

TABLE 5.4 *MAXIMUM LENGTH TO THICKNESS RATIOS FOR FREESTANDING WALLS, FOR SELECTED WIND PRESSURES*

Design Wind Pressure lbs sq in	Maximum L/T Ratio
5	35
10	25
15	20
20	18
25	16
30	14
35	13
40	12

There are two concerns when eccentric loading is present: soil bearing strength and the stress in the footing. When the load shifts to one side of the footing, the pressure exerted on the soil below the footing is increased on that side and decreased on the opposite side. If this load should exceed the bearing strength of the soil, it may fail and allow the wall to rotate or tilt forward and fall. Second, when the load is shifted to one side of the footing, it changes the stress pattern. As long as the downward force acting on the footing is at the center of gravity of the section, all stress in the footing will be uniform and compressive. When the load shifts away from the center of gravity, compressive stress increases at the loaded edge and decreases at the opposite edge. If the load is shifted far enough to one side or the other, tensile stress will develop in the footing and can cause the footing to break apart and fail. The "Principle of the Middle Third" has shown that, as long as the downward acting force is acting within the

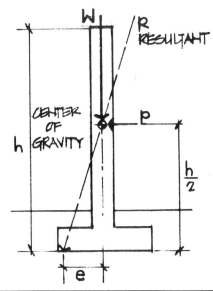

FIGURE 5.34 ECCENTRIC LOADING

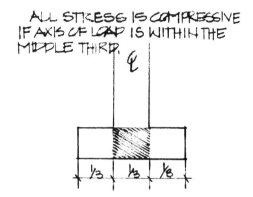

FIGURE 5.35 *PRINCIPLE OF THE MIDDLE THIRD*

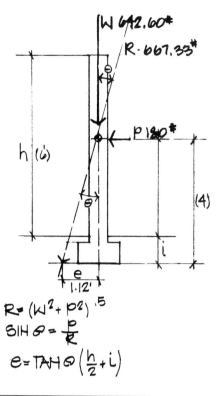

$$R = (W^2 + P^2)^{.5}$$
$$SIN\;\theta = \frac{P}{R}$$
$$e = TAN\;\theta\left(\frac{h}{2} + i\right)$$

FIGURE 5.36 *ECCENTRICITY IN FREESTANDING WALLS*

middle third of the footing, all stress in the footing will remain compressive, Figure 5-35. Since concrete is most often the material used for footings and has little ability to resist tensile stress, eccentric loading should always be kept within the middle third of the footing. In order to be sure that this condition is met, and that the soil bearing pressure is not exceeded, it is necessary to find the point where the eccentric load will act on the footing and to determine the force that will be exerted on the soil. These principles apply to both freestanding walls and retaining walls.

LOCATING THE POINT OF ECCENTRIC LOADING

Figure 5-36 shows the formulas for finding the resultant, the angle θ, and the distance from the centerline of the wall to the point where the eccentric load acts, *e*. To illustrate the application, the same values will be used as the wall in Figure 5-32. These are shown in parentheses in Figure 5-36. The first step is to find the resultant force generated by the weight of the wall (642.60 lbs) and the wind load (180 lbs).

$$R = (W^2 + P^2)^{.5}$$
$$R = (642.60\;lbs^2 + 180lbs^2)^{.5}$$
$$R = (445,334.76)^{.5}$$
$$R = 667.33lbs$$

Next, find θ, the angle between the resultants line of action and the vertical axis of the wall.

$$Sin\;\theta = \frac{P}{R}$$
$$Sin\;\theta = \frac{180\;lbs}{667.33\;lbs}$$
$$Sin\;\theta = 0.2697$$
$$\theta = 15.6483°$$

Now find *e*:

$$e = Tan\;\theta\;\left(\frac{h}{2} + i\right)$$
$$e = 0.2801\;(4\;ft)$$
$$e = 1.12\;ft$$

Given the conditions in the diagram of Figure 5-36, the resultant force is acting at a point beyond the front edge of the footing, and there will be tensile stress in the footing unless it is made wider to include the point of action within the middle third. The other alternative is to design the footing to carry the stress structurally using steel reinforcing. In this case it would be necessary to increase the footing width to 6 ft 9 in, which would be excessive. The best solution is to have a structural engineer check the wall detail and design the appropriate footing.

DETERMINING SOIL PRESSURE FROM ECCENTRIC LOADS

The greatest pressure exerted on the soil is found by the relationship:

$$f_c = \frac{R}{A}\left(1 + \frac{6e}{d}\right)$$

Where:

f_c = the maximum compress force exerted on the soil in lbs/sq in
R = the resultant in lbs
A = the area of the footing in contact with the ground for a typical 1 ft long section
d = the width of the footing's cross section
e = the distance from the centerline of the wall to the point of action of the resultant

To illustrate the application of this relationship, the numbers generated for the wall in Figures 5-32 and 5-36 will be used again. The result was 667.33 lbs, the width of the footing's cross section was 16 in, the value of e was 1.12 ft and the area of the footing for a 1-ft-long section is 192.00 sq in (16 in × 12 in). Solve for f_c as follows:

$$f_c = \frac{R}{A}\left(1 + \frac{6e}{d}\right)$$

$$f_c = \frac{667.33 \text{ lbs}}{192.00 \text{ sq in}}\left(1 + \frac{6 \times 1.12 \text{ ft} \times 12 \text{ in/ft}}{16 \text{ in}}\right)$$

$$f_c = 3.4757 \text{ lbs/sq in} \times 6.04$$

$$f_c = 20.99 \text{ lbs/sq in}$$

Table 5-5 notes some of the bearing capacities of typical soil types. You can see from the table that the bearing pressure computed would be satisfactory for most soils except wet or expansive clays.

Retaining Walls

Retaining walls pose problems of stability similar to those of freestanding walls; that is, they may fail by either overturning, footing failure, or by sliding. What makes them different is that the lateral force acting on the wall is generated by the soil and backfill material behind the wall rather than wind.

The only soil that generates the pressure on the wall is the soil that lies outside the angle of repose. The angle of repose is the angle formed between the stable soil surface and the ground plane, Figure 5-37. The shaded soil area indicates the volume of soil that will contribute to the the lateral pressure on the wall. Since the actual pressure on the wall is the resultant of the horizontal and vertical components of the soil's weight, the pressure is assumed to act at a point one-third the height of the wall as shown in Figure 5-37. The line of action is parallel to the soil surface. If the soil behind the wall is sloping upward, the wall is said to have a surcharge. The amount of surcharge is equal to the weight of the additional soil above the top of the wall.

TABLE 5.5 AVERAGE BEARING CAPACITY OF TYPICAL SOIL TYPES

Soil Type	Bearing Capacity lbs/sq in
Soft or expansive clays	14
Sharp, wet sands	28
Fine, well graded sands	42
Coarse sands	56
Gravels	84
Shales	140

TYPES OF RETAINING WALLS

Retaining walls are classified by their cross section, and there are three types: gravity, cantilever, and counterfort, Figure 5-38. The gravity wall relies on weight and batter to resist the lateral pressure. The term batter refers to sloping the face of the wall back against the slope. The cantilever wall uses a structural cross section and the additional weight of the soil resting on the footing to resist the pressure. The counterfort wall has supports spaced along the face of the wall to stiffen the wall where high lateral pressures are expected. In most cases, low retaining walls (6 ft or less in height) will be either gravity walls or cantilever walls.

LATERAL LOADS ON RETAINING WALLS

It was noted earlier that the lateral load on a retaining wall is generated by the pressure of the soil that lies outside the angle of repose. The formulas in Figure 5-39

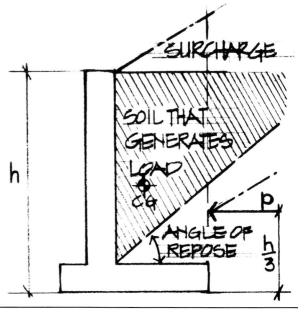

FIGURE 5.37 CHARACTERISTICS OF RETAINING WALLS

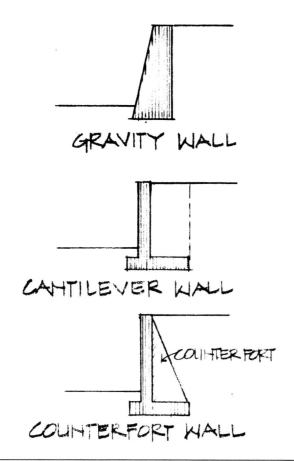

FIGURE 5.38 *TYPES OF RETAINING WALLS*

are generally accepted for making estimates of the lateral loads. The assumption in these formulas is that the soil has an angle of repose of 33 degrees. While this assumption is reasonably safe for most soils from fine sandy loams through tight clays, it will not be valid for materials like fine silts (quartz sands, silica sands), or unstable soils subject to land sliding. In addition, it is also assumed that the soil is in an unsaturated condition, free of excess capillary water. The water can be drained from behind the wall using weep holes, small holes through the base of the wall, or by a subdrainage system.

In addition to the soil and moisture content assumptions, the formulas also assume that there are no building loads included in the angle of repose. If the footing or grade beam of a structure intrudes on the plane of intersection between the angle of repose and the plane of the surface, there will be an additional surcharge that must be taken into account. Building surcharge is one of the most frequently overlooked variables that contribute to stability failures.

CHECKING RETAINING WALLS FOR FOOTING STABILITY

Checking a retaining wall for footing stability follows the same principles as for checking a freestanding wall. The primary differences in retaining walls have already been pointed out, with the exception of the need to

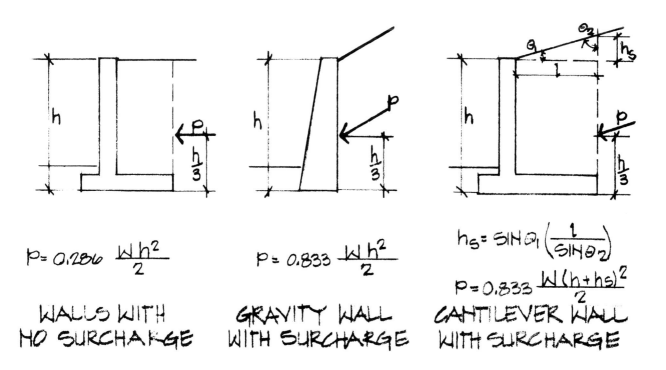

$$P = 0.286 \frac{W h^2}{2}$$

WALLS WITH NO SURCHARGE

$$P = 0.833 \frac{W h^2}{2}$$

GRAVITY WALL WITH SURCHARGE

$$h_s = SIN\,\Theta_1 \left(\frac{1}{SIN\,\Theta_2}\right)$$

$$P = 0.833 \frac{W (h + h_s)^2}{2}$$

CANTILEVER WALL WITH SURCHARGE

FIGURE 5.39 *FORMULAS FOR PRESSURE ON RETAINING WALLS*

locate the center of gravity. Since the wall section is a composite of materials of different weight and the cross section is not a regular geometric shape, it is necessary to locate the center of gravity using the principle of moments.

FINDING THE CENTROID OF THE SECTION BY MOMENTS

The centroid, or center of gravity, is the point in the cross section through which all forces act. In a rectangular cross section of the same material, the centroid lies at the point where the vertical and horizontal axes cross. In a right triangle the centroid lies at a point equal to one-third the distance vertically and one-third the distance horizontally measured away from the 90-degree angle, Figure 5-40.

Given these relationships, the principle of moments states that the sum of the moments of the parts is equal to the moment of the whole. Therefore, it is possible to

find the centroid of any cross section by computing the moments for each component of the section and adding them together. To demonstrate how this principle is applied, consider the retaining wall shown in Figure 5-41. It is a cantilever wall, which means that the soil that rests directly above the footing acts as part of the weight of the wall. The lateral pressure acts through a plane drawn vertically from the back edge of the

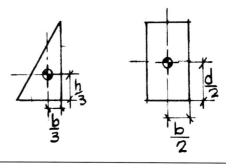

FIGURE 5.40 CENTROIDS OF SECTIONS

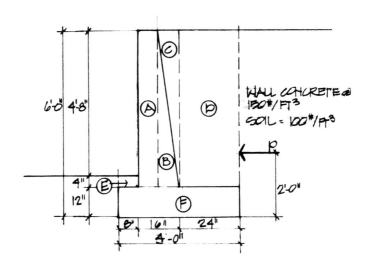

UNIT		WEIGHT	MOMENT ARM	MOMENT
A	.67FT. x 5 FT. x 150 #/FT³ =	50250 # x	1.00 FT.	502.50 FT#
B	.67FT./2 x 5 FT. x 150#/FT³ =	251.25 # x	1.55 FT.	389.44
C	.67FT./2 x 5 FT. x 100#/FT³ =	167.50 # x	1.78 FT.	298.15
D	2 FT. x 5 FT x 100#/FT³ =	1,000.00 # x	3.00 FT	3,000.00
E	.67FT x .33 FT x 100#/FT³ =	22.11 # x	0.33 FT	7.29
F	4 FT. x 1 FT x 150#/FT³	600.00 # x	2.00 FT.	1,200.00
		2,543.36 #		5,397.38 FT#

$$L = \frac{5,397.38}{2,543.36} = 2.12 \text{ FT.}$$

FIGURE 5.41 RETAINING WALL, WEIGHT AND MOMENT CALCULATIONS

footing. The section of the wall has been divided into units, either right triangles or rectangles, and labeled A through F. The front edge of the footing has been designated as the center of moments and the moment for each unit is calculated in tabular form below.

Most students have little trouble finding the weights of the different units, the confusing part is usually finding the moment arms of the various units. For the example in Figure 5-41, the moment arms for each unit are worked out in detail below.

Unit A. The centroid of unit A is half its width of 8 in or 4 in. The distance from the front edge of the footing to the face of A is 8 in. Thus, 8 in + 4 in = 12 in or 1 ft.

Unit B. B is a right triangle so its centroid lies one-third the length of its base from the 90-degree angle. The base is 8 in and one-third of 8 in is 2.64 in. The 90-degree angle of B lies 16 in from the front edge of the footing, so the lever arm for B is 16 in + 2.64 in = 18.64 in, or 1.55 ft.

Unit C. C is also a right triangle with an 8-in base, so its centroid will also lie 2.64 in from the 90-degree angle. The distance from the front edge of the footing to the 90-degree angle is 24 in, and the centroid of C is 2.64 in closer so: 24 in − 2.64 in = 21.36 in or 1.78 ft.

Unit D. D is a rectangle and the center of the rectangle lies 3 ft from the front edge of the footing. The moment arm is 3 ft.

Unit E. E is a small rectangle of soil 8 in wide so its center is 4 in from the front edge of the footing and the lever arm is .33 ft.

Unit F. F is a rectangle 4 ft long, so half its length, 2 ft, is the lever arm for unit F.

Now since the total weight of the composite cross section is known and the total moment is known, it is possible to determine the distance from the front edge

of the footing, the center of moments, to the centroid of the section by dividing the moment in ft/lbs by the weight in lbs to find L in ft, as shown.

FINDING ECCENTRICITY

The next step is to locate the point where the resultant force (R), caused by the weight of the wall (W), and the lateral pressure (P), cuts the plane of the base of the footing. Figure 5-42 shows the information computed to this point, along with the formulas necessary to find P and R. The value of P is computed using the formula for a wall with no surcharge, with the assumption that the soil's angle of repose is 33 degrees or more, as follows:

$$P = 0.286 \frac{Wh^2}{2}$$

$$P = 0.286 \left(\frac{100 \text{ lbs/cu ft} \times 6 \text{ ft}^2}{2} \right)$$

$$P = 0.286 \times 1800 \text{ lbs} =$$

$$P = 514.80 \text{ lbs}$$

Next find R by:

$$R = (W^2 + P^2)^{.5}$$
$$R = (2,543.36 \text{ lbs}^2 + 514.80 \text{ lbs}^2)^{.5}$$
$$R = 2,594.94 \text{ lbs}$$

Find the angle θ by:

$$\text{Sin } \theta = \frac{P}{R}$$

$$\text{Sin } \theta = \frac{514.80 \text{ lbs}}{2,594.94 \text{ lbs}}$$

$$\text{Sin } \theta = 0.198386$$

$$\theta = 11.4426°$$

Find e as follows:

$$e = \text{Tan } \theta \frac{h}{3}$$

$$e = \text{Tan } 11.4426° \frac{6 \text{ ft}}{3}$$

$$e = 0.2024 \times 2 \text{ ft}$$

$$e = 0.40 \text{ ft}$$

All of this information is plotted to scale in Figure 5-42. Notice that the resultant point of action is within the middle third. This means that the footing will not have any tensile stress. This is typical of most pre-designed wall sections; however, predesigned sections do not necessarily allow for plastic or expansive soil

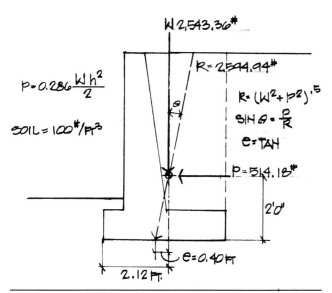

FIGURE 5.42 FINDING ECCENTRIC LOADING

loads, which can be formidable. For this reason, it is usually wise to have the wall section looked at by a structural engineer.

To complete the footing stability investigation procedure, the maximum soil pressure is computed as follows:

$$f_c = \frac{R}{A}\left(1 + \frac{6e}{d}\right)$$

$$f_c = \frac{2{,}594.94 \text{ lbs}}{(48 \text{ in} \times 12 \text{ in})}\left(1 + \frac{6 \times 0.40 \text{ ft} \times 12 \text{ in/ft}}{48 \text{ in}}\right)$$

$$f_c = 4.5051 \text{ lbs/sq in} \times 1.60)$$

$$f_c = 7.21 \text{ lbs/sq in}$$

This is a very light footing pressure and should pose very little problem in almost any soil condition. Light soil bearing pressure is characteristic of the cantilever retaining wall and, for this reason, most walls of any substantial height are cantilever-type walls.

CHECKING RETAINING WALLS FOR OVERTURNING

The procedure for checking retaining walls for overturning is the same as for freestanding walls. The major difference, as already seen in the discussion of footing failure, is that the center of gravity of the wall must be computed. Figure 5-43 shows the computations for the weight of the wall and the location of the center of gravity using moments as before. The lateral pressure on the wall is found as follows, using the formula for retaining walls with no surcharge, assuming an angle of repose of 33 degrees or greater.

$$P = 0.286 \frac{Wh^2}{2}$$

$$P = 0.286 \times \frac{100 \text{ lbs/cu ft} \times 6 \text{ ft}^2}{2}$$

$$P = 0.286 \times 1{,}800 \text{ lbs}$$

$$P = 514.80 \text{ lbs}$$

With the weight and lateral load known, proceed to compute the overturning moment and the righting moment as follows:

$M_o = 514.80 \text{ lbs} \times 2 \text{ ft} =$
$M_o = 1{,}029.60 \text{ ft lbs}$
$M_r = 2{,}002.09 \text{ lbs} \times 1.52 \text{ ft} =$
$M_r = 3{,}043.18 \text{ ft lbs}$

The righting moment is approximately three times greater than the overturning moment, so there is little danger that the wall would overturn.

CHECKING RETAINING WALLS FOR SLIDING

The lateral pressure on the wall is the force that would cause the wall to slide. The force that resists sliding is the friction between the footing and the soil and the horizontal shear strength of the soil in front of the wall. Table 5-6 gives some average friction coefficients for various soil types. The weight of the wall multiplied by the friction coefficient gives a reasonable estimate of how well the wall will resist sliding. As an example, assume that the wall in Figure 5-43 is being proposed in a nonplastic clay, friction coefficient 0.50.

2,002.09 lbs × .50 = 1001.05 lbs

The lateral pressure (514.80), is still about half of the friction value, so the wall would not be likely to slide. In a plastic clay condition the value would be:

2,002.09 lbs × 0.30 = 600.61 lbs

This value is still greater than the lateral pressure of 514.80 lbs.

In most cases, the shear strength of the soil is going to be low, and it is not wise to rely on soil strength in shear to maintain wall stability. The walls most likely to have a tendency to slide are those that carry a surcharge because the resulting lateral pressure is much greater.

RETAINING WALLS WITH A SURCHARGE

To complete the discussion of retaining walls, a complete stability investigation will be worked through for a retaining wall with a surcharge. As noted earlier, this condition is the most extreme and should always be checked carefully. For the example problem, consider the wall in Figure 5-44. It is assumed that the wall is placed in soil with an angle of repose of 33 degrees or greater and that the soil weighs 100 lbs/cu ft. The computations for weight and moment are shown as in previous examples. The one new situation not encountered in previous examples is finding the value of h_s, the height of the triangular soil volume that makes

TABLE 5.6 AVERAGE FRICTION COEFFICIENTS OF SOIL

Soil Type	Friction Coefficient
Sharp sand and gravel	0.60
Sand and sandy loam	0.40
Silts and nonplastic clay	0.50
Plastic clays	0.30

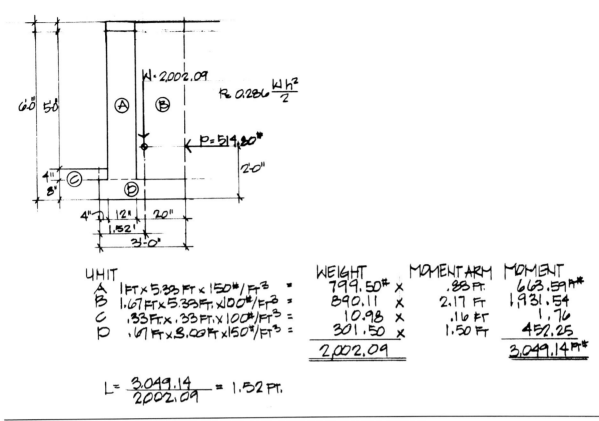

UNIT
A   1 FT × 5.33 FT × 150#/FT³   =
B   1.67 FT × 5.33 FT × 100#/FT³ =
C   .33 FT × .33 FT × 100#/FT³ =
D   .67 FT × 3.00 FT × 150#/FT³ =

WEIGHT		MOMENT ARM	MOMENT
799.50#	×	.83 FT.	663.59#*
890.11	×	2.17 FT	1,931.54
10.98	×	.16 FT	1.76
301.50	×	1.50 FT	452.25
2,002.09			3,049.14 FT#*

$$L = \frac{3,049.14}{2,002.09} = 1.52 \text{ FT.}$$

FIGURE 5.43   RETAINING WALL, WEIGHT AND MOMENT CALCULATIONS

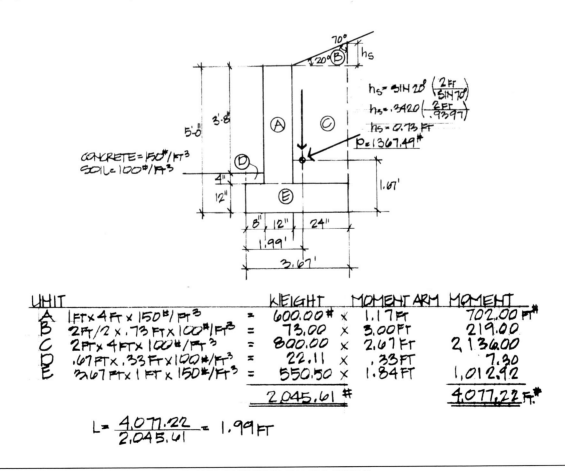

UNIT
A   1 FT × 4 FT × 150#/FT³   =
B   2 FT/2 × .73 FT × 100#/FT³ =
C   2 FT × 4 FT × 100#/FT³ =
D   .67 FT × .33 FT × 100#/FT³ =
E   3.67 FT × 1 FT × 150#/FT³ =

WEIGHT		MOMENT ARM	MOMENT
600.00#	×	1.17 FT	702.00 FT#*
73.00	×	3.00 FT	219.00
800.00	×	2.67 FT	2,136.00
22.11	×	.33 FT	7.30
550.50	×	1.84 FT	1,012.92
2,045.61 #			4,077.22 FT.#*

$$L = \frac{4,077.22}{2,045.61} = 1.99 \text{ FT}$$

FIGURE 5.44   RETAINING WALL, WEIGHT AND MOMENT CALCULATIONS

makes up the surcharge. This is noted as unit B in Figure 5-44. The formula for finding hs is in Figure 5-39.

Since the angle between a level plane and the sloping surface (θ_1) is 20 degrees, the opposite angle is 70 degrees.

$$h_s = \text{Sin } \theta_1 \left(\frac{L}{\text{Sin } \theta_2}\right)$$

$$h_s = \text{Sin } 20° \times \left(\frac{2 \text{ ft}}{\text{Sin } 70°}\right)$$

$$h_s = 0.3420 \left(\frac{2 \text{ ft}}{0.9397}\right)$$

$$h_s = 0.73 \text{ ft}$$

This was noted in the figure and the weight calculations were completed as shown.

In the moment arm calculations, remember that in a right triangle the center of gravity lies one-third the length of the base from the 90-degree angle. The base is 2 ft so 0.33 × 2 ft is 0.67 ft. The footing is 3.67 ft long so 3.67 ft − 0.67 ft is 3.00 ft, as shown.

The next step was to find the lateral pressure (P), on the wall, as follows:

$$P = 0.833 \frac{W (h + h_s)^2}{2}$$

$$P = 0.883 \frac{100 \text{ lbs/cu ft} \times (5 \text{ ft} + 0.73 \text{ ft})^2}{2}$$

$$P = 0.883 \times 100 \text{ lbs/cu ft} \times 16.42 \text{ ft}$$

$$P = 1367.49 \text{ lbs}$$

The basic data are now complete and the wall can be checked for footing stability, as follows:
Find the resultant R:

$$R = (W^2 + P^2)^{.5}$$
$$R = (2{,}045.61 \text{ lbs}^2 + 1367.49 \text{ lbs}^2)^{.5}$$
$$R = 2{,}460.60 \text{ lbs}$$

Next θ is found:

$$\text{Sin } \theta = \frac{P}{R}$$

$$\text{Sin } \theta = \frac{1367.49 \text{ lbs}}{2460.60 \text{ lbs}}$$

$$\text{Sin } \theta = 0.5558$$

$$\theta = 33.7658°$$

The value of eccentricity is found:

$$e = \text{Tan } \theta \frac{h}{3}$$

$$e = .6686 \times 1.67$$

$$e = 1.12 \text{ ft}$$

The footing pressure can now be found by:

$$f_c = \frac{R}{A} \left(1 + \frac{6e}{d}\right)$$

$$f_c = \frac{2460.60}{(44 \text{ in} \times 12 \text{ in})} \left(1 + \frac{(6 \times 1.12 \text{ ft} \times 12 \text{ in/ft})}{44 \text{ in}}\right)$$

$$f_c = 4.66 \text{ lbs/sq in} \times 2.83$$

$$f_c = 13.18 \text{ in}$$

This is a reasonable value for most soil conditions, so the wall would be considered stable.

Next check for overturning stability:

$$M_o = 1{,}367.49 \text{ lbs} \times 1.67 \text{ ft}$$
$$M_o = 2{,}283.71 \text{ ft lbs}$$
$$M_r = 2{,}045.61 \text{ lbs} \times 1.99 \text{ ft}$$
$$M_r = 4{,}070.76 \text{ ft lbs}$$

The righting moment is again almost twice the value of the overturning moment; therefore, the wall should not overturn.

Finally, check for the friction factor and for sliding. For this example assume a nonplastic clay, friction coefficient of 0.50.

2045.61 lbs (the weight of the wall) × 0.50 = 1,022.81 lbs

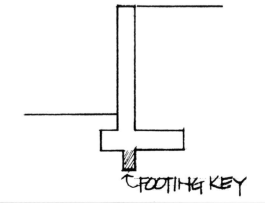

FIGURE 5.45 RETAINING WALL WITH KEY TO RESIST SLIDING

The value of P is 1,367.49 lbs, which is greater. Thus, this wall is in danger of sliding. As noted earlier, this is the danger with any retaining wall that carries a surcharge. The solution to the problem is to add to the mass of the wall to increase the relative weight. This is usually done by extending the footing to capture more soil, rather than adding more concrete to the face of the wall. The other method employed is to add a key to the base of the footing to increase the relative friction, Figure 5-45. This solution should not be used in plastic clays or in platey soils that have little or no shear strength.

Retaining walls are used in all types of landscape construction projects for functional and design reasons. It is important that this discussion be concluded with a final reminder about the assumptions made in checking a wall for stability. All of the formulas used to estimate lateral pressure assume an angle of repose of 33 degrees or more. In addition, it assumes that there is no excess capillary moisture in the soil. Water must be drained from behind the wall using weep holes or a subsurface drain. If positive drainage is not provided, lateral pressures will be increased to as much as three times the pressure of dry soils. Also remember that the footing must be set below the frost line to avoid damage from frost heave. These points are stressed because most retaining wall failures can be directly attributed to loading- and drainage-related problems, not structural failures.

CARPENTRY
AND DESIGN
WITH WOOD

Introduction

Wood and wood products are used extensively in all types of landscape architecture projects. Wood appears most often in structures such as shelters, benches, fences and the like, but it is also used as a paving material, for planters, and even for retaining walls. In short, wood has applications in the landscape limited only by the imagination of the designer. To use wood effectively as a construction material, it is essential to have a working knowledge of the structural properties of wood, its endurance characteristics, availability, grades and grading standards, and typical construction practices.

The first part of this chapter provides some background information about the most common wood species, their advantages and limitations, how they are graded, and how they are usually used in the landscape. This is followed by a discussion of wood fasteners used with wood and how they are applied. The final part of the chapter is devoted to wood detailing, how wood structures are assembled, and why.

Softwood Lumber Species

Wood materials used in construction are usually milled from soft woods. This is wood obtained from narrow leaf trees (gemnosperms), such as pines, cedar, fir and cypress. Wood obtained from broadleafed trees (angeosperms), is called hardwood. Hardwoods are used most frequently in furniture, millwork, and as veneers. The hardwoods that do show up in landscape construction are found in timbers or, more frequently, as railroad ties. Since the use of hardwoods is so limited, they are not considered in any detail.

Many different species of softwood are utilized in the manufacture of lumber, and the availability of species varies widely with the geographic region of the country. The important thing to remember is that each wood species varies in its workability, structural quality, appearance, hardness, and durability. Workability refers to how easily a particular wood species can be cut, shaped, and attached to other structural members. Structural quality is the relative strength of a wood species. Appearance has to do with the visual characteristics of the species such as wood grain (relative coarseness or fineness), wood color, number and the characteristics of knots. Hardness is the relative density of the wood.

To provide some background, a brief description of some of the most popular softwoods is included here.

CEDARS

Two different species of cedar are harvested and used for lumber: northern white and western red. These woods are characteristically soft, low-density woods, very easily worked, and resist warping. Structurally, they are among the weakest of all the wood species, as noted in Chapter 4 and, because they are so soft, they do not hold nails well.

Cedars are pleasant, medium- to fine-grained woods and range in color from a deep red to a very pleasant off-white. Some cedar species and grades are very knotty, and it may be hard to obtain good, clear boards.

Cedars have a natural rot resistance found in no other wood species, which makes cedar a prized material for shingles and siding. In fact, the majority of all cedar harvested each year is used for shingles. It is also noted for its distinct fragrance, which lasts as long as the wood.

Because of its resistance to rot and aesthetic appeal when allowed to weather naturally, cedar is one of the most used wood species. In many cases, cedar could be considered as a possible alternative to redwood, as long as strength, hardness, and nail-holding ability are not critical factors.

CYPRESS, SOUTHERN BALD

Southern bald cypress is a tough, medium-density wood with good workability. It is resistant to shrinking, does not warp as much as pine, and is relatively strong. Because of the tree's growth characteristics it is relatively knotty wood, but the knots are usually small and very tight. Like cedar, cypress is naturally resistant to rot and requires little or no treatment to ensure its durability.

Cypress varies in color from a pale golden yellow to a deep reddish tan. It is a pitchey wood, particularly around the knots, and will not hold some paints well; however, if left totally untreated it will weather to a striking silver-grey. This will usually take about three years of exposure.

Cypress is an excellent landscape material because of its natural rot resistance and its character. Its most frequent applications are as a deck surface, siding, shingles, and as an exterior trim. Because of a fluctuating supply, it can be very expensive at times, and at other times very reasonable, so it pays to check availability and price before specifying cypress. Most of the wood that is milled is cut into 1-in nominal material and 2-in thicknesses can be hard to find.

DOUGLAS FIR

Douglas fir is a hard, dense wood, which makes it somewhat difficult to work. It has a moderate resistance to shrinkage and warping if it is properly cured. As a structural material, fir is one of the strongest of the common softwood species, but it has little natural resistance to rot. For this reason, fir should never be used in an exposed condition.

Fir is a medium- to fine-grained wood that has a pleasant off-white color, and the knots are usually small and tight. Douglas fir does not hold paint well, so it is not a good material for finished surfaces. Most of the fir harvested is cut into 2-in nominal material for use in framing.

PINE, SOUTHERN YELLOW

Southern yellow pine is a hard, dense wood, which makes it very hard to work. It has a very high pitch content; this makes it subject to shrinkage and extreme warping if not carefully cured, and it has little natural resistance to rot. Even properly cured, it may still warp if left unprotected and exposed to moisture. Southern yellow pine also splinters parallel to the grain, which limits its use as a finished surface. On the plus side, southern yellow pine is the strongest of all the commercially harvested softwood species and, when pressure treated with preservatives, will be very rot resistant.

Southern yellow pine is somewhat lacking in appearance. It frequently has large, loose knots that are surrounded with pitch, and the wood color varies from an off-white to a dark yellow tan. The wood grain is coarse and, because of the pitch content, it will not hold paint well. It will, however, take penetrating oil-base stains well.

As a landscape material, southern yellow pine has a lot to offer because it is available in quantity and is among the least expensive of all the commercial species. It is strong, holds nails very well and, because it can be treated to prevent rot and takes stains well, it is a good choice for the budget-minded project.

WESTERN WHITE PINES

White pines, unlike their southern cousins, are soft, medium-density woods that are very easy to work. They resist warping when well cured, and the knots are usually small and tight. They are also weaker than fir or southern yellow pine, and have little resistance to rot when exposed.

White pines are smooth, fine-grained woods that range in color from eggshell white to a light tan. They do not have a tendency to splinter and can be milled to a very smooth, even surface. White pines are superior in their ability to take stains and hold paint. This makes them prized as a finished surface material but, because they are very soft, they will not stand abuse.

As a landscape material, white pines must be viewed with caution because of their lack of rot resistance and softness. In most cases, other species offer more longevity.

REDWOOD

Redwood is a moderately dense wood that is easily worked. It resists shrinkage and is not easily warped.

Redwood has good structural properties and a natural resistance to rot and insect attack. Redwood is characteristically knotty, but the knots are usually small and tight. Redwood was popularized as a landscape material in the 1950s in California; however, since that time, dwindling supplies, increased cost, and decreased quality have made redwood less common.

Redwood has a broad range of colors from almost white to deep sienna and umber. Good quality wood can be finished to a very fine surface, and the wood is not prone to splintering. This makes it an ideal surface for benches and handrails. Naturally weathered redwood has a very pleasant, dark, warm gray to gray red color.

In landscape construction, redwood is still an outstanding material if good quality wood can be obtained at a reasonable cost. But before specifying redwood for a project, designers are advised to check on the quality and availability.

Grading of Wood Products

Wood materials manufactured for construction are classified by size as boards, lumber, or timber. Boards are less than 2 in nominal thickness, lumber is from 2 in to 5 in nominal, and timber is anything greater than 5-in thickness. The term nominal refers to the approximate dimension of the wood cut from the saw log. It is always greater than the actual finished dimension of the lumber.

Wood cut from the saw log is called rough lumber. The rough lumber is then planed down to obtain a smooth, even surface on one or more sides. After planing, the lumber is called dressed lumber. Dressed lumber is then stacked on pallets to allow good air circulation and is placed in a drying yard or a drying kiln.

During the curing process the wood will shrink more, reaching its final dressed dimensions. Since wood is an organic material, the shrinkage from water loss will vary from piece to piece. But for most dressed lumber the dimensions can be taken as ½ in less on dimensions up to 8 in, and ¾ in less on dimensions over 8 in. For board stock, the dressed dimension is usually ¼ in less than the nominal dimension. For example, a 2 × 10 has a dressed dimension of 1½ in × 9¼ in and a 1 × 8 board would be ¾ in × 7½ in. These dimensional differences are important and must be taken into account in doing construction details.

COMMON YARD LUMBER

Common yard lumber is graded visually, rather than mechanically, by standards promulgated by the industry for the particular wood species. Most all grading systems have two broad classifications called select

and common. The select grades are for finished woods, appearance, or structural purposes. Common grades are for light framing and general construction. Most of the western wood products associations, western white pine, fir, spruce, hemlock, etc., grade their select materials as "select," "structural," and "appearance," or No. 1, No. 2, and No. 3. Their common lumber grades are "construction," "standard," and "utility." The Southern Forest Products Association, which sets the grading standards for southern yellow pine, classifies its select materials as B&B, C, D, and "select structural." Common lumber is graded as No. 1, No. 2, No. 3, No. 4, and No. 5. Wood may also be classified as Kiln Dried (KD), or "dense"; this material has a much lower moisture content as specified by the individual wood products association.

Regardless of the name of the wood grade, No. 1, or construction, will be relatively smooth with few tight knots; No. 2, or standard, will be rougher with more knots and some rough edges, but the wood is sound and good for construction framing. Grades No. 3 through No. 5, and utility are not very good quality. They will likely be warped, have rough edges, loose knots, and are not generally suitable for permanent construction work.

The select materials are usually stamped as finish or stress-graded lumber. These grades are given most often after careful visual inspection and some nondestructive testing. The actual requirements vary from association to association and from species to species. For the most part, there is little need for the use of select or stress-graded lumbers in landscape construction projects, so select grades are not considered further.

LUMBER MEASUREMENT

Lumber is sold in units called board feet. A board foot is equal, by definition, to a board 12 in × 12 in × 1 in, nominal, which is 144 cu in. By this definition, any piece of wood that contains 144 cu in is a board foot. To find the relative board foot value for any standard lumber size, simply divide the volume of a typical one-foot length by 144 cu in. For example, a standard 2 × 4 would be:

2 in × 4 in × 12 in = 96 cu in
96 cu in ÷ 144 cu in = .67 bf

When prices are quoted from a lumber supplier, the price will most often be quoted in dollars per 100 board feet.

Wood Fasteners

A very basic and important part of all wood structures is the fasteners used to hold it together. The fasteners

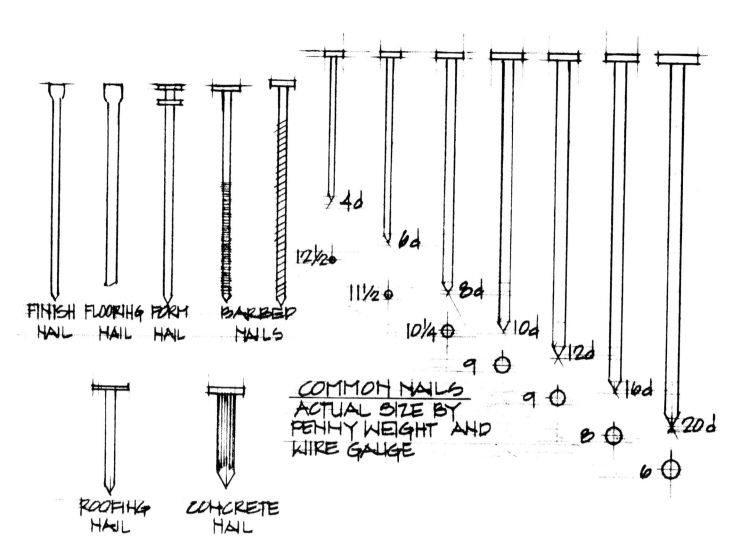

Length In Inches	AM. Steel & Wire Co.'s Steel Wire Gauge	Approx. No. to Lbs.	Nail ings	Sizes and Kinds of Material		Trade Names	Pounds Per 1000 Feet B.M. On Center As Follows				
							12"	16"	20"	36"	48"
									Pounds		
2½	10¼	106	2	1× 4	Used square	8d common	60	48	37	23	20
2½	10¼	106	2	1× 6	edge, as plat-	8d common	40	32	25	16	13
2½	10¼	106	2	1× 8	forms, floors,	8d common	31	27	20	12	10
2½	10¼	106	2	1×10	sheathing or	8d common	25	20	16	10	8
2½	10¼	106	3	1×12	shiplap.	8d common	31	24	20	12	10
4	6	31	2	2× 4	When used	20d common	105	80	65	60	33
4	6	31	2	2× 6	D. & M. blind	20d common	70	54	43	27	22
4	6	31	2	2× 8	nailed, only	20d common	53	40	53	21	17
4	6	31	3	2×10	½ quantity	20d common	60	50	40	25	20
4	6	31	3	2×12	named	20d common	52	41	33	21	17
6	2	11	2	3× 4	required.	60d common	197	150	122	76	61
6	2	11	2	3× 6		60d common	131	97	82	52	42
6	2	11	2	3× 8		60d common	100	76	61	38	34
6	2	11	3	3×10		60d common	178	137	110	70	55
6	2	11	3	3×12		60d common	145	115	92	58	46

FIGURE 6.1 TYPES OF NAILS

used in wood construction can be grouped under four headings: nails, bolts, screws, and special fasteners. Nails are the most common fasteners, but bolts, screws and other types of fasteners have applications where weathering, racking, or tensile stress become a problem. Racking is a term used to describe the tendency of a structure to move laterally at the joints. Weathering will cause the wood to expand and contract and in doing so, it will actually pull the nails out of the joint.

NAILS

Nails are used to connect the basic framing members to the superstructure, and for attaching siding, shingles and decking. Nails are available in aluminum, nonferrous alloys, galvanized steel and steel. Steel, or bright-finished nails, should not be used in exterior construction because they will rust and weaken very rapidly. The rust will also damage the finish of the surface. For outdoor applications, galvanized or alloy nails are the best choice. Figure 6-1 shows some of the most common shapes and sizes of nails used in construction. The size of common, box, and finish nails is usually given by their "penny weight," designated by the lower case letter "d." The term penny has its origin in the cost per 100 nails but, as you can imagine, this no longer means anything except size. The "penny weight" designations are also shown in Figure 6-1. With the development of the pneumatic nail gun, nail sizes are now given by length in inches and wire gauge.

SCREWS

There are two types of screw used in wood construction: wood screws and lag screws. They both have a tapered inclined thread; the primary difference is size and the head. Wood screws are small, from ⅛ in long to 5 in long, and they may have several different head configurations. The lag screw has a machine head, square or hex, and comes in lengths of up to 12 in.

The size of a wood screw is given by its diameter in inches by some length in inches. Common wood screws and sizes are shown in Figure 6-2.

Wood screws, like nails, are available in a number of different materials. For outdoor applications the best materials are either brass, nonferrous alloys or chrome-plated steel. Lag screws are available in hot-dipped galvanized finish and nonferrous alloys.

Screws are most useful for attaching things like railings, bench slats, and other pieces that are subject to loads that put a lot of tensile stress on the fastener at a joint. They should not, however, be used to carry loads that involve shear stress.

BOLTS

Bolts are used at major structural joints, such as the attachment of beams and posts, and stringers for steps. The kinds of bolts used most often are carriage bolts and machine bolts. The kinds of bolts and their sizes are shown in Figure 6-3. Bolts are available in the same range of materials as are wood screws.

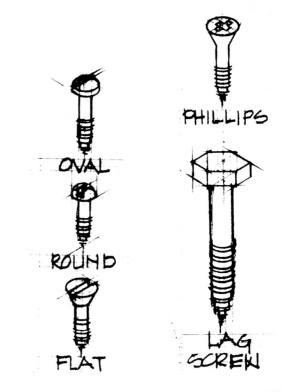

Size	Shank Diameter (D)	Root Diameter (% D)	Lengths
0	.060	.040	¼–⅜
1	.073	.049	¼–½
2	.086	.057	¼–¾
3	.099	.066	¼–1
4	.112	.075	¼–1½
5	.125	.083	⅜–1½
6	.138	.092	⅜–2½
7	.151	.101	⅜–2½
8	.164	.109	⅜–3
9	.177	.118	½–3
10	.190	.127	½–3½
12	.216	.144	⅝–4
14	.242	.161	¾–5
16	.268	.179	1–5
18	.294	.196	1¼–5
20	.320	.213	1½–5
24	.372	.248	3–5

FIGURE 6.2 COMMON WOOD SCREWS

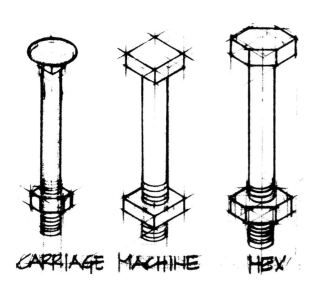

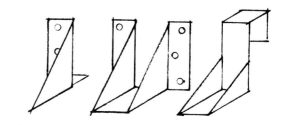

FIGURE 6.4 BRACES AND JOIST HANGERS

Hollow wall fasteners, Figure 6-6, are used to attach things to materials that will not hold a threaded fastener, such as sheet rock or masonry. They work by either filling a hole with a material that will expand as the fastener is threaded into the opening or by having a device that opens into the cavity behind the surface material. The shield type devices are made of plastic, lead or brass alloys. The expanding type devices are made of soft metals or alloys.

Diameter (In)	Lengths (In)
1/4	1/2–8
5/16	3/4–10
3/8	3/4–12
5/16	1–12
1/2	1–16
5/8	1–16
3/4	1–16
7/8	1 1/2–16
1	1 1/2–16
1 1/8	3–16
1 1/4	3–16

FIGURE 6.3 BOLTS: SIZES AND LENGTHS

Bolts are used most often where joints will place most of the load on the fastener or where racking or extreme tensile stress would render a wood screw ineffective. The most common use of bolts is in post-to-beam attachments and handrail post attachments.

SPECIALIZED FASTENERS

Some other types of fasteners used in wood construction are shown in Figure 6-4. The sheet metal fasteners are used to reinforce joints, particularly those subject to racking, or to support joists. They are available in a variety of shapes and sizes for all sorts of applications.

Explosive driven fasteners, Figure 6-5, are made of tough alloy materials and are set with a tool that uses a .22 cal or or .32 cal blank cartridge to drive the fastener. These types of fasteners are very handy for attaching plates and ledgers to concrete or steel.

Wood Preservatives

Woods that do not have a natural resistance to rot will have to be treated with some type of a preservative material if they are to be used outside. The chemicals used to preserve wood are either petroleum-base materials or water-soluble chemicals.

The most common of the petroleum-base chemicals is creosote. It is widely used to treat posts, bridge timbers, poles, and railroad ties. Wood treated with creosote is usually long lived, but it cannot be painted. Another of the popular petroleum-base chemicals is pentachlorophenol (penta). Penta, like creosote, is also a caustic material, but it does not prevent the use of paints or stains after treatment. None of the petroleum-based chemicals should be used where people will come in contact with the surface. Most of these chemicals will weep from the wood during normal

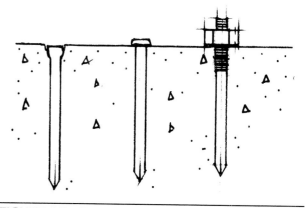

FIGURE 6.5 EXPLOSIVE DRIVEN FASTENERS

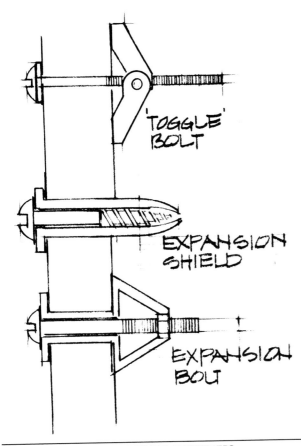

'TOGGLE' BOLT

EXPANSION SHIELD

EXPANSION BOLT

FIGURE 6.6 HOLLOW WALL FASTENERS

daytime heating, and contact with the bare skin will result in a sometimes serious chemical burn.

The water-borne preservatives are complex chemical compounds that contain copper, zinc, arsenic, chrome, or chlorides as the major preservative. Most of the various chemical compounds are proprietary patented materials that carry trade names. One of the most widely known of these is marketed under the trade designation of Wolmanized Lumber.

Some of the water-borne preservatives are recommended by the manufacturers for treatment of woods that may have direct skin contact. Since the designer can be subject to liability suits if a person is injured by a chemical preservative, be sure that the manufacturer of the preservative specifically recommends the material for the intended use.

APPLICATION OF PRESERVATIVES

Preservatives can be applied in a number of ways, most simply by direct application to the surface with a brush or a mop. This method provides the least protection because the material does not penetrate deeply and will soon wear off.

Creosote is usually applied by a dipping process. The wood is first placed in a tank of high-temperature creosote. In this process the heat causes the cells of the wood to expand and absorb the material. Then the wood is placed in a tank of cool water which shrinks the cells and drives the chemical further into the wood.

The most sophisticated treatments involve application of the preservative material under pressure in large tanks or retorts. Pressure treatment forces the chemical material deep into the wood structure so the entire cross section is treated. Wood that has been pressure treated will be designated as either full cell treated or empty cell treated. Full cell treated material is removed directly from the pressure vat and allowed to dry. Empty cell material is left in the vat at a negative pressure and the excess preservative material is drawn off. Full cell material is easily distinguished from empty cell material by the weight. As would be expected, the full cell material is much heavier. Each piece of treated lumber will be stamped with a letter-number designation to indicate the preservative material, the type of treatment, and the recommended use. The code numbers are assigned by the American Wood Preservatives Institute, (AWPI) and are shown in Table 6-1.

Frame Construction

Landscape structures that employ wood are usually designed using the plank-and-beam framing system or some variation of the platform framing system. The platform system began evolving with the introduction of standard size manufactured lumber in the nineteenth century. Today it is the recognized standard for most residential and light commercial construction in this country. Figure 6-7 illustrates a typical deck arbor structure using the platform framing system, with the appropriate names of all the structural members.

The plank-and-beam system simplifies the platform system by eliminating the joists. This system evolved in the post-war period as the variety and sizes of lumber increased and became more available. Because the plank-and-beam system has no joists, the beams must be closer together, and the decking must have a 3-in nominal thickness. Figure 6-8 illustrates the basic principle of the plank-and-beam system.

The merits of using either system is mostly a matter of designer preference. The plank-and-beam system has a lighter, more contemporary feel than the platform system. At first glance it might also appear to require less material, This is not the case, however. The added thickness of the planks and the narrower spacing of the beams, in most cases, uses more material. The cost reduction, if any, is usually accrued in a savings on labor, since there are fewer pieces to the structural system. One other disadvantage of the platform system is the availability of material. Three-inch nominal

TABLE 6.1 *AWPI STANDARD QUALITY MARKS FOR LUMBER, TIMBER AND PLYWOOD*

AWPI Mark*	Treatment or Use Recommended
LP 2 LP 22	Water-borne salts
LP 3 LP 33	Penta, light hydrocarbon solvent (Type C)
LP 4 LP 44	Penta, Volatile hydrocarbon solvent (Type B or D)
LP 5 LP 55	Creosote or creosote/coal-tar solution
LP 7 LP 77	Penta, heavy hydrocarbon solvent (Type A)
FDN	For all lumber and plywood in residential and light commercial structural foundations pressure treated with water-borne salts.
MLP	For lumber and plywood in marine use; pressure treated with creosote or creosote/coal-tar; water-borne salts; dual treatment (salts plus creosote).
MP1	Marine piles pressure-treated with dual treatment
MP2	Marine piles pressure-treated with creosote
MP3	Marine piles pressure-treated with water-borne salts.

*Single digit designation is for above ground use; double digit for soil or fresh water contact.

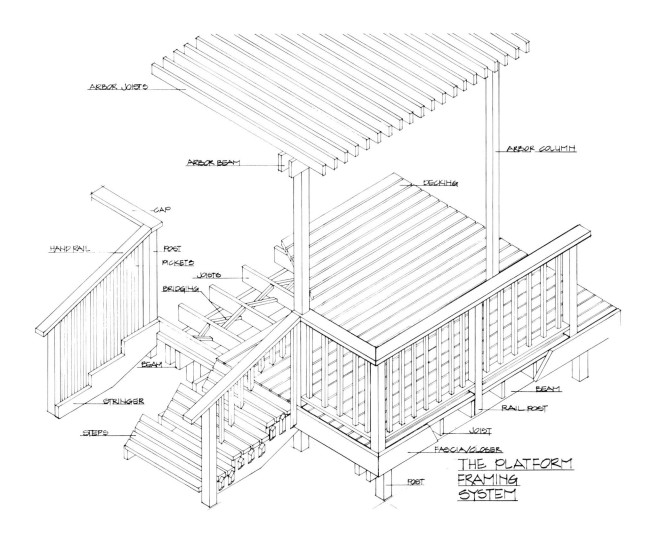

FIGURE 6.7 PLATFORM FRAMING SYSTEM

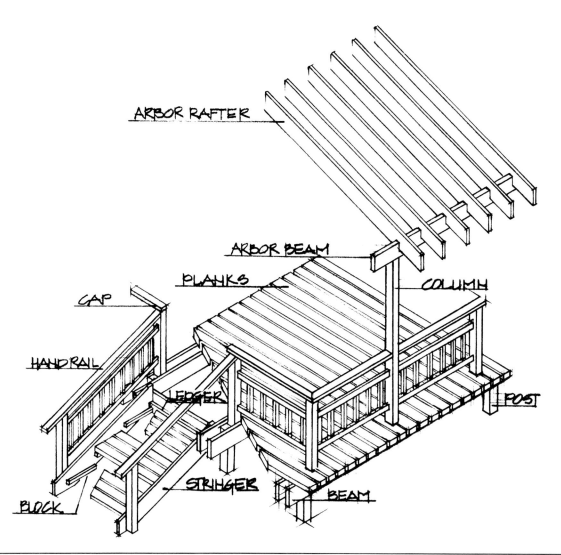

ARBOR RAFTER

ARBOR BEAM

PLANKS

CAP

COLUMN

HANDRAIL

LEDGER

POST

BLOCK

STRINGER

BEAM

FIGURE 6.8 PLANK AND BEAM FRAMING SYSTEM

lumber is not readily available in all parts of the country. If the material has to be special ordered for a small job, the cost may be prohibitive.

The platform system is a heavier looking structure, and uses all 2-in nominal lumber, which is more readily available. Because the structure is composed of three layers, beams, joists and decking, it is much more rigid than the plank-and-beam system and has very little racking tendency. The two illustrations provide a ready reference of basic framing details. Beginning students should study these drawings and become familiar with the terminology and how each system is put together.

Carpentry and Detailing of Wood Structures

The details of how a wood structure is assembled are just as important to the longevity and serviceability of the structure as the ability of the structure support the design loads and the weight of materials in the struc-

ture. Improper placement of members, using poor jointing details, improper or inappropriate fasteners, or poor foundation supports can all lead to the early deterioration of the structure. In addition to the purely functional aspects of the structure, construction detail can also measurably add or detract from the utility and enjoyment of the structure. Some examples of the kinds of details that require close attention are steps, handrails, and seats. Steps must be properly proportioned, and provide good footing to ensure safety. Handrails must be smooth, set at the appropriate height, and proportioned and finished in a way that makes them comfortable to the touch. Seats need to be properly proportioned, at the appropriate height, and finished so that they will not stay wet or provide surprises in the form of splinters or edges that catch clothing. In short, a well-detailed structure should be a delight to the eye as well as the touch.

Too often, construction detailing is approached as a purely mechanical exercise by selecting a general reference detail, such as the ones in the reference manual of this text, and then redoing it to meet a new set of conditions. This approach is analogous to someone trying to design a house by pasting it together from the Sunday home section of the newspaper. The result will likely be a patchwork of poorly related pieces—a residential stew.

The detailing of any structure must be approached as a part of the total design process, building on the overall concepts and vision of the whole. The small details of a structure are often as much a challenge as the big picture, and opportunities abound for design expression and innovation. Attention to the fine details often adds that last measure of sparkle to a job that makes the difference between an outstanding job or just another project.

The first step to good detailing is an understanding of the character and limitations of the material selected. Wood is a modular material, with a rectangular geometry. This means that it will have very limited application to irregular or flowing forms. While it can be bent and shaped, it will always be difficult to make transitions to edges of other parts. Forms with acute angles or circular forms, for example, will always be a problem.

The following are some general rules that will make wood detailing much cleaner and help the beginning student avoid some of the common mistakes.

• Use a 4-in module as the base for all dimensioning. This will usually let the number of pieces of wood required for a project work out evenly.
• Forms should be either rectangles, 90-degree angles or have 45-degree angles. The 45-degree angle will allow all joints to be mitered and pieces will fit at the joints. Use of any other angle will result in unmatched joints.
• If curved edges are used, be sure that the edges are designed around a base grid. This will simplify the support system and limit the fitting of edges to a simple saw cut.

If these simple rules are followed, there will be little problem in developing good details for wood structures.

The remaining discussion in this chapter concentrates on the basic techniques for putting a basic frame structure together. The methods described are common practices used to make basic connections and joints. In each case, the reasons for using a particular method over another will be noted.

PIERS AND FOOTINGS FOR WOOD STRUCTURES

When wood columns or posts are used to support a structure, the primary concern is the longevity of the wood. The zone of rapid deterioration for any wood support is at the soil line. This is the point of frequent

wetting and drying that will accelerate the decomposition of the wood. Therefore, the goal of any footing detail is to reduce the potential for wetting and drying as much as possible.

The first precaution against rot is to be sure to specify a full cell treated wood (AWPB LP-22) for all posts and columns. Then the design of the footing should be such that excess moisture is drained away from the post. Figure 6-9 shows four common details for setting wood posts. The first two are posts set directly into the ground. Notice that in both cases the top of the concrete is above the ground surface and sloped away from the post to minimize moisture penetration. The difference in the two details is not so much a matter of function as it is a matter of construction technique. The detail that shows the post beyond the base of the concrete is the most common situation since the posts are usually set in the hole and plumbed before the concrete is poured. The detail that shows the post cased in concrete requires that the posts be plumbed after the concrete is poured to be sure the

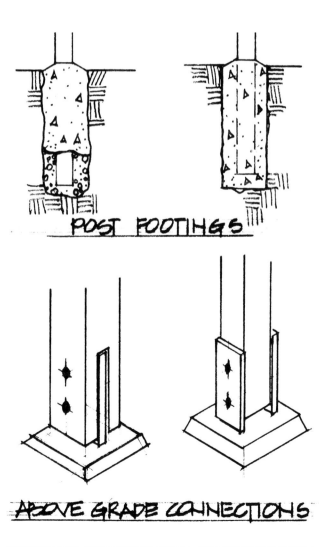

FIGURE 6.9 POST TO GROUND CONNECTIONS

concrete is worked under the post. Some designers believe that having the concrete under the post prevents capillary water from entering the bottom of the post and allowing the wood to rot internally. This logic assumes that no water will penetrate the joint between the post and the concrete footing. The use of posts set directly in the ground is most often seen with fences and screens. These techniques are not recommended for other structures.

For structures other than fences and screens, some type of above-ground post connection is preferred. The two details shown in Figure 6-9 are simple and very effective at keeping the water away from the post. The detail to the left uses a single steel plate set in a concrete base and the post is simply slotted and slipped over the plate and bolted into place. While this detail has a very clean appearance since it hides the plate, it is not as stiff as the detail on the right. The double plate offers a little more support against lateral loads and racking. It is also stronger because it does not require the post to be slotted. Remember that the bolts in this type of detail are very important because it is the bolts that transfer the load to the concrete footing below. Bolts of at least ½ in diameter are necessary. Notice that in both details the post does not contact the ground or the concrete base. This allows air circulation around the post to keep it dry. The primary advantage of the above-ground connection is that, if a post should rot out, it can easily be replaced.

POST-TO-BEAM CONNECTIONS

There is a great deal of variation in the way a beam is attached to a post. Most of the variation occurs because the design of a beam is quite flexible and the post-to-beam connection is often exposed as a feature of the design. Figure 6-10 shows three examples of how a beam is commonly attached to a post. The first illustration shows a two-piece beam bolted directly to the post. In light structures, a single-piece beam can be handled in the same way. It is not absolutely essential that a beam be centered on the column. Two other things that should be pointed out in this first example are the post and the spacer. When the top of a post is exposed, as it is in this case, it is wise to install a sheet-metal cap or cut the top at an angle to shed water. The spacer set between the beam is necessary to help the two-piece beam act as a single member. These are usually placed at 12-in to 16-in intervals.

The beam attached with a plate is a common detail when the beam is set directly on the top of the post. The main reason for the plate is to prevent any lateral load from causing the beam to slide off the post. Elaborate plate details are not necessary to handle the post-to-beam connection, since the weight of the structure above is quite enough to keep the beam on the post for all but the most unusual conditions.

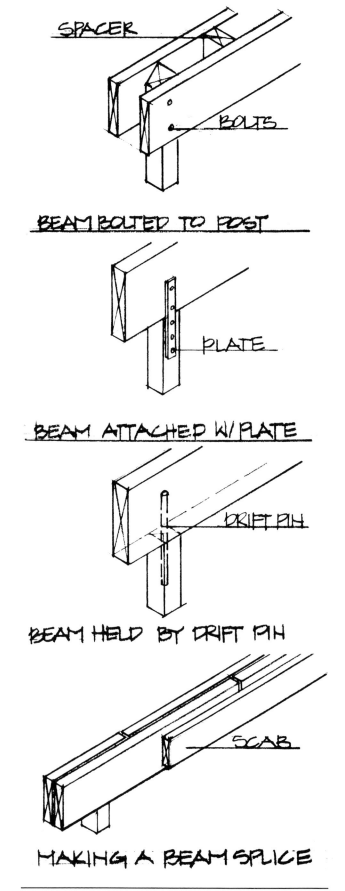

FIGURE 6.10 POST TO BEAM CONNECTIONS

A variation of the plate detail for attaching a beam that rests on the top of a column is the drift pin attachment. A drift pin is simply a steel dowel that is inserted in a hole drilled in the top of the post and the bottom of the beam. This is a particularly nice detail if the beam post connection is exposed and very clean appearance is called for.

Another problem associated with the post-to-beam attachment occurs when making a splice. If a splice is necessary, the joints should be offset as much as possible. Then each joint should be overlapped with a second piece called a scab. The proper way to make a splice is shown in the last drawing of Figure 6-10.

JOIST-TO-BEAM CONNECTIONS

The most common method of attaching the joists to the beams is to rest the joists on the beams and toe-nail them to the beam. This is shown in the first drawing of Figure 6-11. If this method is used and the design loads are in the 40 lbs/sq ft range, it is also wise to provide some form of lateral support in the form of bridging or blocking. Bridging is shown in the top drawing, blocking is shown in the bottom drawing. This bracing is to prevent a lateral force from causing the joists to fold or topple like dominoes. The illustration also shows the use of a closer to fill in the space between the joists. This detail is sometimes used when the ends of the joists are exposed as a part of the design detailing, rather than using the fascia detail shown in Figure 6-7.

The other two details in Figure 6-11 are methods that can be used to reduce the apparent thickness of the structure, or minimize the overall height of the structure where it might be necessary to match the finished floor elevation of an existing building. The center drawing shows the use of joist hangers. Joist hangers are fabricated from a nonferrous alloy sheet metal or they will be hot-dipped galvanized to prevent rust. The joist hangers shown in the illustration are fastened to the face of the beam with nails. There are other types that actually hang from the beam and do not require any fasteners. Joist hangers are available at any building materials supply house.

The alternative to the joist hanger is the use of a ledger. The ledger is usually a 2×4 attached to the face of the beam. The joists are sometimes notched, as shown in the illustration, or are allowed to rest directly on the ledger. The decision about which method is appropriate is a function of local building codes, material availability, and preferred local practice.

STEP AND STRINGER DETAILS

Figures 6-7 and 6-8 show two different ways of detailing the steps. One uses a standard stringer that is cut from a

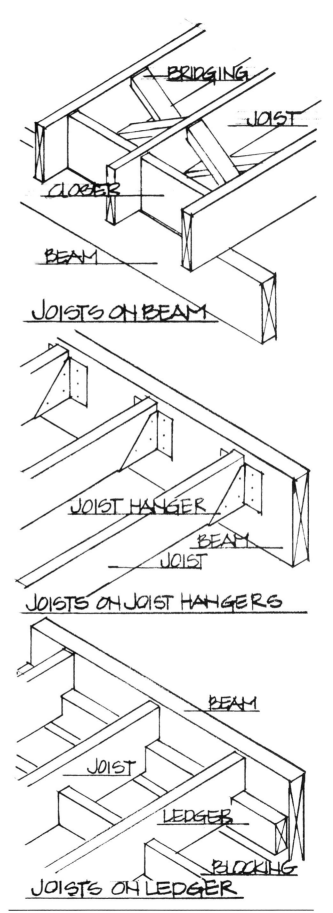

FIGURE 6.11 JOIST CONNECTIONS

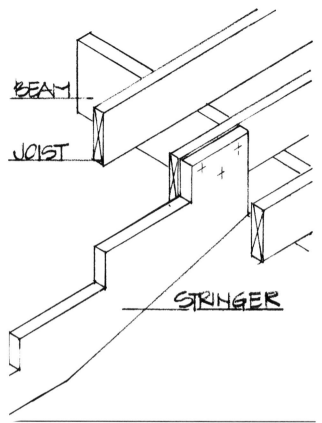

FIGURE 6.12 STRINGER BOLTED TO JOIST

piece of 2 × 12. The other uses a solid 2 × 10 with blocks or steel angles to support the tread. Both illustrations show the stringer supported by a ledger strip attached to the face of the joist or beam face. This is a good solution if there is a joist or beam handy; however, steps may have to be placed on the side of the structure where the joists overhang. In this case, the stringer is attached to the joist ends as shown in Figure 6-12. Steps are a very important feature of any wood frame structure and a lot of interest can be added in the step detail. Some other examples of steps are shown in the reference manual.

RAILINGS AND HANDRAILS

Rails are another important detail for a frame structure; they must be sturdy and at the same time should add to the character of the structure. The two pieces common to all railing details are the cap, or top rail, and the posts. The posts that support a rail should always be bolted to the joists or the beams. Posts that rest on plates on the surface of the deck are too easily pushed over. The top rail should always be of good quality wood that has had the edges chamfered or beveled to prevent splinters. Remember, the rail cap is to touch as well as look at, so it should feel good.

The same types of conditions apply to the handrail along steps: good wood, smooth surface. In addition, the handrail must be set at a comfortable height above the riser. In this regard there is no general agreement as to the ideal height, probably because everyone has different arm lengths. The heights most quoted are between 30 in and 36 in. Our own preference is 32 in. Handrails are required on all steps in public places, and they are recommended on all steps. Failure to provide a handrail carries with it some liability on the part of the designer that should be avoided. The decision to delete a handrail on steps should be left to the client.

One of the most problematic details in wood structures is the transition from the sloped portion of the handrail to the level section of the rail. Figures 6-7 and 6-8 show two solutions to the problem. The solution in Figure 6-7 requires some very careful cutting and fitting to accomplish a smooth transition. Since some of the pieces are relatively small, all attachments have to be made with wood screws. The solution in Figure 6-8 gets around the problem by letting the rail cap of the horizontal portion overlap the sloped section of the handrail. Another alternative to these solutions is to use a vertical handrail for the sloped sections as shown in Figure 6-13.

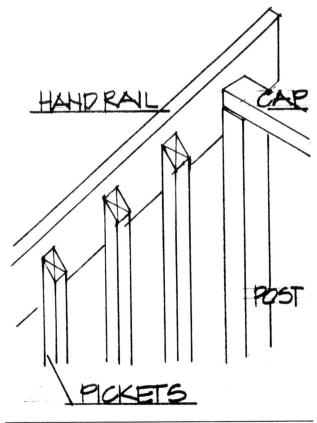

FIGURE 6.13 VERTICAL HANDRAIL

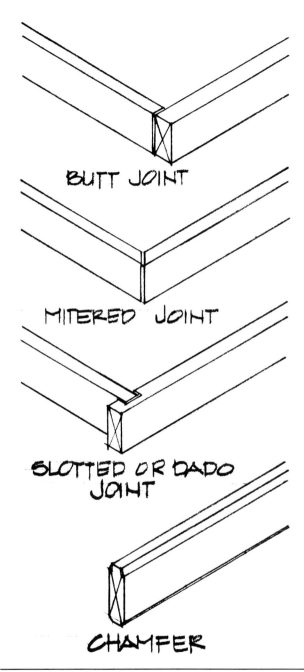

FIGURE 6.14 FINISH AND JOINTS

Joint and Finish Detail

The care and detail used in joining the pieces of a structure are very noticeable, even to the untrained eye. A good carpenter will take the responsibility to do the job right but that does not mean that it is the carpenter's responsibility to know what the designer wants. Figure 6-14 shows the three most common types of joint used in frame structures. The butt joint is usually limited to use in the rough framing of a structure. It is a relatively weak joint and cannot be used to connect pieces subject to racking without some provision for diagonally rein-

forcing the joint. The mitered joint is the most common jointing technique for joining pieces in finished work. It provides a neat, clean edge and does not expose the end of the wood as the butt joint does. The slotted or dado joint allows one piece to slide into the other. This is often used to assemble railings and handrails. In most cases, a dado type joint will be glued and fastened with nails or screws.

The edges of most wood are prime locations for splinters and splits. The edge of a board is also very vulnerable to sharp blows that will take chunks out of the wood and detract from the appearance of the finish. The best way to avoid this hazard is to remove the sharp milled edge of the wood used for rails, caps, and bench slats; this is called chamfering.

FASTENER DETAILS

Bolt, screw and nail heads are sometimes a problem, especially on the walking surface of a deck. Nails that are driven into a surface vertically will have a tendency

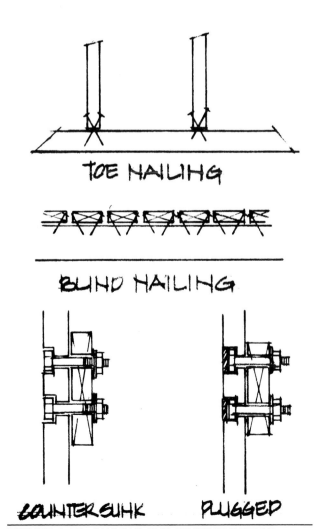

FIGURE 6.15 NAILING AND BOLTING DETAILS

to work their way back out of the hole over time. This is caused by the natural expansion and contraction of the wood caused by temperature and moisture. Any nail sticking up as much as ¼ in from a surface can be a big hazard. One technique used to prevent nail withdrawal from being a hazard is blind nailing. In blind nailing the nails are driven through the side of the board instead of the top so that as they work back out of the hole they will not be a hazard.

Toe-nailing is another technique mentioned earlier. This technique is used to make attachments where it is not possible to drive nails at a 90-degree angle. Joists are usually attached to a beam by toe-nailing.

The other technique used to hide fasteners is called counter-sinking. Nails can be countersunk using a nail punch to drive the nail head into the surface of the wood. Countersinking screws and bolts requires drilling two holes, one for the bolt and a second larger hole to receive the head. Special countersinking bits are available to accomplish this in one step. Depending on the kind of finish, the fasteners may be countersunk and left exposed, or the holes can be plugged. These details are shown in Figure 6-15.

DETAILING FENCES AND SCREENS

Fences and screens are some of the most common of all landscape structures. They are used to provide privacy, security, or sometimes just background. The actual design composition and detail of the individual fence panels may be very simple and open or they may be very complex, even sculptural in quality. This is a matter of designer preference and not the subject of the discussion here. This discussion is limited to consideration of the basic structural components of the fence: the posts and footings, stringers, and gates.

Fence and Screen Posts

The materials used for fence posts will either be wood or metal. Wood fence posts will usually be 4 × 4s, and should always be a full cell treated material. Sometimes 3-in or 4-in round pealed posts are available treated with either creosote or one of the water-borne preservatives. These posts should not be overlooked since they are often less expensive than dimensioned lumber and they are an excellent material. One problem common to dimensioned wood posts is warping. Posts can be set in the ground that are quite straight when installed and then, due to moisture gain, will bow or twist. While wood posts will usually be the least expensive of the materials available for fence posts, they are much shorter lived.

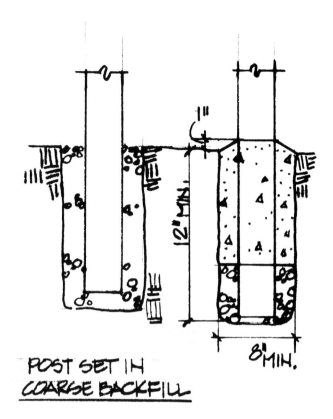

POST SET IN COARSE BACKFILL

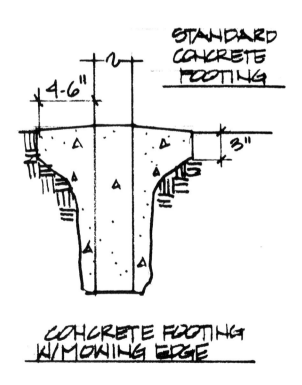

STANDARD CONCRETE FOOTING

CONCRETE FOOTING W/ MOWING EDGE

FIGURE 6.16 FENCE POSTS AND FOOTINGS

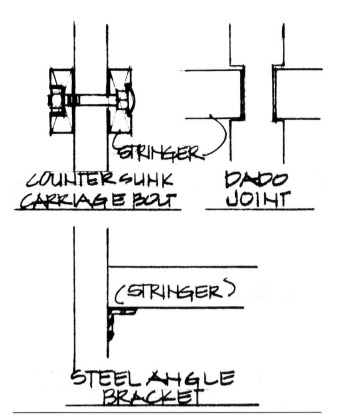

FIGURE 6.17   STRINGER ATTACHMENTS

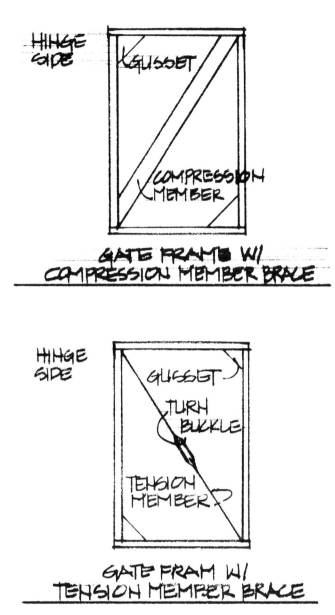

FIGURE 6.18   GATE FRAMES

The alternative to wood fence posts is galvanized steel or alloy posts. The metal posts that are used to install chain link fences are of tubular steel material manufactured specifically for use as fence posts. The material does not have the wall thickness of standard schedule 40 steel pipe but it is very durable under normal loads. It is also less expensive than schedule 40 steel pipe. Metal fence posts are by far the most durable material and they are as easy to work with as wood. Keep in mind that they can be covered with wood if the round post would be out of place in the overall design. Figure 6-16 illustrates some different ways of setting fence posts for different materials.

Stringer and Stringer Attachments

The stringer is the horizontal member that supports the fencing boards or pickets. The size of the stringer and its attachment detail should be considered carefully, particularly if wood is used. Using overloaded 2 × 4s is a very common cause of fence failure, or sag. In most cases it is wise to bolt the stringers onto the posts since exposure to weather will sometimes cause nails to withdraw. If nails are used, they should be galvanized ring-shanked, or barbed. Figure 6-17 shows some different stringer attachments.

GATES

Gates, like fence panels, are usually a matter of design preference. The important structural part is the frame. For reasons of weight, the gate frame should always be as light as possible and very rigid. The basics of providing a very rigid gate frame are shown in Figure 6-18.

The other important part of a successful gate is the type of hinge used to hang the gate. There are any number of different hinges available but the hinge must be matched to the weight of the gate. As a rule, gates should be supported by at least three hinges,

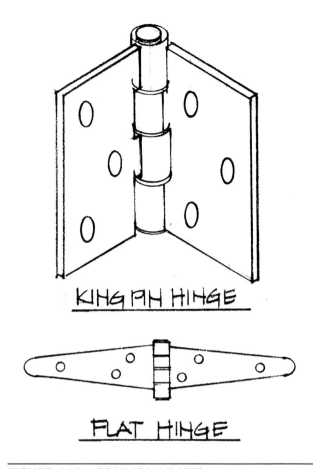

KING PIN HINGE

FLAT HINGE

FIGURE 6.19 COMMON HINGES

particularly if there is a chance that any excess load will be put on the gate, and soft metal hinges should be avoided. Small children are one of the most common excess loads. Figure 6-19 shows some of the most common gate hinges.

Good detailing is a matter of good design and requires a thorough understanding of building materials. Wood is a versatile material and has possibilities and applications far beyond the scope of this discussion. It is also one of the most pleasing of all the common landscape construction materials. People in general seem to be drawn to wood in much the same way as they are drawn to water.

The reference manual of this text is intended to supplement this discussion and help the student develop a better understanding of how things are put together.

C H A P T E R   S E V E N

CONCRETE

AND MASONRY

DESIGN

Introduction

Concrete and unit masonry are among the most versatile and widely used materials in landscape construction. Concrete or masonry units are used for most paved surfaces, such as walks, drives, and terraces. These materials are also used for walls, planters, steps, pools, fountains, and as sculptured features.

Of these two groups, concrete is possibly the most versatile, since it is a plastic material in its delivered state and can be poured and formed into almost any shape the designer can imagine. The finishing of the material offers equal flexibility, providing the designer the opportunity to vary line, textural quality, and to a lesser degree, the color. Concrete has been used for everything from bridges, dams, and buildings to boats and barges; the applications can be considered limitless.

Unit masonry, which includes all types of cast, quarried, and extruded modular building materials, is an equally flexible material. Modular units are available in an almost limitless variety of shapes sizes, colors, and finishes. Various types of building stone, for example, can be quarried, shaped, planed, and polished to meet the needs of any situation. Clay and concrete masonry units can be cast or extruded in almost any shape since the basic materials used to manufacture the units is plastic prior to curing.

Factors that may limit the flexibility of these materials are material availability, access to a skilled

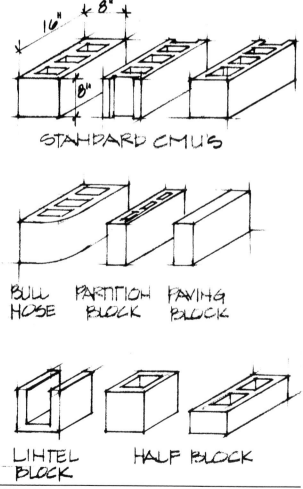

FIGURE 7.1   CONCRETE MASONRY UNITS

235

labor pool, and climate. For example, concrete masonry units are manufactured in many shapes and sizes as shown in Figure 7-1. But from one trade area to another you will find that many of the shapes illustrated are not available. In addition, the units themselves will vary widely in color, surface texture, weight, and porosity.

These same problems also occur with brick and clay masonry units. Brick size, for example, will differ from place to place depending on the manufacturer, the availability of raw materials, and local building conventions. The color and hardness of clay masonry units is also subject to wide variation.

The solution to these problems is knowing the materials available in the trade area of the job and knowing how to use concrete and masonry effectively. The discussion in this chapter is directed to helping the student understand basic concrete and masonry materials and how they are used. The first part of the chapter is devoted to a discussion of the common materials used in the landscape and the final section looks at the basic construction details for concrete and masonry structures.

Concrete and Masonry Materials

CONCRETE

Concrete is classified as either structural concrete or plain concrete, based on how the material is supported. Both structural concrete and plain concrete have steel reinforcing bars or mesh. Structural concrete is any structural member made of concrete that has predetermined points of support, and predictable loading characteristics such as concrete beams, suspended concrete slabs, or concrete piling. Reinforcing steel is used in the concrete to resist predictable tensile stresses that result from the forces acting on the structural member. Plain concrete is any structure or structural member that is supported entirely by the ground surface such as walks, slabs, and common spread footings used to support masonry walls. Steel reinforcing is used in plain concrete to resist the tensile stress of expansion and contraction caused by temperature fluctuation. No structure that is supported entirely by the ground surface can be designed as structural concrete, because the points of support cannot be defined.

Concrete is made of three materials: portland cement, water, and inert granular materials called aggregates. The portland cement and water form a cementitious paste that fills the voids between the aggregate materials ultimately binding it together in a single, rocklike mass.

Portland Cement

Portland cement is a man-made material manufactured from lime, silica, and alumina. The raw materials are processed, mixed in the proper proportions, and then fired and reduced to clinkers. The clinkers are then cured and processed to regulate color, curing time and heat discharge, then they are crushed into fine powder. When water is added to portland cement, a chemical reaction called hydration takes place causing the paste to bond with the aggregates and harden. Initial set will take place in about 45 minutes, and final set is reached in about 10 hours. After setting, concrete continues to cure, becoming harder and stronger. The base measure of hardness, which is the cured strength, is reached in a period of 28 days. This is when concrete will be tested to see if it meets the strength requirements of the specifications.

Portland cements are blended for a wide variety of applications. The color of standard portland cement is gray, but it is also available in white and a variety of earth tones. The colored cements are used for special applications like terazzo—marble chips usually set in white portland and then polished. The earth-tone cements are used frequently in architectural tilt panel construction for walls that will require no additional finish. The earth-tone cements are very good for adding a touch of color to walks and drives in the landscape as well.

In addition to colors, portland cements are manufactured in five structural blends, called types. Type I is a general purpose cement used for paving, buildings, and bridges. Type II is a low-heat cement that is used where the heat given off by the hydration process could cause imperfections in the curing and affect the strength of the material. Concrete made with Type II cement will take longer to cure because the hydration process is retarded. Type III is a high, early-strength blend (HES) that is used when it will be necessary to put heavy loads on the concrete shortly after it has been placed. High, early-strength cement is used frequently in concrete placed in the winter season. Type IV is a very low heat material that is used in concrete pours of extreme thickness, such as dams or reactor walls. Type V is a sulfate resistant blend used in concrete that will be set in soils with high pH or corrosion potential. Type V cement is often used in the manufacture of reinforced concrete pipe.

Air entraining additives can also be used with portland cement to increase the strength and improve the curing uniformity of the concrete. These additives cause air to be trapped in the cement paste; this acts as a natural insulation. Because of this added insulation value, air entrainment is used in concrete that is poured in near freezing temperatures to prevent improper curing. It should also be used in any concrete structure that will be subject to frequent freeze/thaw cycles.

Water

The water used in concrete must be free of minerals, acids, alkali, or other foreign material. Usually, water suitable for drinking is considered satisfactory for concrete.

The amount of water used in concrete will directly affect the final strength of the concrete. The actual water required for the hydration process is much less than the water required to make the concrete mixture easily workable. The introduction of excess water into the concrete mix, beyond the water required to make the material easy to handle, dilutes the cement paste and results in a reduction of strength.

A simple test used to check the cement-to-water ratio of concrete mixes is called a slump test. The slump test uses a 12-in-high cone with an 8-in-diameter base and a 4-in-diameter top. A concrete sample is worked into the cone with a steel rod, and then the cone is removed, allowing the concrete to settle or slump. After the concrete settles, the height is measured. The difference between the original 12-in height and the measured height is the slump. For most construction applications, a slump of between 2 in and 5 in is considered satisfactory, depending on the design and use of the concrete mix. A good guide to the acceptable limits of a slump test for various concrete mixtures can usually be found in the concrete specifications of the state department of highways or transportation.

Aggregates

The aggregates used in concrete are usually dictated by the materials available locally, and whether the aggregate will be exposed in the finished surface. When aggregates of a specific size, color, or weight are required, it is usually necessary to have the concrete mix designed for that particular application by a qualified engineer; however, if there are no special requirements, the concrete supplier will use a predesigned mix based on available materials to meet the strength requirements specified.

Good concrete requires careful blending under controlled conditions of moisture and temperature, with good quality materials. The current state of technology in this country and a very competitive market in the concrete industry have combined to maintain a relatively high quality control standard on concrete products. Designers and construction man-

agers should not, however, be complacent about the quality of the concrete. Quality and mix specifications should always be included in the project manual as well as provisions for laboratory testing.

CONCRETE STRENGTH

The cured strength of concrete is the usual measure of concrete quality. The cured strength is the ultimate strength reached by the concrete in a period of 28 days. Strength is determined in laboratory testing using concrete samples taken from the material delivered to the job site. Samples are placed in cardboard cylinders 6 inches in diameter and 12 in tall. After the specified 28-day curing period these samples are placed in compression until they fail. Laboratory instruments measure the amount of compressive stress at the time the cylinders fail.

For general construction, concrete with a strength of 2,000 to 2,500 psi is satisfactory. For heavier work like pavements, footings and slabs, 3,000 psi material is preferred. Specifying concrete in excess of 3,000 psi is seldom, if ever, necessary for landscape construction.

MORTARS

Mortar is the generic term used to describe the cementitious material used to bond masonry units together. It is very much like concrete in its physical appearance but it is really quite different. The overriding consideration for a masonry mortar is the strength of the bond it forms between itself and the masonry units, not necessarily the strength of the mortar. In fact, it is interesting to note that mortars with higher water-cement ratios generally bond better than stiffer mixtures, just the opposite of concrete.

There are two different types of mortar used in construction based on the materials used in the mix: portland-lime mortars, and masonry cement mortars. The portland-lime mortars are mixtures of portland cement, hydrated lime or lime putty, sand, and water. These mortars do not form as strong a bond between the materials as other mortars but they are stronger. For this reason, portland-lime mortars are often used in heavy stone construction where the weight carried by the mortar joints will be high. Masonry cement mortars are premixed materials that are mixed directly with sand and water and require no additional additives. Most of these materials will be used for general brick and clay unit masonry and for setting ceramic tile.

The American Society for Testing Materials (ASTM) lists five classifications for masonry mortars, based on mixture proportions and their compressive and tensile properties. The classes are designated by the letters M,

N, S, O, K. Of primary importance to the landscape architect are M, N, and S.

Type N mortar is a moderate strength mortar that can be made up from premixed materials or from portland cement and lime. It is best suited to exterior work of a general nature such as nonload bearing walls, pointing, and for grouting the joints in pavement made of masonry units.

Type S mortar is most commonly made up only as a portland-lime mix and has the highest bonding strength of the mortar classifications. Type S mortar is used where the mortar must be relied upon to bond facing materials to a backing. The best example of this application is bonding ceramic units to a wall face.

Type M mortar is made up from a portland-lime mix or can be obtained as a premixed material. This is the strongest mortar classification. Type M mortar should be used on load bearing walls or in walls that are made of heavy materials. It is also the best overall material for masonry structures exposed to moisture and extreme fluctuations in temperature.

The recommended proportioning and approximate strength developed by each type of mortar is given in Table 7-1.

STONE

Stone is a natural material used extensively in all kinds of landscape construction. It appears as a paving material, a veneer surface, as dry stone retaining walls, steps, and sometimes as a decorative feature. Like any natural material, stones vary widely in composition, color, strength and durability. For the most part, the stone used in landscape construction will be granite, sandstone, or limestone. Other types of stone such as slate or marble are also used, but they are generally limited to specific applications rather than general construction work. In most cases, the variety of stone used on a project will be the native stone of the region since the freight cost associated with transporting stone for long distances is usually prohibitive.

Granite

Granites are harder and more dense than any of the other common building stones. Because of their weight and hardness, they are very difficult to work on the job site. In most cases, granite will be precut to the job specification at the quarry before delivery. Because of their hardness and durability, granites are ideal for use in areas of heavy traffic and for surfaces exposed to extreme weathering conditions. It must be pointed out, however, that all granites are not equal. Many granites have ferrous materials, or pyrites, in their structure. The presence of these minerals in the stone will result in rapid chemical weathering and rapid deterioration of

TABLE 7.1 RECOMMENDED PROPORTIONS AND STRENGHTS OF VARIOUS MORTAR MIXES

Mortar Type	Mix (Cement,Lime,Sand)	Strength (psi) Tension	Compression
M	1: ¼ : 3	457	5,492
S	1: ½: 4½	300	2,758
N	1: 1: 6	180	1,173

the stone. It can also lead to unwanted staining of other adjacent surfaces. Most operating quarries have documentation of the chemical composition of their stone and can make suggestions about the proper application.

Some of the most common uses of granite in landscape construction are as rip rap for erosion control, paving stone, or as a veneer stone. Some cities still use granite as a curb material for streets because it has good resistance to chemical and physical abuse. One very popular use is granite paving setts. These are small granite blocks, roughly 2¾ × 2¾ × 3½ in, used for walks, streets and drives.

Limestones

Limestones are quite common in most of the coastal and many interior regions of the country, and they vary widely in their color, strength and hardness. The colors range from an eggshell white to a deep cool gray. Some of the weathered limestones will develop a rich yellow ocher to red rust color.

Since the composition of limestone is principally calcium carbonate it is highly susceptible to chemical weathering. This has become a major problem in many urban areas since acid forming compounds, principally from exaust emissions, are carried freely in the air. The problem is not serious enough to threaten the usefulness of limestone as a building material, but any decorative detailing cut into the stone could be short-lived under certain conditions.

Compared to granite, limestones are very easy to work. The softer stones can be cut with saws and shaped with planes, rasps, and lathes. Because of this workability, it can be cut into thinner sheets and used for paving and wall veneer more easily than granite. In many parts of the country, limestone appears as independent stones and boulders floating free in the upper soil profile. This material is usually called field stone, and is much sought after as a landscape material. The stones themselves vary a great deal in their shape and character and range in size from mammoth boulders to small cobbles and pebbles.

The most common applications of limestone are as copings for walls, paving stone, veneer stone or, in its native state, for dry stone walls and as landscape features.

Sandstone

Sandstones are widely distributed in most parts of the country. They have good workability and are quite durable. The most common sandstones are earthen color ranging from deep ocher to sienna or umber. Other less common colors include dark gray, blue, and green. Bluestone and brownstone are names given to sandstones found in the east and midwest.

Sandstones are similar to limestones in their application and workability. Depending on their chemical and mineral composition they may also be more duarable than limestones. The decision to use either limestone or sandstone is usually a matter of color preference and local availability.

BRICK AND CLAY UNIT MASONRY

Common clay brick and clay unit pavers are probably among the most readily available and most versatile materials used in landscape construction. Clay masonry units are used in practically every imaginable landscape structure from pools and fountains to paving, steps, and walls.

Clay masonry units are molded from moist clay and then fired in a kiln. The color and hardness of the brick will be determined by the clay material used and the amount of exposure to the direct heat of the kiln. The greater the heat the harder the brick and darker the color. Bricks that are exposed to extremely high temperatures will be burned to the point of warping and cracking; these bricks are called clinkers. Brick that is cured evenly without excessive warping is called hard brick. Other brick, not exposed to sufficient heat to completely cure, is called soft brick.

Soft brick is of little practical use outside because it will not stand traffic or extreme weather conditions, especially freezing. Hard brick is best suited to general applications in the landscape. Clinkers, while usable, are not generally recommended since they are not of uniform size, difficult to lay, and very dark in color.

Like any building material made of natural materials, brick will vary markedly in its structural properties and color. This is particularly true of clay products in general. Color is directly related to the minerals present in the clay used to make the brick. Since these deposits are rarely uniform, the brick will not be precisely uniform in color. This can be a major problem for projects that require large quantities of brick or when it becomes necessary to try to match an existing brick color.

Most clay products are manufactured by small independent plants that service a limited geographic trade area. For this reason, they are usually manufactured to withstand the the local climate and will be available in sizes and shapes to meet local building practices.

Brick Grades

Even though brick will vary according to the clay minerals of a given deposit, the clay products industry does have an industry-wide grading standard for brick used in buildings. These standards are based on the brick's resistance to weathering and hardness. Since most landscape construction is exposed to extreme weathering conditions, the designer should be aware of these grading standards. There are three grades listed by ASTM, for brick: SW, MW, and NW.

Grade SW is recommended for use where a high degree of resistance to frost and freezing action is required. Examples of this are brick used in retaining walls and as paving materials.

Grade MW is used where the brick will be exposed to freezing temperatures but is not likely to be saturated with water. Examples of permissable uses of grade MW are freestanding walls above grade, veneered retaining walls, and well-drained paved surfaces.

Grade NW is a soft brick that should only be used as a backup material that will not come into contact with a moisture-bearing surface. As a general rule, grade NW brick is not satisfactory for landscape construction. The most common application of grade NW brick is in manholes.

Brick Size

Brick dimensions are the least standardized of all common building materials; thus, any discussion of size standards could be misleading. In most trade areas of the country there are two brick sizes available. The most common is the so-called American Standard Brick, or modular brick, which measures 2¼ in × 3¾ in × 8 in, and even this is only approximate. The difference in dimension is largely a function of shrinkage during firing. The other common brick size is the SCR brick which is approximately 2⅛ in × 5½ in × 11½ in. It is intended as a primary structural unit and sized to decrease the labor cost for laying. The SCR brick size is very popular for manufactured concrete brick and is most often seen in regions that do not have natural brick-clay deposits. Figure 7-2 illustrates the two common brick and the other less popular sizes.

Brick Coursing and Terminology

Each horizontal layer of brick is called a course, and each layer of thickness is called a withe. Since brick can be laid in many different patterns, the individual brick is named by the brick face that is exposed. For example, there are two common ways to set a brick in a wall: Laying the brick with the 8-in length horizontal so that the 8 in × 2¼ in face is exposed is called a stretcher. When the brick is set with the 3¾-in face horizontal and the 2¼-in dimension vertical, it is called a header or rolok, (rowlock). Figure 7-2 shows the names associated with each brick position.

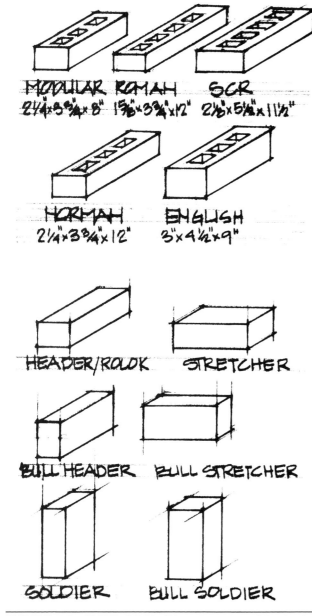

FIGURE 7.2 TYPES OF BRICK AND BRICK POSITIONS

The pattern in which brick is laid, in a wall or paving surface, is called the bond. Some of the more common bond patterns are shown in Figure 7-3.

CONCRETE MASONRY UNITS

Concrete masonry units are manufactured from portland cement, relatively fine aggregates, and sand. Most standard concrete units are rather heavy when compared to clay; however, lightweight units are produced by using very light aggregate materials such as cinders, slag, shale, or vermiculite. The common sizes and shapes of concrete masonry units, CMUs, were shown in Figure 7-1.

Most CMUs have smooth, fine-textured surfaces, and range in color from almost white to very dark gray, In some regions CMUs may be available in buff or eggshell white and other dark earth tones. These block are used as the primary finish of the structure. CMUs are also available with ceramic, glazed surfaces for use as interior or exterior finishes and accent.

The most common unit is the so-called concrete block. It is universally employed as a basic material for structural walls, planters, and pools. The common concrete block is not very attractive in its natural state and will usually be finished with another surfacing material such as stucco, brick, or stone veneer.

A primary disadvantage of all CMUs is that they are very porous, offering little resistance to moisture penetration. Therefore, any CMUs that come into contact

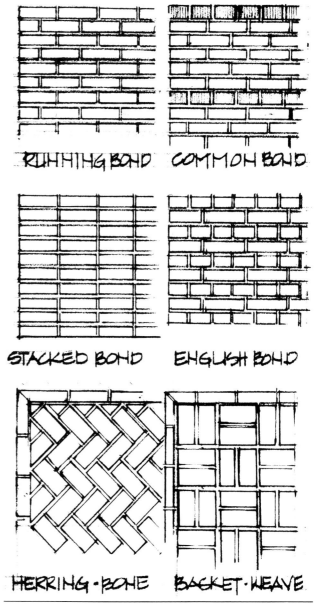

FIGURE 7.3 BRICK BONDS AND PATTERNS

with the ground or are exposed to precipitation must be sealed to prevent moisture penetration. The most common material used for waterproofing concrete masonry units is bituminous cement, asphalt. Exposed surfaces are usually treated with silicone base waterproofing material, or a dense portland cement stucco.

ASPHALT AND BITUMINOUS CONCRETE

Bituminous concrete is a material made from aggregates bound together with bituminous cement and is usually called asphalt or tarmac. The bituminous cement binds the aggregates together to make a concrete-like mass. Since bituminous cements do not cure to a completely solid state, like portland cement, bituminous concretes are considered flexible pavements.

Bituminous cements are water-repellent and frequently used in their raw states as a waterproofing material, as noted earlier; however, they have some distinct disadvantages. Bituminous cements are petroleum-based products manufactured from crude oil and can be dissolved by most petroleum-based solvents like gasoline, oil, or diesel fuel. Therefore, bituminous concretes will usually be damaged by gasoline and oil spills. Asphalts also tend to return to a plastic state when subjected to high temperatures, and heavy traffic loads on the surface can cause the pavement surface to "creep" or "washboard."

Any damage to the surface of an asphalt pavement that allows water to penetrate the road base and will lead to the deterioration of the pavement. The importance of maintaining the waterproof property of asphaltic pavement cannot be overstressed, since any pavement is only as good as the base on which it is placed. Due to their flexible nature, asphaltic pavements will deform to correspond to the shape of the base material. If the surface of the pavement cracks and allows water to reach the base, the base material will become plastic and heavy traffic will destroy the entire pavement. During the winter months, moisture that penetrates the road base will cause frost heave. Frost heave is caused by the growth of ice crystals in the road base and is a common problem in the northern part of the country.

Most bituminous concretes are made by the hot-mix process. Most asphaltic cements must be heated to reach a liquid state so they can be mixed with the aggregates. Then, as the material cools, the asphalt stiffens and forms a concrete-like mass. Other asphaltic cements are manufactured in liquid form that require no additional heat before combining the material with the aggregates. These are called cold-mix asphalts. The primary use of the cold-mix materials is for athletic

court surfaces and as walk surfacing. Cold-mix materials do not have the binding strength of the hot-mix materials and are not suited to pavement surfaces that must carry heavy wheel loads.

Asphalt is still one of the least expensive paving materials available, but it is subject to price fluctuations in the oil market. In periods of high petroleum prices, asphalt may be as expensive as concrete. As a driving surface, asphalt pavements are without a doubt the most desirable. They provide a smooth, quiet driving surface, with very good traction characteristics. Their primary disadvantage is their susceptibility to damage from water penetration of the base and damage from gasoline spills.

Concrete Structures

This section explores the basic details of all concrete structures used in the landscape. The discussion is limited to the generic elements of the details required to prepare basic construction documents. In the course of the discussion some of the regional differences used will be noted, but it will not be possible to touch on all the variations in treatment or material specification.

SLABS AND PAVEMENTS

Bituminous Pavements

The design of bituminous pavements depends on the load to be carried, the native soil condition, and the climate. Light-duty pavements will typically be installed in two layers over a native soil sub-base, while heavier-duty pavements may be laid in as many as five or six layers. The key to a good asphalt pavement begins with the sub-base. This is usually the native soil material of the site, if it can be used. Remember in Chapter 2 it was pointed out that some organic soils and very plastic clays could not be used as a foundation material or for road beds. If peat, muck, or very plastic clays do exist on a site, they will often have to be removed and replaced with a suitable, engineered sub-base material.

A typical treatment of the native soil material on a site involves removing the organic topsoil layer and then scarifying, loosening the surface, the soil to a depth of 6 in to 2 ft and compacting this layer. The amount of compaction of this layer is usually specified to be 95% of optimum density. Optimum density is based on an ideal soil moisture content for a given soil type to reach its optimum compaction density measured by weight. The soil for each site will have different characteristics and the compaction rate must be determined by laboratory testing, using the Standard (ASTM D698, AASHTO T99) or Modified Proctor Density (modified AASHTO) method. The modified AASHTO method is usually specified if the geotechnical report prepared by the soils engineers suggests that T99 will not yield the desired compaction.

Compaction tests are based on soil density (weight), plotted against the percent of moisture, by weight, in the soil. Compaction tests are run on uniform soil samples taken from the building site. Several samples are compacted in the laboratory with different percentages of moisture content, usually between 6% and 16%. The density of the soil, measured by weight, is then plotted against the moisture content of the soil expressed as a percent of the total sample weight. The resulting graph will show the maximum density that can be obtained at a given moisture content. This is then used as the standard for measuring the degree of compaction obtained, for that soil, in the field. The key to obtaining good compaction is moisture content. If too little or too much moisture is present the soil will not reach the required density.

If the native soils of a site are plastic clays that have a high shrink-swell ratio, it is often advisable to treat the subgrade with lime. The lime added to the sub-base combines chemically with the soil to reduce the expansion and contraction properties of the soil. Depending on the soil, lime will usually be added at the rate of 5% to 7% of the soil volume by weight. Application of the lime is usually done at the surface as a dust, or in the form of a liquid slurry, and then incorporated with a rotary tiller. In cases where deep penetration may be necessary to achieve the proper stabilization, the lime may be injected under pressure.

The base of the pavement will usually be an imported material such as gravel, marle, caliche, crushed stone, or shell. Bases can also be prepared by adding portland cement to the native soil to add strength and density. The base and sub-base form the load bearing portion of the pavement. The remaining layer(s) of the section are to waterproof the base and provide a smooth, all-weather surface.

Heavy-duty asphalt pavements are laid in two or more layers. The lower layers are called leveling courses and the top layer is called the wearing surface. The leveling courses are usually very dense, coarse aggregates to add strength to the pavement, and the wearing surface will be made of very fine aggregates to provide a very dense, smooth surface.

Between each layer of an asphaltic pavement there is a layer of bituminous cement called a tack coat. This layer has two purposes: to bind the two layers together and to waterproof the base. Of the two, the waterproofing is the most important.

In regions that experience hard freezes that penetrate the ground below the road base it is common to place a layer of coarse gravel below the road bed and carefully shape the sub-base to keep moisture away from the pavement. This helps limit the possibility of damage to the road from frost heave.

While the recommended thickness of each layer of an asphalt pavement will vary depending on the soil, climate, and load, most light-duty pavements will have a 6-in to 8-in sub-base, a 6-in base, and a 2-in wearing surface. A typical light-duty asphalt pavement is shown in Figure 7-4.

There are two major concerns with any asphalt pavement: the treatment of the edge, and maintanance of the surface. Because asphalt is a pliable material, the edges of the pavement can be damaged easily by traffic and erosion. If there is a chance of frequent traffic crossing the edge of a pavement it is wise to protect that edge with a concrete apron, or mountable curb. The surface of the pavement must also be maintained periodically to keep the pavement surface alive. Continuous traffic over an asphalt surface is the best means of maintenance. The traffic works the pavement surface and keeps it from becoming brittle and cracking. In parking lots the traffic in and out of the parking bays is not usually sufficient to keep the pavement surface from cracking. When cracks do appear they should be sealed, and the entire surface should be treated with a good quality asphaltic sealing material, to keep the pavement from breaking down.

Concrete Slabs and Pavements

Concrete is the most versatile and widely used paving material in the landscape. It can be placed in small areas not easily accessible by large machines, it is

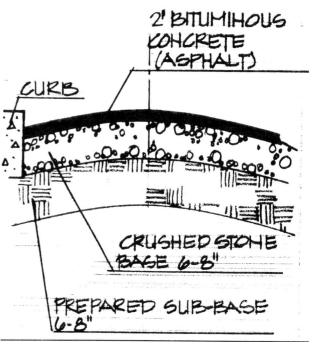

FIGURE 7.4 *LIGHT DUTY ASPHALT PAVEMENT*

durable, and can be finished and textured in a variety of ways. However, concrete does have some limitations that should be considered. Plain concrete has very light surface color that is very reflective. The resulting glare in bright sun can be very uncomfortable and even dangerous, particularly when used for steps. Structurally, concrete has very low tensile strength which makes it very vulnerable to differential soil movement. Very active soils that are not prepared properly can, in a very short period of time, completely destroy a walk or drive. The density of concrete also offers no resiliency, which makes it a very poor selection for surfaces used as athletic courts. Many physicians recommend against playing or running on concrete surfaces.

The detailing of a concrete slab or pavement requires specifying the base treatment, the reinforcing of the concrete, and the finish of the surface.

The preparation of existing soil is just as important to a concrete pavement as it is to asphalt pavement. For most heavy pavement applications the base for concrete should be compacted to 95% of optimum density. For very light-duty concrete pavements, such as walks and light driveways, there may be no need to require special compaction if the soil is well drained and does not have a high shrink-swell ratio.

When clay soils are encountered that have a high shrink-swell ratio, it may be necessary to provide some type of subdrainage at the base of the slab. The objective of the base treatment is to maintain an even soil moisture content under the entire slab.

A final consideration is whether the slab should be moisture proofed. Concrete is a very porous material and soil moisture will be transported upward through the slab. This is no problem on most walks and drives, but if the surface of the slab has to remain dry, or if the surface is to be painted, a plastic moisture barrier should be placed between the sand leveling bed and the natural ground before the concrete is placed.

Concrete slabs on grade are plain concrete and should have steel reinforcing to resist cracking caused by thermal expansion and contraction. The material used for reinforcing is either deformed steel reinforcing bar, (rebar), or welded wire mesh, (wwm).

Rebar is manufactured specifically for use as a concrete reinforcing material. The surface of the bar has numerous surface deformations that help the steel form a bond with the concrete. A good bond between the steel and the concrete is essential for the two materials to work together as a unit. Rebar is plain steel with no surface treatment to prevent rust. Any rust on the surface of the steel will reduce the bond between the steel and the concrete and steel will continue to rust if there is a lot of free moisture moving through the slab. To minimize the contact with moisture, steel is always placed in concrete with a minimum of 2 in of cover over the steel in all directions.

Steel rebar size is given by numbers that correspond to the diameter of the bar in eighths of inches. In other words a #3 bar is ⅜ in, a #4 is ½ in, a #5 is ⅝ in and so on. For most medium- to heavy-duty slabs, #3 or #4 bars are used; #4 bars are used in most spread footings; #3 bars are used as the vertical bars in most unit masonry walls. Larger bars are usually found in structures like pools, heavy-duty footings and piers, or retaining walls.

Welded wire mesh is a smooth steel wire welded together in a 6-in square grid. The rigid grid provides the bond with the concrete rather than using surface deformations. Wire mesh is available in two wire-gauge sizes: 6 ga and 10 ga. The 6-gauge wire has a ³/₁₆-in diameter and the 10-gauge wire has a ⁹/₆₄-in diameter. Wire mesh is most commonly used to reinforce concrete pavements with a 4-in thickness such as walks and light-duty drives.

When determining what type of reinforcing to use and where it should placed in the slab it is important to think about what may happen under the pavement that could cause the surface to crack. There are two types of soil movement that result in surface cracking: end lift, or center lift. In high shrink-swell soils, end lift will occur when excess moisture is allowed to stand at the edge of the slab. The soil at the edge of the slab will expand and lift the entire edge of the slab. Center lift is usually the result of moisture depletion at the edge of the slab caused by vegetation removing large quantities of water. In this case the soil at the edge of the slab shrinks and allows it to drop, Figure 7-5. Since the most visible cracks will result from the center lift condition, steel is usually placed toward the bottom of the slab, if thickness permits.

The amount and type of steel to place in a slab or pavement is a function of the relative mass of the

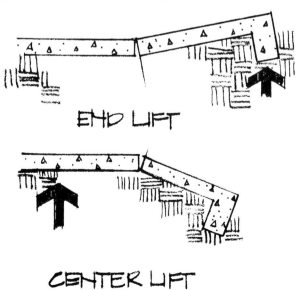

END LIFT

CENTER LIFT

FIGURE 7.5 SLAB CRACKING

TABLE 7.2 SIZE AND AREAS OF COMMON REINFORCING STEEL

No. or Ga.	Diameter in	Area sq in
10 ga.	0.1350	0.014314
6 ga.	0.1920	0.028953
No. 3	0.3570	0.11
No. 4	0.50	0.20
No. 5	0.625	0.31
No. 6	0.750	0.44
No. 7	0.875	0.60
No. 8	1.00	0.79

material, the climate of the area, and the soil. Most standardized building codes require that for thermal reinforcing in plain concrete, the steel should be equal to ¼% (0.0025) of the cross-sectional area of the slab, in both directions. For example, the steel required for a 6-in-thick drive, 16-ft-wide would be found as follows:
The area of the section is:

16 ft × 12 in/ft × 6 in = 1,152 sq in

The steel required is 0.0025 this area or:

1,152 sq in × 0.0025 = 2.88 sq in

Table 7-2 provides the areas of the most common reinforcing materials. Assume that 6 ga wwm is selected as the reinforcing material. There would be a total of 31 6 ga wires in the 16-ft-wide section if a minimum of 2 in is allowed at each edge of the slab, Figure 7-6. Since the area of 6 ga wire is 0.028953 sq in, the total area is:

31 × .028953 sq in = 0.90 sq in

This would only provide about a third of the actual requirement. So, try #3 rebar on 12 in centers, 15 pieces, the area is:

15 × 0.11 sq in = 1.65 sq in

Still insufficient, so try #4 rebar on 12 in centers as follows:

15 × 0.20 sq in = 3.00 sq in

Thus, #4 rebar, spaced 12 in on center in both directions would be the appropriate thermal reinforcing.
In very mild climates, in areas that have sandy well-drained soils, the requirement of 0.0025 of the cross-sectional area is seldom used. This is because the

temperature fluctuations are not so great as to warrant that amount of steel for light-duty applications. In fact, it is not at all uncommon to use no steel at all in 4-in-thick concrete walks.
In general construction it is usual to use 6 × 6 × 10 × 10 wwm in 4 in concrete walks, 6 × 6 × 6 × 6 wwm in 5 in heavy-duty walks and light drives, and reinforcing bar in all 6-in-thick concrete used for street pavements and heavy-duty drives. In any area where the frost line goes deeper than the base of the slab, or where there are expansive soils, the rule of 0.0025 of the cross-sectional area should be applied as a minimum.
Placing of concrete requires the setting of forms that are adjusted to the proper grades, and they assist in the finishing of the surface. After the forms are set and the rough excavation is complete, the forms will be dressed with coarse sand to level the base and ensure that the concrete will be a uniform depth.

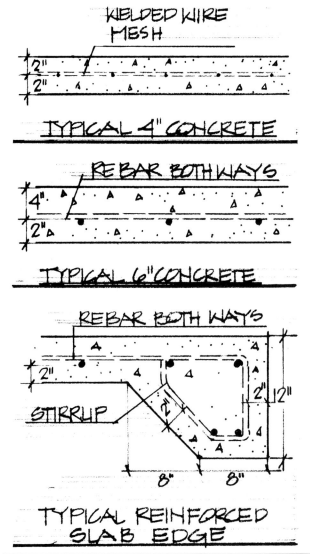

FIGURE 7.6 STEEL PLACEMENT IN CONCRETE SLABS

Before the concrete is placed in the forms, the finished base and the form should be sprayed with water until all surfaces are damp. If the concrete is placed in dry forms, the water will be drawn out of the concrete and it will not cure properly. Concrete cannot be poured when the ground or the forms are frozen. If the mixture freezes, the water is not available to maintain the hydration process and the concrete will not bond.

As the concrete is placed into the forms, it must be carefully worked into all parts of the form so that no voids or air pockets are left. On large pours, mechanical vibrators are used to work the concrete into the forms, but on smaller pours the concrete can be worked into the forms adequately with a shovel or hand tamp. If voids (called honeycombs) do occur, the slab will be weakened and will likely fail in a short time period. Honeycomb conditions can usually be spotted when the forms are first removed from the concrete. If they are present, the concrete should be removed and replaced with new pour.

After the concrete has been placed in the form, it is leveled with a long board called a screed, which is drawn back and forth across the forms. This process levels the concrete in the form. After screeding, the surface will be tamped to drive the coarse aggregates deeper into the surface, and then the surface is smoothed with a mechanical trowel or a float. This step levels the surface again and brings a uniform cement paste to the surface. When this step is completed the concrete is allowed to reach its initial set before final finishing begins.

The most common surface finishes are: the steel trowel finish, wood float finish, and the broom finish. The steel trowel finish is a very smooth, almost slick, surface that is not recommended outside. When a steel trowel surface is wet it is very slippery and is dangerous to vehicles and pedestrians alike. The wood float finish is also quite smooth but is not as slick as the steel trowel surface when it is wet. It is used on covered areas and on some walks because it is much easier to clean. The broom finish is the most common outdoor finish used because it will provide good footing when it is wet, and the textural quality is generally more pleasant.

A wide variety of other decorative finishes are used to achieve the desired surface quality. Some of the more popular finishes are outlined below:

1. **Exposed aggregate:** Exposed aggregate finishes are done in two ways. The aggregate may be exposed by allowing the concrete to reach its initial set, and then, using a stiff broom and water, the grout paste is removed from the surface, exposing the aggregate. This method is only used when the aggregate material in the concrete mix is pleasant. Concretes that use crushed limestone, slag, or cinder as the aggregate will not have an attractive surface.

   The other method of achieving an exposed aggregate finish is by seeding the decorative aggregate material into the surface after the concrete has been screeded and floated. Then after the concrete reaches its initial set, the seeded surface is washed and swept to clean the grout off the aggregate surface.

2. **Sandblasted finishes:** Sandblasting the concrete surface produces a much different looking surface than exposed aggregate. The sandblasting is usually done after the concrete has reached its final set but before the pavement has completely cured. Sandblasting produces a pitted surface that resembles a fine weathered stone or coral. The coarseness of the finish can be controlled by the amount of sandblasting and by how long the concrete is allowed to cure before it is sandblasted.

3. **Rock salt finish:** A rock salt finish is obtained by spreading coarse grained rock salt, like the salt used to make homemade ice cream, on the surface of the concrete as it reaches its initial set. The salt draws off the water around it and leaves a very pitted surface that resembles fossiliferrous limestone or marble. The effect can be quite striking but it must be done by an experienced concrete finisher.

4. **Textured finishes:** There are several patented concrete finishing processes that use special tools to texture concrete to look like almost any kind of material. Some examples of patterns include: quarry or Mexican tile, brick, cobblestone, Belgian block (fish scale), and slate. Each process uses dyes to achieve the desired surface color. When these finishes are applied properly, they are durable and are hard to tell from the real thing from a distance.

5. **Applied finishes:** There are a number of different materials available to apply to the surface of concrete to get different color and textural effects. These finishes are very popular for pool decks and athletic surfaces. The applied finish products are placed on the concrete after it has cured for several days. Most materials go on in a liquid state to form a topping about ⅛ in thick. The surface is then worked with a trowel or squeegy to achieve the desired texture.

6. **Manufactured form liners:** Form liners are available to provide a variety of different textured finishes to cast-in-place concrete walls such as simulated wood grain, vertical or horizontal fluting, and rough brush hammer texturing. Most form liners are made of styrofoam or a lightweight plastic and can only be used one time.

Paving Joints

Concrete pavements use two kinds of joints to control cracking caused by soil movement and thermal expansion and contraction. Expansion joints, Figure 7-7, are placed between separate concrete pours at regular intervals to permit the concrete to expand and contract with changes in temperature. The joints are filled with a resilient material, such as wood or a bituminous impregnated fiberboard, to seal the joint. In regions that have expansive soils, the expansion joints should also be dowled to keep the edges of the adjoining slabs from moving vertically. Even a small change in the vertical relationship of two adjoining panels can cause people to trip and fall.

There are any number of standards for placing of expansion joints depending on which reference is consulted. Most recommendations suggest that 30 ft is the maximum distance between expansion joints. Others use 24 ft as the maximum. Yet there are many cases where expansion joints exceed these maximums with no ill effect. Current thinking seems to favor the notion that the placement of joints should be based on the separation of concrete panels of different mass, since large masses will expand and contract more slowly than smaller masses. Therefore, the joints should be placed to isolate unlike elements and to divide the construction into workable units.

The second type of joint is the control joint, Figure 7-8. The control joint is used to control cracks in the slab. As a rule, concrete laid on the ground is going to crack, simply because heating and cooling is not going to be uniform over the entire surface. The control joint is cut into the surface of the concrete to provide a weak place, similar to the perforations in the paper of your checkbook. As cracks occur they will grow to the control joint and then turn and run with the joint.

The provision of expansion and control joints is essential in any concrete pavement for structural

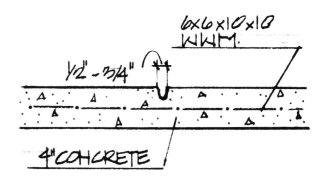

FIGURE 7.8 TYPICAL CONTROL JOINT

reasons, but they should also be considered in their design context as well. The joint pattern in a pavement sets up a visual rhythm and geometry for the site that helps add scale and character to the overall composition. Thus, if the joint pattern is not well thought out or is done in a haphazard manner, it will detract measurably from the overall appearance. Figure 7-9 shows some simple recommendations for the placement of expansion joints and control joints in concrete surface.

UNIT MASONRY PAVEMENT

Masonry pavements provide an interesting and flexible alternative to concrete or asphalt pavements. The use of masonry as a primary paving surface adds color, texture, and scale that is just not available with other materials. The usual drawback to the use of masonry pavements is the cost of installation, which is usually much higher than concrete.

Like any other pavement, a masonry pavement is only as good as its base, so the treatment of the base should be the same as for asphalt or concrete. There are two ways to install masonry units: in a sand leveling bed on grade, or as a veneer surface on concrete. In the first case, the units are set directly on sand with no mortar joint, so the units essetially form a flexible pavement. In this case the base should be prepared in much the same manner as for asphalt. When they are laid as a veneer on a slab, the base is provided by the concrete. The depth and detail of the pavement base depends on the use of the pavement. If masonry units are used for a street or drive they must be set on a well-prepared road bed. For light-duty walks and pavements in nonplastic soils that will have no vehicular traffic, the native soil is usually compacted with a hand or mechanical tamp and then leveled with sand. The installation of masonry units on sand is shown in Figure 7-10.

If a site has very active soils, masonry pavements should be laid on a concrete base. Since the joints of the units laid on grade are not sealed, moisture will pene-

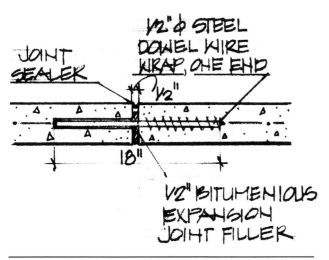

FIGURE 7.7 TYPICAL EXPANSION JOINT

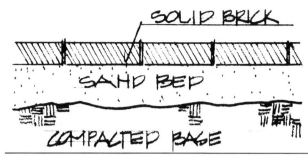

FIGURE 7.10   MASONRY UNITS ON SAND

trate the base and the resulting soil movement will usually destroy the surface in a very short time. Figure 7-11 shows the installation of unit pavers on a slab. Notice the detail of the expansion joint. This method is employed to keep the joints from being visible at the surface.

There is a variety of masonry paving materials on the market that adds a great deal to the appearance of a project. Most of this new generation of materials are made of concrete with an integral color in the mix. They are produced in interlocking modules so that traffic cannot dislodge them easily, which is a problem with rectangular brick. There are also some materials designed with holes in the interlocking units to allow grass to grow and cover the surface. These materials have not proved successful for heavily used parking surfaces, and most of them are not pleasant to walk on, particularly for women with narrow heels. They are useful as an erosion stabilization material. Figure 7-12 shows an example of these materials.

Masonry pavements offer one of the richest palletes of color, texture, and quality of scale available to the designer, but their modular qualities must be recognized in the development of the design details. Brick, for example, are rectangular units and fit best into a design geometry based on a 4-in grid. If angles

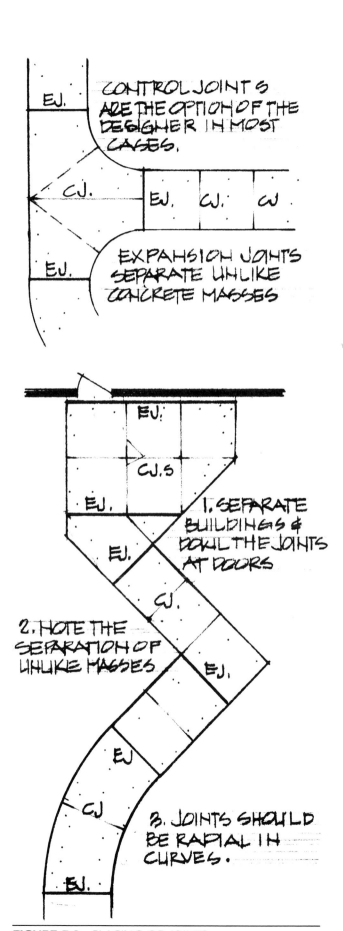

FIGURE 7.9   PLACING OF JOINTS

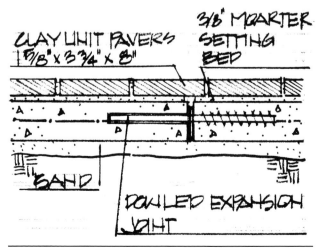

FIGURE 7.11   CLAY PAVERS ON CONCRETE

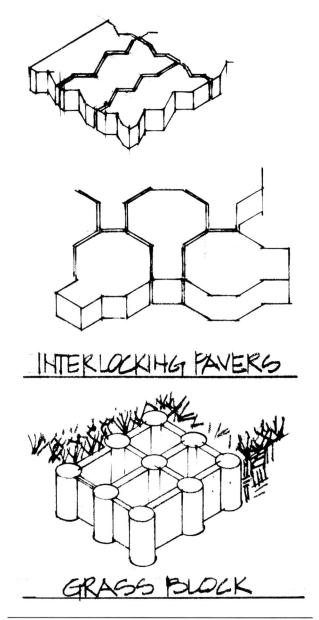

FIGURE 7.12 PAVING SYSTEMS

UNIT MASONRY WALLS

Walls have two parts: the footing and the wall stem. The footing is almost always made of concrete, and transfers the load of the wall to the ground. The stem is the exposed portion of the wall. Chapter 4 explains the mechanics of wall stability. This discussion looks only at the structural details of the wall.

Footings

There are two types of footing used for wall support: the standard grade beam and the post-and-beam foundation. The grade beam, so called because it is essentially a continuous beam set at or just below grade. This is the most common and least expensive method of supporting a wall. The depth of the beam is usually between 8 in and 12 in depending on the weight of the wall and the temperature extremes of the site. For most masonry walls in warm climates up to 6 ft in height, the 8 in thickness is sufficient. In cold climates the footing must be set with the bottom surface below the frost line and should be 12 in thick. The 12-in thickness is also advised in clay soils.

The width of the footing for freestanding, nonload-bearing walls is by convention twice the width of the wall. So the footing for a typical 8-in thick brick wall should be 16 in wide. The typical grade beam footing is illustrated in Figure 7-13.

introduced into the design geometry it will require cutting and fitting of the brick. While this is not altogether wrong, it can lead to some very small fitted pieces at joints and edges that look out of place. These small pieces are also easily dislodged by freezing weather, or from heavy traffic at the edge of the joint. As with wood, if angles are introduced into brick work they should be 45 degrees to be sure that the joints can be matched. If the design geometry uses 30-degree or 60-degree angles there are other paving modules available that will fit these geometries very well. The key to a clean looking pavement is to select a unit that is made to fit the design geometry.

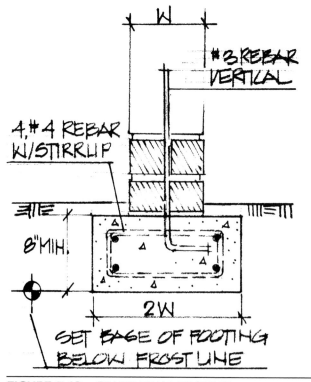

FIGURE 7.13 GRADE BEAM FOOTING

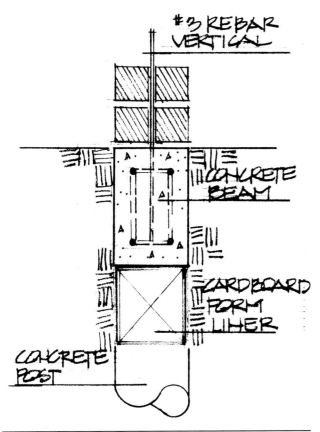

FIGURE 7.14 POST AND BEAM FOOTING

The post-and-beam footing shown in Figure 7-14 is employed when expansive soils are encountered. If a wall were placed on a grade beam footing in these soil conditions, the soil pressure acting on the wall would soon crack the footing and the cracks would be transferred upward through the wall. The cracks would weaken the wall and in time it will begin to fall apart. Walls will also tilt at odd angles as the soil movement takes place and can overturn.

The post-and-beam footing is a structural beam resting on posts drilled past the active zone of the soil. The depth of this zone varies but is usually on the order of 3 to 5 ft. When the beam is formed, a wax-coated cardboard box is placed in the bottom of the form and left in place. This provides a void under the beam so that the soil is never in contact with the bottom of the beam. Special care must be used in backfilling around the base of the wall to be sure that no soil is allowed to get under the beam, and the surface should be graded to carry water away from the foundation of the wall.

The steel reinforcing placed in a standard grade beam should meet the minimum requirements for thermal reinforcement. For a standard 12-in-deep by 16-in-wide footing this is usually four #4 rebars placed as shown in Figure 7-13. In addition to the horizontal

steel placed in the footing, vertical bars should be placed on 30- to 36-in centers along the entire footing. These vertical bars are used to tie the stem of the wall to the footing. In most cases, #3 bars are used.

Masonry Wall Details

There are five different details used for unit masonry walls. These are shown in Figure 7-15. The pier and panel wall is a single withe of masonry held between piers. These walls require the use of double-faced masonry units, and should only be used with a pier and

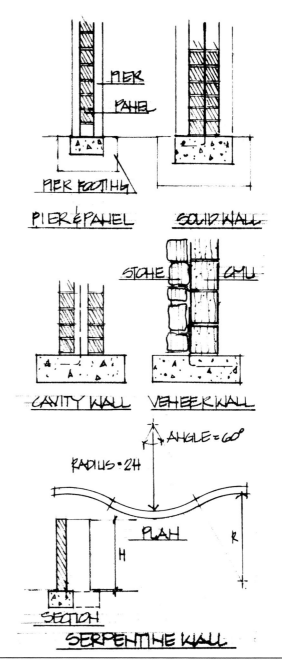

FIGURE 7.15 TYPES OF MASONRY WALLS

beam foundation. The single withe panel is not as stiff as double withe panels and any structural movement could cause the wall to fail.

A serpentine wall may be a double withe panel or a single withe panel if piers are provided. If a two withe panel is used, the wall does not require piers since the curve of the wall provides the necessary stability to resist lateral loads. The rules for determining the radius of the curved faces and the distance between the panel faces is shown below the sketch of the wall in Figure 7-15.

The solid masonry wall is the most common of all details used for exterior walls. It does require more material than either the pier and panel wall or the serpentine wall with a single withe, but it is a heavier more durable wall. It also lends itself to more intricate detailing of the wall face since the brick can be set in many different positions to generate a variety of patterns. The solid wall only requires the use of single face brick, which is more readily available and less expensive.

The cavity wall is most often used to give the visual effect of mass and to hide the piers. The piers are still required at regular intervals (see Chapter 5), but they can be laid in such a way that they cannot be detected. The cavity wall also provides even more flexibility in the placement of units in the face of the wall. Units can be set to achieve deeply shadowed reveals or to even incorporate other materials, such as cut stone, as a part of the wall detail.

The veneered wall is most often built using CMUs as the backing material with a facing material of rough or cut stone. It can also be used to provide two different surface finishes, such as stucco on one face and brick on the other.

There are several important decisions that have to be made in the preparation of a masonry wall detail: vertical and horizontal reinforcing, pier spacing and detail, cap and end details, brick pattern and bond, and the joint thickness and type.

Just like concrete, masonry structures need steel reinforcing to tie them together and help protect the structure from tensile stress caused by temperature fluctuations. Reinforcing is placed in the wall panel in both the vertical and horizontal planes. The vertical steel is usually #3 rebar spaced on 30- to 36-inch centers. In a single withe panel the rebar has to be extended through the brick cores, and in other walls it is extended through the space between the withes. The vertical steel is tied to the steel bars left extending from the top of the footing. The general rule is that the overlap of the bars is equal to 20 bar diameters. This is about 7½ in for #3 bars.

Horizontal reinforcement for masonry walls is provided by welded wire mesh laid in the mortar joints. This material is made of 6-ga wire sized to fit the width of the wall. Usually, reinforcing is placed in every fifth

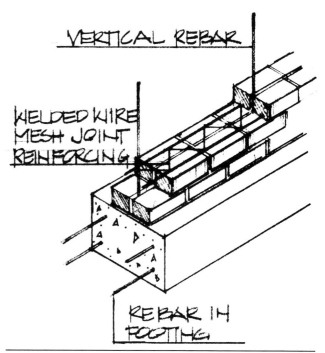

FIGURE 7.16 MASONRY WALL REINFORCING

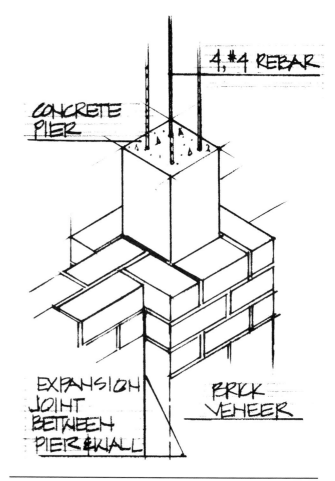

FIGURE 7.17 TYPICAL MASONRY WALL PIER

or sixth mortar joint. Another method of stiffening the wall panel is the use of roloks. These are headers set to tie the two withes of the wall together. Reinforcing for masonry panels is shown in Figure 7-16.

The spacing of piers can be determined using the formula in Chapter 5. The piers used to reinforce masonry walls are usually made of concrete and poured at the same time as the footing. As a rule, the finished dimension of the pier will be twice the width of the wall. In the case of a standard double withe wall, the piers have a finished dimension of 16 in × 16 in. The concrete portion of the pier is 8 in × 8 in, then it is veneered with brick. The pier is reinforced with a minimum of four #4 rebars, and should extend to a depth of twice the depth of the footing. The most common pier detail is shown in Figure 7-17.

Cap and end, or joint details should always be clearly thought out, and detailed for any wall. A

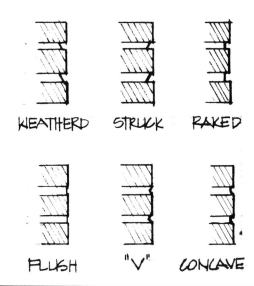

FIGURE 7.19 MORTAR JOINTS

majority of the brick and masonry units are manufactured with holes or open cores to reduce the weight of the unit. While this is logical, it also presents a problem when it becomes necessary to use the units to finish the top and ends of the wall. In many cases, manufacturers will produce special units or solid brick to simplify the detailing of these problem spots, but it is up to the designer to clearly show how ends joints and wall caps are to be done. Figure 7-18 shows some common methods for handling cap and end details of masonry walls.

Masonry walls offer many opportunities to create variety and add a special touch of detail to a project. Figure 7-3 illustrated some of the more popular bond patterns that can be used with brick and masonry units, and these are only a few of the possibilities. Students are encouraged to use the modular nature of masonry materials and explore the many possible combinations of units.

The final consideration of the wall detail is the choice of type and thickness of the mortar joint. Figure 7-19 shows some of the most common types of mortar joints used in masonry walls. Struck joints and raked joints are not recommended in climates that experience frequent freezing temperatures because water may be held in the joint. Brick is usually laid with a ⅜-in mortar joint, block and cut stone will usually be laid with a ½-in joint and rough stone will be laid with a ¾-in joint or more, depending on the roughness of the stone.

Beginning students are encouraged to observe masonry details in the walls and buildings that they see every day. Pay particular attention to how the materials are laid, the patterns that are used and the finish details at joints, caps and corners. You will be surprised at the variety and richness of detail that exists from structure to structure.

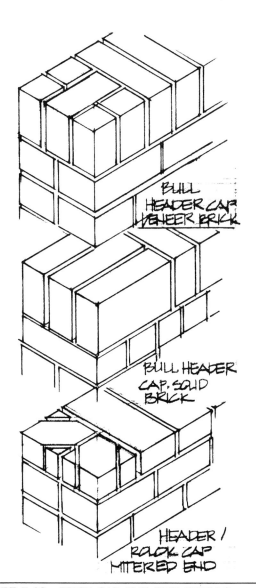

FIGURE 7.18 BRICK CAP AND END DETAILS

IRRIGATION
DESIGN

Introduction

Irrigation systems are essential to the successful maintenance of most landscape development projects. The irrigation system is necessary to provide supplemental water to the landscape development in periods of low rainfall. The need for an irrigation system is easily understandable in a desert environment, but often overlooked in areas of high annual rainfall. Even in these regions, irrigation is still desirable. A good example of this need is the Pacific northwest around Seattle, Washington. Seattle receives an average annual rainfall of about 94 in and has a plant water demand of only about 25 in per year. At first glance, this appears to be in excess of almost four times what the plant material of the region would require, but there is a problem. The peak plant water demand of 20 in occurs between the months of May and September, and during this period the Seattle area only gets about 8 in of rainfall. Thus, in one of the wettest areas of the entire continental United States there is still a rainfall deficit of 12 in during the spring and summer growing months, which means supplemental water is necessary.

The decision about what type of irrigation system is appropriate for a project is a matter of understanding the climate of the region, the characteristics of the soil, a knowledge of the plant materials used on the project, and the cost of installation and maintenance. The purpose of this chapter is to look at all these considerations and provide the student with the background information necessary to make sound decisions about the design and installation of irrigation systems for a variety of different problems. The emphasis throughout the chapter will be on principles rather than specific techniques or equipment. Irrigation technol-

ogy is still developing at a space-age pace, and any effort to point to specific examples would quickly become dated.

The chapter is covers four main topics. The first portion of the chapter covers the design considerations of an irrigation system related to plant materials and soil. This foundation information is the essence of making good decisions about the design of an irrigation system. The second portion of the chapter is an overview of the various components of an irrigation system. The third portion is a discussion of basic pressure hydraulics as it relates to the design of an irrigation system. The final portion leads the student through the design of a simple, small-scale irrigation system.

Agronomic Principles of Irrigation

Design decisions about an irrigation system must be made with a knowledge of the soil condition and the plant materials that will require the supplemental water. The soil at the site acts as a reservoir that stores water and the plants are the primary consumers.

SOIL CHARACTERISTICS

Soil has three properties that need to be taken into account in the design of an irrigation system: infiltration (percolation) rate, field capacity, and available moisture.

The infiltration rate of a soil is related directly to the particle sizes and relative proportion of sand, silt, and clay in the soil, the amount of moisture present in the soil, and the slope of the surface. Infiltration rates are expressed in inches per hour, which is the number of vertical inches of water that will be absorbed by a soil in one hour. In general, coarse-grained soils (sands) have the highest infiltration rates, while dense clay soils have the lowest infiltration rates. The amount of moisture in the soil also has an influence on the infiltration rate. A dry soil has a relatively high initial infiltration rate that will decrease continuously as the soil approaches saturation. Saturation is when the pore space of the soil is completely filled with water. Slope also affects infiltration since it is easier for water to move along the surface rather than down into the soil profile. In general the steeper the slope the lower the infiltration rate. Table 8-1 gives the maximum infiltration rates that can be expected for various soil and slope conditions. The values in this table are conservative and can be used as a design guide in lieu of more accurate data.

The infiltration rate of a soil is important in making decisions about how fast water can be applied to a site. If the application rate of the irrigation system exceeds the infiltration rate, the additional water will be lost as runoff. This is not to be taken lightly since water costs for a large system can be very high if it is using the municipal water supply, and this is poor management of a very valuable resource.

The field capacity of a soil is the amount of water the soil will hold after gravity has drained off any excess. Water is held in the soil profile by the attraction of the soil particles to the water. The water is held in a film that surrounds each soil particle. Fine-particle soils, like silts and clays, have a much greater surface area in proportion to the volume and have correspondingly higher field capacities. The relationship between field capacity and irrigation practice is related to the actual volume of water applied at one time. Soils with a high field capacity can hold greater volumes; therefore, more water can be applied at one time. High field capacity is not a measure of how much water is available for plant use, however. A clay soil, for example, may have a very high field capacity but only a small portion

TABLE 8.2 *AVAILABLE MOISTURE FOR VARIOUS SOIL TEXTURES IN INCHES*

Soil Texture	Available Moisture In Inches Per Foot of Depth
Sand	0.5–1.0
Sandy Loam	1.0–1.5
Silt Loam	1.5–2.5
Silty Clay Loam	2.0–2.5
Clay	2.5

These numbers assume that the soil profile, equal to the root depth of the plant, is at field capacity.

of that water may be available to the plant due to the strong attraction of the clay particles to the water.

The amount of water available to the plant for use is called available moisture and is expressed as a percentage of the the soil's field capacity. In most soils, only 5-10% of the soil moisture is actually available for plant use. Therefore, the available moisture is a critical consideration in deciding how often to water. For example, if plant demand was 1 in of water per week, and the soil had a field capacity of 2 in and an available moisture value of 0.15, then only 0.3 in of water would be available when the soil was at field capacity. A water demand of 1 in per week is equal to 0.14 in per day, which means that the plants will remove the available moisture in a little more than two days. Therefore, it will be necessary to irrigate at least every third day.

Table 8-2 gives the approximate available moisture for various soil textures.

PLANT CHARACTERISTICS

Plants have three characteristics that must be taken into account when considering an irrigation system: depth of root zone, evapotranspiration (E.T.) in peak growing periods, and the water requirement for good appearance. The first two properties are reasonably well documented for turf grasses, while the third still requires close observation. Unfortunately there is little known about the BT rate of woody ornamentals.

The rooting depth of a plant is important to determine how deep the soil profile will have to be watered. Most ornamental turf grasses have root depths of 9-18 in. This characteristic is not only dependent on the species but also on the cultural practice. Turf grasses will have shallower root systems in response to the mowing height. Most ornamental woody shrubs will have root depths between 18 in and 36 in. An assumed depth of 24 in is usually satisfactory for most irrigation applications. Small ornamental trees will have a root zone of about 36 in and large trees will root to depths in excess of 48 in.

TABLE 8.1 *MAXIMUM INFILTRATION RATES FOR SLOPE AND SOIL TYPE IN INCHES PER HOUR*

Slope	Sandy Soil	Medium Soil Volume in in/hr	Heavy Soil
0–5%	0.75	0.50	0.25
6–8%	0.60	0.40	0.20
9–12%	0.55	0.30	0.17
13–20%	0.35	0.20	0.10
over 20%	0.25	0.15	0.07

Source: Adapted from *Sprinkler Irrigation Handbook,* Crawford Reid, Editor, Rainbird, Glendora, California, 1961.

TABLE 8.3 SURFACE INCHES OF WATER REQUIRED TO WET THE SOIL TO A DESIRED DEPTH

Depth of Wetted Profile, Inches	Surface Depth Required by Soil Type		
	Sand	Silt	Clay
6	0.4	0.9	1.3
12	0.9	1.8	2.6
18	1.3	2.8	4.0
24	1.7	3.5	5.1
30	2.0	4.2	6.3
36	2.4	4.9	7.3

As mentioned, root zone has an impact on how much water needs to be supplied to wet the soil profile to the appropriate depth. Table 8-3 gives the number of inches of water required at the surface to wet the soil to a given depth for various soil textures. Since the relationships are essentially linear, it is possible to interpolate the values for conditions that fall between the values given in the table.

Moisture is lost from the soil profile in two ways. First there is normal evaporation that responds to the air movement and temperature, the amount of solar radiation, and the relative humidity of the the atmosphere. The second loss is due to plant transpiration, water taken up and used by the plant and given off through the foliage. These two activities are referred to as evapotranspiraton, and gives a single measure of evaporation and plant transpiration. Much of the early research done in irrigation used the soil moisture measure as the determinant of when and how much to water. Current thinking now seems to favor the evapotranspiration measure as a more accurate means of making these determinations. The logic behind this recommendation is that soil moisture measurements can only determine the relative moisture content of the soil at a given point, and makes the assumption that the soil moisture will be uniform, which is not necessarily true. Evapotranspiration measures, however, are made based on the amount of moisture being released into the atmosphere over a broad area. Logically then, this method should better estimate the amount of water that needs to be replaced each day. Application of the evapotranspiration measure requires the installation of sophisticated measuring instruments, and this is being done in some of the irrigated croplands of the west. Average evapotranspiration rates for various ornamental materials are given in Table 8-4. These are evapotranspiration rates for the peak of the growing months.

WATER FOR IRRIGATION

Water quality should also be considered in the design of an irrigation system, in relation to the soil and plant materials. A water supply, regardless of whether it is groundwater or surface water, may have harmful minerals or elements in the water that can damage the irrigation equipment and or the plant material. One of the most common of all water impurities is salt. Water with salt contents larger than 500 parts per million is generally not recommended for use as irrigation water, depending on the character of the soil. High salt content waters can be used if the soil will allow the salt buildup to be leached out of the root zone by periodic heavy irrigation. Salt contents of as high as 800-900 parts per million can be used if the plants are resistant to salt burn. There are soils that will not respond to this management technique and cannot be irrigated with high saline content water.

Other water-borne impurities that will cause problems are gas and oil, heavy metals, iron, sulfur, and calcium carbonate. Any of these minerals, if present in sufficient quantity, will cause damage to turf grasses, discoloration of foliage, paved surfaces and walls, corrosion of metal parts in the irrigation system, and the clogging of sprinkler nozzles. The designer needs to be aware of these possibilities and select equipment that will not be affected by the water quality.

The key to a good irrigation system design is in giving appropriate consideration to the soil, plant material, and the water resource. The soil determines the frequency of watering based on the infiltration rate and the available moisture. The volume of water required is determined by the plant material, based on the evapotranspiration rate. Water, in turn, will affect the kinds of material used in the irrigation system and, to some degree, the cultural practices required in the maintenance of the landscape.

Irrigation Equipment

An irrigation system is composed of three subsystems: the water supply system, the delivery system, and the distribution system. Each of these subsystems needs to be considered in the overall design.

TABLE 8.4 EVAPOTRANSPIRATION RATES FOR SELECTED MATERIALS AND CLIMATES, IN INCHES PER DAY

Plant Type	Peak Evapotranspiration Rate	
	Temperate Zone	Warm Zones
Turf Grasses	0.15	0.25
Annuals	0.15	0.20
Small Woody Shrubs	0.15	0.20
Large Woody Shrubs	0.20	0.25
Small Trees	0.20	0.30
Large Trees	0.25	0.35

TABLE 8.5 *MAXIMUM RECOMMENDED CAPACITIES OF STANDARD WATER METERS*

Meter Size Inches	Available Volume in Gallons per Minute (gpm)
⅝	20
¾	30
1	50
1½	100
2	160
3	300
4	500

WATER SUPPLY

Three types of water supply system are employed in irrigation design: public water supply, wells, and reservoirs.

Municipal Water Supply

The most frequently used water supply is the public water distribution system that also supplies potable drinking water. Access to this system usually requires making a direct tap to a water main and installing a new water meter. Tapping an existing public water supply will require a special permit from the water utility and they will most often provide the tap and meter. Tapping an existing water line, that is under pressure, requires special tools and most utilities require that the tap be made by a master plumber.

In most cities it is wise to install a separate meter for the irrigation system since sewer service charges are based on the volume of water used. A meter dedicated to irrigation will not have a sewer service charge.

The main considerations for the designer, when using the city water supply, are the volume of water available and the pressure. The water volume available will be determined by the size of the water main providing the service and the size of the meter. Table 8-5 gives the maximum recommended volumes available through standard size water meters. The volumes shown will be affected to some degree by the size of the supply main, but are reasonable values. Most residential water services will be either a ⅝- or ¾-in meter, commercial and institutional services will usually be 1-in services or larger depending on the number of square feet in the building.

The pressure available at a water meter can vary over a wide range and depends on all kinds of system variables. The only way to be sure of the pressure is to have it checked in the field. It is best to check the pressure more than once and at different times of the day. In most cases, the nighttime pressure will be significantly higher since it is a lower water use period.

If a low pressure condition is found, it may become necessary to add a booster pump to the irrigation system to make it operate efficiently. The use of pumps will be discussed later in this section.

Wells

One of the most desirable water supplies for an irrigation system is a well, if good quality water is available in sufficient quantity. In parts of the country where groundwater can be found at a reasonable depth, about 500 ft or less, a well is worth considering since it will usually pay for itself by eliminating the need to purchase water from the municipal utility.

The equipment necessary to use a well includes a pump and a pressurization system. There is a variety of pumps available for use on irrigation systems. The choice of which type to use depends on the depth of the well, the volume of water required by the irrigation system, and quality of the water. For shallow wells and systems that have low volume and pressure requirements, the best pump is a self-priming pump, sometimes called a jet pump. For deeper wells and higher gallonage and pressure requirements, submersible pumps are the best solution. Submersible pumps fit entirely into the well casing and the only thing that is visible at the surface is the electrical wire that services the pump. For very deep wells and systems with high gallonage and pressure demands, it will probably be necessary to use a turbine pump. A turbine pump also is set in the well casing but the drive motor is mounted over the well casing at the surface. The motor drives the pump with a long shaft that extends the entire depth of the well. When a turbine pump is to be used, it is essential that the well casing be driven vertical with no deviations. The kinds of pumps used for irrigation are shown in Figure 8-1.

When a well is used, it is usually desirable to have some means of maintaining pressure on the system at all times, for such tasks as washing down paved surfaces and normal hand watering chores. Pressure can be generated in the system in two ways. Small systems can use a device called a pressure cell. The pressure cell works on the same principle as a water balloon. Water is put into an elastic membrane that mechanically places the water under pressure. Pressure cells are small and can be used singly or in groups, depending on the need. They will generally be successful until the demand is greater than 30 gpm.

At flow rates greater than 30 gpm, pressurization is usually accomplished with a hydropneumatic pressure tank. These systems use air to generate the pressure. When water, which is not compressable, is forced into a tank full of air, the air is compressed and exerts a corresponding pressure on the water. Pressure cells and hydropneumatic tanks are shown in Figure 8-2.

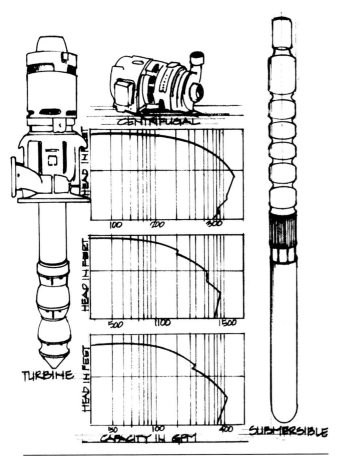

FIGURE 8.1 IRRIGATION PUMPS

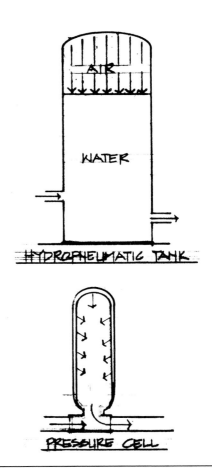

FIGURE 8.2 PRESSURE SYSTEMS

Information about the design and sizing of specific pumps, pressure cells, and hydropneumatic tanks can be obtained from any large plumbing supply house or directly from the manufacturers. The literature they provide is sufficient to match the equipment to the pressure and water demand requirements of the system. They can also provide technical assistance to detail more complicated pumping and pressurization systems.

Reservoirs

Surface water impoundments are also a frequently used option for irrigation water supplies. They may be natural or man-made lakes or even concrete vaults used to store stormwater or even effluent water from wastewater treatment plants. Regardless of the water source, the designer has to be sure that the water quality and the water quantity is sufficient to support the system being designed.

Moving the water from a reservoir into the irrigation system also requires a pump and a pressurization system. The means of providing the pressurization are the same as for a well. The pumps used, however, are usually centrifugal type pumps. Centrifugal pumps are the least expensive pumps for the volume and pressure

generated but they have very limited suction capacity. In general, a centrifugal pump cannot lift water over 6 to 10 ft. In most applications, it is best to try to keep the pump very close to the elevation of the water supply. This will usually keep the pump from losing its prime. The danger in allowing a centrifugal pump to lose its prime is that the pump depends on the water for cooling and lubrication. If prime is lost and the pump operates dry for an extended period, it may damage the pump motor.

Centrifugal pumps are also used to add pressure to systems using city water that have very low pressure. They are simply placed between the water supply and the system and are operated any time the increased pressure is required. Figure 8-1 shows a typical centrifugal pump.

THE DELIVERY SYSTEM

The delivery system is the network of channels and conduits with the attendant controls that move the water from the water supply to the water distribution components of the irrigation system. Today, most sprinkler or drip irrigation systems use a network of pipe, with remotely controlled valves to regulate and direct the flow of water in the system. The remote control valves are operated by a clock-operated device called a controller.

Irrigation Pipe and Fittings

The pipe used in irrigation systems will be either polyvinyl chloride (PVC) pipe or polyethylene tubing. For special applications, copper, galvanized steel, or cast iron pipe may be required, but today these are exceptions rather than the rule. The situations requiring the use of metal pipe may include pipe under pavements that carry heavy wheel loads, pipe in planters on roof decks or buildings, or long runs of pipe that must remain under very high pressure and back flow prevention device mountings.

PVC pipe is identified by the grade and type of plastic compound used to manufacture the pipe and by the working strength of the pipe or the wall thickness. All pipe must be continuously marked with the grade and class, or schedule. The grade of a PVC compound is either 1120, or 1220. The first digit is the grade of PVC compound, (grade 1). The second digit is the type of compound. Type 1 compound is for normal applications, type 2 compound is for high heat and caustic water applications. The last two digits (20) are the ultimate strength rating of the plastic compound times 100. In other words, the pipe has an ultimate strength of 2,000 lbs/sq in. The class rating of a pipe is the recommended working pressure of the pipe. The most common classes are: 160, 200, and 315. In most cases, class 160 pipe is used for residential and light commercial systems. Class 200 and 315 is used for larger systems with higher operating pressures.

Schedule-rated pipe is heavy wall pipe. The actual wall thickness varies with the diameter of the pipe. There are two types of schedule-rated pipe, schedule 40 and schedule 80. Schedule 80 has the heaviest wall. Heavy wall pipe is usually used where additional pipe stiffness is desired, or where the pipe may be subject to damage from excavation or from sharp materials like crushed stone in a road bed. Heavier wall pipe can also be threaded to make connections to other threaded fittings, such as pumps, valves, and irrigation heads.

The PVC compounds used in most plastic pipe are very sensitive to ultraviolet radiation and, if exposed to direct sun for extended periods, the pipe will become brittle and break. It will also expand dramatically as temperatures increase. For this reason, common PVC should not be used above ground. There are some new plastic compounds on the market that no longer have these problems and the pipe is especially marked for above ground, full sun application.

The fittings used to join lengths of pipe together are either slip type fittings or threaded fittings. Slip joint fittings are either solvent welded or heat welded joints.

It is important when using slip type joints that the PVC compound of the fittings be the same as that of the pipe to ensure a proper bond. The common types of pipe fittings are shown in Figure 8-3.

Two important types of fitting are the dresser coupling and the union. Both of these fittings allow the pipe to be broken without cutting the pipe. The union is a threaded joint, and the dresser coupling simply slips onto the ends of the pipe and uses O-rings to seal the joint. The dresser coupling is a very effective means of isolating the pipe in the system from vibration since the rubber O-rings in the fitting will damp out the vibration.

Valves

Valves are used to control the flow of water in the system, from the supply to the individual heads, and to drain or maintain water in the pipe. The control valves may be operated manually or by remote control. Large, manually operated valves are usually placed in the system so that all or part of the system can be shut down for maintenance or repair while the remaining parts of the system can still be operated. Remote control valves are used to turn the water on and off at specific points in the system.

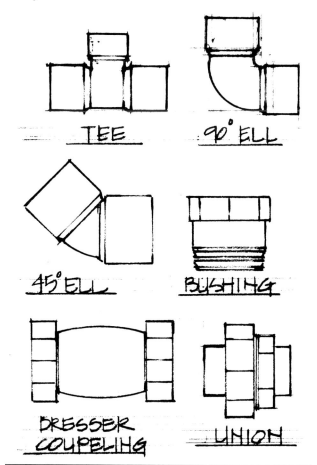

FIGURE 8.3 *COMMON PIPE FITTINGS*

The most common of the manually operated valves are the gate valve and the globe valve. The globe valve was once preferred in dirty water since the washer and seat that form the seal could be replaced, and this was not possible in a gate valve. Now there are gate valves being manufactured with replaceable seals and they are now the most common of all the manual valves. They are preferred since the flow through the valve is in line with the pipe so there is very little pressure loss through the valve.

The third type of manual valve is the so-called quick coupling valve. This valve was originally developed and used for manually operated irrigation systems. Sprinkler heads were attached to the key; then, when the key was inserted into the valve, the water came on. Manual, quick coupling systems are seldom used for irrigation now because their operation is labor-intensive; however, the quick coupling valve is very useful to provide outlets for hand watering and washdown operations. They are mounted in boxes below grade and, since they require a special key to operate, they are less subject to vandalism than a standard hose bibb. These valves are shown in Figure 8-4.

Remote control valves are operated either hydraulically or electrically. Hydraulically operated valves are controlled by a small tube that supplies water to the valve. When the water supply to the valve is on, the valve is closed. If the pressure on the tube is released, the valve will open. Since a positive water supply is required to keep the valve closed, the hydraulic valve is called a normally open valve. The electrically operated valve uses a solenoid to turn the valve on and off. When the power to the valve is on the solonoid retracts and allows the pressure to drop in the bonnet of the valve. The water pressure in the line forces the seal open and the water is on. When the power is off, the solenoid closes and the pressure in the valve bonnet equalizes, and the valve closes. The electrically operated valves are therefore called normally closed valves.

Hydraulically controlled valves are generally less expensive than electrically controlled valves of the same size, and they are useful on large systems where long runs of wire are not practical or where dirty water could clog the small openings in a solenoid operated electric valve. Hydraulic valves can also be an asset where frequent electrical storms are a problem. Very large turf heads often incorporate a hydraulic valve in the head so that each head of the system can be operated independently. This scheme reduces the size of pipe required in the system, resulting in a substantial reduction in initial cost.

Electrically operated valves are used on the majority of residential and large commercial projects. The normally closed feature of the valve makes it attractive from a maintenance viewpoint because the valve remains closed if the wire to the valve is cut. Likewise,

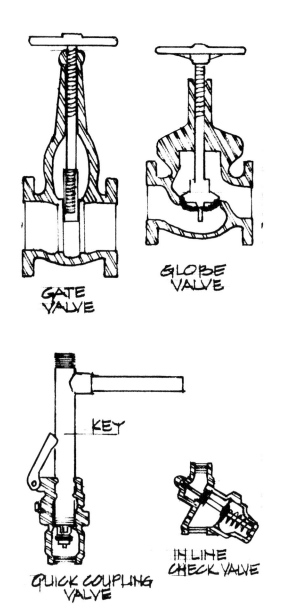

FIGURE 8.4 SPECIALIZED VALVES

the cut in an electrical line is usually easier to find and repair than a leak in a hydraulic tube.

Remote control valves are available with plastic or brass bodies, with or without pressure regulation devices and other special features. The improvements in plastic compounds have made plastic body valves very attractive for normal applications because they are much less expensive than brass valves. In most cases, plastic valves are a good choice for sizes up to 3 in and water pressures to 100 psi. For larger valves and higher water pressures, brass body valves are probably a better choice. Two typical remote control valves are shown in Figure 8-5.

There are a number of special valves used in irrigation systems to either maintain the direction of flow in a

RAIN BIRD

150-PE

150-PE-PRS

FIGURE 8.5 ELECTRIC REMOTE CONTROL VALVES

system, or allow the system to drain or not drain, and to regulate the pressure on the system. Some of the more common specialized valves are noted here along with their application.

1. **Check valves:** Check valves come in a variety of shapes and sizes for various situations. The purpose of a check valve is to keep water from draining out of the system by gravity flow when the operating pressure is taken off the system, see Figure 8-4. Some of the most common applications of the check valve are use at the base of a pump suction line to keep the pump from losing its prime, and at the base of low-lying irrigation heads to keep the water in a zone from draining

out through the head when the pressure is off. If a zone is allowed to drain through a low head, it will usually result in a very wet zone around the head, which can damage the turf-especially if there is any traffic over the area. It can also present a problem when pressure is put back on the system. Water entering an empty pipe will pick up speed and begin compressing the air in front of the water. When the water and the compressed air reach the end of the pipe it results in a very high pressure called surge pressure, which can break the pipe and blow the head off the end of the line. It can also result in another condition called water hammer. Water hammer results when the pressure from the compressed air in front of the water becomes greater than the water pressure. When this happens, the water is forced backward in the pipe until the water pressure is again greater than the pressure of the compressed air. Under the right conditions, these cycles will continue until the air is released from the line or the water volume and pressure becomes sufficient to drive the water from the line. Water hammer actually sounds like someone is beating on the pipe with a hammer and it can cause damage to the system if the condition is allowed to persist.

2. **Drain Valves:** Drain valves are used to purge water from the lines. They can be either automatic or manually operated. They are most often used to drain water from pumps and lines that are subjected to freezing temperatures.

3. **Pressure Regulating Valves:** Pressure regulating valves are most frequently used to reduce pressure on parts of the irrigation system. Small turf and shrub heads and drip irrigation emitters operate at much lower pressures than most large turf heads. Therefore, pressure regulating valves are used to reduce the pressure on these zones in the system. They also have application on multistage pump systems. The actual pressure generated by a pump at any one time is related directly to the flow. At low flows the pressure generated by the pump will be higher, dropping as the volume increases. Quite often it is necessary to install a pressure regulating valve downstream of the pump to reduce these differences and keep the pressure on the system constant.

4. **Master Valves:** A master valve is actually just a remote controlled valve placed at the water supply that feeds the entire system. In some cities, the master valve is required to keep pressure off the irrigation system when it is not operating. This regulation is usually an effort to help protect the potable water supply from contamination, and prevent the waste of water that can result if there is a break in an irrigation main.

Other Fittings

Other important devices that are employed on irrigation systems include backflow prevention devices and strainers. There are three types of backflow prevention used to protect potable water supplies from potential contamination by an irrigation system. Since an irrigation system is usually set at a higher elevation than a potable water main, gravity can cause contaminated water in the irrigation system to flow backward into the potable water supply if the pressure on that line drops.

Since the risk of contaminating a potable water supply is relatively high, most municipal building codes require some type of backflow prevention device on an irrigation system. Unfortunately, there is no uniform opinion regarding the type of backflow prevention device that is best, so it is advisable to contact the local building department before specifying a piece of equipment.

The principles of the most common backflow preventers are outlined below.

1. **The Atmospheric Vacuum Breaker and Pressure Vacuum Breaker:** These devices are the most commonly recognized by the standard plumbing codes. They are operated by atmospheric pressure and remain closed as long as there is no water demand on the system. These backflow prevention devices must be mounted above grade at least 6 in higher than the highest head in the

RAIN BIRD

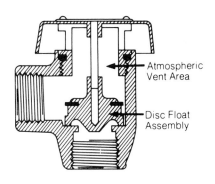

RAIN BIRD AVB Series
Atmospheric Vacuum Breaker

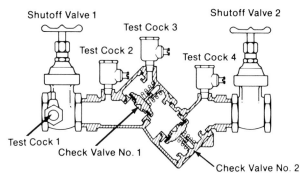

RAIN BIRD DCA Series
Double Check Valve Assembly

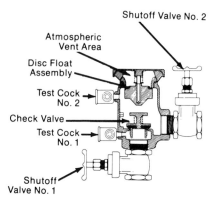

RAIN BIRD PVB Series
Pressure Vacuum Breaker

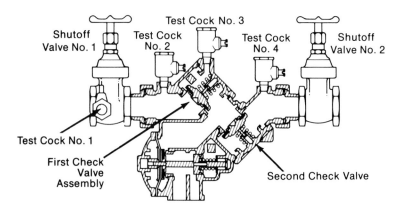

RAIN BIRD RPA Series
Reduced Pressure Principle Backflow Preventer

FIGURE 8.6 BACKFLOW PREVENTERS

irrigation system to prevent backflow. In cases where the water supply is at the low point of the site, the vacuum breaker may have to be mounted a substantial height above grade. This is often unsightly and equally expensive. The standard atmospheric vacuum breaker is used on lines that are not under constant pressure, and the pressure vacuum breaker is used on lines that are under constant pressure.

2. **Reduced Pressure Backflow Preventers:** These devices are generally recognized as the best form of backflow prevention. Reduced pressure devices can be installed in a box below the ground as long as the body of the device is exposed to the atmosphere and there is positive drainage away from the sump; i.e., a connection to a storm sewer or wastewater line. These devices work on the the reduced pressure principle. If the pressure drops on the inlet side of the device it closes, and the water flowing from the system is drained into a sump under the backflow preventer.

3. **Double Check Valves:** The double check valve operates on the same principle as any check valve, which is simply a flap inside the valve that only allows the water to flow in one direction. Any back pressure on the line will cause the flap to close and water cannot move. The double check valve is not an approved backflow device in most standardized plumbing codes. It has, however, been accepted as a backflow prevention device in many parts of the country. The only way to be sure is to check with the local building authorities to see which of these devices is approved for use. The three types of backflow preventers are shown in Figure 8-6.

Strainers are used on irrigation systems to filter out solid particles in the water supply that can clog the nozzles of sprinkler heads or drip irrigation emitters. Large particles are usually filtered out at the water supply using a standard "Y" strainer. Very fine particles that will damage drip emitters are filtered out with small in-line filters placed at each individual zone of the system. Strainers are absolutely essential on drip irrigation systems and should always be mounted to allow easy access because they must be serviced regularly.

CONTROLLERS

The controller is the brain of the automated irrigation system. There are two kinds of controller in general use: the electromechanical controller and the solid state

controller. The electromechanical controller has a gear-driven mechanical operating system to turn the irrigation valves on and off. These are now considered older technology, but they have some very nice features that still make them popular for applications like golf courses and large parks and campuses. One feature is that a loss of power does not cause the controller to forget the program. There are also some hybrid controllers that combine the best features of the electromechanical controllers and solid state controllers.

The solid state controllers are a result of advances in silicon technology. They are essentially programmable microcomputers with solid state clocks. The early models were not as versatile as the electromechanical controllers, but this is changing rapidly with continued developments in technology. As noted earlier, the one problem with the solid state controllers is that they

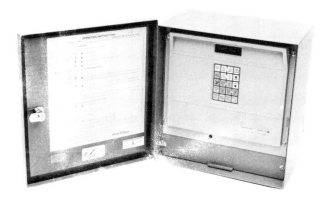

FIGURE 8.7 *IRRIGATION CONTROLLERS*

RAIN BIRD

1802

1804

1806

Pop-Up Spray Sprinklers
Nozzles and Shrub Adapters

1812

Full Circle Bubbler

**Full or Part Circle Mini-Paw®
Impact Rotor Pop-Up
Sprinklers**

Shrub Adapter

TORO
Excellence in Irrigation®

Shrub   **Lawn**   **High-Pop**

Gear Driven Multiple Nozzle Sprinkler

FIGURE 8.8 IRRIGATION HEADS

forget the program if there is a power failure. Some controllers do have backup batteries but these are only good for short-duration power failures and the battery will need to be replaced periodically. Two types of controllers are shown in Figure 8-7.

The next step in controller technology and water management will be the introduction of the micro-computer as a means of programming the controllers' functions. These computers will be linked to weather information gathering stations and will be able to inter-pret the data and program the controllers for each set of events. They will be able to replace water based on evapotranspiration rates, turn the system off during wet periods, and automatically initiate syringe cycles to control surface temperatures and remove dew. Most of the major irrigation companies are already marketing this type of technology.

THE WATER DISTRIBUTION SYSTEM

The water distribution system is composed of the sprinkler heads, drip emitters, and other devices used to distribute irrigation water to the plant materials. There is such a variety of equipment available for water distribution that it would not be possible to cover all the proprietary types and features of the equipment on the market. The discussion here will be limited to the more generic types of equipment that are used for ornamen-tal landscape development.

Sprinkler Irrigation Heads

Sprinkler heads will either be a fixed, spray-pattern type head or a rotary head. The head will either be fixed or set in a pop-up body.

Fixed irrigation heads, heads that do not pop up, are normally used only in shrub beds or to provide supplemental water to trees. All other heads are usually pop-up type heads. A pop-up head is a nozzle mounted on a pipe, called a riser, that will pop-up above the surface when watering and then retract into the body when the water is turned off.

A spray head, or fixed-pattern irrigation head, is one that distributes water in a fixed sheet of spray over a predetermined pattern. The common patterns are full circle, half circle, quarter circle, third circle, and three-quarter circle. Other special patterns are available such as strip heads, for watering very narrow rectangular areas, and square pattern heads. Most manufacturers provide these nozzle patterns for fixed shrub heads and for pop-up bodies with 4-in, 6-in, 12-in, and 18-in riser. The longer risers are used in shrub and ground cover beds. The fixed pattern spray heads are now available from some manufacturers with matched precipitation rates. In other words, regardless of the spray pattern,

each head will apply the same amount of equivalent precipitation.

Spray heads are most often used for small turf areas and for shrub and ground cover plantings. Depending on the nozzle, they have an average radius of between 12 ft and 15 ft, and some of them can be adjusted to reduce the radius. The major disadvantages of the the spray head is that they almost always have relatively high precipitation rates and the spray pattern is much affected by wind. Some manufacturers offer a line of stream spray nozzles for their spray heads that help reduce the effect of wind on the spray pattern, but these are not recommended for turf application.

A variation of the spray head is the bubbler head. The bubbler heads are used to gradually soak an area rather than spray it. Bubblers are most often used to water annual beds where the impact of spray could damage the flowers or to provide supplemental water to trees or other large plants. Very low gallonage bubblers are now available that offer a very attractive alternative to the more temperamental drip irrigation emitters.

Rotary irrigation heads are most often either gear driven or impact driven. The gear driven rotary head uses water flow to drive a gear box in the head that causes the nozzle of the head to rotate. The impact driven head uses a spring-loaded arm that oscillates when it is contacted by the water from the spray nozzle, and centrifugal force of the oscillations causes the head to rotate. Rotary heads have one or more nozzles that deliver water in streams. This characteristic sometimes allows them to cover larger areas and they are some-what less affected by wind. Rotary heads are available in both fixed or pop-up bodies, and are most often used to cover large turf areas. The one problem with the large rotary heads is that very few of the heads are available with matched precipitation rates. Most manufacturers do provide a variety of nozzles that will allow the designer to adjust the relative precipitation rate of each head to meet different conditions, but the nozzles must be selected carefully. Figure 8-8 illustrates some typical sprinkler irrigation heads.

Drip Irrigation Emitters

Drip emitters, as the name suggests, apply water at very low rates to the root zone of the plant. To demonstrate the contrast in application rates, standard sprinkler heads measure their delivery rates in gallons per minute, while drip emitters measure their delivery rates in gallons per hour. Some typical drip irrigation emit-ters are shown in Figure 8-9.

In addition to the standard drip emitters, many manufacturers also offer a line of very small spray heads that cover areas almost as large as standard fixed spray heads but at very low gallonage. These so called micro-spray heads are much more water efficient than

Single Outlet Pressure Compensating Emitters

Mirco-Bird Spray Jet   **Pressure Regulator**

Y-Filters

FIGURE 8.9   *DRIP IRRIGATION EQUIPMENT*

the standard spray head, but they are subject to clogging and wind distortion. Continued advances in microspray technology may provide the solution to some of the problems of drip irrigation for ornamental applications.

Basic Irrigation Hydraulics

Hydraulic design of an irrigation system depends on the delivery of specific volumes of water to the irrigation heads and emitters at a predetermined operating pressure. Since the water in an irrigation system is under pressure, the hydraulic principles that govern

flow are different from those that control flow in open channels.

PRESSURE

Pressure is the resistance to flow in an irrigation system. Flow is generated by gravity, pumping, air pressure, or a pressure cell. Gravity is used to generate flow on most large water utility systems by means of an elevated water storage tank. The gravity pressure generated by a water tank is equal to the elevation of water above a given point on the ground. The actual pressure can be expressed as either feet of head, or in pounds per square inch. One foot of head is equivalent to 0.433 lbs/sq in. If pressure is given in feet of head it is the pressure that would result from a column of water of the same height. For example, if a pump has a pressure rating of 200 ft hd, the equivalent pressure in psi is 200 ft hd × 0.433 ft hd/psi = 86.60 psi. The other pressure generating devices were explained earlier.

When pressure is discussed in relation to an irrigation system it is important to distinguish between static pressure, dynamic pressure, and relative operating pressure. Static pressure is a measurement of pressure taken at a specific point in the system when there is no water flow. Static pressure measures are usually given for water pressure in a water main at a water meter, or the pressure delivered at the discharge side of a pump. Dynamic pressure is a measure of pressure at a designated point in an irrigation line at a specified delivery rate. As water begins to move in a line, the friction between the wall of the pipe and the water will cause an energy loss and a corresponding drop in pressure. The longer the run of pipe the greater the decrease in the dynamic pressure. Since dynamic pressure is related to flow and distance, the pressure is different at every point in the irrigation system.

Operating pressure is the optimum pressure required for irrigation equipment to perform at the level given by the manufacturer. Most heads have a wide operating pressure range, usually 30 to 40 psi, but the performance of the head will be different at each pressure level. In order to keep the head performance reasonably matched, manufacturers recommend that the pressure difference between the first operating head on a line and the last head be a maximum of 10%. Thus, if the pressure delivered to the first head on the line is 30 psi, the minimum acceptable pressure at the last head on the line is 27 psi.

VELOCITY

Water velocity in a pressure system is an important concern since it is related to the potential energy in the system. Water traveling at high velocities in a pipe can cause scour at the joints and, under certain extreme conditions, actually damage the pipe and other equipment on the system. In general, most manufacturers recommend that velocities be kept under 5 ft per second to be safe. Velocity can be found by:

$$V = 0.408 \frac{Q}{D^2}$$

Where:

V = velocity in ft/sec
Q = gallons per minute
D = the diameter of the pipe in inches

PRESSURE LOSS

The amount of pressure lost in a system is dependent on the pipe size, the pipe material, and the volume of water being moved in the pipe. The formula used to determine the pressure loss in a a closed system is the Hazen and Williams model:

$$h_f* = 0.2083 \left(\frac{100}{c}\right)^{1.852} \frac{Q^{1.85}}{d^{4.866}}$$

h_f* = friction loss in ft hd
q = water flow in gpm
d = inside pipe diameter
c = the friction coefficient of the pipe
*Multiply by 0.433 for psi loss per 100 ft of pipe.

Regular use of the Hazen and Willams model and the formula for velocity would be cumbersome, at best. So, to simplify the process of finding pressure loss and velocity in pipe, a set of tables has been developed that gives the pressure loss for pipe runs from 5 ft to 100 ft, and the velocity for selected flows. There is a table for each different pipe material since the flow characteristics are different for each. The table included at the end

of this chapter is for PVC 1120-1220 Class 160 pipe. This table will be used for all the examples in this chapter. A complete set of these tables can be obtained, free, from most of the major irrigation pipe or equipment manufacturers. The formulas cited here are the basis for the preparation of the tables.

Pressure Loss Computations

Proper design of an irrigation system must account for the pressure loss in all of its parts. Every time water passes through a meter, a valve, a fitting, or a run of pipe, there will be a pressure loss. The design of the system must account for all of these pressure losses. Accounting for these losses is usually accomplished in two stages. The first stage accounts for the pressure loss in the delivery system, from the water supply to the valve that controls the individual irrigation zone. The second stage accounts for the pressure loss between the first and last head of a zone. Remember, there should be no more than a 10% pressure loss between the first and last head.

PRESSURE LOSS IN THE DELIVERY SYSTEM

The amount of pressure lost in the delivery system depends on the piping strategy used. There are three ways that the delivery system can be piped: an inline system, a dual source system, or a loop system. These strategies are illustrated in Figure 8-10. The inline strategy is simply a single main that distributes water to demand points along its entire length. With this system there is a constant pressure decrease equal to the distance from the water source. When an inline strategy is used to deliver water to an irrigation system, the pipe usually has to be quite large to minimize the pressure lost in the line.

The dual source and loop systems are strategies that equalize the pressure loss in the distribution system by providing two paths for the water to travel from the source to the demand point. In either the dual source system or the loop system, the pressure at any demand point on the system will be equal. This has a distinct design advantage because the pressure delivered to each valve of an irrigation system will be the same regardless of its distance from the water supply. To demonstrate how this works, consider the diagrams in Figure 8-11. The top diagram shows two 1½-in pipes each carrying 20 gpm to the same demand point 300 ft from the water supply. If we assume that a flow of 20 gpm will lose 0.7 psi for each 100 ft of pipe the pressure loss in either line is:

300 ft × 0.7 psi/100 ft =
3.0 × 0.7 = 2.10 psi

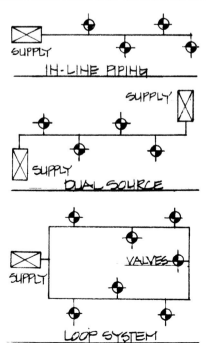

FIGURE 8.10 *DELIVERY SYSTEM PIPING*

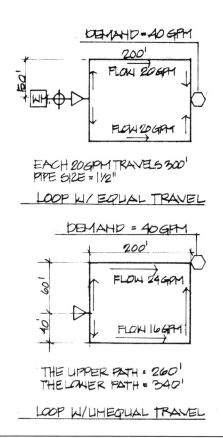

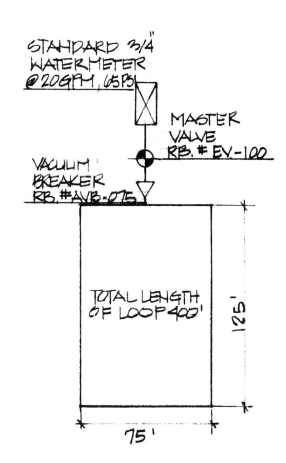

FIGURE 8.11 PRESSURE LOSS IN LOOPS

If the static pressure at the water supply was 90 psi the 40 gpm are delivered to the demand point at:

90 psi − 2.10 psi = 87.90 psi.

Now, to illustrate the pressure equalizing effect of a loop system, move the demand point so the paths that the water will travel to the demand point are not equal, as shown in the bottom diagram of Figure 8-11. In this situation, more water will flow through the shorter pipe and the balance of the volume will travel the longer route as shown. Now find the pressure loss for 24 gpm traveling 260 ft in a 1½-in line as follows:

The pressure loss for 24 gpm in a 1½-in pipe is 0.81 psi/100 ft.

260 ft × 0.81 psi/100 ft =
2.6 × 0.81 = 2.11 psi

The pressure loss for 16 gpm flowing in a 1½-in pipe is 0.62 psi/100 ft.

340 ft × 0.62 psi/100 ft
3.4 × 0.62 = 2.11 psi

Again the pressure loss is equal, and the 40 gpm are delivered to the demand point at the same pressure as in the first example. This principle applies regardless of the position of the demand point on the loop system.

Valve Pressure Loss (PSI)

Flow (GPM)	EV-100 EV-100F
5	3.0
10	3.0
15	3.5
20	3.5
25	4.0
30	4.7

Pressure Loss*

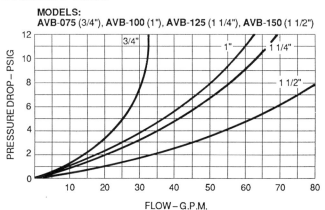

FIGURE 8.12 PRESSURE LOSS IN THE DELIVERY SYSTEM

For most situations, the loop system is by far the most efficient water delivery strategy and there is very little difference in cost of installation or materials, primarily because the pipe size for a loop system is smaller. But on linear irrigation systems like highway rights-of-way, the inline delivery strategey may be the more practical solution.

Estimating Pressure Loss in the Delivery System

To illustrate the procedure for computing pressure loss in the water delivery system, consider the diagram in Figure 8-12. The pressure losses that have to be taken into account are the water meter, the master valve, the vacuum breaker, and the loop itself. The pressure at the water meter is assumed to be 65 psi. The other information that is necessary to find the accumulated pressure loss is the volume of flow, the length of the loop and actual size and flow characteristics of the master valve, the water meter and the vacuum breaker. These data are obtained from the equipment manufacturer's specifications. The pressure loss through the water meter can be estimated from Table 8-6.

The delivery rate for the system was set at 20 gpm. This is the maximum amount of water that will be allowed at any single valve on the system. This is purely a design decision. Greater or lesser volumes can be used so long as the demand does not exceed the capacity of the water supply. The pressure loss for the delivery system is summarized as follows:

Component	Pressure loss (psi)
¾ in water meter @20 gpm	6.5
Master valve, Rainbird EV 100-F @20 gpm	3.5
Vacuum breaker, Rainbird AVB 075 @20 gpm	3.0
Total pressure loss	13.0

The pressure in the loop is found by simply taking half the length of the loop and half the total water demand and finding the equivalent pressure loss as follows:

The total length of the loop in Figure 8-12 is 400 ft, half the length is 200 ft. The maximum water demand is 20 gpm; half of 20 gpm is 10 gpm. The pressure loss for 10 gpm flowing in a ¾-in pipe is 4.3 psi per 100 ft and the flow velocity is 4.7 ft/sec, which is below the maximum of 5 ft/sec. The total pressure loss for a ¾-in loop is:

200 ft $\times$ 4.3 psi/100 ft =
2.0 $\times$ 4.3 psi = 8.6 psi

Thus, the total loss for the delivery system will be:

Equipment loss	13.00 psi
Loop loss	8.60 psi
	21.60 psi

TABLE 8.6 *PRESSURE LOSS THROUGH WATER METERS*

Flow gpm	Meter Size				
	⅝	¾	1	1½	2
15	8.3	3.6	1.2		
16	9.4	4.1	1.4	0.4	
17	10.7	4.6	1.6	0.5	
18	12.0	5.2	1.8	0.6	
19	13.4	5.8	2.0	0.7	
20	15.0	6.5	2.2	0.8	
22		7.9	2.8	1.0	
24		9.5	3.4	1.2	
26		11.2	4.0	1.4	
28		13.0	4.6	1.6	
30		15.0	5.3	1.8	0.7
32			6.0	2.1	0.8
34			6.9	2.4	0.9
36			7.8	2.7	1.0
38			8.7	3.0	1.2
40			9.6	3.3	1.3
42			10.6	3.6	1.4
44			11.7	3.9	1.5
46			12.8	4.2	1.6
48			13.9	4.5	1.7
50			15.0	4.9	1.9
55				6.0	2.1
60				7.2	2.7
65				8.3	3.2
70				9.8	3.7
75				11.3	4.3
80				12.8	4.9
90				16.1	6.2
100				20.0	7.8

*The pressure losses and flow rates are for water meters dedicated to irrigation use only. If the meter is also serving a building, water use from the meter should be limited to approximately 50% of the meter's optimum flow capacity.

The pressure delivered to each valve on the loop would be:

Static pressure at the meter	65.00	psi
Less delivery system loss	−21.60	psi
	43.40	psi

So far, no consideration has been given to the pressure loss caused by pipe fittings. Each fitting placed in the pipe system will cause some additional pressure loss because of turbulence that occurs when water moves over an uneven surface or changes direction. An effort to estimate the pressure loss at each fitting in the system is not really possible in most cases because it is difficult to prepare a drawing that is dimensionally accurate. For this reason, it is customary to make an approximate allowance for pressure loss in the fittings equal to 10% of the loss computed for the pipe, water meter, vacuum breaker, and other major fittings. For this example, the allowance for pressure loss in fittings would be:

fittings. For this example, the allowance for pressure loss in fittings would be:

$$0.10 \times 21.60 \text{ psi} = 2.16 \text{ psi}$$

Subtracting the additional 2.16 psi from the 43.40 psi estimate gives a final delivery pressure of 41.24 psi. For most small systems this is quite adequate. If the static pressure at the water meter had been 10 to 15 psi lower it would have been advisable to use a larger size pipe for the loop.

Estimating Pressure Loss in Irrigation Zones

Once the pressure loss is accumulated for the water delivery system the pressure that is delivered to the valves that control each zone in the system is known. The next step is to size the pipe in each of the irrigation zones and check the pressure loss to be sure that the pressure delivered to each head is within its operating range, and that the pressure difference between the first head and the last head is not more than 10%. This procedure is followed for each zone of the irrigation system. There are five steps to sizing the pipe and checking the pressure loss in an irrigation zone:

1. Determine the operating pressure of the heads in the zone. This decision is based on the irrigation equipment manufacturers' data and the pressure available at the valve.
2. Find the total water demand for the zone. This is done by accumulating the water demand in gpm for each of the irrigation heads in the zone.
3. Size the pipe in the zone, working from the last heads of the zone to the first head, accumulating the pressure loss for each pipe run.
4. Check the total pressure loss to be sure that the pressure loss between the first and last head on the system is within the allowable 10% limit.
5. Select and size the valve to supply the zone and size the final run of pipe from the valve to the first head.

To illustrate the application of this procedure consider the typical irrigation zone in Figure 8-13. For the example, it is assumed that the available pressure and volume at the valve is the same as the values used in the previous example. The volume was 20 gpm and the estimated delivery pressure was 41.24 psi. These values are noted in the figure.

The heads used in the example are Rainbird 1800 series pop-ups. The appropriate manufacturers' data is shown as an inset in the figure. Since the pressure available at the valve is 41.24 psi, the performance data for an operating pressure of 30 psi will be used. The total water demand for the seven half-circle heads and two full-circle heads, based on the 30 psi operating pressure

is 20.35 gpm, see Figure 8-13. Note that the volume demand is slightly higher (20.35 gpm), than the design volume of 20 gpm used in the previous example. The additional 0.35 gpm is not of sufficient magnitude to cause any problem.

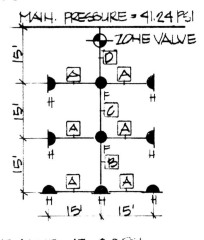

DEMAND AT 30 PSI

7 - 1/2 @ 1.85 GPM EA.   12.95 GPM
2 - F @ 3.70 GPM EA.   7.40 GPM
TOTAL DEMAND = 20.35 GPM

RAIN BIRD

15 Series				Standard 30° Trajectory	
Nozzle	PSI	Radius	GPM	Precip.■	Precip.
15F	15	11	2.60	2.07	2.39
	20	12	3,00	2.01	2.32
	25	14	3.30	1.62	1.87
	30	15	3.70	1.58	1.83
15TQ	15	11	1.95	2.07	2.39
	20	12	2.25	2.01	2.32
	25	14	2.48	1.62	1.87
	30	15	2.78	1.58	1.83
15TT	15	11	1.74	2.07	2.39
	20	12	2.01	2.01	2.32
	25	14	2.21	1.62	1.87
	30	15	2.48	1.58	1.83
15H	15	11	1.30	2.07	2.39
	20	12	1.50	2.01	2.32
	25	14	1.65	1.62	1.87
	30	15	1.85	1.58	1.83
15T	15	11	0.87	2.07	2.39
	20	12	1.00	2.01	2.32
	25	14	1.10	1.62	1.87
	30	15	1.23	1.58	1.83
15Q	15	11	0.65	2.07	2.39
	20	12	0.75	2.01	2.32
	25	14	0.83	1.62	1.87
	30	15	0.93	1.58	1.83

1804

FIGURE 8.13 *PRESSURE LOSS IN IRRIGATION ZONES*

The head spacing in the example is 15 ft, so each run of pipe between the heads is 15 ft, as noted. The next step is to establish a trial pipe size for each length of pipe, beginning with the last heads on the line, working back to the valve. For this initial example, the sizing of each segment will be explained in detail.

For reference, each pipe run that carries a different volume of water has been assigned a different letter. If a pipe carries the same volume of water as any other pipe in the system, it has been assigned the same letter. The pipe sizing begins with "A."

A. All of the pipes designated by letter A carry a volume of 1.85 gpm, because they service a single half-circle head. This is a low volume and the appropriate pipe size would be a ½-in pipe, since it is the smallest size pipe available for this type of work. The pressure loss for a ½-in pipe carrying 1.85 gpm (use the value for 2 gpm) is:

Pressure loss from the table at the end of the chapter for 2 gpm in a ½-in pipe is 0.74 psi/100 ft. The pressure loss for 15 ft of pipe is:

.15 (100 ft) × 0.74 psi/100 ft = .11 psi

Thus, all pipes designated A would be ½-in pipe and have a pressure loss of .11 psi.

B. Pipe run B carries the water that goes to the last three heads on the line, which are half-circle heads using 1.85 gpm each. The total volume carried by pipe run B is:

3 × 1.85 gpm = 5.55 gpm (use 6 gpm)

In the pressure loss table at the end of the chapter, note that 6 gpm in a ½-in pipe is approaching a velocity of 5 ft/sec, but is still not over the 5 ft/sec limit so ½-in pipe

would be safe. The pressure loss for a 15 ft run of pipe at the assumed 6 gpm is:

6 gpm flowing in a ½-in pipe loses 5.76 psi/100 ft, thus,

.15 (100 ft) × 5.76 psi/100 ft = .86 psi

C. Pipe run C carries the water for all the heads downstream which are: five half-circle heads at 1.85 gpm and one full-circle head at 3.70 gpm. Thus, the total gallonage in run C is:

$$\begin{array}{r} 5 \times 1.85 \text{ gpm} = 9.25 \text{ gpm} \\ +1 \times 3.70 \text{ gpm} = \underline{3.70 \text{ gpm}} \\ 12.95 \text{ gpm (use 13 gpm)} \end{array}$$

In the table, note that there is no value given for 13 gpm, and that the velocity for a ¾-in pipe at 12 gpm is greater than 5 ft/sec. This means that a 1-in pipe will be required and the value for the pressure loss per 100 ft of pipe will have to be interpolated, as follows:

The pressure loss for flows of 12 gpm and 14 gpm through a 1-in pipe are respectively: 1.78 psi and 2.36 psi. The difference is:

$$\begin{array}{r} 2.36 \text{ psi} \\ -\underline{1.78 \text{ psi}} \\ 0.58 \text{ psi} \end{array}$$

0.58 psi ÷ 2 = .29 psi

$$\begin{array}{r} 1.78 \text{ psi} \\ +\underline{0.29 \text{ psi}} \\ 2.07 \text{ psi/100 ft} \end{array}$$

The pressure loss for pipe run C is:

.15 (100 ft) × 2.07 psi/100 ft = .31 psi

The pressure loss between the first and last head on the line is represented by the accumulated pressure loss in pipe runs A, B, and C. The pipe sizes and the accumulated pressure loss for the appropriate runs are shown in Figure 8-14. The first head on the line is the full-circle head at the end of pipe run D. The last head on the line is represented by either of the half-circle heads at the end of pipe runs designated A that lie downstream of pipe run B. The cumulative pressure loss, equal to 1.28 psi, is shown in tabular form in the same figure. Since the operating pressure selected was 30 psi, the permissible loss would be 10% of 30 psi, or 3 psi. Thus, the 1.28 psi loss is within acceptable limits and no portion of the zone exceeds a velocity of 5 ft/sec.

To complete the design of the zone, the final pipe run, D, has to be sized and then the valve to operate the zone can be selected and sized.

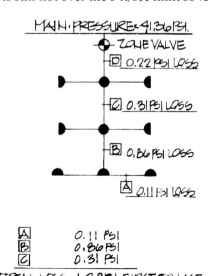

FIGURE 8.14 PRESSURE LOSS FIRST TO LAST HEAD

D. Pipe run D is also 15 ft long and carries the full 20.35 gpm, (assume 21 gpm) for all the heads of the zone. Again, there is no value for 21 gpm in the table, so a value will have to be interpolated, and based on a velocity of less than 5 ft/sec the pipe size should be 1¼ in. Interpolate the pressure loss per 100 ft as follows:

The pressure loss for 20 gpm and 22 gpm flowing in a 1¼-in pipe are, respectively: 1.36 psi and 1.62 psi.

$$
\begin{array}{r}
1.62 \text{ psi} \\
-1.36 \text{ psi} \\
\hline
0.26 \text{ psi}
\end{array}
$$

$$0.26 \text{ psi} \div 2 = 0.13 \text{ psi}$$

$$
\begin{array}{r}
1.36 \text{ psi} \\
+0.13 \text{ psi} \\
\hline
1.49 \text{ psi}/100 \text{ ft}
\end{array}
$$

The pressure loss for the final run of pipe D is:

$$.15 \ (100 \text{ ft}) \times 1.49 \text{ psi}/100 \text{ ft} = 0.22 \text{ psi}$$

The final step is to select and size the valve to service the zone. For the example, a Rainbird PE-PRS series valve will be used, and the pressure loss data for these valves is shown in Figure 8-15. The PE-PRS is available in 1-in, 1½-in, and 2-in sizes. In the 1-inch size, with a flow of 21 gpm there would be a 2.75 psi loss through the valve. This value was obtained, again, by simple interpolation.

The final pressure loss data, all the pipe sizes, and valve size are shown in the appropriate final form in Figure 8-15. Notice that the estimated pressure delivered to the first head on the line is 38.27 psi instead of the 30 psi design pressure given earlier. This additional pressure is not a major concern since there will be additional pressure losses in the fittings of the zone and the inlet pressure to the zone will probably fluctuate from time to time. Had the pressure delivered to the head been as much as 20 psi greater than the design pressure, however, the excess pressure could cause the head to fog. Fogging is caused by high pressure at the nozzle which breaks the water into a fine fog-like mist, rather than distributing it in the intended pattern. It would have been wise to use the pressure reducing feature of the PE-PRS series valve. The pressure reduction feature is available on valves from other manufacturers as well.

The procedure followed here is the same for any irrigation zone in any irrigation system. The head patterns will vary and the pipe runs may be more complex but the principles are exactly the same. This will be demonstrated in the design illustration problem at the end of the chapter.

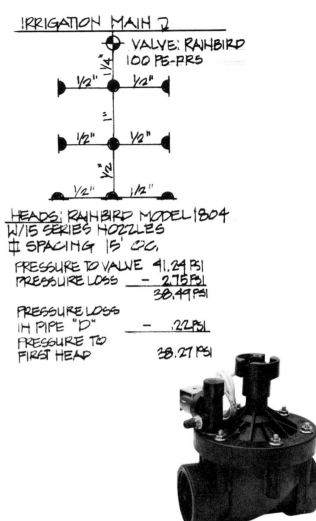

Valve Pressure Loss (PSI)

Pressure loss through the valve with PRS module completely open—NOT regulating pressure.

Flow (GPM)	100-PE 1″ 100-PE-PRS 1″	150-PE(1½″) 150-PE-PRS(1½″)	200-PE(2″) 200-PE-PRS(2″)
.25*	3.0	—	—
.50*	3.0	—	—
1*	3.0	—	—
5*	2.0	—	—
10*	1.5	—	—
20	2.5	1.2	0.7
30	5.0	1.6	0.8
40	9.3	1.9	1.0
50	15.5	2.3	1.3
75	—	5.0	2.6
100	—	7.7	4.7
125	—	13.9	7.4
150	—	20.0	11.0
175	—	27.5	15.5
200	—	36.0	21.3

*Flow rate recommended only for PE valves without PRS module.

FIGURE 8.15 COMPLETE IRRIGATION ZONE

COMPENSATING FOR GRAVITY LOSS OR GAIN IN THE SYSTEM

In addition to the pressure losses caused by friction between the moving water and the pipe, there are frequently pressure losses or gains caused by differences in the elevation of the site. Pressure losses or gains caused by gravity are constant throughout the system. Each foot of vertical rise or fall in elevation above or below the elevation of the water supply will result in an increase or decrease in pressure of 0.433 psi. For example, an irrigation line that lies 20 ft below the water source will experience a pressure gain of 8.66 psi (0.433 psi/ft × 20 ft vertical = +8.66 psi). A point 10 ft above the water supply will experience a pressure loss of 4.33 psi (0.433 psi/ft × 10 ft vertical = −4.33 psi). On very hilly sites with grade changes in excess of 20 ft vertical, it is wise to try and locate the water source at the higher elevations of the site, since it is much easier and less expensive to reduce the pressure in the system than it is to generate a corresponding increase in pressure. On most compact sites common to residential and commercial design, there is usually little problem with gravity loss or gain, but it almost always comes into play on large systems for parks, golf courses and highway irrigation projects.

Design and Layout of the Irrigation System

To begin making the preliminary design decisions, the following information must be in hand.

1. Soil properties: The infiltration rate and the available soil moisture characteristics of the soil will be the basis for deciding the desirable precipitation rate of the sprinkler equipment used, and later the frequency of water application.
2. Planting plan and plant list: This information is necessary to determine the peak evapotranspiration rate that is the basis for deciding how much supplemental water the system must be capable of delivering in one week. For example, if a project is located in a warm climate and is using a lot of turf area, the capacity of the system would be based on the estimated peak evapotranspiration of the turf. If no better information were available, the value of 0.25 in/day could be used from Table 8-4. For this condition, then, the weekly capacity of the system should be: 0.25 in/day × 7 days/week = 1.75 in/week. The planting plan should always be the base drawing on which the irrigation plan is prepared.

3. The grading plan: The grading plan or some information about the elevation difference will be required. Remember that gravity will cause losses or gains in the water pressure depending on the location of the water supply. Also remember that the slope of the surface will affect the infiltration rate of the soil.
4. Water supply information: The pressure at the water meter or pump and the size of the water meter or pump must be known if the system is to be operated using the existing water system. If the system will use a new water supply it can be designed after the system has been designed and its demands are known.
5. The next item to be determined is the amount of time it will take to water the entire project. This can be critical on some larger projects with limited water supplies or with a limited timeframe in which to accomplish the water application. The following formula can be used to estimate the amount of time that will be required to apply any volume of water to a site of a known area.

$$t = P \left(\frac{453.024 \, A}{Q} \right)$$

Where:

t = the watering time required in hours
P = the volume of water to be applied in inches
Q = the maximum volume available from the water supply in gpm
A = the area to be irrigated in acres

To illustrate the application of this formula assume that the conditions noted in number 2 required the application of 1.75 in/week, and that it was a residence with an area of ½ acre to be watered from a ¾-in water meter at about 20 gpm. Find t as follows:

$$t = 1.75 \text{ in/week} \times \frac{(453.024 \times .5 \text{ acres})}{20 \text{gpm}}$$

$$t = 19.82 \text{ hr/week}$$

If this system were operated three times each week, each period of operation would have to be 19.82 ÷ 3 = 6.61 hours. For a residential job this would pose little problem. The projects that are frequently a problem and have to be carefully considered are commercial and institutional projects that might wish to expand their site development over the years. When this is likely, watering time estimates should be made for the entire project and not just the first phase of development.

Once all these data are in hand, the next step is to make the preliminary design decisions which are:

1. What will be the maximum design flow from the water supply? The figure of 20 gpm from a ¾-in meter is an example of this decision. If a ¾-in meter is the supply, 20 to 25 gpm is the recommended design value. Using the maximum available flow of 30 gpm will usually result in too much pressure loss through the meter, and it will cause a very noticeable pressure drop if the water is turned on in the building using the supply line.
2. What will be the maximum operating pressure used on the system? This may be determined by the water supply if the available pressure is low, in the range of 35 to 45 psi. If the available pressure is not a problem, the operating pressure will be determined by the equipment selected.
3. The final decision, then, is to determine what irrigation equipment will be used for the project. This is a major decision and is covered in detail in the discussion that follows.

SELECTING THE IRRIGATION EQUIPMENT AND THE TYPE OF SYSTEM

Several things must be taken into account when selecting the irrigation equipment to be used. In general, the following items should be considered: the type of system, type of project, parts and maintenance, water quality, flexibility, and performance.

Selecting the Type of System

Two types of irrigation system are in general use for ornamental landscape development: sprinkler irrigation and drip irrigation. Either type may be used on a project or, more frequently today, they will be mixed. The best way to understand the differences in the two types of system is to look at the advantages and disadvantages of each.

Advantages of Drip Irrigation

a. Drip irrigation is the most water-efficient system available if it is placed in the proper relationship to the plant.
b. There is little evaporation loss of water and there is no runoff or overspray.
c. Only plants that need water are irrigated.
d. Drip systems are not subject to wind distortion.

Disadvantages of Drip Irrigation

a. Drip irrigation cannot be used on turf.
b. Because of the small size of the parts and the surface exposure of the distribution system, drip irrigation systems are subject to higher rates of vandalism and mechanical damage from normal maintenance operations.
c. The cost of proper installation of drip irrigation will be higher per square foot than for sprinkler irrigation, assuming the same general area is watered.

Advantages of Sprinkler Irrigation

a. Sprinkler equipment has been designed to handle practically every landscape situation, and can be used on all types of plant material.
b. Sprinklers can cover large landscape areas with a very small amount of equipment and material.
c. Sprinklers most closely simulate natural rain, and do help keep the plant foliage clean.
d. The initial installation cost is less per square foot than for drip irrigation, and it is somewhat less expensive to maintain.

Disadvantages of Sprinkler Irrigation

a. Sprinkler irrigation is not water-efficient. As much as 50% of the water applied by a sprinkler irrigation system may be lost to runoff or evaporation.
b. Even with the most careful design and equipment selection it is hard to prevent overspray of walks, parking areas, and building walls.
c. Sprinklers are very sensitive to wind, which will distort the pattern of coverage. In some oceanfront locations this can practically render a sprinkler system useless if the prevailing winds persist for long seasonal periods.

In general, it is safe to say that sprinklers must be used on turf areas, and they do work much better than drip irrigation on most dense and creeping groundcovers. Drip irrigation is best used for watering larger shrub masses, sparse groundcover plantings, and trees. This kind of mix is very much in evidence in the desert southwest regions of the country, where water conservation practices are a must.

Selecting Equipment to Fit the Project

The type of project is a factor in selecting the right irrigation equipment. Several general topics should be considered:

1. Will the equipment be exposed to vandalism or damage from heavy mowing machinery? The

materials used in heads and other components used in residential irrigation are usually not heavy enough to take the beating handed out by large tractor-type mowing machines.

2. Will the owner have the skills and the ability to provide the necessary maintenance and to operate the system properly? Irrigation systems must be maintained and operated properly to be of value. It is possible with today's technology to design a very sophisticated system that will be of little use because the owner cannot or will not properly operate or maintain the system.

3. Will parts for the equipment used be available? Good deals on equipment should be avoided if there is not a local distributor that handles the parts and supplies needed for operation.

4. Water quality is a major concern when considering maintenance. If the water supply is likely to be dirty; i.e., full of sand and gravel, organic materials, acid or caustic minerals, maintenance is going to be a problem. If the water is dirty, avoid spray heads and small nozzles as much as possible, and be sure to use appropriate filters and strainers. If unwanted minerals are found in the water, plastic materials will usually be less effected than metal parts. Be very sure that the valves selected are recommended by the manufacturer for dirty water applications.

Selecting Equipment for Flexibility and Performance

The performance qualities that must be considered in the equipment selected are outlined below:

1. Precipitation rate: The heads selected should have a precipitation rate equal to or less than the infiltration rate of the soil.
2. The distribution patterns available should reasonably match the geometry of the project at hand.
3. The heads should have either compatible precipitation rates or a variety of nozzle options that allow the matching of precipitation rates within irrigation zones.
4. There should be a certain margin in the operating pressure limits of the heads that will not measurably affect the performance characteristics.
5. Look for the adjustment characteristics of the heads and valves. Adjustability is usually very important close to buildings and in complicated planting schemes, but it usually costs more.

In the example problem that follows this discussion, decisions regarding the selection of the equipment will be pointed out. It will not be possible to touch on all of the issues raised in this discussion, however, so students are encouraged to review this outline when making irrigation equipment decisions for any project.

GETTING READY TO DESIGN THE SYSTEM

The remaining part of this chapter is devoted to working through a design example of an irrigation system for a small institutional project. The discussion will touch on all the concerns that have been raised in previous sections to demonstrate their application. To begin, consider the base plan in Figure 8-16. It is a small branch library located in the semi-arid belt of west-central California. The crosses on the plan indicate tree locations and the dashed lines indicate the bed lines.

Before the irrigation system can be laid out it will be necessary to study the planting plan and determine the relative water needs, determine the volume and pressure of the water source, and the properties of the soil. The following remarks are numbered to correspond to the brief notes on the plan in Figure 8-17. Most of the notes relate to the plant material and the appropriate method of irrigation; notes 6, 11, and 12 refer to controller location, water source, and the soil. It should be understood that the type of equipment used in each case is a matter of professional judgment based on experience. There is little in the way of sound empirical research that can be used to guide the selection of irrigation equipment or methods for ornamental plant materials.

1. The boundary of the parking lot is screened by a mass of large flowering shrubs, spaced 5 ft, and trees, spaced 20 ft apart. The plan calls for the ground to be mulched with bark. The spacing and cover make this area good for drip irrigation.
2. The bed on the north property line near Grenada Blvd. has a clump type ground cover that will cover the entire bed. This bed will have to have spray irrigation because drip irrigation would not be effective on this type of ground cover.
3. The traffic islands of the parking lot are planted with trees and a spreading ground cover that is planted on 24-in centers. The trees and the ground cover will require only drip irrigation.
4. There are three beds at the north side of the building planted with a flowering groundcover that is dense-growing and requires a lot of water to maintain the bloom. These beds will have to be spray irrigated.
5. All of the beds near the face of the building, designated by the number 5, are planted with

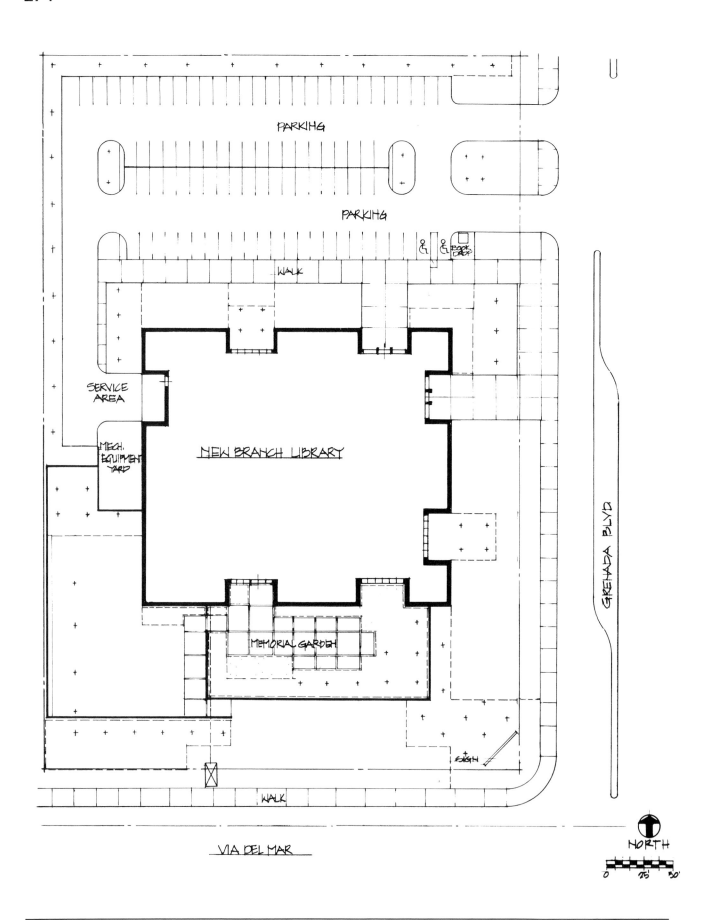

PARKING

PARKING

WALK

BOOK DROP

SERVICE AREA

MECH. EQUIPMENT YARD

NEW BRANCH LIBRARY

MEMORIAL GARDEN

SIGN

GRENADA BLVD

WALK

VIA DEL MAR

NORTH

0   25'   50'

FIGURE 8.16 IRRIGATION PROBLEM

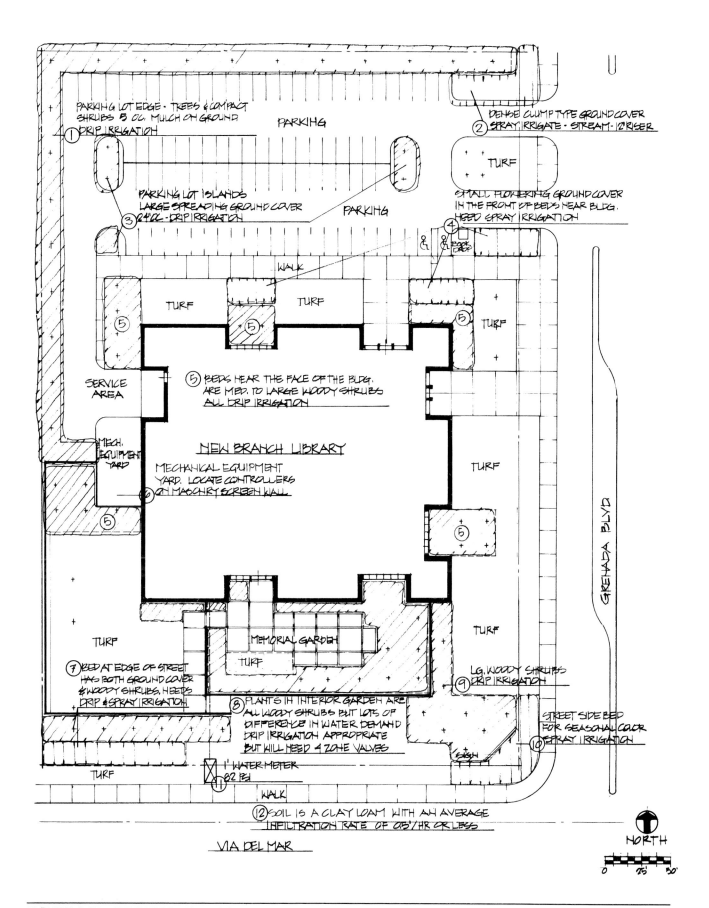

FIGURE 8.17 IRRIGATION ANALYSIS

woody shrubs planted on 24-in to 48-in centers. These beds can all be drip irrigated.

6. The mechanical equipment yard at the rear of the building will provide a good place to locate the irrigation controllers. They will be secure, but accessible to the groundskeepers without going into the building.

7. The bed at the southwest corner near Via Del Mar is mixed with small flowering shrubs and dense groundcovers near the front of the bed, with large woody shrubs and trees to the back of the bed. In this case it is best to split the irrigation and spray the front of the bed and drip irrigate the back portion of the bed.

8. The interior part of the memorial garden is a complex planting and has a little bit of turf in one place. The turf here, as in all other areas of the site, will have to be spray irrigated. The remaining plant material can all be drip irrigated, but the complexity of the planting and difference in water requirements will require that the planting be broken into four different zones.

9. The large bed behind the sign at the southeast corner of the site is all large woody material with a very low water requirement. The trees, however, have a reasonably high water requirement. So, while the whole bed will be drip irrigated, it will have to be split into two zones to regulate the water volume.

10. The bed in front of the sign at Grenada and Via Del Mar is for seasonal planting, which will make spray irrigation preferable. If drip irrigation were used, it would have to be reworked with each new planting.

11. The water supply to the new library is a 1-in meter and is serviced by a 12-in transmission line on the south side of Via Del Mar. Pressure checks were made on the meter at three different times of day that averaged 82 psi.

12. The soil on the site is a uniform deep clay loam. Percolation tests were run in the geotechnical report because the city requires on-site detention of stormwater. The large turf area at the southwest corner of the property is depressed and used for stormwater detention, and has an average percolation rate of 0.5 in/hr. One soil problem noted in the report was that exposed soil has a tendency to form a slight crust when dry, but will begin to drain after the crust becomes moist.

Equipment Selection

Based on this analysis, the following equipment was selected for the project. It should be noted that Toro equipment is used as an example only. Other manufacturers offer equipment of equal quality and with similar performance characteristics.

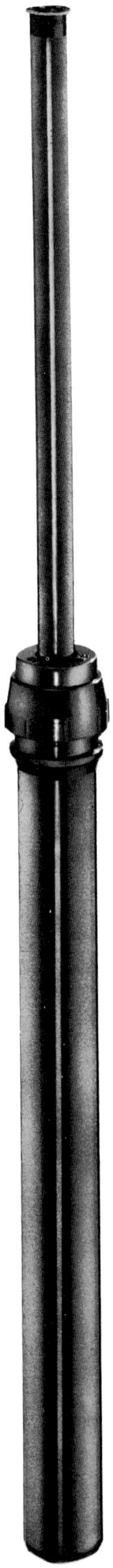

Low Gallonage

Pattern		PSI	GPM	Radius
90°	12'-Q	20	.4	10'
		25	.7	12'
		40	.9	13'
		50	1.0	14'
120°	12'-120°	20	.6	10'
		25	.8	12'
		40	1.0	13'
		50	1.1	14'
180°	12'-H	20	.9	10'
		25	1.0	12'
		40	1.1	13'
		50	1.3	14'
240°	12'-240°	20	1.1	10'
		25	1.2	12'
		40	1.5	13'
		50	1.7	14'
270°	12'-270°	20	1.3	10'
		25	1.5	12'
		40	1.6	13'
		50	1.7	14'
360°	12'-F	20	1.7	10'
		25	2.0	12'
		40	2.3	13'
		50	2.6	14'

570-HP

2 Excellent for high traffic areas where vandalism or injury are a concern
• 12-inch pop-up for flower beds, ground cover or other areas where you need full retraction.
• Accepts all Toro spray nozzles
• Body height, 16"
• ½-inch female N.P.T. threads
• Average flush rate less than .8 G.P.M.

FIGURE 8.18 *SPRAY IRRIGATION HEAD PERFORMANCE*

1. Small spray heads: For small areas that require spray irrigation, the 570 series heads will be used with the low gallonage nozzles to keep the precipitation rate as low as possible. For turf areas the 570P, a 3-in pop-up, will be used and for the ground cover areas the 570HP, a 12-in pop-up is used, Figure 8-18.

2. Rotary turf heads: For larger turf areas the 300 series head was selected. This is a gear-driven rotary head with small multiple nozzles that have a very low water requirement and, therefore, have a very low precipitation rate. The heads are available in the patterns that are needed and they have matched precipitation rates regardless of the pattern. This is a very important feature to look for in larger turf heads. All the heads used will have the standard 3-in pop-up, and will use either the −63 or −01 nozzle. Changing nozzles in this particular head will adjust the radius of throw. The 300 series heads are shown in Figure 8-19.

3. The drip emitters will be Toro's 700 series emitters. These are either six-outlet type for shrub applications or single-outlet emitters for trees. These emitters have to be selected for the desired flow. Both emitters are available in ½-, 1-, and 2-gph flow rates. The emitters are shown in Figure 8-20.

4. Valves: The valves selected for the system are the electric 250 series valves for the spray irrigation zones and the 260-06-03 series valves for the drip zones. It is important to note that different valves have to be used for drip and spray irrigation. Standard spray irrigation valves will only work well at flows of over 5 gpm, and most drip irrigation zones will have flows of 1 gpm or less. The valves and valve performance are shown in Figure 8-21.

5. Controllers: The controllers selected for the project are the IC, enhanced series controller. These are an improved solid state controller that are flexible enough to run both drip and sprinkler irrigation equipment. The controllers are shown in Figure 8-22.

6. Other equipment: For backflow prevention, the city will allow a double check valve, so that is the preferred choice. The drip equipment will require the use of pressure reducers and "Y" strainers on all zones. These will be the ones that are recommended by Toro.

Head Spacing

Head spacing can be either square or triangular. Triangular spacing is more efficient as far as the even distribution of water but it is very difficult to use when it becomes necessary to keep water off walks and other landscape areas. In general triangular spacing is best suited to parks, golf courses, athletic fields, and other areas that do not have hard edges.

TORO SERIES 300—STREAM ROTOR®

Stream Rotor (Body Only)
300-00-00 (3″ for turf)
300-10-00 (shrub head—no pop)
300-12-00 (12″ high pop)
- Accepts all Stream Rotor arc discs and nozzles
- Simply insert desired arc plate and nozzle (no tools required)
- Plastic plug protects the drive assembly from debris and retains seal

			360°	180°	90°	270°
						ARC DISC 312-00
			F	H	Q	
Nozzle	**P.S.I.**	**Radius**				G
-01	35	16′	2.28	1.14	0.57	1.71
	50	18′	2.88	1.14	0.72	2.16
-02	35	21′	2.88	1.44	0.72	2.16
	50	24′	3.41	1.71	0.85	2.56
-03	35	28′	5.43	2.72	1.36	4.07
	50	30′	6.45	3.23	1.61	4.84
-63	35	28′	2.72	1.36	0.68	2.04
	50	30′	3.23	1.62	0.81	2.42
-93	35	28′	4.07	2.04	1.02	3.05
	50	30′	4.84	2.42	1.21	3.63

FIGURE 8.19 *ROTARY IRRIGATION HEAD PERFORMANCE*

Emitters with Lime Cap

Installs directly into drip hose at the planting area. Excellent for areas where water contains minerals which could build up and clog the small outlet orifice.

700-04 (Brown) ½ GPH, 700-02 (Black) 1 GPH, 700-08 (Green) 2 GPH

6 Outlet Emitter

Ideal for bubbler or shrub spray conversion. Mounts directly into 710-06 or 710-07 emitter holders for ½″ risers. Excellent for closely-planted shrub areas where more than one single-outlet emitter will be required. Saves time and money. Distribution tubing goes directly to the plants.

700-06 (Brown) ½ GBH, 700-03 (Black) 1 GPH, 700-09 (Green) 2 GPH

FIGURE 8.20 DRIP IRRIGATION EMITTERS

In a case such as the example problem, triangular spacing would not be efficient because the site is broken into too many small zones and the shapes are essentially rectangular as well. When square spacing is used, heads should be placed so that spray from one head reaches the adjacent head. This means that if a head has a radius of 14 ft, which is the case with the 570P with the low gallonage nozzle, then the head spacing is 14 ft. Trying to spread heads farther than this will result in dry spots.

Operating Pressure

The operating pressure selected for the system is 50 psi. The pressure available at the meter will support this level and both the 300 series and 570 series heads operate well at this pressure. It does mean that pressure reducers will have to be used on the drip irrigation zones, but this is the rule rather than an exception.

Precipitation Rate

The final check before going to the drawing board to lay out the head pattern is to find the precipitation rate for each of the heads used. The formulas for finding precipitation rate are:

Friction Loss

Type	5	10	15	20	25	30	40
				G.P.M			
1″ Hydraulic	<1	1.0	2.0	3.0	4.0	6.0	9.5
1″ Electric	3.0	4.4	4.5	5.0	5.4	7.0	9.5

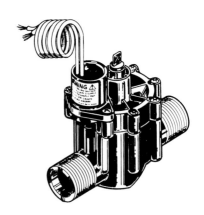

Friction Loss

Type	5	10	15	20	25	30	35	40	45
					G.P.M				
With flow control	2.0	2.0	2.3	3.1	4.0	5.4	7.0	8.7	10.5
Without flow control	2.0	2.0	2.3	3.1	4.0	5.4	7.0	8.7	10.5

FIGURE 8.21 REMOTE CONTROL VALVE PERFORMANCE

Square spacing:

P = gpm of full circle head × 96.3 ÷ spacing²

Triangular spacing:

P = gpm of full circle head × 96.3 ÷
head spacing × (0.866 head spacing)

For the heads used in the example problem the precipitation rates are as follows for square spacing.

570 series heads with low gallonage nozzles:

P = 2.6 gpm × 96.3 ÷ (14 × 14) = 1.28 in/hr

300 series heads −01 nozzles:

P = 2.88 gpm × 96.3 ÷ (18 × 18) = 0.86 in/hr

300 series heads −63 nozzles:

P = 2.72 × 96.3 ÷ (30 × 30) = 0.29 in/hr

It is obvious here that the spray heads are going to apply water at a rate greater than the infiltration rate of the soil, and the 300 series heads with the -01 nozzles will be marginal, while the 300 series heads with the -63 nozzles will be very efficient. The performance values are typical for the types of heads regardless of the brand name.

The only way to cope with the high precipitation rates of the smaller heads is to water more frequently and for shorter periods each time to take advantage of the early high infiltration rate. Some managers suggest cycling the spray heads as much as three times in a single watering cycle to increase the efficiency of water application.

LAYING OUT THE SYSTEM

When all of the important decisions have been made, the layout of the system begins with developing the head pattern that will best fit the project. In this case, the square pattern was selected as noted earlier, and the head spacing is set equal to the radius of the head as recommended. The head pattern for the example problem is shown in Figure 8-23. To illustrate how triangular spacing works, the spray heads at the southwest corner of the site were triangular spaced. Head layout may have to go through many refinements to reach the final pattern. The key to remember is: *Do not spread the heads out!* You can reduce the water volume and throw but you can not increase the performance.

Areas that receive drip irrigation will not usually be laid out for reasons of scale. In most cases it is only necessary to indicate the zone to be drip irrigated and

Toro IC 4x4, IC 6x6, IC 8x8, IC 12x12 Enhanced IC Controllers

Here are the new-concept Toro IC Controllers, offering you the greatest versatility capability to program each station independently, you can solve almost any special control problem. And even with their wide-ranging control capabilities, these new Toro controllers are simple to program. Try them and discover that Toro is the only way to go for full, versatile, affordable control.

Features
• Multiple programs
• 12-key keyboard
• Variable 12- or 14-day clock
• Variable minute or hour station timing
• Variable 12- or 24-hour clock readout
• 6 start times per day
• Each station programmed independently
• Battery back-up providing programming protection in case of power failure
• Recharging unit—Nicad battery only
• Fail-safe program
• Variable fail-safe station timing 0,7,12,25 minutes
• Pump/master valve circuit
• Locking cabinet
• "Line Gard"
• Permanent cancel
• Rain switch

Specifications
• UL listed
• 120 V.A.C.
• 30 V.A. plug-in or internal transformer—(residential)
• ½″ inlet for 115 V.A.C. primary line
• Up to 60-minute timing per station
• 1 to 15 hour timing for drip programs
• 11″ high, 9″ wide, 5″ deep (residential)
• 12″ high, 11″ wide, 5″ deep (commercial)
• 40 V.A. internal transformer (commercial)
• Heavy duty metal cabinet (commercial)

FIGURE 8.22 *IRRIGATION CONTROLLERS*

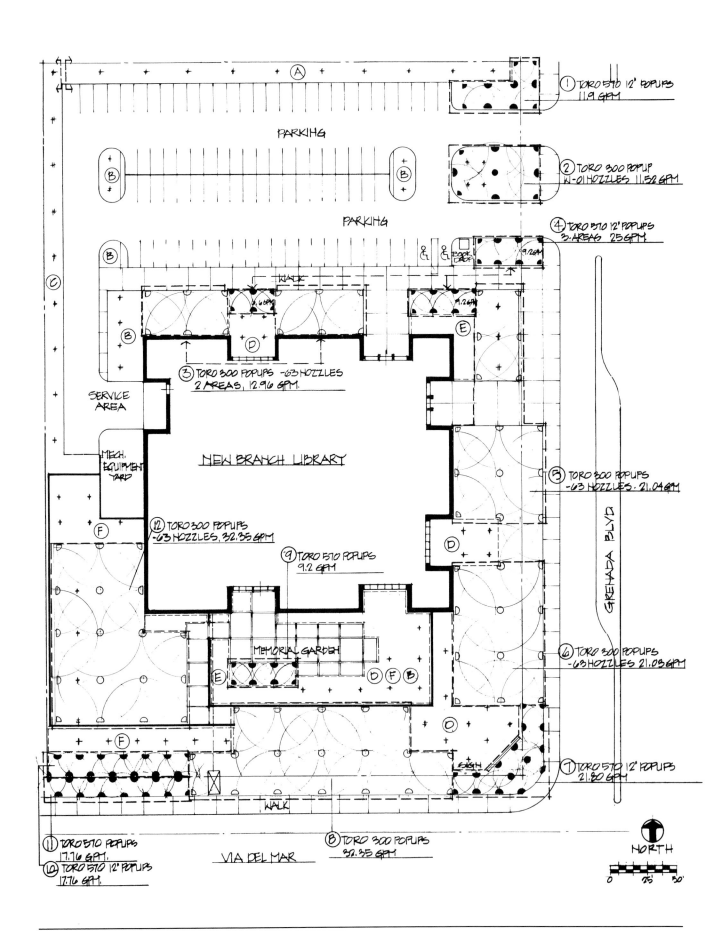

FIGURE 8.23 HEAD LAYOUT AND WATERING ZONES

to note the type of emitter to be used for each situation. Figure 8-24 shows the layout of a typical drip irrigation zone as an example of how these zones will be handled. The thing to note in this figure is the inclusion of a "Y" strainer before the remote control valve, and the provision of a pressure reducer downstream of the valve. The strainer is essential to keep grit and other solid material out of the drip emitters, and the pressure reducer is necessary to ensure that the emitters will perform at the specified flow. This information is usually called out by notes on the plans and by a section in the technical specifications of the project manual.

Upon completion of the head layout, the next step is to group the heads into individual watering zones. Two things are considered in grouping the heads: plant type and total water demand of the zone. The plant type governs the water demand. Turf areas must be separated from shrub areas, and shrubs with high water requirements should be separated from shrubs with lower water requirements, as noted earlier. The heads must also be grouped into zones so as not to exceed the volume of water available from the water supply and heads of different series; i.e., spray and rotary cannot be mixed. In this case there is a 1-in water meter that is capable of providing up to 50 gpm, if necessary. In this case it was decided that zones of 30 to 35 gpm would be the maximum used.

Figure 8-23 shows how the heads were grouped for the example problem, and the gallonage requirement for each zone. The gallonage requirements are found by simply accumulating the water demand of each head in the zone. To illustrate this, consider zone 1 at the northeast corner of the property. This zone uses 570 series heads with low gallonage nozzles. The water requirements for each head pattern are from Figure 8-18, and the number of each in zone 1 are as follows:

1 Three-quarter circle @ 50 psi (1.7 gp) =	1.7 gpm
4 Half circles @ 50 psi (1.3 gpm) =	5.2 gpm
5 Quarter circle @ 50 psi (1.0 gpm) =	5.0 gpm
Total water demand zone 1	11.9 gpm

This procedure is followed for each zone of the system. The highest water demands for this system are zones 8 and 12 with demands of 32.35 gpm. The lowest water demand is zone 9 at 9.2 gpm. The difference in the high and low demand for a system is sometimes a matter of concern since the pressure loss in the water delivery system will be less than at higher flows. This means that the low flow zones will usually operate at somewhat elevated pressures. If the increase in pressure is sufficiently high the head may fog. Fogging conditions can be eliminated by installing a pressure reducing device under each head on a line or by using a pressure reducing or flow regulating feature on the remote control valve for the zone. In this case, the

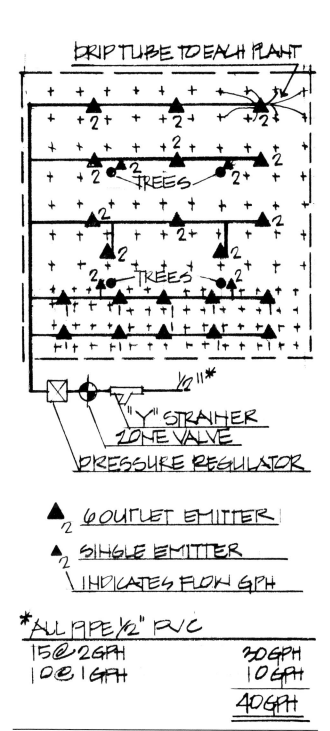

FIGURE 8.24 TYPICAL DRIP ZONE

valves used have a flow regulating feature that should be sufficient to reduce the chance of fogging in any of the low flow zones.

Piping the System

Once the head layout is complete and the zones have been designated, the piping schematic is prepared. Figure 8-25 shows the piping layout for the example problem. There is no absolute best way to lay out the

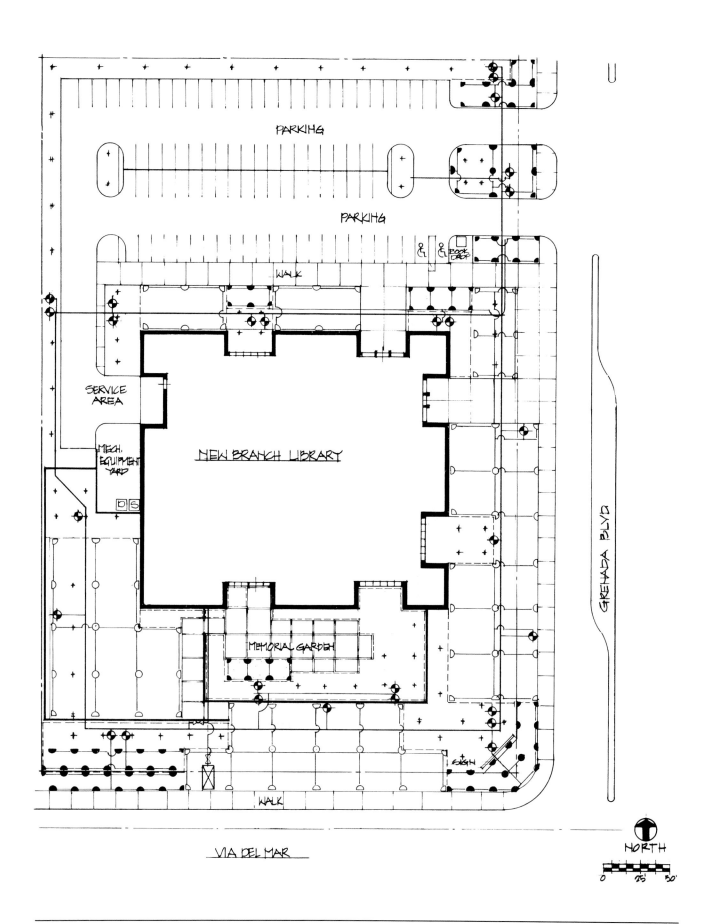

FIGURE 8.25 PIPING LAYOUT

piping for an irrigation system; however, there are some general guidelines that can be used to plan the overall layout.

1. Try to locate the valves in clusters so they can be found easily. The best locations are along the edges of walks, or at the edges between turf and shrub beds. Always put the valves in a valve box so they can be accessed from the surface for maintenance.
2. The main supply line from the valve to the heads of a zone should be located in the center of the zone. (See zones 8 and 12.) This splits the water load and will help reduce the total pressure loss between the first and last head on the line. It will also minimize the size of pipe required.
3. Keep the runs of pipe straight. This will aid in finding the pipe later for maintenance and repairs.

A good piping system usually looks very clean and simple. If a system looks complicated then it usually is not efficient.

4. In shrub beds, try to keep the pipe to the edge of the bed, only crossing the bed when necessary. Insofar as possible, try to keep the pipe located between the balls of plants rather than under the plant. This will at times take a bit more pipe, but the lines are much less likely to be cut by normal maintenance activities.

Sizing the Pipe

Once the pipe layout is complete, the pipe is sized in each zone. This is done by zone, following the procedure outlined earlier in the chapter. To review the procedure, the detailed pressure loss tabulations for the loop and irrigation zone 12 are included here. Students

DELIVERY SYSTEM PRESSURE LOSS

Part	Pressure Loss
1 in. Water meter @ 33.0 gpm	6.5 psi
1 in Double check valve.	6.0 psi
Pressure loss in 1 in loop. Loop length is 1,140 ft and the maximum flow is 33 gpm. The pressure loss is based on ½ the length and ½ the flow. The pressure loss of .95 psi/100 ft was interpolated for a flow of 16.5 gpm in a 1¼ in pipe. Thus, 5.7 × 0.95 =	5.42 psi
Subtotal	17.92 psi
Allow 10% for fittings including the gate valve.	1.79 psi
Total pressure loss in delivery system	19.71 psi
Pressure available at each zone valve	
Pressure at meter	82.00 psi
Less loss in the delivery system	19.71 psi
	62.29 psi

ACCUMULATED PRESSURE LOSS FOR ZONE 12*

Pipe Size In.	Flow in gpm	Pipe Run in Hundreds of Feet	Pressure Loss per 100 ft in psi	Pressure Loss in psi
½	1	0.3	0.20	0.06
½	3	0.3	1.56	0.47
¾	4	0.3	0.78	0.23
1	13	0.3	2.07	0.62
1¼	26	0.3	2.22	0.66
			Total loss first to last head	2.04 psi
1½	33	0.25	1.78	0.45
1 in. valve	33	—	—	7.75
			Total loss from main to first head	8.20 psi

*Note in Figure 8-28 that the pipe sizes are shown for the pipe runs that represent the loss between the first and last head in zone 12. The computations are shown in order from the last run of pipe back to the zone valve. Pressure loss is based on flow at the next full gallon per minute that the line carries; i.e., a flow of 0.81 gpm is taken as 1 gpm. Pressure losses are in psi/100 ft, and were interpolated if the value could not be taken directly from the table. The head spacing for the 300 series heads is 30 ft so each pipe run is 30 ft.

should look over each of these examples to be sure the procedure is understood.

Pressure delivered to first head:

Pressure at valve:	62.29 psi
Pressure loss to first head:	8.20 psi
	54.09 psi

Using the design pressure of 50 psi, the allowable pressure drop between the first and last head is 5 psi. Therefore, the 2.67 psi loss calculated is acceptable. The actual pressure delivered to the first head on the line is higher than the 50 psi design pressure. But also remember that there has been no allowance made for additional pressure loss through the pipe fittings, so the actual excess pressure will be somewhat less. Overall, there is not a sufficient difference in pressure to seriously affect the performance of the heads.

The procedure followed here would be followed for each zone of the system in turn until all the pipe had been sized as shown in the final irrigation plan, Figure 8-26.

Stationing and the Controller Program

The final step in completing the irrigation plan is the assignment of station numbers to each irrigation zone and the development of the controller program.

In the example problem there were 12 different sprinkler irrigation zones, so an IC-12 $\times$ 12 controller will be used to control all the sprinkler zones. The drip irrigation will require 16 different valves to operate the various zones; however, since the gallonage demands are very low, it is possible to operate several of these valves at one time on the same controller station, so an IC-4 $\times$ 4 will be used to control the drip irrigation. The numbered stations on the plan are the sprinkler zones and the stations designated by letters are for drip irrigation.

Once the individual stations have been designated, the controller program is developed to deliver the right amount of supplemental water to each zone. To decide how long a station should be run, it is necessary to know the precipitation rate or delivery rate of the zone, the frequency of watering, and the amount of supplementary water that is to be applied. To illustrate how this is done, the time will be computed for a typical drip zone, a shrub zone, and a turf zone for the peak water use period.

Typical drip irrigation zone:

Water requirement of shrubs	10 gpd
Water requirement of trees	20 gpd

Water delivery will be controlled by the type and number of emitters used on trees and shrubs. In other words, trees will have one or more emitters rated at 2

gph and shrubs will be served by emitters with a 1 gph rate. The available moisture characteristic of the soil is such that every-other-day watering will be satisfactory, so the operating time for the drip stations based on the shrub delivery rate of 1 gph will have to operate 20 hours to deliver the required 20 gallons for the two-day cycle.

These long operating times are typical of drip irrigation systems, and you will notice that the controller selected will only allow a program time of up to 15 hours. This being the case, it would probably be just as well to operate the drip stations 10 hours each day during the peak growing season and then drop the watering time to 10 to 15 hours every other day during the fall and winter months.

Typical shrub zone, 570 series spray heads:

Evapotranspiration rate is .2 in/day or 1.4 in/week (Table 8-4). The precipitation rate of the 570 series head found earlier in the chapter was 1.28 in/hr.

The total operating time to apply 1.40 inches of water is:

1.40 in/hr ÷ 1.28 in/wk = 1.09 hr/wk

At this point it is necessary to make a judgment about the sequence of watering because the precipitation rate of the 570 series head is almost three times greater than the infiltration capacity of the soil. As noted earlier, in cases like this it is best to water more frequently for shorter periods of time to reduce the amount of water lost to runoff. Even when this is done, the time of operation will have to be extended to compensate for the water lost to evaporation and runoff. The exact amount of time necessary to compensate for this loss is very difficult to predict but a good place to start is by assuming an efficiency of about 50%. Given this assumption, heads will be operated twice as long as the time calculated to apply the required water. In this case, it would be 2.18 hours per week.

Since the available moisture indicates that every-other-day watering is desirable, the time of operation is based on 3.5 operating periods per week, which yields seven watering periods in a two week period. The time of operation required for each cycle is:

2.18 hr/week ÷ 3.5 cycles per week = 0.62 hr per cycle, or about 37.4 minutes per cycle

To further increase the efficiency of each watering cycle, the 38 minute period can be broken down into four to six different watering periods during the course of the day. For example, if each watering cycle were broken into four different periods the time for each period is:

38 min/cycle ÷ 4 periods/cycle = 9.5 min/period

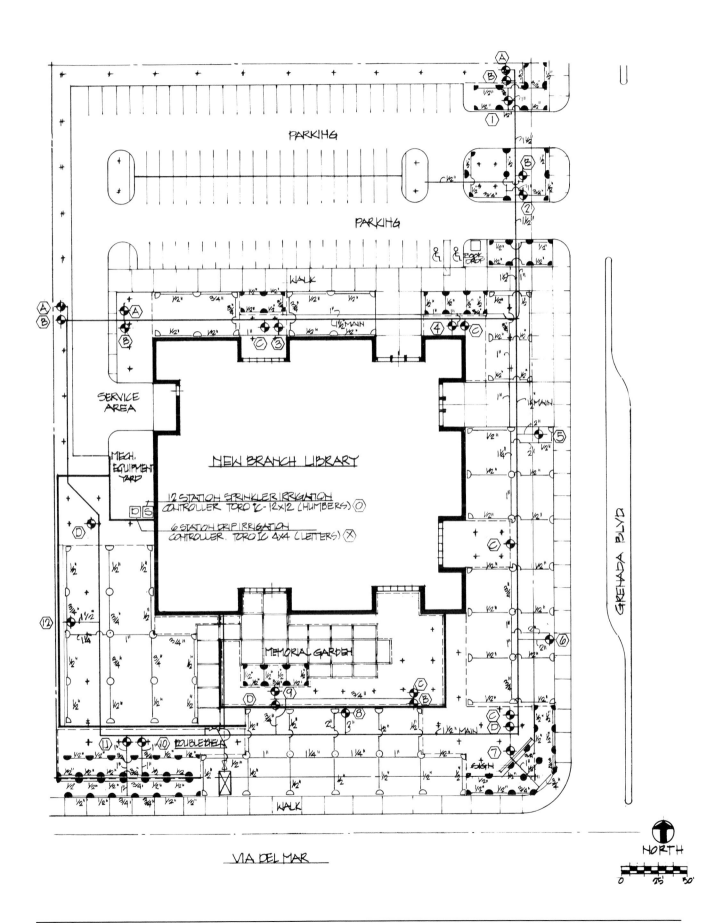

FIGURE 8.26 IRRIGATION PLAN

FRICTION LOSS TABLE
PVC 1120-1220   CLASS 160
P.S.I. LOSS PER PIPE LENGTH NOTED

PIPE SIZE	GPM	100	90	80	70	60	50	40	30	20	10	5	VEL.	GPM
1/2" .720" I.D.	1	.20	.18	.16	.14	.12	.10	.08	.06	.04	.02	.01	.8	1
	2	.74	.67	.59	.52	.44	.37	.30	.22	.15	.07	.04	1.6	2
	3	1.56	1.40	1.25	1.09	.94	.78	.62	.47	.31	.16	.08	2.4	3
	4	2.68	2.41	2.14	1.88	1.61	1.34	1.07	.80	.54	.27	.13	3.2	4
	5	4.04	3.64	3.23	2.83	2.42	2.02	1.62	1.21	.81	.40	.20	4.0	5
	6	5.76	5.18	4.61	4.03	3.46	2.88	2.30	1.73	1.15	.58	.29	4.8	6
	7	7.66	6.89	6.13	5.36	4.60	3.83	3.06	2.30	1.53	.77	.38	5.6	7
	8	9.78	8.80	7.82	6.85	5.87	4.89	3.91	2.93	1.96	.98	.49	6.4	8
3/4" .930" I.D.	2	.22	.20	.18	.15	.13	.11	.09	.07	.04	.02	.01	.9	2
	4	.78	.70	.63	.55	.47	.39	.31	.23	.16	.08	.04	1.9	4
	6	1.66	1.49	1.34	1.16	1.00	.83	.66	.50	.34	.17	.09	2.8	6
	8	2.84	2.56	2.27	2.01	1.70	1.42	1.14	.85	.56	.28	.14	3.7	8
	10	4.30	3.87	3.45	3.01	2.58	2.15	1.72	1.29	.86	.43	.22	4.7	10
	12	6.00	5.40	4.80	4.20	3.60	3.00	2.40	1.80	1.20	.60	.30	5.7	12
	14	8.00	7.20	6.40	5.60	4.80	4.00	3.20	2.40	1.60	.80	.40	6.6	14
1" 1.195" I.D.	6	.48	.44	.39	.34	.29	.24	.20	.15	.10	.05	.03	1.7	6
	8	.84	.76	.67	.59	.50	.42	.34	.25	.16	.08	.04	2.3	8
	10	1.28	1.13	1.02	.88	.76	.63	.51	.38	.26	.13	.07	2.9	10
	12	1.78	1.60	1.43	1.25	1.07	.89	.71	.53	.36	.18	.09	3.4	12
	14	2.36	2.12	1.89	1.65	1.42	1.18	.94	.71	.48	.24	.12	4.0	14
	16	3.04	2.73	2.43	2.12	1.82	1.52	1.21	.91	.60	.30	.15	4.5	16
	18	3.76	3.38	3.01	2.63	2.26	1.88	1.50	1.13	.76	.38	.19	5.1	18
	20	4.56	4.10	3.65	3.19	2.74	2.28	1.82	1.37	.92	.46	.23	5.7	20
	22	5.50	4.95	4.40	3.85	3.30	2.75	2.20	1.65	1.10	.55	.28	6.3	22
	24	6.46	5.81	5.23	4.52	3.88	3.23	2.58	1.94	1.30	.65	.38	6.8	24
1-1/4" 1.532" I.D.	10	.38	.34	.31	.27	.23	.19	.15	.11	.08	.04	.02	1.7	10
	12	.52	.47	.42	.37	.32	.26	.21	.16	.10	.05	.03	2.1	12
	14	.70	.63	.56	.49	.42	.35	.28	.21	.14	.07	.04	2.4	14
	16	.90	.81	.72	.63	.54	.45	.36	.27	.18	.09	.05	2.8	16
	18	1.12	1.01	.90	.78	.67	.56	.45	.34	.22	.11	.06	3.1	18
	20	1.36	1.22	1.09	.95	.82	.68	.54	.41	.28	.14	.07	3.5	20
	22	1.62	1.46	1.30	1.13	.97	.81	.65	.49	.32	.16	.08	3.9	22
	24	1.90	1.71	1.53	1.33	1.14	.95	.76	.57	.38	.19	.10	4.2	24
	26	2.22	2.00	1.78	1.55	1.33	1.11	.89	.67	.44	.22	.11	4.5	26
	28	2.54	2.29	2.04	1.78	1.52	1.27	1.02	.76	.50	.25	.13	4.9	28
	30	2.90	2.61	2.32	2.03	1.74	1.45	1.16	.87	.58	.29	.15	5.2	30
	32	3.26	2.93	2.62	2.28	1.96	1.63	1.30	.98	.66	.33	.17	5.6	32
	34	3.64	3.28	2.91	2.55	2.18	1.82	1.46	1.09	.72	.36	.18	5.9	34
	36	4.04	3.64	3.23	2.83	2.42	2.02	1.62	1.21	.80	.40	.20	6.2	36
	38	4.48	4.03	3.59	3.14	2.69	2.24	1.79	1.34	.90	.45	.23	6.6	38

Tables on pages 286–287 courtesy of the Toro Company, Irrigation Division, P.O. Box 439, Riverside, California 92502.

PVC 1120-1220 CLASS 160

1-1/2" (1.754" I.D.)

GPM												Vel	GPM
20	.70	.63	.56	.49	.42	.35	.28	.21	.14	.07	.04	2.7	20
25	1.06	.95	.86	.74	.64	.53	.42	.32	.22	.11	.06	3.3	25
30	1.50	1.35	1.20	1.05	.90	.75	.60	.46	.30	.15	.08	4.0	30
35	1.98	1.78	1.59	1.39	1.19	.99	.79	.59	.40	.20	.10	4.7	35
40	2.54	2.29	2.04	1.78	1.52	1.27	1.02	.76	.51	.25	.13	5.3	40
45	3.16	2.84	2.53	2.21	1.90	1.58	1.26	.95	.64	.32	.16	6.0	45
50	3.84	3.46	3.07	2.69	2.30	1.92	1.54	1.15	.76	.38	.19	6.6	50

2" (2.193" I.D.)

GPM												Vel	GPM
30	.50	.45	.40	.35	.30	.25	.20	.15	.10	.05	.03	2.6	30
35	.68	.61	.54	.47	.40	.34	.27	.20	.13	.07	.04	3.0	35
40	.86	.77	.69	.60	.52	.43	.34	.26	.17	.09	.05	3.4	40
45	1.08	.97	.86	.75	.64	.54	.43	.32	.21	.11	.06	3.8	45
50	1.30	1.17	1.04	.91	.78	.65	.52	.39	.26	.13	.07	4.3	50
55	1.54	1.39	1.23	1.08	.92	.77	.62	.46	.31	.15	.08	4.7	55
60	1.80	1.62	1.44	1.26	1.08	.90	.72	.54	.36	.18	.09	5.1	60
65	2.10	1.89	1.68	1.47	1.26	1.05	.84	.63	.42	.21	.11	5.5	65
70	2.40	2.16	1.92	1.68	1.44	1.20	.96	.72	.48	.24	.12	6.0	70
75	2.74	2.47	2.19	1.92	1.64	1.37	1.10	.82	.55	.27	.14	6.4	75
80	3.10	2.79	2.48	2.17	1.86	1.55	1.24	.93	.62	.31	.16	6.8	80

2 1/2" (2.655" I.D.)

GPM												Vel	GPM
50	.50	.45	.40	.35	.30	.25	.20	.15	.10	.05	.03	2.9	50
60	.70	.63	.56	.49	.42	.35	.28	.21	.14	.07	.04	3.5	60
70	.96	.86	.77	.67	.58	.48	.38	.29	.19	.10	.05	4.1	70
80	1.22	1.10	.98	.85	.73	.61	.49	.37	.24	.12	.06	4.6	80
90	1.52	1.37	1.22	1.06	.91	.76	.61	.46	.30	.15	.08	5.2	90
100	1.84	1.66	1.47	1.29	1.10	.92	.74	.55	.37	.18	.09	5.8	100
110	2.20	1.98	1.76	1.54	1.32	1.10	.88	.66	.44	.22	.11	6.4	110
120	2.58	2.32	2.06	1.81	1.55	1.29	1.03	.77	.52	.26	.13	7.0	120

3" (3.230" I.D.)

GPM												Vel	GPM
80	.46	.41	.37	.32	.28	.23	.18	.13	.09	.05	.02	3.1	80
90	.58	.52	.46	.41	.35	.29	.23	.17	.12	.06	.03	3.5	90
100	.70	.63	.56	.49	.42	.35	.28	.21	.14	.07	.03	3.9	100
110	.84	.76	.67	.59	.51	.42	.33	.25	.17	.08	.04	4.3	110
120	.98	.88	.78	.69	.59	.49	.39	.30	.20	.10	.05	4.7	120
130	1.14	1.03	.91	.80	.68	.57	.46	.34	.23	.11	.06	5.1	130
140	1.32	1.18	1.05	.92	.79	.66	.52	.39	.26	.13	.07	5.5	140
150	1.50	1.35	1.20	1.05	.90	.75	.60	.45	.30	.15	.08	5.9	150
160	1.68	1.51	1.34	1.18	1.01	.84	.67	.50	.34	.17	.09	6.3	160
170	1.88	1.69	1.51	1.32	1.13	.94	.75	.56	.37	.19	.10	6.7	170

4" (4.154" I.D.)

GPM												Vel	GPM
150	.44	.39	.35	.31	.26	.22	.17	.13	.09	.04	.02	3.6	150
160	.50	.45	.40	.35	.30	.25	.20	.15	.10	.05	.03	3.8	160
170	.56	.51	.44	.39	.33	.28	.22	.17	.11	.05	.03	4.0	170
180	.62	.56	.49	.43	.37	.31	.25	.18	.12	.06	.03	4.3	180
190	.68	.62	.55	.48	.41	.34	.28	.21	.14	.07	.04	4.5	190
200	.74	.67	.59	.52	.44	.37	.30	.22	.15	.07	.04	4.7	200
210	.80	.72	.64	.56	.48	.40	.32	.24	.16	.08	.04	4.9	210
220	.88	.80	.71	.62	.53	.44	.36	.27	.18	.09	.05	5.2	220
230	.96	.86	.77	.67	.58	.48	.38	.29	.19	.09	.05	5.4	230
240	1.04	.94	.83	.73	.62	.52	.42	.31	.21	.10	.05	5.7	240
250	1.12	1.01	.90	.78	.67	.56	.45	.34	.22	.11	.06	5.9	250
260	1.20	1.08	.96	.84	.72	.60	.48	.36	.24	.12	.06	6.2	260
270	1.28	1.16	1.03	.90	.77	.64	.52	.39	.26	.13	.07	6.4	270
280	1.38	1.24	1.10	.97	.83	.69	.55	.41	.28	.14	.07	6.6	280

The flexibility to do this is built into most good irrigation controllers such as the Toro IC-series controllers used in the example. It is important that designers think about their water demands and use the features of the available equipment to ensure the most efficient use of the water.

Typical turf zone 300 series heads:

The watering time for the turf areas using the 300 series heads is a very simple calculation since the precipitation rates of these heads is well below the infiltration rate of the soil, which was 0.29 in/hr. Given the evapotranspiration rate of 0.25 in/day for turf grasses in warm zones, the weekly demand is:

0.25 in/day × 7 days = 1.75 in/week

The weekly operating time is:

1.75 in/week ÷ 0.29 in/hr = 6.03 hr/week

Based on 3.5 watering cycles per week, the watering time for each cycle would be:

6.03 hr/week ÷ 3.5 cycles per week = 1.72 hr/cycle or about 103 minutes per cycle

Most irrigation controllers will only allow stations to be programmed for up to 60 minutes for each watering period, so in this case the turf stations would be programmed to operate for two periods during each cycle, 52 minutes each time.

The program times noted here are for peak growing periods in each case. Keep in mind that these times need to be reduced during the fall and winter months when plants will be dormant. Depending on the controller this may mean reprogramming the controller, or in some cases, just switching to another program. Figure 8-27 is a completed controller program for the example problem.

CONTROLLER PROGRAM

STATION NUMBER	HEAD TYPE	PRECIPITATION RATE IN/HR	WATER REQUIRED IN/WK	CYCLES PER WEEK	PERIODS PER CYCLE	TIME PER PERIOD MINUTES
1	570	1.28	1.40	3.5	4	9.5
2	300-01	0.86	1.75	3.5	4	9
3	300-63	0.29	1.75	3.5	2	52
4	570	1.28	1.40	3.5	4	9.5
5	300-63	0.29	1.75	3.5	2	52
6	300-63	0.29	1.75	3.5	2	52
7	570	1.28	1.40	3.5	4	9.5
8	300-63	0.29	1.75	3.5	2	52
9	570	1.28	1.75	3.5	4	9.5
10	570	1.28	1.40	3.5	4	9.5
11	570	1.28	1.75	3.5	4	9.5
12	300-63	0.29	1.75	3.5	2	52

STATION	EMITTER	WATER RATE GPH	WATER REQUIRED GPH	CYCLES PER WEEK	TIME PER CYCLE HOURS	HOURS PER WEEK
A	700-01	2	70	3.5	10	35
B	700-01 x2	4	105	3.5	7.5	26.25
C	700-02	1	70	7	10	70
D	700-03 x2	4	140	7	5	35

FIGURE 8.27 CONTROLLER PROGRAM

LIGHTING

DESIGN

Introduction

Site lighting is a practical consideration as well as a design consideration in any new project. Good lighting can extend the use of outdoor environments, contribute to the safety of many areas, and add charm and drama to the nighttime landscape.

The field of lighting design is a highly developed and specialized technology that is constantly changing with new discoveries in optics, light sources, and the understanding of light energy. For these reasons, our discussion in this chapter will be limited to those general considerations that are not likely to change rapidly. The objective of this chapter is to present a foundation of basic materials that can be expanded to meet the needs of the individual practitioner. The chapter is organized into four sections that discuss the kinds of lighting equipment, basic lighting techniques, the fundamentals of electricity, and the preparation of electrical plans.

Lighting Equipment

The lighting industry produces lighting equipment to serve three functional levels: utility and security lighting, area lighting, and effect lighting. Utility and security lighting is a practical consideration that enters every landscape project and may be associated with area or effect lighting. The major objective of utility lighting is to increase the efficiency of the driver or pedestrian in the nighttime environment. Characteristically, light levels are minimal and color and uniformity are minor considerations. Area lighting as used here refers to lighting systems designed to permit

the use of an area with near daylight conditions. These are the systems normally associated with athletic fields, complex highway interchanges, or high-use public spaces. These kinds of lighting systems typically require special attention to the lighting distribution pattern, light source, and color. Effect lighting is the most demanding of the three lighting levels, because it must satisfy the objectives of security and utility lighting with the added objective of creating an interesting visual environment.

The fixtures used for lighting in the landscape can be classified in two ways: light source and the light distribution pattern of the light fixtures (luminaire). Within these broad classifications there are innumerable shapes, sizes, colors, and suggested applications. These are a matter of taste and designer preference. For this reason, specific examples or references to equipment will be avoided in this discussion. There are two families of light source common to outdoor lighting applications: incandescent filament lamps and electric-discharge lamps. Within each family there is a host of variation in the lamps themselves. These differences result in a wide variety of light color, lamp life, energy efficiency, and suitability for specific uses.

INCANDESCENT LAMPS

Incandescent filament lamps produce light by passing an electric current through a filament, usually tungsten, which heats to an incandescent (glowing) state. Incandescent lamps common to landscape applications include the common light bulb; sealed-beam lamps; low-voltage lamps; and tungsten-iodine lamps, frequently called quartz-iodine lamps. Incandescent lamps characteristically produce a more pleasing light color and are free of strobe effect. Strobe effect is a flickering of the light caused by the cycling of electric current. Strobe effect generally rules out the use of electric-discharge lamps for athletic courts and fields.

The primary disadvantage of the incandescent lamp is that it is the least energy efficient of the light sources, and much shorter-lived.

The types of incandescent lamps of the most interest to the landscape architect are the low-voltage incandescent lamps, and the standard voltage lamps made specifically for outdoor applications. The low-voltage lamps are usually sealed-beam lamps, similar to the headlights of an automobile, and operate on 12-volt direct current supplied by a centrally located transformer. Low-voltage lamps have the advantage of simple installation, wide availability, and they are much safer and less expensive than conventional lamps that operate on high-voltage alternating current. This is especially true when lights must be mounted below the ground where moisture could cause a hazard. Several major companies manufacture lines of low-voltage lighting equipment and fixtures are available in a variety of shapes, sizes, and lamp wattages. Color lenses and filters are also available with most lighting systems, which add another dimension to the design flexibility.

When it is necessary to use higher voltage lamps the designer must be sure that the fixture has been manufactured for, and approved for, the use intended. These fixtures may be much more expensive than a standard light fixture because the materials and quality control requirements are much more exacting.

ELECTRIC DISCHARGE LAMPS

Electric-discharge lamps is a large family of lamps that produce light by passing an electrical current through a gas or metallic vapor. Lamps most common to landscape applications are mercury vapor, metallic halide, fluorescent, high-pressure sodium, and low-pressure sodium.

The fluorescent lamp is probably the most familiar of these lamps. It is inexpensive and available for a wide range of applications. Its chief disadvantages are the length of the bulb, short life, and low energy efficiency. However, its adaptability, color flexibility, and availability many times make it a good choice. The mercury vapor lamp became quite popular in this country in the post-war period as the primary lamp used for highway and general lighting. The reason for its popularity is its longevity of 24 to 26 thousand hours. Its major drawbacks are in color and energy efficiency. The light produced is in the green to blue-green spec-

trum, which is not particularly flattering to many natural colors. Continuing research and development programs have been able to produce several hybrid lamps that have much improved color qualities. Metal halide is probably the most notable of these improved lamps; however, where purity of color is essential, mercury vapor lamps are still lacking.

Sodium lamps are becoming more popular than mercury vapor because of their energy efficiency. Note in Table 9-1 that mercury vapor lamps produce fewer lumens per watt than the sodium lamps, which means they are less efficient; however, this increased efficiency must also be weighed against the life of the lamp. When using the sodium lamp, there is a loss of as much as 10 thousand hours of lamp life.

While sodium lamps are very attractive in terms of energy, they also have some distinct disadvantages. They are relatively short-lived compared to mercury vapor lamps, and the light color is in the pink to orange spectrum, which is even less flattering than mercury vapor. In years to come some improvements may be made in color quality, but for now it is at the bottom of the list.

The other means of classifying lighting equipment is by the light distribution pattern. This feature is related to the characteristics of the light fixture and the lens rather than the type of lamp used. Light fixtures are often designed with reflectors and lenses that collect and focus the light in a specific pattern. The lamp produces the light energy and the light fixture determines how the light is distributed. For this reason, most fixtures are available with a number of different lamp options, allowing the designer to control the intensity and color of the light. Figure 9-1 shows the five standard light distribution patterns available for fixtures manufactured or distributed in this country.

The Type I luminaire is used for overhead applications that might occur in parking facilities or on some athletic facilities such as shuffleboard. It is also used for low-level fixtures that are employed for lighting walks, steps, and planted areas.

TABLE 9.1 COMPARISON OF LIFE AND EFFICIENCY OF LIGHT SOURCES

Light Source	Energy Efficiency Lumens per Watt	Life Hours
Incandescent, standard	10–18	750–1,000
Tungsten-iodine	18–20	2,000
Mercury vapor	55	24–26,000
Fluorescent	70	6,000
Metal halide	90	14–15,000
High pressure sodium	130	16,000
Low pressure sodium	190	11,000

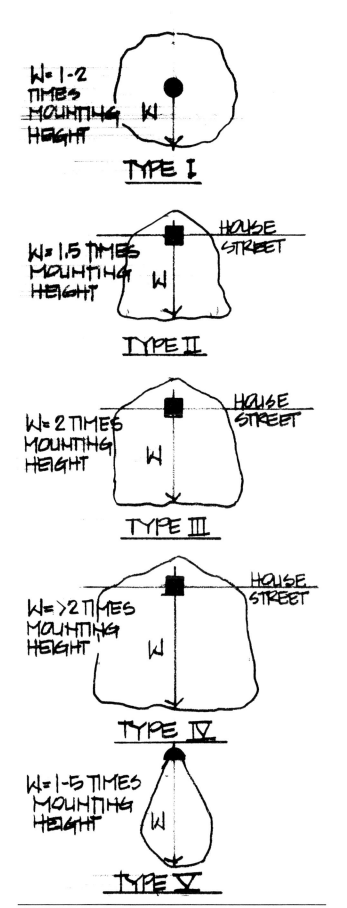

W= 1-2 TIMES MOUNTING HEIGHT

TYPE I

W= 1.5 TIMES MOUNTING HEIGHT

HOUSE STREET

TYPE II

W= 2 TIMES MOUNTING HEIGHT

HOUSE STREET

TYPE III

W= >2 TIMES MOUNTING HEIGHT

HOUSE STREET

TYPE IV

W= 1-5 TIMES MOUNTING HEIGHT

TYPE V

FIGURE 9.1 FIXTURE LENSES

Types II, III, and IV are luminaires that are used for street lighting and most general utility lighting applications. The only thing that distinguishes between the three is the ratio of light spread to mounting height. The larger the number, the greater the spread of the light.

The Type V luminaire is most commonly called a floodlight. The light beam is concentrated and can be aimed precisely to control illumination levels. Floodlights are most often used for lighting sports areas, building facades, signs, and for other decorative effects. Floodlights are available with a wide variety of light source, beam distribution, and lamp wattages for almost any application.

Designing Lighting Systems

The design of light distribution is a complex technology and many of the detailed concepts are beyond the scope of this discussion; however, there are some basic principles and methodologies that are useful to the landscape architect in making decisions about lighting. The background presented here will allow the designer to make most of the basic lighting decisions necessary for the average project. In addition, a good understanding of these principles will help in discussions with lighting consultants.

The primary concerns in the design of a lighting system are the level of light (brightness) to be maintained on a surface, the uniformity of the light distribution, the light color, and the aesthetic value of the lighting scheme.

The proper level of illumination is determined by the lighting function. Various standards for lighting levels have been established as guidelines to making these decisions, but there is little agreement among sources. Table 9-2 is a summary of recommendations, but users are cautioned to check with governing agencies before accepting the values given here.

DETERMINING LIGHT DISTRIBUTION

The primary measure of light intensity is the footcandle (fc). One footcandle is equal to one lumen of light energy distributed over one square foot.

There are several ways to determine how much light will be cast on any surface, but the two methods presented here are of the most use to the landscape architect. The point-by-point method for finding light distribution is the most popular method among most lighting specialists when accuracy is essential. In most cases, it is the preferred method for doing the design of sports fields. A less accurate but much less demanding method is the average illumination method. This system can be used for general lighting design such as

TABLE 9.2 RECOMMENDED LIGHTING LEVELS FOR SELECTED ACTIVITIES

Use	Recommended Illumination in Footcandles	
	Maximum	Minimum
Utility Lighting		
Minimum visibility	—	0.5
Driving	1.0	0.5
Pedestrian ways	1.0	0.5
Gardens, general	2.0	1.0
Area Lighting		
Parking lots	2.0	1.0
Tennis and handball	50.0	20.0
Baseball		
Infields	150.0[a]	50.0[b]
Outfields	100.0	20.0
Football	100.0	20.0

[a] For color telecasts.

[a] These values are sometimes called club class lighting and are preferred by the author. Lower values are sometimes used called recreation class lighting, but technology has increased light efficiency to the point that lower values are seldom justified even for reasons of cost.

the spacing of walk lights and lights for parking facilities. It should not be used for locating street lights, since there is no basis for determining the uniformity of the light distribution.

The Point-by-Point Illumination Method

The formula for the point-by-point method is

$$E_h = \frac{I \cos \theta}{d^2}$$

Where:

E_h = the illumination on the horizontal surface in footcandles

I = the lamp intensity in lumens

θ = the angle between the fixture and some known point on the ground

d = the distance from the luminaire to the point (see Figure 9-2)

To properly apply the point-by-point method, several other factors must be considered to produce accurate results. First, the light source will not retain its initial output over its entire life. Most lamps will deteriorate as much as 75% over their lifetime. This means that some adjustment for deterioration of the lamp should be made. In addition, outdoor fixtures will accumulate dust and oil films on the lenses that will further reduce the output, so an additional adjustment has to be made. In addition to loss of light from deterioration, the light intensity of any fixture will vary within the angle of the vertical plane. This means that

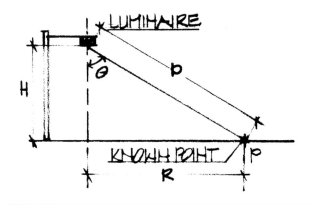

FIGURE 9.2 ELEMENTS OF POINT-BY-POINT METHOD

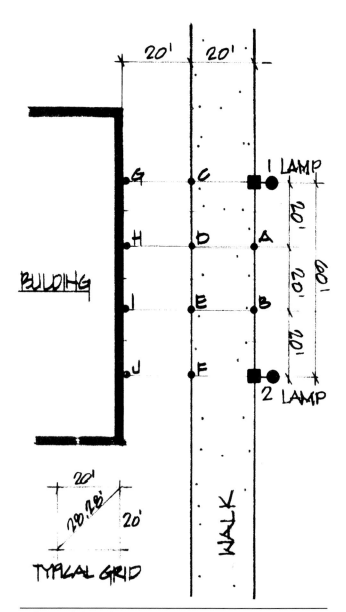

FIGURE 9.3 USING THE POINT-BY-POINT METHOD

the light intensity (I) will be different for each angle (θ) taken from the lens. The information about differences in light intensity can be found in the photometric data for the light fixture furnished by the manufacturer.

To illustrate the application of the point-by-point method, a simple problem using two luminaires will be solved. The basic information is shown in the schematic plan, Figure 9-3. Assume that the walk area in the plan is to be illuminated at a maintained level of 2 footcandles. The fixtures used in this example are Kim 400 watt, metallic halide, Type II luminaires. To determine the average maintained horizontal illumination it is necessary to calculate the actual illumination at several points on the ground. These points are labeled A-J in the figure. The photometric data for the fixture used is shown in Figure 9-4. The calculation for point A is worked out in detail.

The illumination at point A for fixture one is

$$E_h = \frac{I \cos \theta}{d^2}$$

First find that:

$$d^2 = h^2 + r^2$$
$$d^2 = 20^2 + 20^2$$
$$d^2 = 800 \text{ sq ft}$$
$$d = 28.28 \text{ ft}$$

Next find θ where

$$\sin \theta = \frac{r}{d}$$

$$\sin \theta = \frac{20 \text{ ft}}{28.28 \text{ ft}}$$

$$\sin \theta = 707213579$$

$$0 = 45°$$

From Figure 9-4 B, find the light intensity for an angle of 45 degrees is 5,430, and find E_h as follows:

$$E_h = \frac{I \cos \theta}{d^2}$$

$$E_h = \frac{5430 \times 0.707106781}{28.28^2}$$

$$E_h = 4.80 \ F_c$$

The values of E_h for the remaining points were found by the same procedure and are summarized in Table 9-3.

Notice the maximum to minimum ratio and the maximum to average ratio at the bottom of Table 9-3. These ratios offer a means of comparing the relative uniformity of light distribution over the area checked. For very sensitive areas, the maximum to minimum ratio should govern, and should not exceed, a ratio of

6:1. This is particularly important on major streets where traffic is traveling at speeds of 40 mph or greater. In these situations, if the light is uneven it can cause a condition known as "flicker vertigo" where a driver becomes disoriented. For less sensitive areas, the maximum to average ratio can be used and it should never exceed 10:1. When the ratio is greater than 10:1, there will be dead spots in the lighting that are completely dark and the area will be visually disconcerting.

Based on the maximum to average ratio, the lighting solution for Figure 9-3 is acceptable, but as yet there has been no allowance made for lamp deterioration or accumulation of dirt on the luminaire. A good round depreciation figure for most work is 50%. But in some areas, such as heavy industrial zones and on major freeways, a figure as high as 70% is advised. If the 50% adjustment is applied to the problem at hand, the average maintained illumination would be: 4.21×0.50 (the depreciation factor) $= 2.10 \ F_c$, maintained illumination.

Before leaving this example, it should be noted that most lighting solutions can be based on a 2-luminaire setup such as the one shown, since the addition of other fixtures on the same grid will repeat the same lighting pattern.

The Average-Illumination Method

The average-illumination method is less exacting than the point-by-point method but it is much faster to use, and gives reasonable results for general area lighting and utility lighting. The most useful application is for finding the desired spacing for fixtures along walks and in parking lots. The primary disadvantage of the method is that there is no basis for checking the uniformity ratio of the solution. Average illumunation is found by the equation

$$F_c = \frac{IuM}{LW}$$

Where:

F_c = average illumination in footcandles
I = lamp intensity in lumens
u = the coefficient of utilization
M = the maintenance factor
L = the horizontal distance between fixtures
W = the width of the area to be illuminated

The expression solved for L is

$$L = \frac{IuM}{F_c W}$$

To illustrate this method, the same problem used in the point-by-point method will be repeated so the results can be compared. All the equipment and conditions remain the same for the problem. The first

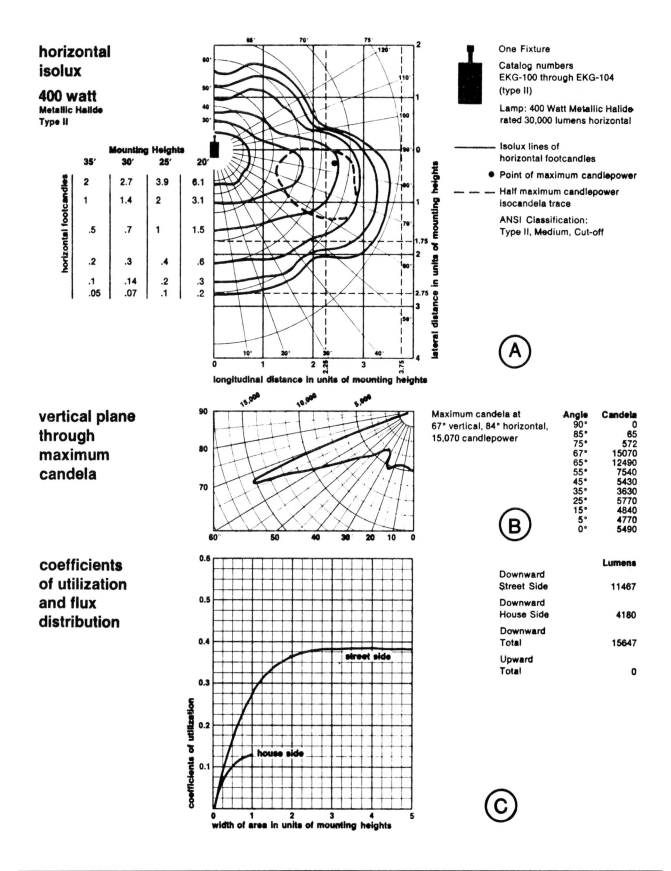

FIGURE 9.4 PHOTOMETRICS

TABLE 9.3 SUMMARY OF ILLUMINATION
INTENSITY FOR ALL POINTS Figure 9-3

Point	Luminaire 1	Luminaire 2	Total
A	4.80	2.41	7.21
B	2.41	4.80	7.21
C	4.80	0.04	4.84
D	3.61	0.81	4.42
E	0.81	3.61	4.42
F	0.04	4.80	4.84
G	2.41	0.03	2.44
H	2.21	0.53	2.74
I	0.53	2.21	2.74
J	0.03	2.41	2.44

Minimum to Maximum Ratio = 7.21 / 2.44 = 2.95: 1
Maximum to Average Ratio = 7.21 / 4.21 = 1.71: 1

step is to find all the values for each expression in the formula from Figure 9-4 and from the previous problem statement. The value of I is found in Figure 9-4 at the upper right-hand corner of the page (Lamp: 400 watt metalic halide rated 30,000 lumens horizontal). The value of u is found in the graph designated C in Figure 9-4, based on a mounting height of 20 ft and a space two mounting heights wide, (Fit 2 mounting heights read up to the street side graph then left to read $U = .3625$). The maintenance factor is assumed to be $M = 0.50$, which is the same value applied in the previous example. $L = 60$ ft, and W is 40 ft. Both values are taken from the problem statement.

$$F_c = \frac{IuM}{LW}$$

$$F_c = \frac{30,000 \text{ Lumens} \times .3625 \times 0.50}{60 \text{ ft} \times 40 \text{ ft}}$$

$$F_c = \frac{5,437.50}{2,400 \text{ sq ft}}$$

$$F_c = 2.27$$

The value for the adjusted point-by-point method was 2.10, which is very close to the value just computed. Typically, the values using the average-illumination method will be higher than values computed using the point-by-point method. In either case, the requirement for 2 F_c average maintained illumination has been satisfied.

The more common application of the average-illumination method is to find the appropriate spacing between fixtures for a preferred average illumination. Again, the same problem conditions will be used but this time the expression will be solved for L. This value will yield the maximum allowable spacing for the fixtures that will still provide the required 2 F_c average illumination.

$$L = \frac{IuM}{F_cW}$$

$$L = \frac{30,000 \text{ Lumens} \times 0.3625 \times 0.50}{2 \times 40 \text{ ft}}$$

$$L = \frac{5,437.5}{80}$$

$$L = 67.96 \text{ ft}$$

Thus, the maximum spacing that would be allowed and still maintain the required light level is about 68 ft. This also agrees with the previous figures. The spacing application is also very handy when trees and other plant material may interfere with the lighting. After determining the spacing, minor adjustments can be made in the lighting pattern, and then supplemental lighting can be added to correct any critical areas.

Designing Lighting for Effect

To this point in the discussion, only the principles of light distribution for area and utility lighting have been presented. These techniques work well and are accurate, but they are of limited value when lighting effect is the primary concern. Effect lighting is the technology of controlling the light intensity, direction, and color to achieve a desired composition. The kinds of effects that can be achieved by proper lighting quite often make a project feel and look quite different from its appearance in daylight. This can be both an advantage and a disadvantage.

On the one hand, the lighting designer can develop a system that will emphasize and highlight desirable parts of an outdoor composition and play down others. For example, single plants or features can be lighted to stand out against a dark background. Color can also be added as an ingredient to further emphasize the mood. The danger comes in planning only for the nighttime environment. A landscape composition that relies on light alone to achieve its charm may run the risk of being visually stale in the daylight hours. In some cases, such as lighting an entertainment spot or restaurant used mostly at night, this means of approaching a problem may be valid. But for most situations, the landscape must work in both daylight and darkness.

Effect lighting is a matter of designer preference; there is no absolute best answer for a given situation. Therefore, the objective of this section is to discuss a palette of lighting effects, how they are achieved, and some examples of how they are used. The basic palette of effects includes:

- Uplighting
- Downlighting
- Moonlighting
- Shadow and texture lighting
- Accent lighting
- Silhouette lighting
- Bounce lighting

Uplighting

Uplighting is one of the most striking of all lighting effects, because the light direction is counter to the normal daylight experience. It is most often used to accent plants or other landscape features. This lends a glowing silhouette effect to the object since there is a high contrast between outline and horizontal surfaces. One word of caution about using uplighting: Some cities will not permit the use of uplighting, because enough stray light at night will affect upward visibility.

Downlighting

Downlighting is not as unusual as uplighting because the eye is more accustomed to this condition. The primary feature is the ability to create texture patterns on the ground plane by directing the light through foliage or other overhead structures. It also provides a high contrast between upper and lower surfaces of foliage that can sometimes be used to good advantage.

Moonlighting

Moonlighting is an effect achieved by mounting lights high above the ground surface so that the light becomes diffused and casts hardly any shadow. In cases where there is no way to mount the lights high enough to reduce the shadow, a diffusion screen can be used and the wattage of the lamp can be reduced. The effect, if properly done, is very much like moonlight where objects are visible, but there is a minimum contrast between objects and colors are muted. Moonlighting gives an interesting effect along paths, in transition zones, and for intimate spaces like small view gardens. Moonlighting is not easy to achieve in some situations because it is very vulnerable to light spill from other areas of the project with higher light levels.

Shadow and Texture Lighting

Shadow and texture lighting are achieved by directing the light on, or through, an object. Many interesting texture effects can be generated by passing light through foliage or structures with small openings. It must be remembered that the coarseness of a shadow pattern will be related to the distance of the light source from the ground. The higher the light and its screen is from the ground the coarser the shadow pattern will be. As a general rule, objects with well-spaced, slender parts make the best subjects for generating light texture.

Texture lighting can be used to add interest to turf areas, and can be especially interesting on paved surfaces with little natural character. In many cases, texture effects are a by-product of downlighting in trees, which may or may not work to the advantage of the overall mood.

Accent Lighting

Accent lighting is most frequently associated with spot lighting a landscape subject; however, accents can be accomplished by any number of techniques. The chief component of any accent effect is sharp contrast with the surrounding elements. For this reason, accents can be achieved not only by spotlighting, but by uplighting, downlighting, or any other combination of methods that will provide a sharp contrast.

Silhouette Lighting

Silhouette lighting is achieved by lighting the background so the objects in the foreground appear as only outlined mass. In order to be effective, it usually requires that spotlights or floodlights with concentrated beams be used and that the background be reasonably close to the objects relative to the distance scale. If too much light spills out of the light fixtures used on the background, the subjects will lose the silhouette image. Likewise, if the background is too far from the object it will be difficult to generate the necessary contrast in light and dark.

Bounce Lighting

Bounce lighting is achieved by directing the light source against a reflective surface that redistributes the light to the desired area. This effect is often called indirect lighting. Many times this is a very exciting way to achieve the utility lighting requirements on a project. It can also be used to fill the areas between other lighting effects without directly exposing the actual light source.

LIGHT COLOR

The second important component of effect lighting is color. Color is a powerful tool that can be used to create mood or add emphasis and contrast. It can also cause some undesirable effects if not carefully handled.

The colors of the light spectrum are not the same as the primary colors of pigments; red, blue, and yellow. The primary colors of the light spectrum are red, blue, and green. The light colors that result by mixing the primary light colors are shown in the Maxwell Color Triangle in Figure 9-5. When the three primary light

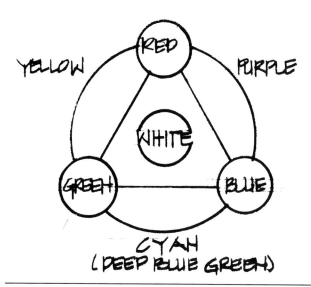

FIGURE 9.5 *MAXWELL LIGHT COLOR TRIANGLE*

colors are mixed the result is pure white light, which is the apparent absence of color.

Misconceptions about color pigments and light color often arise because of the different chromatic relationships. A very simple way to get at the relationship between object pigmentation and light color is to remember that the color of an object is the result of the surface reflecting certain colors in the light spectrum.

For example, a leaf appears green in the daylight hours because most of the reds and blues of the light spectrum are absorbed and the green light is reflected. If the same leaf is placed in yellow light; however, the blue light component is not present, and the leaf will appear brown.

As a rule, objects will look best if they are featured in light of the same color. Foliage looks best in green light, reds look best in red light, and so on. On the other hand, white objects sometimes appear cold and artificial in pure white light. In most cases, white or light color objects will look best in yellow or amber light. Amber is also a good choice for lighting water features.

The watchword in preparing plans that involve effect lighting is flexibility. The outdoor setting is in a perpetual state of change because of the season and growth of plant materials. Any lighting system should be designed to recognize these changes and be capable of future adjustment. Even initial installation will have to be fine-tuned in the field to be sure that the overall appearance matches the design concept.

Principles of Electricity

Electricity is a phenomenon that is still not fully explained. It can be said that all matter is composed of very small particles called protons and electrons. These small pieces make up an atom and the small particles themselves are electrical energy held together by magnetic attraction.

Protons carry a positive charge and form the nucleus of the atom. The electrons are negative charges that are attracted to the nucleus of positive charges. In the complex structure of some atoms like copper, iron, or aluminum, there is a large number of electrons in the outer shell that are not held tightly to the nucleus. These are called free electrons. Free electrons will move from one atom to another and they are the basic component of electric current. Materials that have a large number of free electrons are called conductors, and materials that have few free electrons are called insulators. The flow of free electrons through a conductor is electric current. Energy in this form can be converted to light, heat, or mechanical energy and captured to perform work.

POWER GENERATION

Figure 9-6 is a schematic of a simple electric power generator. When the conductor is rotated in the magnetic field, a flow of free electrons is set up. By convention, the flow is from the positive to the negative pole in a clockwise direction. As long as the line from the generator to the consumer (in this case a light bulb) is continuous, the flow of electricity will continue. This loop principle is called a circuit.

Large power generators used to produce power for the consumer market are more complex than the one shown in Figure 9-6, but the principles are exactly the same. Commercial power produced by a generator of this type is alternating current. The current alternation is caused by the rotation of the conductor coils inside the magnetic field, changing the position of the magnetic poles in relation to the conductor.

Commercial power generators are three-phase generators, because there are three sets of conductors

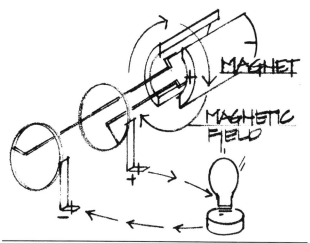

FIGURE 9.6 *GENERATOR SCHEMATIC*

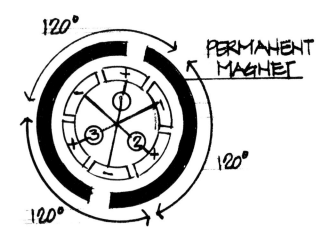

FIGURE 9.7 THREE PHASE GENERATOR

instead of the single set of conductors shown in the simple schematic. Figure 9-7 is a schematic of a three-phase generator. Each set of conductors in the generator produces electric current independent of the other two. The number of alternating current cycles produced by an alternating current generator is directly related to the speed of rotation. The standard cycling rate of electricity in this country is 60 cycles per second, or 60 Hz.

The reason for the three-phase generator is that a number of different power outputs can be obtained by using different combinations of the three phases. When all three phases of the generator are combined, it is called three-phase power; if only a single phase of the generator is used it is single-phase power. This characteristic of electric power is important when considering the cost, availability, and efficiency of an electrical system.

MEASUREMENT OF ELECTRIC POWER

Electric energy has two variables: volts and amps. These variables are best understood by drawing an analogy between electricity and water.

The ampere (amp) is a measure of current intensity, (the number of free electrons passing through the cross-sectional area of a conductor). This is analogous to a volume of water flowing through the cross section of a pipe. In a pipe, flow is measured in gpm or cfs; in an electrical system the volume is measured in amps.

Voltage is a measure of the force driving the free electrons in the system, or the electromotive force (emf). The emf is similar to the pressure in a hydraulic system. The magnitude of the pressure that moves water through a system is given in psi; emf is given in volts.

Since electric energy is transmitted at the speed of light (186,000 miles per second) the velocity of flow in an electrical circuit is taken as a constant; however, just

as there is resistance in a hydraulic system, there is a resistance to flow in an electrical conductor. As the flow of electrons occurs, there is a corresponding loss of voltage in proportion to the distance of travel. The resistance to electrical flow is measured in ohms.

The relationship between these three variables is expressed by Ohm's Law, which states the current that will flow through a given resistance is directly proportional to the voltage. This relationship is expressed as

$$I = \frac{E}{R}$$

Where:

I = the intensity of current in amps
E = the emf in volts
R = the resistance in ohms

Electric power, which is the potential energy present, is measured in units of watts. The energy input into any electrically operated appliance can be found by the expression

$$P = IE$$

Where:

P = power in watts
I = the intensity of flow in amps
E = the electromotive force in volts

This relationship is called the power formula. Since power is the product of volts times amps, the potential power of a system can be rated in terms of volt-amps (va) or, more often, thousands of volt-amps (kva).

POWER DISTRIBUTION

Power distribution is handled in two stages: There is the primary power distribution system that transmits power from the primary generating plant, and the secondary distribution system that serves the end consumer.

The primary power distribution system is operated at very high voltages from all three phases of the generator. The high voltage transmisson is done for simple reasons of economy. By operating at high voltage, the intensity of electron flow is reduced and the loss of energy is significantly reduced over great distances. Once the power reaches a consumer center it is stepped down to a lower voltage, primarily for reasons of safety. As power is transitioned from the primary distribution system to the secondary distribution system, it may be broken down to single-phase power or left as three-phase power.

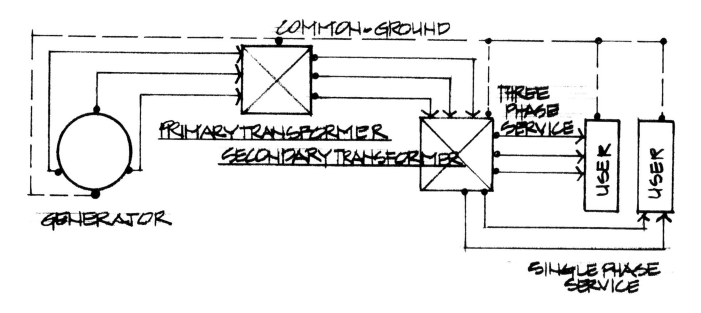

FIGURE 9.8 POWER DISTRIBUTION SYSTEM

Single-phase service uses only a single phase of the generator and is stepped down to service voltages of 240 or 480 volts. If a transformer is mounted above ground on a power pole, a single-phase system is easy to spot because there are only two insulator connections to the transformer—one linked to one of the primary generator phases and one tied to the common lead of the system. The standard service to a small electrical consumer, like a residence, is a 240-volt circuit that has three wires. One of the wires is the common lead called the ground, and the other two wires are power leads called hot wires that have an operating voltage of 120 volts. To operate a 120-volt appliance, a single lead and the ground are used; to operate a 240-volt appliance, two leads and the ground are required.

If a three-phase power secondary system is used, the power will be available as either a 208- or 277-volt operating system. Three-phase systems are also easy to identify because they have a four lead connection at the transformer: one wire for each phase of the generator and one common lead.

On large projects, three-phase power is the preferred operating system for site lighting and the operation of other site electrical systems because it is more efficient than single-phase power. If only single-phase power is available, it is wise to use high voltage equipment (240-volt or 480-volt) for the heavier electrical demands, to maintain the efficiency of the system. Practically all electrical equipment made for outdoor application is available in both three-phase and single-phase models, and for the standard operating voltages. Figure 9-8 is a diagram of the basic parts of the distribution system.

ON-SITE ELECTRICAL SYSTEMS

The on-site electrical service begins at the power meter and will often be both three-phase and single-phase service. Single-phase power is always used for the ordinary building service to operate the normal interior lighting system and other light-duty appliances. The three-phase system will only be used to operate other heavy systems that involve large, electric motors like pumps, large air-conditioning systems, heavy refrigeration, and large outdoor lighting systems. Figure 9-9 is a diagram of the the parts of a typical on-site power distribution system.

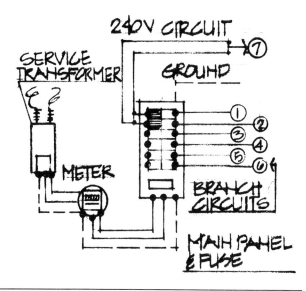

FIGURE 9.9 ON-SITE ELECTRIC SERVICE

branch circuit in the panel is protected by a fuse or circuit breaker that is also rated in amps. The usual amperage rating for a standard 120-volt circuit is 20 amps, and the rating for a 240-volt branch circuit will be 40 amps. There are appliances that require larger amperage capacity but these circuits will require heavier wire, and usually have a different type of outlet. Figure 9-10 is a diagram of a typical single phase branch circuit.

Standard building codes now require that all branch circuits in a building be installed with a system ground, or ground fault interrupter. This is to protect people from being electrocuted if the system or an appliance suffers a short. In these grounded circuits, the electric current will pass from the short to the ground rather than passing through the person touching the shorted appliance, as illustrated in Figure 9-11.

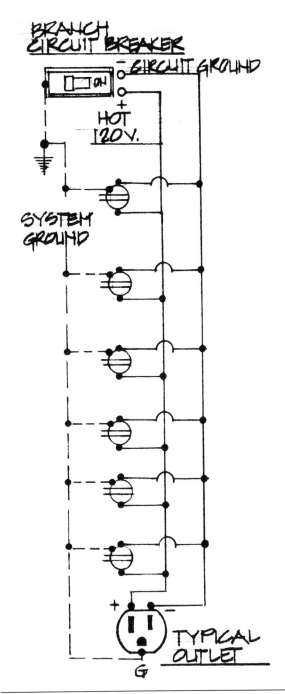

FIGURE 9.10 *TYPICAL BRANCH CIRCUIT*

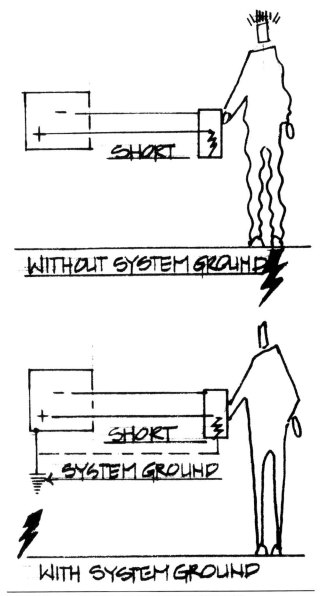

FIGURE 9.11 *120v THREE WIRE SERVICE*

The main power supply for a site is brought from the meter to a main power supply panel where distribution of the power is broken down into branch circuits. These branch circuits feed the various subsystems of the site. The size of the electrical service at the panel is always rated in amps. This rating is based on the voltage being supplied to the panel. For example, a main panel with a rating of 200 amps on a standard single-phase 240-volt service is capable of handling a peak power load of 48,000 watts, 240 volts × 200 amps = 48,000. Each

Wiring and Electrical Plans

The first parts of the chapter have looked at lighting equipment, basic lighting design, and some of the basic principles of electricity and power distribution. The objective of this section is to demonstrate the application of some of this theory in the preparation of simple electrical plans.

Electrical plans are one of the simplest of all working drawings to prepare because the information about wiring and layout is presented as a diagram rather than a scale representation of the finished product. Fixtures and appliances incorporated into the project are represented by simple symbols, and wiring is shown in simple schematic form. The specifications and performance characteristics of the various components are called out in schedules on the plans. The symbols used to do electrical plans should always conform to the nationally accepted standards for the electrical trades. Some of the most-used symbols are shown in Chapter 1. Proper use of these symbols is essential to avoid confusion in the bidding and construction process.

The electrical plan is usually prepared on a very simple schematic site plan that only shows the important structures, plant masses, roads and drives, and any underground utilities that may be affected by the electrical system. In some cases where the electrical work is only a minor part of the project, the electrical information may be included on other drawings. When this is done, be sure that the information is clear and will not be lost in the detail of other systems.

A procedure for the preparation of electrical drawings is provided below. This procedure is recommended as a checklist and guide for the student.

1. Check the local electrical codes and obtain copies of the requirements that will govern the work.
2. Contact the local power company and determine what kind of electrical service will be available at the project site. This is particularly important if high-voltage or three-phase equipment may be needed on the project. It is also wise to find out which services and equipment will be provided by the power supplier, and which will be required of the owner. The client's responsibility to pay for the extention of power lines and furnish switch gear and transformers can sometimes lead to budget disasters if not taken into account at an early date. Many times, the power company will be able to offer suggestions that can result in substantial savings in time and money.
3. Check the on-site power supply and determine what new service or system revisions will be necessary to operate the the new electrical equip-

ment. This is a very important step if the new work is an addition to an existing electrical system.
4. Prepare a schematic base map of the site. Indicate any on-site obstructions or other utilities that might interfere with the installation of the electrical work. Trees and roof overhangs are the most common offenders.
5. Locate all the required fixtures, appliances, switches, and panels on the plan using the proper symbols. Be sure that it is clear what equipment is new and what equipment is existing or furnished by others.
6. Size the wire to carry the load on each circuit and prepare an equipment and panel schedule.

To illustrate the preparation of a typical electrical plan, a large residential project is used as an example. Since much of the lighting for a residence is done for effect as well as utility and security, the base map in Figure 9-12 shows the outline of plant masses and location of trees.

For the purpose of the example, it is assumed that the local electrical code has been reviewed, and that the local power company has been consulted. A check of the existing power panel shows that the residence has a 200-amp service and there is room in the existing panel to add up to five additional 20 amp circuits. This means that no additions will have to be made to the the existing system. The equipment that is selected for the job includes eight 200-watt, 120-volt floodlights for downlighting in the trees. The downlighting is supplemented by six weatherproof duplex outlets located in the planting beds to operate spike mounted, 100-watt flood lamps. These provide flexibility for seasonal change.

In addition to the 120-volt equipment, several low voltage lamps have been used in the areas adjacent to the residence. These lamps were selected to do the permanent effect lighting at the entrance and near the terrace. Figure 9-12 shows the schematic layout of the lighting with the equipment legend.

The next step is to compute the load requirements and work out a panel schedule. To find the load, calculate the amperage load of each of the different fixtures as follows:
The 200 watt floods

$$I = \frac{P}{E}$$

$$I = \frac{200 \text{ watts}}{120 \text{ volts}}$$

$$I = 1.67 \text{ amps}$$

The duplex outlets will also equal 1.67 amps since each outlet will operate two 100-watt floods. The transfor-

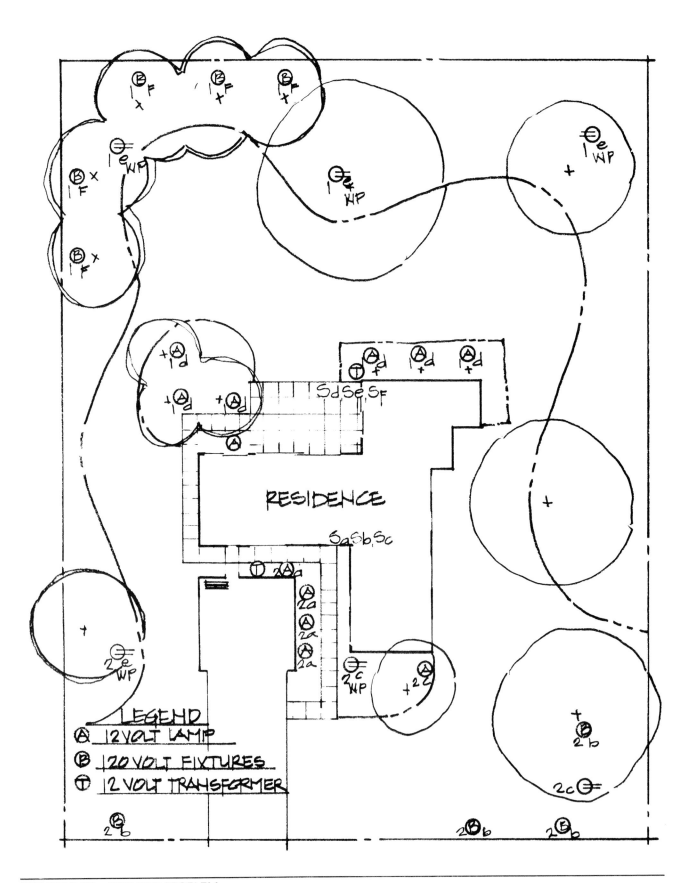

FIGURE 9.12 EXAMPLE PROBLEM

mers that operate the low voltage lighting are each rated at 126 watts

$$I = \frac{126 \text{ watts}}{120 \text{ volts}}$$

$$I = 1.05 \text{ amps}$$

The accumulated totals for the lights in the back yard and the front yard are tabulated below.

Amperage of back yard fixtures:

8–200 watt fixtures @ 1.67 amps	13.36 amps	
1-Transformer @ 1.05 amps	1.05 amps	
	14.41 amps	

Amperage of front yard fixtures:

7–200 watt fixtures @ 1.67 amps	11.69 amps	
1-Transformer @ 1.05 amps	1.05 amps	
	12.74 amps	

The maximum safe load on a branch circuit, as noted earlier, is 20 amps. This means that two additional branch circuits will have to be added to the existing panel to carry the additional load. Notice that even though the lights in the rear of the house are operated on the same panel circuit, the lighting system will be wired to allow separate operation of the three components. The operation will be controlled by three switches located near the terrace. The front section is also controlled by three switches located near the front door. All of this information is shown on the plan by symbols, Figure 9-12.

The final step is to size the wire. The process is quite similar to sizing pipe. As noted earlier, the flow of electricity through the wire will result in a loss of voltage similar to the pressure loss in a pipe. In an electrical system, the maximum allowable voltage drop in a line is 2% of the operating voltage. This amounts to 2.4 volts in a 120-volt electrical system. Table 9-4 gives the voltage drop in standard copper wire per 100 lf of run per   amp.

To illustrate how the wire sizing is checked, consider Figure 9-13. For the purpose of illustration, the approximate location of the wire and the length of run has been noted on the plan. Beginning at the panel branch, circuit one carries a load of 14.41 amps approximately 100 ft to the switches in the rear. From Table 9-4, find that a #10 wire loses 0.21194 volts per amp per 100 ft. Therefore, 14.41 amps × 0.21194 amps/100 ft = 3.05 volts. This is more than the allowable 2%. So a #8 wire is tried. A #8 wire loses 0.13325 volts per 100 ft per amp, so: 0.13325 × 14.41 = 1.92 amps, which is satisfactory.

From switch *e* to the first duplex outlet, the load will be 3 × 1.67 amps, or 5.01 amps. The load must travel

TABLE 9.4 VOLTAGE DROP PER 100 FT OF COPPER WIRE

Wire Size (awg)	Voltage Drop per 100 ft per Amp
3/0	0.01311
2/0	0.01652
1/0	0.02085
1	0.02628
2	0.03314
3	0.04179
4	0.05270
6	0.08380
8	0.13325
10	0.21194
12	0.33690
14	0.54767

about 40 ft. For the first effort, try a #12 wire at a loss of 0.33690 volts per 100 ft per amp. Therefore, 5.01 amps × 0.33690 volts × .40 100 ft = 0.675 volts. This appears to be satisfactory.

From the duplex outlet, the line splits and carries 1.67 amps 60 ft to the other duplex outlets. From Table 9-4 find that a #14 wire loses 0.54767 volts per amp per 100 ft. Therefore, 1.67 amps x 0.54767 volts × 0.60 100 ft = 0.548 volts. The total voltage loss for the circuit is tabulated below.

The accumulated voltage drop from the panel to the last duplex outlet is 3.14 volts, again greater than the allowable 2%. If #12 wire were used for the duplex outlet, the total drop would be reduced to 2.93 volts, which is still not enough. The best solution and the most common is to make the entire wire run in the back yard #12 wire. This will bring the voltage drop into acceptable limits.

Run	Voltage Drop	Wire Size
Panel to switch	1.92 volts	#8
Switch to first outlet	0.675	#12
First outlet to last outlet	0.548	#14
	3.143 volts	

It should also be noted that most electrical appliances have a safety range for low voltage operation. The average light bulb, for example, is rated for operation between 110 and 120 volts.

The wire sizes for the other zones of the project would be accomplished in the manner just illustrated: simple trial and error. It is not necessary to size the wire for the low voltage lamps since the manufacturer usually furnishes the proper wire with the lamps. If single components are purchased, or if it is necssary to use more wire than that supplied with the fixtures, the

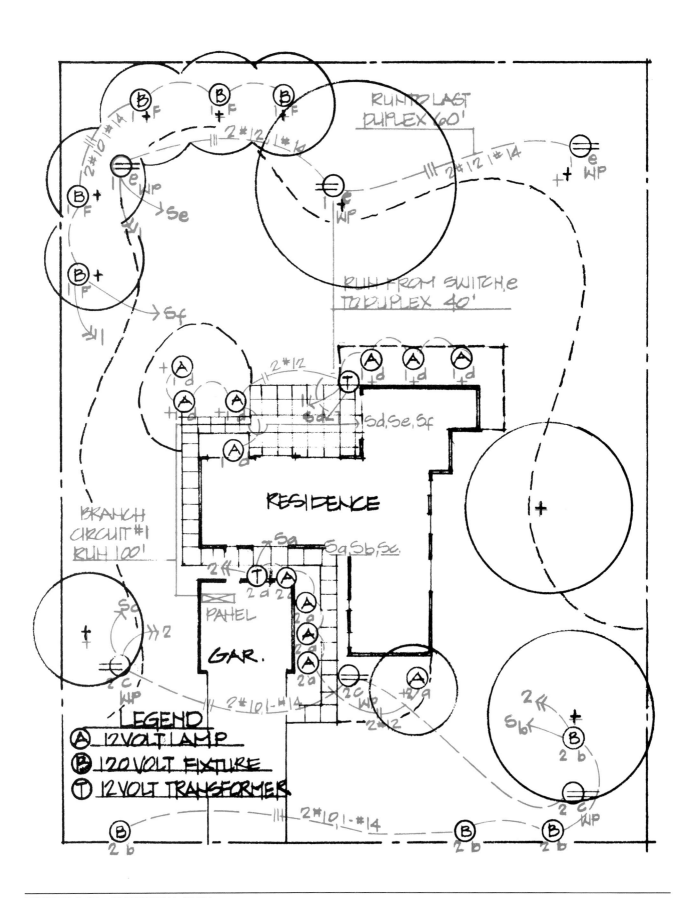

FIGURE 9.13 ELECTRICAL PLAN

ELECTRICAL FIXTURE & PANEL SCHEDULE

KEY	PANEL	CIRCUIT	LOAD AMPS	FIXTURES
Ⓑ Ⓐ	1 1	1 1	14.41	STANDARD DUPLEX OUTLET WP. 200 WATT FLOODS PRESTO LIGHT #200 BK. 12v 100WATT FLOOD CALIGHT #100-G2-A
Ⓑ Ⓐ	1 1	2 2 2	12.74	STANDARD DUPLEX OUTLET WP 200 WATT FLOODS PRESTO LIGHT #200BK 12v 100WATT FLOOD CALIGHT #100-G2-A
				PROVIDE 12.120v 100W. SPIKE MOUNT FLOODS PRESTO LIGHT #100.WP-SM

FIGURE 9.14 TYPICAL ELECTRICAL SCHEDULE

literature supplied by the manufacturer will provide information about the wire size required to install the equipment.

The basics of the final electrical plan are shown in Figure 9-13, and the typical electrical schedule, Figure 9-14. When space is available on the electrical plan, the schedule is usually placed on the same sheet as the plan. Students and professionals alike are cautioned to read the manufacturers' literature carefully when preparing the final materials schedule for the plan. The model numbering system used by most suppliers contains a lot of information including bulb type and wattage, lens type, case type, color, pole type, and other mounting accessories. Always double check these numbers to be sure that they are right for the job at hand.

FOUNTAIN
AND POOL
DESIGN

Introduction

The use of water in the landscape is one of the most challenging and delightful ways to add punctuation and interest to any landscape. Water, it seems, has the ability to attract attention and alter the mood of a space more quickly than any other feature. The reflective quality of a pool adds serenity to a space, the play of running water will cheer and make even a hot space feel cooler, and the intricate play of water jets adds visual interest that can be accomplished in no other way.

The design of good water features involves a working knowledge of three basic elements: equipment, basic hydraulics, and the structural requirements of pools. As with light and irrigation, our discussion of equipment will be limited to the basic components used in fountains and pools. There will be a brief discussion of hydraulics, related to weirs and water jets, and finally a consideration of the actual structural requirements of pools.

The subject of swimming pools is not considered in this discussion because, in the opinion of the author, the development of the pool industry makes it possible for a designer to select a pool package and type to fit almost any situation. The materials are plastic and lend themselves to many shapes and forms. The equipment is of high quality, for the most part, and is usually packaged in a fashion that requires little expertise to make a good selection for the problem at hand. Where large

swimming pools are concerned, the technical considerations reach far beyond the scope of this text, and will require the services of a good engineer.

Equipment for Fountains and Pools

There is a variety of fountain and pool equipment available on today's market specifically engineered to accomplish a variety of visual effects. Much of the equipment is furnished in kit form and will require very little in the way of additional fittings or equipment to achieve a very nice end product. Likewise, the manufacturers and their representatives are usually able to give technical assistance in the design and installation of fountains that use their equipment. In fact, it is wise early on in the development of a project to contact various equipment suppliers, find out what they have to offer, and let them know what the client has in mind. Many times they can offer valuable guidance.

NOZZLES

The heart of any fountain is the nozzle. The shape of the water jet and its performance is a function of the nozzle design. Fountain nozzles are precision components specifically developed to create certain effects. Some of the most basic types described in the following paragraphs.

Smooth-Bore Nozzles

Smooth-bore nozzles are used to achieve clear, smooth water columns. If a smooth-bore nozzle is placed in a vertical position it will give the appearance of a crystal or glass-like shaft supporting a frothing cascade at its summit. This is a particularly interesting effect when lighted but lacks visual appeal in daylight. Smooth-bore nozzles placed at an angle will maintain a clear shaft of water over the first part of the trajectory, gradually breaking into finer spray in its downward path. These basic effects are illustrated in Figure 10-1.

Aerating Nozzles

Aerating nozzles create water columns mixed with thousands of air bubbles. The diameter is usually larger than a comparable smooth-bore nozzle and they require higher operating pressures. The aerated water column has a much greater visibility in daylight or in other forms of high illumination. For this reason, it is usually preferred if only a single jet is used in a water

display or if the display is designed to be seen from a great distance.

The aerating nozzle operates by discharging water through several small jets near its base, or by an aeration sleeve. The stream picks up air, incorporates it into the water, and then the aerated stream is discharged as a single column. To achieve a proper air-water mixture, the water level around the nozzle is critical. At low levels, proper aeration will not take place and at high levels the column height will be markedly reduced. Since the water-level tolerance is usually less than 2 in, some kind of water level control is essential for any fountain with an aerating nozzle. Typical aerating nozzles are shown in Figure 10-2.

Multi-Jet Nozzles

Multi-jet nozzles are used to sculpture the water into a pattern, or they can be grouped to give the appearance of a large, single stream. Multi-jet nozzles can be most effective when water sound and pattern are the primary design objectives. Since the water pattern is controlled and more compact, these nozzles are frequently used where either wind or space could be a limiting factor. A variety of multi-jet nozzles is shown in Figure 10-3.

N112   N123

N112

FIGURE 10.1   SMOOTH BORE NOZZLES

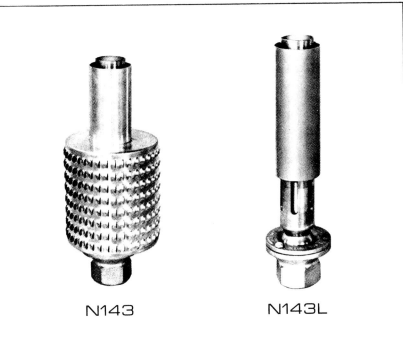

N143   N143L   N143

FIGURE 10.2 AERATING JET NOZZLES

PUMPS

The pumps used for fountains are similar to those used for irrigation systems. In most cases, small fountains will employ a small submersible pump that sits in the pool with the fountain equipment. These pumps simply take water directly from the pool and require no special plumbing to install. In larger fountains, where large water volumes and or high pressures are required, centrifugal pumps are used. These are mounted outside the pool at or below the elevation of the pool.

Large centrifugal pumps are noisy when they are operating and this is sometimes a problem if the pump is located in a pedestrian area near the pool. They also need to be protected from the weather, and must be accessible for periodic maintenance. The small submersible pumps mounted in the pool are sometimes visible, detracting from the overall appearance of the fountain. But the pump itself is not often as much an eyesore as the pipe that feeds the fountain nozzle and the electric cable that supplies the power to the pump. Often these items are just strung around on the bottom of the pool which in some cases looks like a junk pile. If a submersible pump is to be used, be sure that attention is given to the location of the pump, and the attendant plumbing.

Submersible pumps are also sensitive to water level. In most cases they must have at least 16 in of water over the top of the pump. If the pump is operated in shallower water, a vortex may develop over the pump and allow air to be drawn in, which can cause the pump to overheat and fail.

WATER LEVEL CONTROL DEVICES

There are two kinds of water level control devices: electronic sensors, and float-type valves. The electronic sensor is a small device with two electronic probes mounted in the side of the pool to mark the upper and lower water level. When the water level drops below the lower probe, the sensor sends a signal that opens a solenoid-operated valve to add water to the pool. The solenoid valves are exactly the same as those used for controlling an irrigation system. Electronic sensors are usually the best solution for pools that have a capacity of more than 1,000 cu ft of water, because it will be necessary to add large volumes of water quickly.

The float valve is just like the valve that operates the water closet at home. A float attached to an arm will rise and fall with the water level; when the float is sufficiently depressed, the valve opens and begins adding water to the pool. These valves are only good for pools with small volumes because they have very low delivery rates. They are seldom suited to pools in arid areas where high evaporation rates require almost constant addition of water. Another problem with these valves is that they must be mounted at the water line of the pool and they are visible. Care must be taken in locating a float valve to be sure it does not detract from

FIGURE 10.3 MULTI-JET NOZZLES

the appearance of to pool. Water level control devices are shown in Figure 10-4.

FILTERS

Large fountains should always be equipped with a filter system. Any outdoor pool is going to collect trash, sand and silt and, in warm weather, algae will be a constant problem. Dirt and algae in the water is not just an appearance problem. Pumps will be damaged by any solids in the water; coarse sand, for example, can ruin a pump in a very short period of time.

The filter systems are the same as those used for residential swimming pools. They are packaged systems that include the pump filter and the cleaning manifold already in place. A typical filter is shown in Figure 10-5. Careful consideration should be given to the location of the filter system because it requires frequent maintenance and is not particularly attractive.

OTHER ACCESSORIES

Wind Sensors

In small spaces where there is a lot of pedestrian traffic, it is often necessary to put a wind sensor on the fountain pump to shut it down when high winds occur. Spray from a fountain can waterspot glass and make

pavement very slippery to walk on. When this occurs, the fountain is no longer an asset.

Pattern and Light Displays

Many equipment manufacturers offer fountain controllers that regulate the water and light display. Any system that uses multiple nozzles is a candidate for such a controller. It can add measurably to the interest of the fountain. These controllers are sometimes used in conjunction with a wind sensor to adjust the water display for the wind conditions so that the whole water display will rarely be shut down.

LIGHTING

Pool lights are available with the same kinds of lamps discussed in Chapter 9. The primary difference in pool lights is the housing; it must be waterproof and of material that will not oxidize. Some light fixtures are made to be mounted into the pool wall or floor, but the more popular types are made to rest on the bottom of the pool. These are usually favored because any fixture mounted in the wall or bottom of the pool is a point of weakness where a leak might occur. The only thing that is critical when selecting pool lighting equipment is to be sure that the water level of the pool will provide sufficient water cover over the light fixture. Pool lights rely on the water in the pool to dissipate the heat generated

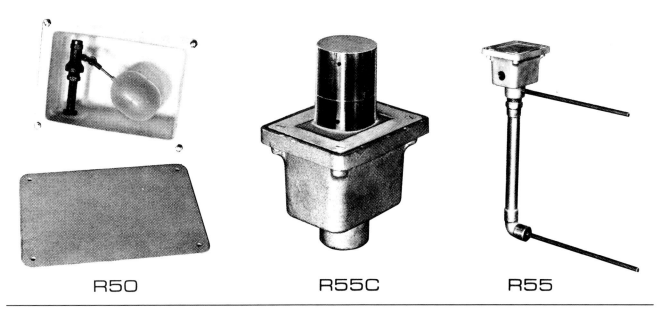

R50   R55C   R55

FIGURE 10.4 *WATER LEVEL CONTROL EQUIPMENT*

by the lamps. If the lens ever becomes exposed, the heat will break the lens and the lamp will leak. This will ruin the fixture and can be an electrical hazard.

Fittings

The utility fittings that are incorporated into a pool or fountain must be able to stand harsh chemicals and must not be subject to oxidation. Rust or oxidization of any kind can break the bond between the concrete and the fittings installed through the wall or bottom of the pool and it will begin to leak. The material most often used to machine or cast pool fittings is called "red

R-62-1

FIGURE 10.5 *POOL FILTER*

brass." Red brass is a copper-brass alloy that will not oxidize and lose its bond with the concrete. Things like stand pipes, anti-vortex plates, junction boxes, and other metal housings should be made of red brass.

Basic Hydraulics of Fountains

There are two types of water display used in ornamental fountains: water jets and cascades. Each of these effects is governed by a different set of hydraulic principles. The designer must have some knowledge of the general operational principles of each in order to achieve successful results.

WATER JETS

Water jets are the result of forcing water through a restricted orifice (nozzle) to increase the water velocity and create a uniform stream. As seen earlier in the discussion of equipment, there are several types of nozzles available to the designer to achieve a variety of effects. In each case, the performance of the nozzle is related to a specific volume of water at a given pressure.

When the initial design of a fountain has been completed with respect to the size of the pool and character and height of the of water display, the next major task is picking and sizing the pump. To illustrate the procedure, consider the fountain in Figure 10-6.

The water display is to be a single aerating nozzle that will produce a water column of 20 ft. The hydraulic requirements furnished in the manufacturer's literature, Figure 10-7, indicate that this requires a pump that will deliver 136 gpm at 45 ft of head. This volume and demand is at the upper limit of most submersible pumps, so a centrifugal pump will be the best choice.

Figure 10-8 is an example of typical pump data taken from a Kim fountain equipment catalog. The pump curves illustrate the pump performance in feet of head at specified delivery volumes. The actual performance requirements of the nozzle selected are slightly more than the performance of the KP4 series pumps, so the KPL series pumps appear to be the best choice. The KPL-300 would appear to be an almost perfect match operating at the peak of the pump's efficiency; at a flow of 136 gpm, it produces almost exactly 45 ft of head; however, no allowance has yet been made for head loss between the pump and the nozzle, and it will be very difficult to design the delivery system with no loss of head. Several things can be done at this point. Kim could be contacted directly, to recommend a different pump, or the design parameters can be reconsidered. Looking back at the specifications of the nozzle, it is clear that the nozzle will perform at pressures as low as 37 ft of head at a height of 15 ft so, in all likelihood, the actual height of the aerated column generated using the model KPL-300 pump with the N-146 nozzle will be somewhere between 15 and 20 ft. The question is whether the 20-ft height is that important. In either case it would be wise to contact a Kim representative directly

and find out if the use of that particular pump is recommended.

The problem of matching pumps to nozzles, as illustrated here, is typical, and the solution usually involves calling the manufacturer to find out what the best course of action would be. Pumps are available for practically any performance combination of pressure and volume that can be imagined. For this reason, catalogs such as Kim's only show a few of the more common performance ranges of the pumps they sell.

Computations with respect to the pressure loss in the suction line and discharge lines of the water delivery system are done in exactly the same way as for irrigation systems. The only word of caution is that pressure loss should be considered for every component of the delivery system, since a fountain nozzle will respond to any variation in the delivery pressure. This is very important when designing a water display that has more than one nozzle operated by a single pump. The piping that distributes the water to the nozzles should be laid out in a way that will equalize the pressure delivered to each head. This often requires the installation of pressure compensating valves in the delivery lines or at the base of the nozzle. One fact that will always help in making decisions about pump selections is that excess pressure can be taken care of in the system, but generating more pressure is seldom possible.

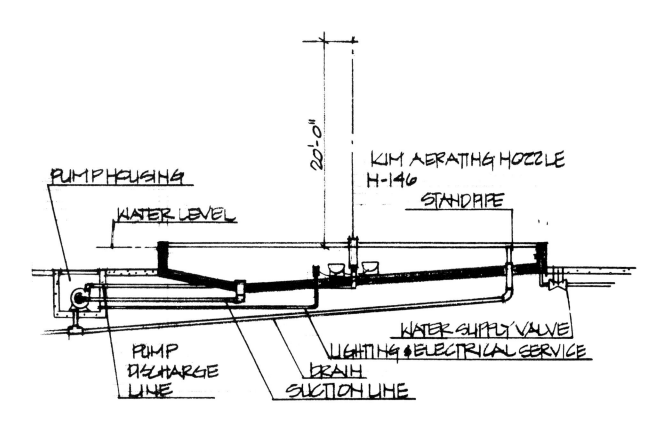

FIGURE 10.6 POOL AND FOUNTAIN SCHEMATIC

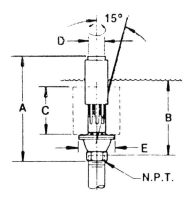

| Model | | | | Trash Screen | | | |
Number	N.P.T	A	B	C	O.D.	D	E
N-140	1/4"	7	5"	$3^{13}/_{16}"$	$3^5/_{16}"$	1/4"	2 1/4"
N-141	1/2"	$7^{15}/_{16}"$	5 1/2"	$3^{13}/_{16}"$	$3^6/_{16}"$	1/2"	2 1/2"
N-142	1"	$9^9/_{16}"$	6 1/2"	4 1/4"	4 1/2"	1"	2 1/4"
N-143	1 1/4"	$11^3/_{16}"$	8"	4 1/2"	4 1/2"	1 1/4"	3 1/4"
N-144	1 1/2"	$13^3/_{16}"$	9"	5 1/8"	$5^{13}/_{16}"$	1/8"	3 3/4"
N-145	2"	$15^9/_{16}"$	11"	$7^{15}/_{16}"$	$8^1/_{16}"$	2"	4 1/2"
N-146	3"	20 1/4"	14 1/2"	8 5/8"	$9^1/_{16}"$	2 1/4"	6 1/8"
N-147	4"	25 3/4"	18"	NOT AVAILABLE		4"	8 1/4"

Model Number	Spray Height	2'	3'	4'	5'	6'	8'	10'	12'	15'	20'	25'	30'	35'	40'	45'	50'
N-140	GPM	2.5	3	3.54	4	4.5											
	Head	21'	23'	28'	35'	42'											
N-141	GPM		4.5	6	7	7.5	8										
	Head		16'	24'	27'	35'	40'										
N-142	GPM			9	11	12	13										
	Head			22'	26'	30'	35'										
N-143	GPM			13	14	16	18	19	20								
	Head			16'	20'	26'	30'	37'	45'								
N-144	GPM			28				37		43	48	53	57	60			
	Head			25'				35'		50'	64'	78'	94'	112'			
N-145	GPM			40				50		59	68	73	78	83	87		
	Head			25'				35'		45'	56'	68'	82'	100'	120'		
N-146	GPM			75				104		123	136	148	157	165	173	180	186
	Head			22'				30'		37'	45'	53'	62'	70'	80'	90'	105'

FIGURE 10.7 NOZZLE PERFORMANCE SPECIFICATIONS

WEIRS AND CASCADES

A water cascade falling from level to level is an interesting detail that is frequently employed in water displays. Several different visual effects can be obtained with the cascade, depending on the design detail of the face of the weir and the water volume passing over it.

Smooth-faced weirs allow the water to pass over them in a clear sheet; as the water falls from the upper to the lower pool, it will begin to break up as air is mixed with the water. The amount of break-up of the water sheet is dependent on the volume of water passing over the weir and the vertical distance between the upper and lower pool. The greater the volume of water passing over a smooth faced weir the greater the distance it will travel before breaking up.

Rough-faced weirs break up the water as it passes the top and this forms an opaque sheet. Depending on the volume passing over the weir, the water will break up more as it falls and leave gaps in the sheet as it reaches the lower pool. The gaps in the sheet produce a more irregular sound than water flowing over a smooth-faced weir, which will remain an almost con-stant rush. For this reason, rough-faced weirs are most often used where the sound is the primary design effect.

ESTIMATING WATER VOLUME OVER WEIRS

The volume of water required to maintain a desired depth of flow over a rectangular weir can be estimated by Bazin's formula:

$$Q = \left(.405 + \frac{.00984}{H}\right)\left[1 + \left(.55 \frac{H^2}{(P+H)^2}\right)\right]LH\,(2gH)^{.5}$$

Where:

Q = water volume in cubic feet per second

H = head in feet (the depth of the water taken at a distance of $4 \times H$ from the face of the weir, see Figure 10-9)

P = the height of the weir above the upper pool level in ft

L = the length of the weir in ft

g = 32.17 (the universal gravity constant)

Model Number	HP	A	B	C	D	E	R	S
KPL-50-1 KPL-50-3	½	20⅜"	6⅛"	11½"	8"	11"	1½"	1½"
KPL-70-1 KPL-70-3	¾	21⅜"	8⅜"	12½"	8"	11"	1½"	1½"
KPL-100-1 KPL-100-3	1	21¾"	9¾"	12¾"	8"	11"	2"	2"
KPL-150-1 KPL-150-3	1½	22½"	9¾"	13⅛"	8"	11"	2"	2"
KPL-200-1 KPL-200-3	2	22½"	9¾"	13⅛"	8"	11"	2"	2"
KPL-300-1 KPL-300-3	3	23"	9¾"	14⅛"	8"	11"	2"	2"

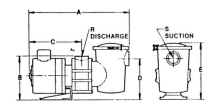

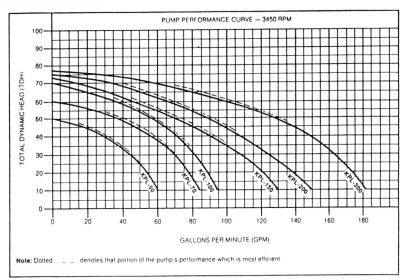

Note: Dotted _ _ _ denotes that portion of the pump's performance which is most efficient

Note: Performance for -1 (single phase) and -3 (three phase) pumps are the same

Model Number	HP	A	B	C	D	E	F	G	H
KP4-30-3	3	22"	10"	7½"	6"	4⅞"	4⅛"	2½"	3"
KP4-50-3	5	23"	10"	7½"	7½"	6⅞"	4¼"	3"	4"
KP4-75-3	7½	25"	12"	7½"	7½"	6⅞"	4¼"	4"	5"
KP4-100-3	10	27"	12"	7½"	7½"	6⅞"	4¼"	4"	5"
KP4-150-3	15	30"	14"	6⅞"	7½"	6⅛"	4¼"	4"	5"

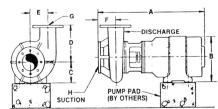

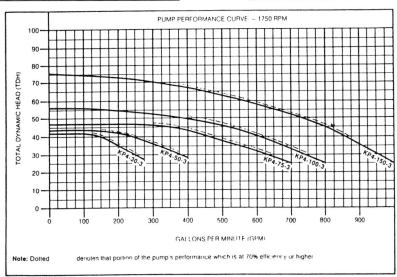

Note: Dotted _ _ _ denotes that portion of the pump's performance which is at 70% efficiency or higher

FIGURE 10.8 PUMP CURVES

To illustrate the application of the formula, consider the cascade in Figure 10-9. The dimensions and the letters of the appropriate terms are shown on the drawing. The solution is as follows:

$$Q = \left(0.405 + \frac{0.00984}{0.33\text{ft}}\right)$$
$$\left[1 + \left(0.55\ \frac{0.33\text{ ft}^2}{(1\text{ ft} + 0.33\text{ ft})^2}\right)\right]$$
$$3\text{ ft} \times 0.33\text{ ft } (2 \times 32.17 \times 0.33\text{ ft})^{.5}$$
$$Q = 0.4348 \times 1 + 0.03386 \times .99 \times 4.6078$$
$$Q = 0.4348 \times 1.033860 \times .99 \times 4.608$$
$$Q = 2.05\text{ cfs}$$

To convert cfs to gallons per minute multiply cfs by 448.831:

$$2.05\text{ cfs} \times 448.831\text{ gpm/cfs} = 920.10\text{ gpm}$$

The 920 gpm figure represents the water required to maintain approximately a 4-in-deep cascade flowing over the weir. The 4-in depth was used for illustration purposes to make the point that the cascade water effect will usually require a larger volume of water than might be expected. If the water depth is reduced to 1 in, the cascade would only require a volume of around 130 gpm and a ½-in depth would reduce the requirement to about 60 gpm. The drop from the upper pool to the lower pool must be considered in the final selection of depth of flow over the weir. As a rule of thumb, the depth should be about ¼ in for each vertical foot of fall if the sheet of water is to be maintained.

The use of this formula assumes that the elevation of the weir is above the downstream water level and that the front edge of the weir is open to the atmosphere. If either of these conditions is not met, the volume of water required to maintain the desired depth will be greater than the volume calculated. It should also be noted that the actual depth of the water at the edge of the weir will be somewhat less due to the constantly increasing velocity of the water sheet as it travels over the weir crest.

The head requirement for pumps used to generate a cascade is very low since it only needs to be enough to lift the water from the lower pool to the upper pool. Excess head will cause the water in the upper pool to boil and this can interfere with the flow over the weir. In most cases, it will be necessary to provide a valve at the inlet to the upper pool to regulate the flow and pressure.

Pool Construction

The pool is the heart of a successful water feature in the landscape. A well-designed pool can reduce maintenance, complement the active water display, and accent the overall landscape composition. If the pool is poorly designed, the life of the water feature will be short indeed.

The most common reason for abandoning a water feature is pool leakage. Mechanical equipment can be repaired or replaced, but a leak in a pool is difficult to locate and often impossible to repair. Therefore, no expense should be spared in the design of the pool. The things that should be considered in developing the details of a pool are water depth, surfacing, structural material, water level control, and the drain.

Pool Depth

The minimum recommended pool depth is 16 in. This seems to be the best depth to achieve a good reflective

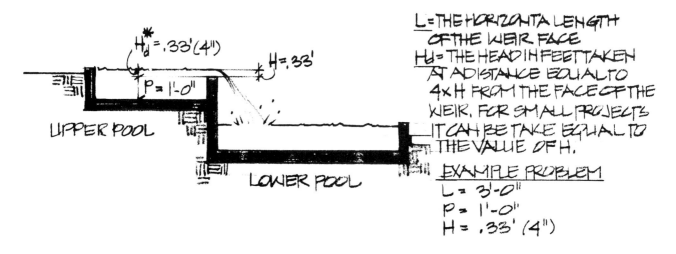

FIGURE 10.9 ESTIMATING FLOW OVER WEIRS

surface, prevent excessive algae growth, and satisfy the requirements of most domestic fountain equipment; i.e., lamps and submersible pumps. Depths of less than 16 in should always be used advisedly since algae will develop quickly in shallow, warm water. Similarly, deeper pools seem to offer no great advantage unless there is some specific reason for the greater depth, such as a pump that might require more water over the intake orifice. In these cases, it is wise to cast a special sump in the bottom of the pool and keep the rest of the pool at about 16 in deep.

POOL SURFACING

The pool surfacing should be selected with two things in mind: the ease of cleaning and the desired appearance of the water surface. For ease of maintenance, the interior surface of the pool should be as smooth as possible with all rounded corners. The best finishes are ceramic tile and or steel trowled portland stucco.

The appearance of the water surface is affected by the color of the bottom of the pool. Light colors will make the water appear transparent, dark colors cause the surface to be reflective. In most situations, the dark colors are preferred, particularly when there are vertical structures that could be reflected to good advantage. Keep in mind that when light-colored finishes are used, everything in the pool is visible.

STRUCTURAL MATERIALS

A number of materials can be used to make a pool that will hold water. Among these are copper, PVC, fiberglass, and concrete. Copper is an interesting material that is frequently used for small indoor pools. In fact, building codes often require the use of copper. PVC has been used as a liner on sand to generate large free-form water features. These have been reasonably successful as long as there is no traffic in the pool that might puncture the lining. Some of the newer lining materials used to line agricultural ponds are very tough and make an excellent lining material for water features of this kind, but they are very expensive. Some liner materials may cost as much as or more than concrete. Fiberglass has been employed as a material for prefabricated pools of all shapes and sizes, and for small jobs this may be a very good choice of material. It is durable, easy to maintain, and lightweight. The sometimes makes a good choice for rooftop or interior applications.

Concrete is still the most common of all the materials used for pools, and is probably the best for most situations. Concrete is durable and can be formed and finished in a wide range of shapes and colors.

While concrete offers distinct advantages, keep in mind that it is not waterproof unless it is properly proportioned and finished. For most pool work, a special concrete mix should be used with small-graded aggregate and very rich in portland cement. It is often referred to in the trade as five-sack concrete. This simply means that five sacks of portland cement are used for each cubic yard of concrete. After the concrete is cured it must be plastered with a good quality portland cement stucco to fill the surface pores of the concrete and prevent leaking. The finish coat is necessary regardless of how the concrete is placed. If a color is used, it is usually incorporated into the finish plaster.

WATER LEVEL CONTROLS

For very small pools, it may not be necessary to provide a special valve for filling the pool. But for larger pools, over 35 cubic feet, a special fill line and an automatic water level control should be provided. The size of the fill line is determined by the volume of the pool. For medium-sized pools (40 to 80 cubic feet) a ¾-in line is sufficient; for larger pools, a 1- to 1½-in line should be provided.

The fill line should be brought to the pool next to the automatic level control valve, at a point that is easily accessible for maintenance. If a float valve is used, it is best located in the front edge of the pool, since this is the part of the pool that is least seen.

All pools should have an overflow control. This is accomplished by simply providing a standpipe threaded into the pool drain that extends to the desired water level. The pipe is open so that any excess water will simply drain out of the pool. To drain the pool, the standpipe is simply removed. See Figure 10-10.

The pool drain must be connected to either a storm sewer or a sanitary sewer. The requirements vary from city to city. Most cities seem to prefer connection to the sanitary sewer. Always be sure to check the elevation of the pool in reference to the sewer line. Pools are often located in low lying areas that will not allow them to gravity drain. In these situations, a pump must be used to drain the pool. This is not a big problem if the pool has a filter system, since the filter pump can be used to perform the draining function.

In cold climates where pools must be shut down in the winter, it is essential that all piping be designed so that it can be drained when the pool is drained. Residual water left in pipes or in the pump and filter can cause considerable freeze damage.

The structural design and detailing of pools is largely a matter of designer preference and the wishes of the client, so this discussion has been limited to general considerations. The pool details in the reference manual show many options for coping and edge details, finishes and equipment location. Pay particular attention to the material thicknesses and placement of steel reinforcing. The 6-in material thickness and double row of steel reinforcing is a generally accepted standard for all shallow decorative pools regardless of the surface area.

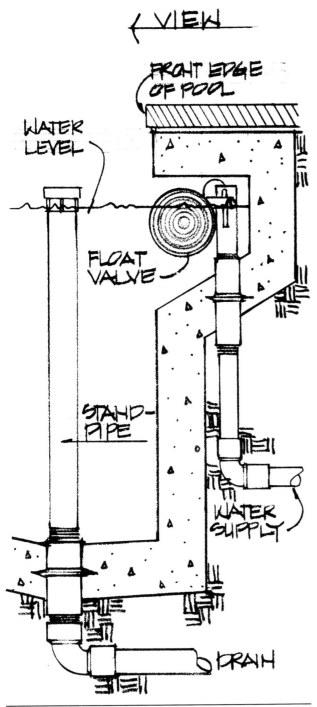

FIGURE 10.10 WATER LEVEL CONTROLS

LANDSCAPE

CONSTRUCTION

MANUAL

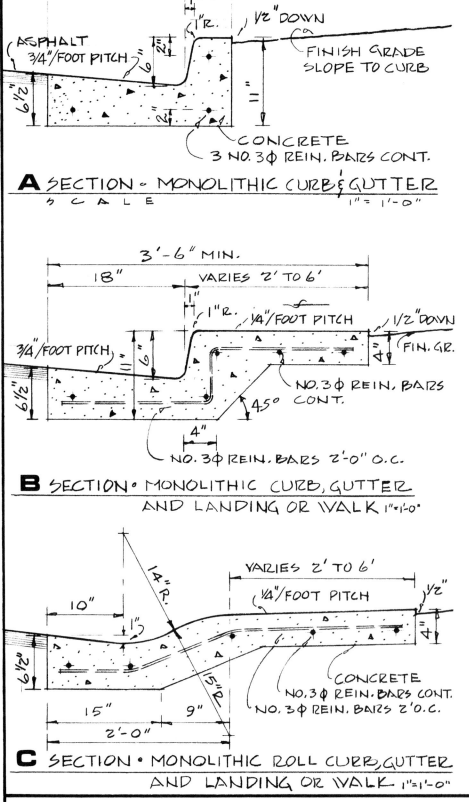

A SECTION · MONOLITHIC CURB & GUTTER

SCALE   1"= 1'-0"

B SECTION · MONOLITHIC CURB, GUTTER
AND LANDING OR WALK 1"=1'-0"

C SECTION · MONOLITHIC ROLL CURB, GUTTER
AND LANDING OR WALK 1"=1'-0"

A ONE OF THE MOST USED CURB & GUTTER DETAILS. WORKS WELL TO CONTROL VEHICLES. SLOPE ON FACE OF CURB PREVENTS WEAR ON TIRES. SQUARE EDGE ON BACK OF CURB ALLOWS A TURF EDGER TO BE USED.

B A MINIMUM TWO FOOT WIDTH AT THE TOP OF THE CURB WILL PERMIT MOWING WHILE CARS ARE PARKED. THIS WILL ALSO PROVIDE A REASONABLE LOCATION FOR SPRINKLER HEADS FOR TURF OR GROUND COVER. THE TOP PORTION MAY BE EXTENDED TO PROVIDE WALK SPACE ALONG THE CURB. THE MONOLITHIC POUR ELIMINATES A JOINT BETWEEN WALK AND CURB; THUS WALK AND CURB STAY EVEN. MORE SKILL WILL BE REQUIRED TO INSTALL A MONOLITHIC POUR.

C THIS DETAIL PROVIDES ACCESS ALONG ITS ENTIRE EDGE, ALLOWING DRIVES TO BE ADDED WITHOUT BREAKING CURB. IT DOES NOT CONTROL TRAFFIC VERY WELL (SHOULD NOT BE USED FOR HEAD IN PARKING) AND WILL NOT CARRY THE WATER VOLUME OF VERTICAL CURBS

D THIS DETAIL IS USED FREQUENTLY WITH ALL TYPES OF CONCRETE PAVING. THE EDGE OF THE PAVING CAN BE DOWELED AND THE CURB IS ADDED AFTER PAVING HAS HARDENED. THIS CURB WILL CONTROL VEHICLES AND PROVIDE A CHANNEL FOR STORM WATER.

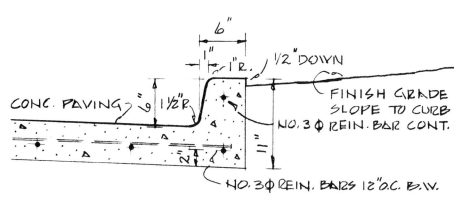

D SECTION · MONOLITHIC CURB & PAVING
SCALE   1" = 1'-0"

E A 6" HIGH ROLL CURB WILL CONTROL VEHICLES TO SOME DEGREE, YET ALLOW ACCESS OVER IT. STORM WATER CAPACITY WILL ALMOST EQUAL THAT OF THE VERTICAL CURB.

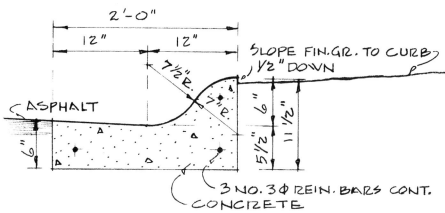

E SECTION · ROLL CURB & GUTTER
SCALE   1" = 1'-0"

F THIS DETAIL SHOULD ONLY BE USED WHERE THE SLOPE IS DIRECTED AWAY FROM THE CURB. WHEN USED AS A GUTTER, THE JOINT BETWEEN THE ASPHALT PAVING AND CONCRETE CURB WILL ALLOW WATER TO MOVE UNDER THE PAVING AND CURB CAUSING BOTH TO FAIL.

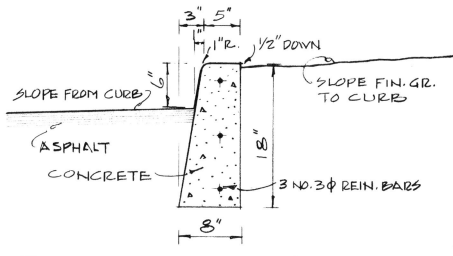

F SECTION · CURB W/OUT GUTTER
SCALE   1" = 1'-0"

CONCRETE CURB & GUTTER DETAILS

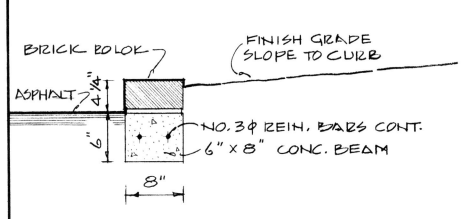

BRICK BOLOK

ASPHALT

FINISH GRADE
SLOPE TO CURB

4¼"

6"

NO. 3∅ REIN. BARS CONT.
6" X 8" CONC. BEAM

8"

A SECTION · BRICK CURB ON BEAM
SCALE   1" = 1'-0"

A THE USE OF ANY ASPHALT TYPE PAVING WILL REQUIRE A STRUCTURAL EDGE TO KEEP IT FROM BREAKING OFF AND PRODUCING AN EDGE THAT IS DIFFICULT TO MAINTAIN. WHERE BRICK IS DESIRED, THIS DETAIL SHOWS A CURB OF BRICK THAT WILL ALSO HELP TO CONTROL WATER RUN OFF.

5"X8"X 12"TO 18"
STONE CURB

FINISH GRADE
SLOPE TO CURB

DRIVE

5"

6"

2 NO. 3∅ REIN. BARS CONT.
6" X 8" CONCRETE BEAM

8"

B SECTION · STONE CURB ON BEAM
SCALE   1" = 1'-0"

B ANY MATERIAL MAY BE USED FOR THE CURB IF IT WILL WITHSTAND THE FORCE OF A TIRE BUMPING IT. DUE TO THE CRACK THAT WILL FORM BETWEEN THE CONCRETE BEAM AND ASPHALT, IT IS RECOMMENDED THAT WATER NOT BE DIRECTED TO THIS CURB.

BRICK BOLOK

CONC.

FINISH GRADE
SLOPE TO CURB

4¼"

2" 5" 7"

8"

NO. 3∅ REIN. BARS 12"O.C. B.W.

C SECTION · BRICK CURB AT CONC. PAVING
SCALE   1" = 1'-0"

C THIS DETAIL WILL WORK WELL AS AN EDGE TO A DRIVE WAY OR A MAJOR WALK WAY. FOR A WALK 4" OF CONCRETE IS ENOUGH FOR MOST SITUATIONS.

D CURBS WITHIN A LARGE PAVED AREA WILL HELP FACILITATE GRADING FOR DRAINAGE, IN THAT THE CURB WILL NOT ALLOW THE WATER TO FLOW INTO PLANTED AREAS. WEEPS ARE IMPORTANT IN THESE CURBS FOR AN AREA OF HIGH RAIN FALL.

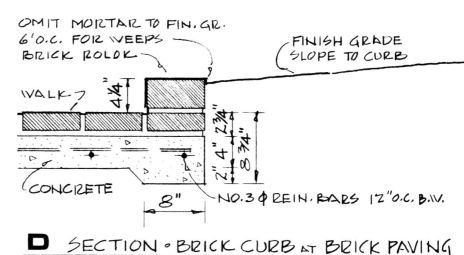

OMIT MORTAR TO FIN. GR. 6'O.C. FOR WEEPS
BRICK ROLOK
FINISH GRADE SLOPE TO CURB
WALK
4¼"
2¾"
2" 4" 8¾"
CONCRETE
8"
NO. 3 ⌀ REIN. BARS 12"O.C. B.W.

D SECTION · BRICK CURB AT BRICK PAVING
SCALE   1" = 1'-0"

E A MONOLITHIC CONCRETE CURB AND PAVING LOOKS NEAT AND WILL PROHIBIT WATER FLOWING INTO PLANTED AREAS. FINISH SHOULD BE THE SAME FOR CURB AND PAVING. SAND FILL UNDER CONCRETE SHOULD BE USED ON ALL OF THESE DETAILS WHERE HEAVY CLAY SOILS OCCUR.

EXPOSED AGGREGATE CONC. FIN. WALK.
ROLL CURB (EXP. AGGR. FINISH)
3½" R
4"
1" R.
4"
4"
¾" P.V.C. PIPE WEEP 6'O.C.
NO. 3 ⌀ REIN. BAR CONT.
NO. 3 ⌀ REIN. BARS 12"O.C. BOTHWAYS
2" SAND FILL

E SECTION · CURB AT CONCRETE WALK
SCALE   1" = 1'-0"

F THIS SHOULD BE CONSIDERED AS A MINIMUM DETAIL TO ACHIEVE A RAISED PLANT BED. IT IS LIMITED AS A GUTTER AND WOULD NOT WITHSTAND MUCH FORCE AS FROM LAWN MOWERS, ETC.

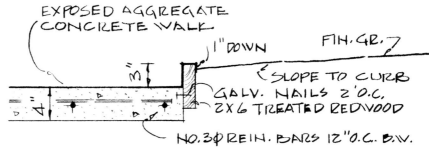

EXPOSED AGGREGATE CONCRETE WALK
1" DOWN
FIN. GR.
3"
4"
SLOPE TO CURB
GALV. NAILS 2'O.C.
2X6 TREATED REDWOOD
NO. 3 ⌀ REIN. BARS 12"O.C. B.W.

F SECTION · WOOD CURB AT CONC. WALK
SCALE   1" = 1'-0"

CURB DETAILS

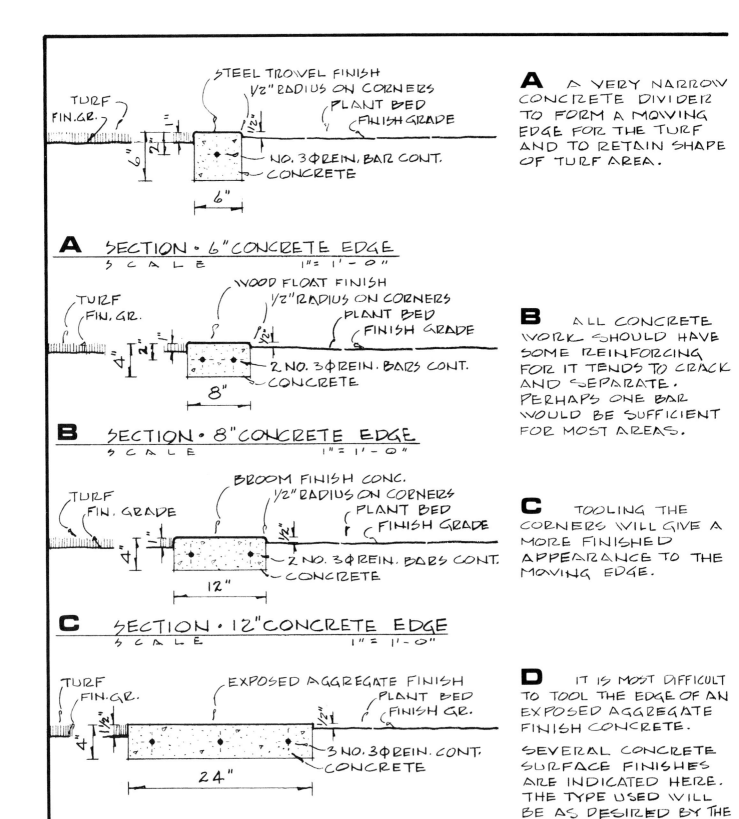

TURF FIN. GR.

STEEL TROWEL FINISH
1/2" RADIUS ON CORNERS
PLANT BED
FINISH GRADE

NO. 3⌀ REIN. BAR CONT.
CONCRETE

6"

A SECTION · 6" CONCRETE EDGE
SCALE   1" = 1'-0"

A A VERY NARROW CONCRETE DIVIDER TO FORM A MOWING EDGE FOR THE TURF AND TO RETAIN SHAPE OF TURF AREA.

TURF FIN. GR.

WOOD FLOAT FINISH
1/2" RADIUS ON CORNERS
PLANT BED
FINISH GRADE

2 NO. 3⌀ REIN. BARS CONT.
CONCRETE

8"

B SECTION · 8" CONCRETE EDGE
SCALE   1" = 1'-0"

B ALL CONCRETE WORK SHOULD HAVE SOME REINFORCING FOR IT TENDS TO CRACK AND SEPARATE. PERHAPS ONE BAR WOULD BE SUFFICIENT FOR MOST AREAS.

TURF FIN. GRADE

BROOM FINISH CONC.
1/2" RADIUS ON CORNERS
PLANT BED
FINISH GRADE

2 NO. 3⌀ REIN. BARS CONT.
CONCRETE

12"

C SECTION · 12" CONCRETE EDGE
SCALE   1" = 1'-0"

C TOOLING THE CORNERS WILL GIVE A MORE FINISHED APPEARANCE TO THE MOWING EDGE.

TURF FIN. GR.

EXPOSED AGGREGATE FINISH
PLANT BED
FINISH GR.

3 NO. 3⌀ REIN. CONT.
CONCRETE

24"

D SECTION · 24" CONCRETE EDGE
SCALE   1" = 1'-0"

D IT IS MOST DIFFICULT TO TOOL THE EDGE OF AN EXPOSED AGGREGATE FINISH CONCRETE.

SEVERAL CONCRETE SURFACE FINISHES ARE INDICATED HERE. THE TYPE USED WILL BE AS DESIRED BY THE DESIGNER.

LANDSCAPE CONSTRUCTION - MANUAL

E SHOWING A TYPICAL SECTION FOR A WALK WAY. 4" THICKNESS SHOULD BE CONSIDERED MINIMUM BUT WILL BE SUFFICIENT FOR MOST SITUATIONS WHERE HEAVY VEHICLES WILL NOT DRIVE OVER IT.

THE 2" SAND FILL MAY BE USED IN AREAS WITH VERY ACTIVE SOILS OR TO ASSURE FOUR FULL INCHES OF CONCRETE.

F SHOWING A 1X4 DOWELED JOINT. WITH OUT THE DOWEL THE CONCRETE WILL OFTEN SHIFT, PRODUCING TWO LEVELS AT THE JOINT.

ALL REDWOOD JOINTS TO BE SELECT HEART, AND TREATED WITH A WOOD PRESERVATIVE.

G USING A 2X4 FOR MORE DEFINITION OF THE JOINTS IN THE DESIGN.

H SHOWING A TYPICAL SECTION FOR A DRIVE WAY. IN MOST AREAS THE ADDITIONAL INCH OF CONCRETE IS ALL THAT IS NECESSARY FROM A WALK DETAIL TO A DRIVE.

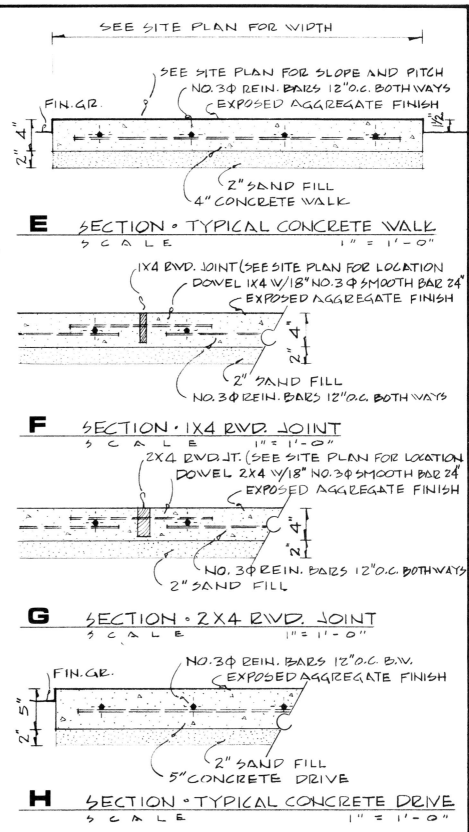

SEE SITE PLAN FOR WIDTH

FIN. GR.

SEE SITE PLAN FOR SLOPE AND PITCH
NO. 3∅ REIN. BARS 12" O.C. BOTH WAYS
EXPOSED AGGREGATE FINISH

2" SAND FILL
4" CONCRETE WALK

E SECTION · TYPICAL CONCRETE WALK
SCALE 1" = 1'-0"

1X4 RWD. JOINT (SEE SITE PLAN FOR LOCATION
DOWEL 1X4 W/18" NO. 3∅ SMOOTH BAR 24"
EXPOSED AGGREGATE FINISH

2" SAND FILL
NO. 3∅ REIN. BARS 12" O.C. BOTH WAYS

F SECTION · 1X4 RWD. JOINT
SCALE 1" = 1'-0"

2X4 RWD. JT. (SEE SITE PLAN FOR LOCATION
DOWEL 2X4 W/18" NO. 3∅ SMOOTH BAR 24"
EXPOSED AGGREGATE FINISH

NO. 3∅ REIN. BARS 12" O.C. BOTH WAYS
2" SAND FILL

G SECTION · 2X4 RWD. JOINT
SCALE 1" = 1'-0"

FIN. GR.

NO. 3∅ REIN. BARS 12" O.C. B.W.
EXPOSED AGGREGATE FINISH

2" SAND FILL
5" CONCRETE DRIVE

H SECTION · TYPICAL CONCRETE DRIVE
SCALE 1" = 1'-0"

CONCRETE EDGES AND PAVING DETAILS

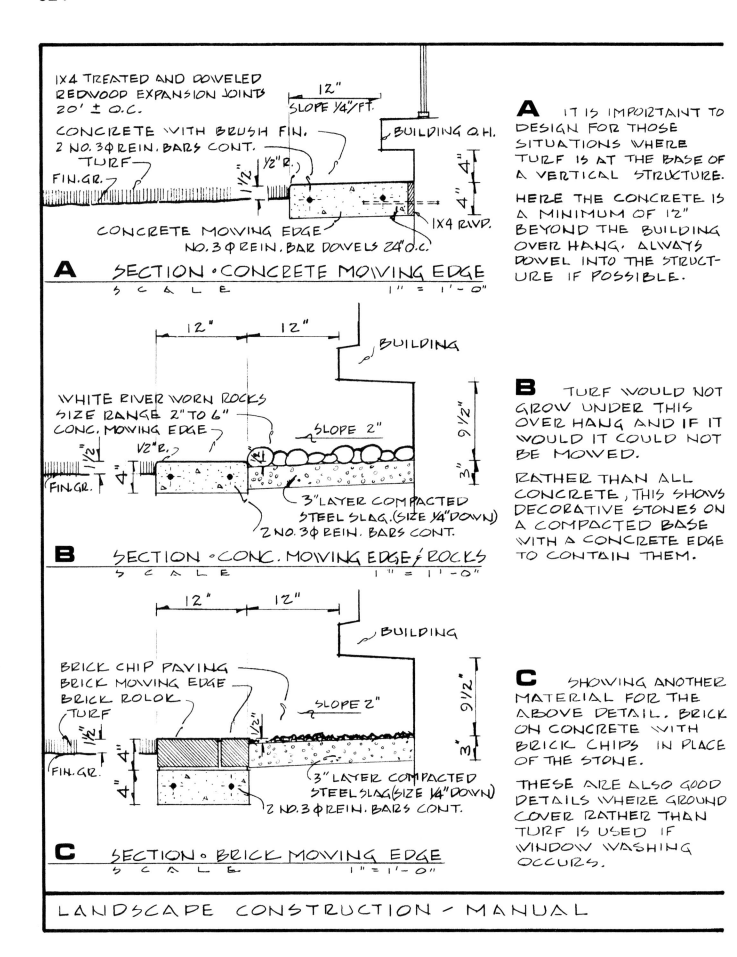

1X4 TREATED AND DOWELED REDWOOD EXPANSION JOINTS 20' ± O.C.

CONCRETE WITH BRUSH FIN. 2 NO. 3⌀ REIN. BARS CONT.

TURF

FIN. GR.

12"

SLOPE 1/4"/FT.

BUILDING O.H.

1/2" R.

4"   4"

1X4 RWD.

CONCRETE MOWING EDGE NO. 3⌀ REIN. BAR DOWELS 24" O.C.

A SECTION · CONCRETE MOWING EDGE
SCALE   1" = 1'-0"

A IT IS IMPORTANT TO DESIGN FOR THOSE SITUATIONS WHERE TURF IS AT THE BASE OF A VERTICAL STRUCTURE.

HERE THE CONCRETE IS A MINIMUM OF 12" BEYOND THE BUILDING OVER HANG. ALWAYS DOWEL INTO THE STRUCTURE IF POSSIBLE.

12"   12"

BUILDING

WHITE RIVER WORN ROCKS SIZE RANGE 2" TO 6" CONC. MOWING EDGE

1/2" R.

9 1/2"   3"

SLOPE 2"

FIN. GR.

4"

3" LAYER COMPACTED STEEL SLAG. (SIZE 1/4" DOWN) 2 NO. 3⌀ REIN. BARS CONT.

B SECTION · CONC. MOWING EDGE & ROCKS
SCALE   1" = 1'-0"

B TURF WOULD NOT GROW UNDER THIS OVER HANG AND IF IT WOULD IT COULD NOT BE MOWED.

RATHER THAN ALL CONCRETE, THIS SHOWS DECORATIVE STONES ON A COMPACTED BASE WITH A CONCRETE EDGE TO CONTAIN THEM.

12"   12"

BUILDING

BRICK CHIP PAVING
BRICK MOWING EDGE
BRICK ROLOK
TURF

SLOPE 2"

1/2"

9 1/2"   3"

FIN. GR.

4"   4"

4"

3" LAYER COMPACTED STEEL SLAG (SIZE 1/4" DOWN) 2 NO. 3⌀ REIN. BARS CONT.

C SECTION · BRICK MOWING EDGE
SCALE   1" = 1'-0"

C SHOWING ANOTHER MATERIAL FOR THE ABOVE DETAIL. BRICK ON CONCRETE WITH BRICK CHIPS IN PLACE OF THE STONE.

THESE ARE ALSO GOOD DETAILS WHERE GROUND COVER RATHER THAN TURF IS USED IF WINDOW WASHING OCCURS.

LANDSCAPE CONSTRUCTION - MANUAL

D SHOWING A MINIMUM WIDTH FOR MOWING AND WINDOW WASHING.

USE 8d GALV. NAILS 24" O.C. PROJECTING FROM THE 1X4 WHERE BUILDINGS CAN NOT BE DOWELED.

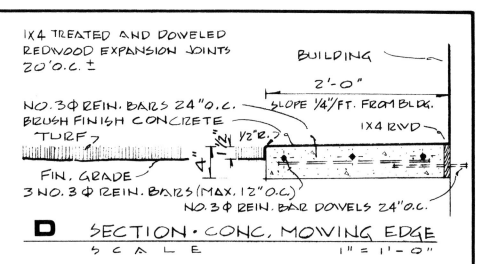

1X4 TREATED AND DOWELED REDWOOD EXPANSION JOINTS 20'O.C. ±

NO.3Φ REIN. BARS 24"O.C.
BRUSH FINISH CONCRETE
TURF

FIN. GRADE
3 NO.3Φ REIN. BARS (MAX. 12"O.C.)
NO.3Φ REIN. BAR DOWELS 24"O.C.

BUILDING
2'-0"
SLOPE 1/4"/FT. FROM BLDG.
1X4 RWD.

D   SECTION · CONC. MOWING EDGE
SCALE   1" = 1'-0"

E SAME DETAIL AS ABOVE WITH BRICK PAVING ON TOP. THIS CHANGE OF MATERIAL COULD ALSO INCLUDE FLAGSTONE, SLATE, ETC.

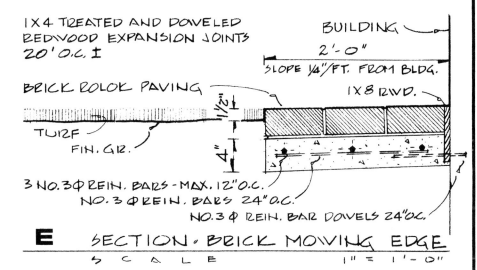

1X4 TREATED AND DOWELED REDWOOD EXPANSION JOINTS 20'O.C. ±

BRICK ROLOK PAVING
TURF
FIN. GR.

3 NO.3Φ REIN. BARS - MAX. 12"O.C.
NO.3Φ REIN. BARS 24"O.C.
NO.3Φ REIN. BAR DOWELS 24"O.C.

BUILDING
2'-0"
SLOPE 1/4"/FT. FROM BLDG.
1X8 RWD.

E   SECTION · BRICK MOWING EDGE
SCALE   1" = 1'-0"

F THIS WOULD SERVE AS A HARD SURFACE FOR A LADDER USED FOR WASHING HIGH WINDOWS.

4' WIDTH ADJACENT TO A STRUCTURE WOULD NOT ALLOW TWO PEOPLE TO PASS COMFORTABLY WHEN USED AS A WALK.

1X4 TREATED AND DOWELED REDWOOD EXPANSION JOINTS 4'O.C.

BUILDING
4'-0"
SLOPE 1/4" PER FOOT FROM BUILDING

EXPOSED AGGREGATE FINISH CONC.
TURF
1X4 RWD.

NO.3Φ REIN. BARS 12"O.C. BOTH WAYS
TREATED 1X4 RWD/NO.3Φ BAR DOWELS 24"O.C.

F   SECTION · WALK AT BUILDING
SCALE   1" = 1'-0"

MOWING EDGE DETAILS

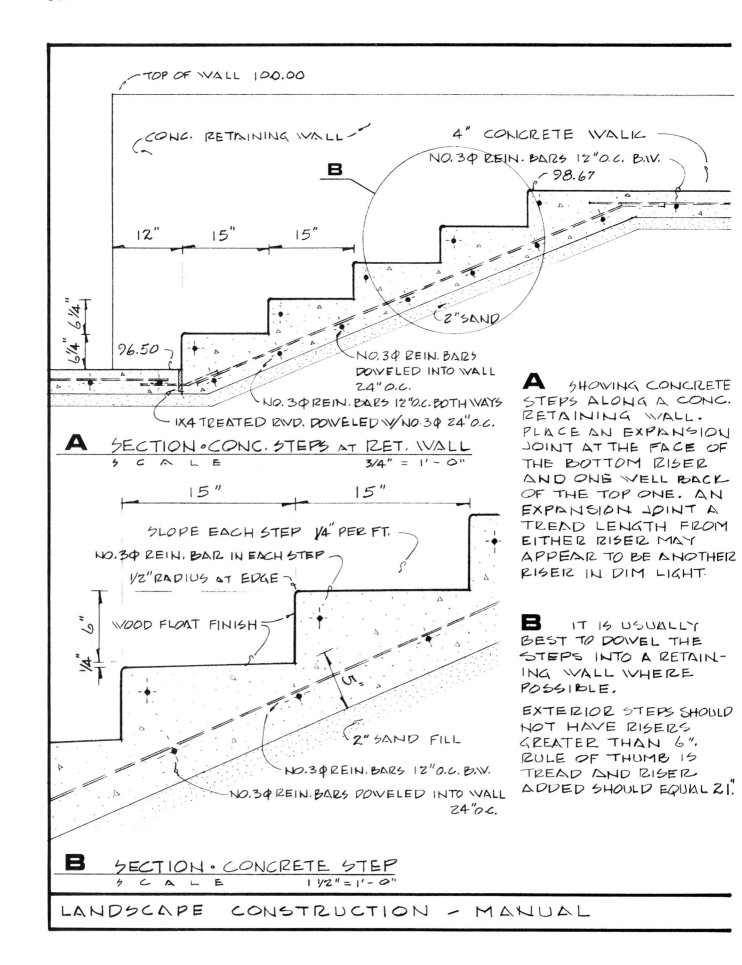

TOP OF WALL 100.00

CONC. RETAINING WALL

4" CONCRETE WALK

NO. 3φ REIN. BARS 12"O.C. B.W.

98.67

B

12"   15"   15"

2" SAND

6¼"   6¼"

96.50

NO. 3φ REIN. BARS DOWELED INTO WALL 24"O.C.

NO. 3φ REIN. BARS 12"O.C. BOTH WAYS

1X4 TREATED BVD. DOWELED W/NO. 3φ 24"O.C.

A SECTION • CONC. STEPS AT RET. WALL

SCALE   3/4" = 1'-0"

15"   15"

SLOPE EACH STEP ¼" PER FT.

NO. 3φ REIN. BAR IN EACH STEP

½" RADIUS AT EDGE

6"

WOOD FLOAT FINISH

¼"

5"

2" SAND FILL

NO. 3φ REIN. BARS 12"O.C. B.W.

NO. 3φ REIN. BARS DOWELED INTO WALL 24"O.C.

B SECTION • CONCRETE STEP

SCALE   1½" = 1'-0"

A SHOWING CONCRETE STEPS ALONG A CONC. RETAINING WALL. PLACE AN EXPANSION JOINT AT THE FACE OF THE BOTTOM RISER AND ONE WELL BACK OF THE TOP ONE. AN EXPANSION JOINT A TREAD LENGTH FROM EITHER RISER MAY APPEAR TO BE ANOTHER RISER IN DIM LIGHT.

B IT IS USUALLY BEST TO DOWEL THE STEPS INTO A RETAINING WALL WHERE POSSIBLE.

EXTERIOR STEPS SHOULD NOT HAVE RISERS GREATER THAN 6". RULE OF THUMB IS TREAD AND RISER ADDED SHOULD EQUAL 21".

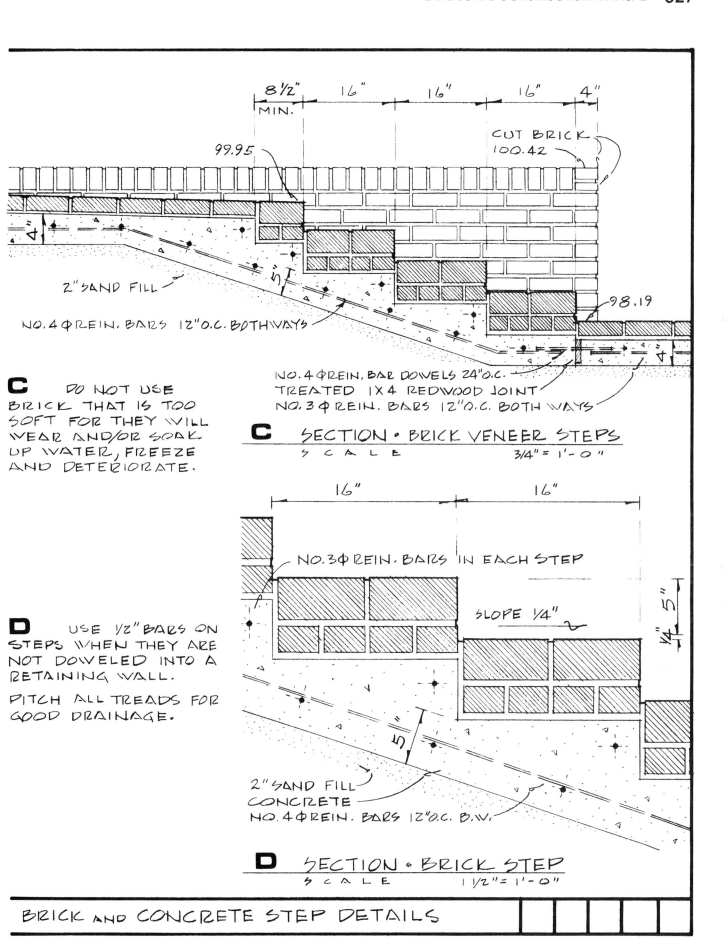

8 1/2" MIN.   16"   16"   16"   4"

99.95

CUT BRICK 100.42

4"

2" SAND FILL

5"

NO. 4 Ø REIN. BARS 12" O.C. BOTHWAYS

98.19

NO. 4 Ø REIN. BAR DOWELS 24" O.C.
TREATED 1 X 4 REDWOOD JOINT
NO. 3 Ø REIN. BARS 12" O.C. BOTH WAYS

C DO NOT USE BRICK THAT IS TOO SOFT FOR THEY WILL WEAR AND/OR SOAK UP WATER, FREEZE AND DETERIORATE.

C SECTION • BRICK VENEER STEPS
SCALE   3/4" = 1'-0"

16"   16"

NO. 3 Ø REIN. BARS IN EACH STEP

SLOPE 1/4"

1/4" 5"

D USE 1/2" BARS ON STEPS WHEN THEY ARE NOT DOWELED INTO A RETAINING WALL.

PITCH ALL TREADS FOR GOOD DRAINAGE.

5"

2" SAND FILL
CONCRETE
NO. 4 Ø REIN. BARS 12" O.C. B.W.

D SECTION • BRICK STEP
SCALE   1 1/2" = 1'-0"

BRICK AND CONCRETE STEP DETAILS

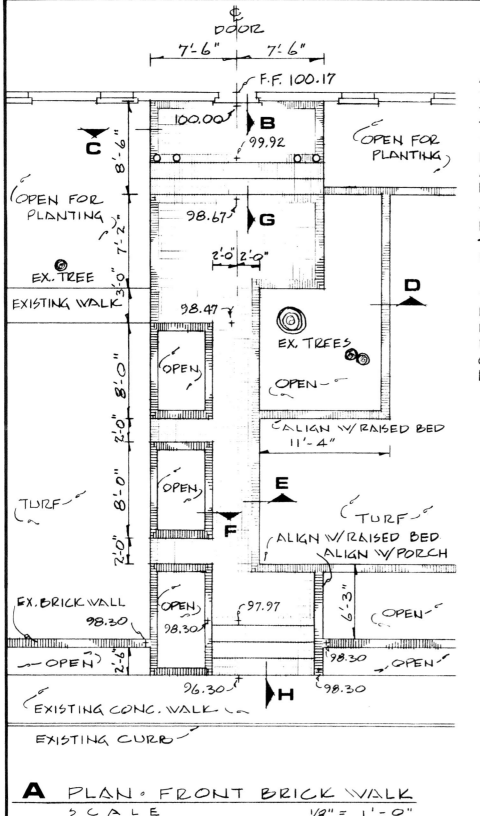

A PLAN · FRONT BRICK WALK
SCALE 1/8" = 1'-0"

A SHOWING A PORCH WITH STEPS TO THE WALK AND STEPS AT THE EXISTING SIDE WALK. ALSO SHOWING RAISED PLANT BEDS AND BRICK MOWING EDGES.

THE SECTIONS, INDICATED BY REFERENCE SYMBOLS ON THE PLAN, WILL OCCUR ON THE NEXT THREE PAGES.

THIS PLAN IS SIGNIFICANT ONLY IN SHOWING A METHOD OF LAY OUT AND TO INDICATE SECTION DRAWINGS.

LANDSCAPE CONSTRUCTION - MANUAL

B EVEN THOUGH THE PORCH IS DOWELED INTO THE FOUNDATION OF THE HOUSE IT IS IMPORTANT THAT THE CONCRETE ALSO BE CARRIED DOWN BELOW EXISTING GRADE FOR ADDITIONAL SUPPORT.

FOR A SMALL AREA SUCH AS THIS THE CONTRACTOR MAY WANT TO POUR THE CONCRETE LEVEL AND HAVE A THICKER MORTAR BED UNDER THE FLAT PAVERS.

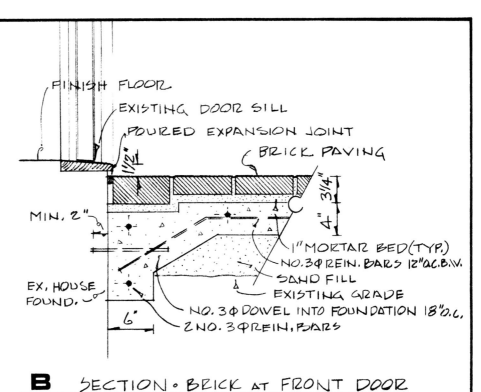

FINISH FLOOR
EXISTING DOOR SILL
POURED EXPANSION JOINT
BRICK PAVING
1 1/2"
4" 3/4"
MIN. 2"
1" MORTAR BED (TYP.)
NO. 3Ø REIN. BARS 12" O.C. B.W.
SAND FILL
EXISTING GRADE
EX. HOUSE FOUND.
6"
NO. 3Ø DOWEL INTO FOUNDATION 18" O.C.
2 NO. 3Ø REIN. BARS

B SECTION · BRICK AT FRONT DOOR
SCALE   1" = 1'-0"

C SHOWING THE TWO SIDES OF THE PORCH WITH ITS PAVING, BOLOK EDGE AND VENEER ON THE SIDE.

THE STEEL MAY ALSO BE BENT AND CARRIED DOWN RATHER THAN A CUT PIECE AS SHOWN.

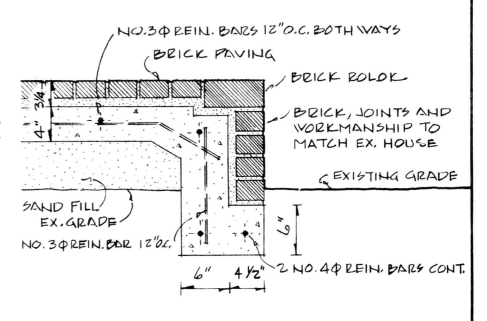

NO. 3Ø REIN. BARS 12" O.C. BOTH WAYS
BRICK PAVING
BRICK ROLOK
BRICK, JOINTS AND WORKMANSHIP TO MATCH EX. HOUSE
4" 3/4"
EXISTING GRADE
SAND FILL
EX. GRADE
NO. 3Ø REIN. BAR 12" O.C.
6"
6" 4 1/2"
2 NO. 4Ø REIN. BARS CONT.

C SECTION · PORCH EDGE
SCALE   1" = 1'-0"

PLAN AND DETAILS FOR BRICK PAVING

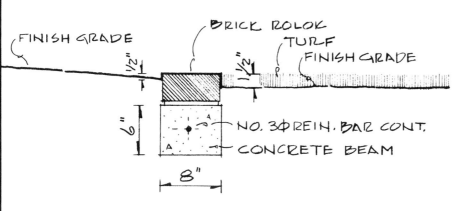

D SECTION · BRICK MOWING EDGE
SCALE   1" = 1'-0"

D A BRICK DIVIDER BETWEEN A GROUND COVER BED AND TURF. THIS MOWING EDGE MUST SLOPE TO GIVE A CONSTANT 1 1/2" ABOVE FINISH GRADE ON THE TURF SIDE. THIS ALLOWS THE LAWN MOWER WHEEL TO ROLL ON THE BRICK.

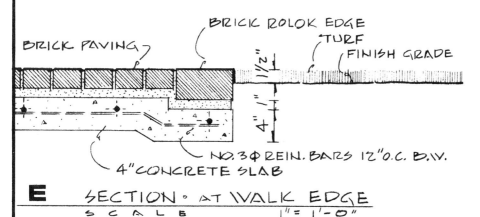

E SECTION · AT WALK EDGE
SCALE   1" = 1'-0"

E SHOWING A TYPICAL BRICK WALK EDGE WHERE A ROLOK IS USED IN THE PATTERN.

A ONE INCH MORTAR BED IS TYPICAL BUT NOT CRITICAL UNLESS IT BECOMES TOO LITTLE AND THE BRICK MUST BE CUT.

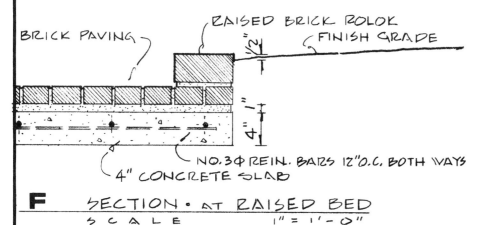

F SECTION · AT RAISED BED
SCALE   1" = 1'-0"

F FOR DRAINAGE IT IS OFTEN DESIRABLE TO RAISE PLANTING AREAS THAT OCCUR IN THE WALK.

THE CONCRETE AND ITS REINFORCING WILL BE THE SAME AS FOR A CONCRETE FINISH WALK. A ROUGH FINISH TO THE CONCRETE IS PREFERRED FOR IT WILL ASSURE BOND WITH THE BRICK.

G A TYPICAL BRICK VENEERED STEP WITH BRICK PAVING CONTINUING AT THE BOTTOM AND TOP.

A DOWELED EXPANSION JOINT IS BEST PLACED AT THE BOTTOM AND IN LINE OF THE FACE OF THE RISER.

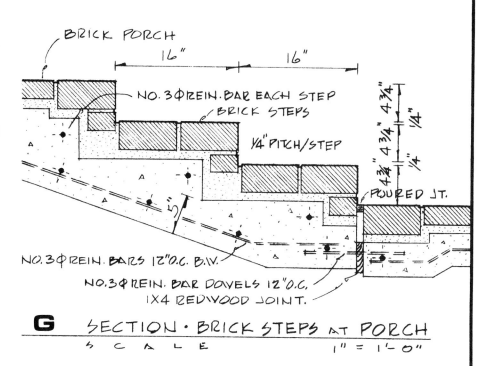

BRICK PORCH

16"   16"

NO.3Ø REIN. BAR EACH STEP

BRICK STEPS

1/4" PITCH/STEP

4 3/4" 4 3/4" 4 3/4" 1/4" 1/4"

POURED JT.

NO.3Ø REIN. BARS 12"O.C. B.W.

NO.3Ø REIN. BAR DOWELS 12"O.C.

1X4 REDWOOD JOINT.

G SECTION · BRICK STEPS AT PORCH
S C A L E   1" = 1'-0"

H UNDER CUT AT JOINING WITH EXISTING PAVING WHEN DOWELING IS NOT PRACTICAL. THIS WILL KEEP THE STEP FROM SHIFTING UP OR THE EXISTING PAVING FROM SINKING.

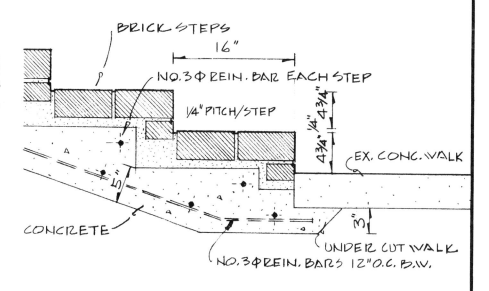

BRICK STEPS

16"

NO.3Ø REIN. BAR EACH STEP

1/4" PITCH/STEP

4 3/4" 1/4" 4 3/4"

EX. CONC. WALK

CONCRETE

UNDER CUT WALK

NO.3Ø REIN. BARS 12"O.C. B.W.

3"

H SECTION · BRICK STEPS AT EX. WALK
S C A L E   1" = 1'-0"

BRICK STEP AND PAVING DETAILS

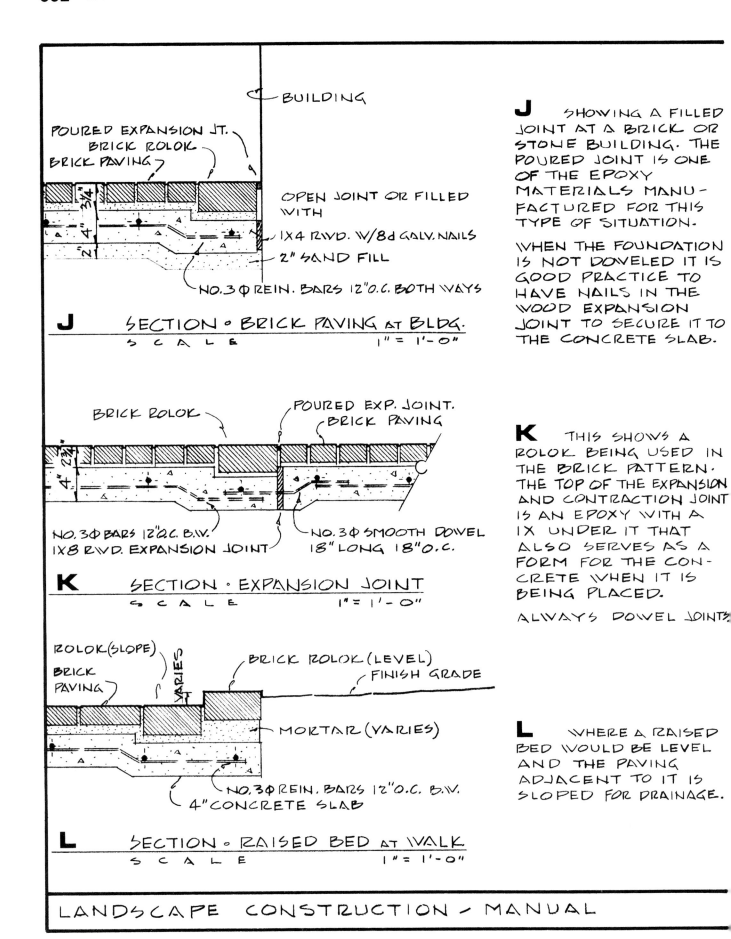

BUILDING

POURED EXPANSION JT.
BRICK ROLOK
BRICK PAVING

OPEN JOINT OR FILLED
WITH

1X4 RWD. W/8d GALV. NAILS

2" SAND FILL

NO. 3 Ø REIN. BARS 12" O.C. BOTH WAYS

J SECTION ∘ BRICK PAVING AT BLDG.
SCALE   1" = 1'-0"

J   SHOWING A FILLED JOINT AT A BRICK OR STONE BUILDING. THE POURED JOINT IS ONE OF THE EPOXY MATERIALS MANU- FACTURED FOR THIS TYPE OF SITUATION.

WHEN THE FOUNDATION IS NOT DOWELED IT IS GOOD PRACTICE TO HAVE NAILS IN THE WOOD EXPANSION JOINT TO SECURE IT TO THE CONCRETE SLAB.

BRICK ROLOK

POURED EXP. JOINT.
BRICK PAVING

NO. 3 Ø BARS 12" O.C. B.W.
1X8 RWD. EXPANSION JOINT

NO. 3 Ø SMOOTH DOWEL
18" LONG 18" O.C.

K SECTION ∘ EXPANSION JOINT
SCALE   1" = 1'-0"

K   THIS SHOWS A ROLOK BEING USED IN THE BRICK PATTERN. THE TOP OF THE EXPANSION AND CONTRACTION JOINT IS AN EPOXY WITH A 1X UNDER IT THAT ALSO SERVES AS A FORM FOR THE CON- CRETE WHEN IT IS BEING PLACED.

ALWAYS DOWEL JOINTS

ROLOK (SLOPE)
BRICK PAVING

BRICK ROLOK (LEVEL)
FINISH GRADE

MORTAR (VARIES)

VARIES

NO. 3 Ø REIN. BARS 12" O.C. B.W.
4" CONCRETE SLAB

L SECTION ∘ RAISED BED AT WALK
SCALE   1" = 1'-0"

L   WHERE A RAISED BED WOULD BE LEVEL AND THE PAVING ADJACENT TO IT IS SLOPED FOR DRAINAGE.

M THE JOINT BEHIND THE ROLOK MAY EITHER BE OPEN OR FILLED WITH MORTAR. THIS DETAIL DOES NOT ALLOW FOR INDEPENDENT MOVEMENT BETWEEN THE HOUSE AND PAVING.

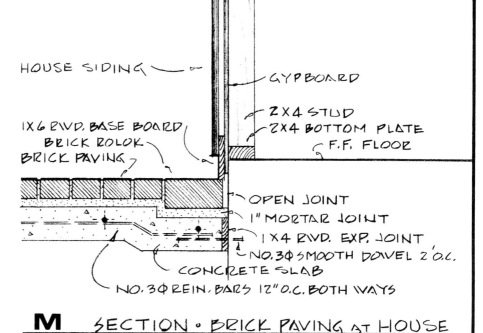

HOUSE SIDING

GYP BOARD

2 X 4 STUD
2 X 4 BOTTOM PLATE
F.F. FLOOR

1 X 6 RWD. BASE BOARD
BRICK ROLOK
BRICK PAVING

OPEN JOINT
1" MORTAR JOINT
1 X 4 RWD. EXP. JOINT
NO. 3Φ SMOOTH DOWEL 2' O.C.
CONCRETE SLAB
NO. 3Φ REIN. BARS 12" O.C. BOTH WAYS

M SECTION · BRICK PAVING AT HOUSE
SCALE   1" = 1'-0"

N A BRICK VENEER DOWN THE SIDE OF THE CONCRETE IS NOT NECESSARY FOR IT WILL NOT BE VIEWED BECAUSE OF THE DECK.

IT IS NOT NECESSARY TO TIE THE PAVING AND DECK TOGETHER, BUT BE SURE THAT THEY MAINTAIN THE SAME LEVEL.

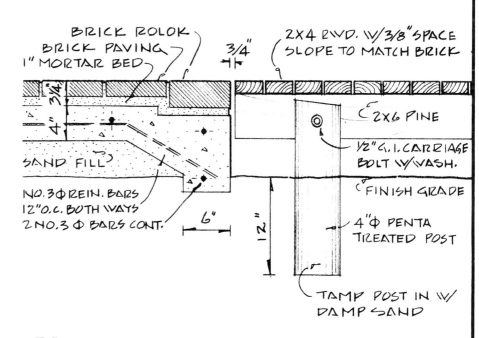

BRICK ROLOK
BRICK PAVING
1" MORTAR BED

2 X 4 RWD. W/ 3/8" SPACE SLOPE TO MATCH BRICK

3/4"

3/4"

4"

SAND FILL

NO. 3Φ REIN. BARS
12" O.C. BOTH WAYS
2 NO. 3 Φ BARS CONT.

6"

12"

2 X 6 PINE

1/2" G.I. CARRIAGE BOLT W/ WASH.

FINISH GRADE

4"Φ PENTA TREATED POST

TAMP POST IN W/ DAMP SAND

N SECTION · BRICK PAVING AT DECK
SCALE   1" = 1'-0"

BRICK PAVING DETAILS

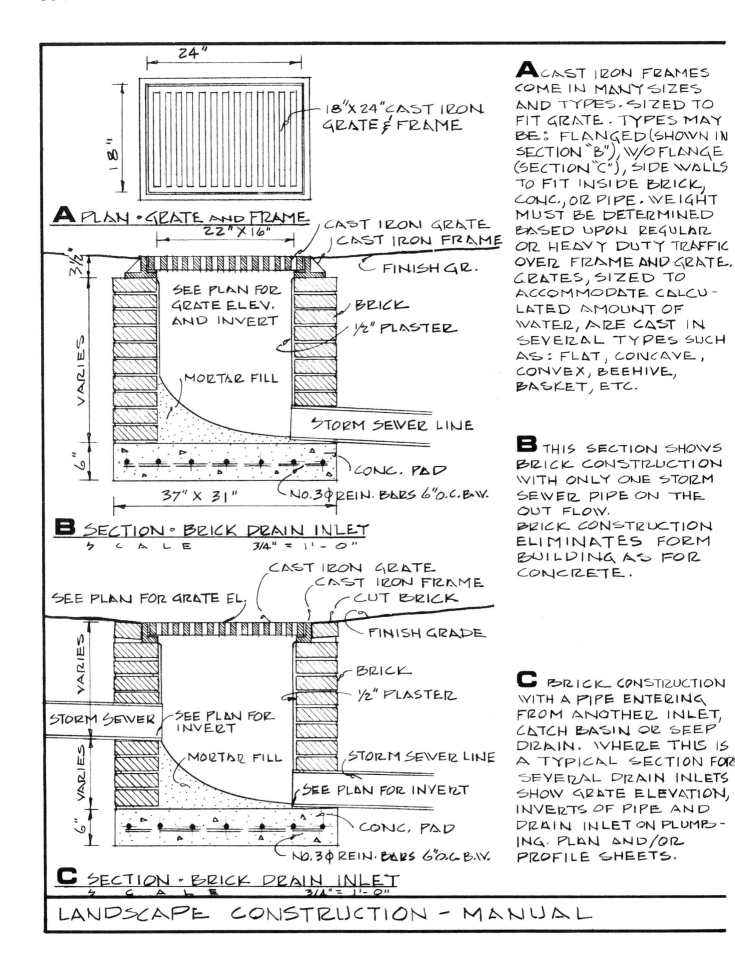

24"

18"X24" CAST IRON GRATE & FRAME

18"

A PLAN · GRATE AND FRAME

22" X 16"

CAST IRON GRATE
CAST IRON FRAME
FINISH GR.

3½"

SEE PLAN FOR GRATE ELEV. AND INVERT

BRICK
½" PLASTER

VARIES

MORTAR FILL

STORM SEWER LINE

6"

CONC. PAD

37" X 31"

NO. 3 φ REIN. BARS 6" O.C. B.W.

B SECTION · BRICK DRAIN INLET
SCALE 3/4" = 1'-0"

CAST IRON GRATE
CAST IRON FRAME
CUT BRICK

SEE PLAN FOR GRATE EL.

FINISH GRADE

VARIES

BRICK
½" PLASTER

STORM SEWER

SEE PLAN FOR INVERT

VARIES

MORTAR FILL

STORM SEWER LINE

SEE PLAN FOR INVERT

6" VARIES

CONC. PAD

NO. 3 φ REIN. BARS 6" O.C. B.W.

C SECTION · BRICK DRAIN INLET
SCALE 3/4" = 1'-0"

A CAST IRON FRAMES COME IN MANY SIZES AND TYPES. SIZED TO FIT GRATE. TYPES MAY BE: FLANGED (SHOWN IN SECTION "B"), W/O FLANGE (SECTION "C"), SIDE WALLS TO FIT INSIDE BRICK, CONC., OR PIPE. WEIGHT MUST BE DETERMINED BASED UPON REGULAR OR HEAVY DUTY TRAFFIC OVER FRAME AND GRATE. GRATES, SIZED TO ACCOMMODATE CALCULATED AMOUNT OF WATER, ARE CAST IN SEVERAL TYPES SUCH AS: FLAT, CONCAVE, CONVEX, BEEHIVE, BASKET, ETC.

B THIS SECTION SHOWS BRICK CONSTRUCTION WITH ONLY ONE STORM SEWER PIPE ON THE OUT FLOW. BRICK CONSTRUCTION ELIMINATES FORM BUILDING AS FOR CONCRETE.

C BRICK CONSTRUCTION WITH A PIPE ENTERING FROM ANOTHER INLET, CATCH BASIN OR SEEP DRAIN. WHERE THIS IS A TYPICAL SECTION FOR SEVERAL DRAIN INLETS SHOW GRATE ELEVATION, INVERTS OF PIPE AND DRAIN INLET ON PLUMBING PLAN AND/OR PROFILE SHEETS.

LANDSCAPE CONSTRUCTION - MANUAL

D CONSIDERATION FOR GRATE DESIGN SHOULD BE GIVEN TO BICYCLES WHERE THEY ARE ALLOWED. SOME SUGGESTIONS ARE:
1. DIAGONAL BARS AT 45° 2. BARS TRANSVERSE TO DIRECTION OF TRAFFIC. 3. SLOTTED GRATES WITH SLOTS 1¼" TO 2¼" AND CROSS BAR SPACING 9" MAXIMUM.

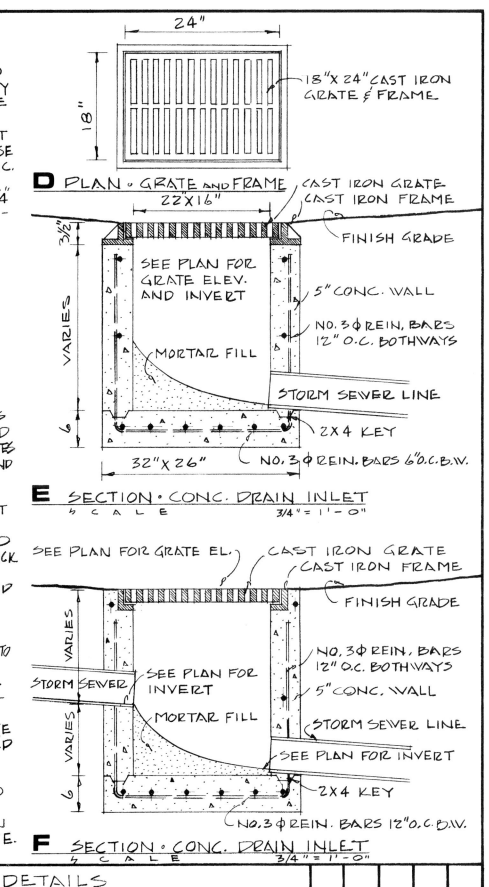

24"

18"

18"X 24" CAST IRON GRATE & FRAME

D PLAN · GRATE AND FRAME

22"X16"

CAST IRON GRATE
CAST IRON FRAME

FINISH GRADE

3½"

SEE PLAN FOR GRATE ELEV. AND INVERT

5"CONC. WALL

NO. 3∅ REIN. BARS 12" O.C. BOTHWAYS

VARIES

MORTAR FILL

STORM SEWER LINE

6"

2X4 KEY

32"X 26"

NO. 3∅ REIN. BARS 6"O.C.B.W.

E SECTION · CONC. DRAIN INLET

SCALE   3/4" = 1'-0"

E THIS SECTION SHOWS CONCRETE BOTTOM AND SIDES. THE KEY INDICATES TWO POURS (BOTTOM AND THEN THE SIDES). THE BOX COULD BE A MONOLITHIC POUR BUT FORMING IS MORE DIFFICULT. THE RAISED FRAME ON EITHER BRICK OR CONCRETE WILL ALLOW PAVING AROUND THE INLET.

F SHOWING A PIPE INTO INLET BOX AND PIPE TAKING WATER OUT. PIPE DEPTH WILL DEPEND UPON OVERALL SUBSURFACE DRAINAGE PLAN; BUT CARE SHOULD BE TAKEN TO PLACE THEM BELOW A MINIMUM DEPTH TO AVOID DAMAGE FROM ACTIVITY ON THE GROUND SURFACE.

SEE PLAN FOR GRATE EL.

CAST IRON GRATE
CAST IRON FRAME

FINISH GRADE

VARIES

NO. 3∅ REIN. BARS 12" O.C. BOTHWAYS

5"CONC. WALL

STORM SEWER

SEE PLAN FOR INVERT

MORTAR FILL

STORM SEWER LINE

VARIES

SEE PLAN FOR INVERT

6"

2X4 KEY

NO.3∅ REIN. BARS 12"O.C.B.W.

F SECTION · CONC. DRAIN INLET

SCALE   3/4" = 1'-0"

DRAIN INLET DETAILS

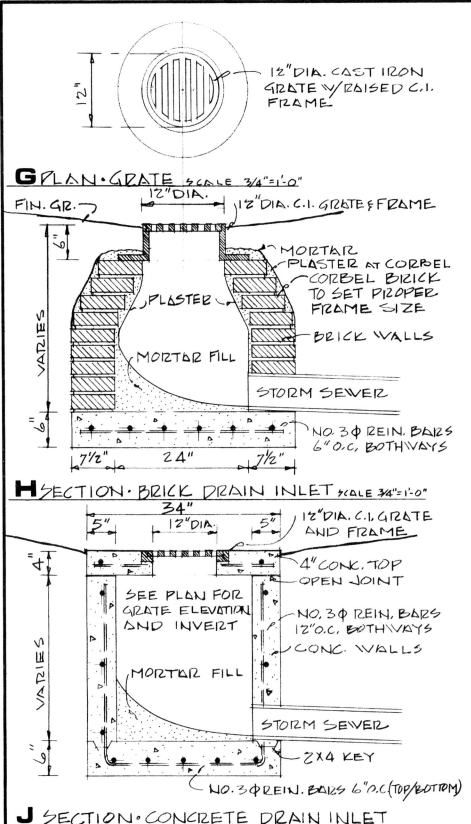

G PLAN · GRATE SCALE 3/4"=1'-0"

12"DIA. CAST IRON GRATE W/RAISED C.I. FRAME

12"DIA.

FIN. GR.

12"DIA. C.I. GRATE & FRAME

MORTAR PLASTER AT CORBEL

CORBEL BRICK TO SET PROPER FRAME SIZE

PLASTER

BRICK WALLS

MORTAR FILL

STORM SEWER

VARIES

NO. 3Ø REIN. BARS 6" O.C. BOTHWAYS

7½" 24" 7½"

H SECTION · BRICK DRAIN INLET SCALE 3/4"=1'-0"

34"

5" 12"DIA. 5"

12"DIA. C.I. GRATE AND FRAME

4" CONC. TOP OPEN JOINT

SEE PLAN FOR GRATE ELEVATION AND INVERT

NO. 3Ø REIN. BARS 12" O.C. BOTHWAYS

CONC. WALLS

MORTAR FILL

VARIES

STORM SEWER

2X4 KEY

NO. 3Ø REIN. BARS 6" O.C. (TOP/BOTTOM)

J SECTION · CONCRETE DRAIN INLET

SCALE 3/4" = 1'-0"

G WHERE LARGE GRATES ARE NOT NECESSARY, THERE ARE SEVERAL WAYS TO REDUCE THE OPENING OF AN INLET OR A CATCH BASIN AND STILL RETAIN A LARGE AREA TO COLLECT AND MOVE WATER. THIS SMALL GRATE WITH NO BRICK OR CONCRETE SHOWING REDUCES THE VISUAL IMPACT.

H GRATES AND FRAMES OF LARGER AND SMALLER DIA. CAN ALSO BE USED WITH THE SECTIONS ON THIS PAGE. THE AREA SHOWN AS MORTAR FILL KEEPS WATER FROM REMAINING IN THE INLET BOX. THE PLASTER WILL SMOOTH THE WALLS, THUS REDUCING ROUGH SPOTS THAT WILL COLLECT DEBRIS.

J A REDUCED GRATE IN A CONCRETE INLET WILL CALL FOR A CONCRETE SLAB ON TOP. THIS IS USUALLY PRECAST AND THEN SET IN PLACE WITHOUT FILLING THE JOINT. IT CAN BE REMOVED FOR REPAIR AND ADDITIONAL CONSTRUCTION. THE FRAME IS CAST INTO THE TOP SLAB.

K FOUNDRIES CAST SEVERAL SIZES AND TYPES OF THE GRATE AND FRAME SHOWN HERE. THE FRAME FITS INTO THE BELL OF A PIPE. A DETAIL WOULD SHOW, IN ADDITION TO THAT INFORMATION SHOWN HERE, A FOUNDRY CATALOG NUMBER FOR BOTH THE GRATE AND FRAME. (THIS WOULD BE TYPICAL FOR ALL GRATES AND FRAMES SHOWN IN THIS DOCUMENT.)

L THIS DETAIL MAY OCCUR AT THE END OF A CAST IRON DRAIN LINE. CAST IRON DRAIN PIPE SHOULD BE USED WHERE IT RUNS UNDER A STRUCTURE, SUCH AS FROM AN INTERIOR COURT.

M CAST IRON GRATES THAT WILL FIT INTO THE BELL OF A DRAIN PIPE ARE AVAILABLE FROM 3¾" DIA. TO OVER 32" IN DIA.

N SOMETIMES REFERRED TO AS A "YARD DRAIN", THESE SMALL SIMPLE DRAIN INLET DETAILS WORK WELL IN MANY SITUATIONS ON RESIDENTIAL PROJECTS.

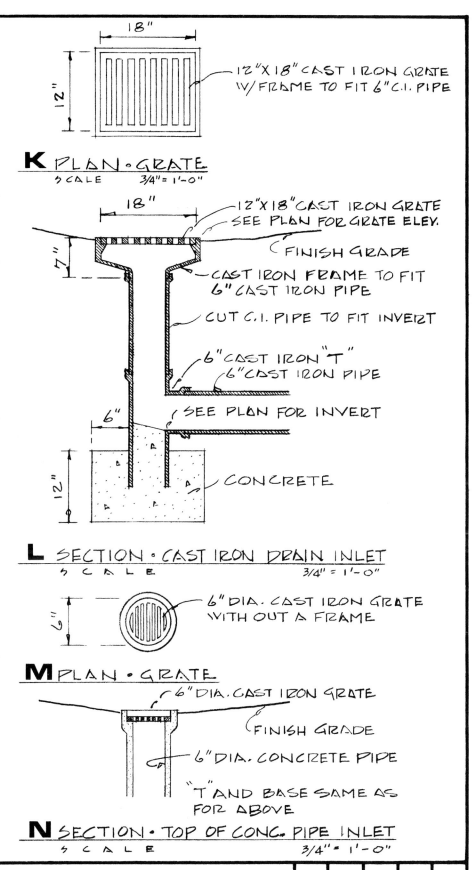

18"
12"

12"X18" CAST IRON GRATE W/FRAME TO FIT 6" C.I. PIPE

K PLAN • GRATE
SCALE   3/4" = 1'-0"

18"
7"

12"X18" CAST IRON GRATE SEE PLAN FOR GRATE ELEV.
FINISH GRADE
CAST IRON FRAME TO FIT 6" CAST IRON PIPE
CUT C.I. PIPE TO FIT INVERT
6" CAST IRON "T"
6" CAST IRON PIPE
SEE PLAN FOR INVERT

6"
12"

CONCRETE

L SECTION • CAST IRON DRAIN INLET
SCALE   3/4" = 1'-0"

6"

6" DIA. CAST IRON GRATE WITH OUT A FRAME

M PLAN • GRATE

6" DIA. CAST IRON GRATE
FINISH GRADE
6" DIA. CONCRETE PIPE
"T" AND BASE SAME AS FOR ABOVE

N SECTION • TOP OF CONC. PIPE INLET
SCALE   3/4" = 1'-0"

DRAIN INLET DETAILS

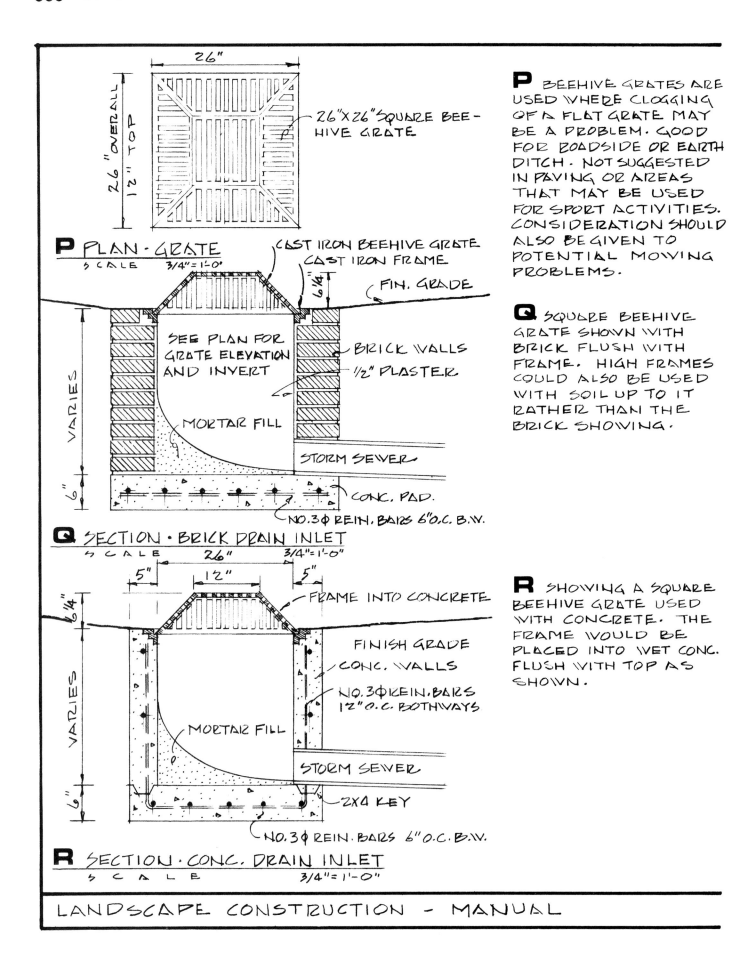

26"

26" OVERALL
12" TOP

26"X26" SQUARE BEE-
HIVE GRATE

P PLAN · GRATE
SCALE   3/4" = 1'-0"

CAST IRON BEEHIVE GRATE
CAST IRON FRAME

6¼"

FIN. GRADE

SEE PLAN FOR
GRATE ELEVATION
AND INVERT

BRICK WALLS
½" PLASTER

MORTAR FILL

VARIES

STORM SEWER

6"

CONC. PAD.
NO.3∅ REIN. BARS 6"O.C. B.W.

Q SECTION · BRICK DRAIN INLET
SCALE   26"   3/4" = 1'-0"

5"   12"   5"

6¼"

FRAME INTO CONCRETE

FINISH GRADE
CONC. WALLS

NO.3∅ REIN. BARS
12" O.C. BOTHWAYS

MORTAR FILL

VARIES

STORM SEWER

6"

2X4 KEY

NO.3∅ REIN. BARS 6" O.C. B.W.

R SECTION · CONC. DRAIN INLET
SCALE   3/4" = 1'-0"

P BEEHIVE GRATES ARE USED WHERE CLOGGING OF A FLAT GRATE MAY BE A PROBLEM. GOOD FOR ROADSIDE OR EARTH DITCH. NOT SUGGESTED IN PAVING OR AREAS THAT MAY BE USED FOR SPORT ACTIVITIES. CONSIDERATION SHOULD ALSO BE GIVEN TO POTENTIAL MOWING PROBLEMS.

Q SQUARE BEEHIVE GRATE SHOWN WITH BRICK FLUSH WITH FRAME. HIGH FRAMES COULD ALSO BE USED WITH SOIL UP TO IT RATHER THAN THE BRICK SHOWING.

R SHOWING A SQUARE BEEHIVE GRATE USED WITH CONCRETE. THE FRAME WOULD BE PLACED INTO WET CONC. FLUSH WITH TOP AS SHOWN.

LANDSCAPE CONSTRUCTION - MANUAL

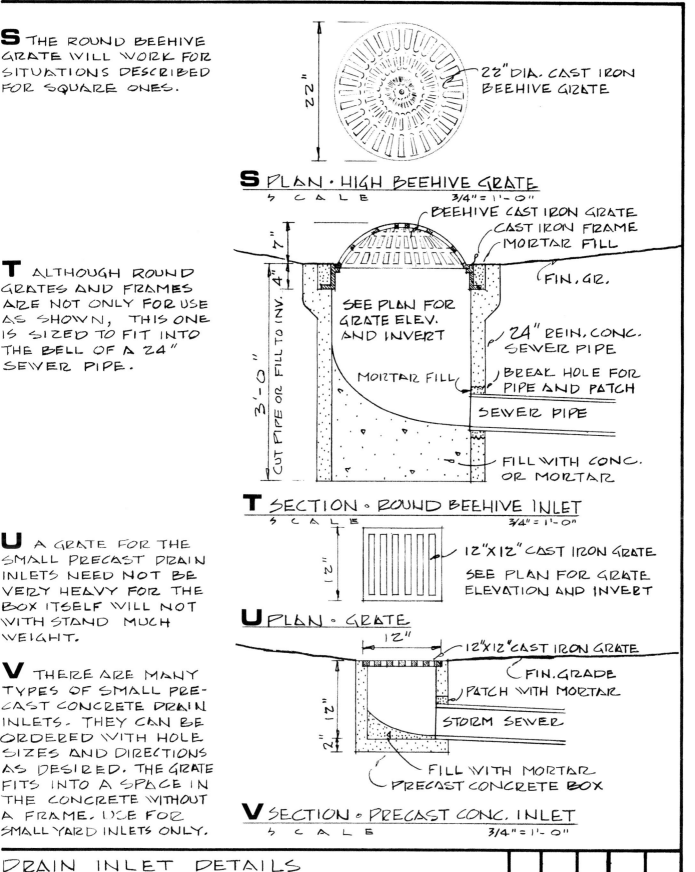

S THE ROUND BEEHIVE GRATE WILL WORK FOR SITUATIONS DESCRIBED FOR SQUARE ONES.

T ALTHOUGH ROUND GRATES AND FRAMES ARE NOT ONLY FOR USE AS SHOWN, THIS ONE IS SIZED TO FIT INTO THE BELL OF A 24" SEWER PIPE.

U A GRATE FOR THE SMALL PRECAST DRAIN INLETS NEED NOT BE VERY HEAVY FOR THE BOX ITSELF WILL NOT WITH STAND MUCH WEIGHT.

V THERE ARE MANY TYPES OF SMALL PRE-CAST CONCRETE DRAIN INLETS. THEY CAN BE ORDERED WITH HOLE SIZES AND DIRECTIONS AS DESIRED. THE GRATE FITS INTO A SPACE IN THE CONCRETE WITHOUT A FRAME. USE FOR SMALL YARD INLETS ONLY.

S PLAN · HIGH BEEHIVE GRATE SCALE 3/4"=1'-0"

22" DIA. CAST IRON BEEHIVE GRATE

BEEHIVE CAST IRON GRATE
CAST IRON FRAME
MORTAR FILL
FIN. GR.
SEE PLAN FOR GRATE ELEV. AND INVERT
24" REIN. CONC. SEWER PIPE
BREAK HOLE FOR PIPE AND PATCH
MORTAR FILL
SEWER PIPE
FILL WITH CONC. OR MORTAR

T SECTION · ROUND BEEHIVE INLET SCALE 3/4"=1'-0"

12"X12" CAST IRON GRATE
SEE PLAN FOR GRATE ELEVATION AND INVERT

U PLAN · GRATE

12"X12" CAST IRON GRATE
FIN. GRADE
PATCH WITH MORTAR
STORM SEWER
FILL WITH MORTAR
PRECAST CONCRETE BOX

V SECTION · PRECAST CONC. INLET SCALE 3/4"=1'-0"

DRAIN INLET DETAILS

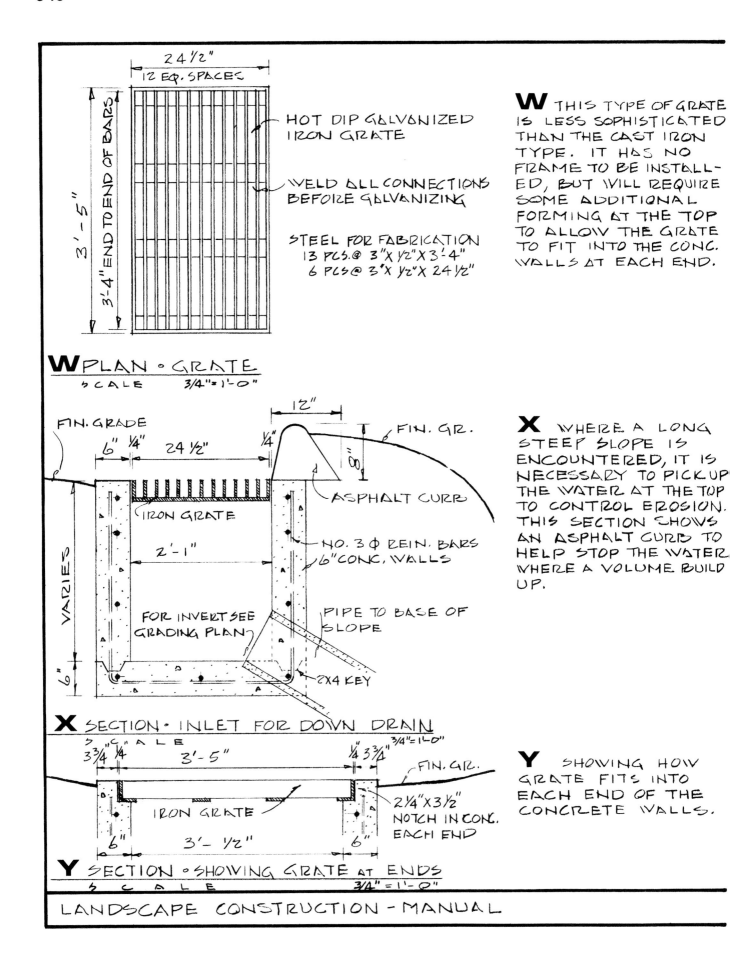

24 ½"
12 EQ. SPACES

HOT DIP GALVANIZED
IRON GRATE

WELD ALL CONNECTIONS
BEFORE GALVANIZING

STEEL FOR FABRICATION
13 PCS.@ 3"X ½"X3'-4"
6 PCS@ 3"X ½"X 24½"

3'-5" END TO END OF BARS
3'-4" END TO END OF BARS

W PLAN • GRATE
SCALE 3/4"=1'-0"

W THIS TYPE OF GRATE IS LESS SOPHISTICATED THAN THE CAST IRON TYPE. IT HAS NO FRAME TO BE INSTALLED, BUT WILL REQUIRE SOME ADDITIONAL FORMING AT THE TOP TO ALLOW THE GRATE TO FIT INTO THE CONC. WALLS AT EACH END.

FIN. GRADE
6" ¼" 24½" ¼"
12"
FIN. GR.
8"
ASPHALT CURB
IRON GRATE
2'-1"
NO. 3 Ø REIN. BARS
6" CONC. WALLS
VARIES
FOR INVERT SEE GRADING PLAN
PIPE TO BASE OF SLOPE
6"
2X4 KEY

X SECTION • INLET FOR DOWN DRAIN
SCALE 3/4"=1'-0"

X WHERE A LONG STEEP SLOPE IS ENCOUNTERED, IT IS NECESSARY TO PICK UP THE WATER AT THE TOP TO CONTROL EROSION. THIS SECTION SHOWS AN ASPHALT CURB TO HELP STOP THE WATER WHERE A VOLUME BUILD UP.

3¾" ¼ 3'-5" ¼ 3¾"
FIN. GR.
IRON GRATE
2¼"X3½" NOTCH IN CONC. EACH END
6" 3'-½" 6"

Y SECTION • SHOWING GRATE AT ENDS
SCALE 3/4"=1'-0"

Y SHOWING HOW GRATE FITS INTO EACH END OF THE CONCRETE WALLS.

LANDSCAPE CONSTRUCTION - MANUAL

Z HERE SPACE ALLOWS A MOUND OF EARTH BEHIND THE INLET. THE "V" TYPE GRATE FITS WELL IN THIS TYPE OF DRAINAGE SWALE. INLETS ARE PLACED PARALLEL TO THE TOP OF THE SLOPE AT LOW POINTS WITH HIGH POINTS IN BETWEEN.

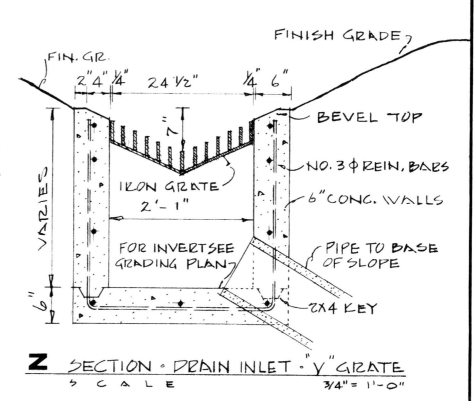

FIN. GR.

FINISH GRADE

2" 4" ¼"   24 ½"   ¼" 6"

BEVEL TOP

IRON GRATE 2'-1"

NO. 3 ∅ REIN. BARS

6" CONC. WALLS

VARIES

6"

FOR INVERTSEE GRADING PLAN

PIPE TO BASE OF SLOPE

2X4 KEY

Z SECTION · DRAIN INLET · "V" GRATE

SCALE

3/4" = 1'-0"

ZZ THIS LONGITUDINAL SECTION OF THE INLET WITH A "V" TYPE GRATE SHOWS ½ OF THE GRATE AND HOW END WALLS MUST SLOPE. THIS TYPE INLET WORKS WELL IN LARGE OPEN FIELDS, PARKS, ETC.

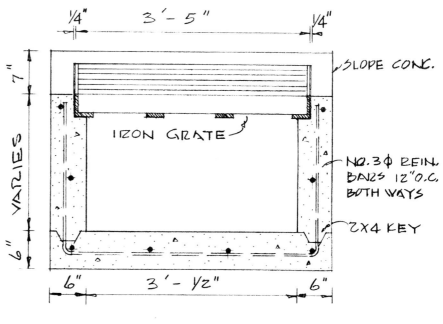

¼"   3'-5"   ¼"

7"

SLOPE CONC.

VARIES

IRON GRATE

NO. 3 ∅ REIN. BARS 12" O.C. BOTH WAYS

2X4 KEY

6"

6"   3'-½"   6"

ZZ SECTION · DRAIN INLET · "V" GRATE

SCALE

3/4" = 1'-0"

DRAIN INLET DETAILS

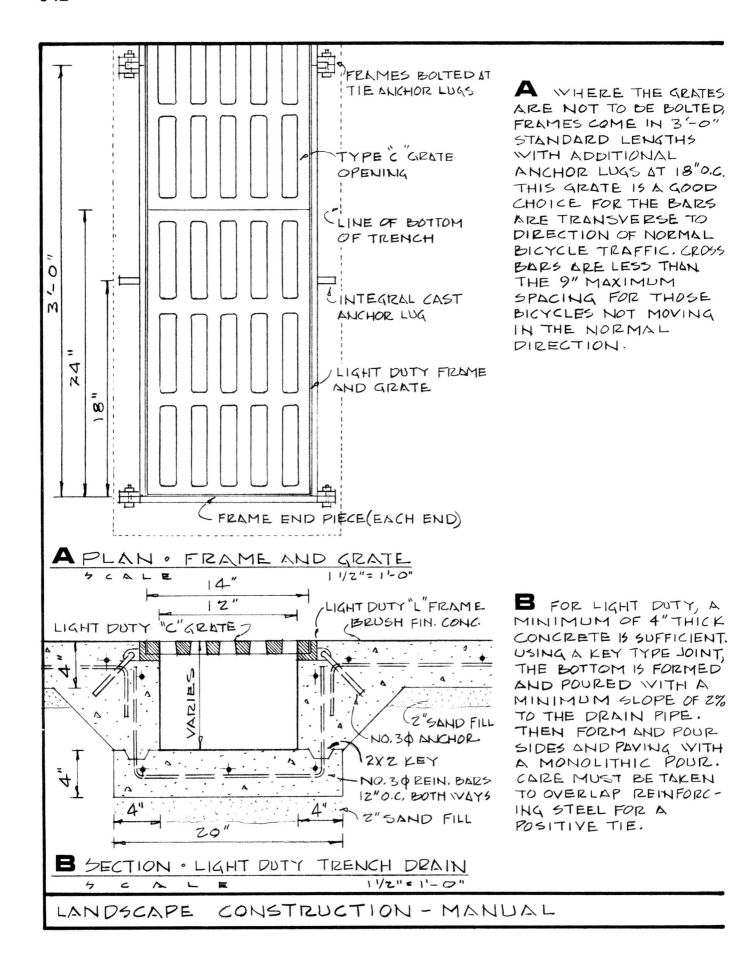

A WHERE THE GRATES ARE NOT TO BE BOLTED, FRAMES COME IN 3'-0" STANDARD LENGTHS WITH ADDITIONAL ANCHOR LUGS AT 18"O.C. THIS GRATE IS A GOOD CHOICE FOR THE BARS ARE TRANSVERSE TO DIRECTION OF NORMAL BICYCLE TRAFFIC. CROSS BARS ARE LESS THAN THE 9" MAXIMUM SPACING FOR THOSE BICYCLES NOT MOVING IN THE NORMAL DIRECTION.

FRAMES BOLTED AT TIE ANCHOR LUGS

TYPE "C" GRATE OPENING

LINE OF BOTTOM OF TRENCH

INTEGRAL CAST ANCHOR LUG

LIGHT DUTY FRAME AND GRATE

FRAME END PIECE (EACH END)

A PLAN • FRAME AND GRATE
SCALE 1 1/2"=1'-0"

B FOR LIGHT DUTY, A MINIMUM OF 4" THICK CONCRETE IS SUFFICIENT. USING A KEY TYPE JOINT, THE BOTTOM IS FORMED AND POURED WITH A MINIMUM SLOPE OF 2% TO THE DRAIN PIPE. THEN FORM AND POUR SIDES AND PAVING WITH A MONOLITHIC POUR. CARE MUST BE TAKEN TO OVERLAP REINFORCING STEEL FOR A POSITIVE TIE.

LIGHT DUTY "C" GRATE
LIGHT DUTY "L" FRAME BRUSH FIN. CONC.
VARIES
2" SAND FILL
NO.3 Ø ANCHOR
2X2 KEY
NO.3 Ø REIN. BARS 12"O.C. BOTH WAYS
2" SAND FILL

B SECTION • LIGHT DUTY TRENCH DRAIN
SCALE 1 1/2"=1'-0"

LANDSCAPE CONSTRUCTION - MANUAL

C IT IS NOT A GOOD IDEA TO ATTEMPT A MONOLITHIC POUR OF TRENCH WALLS AND A RETAINING WALL (WHERE IT OCCURS AS SHOWN). IT IS, HOWEVER, IMPORTANT THAT THE TWO BE TIED TOGETHER. DOWELING, AS SHOWN, IS ONE GOOD WAY TO ACCOMPLISH THIS. TRENCH DEPTHS WILL BE THE SAME AS SUGGESTED IN THE HEAVY DUTY TRENCH DETAILS.

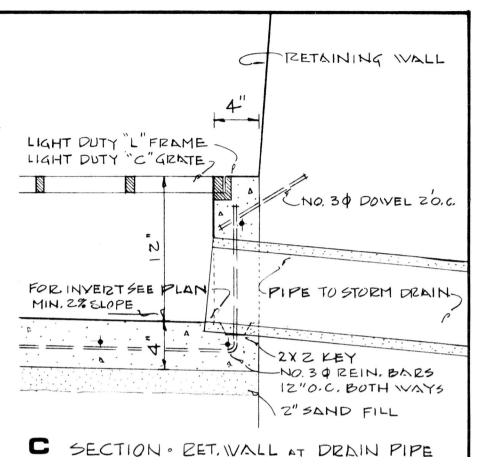

RETAINING WALL

4"

LIGHT DUTY "L" FRAME
LIGHT DUTY "C" GRATE

NO. 3 ∅ DOWEL 2'O.C.

PIPE TO STORM DRAIN

FOR INVERT SEE PLAN
MIN. 2% SLOPE

2X2 KEY
NO. 3 ∅ REIN. BARS
12" O.C. BOTH WAYS
2" SAND FILL

C SECTION · RET. WALL AT DRAIN PIPE
SCALE   1½" = 1'-0"

D WHERE PAVING EXISTS AT AN END OF THE TRENCH, THE DETAIL WOULD BE SIMULAR TO THAT OF THE CROSS-SECTION, WITH THE DRAIN PIPE SHOWN. SEVERAL TYPES OF GRATES AND FRAMES ARE AVAILABLE FOR LIGHT DUTY TRENCH DRAINS. CHECK WITH THE MANUFACTURERS CATALOG FOR ADDITIONAL INFORMATION.

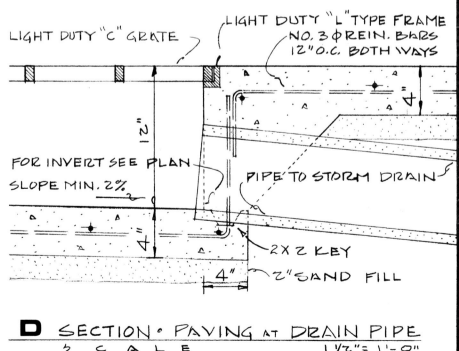

LIGHT DUTY "C" GRATE

LIGHT DUTY "L" TYPE FRAME
NO. 3 ∅ REIN. BARS
12" O.C. BOTH WAYS

FOR INVERT SEE PLAN
SLOPE MIN. 2%

PIPE TO STORM DRAIN

2X2 KEY
4"   2" SAND FILL

D SECTION · PAVING AT DRAIN PIPE
SCALE   1½" = 1'-0"

DRAIN INLET DETAILS (TRENCH)

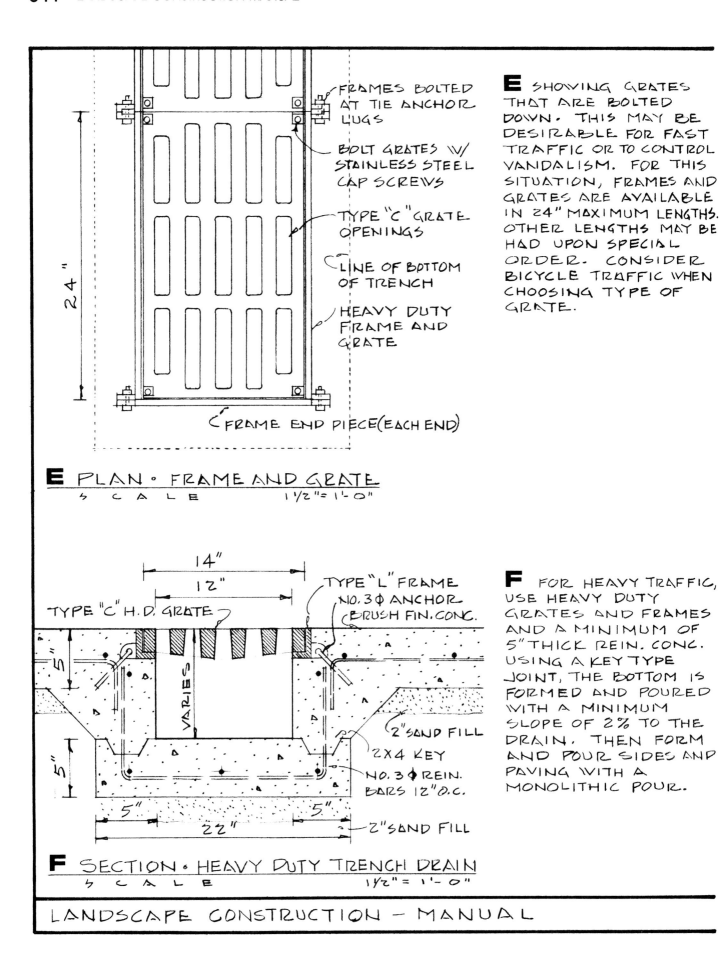

FRAMES BOLTED AT TIE ANCHOR LUGS

BOLT GRATES W/ STAINLESS STEEL CAP SCREWS

TYPE "C" GRATE OPENINGS

LINE OF BOTTOM OF TRENCH

HEAVY DUTY FRAME AND GRATE

FRAME END PIECE (EACH END)

24"

E PLAN · FRAME AND GRATE
SCALE 1½"= 1'-0"

E SHOWING GRATES THAT ARE BOLTED DOWN. THIS MAY BE DESIRABLE FOR FAST TRAFFIC OR TO CONTROL VANDALISM. FOR THIS SITUATION, FRAMES AND GRATES ARE AVAILABLE IN 24" MAXIMUM LENGTHS. OTHER LENGTHS MAY BE HAD UPON SPECIAL ORDER. CONSIDER BICYCLE TRAFFIC WHEN CHOOSING TYPE OF GRATE.

14"
12"

TYPE "C" H.D. GRATE

TYPE "L" FRAME
NO. 3 ⌀ ANCHOR
BRUSH FIN. CONC.

VARIES

5"
5"

2" SAND FILL
2X4 KEY
NO. 3 ⌀ REIN. BARS 12" O.C.
2" SAND FILL

5"
22"
5"

F SECTION · HEAVY DUTY TRENCH DRAIN
SCALE 1½"= 1'-0"

F FOR HEAVY TRAFFIC, USE HEAVY DUTY GRATES AND FRAMES AND A MINIMUM OF 5" THICK REIN. CONC. USING A KEY TYPE JOINT, THE BOTTOM IS FORMED AND POURED WITH A MINIMUM SLOPE OF 2% TO THE DRAIN. THEN FORM AND POUR SIDES AND PAVING WITH A MONOLITHIC POUR.

G CURBS MAY BE
POURED MONOLITHIC
OR DOWELED AND
POURED SEPARATELY.
THE PIPE (SIZED DEPEN-
DING UPON CALCULATED
VOLUME OF FLOW) WILL
BE PLACED BEFORE
THE BOTTOM OF THE
TRENCH IS POURED.
DEPTH OF TRENCH WILL
BE A MINIMUM OF 6"
AT THE HIGH END AND
DEEP ENOUGH AT THE LOW
END TO ACCOMMODATE
ALL OF THE FOLLOWING:
MINIMUM 2% SLOPE,
PIPE SIZE, AND SPECIAL
DEPTH REQUIREMENTS
FOR THE PIPE.

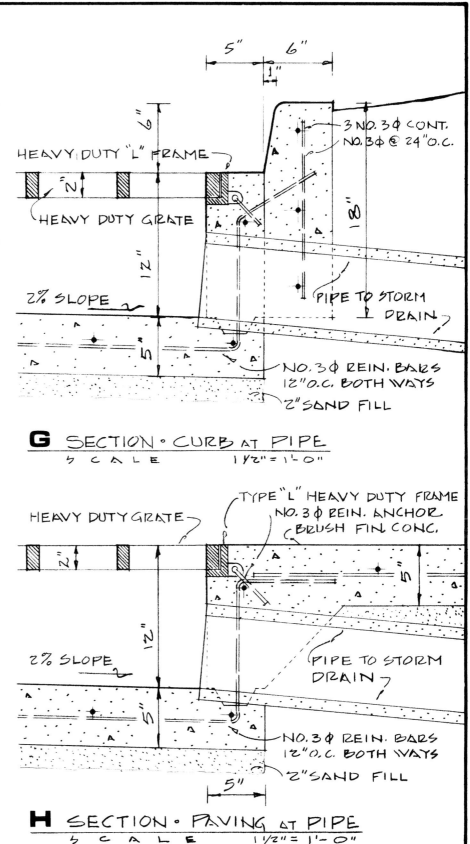

G SECTION · CURB AT PIPE
SCALE   1½"=1'-0"

H PAVING OCCURRING
AT ENDS OR SIDES OF
THE TRENCH SHOULD
BE A MONOLITHIC POUR
WITH THE WALLS.
CHECK WITH MANUFACT-
URERS TO DETERMINE
THE VARIOUS TYPES
OF FRAMES AND
GRATES AND THEIR
STANDARD DIMENSIONS.

H SECTION · PAVING AT PIPE
SCALE   1½"=1'-0"

DRAIN INLET DETAILS (TRENCH)

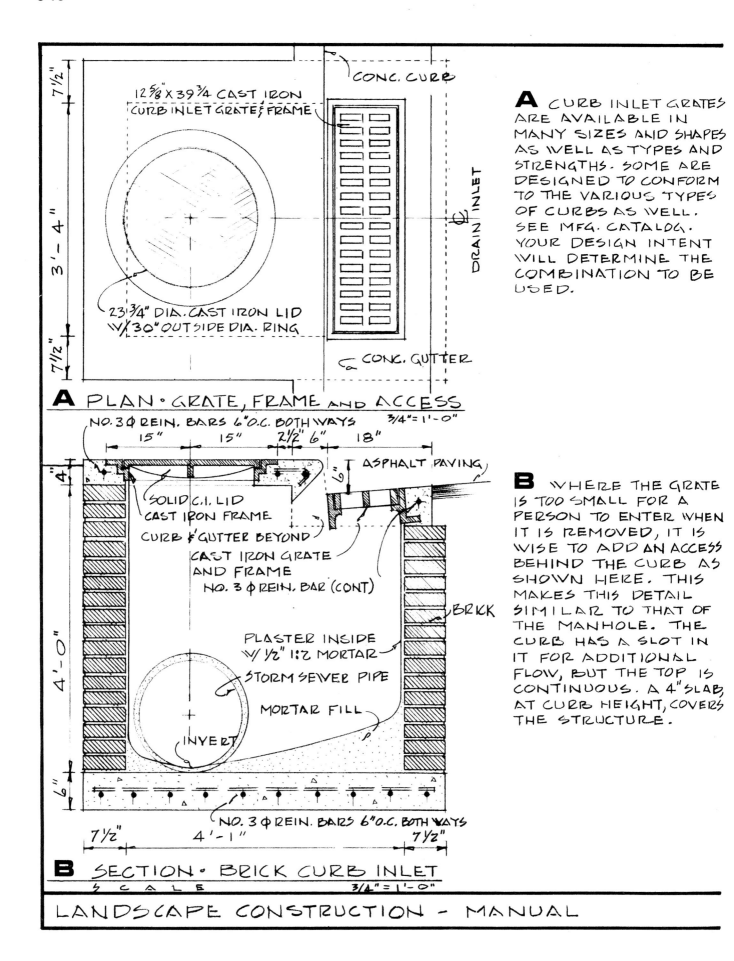

CONC. CURB

12 5/8" X 39 3/4 CAST IRON CURB INLET GRATE & FRAME

DRAIN INLET

23 3/4" DIA. CAST IRON LID W/ 30" OUTSIDE DIA. RING

CONC. GUTTER

7 1/2"
3'- 4"
7 1/2"

A PLAN · GRATE, FRAME AND ACCESS

3/4" = 1'-0"

A CURB INLET GRATES ARE AVAILABLE IN MANY SIZES AND SHAPES AS WELL AS TYPES AND STRENGTHS. SOME ARE DESIGNED TO CONFORM TO THE VARIOUS TYPES OF CURBS AS WELL. SEE MFG. CATALOG. YOUR DESIGN INTENT WILL DETERMINE THE COMBINATION TO BE USED.

NO. 3 φ REIN. BARS 6" O.C. BOTH WAYS

15" 15" 2 1/2" 6" 18"

ASPHALT PAVING

SOLID C.I. LID
CAST IRON FRAME
CURB & GUTTER BEYOND
CAST IRON GRATE AND FRAME
NO. 3 φ REIN. BAR (CONT)

BRICK

PLASTER INSIDE W/ 1/2" 1:2 MORTAR
STORM SEWER PIPE
MORTAR FILL
INVERT

4"
4'-0"
6"

NO. 3 φ REIN. BARS 6" O.C. BOTH WAYS

7 1/2" 4'-1" 7 1/2"

B SECTION · BRICK CURB INLET

SCALE 3/4" = 1'-0"

B WHERE THE GRATE IS TOO SMALL FOR A PERSON TO ENTER WHEN IT IS REMOVED, IT IS WISE TO ADD AN ACCESS BEHIND THE CURB AS SHOWN HERE. THIS MAKES THIS DETAIL SIMILAR TO THAT OF THE MANHOLE. THE CURB HAS A SLOT IN IT FOR ADDITIONAL FLOW, BUT THE TOP IS CONTINUOUS. A 4" SLAB, AT CURB HEIGHT, COVERS THE STRUCTURE.

LANDSCAPE CONSTRUCTION - MANUAL

C ALWAYS CONSIDER SAFETY STANDARDS FOR BICYCLES WHEN CHOOSING A GUTTER GRATE. WHERE BICYCLES ARE NOT ALLOWED, SUCH AS FREEWAYS, ETC. THIS IS OF NO CONCERN. THIS DETAIL SHOWS THE CURB WIDTH CHANGED TO COVER THE STRUCTURE. THIS WILL PRESENT A PROBLEM WHERE TURF IS TO BE EDGED.

D DUE TO THE WIDTH OF THIS GRATE AND FRAME, THE DETAIL WILL ONLY WORK WHERE THE STREET OR PARKING AREA IS PAVED WITH CONCRETE. WHEN USING MORE THAN ONE GRATE IN LINE, OR WHERE HEAVY VEHICLES ARE ANTICIPATED, AN IRON "I" BEAM WOULD BE ADDED UNDER THE INSIDE EDGE OF THE FRAME. PIPE SIZES AND DIRECTIONS WILL BE INDICATED ON THE GRADING PLAN. HOWEVER, IT IS DESIRABLE TO SHOW SOME ON THE DETAIL AS TYPICAL TO INDICATE HOW THEY FIT INTO THE DETAIL.

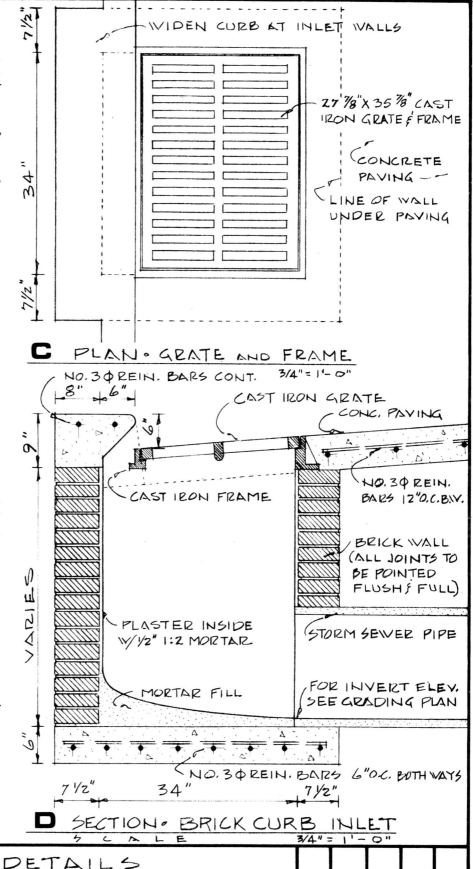

C PLAN · GRATE AND FRAME

D SECTION · BRICK CURB INLET

CURB INLET DETAILS

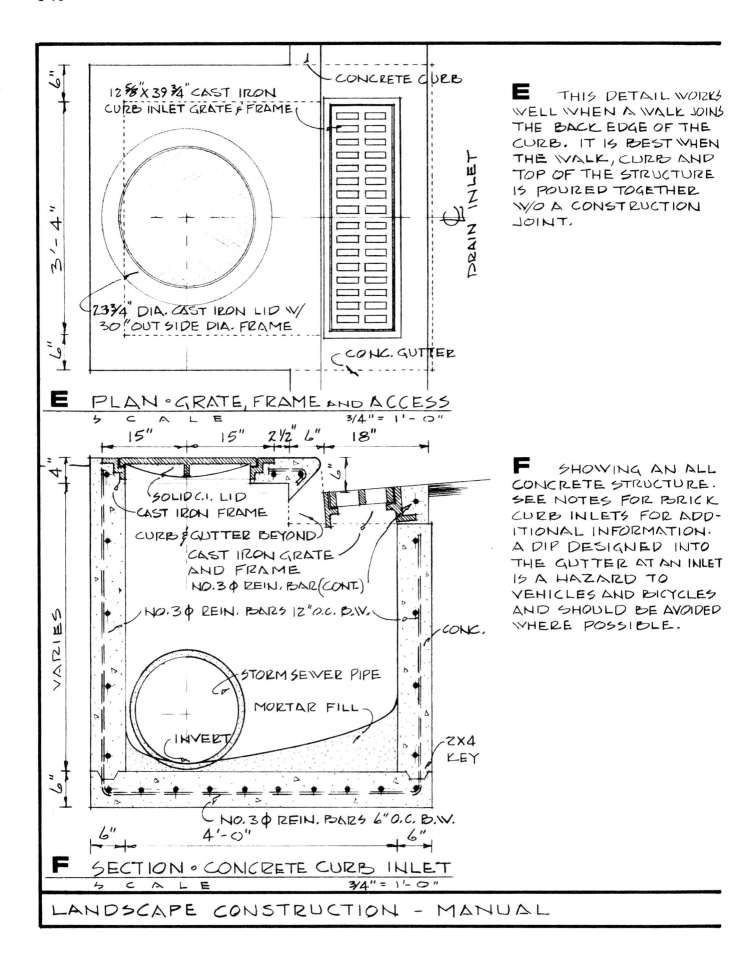

12⅝" X 39¾" CAST IRON CURB INLET GRATE & FRAME

CONCRETE CURB

DRAIN INLET

23¾" DIA. CAST IRON LID W/ 30" OUTSIDE DIA. FRAME

CONC. GUTTER

6" 3'-4" 6"

E PLAN ∘ GRATE, FRAME and ACCESS
SCALE   3/4" = 1'-0"

E THIS DETAIL WORKS WELL WHEN A WALK JOINS THE BACK EDGE OF THE CURB. IT IS BEST WHEN THE WALK, CURB AND TOP OF THE STRUCTURE IS POURED TOGETHER W/O A CONSTRUCTION JOINT.

15"   15"   2½" 6"   18"

4"

SOLID C.I. LID
CAST IRON FRAME
CURB & GUTTER BEYOND
CAST IRON GRATE AND FRAME
NO.3 ∅ REIN. BAR (CONT.)
NO.3 ∅ REIN. BARS 12" O.C. B.W.

CONC.

STORM SEWER PIPE
MORTAR FILL
INVERT

2 X 4 KEY

VARIES

6"

NO.3 ∅ REIN. BARS 6" O.C. B.W.
6"   4'-0"   6"

F SECTION ∘ CONCRETE CURB INLET
SCALE   3/4" = 1'-0"

F SHOWING AN ALL CONCRETE STRUCTURE. SEE NOTES FOR BRICK CURB INLETS FOR ADDITIONAL INFORMATION. A DIP DESIGNED INTO THE GUTTER AT AN INLET IS A HAZARD TO VEHICLES AND BICYCLES AND SHOULD BE AVOIDED WHERE POSSIBLE.

G THIS WOULD BE A GOOD CHOICE OF A GRATE WHERE BICYCLES WILL BE ON THE STREET. REMEMBER GRATE SIZES ARE SET BY THE CALCULATED VOLUME OF WATER AT THAT POINT.

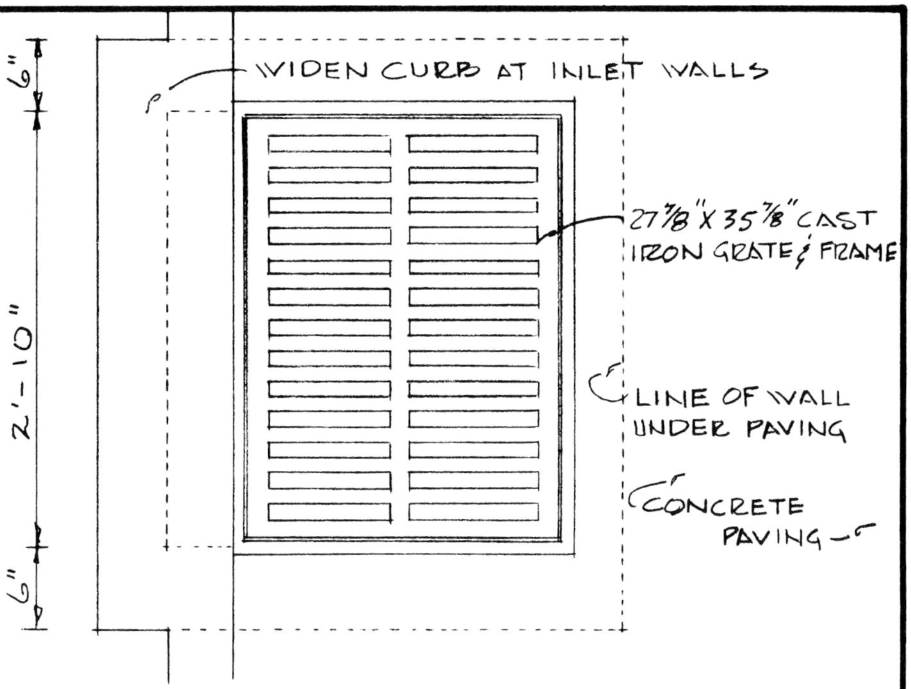

WIDEN CURB AT INLET WALLS

27⅞" X 35⅞" CAST IRON GRATE & FRAME

LINE OF WALL UNDER PAVING

CONCRETE PAVING

6"

2'-10"

6"

G PLAN · GRATE AND FRAME
SCALE   ¾" = 1'-0"

H 1. POUR THE BOTTOM 2. SET PIPE OR PIPES 3. POUR WALLS 4. SET GRATE FRAME 5. POUR STREET PAVING AND CURB 6. MORTAR FILL.

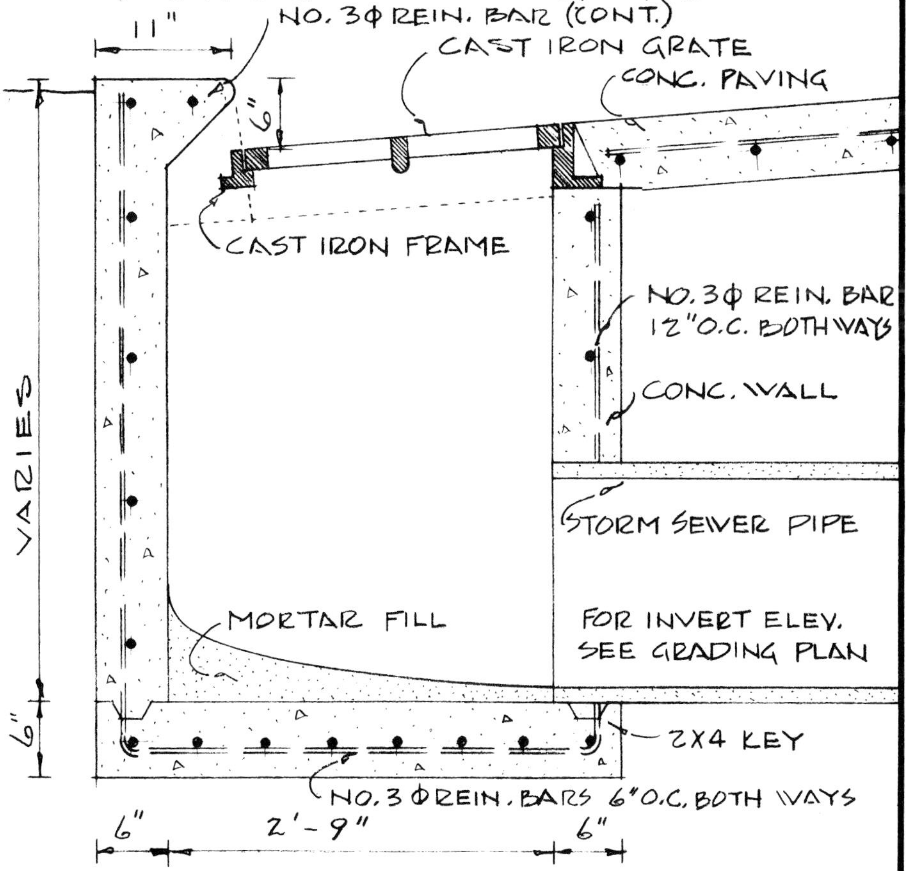

11"

NO. 3 ∅ REIN. BAR (CONT.)

CAST IRON GRATE

CONC. PAVING

6"

CAST IRON FRAME

NO. 3 ∅ REIN. BAR 12" O.C. BOTH WAYS

CONC. WALL

VARIES

STORM SEWER PIPE

MORTAR FILL

FOR INVERT ELEV. SEE GRADING PLAN

6"

2X4 KEY

NO. 3 ∅ REIN. BARS 6" O.C. BOTH WAYS

6"   2'-9"   6"

H SECTION · CONCRETE CURB INLET
SCALE   ¾" = 1'-0"

CURB INLET DETAILS

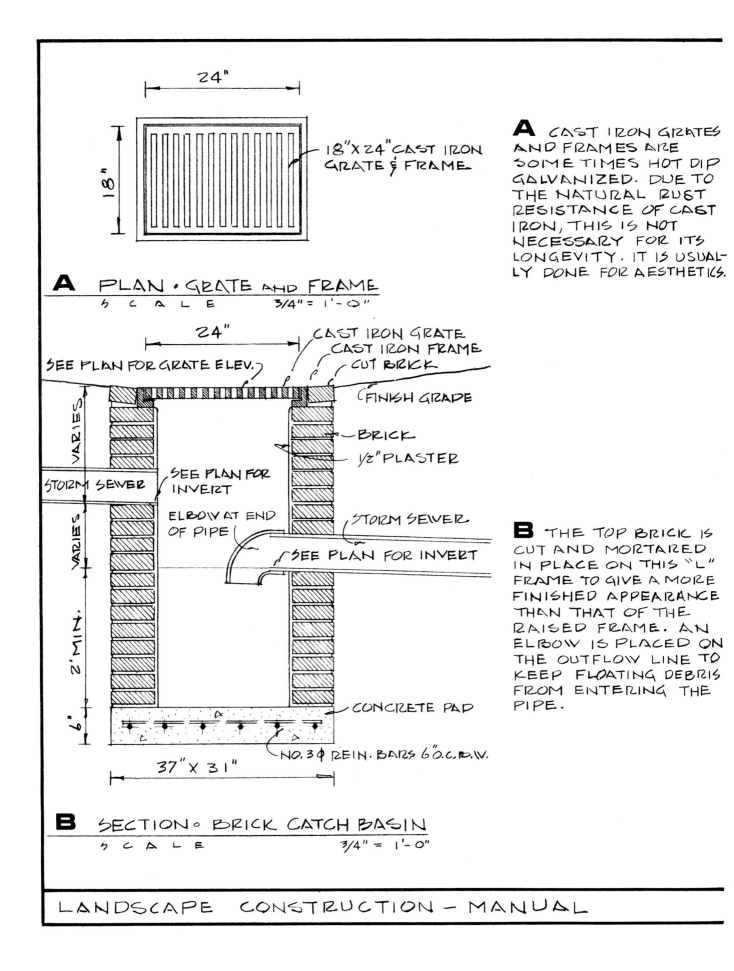

24"

18"

18"X24" CAST IRON GRATE & FRAME

A PLAN · GRATE AND FRAME
SCALE   3/4" = 1'-0"

A CAST IRON GRATES AND FRAMES ARE SOMETIMES HOT DIP GALVANIZED. DUE TO THE NATURAL RUST RESISTANCE OF CAST IRON, THIS IS NOT NECESSARY FOR ITS LONGEVITY. IT IS USUALLY DONE FOR AESTHETICS.

24"

SEE PLAN FOR GRATE ELEV.

CAST IRON GRATE
CAST IRON FRAME
CUT BRICK

FINISH GRADE

BRICK
1/2" PLASTER

VARIES

STORM SEWER

SEE PLAN FOR INVERT

VARIES

ELBOW AT END OF PIPE

STORM SEWER

SEE PLAN FOR INVERT

2' MIN.

6"

CONCRETE PAD

37" X 31"

NO. 3∅ REIN. BARS 6" O.C., B.W.

B SECTION · BRICK CATCH BASIN
SCALE   3/4" = 1'-0"

B THE TOP BRICK IS CUT AND MORTARED IN PLACE ON THIS "L" FRAME TO GIVE A MORE FINISHED APPEARANCE THAN THAT OF THE RAISED FRAME. AN ELBOW IS PLACED ON THE OUTFLOW LINE TO KEEP FLOATING DEBRIS FROM ENTERING THE PIPE.

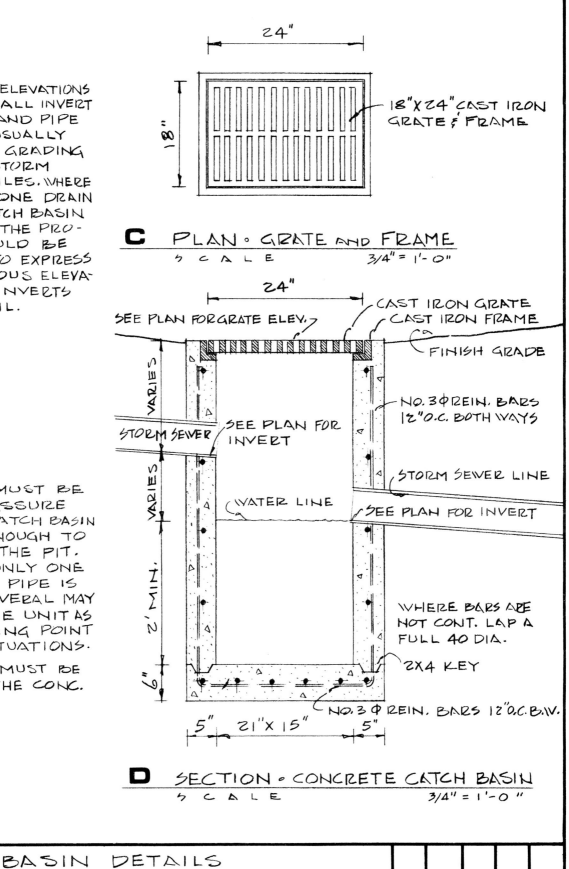

C GRATE ELEVATIONS AS WELL AS ALL INVERT ELEVATIONS AND PIPE SIZES ARE USUALLY GIVEN ON THE GRADING PLAN AND STORM DRAIN PROFILES. WHERE MORE THAN ONE DRAIN INLET OR CATCH BASIN OCCURS ON THE PROJECT, IT WOULD BE DIFFICULT TO EXPRESS THESE VARIOUS ELEVATIONS AND INVERTS ON THE DETAIL.

D CARE MUST BE TAKEN TO ASSURE THAT THE CATCH BASIN IS LARGE ENOUGH TO CLEAN OUT THE PIT. ALTHOUGH ONLY ONE IN-FLOWING PIPE IS SHOWN, SEVERAL MAY FLOW TO ONE UNIT AS A COLLECTING POINT IN SOME SITUATIONS.

THE FRAME MUST BE CAST INTO THE CONC.

C PLAN · GRATE AND FRAME
SCALE 3/4" = 1'-0"

18"X24" CAST IRON GRATE & FRAME

D SECTION · CONCRETE CATCH BASIN
SCALE 3/4" = 1'-0"

CATCH BASIN DETAILS

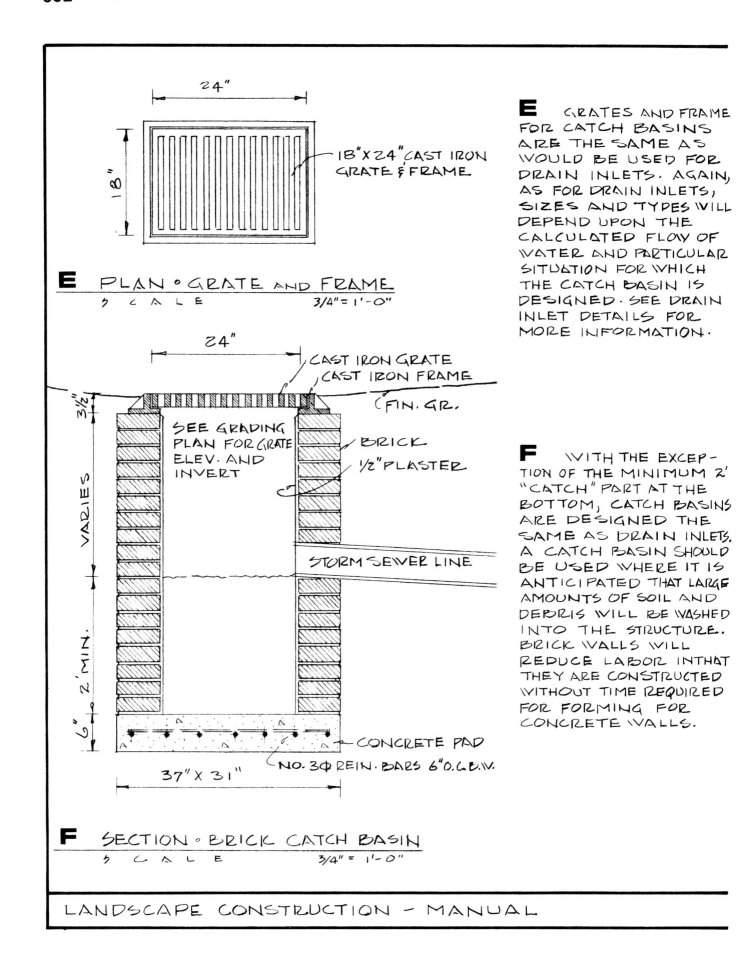

24"

18"X24" CAST IRON
GRATE & FRAME

18"

E PLAN ∘ GRATE AND FRAME
SCALE   3/4" = 1'-0"

E GRATES AND FRAME FOR CATCH BASINS ARE THE SAME AS WOULD BE USED FOR DRAIN INLETS. AGAIN, AS FOR DRAIN INLETS, SIZES AND TYPES WILL DEPEND UPON THE CALCULATED FLOW OF WATER AND PARTICULAR SITUATION FOR WHICH THE CATCH BASIN IS DESIGNED. SEE DRAIN INLET DETAILS FOR MORE INFORMATION.

24"

CAST IRON GRATE
CAST IRON FRAME

FIN. GR.

3/2"

SEE GRADING
PLAN FOR GRATE
ELEV. AND
INVERT

BRICK
1/2" PLASTER

VARIES

STORM SEWER LINE

2' MIN.

6"

CONCRETE PAD
NO. 3∅ REIN. BARS 6"O.C. E.W.

37" X 31"

F SECTION ∘ BRICK CATCH BASIN
SCALE   3/4" = 1'-0"

F WITH THE EXCEPTION OF THE MINIMUM 2' "CATCH" PART AT THE BOTTOM, CATCH BASINS ARE DESIGNED THE SAME AS DRAIN INLETS. A CATCH BASIN SHOULD BE USED WHERE IT IS ANTICIPATED THAT LARGE AMOUNTS OF SOIL AND DEBRIS WILL BE WASHED INTO THE STRUCTURE. BRICK WALLS WILL REDUCE LABOR IN THAT THEY ARE CONSTRUCTED WITHOUT TIME REQUIRED FOR FORMING FOR CONCRETE WALLS.

G THIS MAY BE A BETTER GRATE CHOICE WHERE BICYCLES WILL CROSS IT AT VARIOUS ANGLES. SEE DRAIN INLET DETAILS FOR SUGGESTIONS ON BICYCLE CONSIDERATIONS.

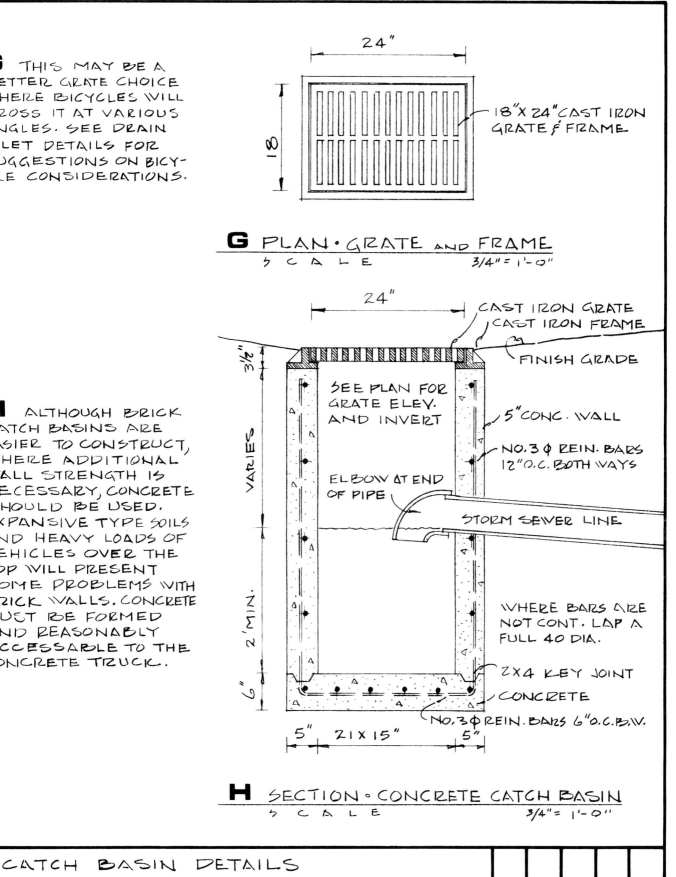

24"

18

18"X 24" CAST IRON GRATE & FRAME

G PLAN · GRATE and FRAME
SCALE   3/4" = 1'-0"

H ALTHOUGH BRICK CATCH BASINS ARE EASIER TO CONSTRUCT, WHERE ADDITIONAL WALL STRENGTH IS NECESSARY, CONCRETE SHOULD BE USED. EXPANSIVE TYPE SOILS AND HEAVY LOADS OF VEHICLES OVER THE TOP WILL PRESENT SOME PROBLEMS WITH BRICK WALLS. CONCRETE MUST BE FORMED AND REASONABLY ACCESSABLE TO THE CONCRETE TRUCK.

24"

CAST IRON GRATE
CAST IRON FRAME
FINISH GRADE

3½"

SEE PLAN FOR GRATE ELEV. AND INVERT

VARIES

ELBOW AT END OF PIPE

5" CONC. WALL

NO. 3 ∅ REIN. BARS 12" O.C. BOTH WAYS

STORM SEWER LINE

WHERE BARS ARE NOT CONT. LAP A FULL 40 DIA.

2' MIN.

6"

2X4 KEY JOINT
CONCRETE
NO. 3 ∅ REIN. BARS 6" O.C. B.W.

5"   21 X 15"   5"

H SECTION · CONCRETE CATCH BASIN
SCALE   3/4" = 1'-0"

CATCH BASIN DETAILS

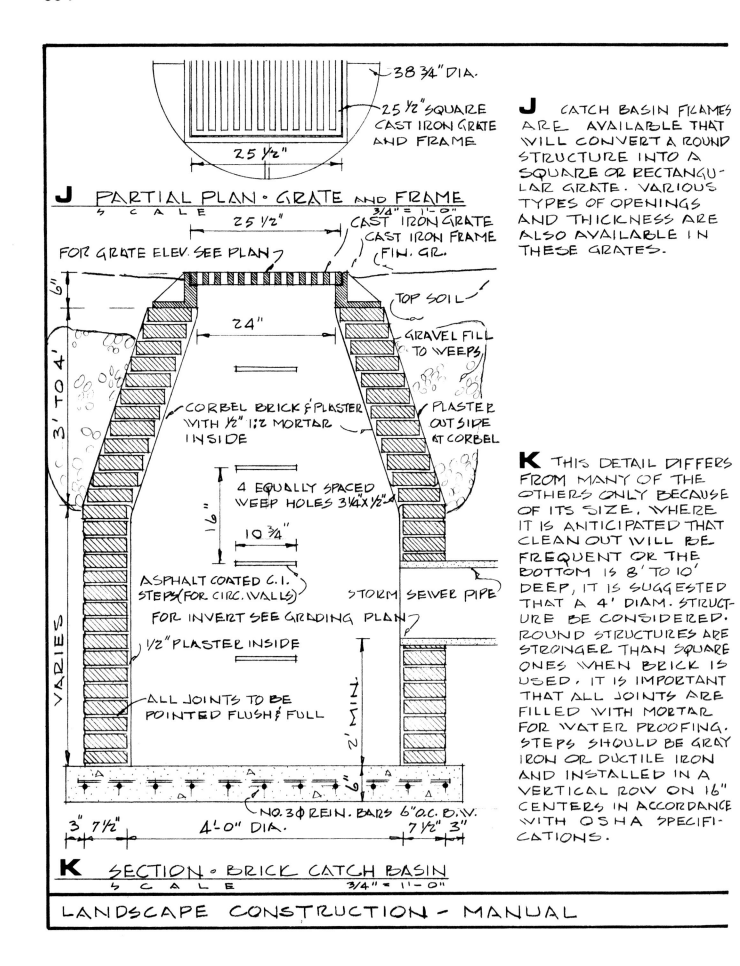

38 ¾" DIA.

25 ½" SQUARE CAST IRON GRATE AND FRAME

25 ½"

J PARTIAL PLAN · GRATE AND FRAME
SCALE ¾" = 1'-0"

25 ½"

CAST IRON GRATE
CAST IRON FRAME
FIN. GR.

FOR GRATE ELEV. SEE PLAN

TOP SOIL

6"

3' TO 4'

24"

GRAVEL FILL TO WEEPS

CORBEL BRICK & PLASTER WITH ½" 1:2 MORTAR INSIDE

PLASTER OUTSIDE AT CORBEL

4 EQUALLY SPACED WEEP HOLES 3¼" X ½"

16"

10 ¾"

ASPHALT COATED C.I. STEPS (FOR CIRC. WALLS)

STORM SEWER PIPE

FOR INVERT SEE GRADING PLAN

½" PLASTER INSIDE

VARIES

2' MIN.

ALL JOINTS TO BE POINTED FLUSH & FULL

6"

NO. 3Ø REIN. BARS 6" O.C. B.W.

3" 7½"

4'-0" DIA.

7½" 3"

K SECTION · BRICK CATCH BASIN
SCALE ¾" = 1'-0"

J CATCH BASIN FRAMES ARE AVAILABLE THAT WILL CONVERT A ROUND STRUCTURE INTO A SQUARE OR RECTANGULAR GRATE. VARIOUS TYPES OF OPENINGS AND THICKNESS ARE ALSO AVAILABLE IN THESE GRATES.

K THIS DETAIL DIFFERS FROM MANY OF THE OTHERS ONLY BECAUSE OF ITS SIZE, WHERE IT IS ANTICIPATED THAT CLEAN OUT WILL BE FREQUENT OR THE BOTTOM IS 8' TO 10' DEEP, IT IS SUGGESTED THAT A 4' DIAM. STRUCTURE BE CONSIDERED. ROUND STRUCTURES ARE STRONGER THAN SQUARE ONES WHEN BRICK IS USED. IT IS IMPORTANT THAT ALL JOINTS ARE FILLED WITH MORTAR FOR WATER PROOFING. STEPS SHOULD BE GRAY IRON OR DUCTILE IRON AND INSTALLED IN A VERTICAL ROW ON 16" CENTERS IN ACCORDANCE WITH OSHA SPECIFICATIONS.

L CONCRETE STRUCT-
URES ARE MORE EASILY
FORMED SQUARE RATH-
ER THAN ROUND. THUS
A SQUARE GRATE AND
FRAME IS USED HERE.

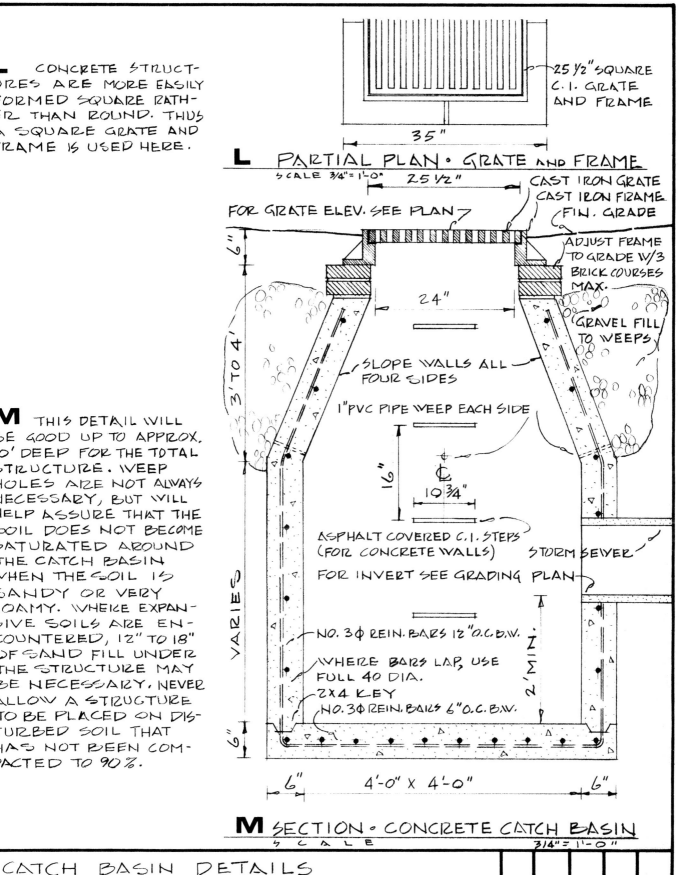

L PARTIAL PLAN · GRATE AND FRAME
SCALE 3/4"=1'-0"

25 1/2" SQUARE
C.I. GRATE
AND FRAME

35"

25 1/2"

CAST IRON GRATE
CAST IRON FRAME
FIN. GRADE

FOR GRATE ELEV. SEE PLAN

ADJUST FRAME
TO GRADE W/3
BRICK COURSES
MAX.

GRAVEL FILL
TO WEEPS

24"

SLOPE WALLS ALL
FOUR SIDES

1" PVC PIPE WEEP EACH SIDE

16"

10 3/4"

ASPHALT COVERED C.I. STEPS
(FOR CONCRETE WALLS)

STORM SEWER

FOR INVERT SEE GRADING PLAN

NO. 3∅ REIN. BARS 12" O.C. B.W.

WHERE BARS LAP, USE
FULL 40 DIA.

2X4 KEY
NO. 3∅ REIN. BARS 6" O.C. B.W.

6"

4'-0" X 4'-0"

6"

2' MIN.

VARIES

6"

3' TO 4'

M THIS DETAIL WILL
BE GOOD UP TO APPROX.
10' DEEP FOR THE TOTAL
STRUCTURE. WEEP
HOLES ARE NOT ALWAYS
NECESSARY, BUT WILL
HELP ASSURE THAT THE
SOIL DOES NOT BECOME
SATURATED AROUND
THE CATCH BASIN
WHEN THE SOIL IS
SANDY OR VERY
LOAMY. WHERE EXPAN-
SIVE SOILS ARE EN-
COUNTERED, 12" TO 18"
OF SAND FILL UNDER
THE STRUCTURE MAY
BE NECESSARY. NEVER
ALLOW A STRUCTURE
TO BE PLACED ON DIS-
TURBED SOIL THAT
HAS NOT BEEN COM-
PACTED TO 90%.

M SECTION · CONCRETE CATCH BASIN
SCALE 3/4"=1'-0"

CATCH BASIN DETAILS

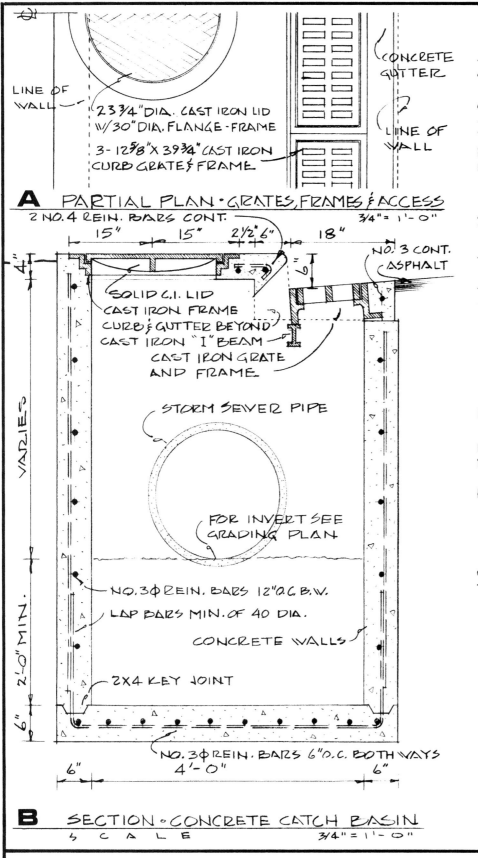

CONCRETE GUTTER

LINE OF WALL

LINE OF WALL

23¾" DIA. CAST IRON LID W/ 30" DIA. FLANGE - FRAME

3 - 12⅝" X 39¾" CAST IRON CURB GRATE & FRAME

A PARTIAL PLAN · GRATES, FRAMES & ACCESS
¾" = 1'- 0"

2 NO. 4 REIN. BARS CONT.

15" 15" 2½" 6" 18"

NO. 3 CONT.

ASPHALT

SOLID C.I. LID
CAST IRON FRAME
CURB & GUTTER BEYOND
CAST IRON "I" BEAM
CAST IRON GRATE AND FRAME

STORM SEWER PIPE

FOR INVERT SEE GRADING PLAN

VARIES

2'-0" MIN.

6"

NO. 3 Ø REIN. BARS 12" O.C. B.W.
LAP BARS MIN. OF 40 DIA.

CONCRETE WALLS

2 X 4 KEY JOINT

NO. 3 Ø REIN. BARS 6" O.C. BOTH WAYS

6" 4'- 0" 6"

B SECTION · CONCRETE CATCH BASIN
S C A L E   ¾" = 1'- 0"

A WHEN MORE THAN ONE CURB OPENING AND GRATE IS RE-QUIRED FOR THE CALCULATED WATER VOLUME, IT IS COMMON PRACTICE TO LINE THEM END TO END. ONLY ONE ACCESS IS NECESSARY, HOWEVER, FOR THERE ARE NO WALLS WITHIN THE CATCH BASINS. IT IS NOT GOOD PRACTICE TO SHOW LESS THAN ONE HALF OF THE FULL PLAN WHEN DRAWING A PARTIAL PLAN. SPACE PROHIBITED IT HERE.

B WHEN MORE THAN ONE GRATE AND FRAME IS USED, IT IS NECESSARY TO INCLUDE AN "I" BEAM AS SHOWN HERE. 6" THICK WALLS ARE USUALLY USED RATHER THAN 5" WHEN THE INLET OR CATCH BASIN IS LOCATED IN OR NEAR VEHICULAR TRAFFIC.

C VARIOUS TYPES OF CAST IRON CURB INLET FRAME, GRATE AND CURB BOX COMBINATIONS ARE AVAILABLE. SEE MFG. CATALOG FOR THE ONE THAT FITS BEST YOUR PARTICULAR SITUATION.

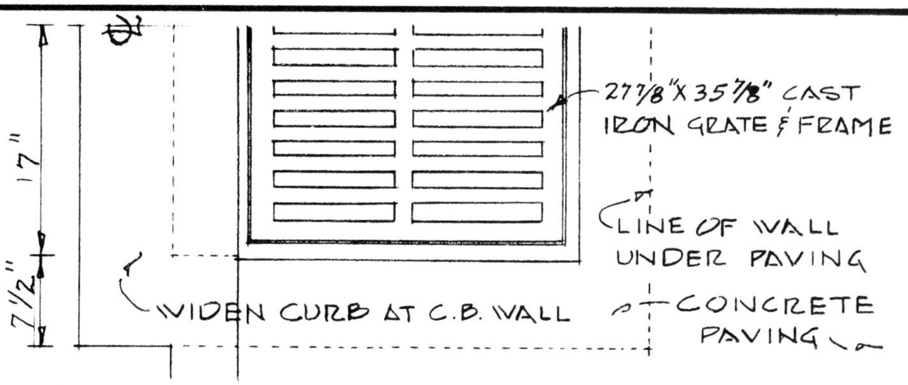

27⅞"X35⅞" CAST IRON GRATE & FRAME

LINE OF WALL UNDER PAVING

CONCRETE PAVING

WIDEN CURB AT C.B. WALL

C PARTIAL PLAN· GRATE AND FRAME
3/4" = 1'-0"

NO.3∅ REIN. BARS CONT.
8" 6"
9"
CAST IRON GRATE
CONC. PAVING
CAST IRON FRAME
NO.3∅ REIN. BARS 12"O.C.B.W.
BRICK WALL

D CURB CUTS ARE NECESSARY ONLY WHERE THE CATCH BASIN OR INLET IS LOCATED ALONG THE FLOW LINE RATHER THAN AT A LOW POINT OF A STREET OR PARKING AREA. THE INVERT ELEVATION VARIES AS SHOWN (DEPENDING UPON THAT NECESSARY AS INDICATED ON THE GRADING PLAN OR STORM SEWER PROFILES). WHEN THE PIPE IS UNDER THE STREET AS SHOWN HERE, A MINIMUM COVER SHOULD BE MAINTAINED. THIS MINIMUM DISTANCE WILL DEPEND UPON THE TYPE OF ROAD WAY CONSTRUCTION AND TRAFFIC.

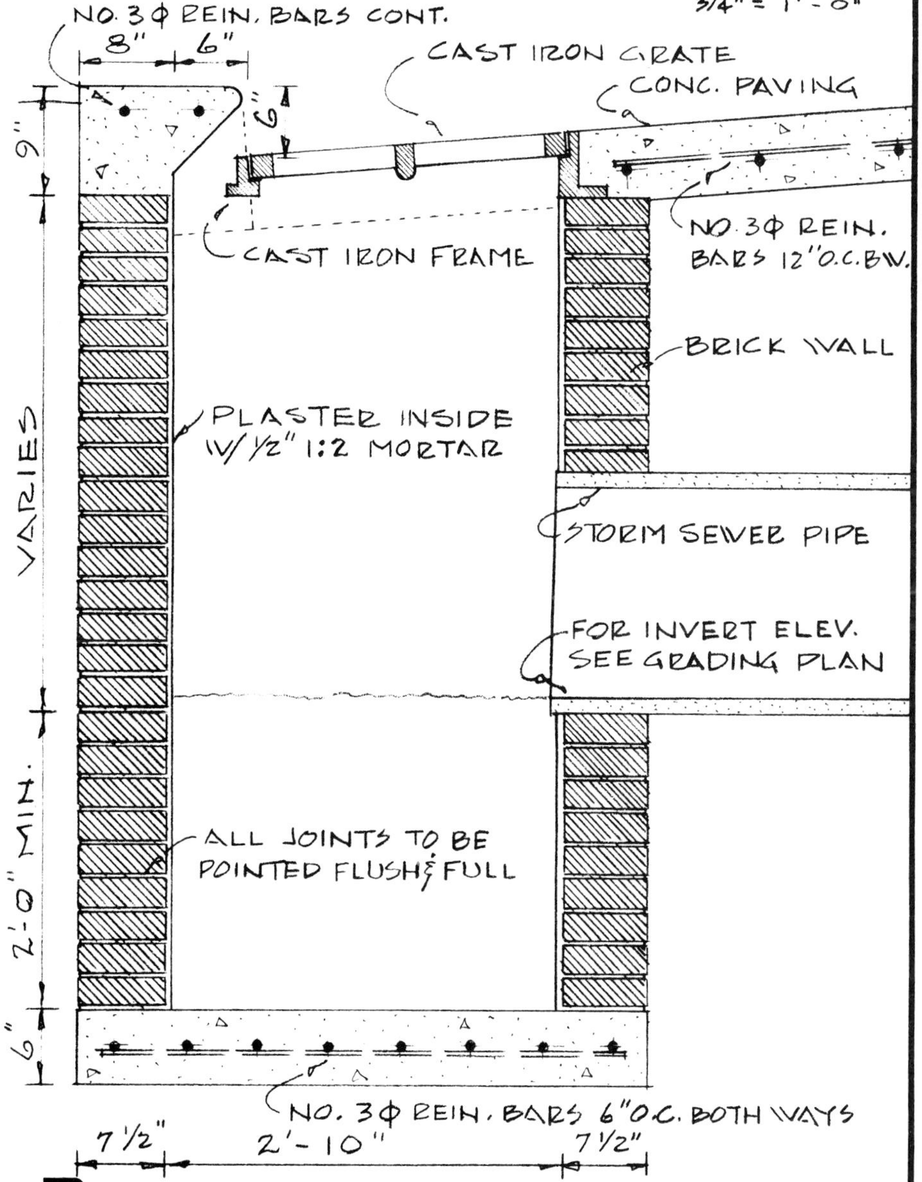

VARIES
PLASTER INSIDE W/ ½" 1:2 MORTAR
STORM SEWER PIPE
FOR INVERT ELEV. SEE GRADING PLAN
ALL JOINTS TO BE POINTED FLUSH & FULL
2'-0" MIN.
6"
NO.3∅ REIN. BARS 6"O.C. BOTH WAYS
7½" 2'-10" 7½"

D SECTION· BRICK CATCH BASIN
SCALE   3/4" = 1'-0"

CURB CATCH BASIN DETAILS

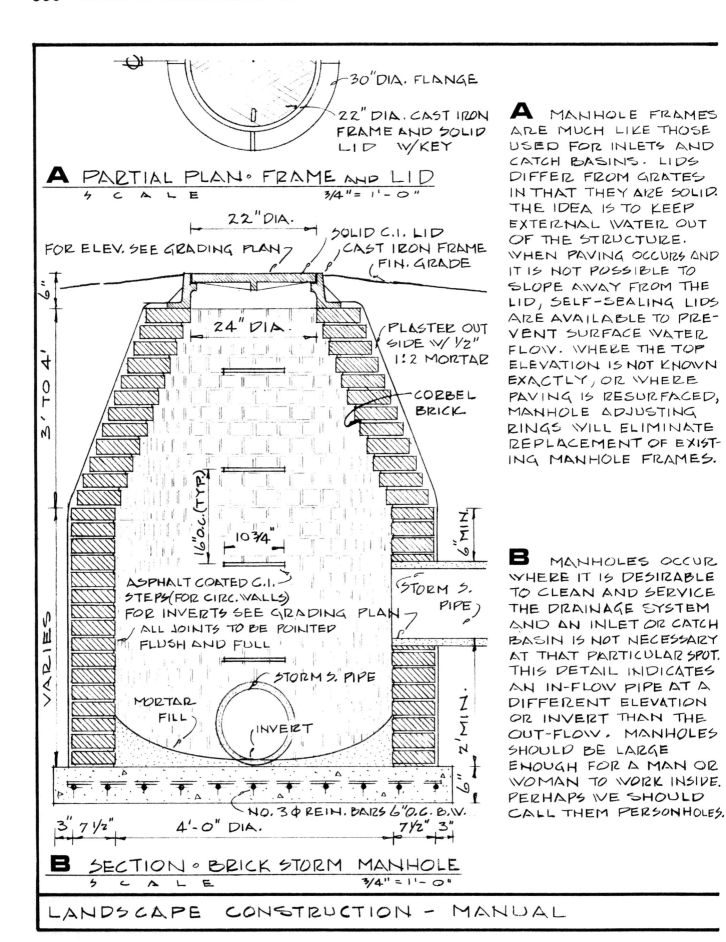

30" DIA. FLANGE

22" DIA. CAST IRON FRAME AND SOLID LID W/KEY

A PARTIAL PLAN ∘ FRAME AND LID

SCALE   3/4" = 1'-0"

A MANHOLE FRAMES ARE MUCH LIKE THOSE USED FOR INLETS AND CATCH BASINS. LIDS DIFFER FROM GRATES IN THAT THEY ARE SOLID. THE IDEA IS TO KEEP EXTERNAL WATER OUT OF THE STRUCTURE. WHEN PAVING OCCURS AND IT IS NOT POSSIBLE TO SLOPE AWAY FROM THE LID, SELF-SEALING LIDS ARE AVAILABLE TO PREVENT SURFACE WATER FLOW. WHERE THE TOP ELEVATION IS NOT KNOWN EXACTLY, OR WHERE PAVING IS RESURFACED, MANHOLE ADJUSTING RINGS WILL ELIMINATE REPLACEMENT OF EXISTING MANHOLE FRAMES.

22" DIA.

FOR ELEV. SEE GRADING PLAN

SOLID C.I. LID
CAST IRON FRAME
FIN. GRADE

6"

3' TO 4'

24" DIA.

PLASTER OUTSIDE W/ ½" 1:2 MORTAR

CORBEL BRICK

16" O.C. (TYP.)

10¾"

6" MIN.

ASPHALT COATED C.I. STEPS (FOR CIRC. WALLS) FOR INVERTS SEE GRADING PLAN. ALL JOINTS TO BE POINTED FLUSH AND FULL

(STORM S. PIPE)

VARIES

STORM S. PIPE

MORTAR FILL

INVERT

2' MIN.

6"

NO. 3 ∅ REIN. BARS 6" O.C. B.W.

3" 7½"

4'-0" DIA.

7½" 3"

B SECTION ∘ BRICK STORM MANHOLE

SCALE   3/4" = 1'-0"

B MANHOLES OCCUR WHERE IT IS DESIRABLE TO CLEAN AND SERVICE THE DRAINAGE SYSTEM AND AN INLET OR CATCH BASIN IS NOT NECESSARY AT THAT PARTICULAR SPOT. THIS DETAIL INDICATES AN IN-FLOW PIPE AT A DIFFERENT ELEVATION OR INVERT THAN THE OUT-FLOW. MANHOLES SHOULD BE LARGE ENOUGH FOR A MAN OR WOMAN TO WORK INSIDE. PERHAPS WE SHOULD CALL THEM PERSONHOLES.

C MANHOLE FRAMES AND LIDS ARE AVAILABLE IN ROUND OR SQUARE, VARIOUS SIZES, AND VARIOUS HEIGHTS. CHECK MFG. CATALOGS.

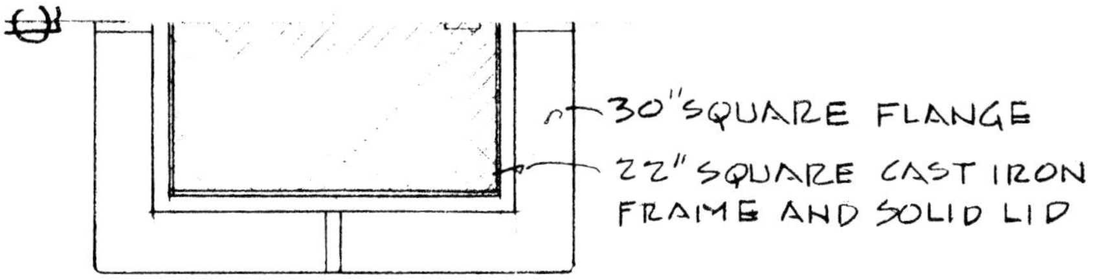

30" SQUARE FLANGE

22" SQUARE CAST IRON FRAME AND SOLID LID

C PARTIAL PLAN • FRAME AND LID

SCALE   3/4" = 1'-0"

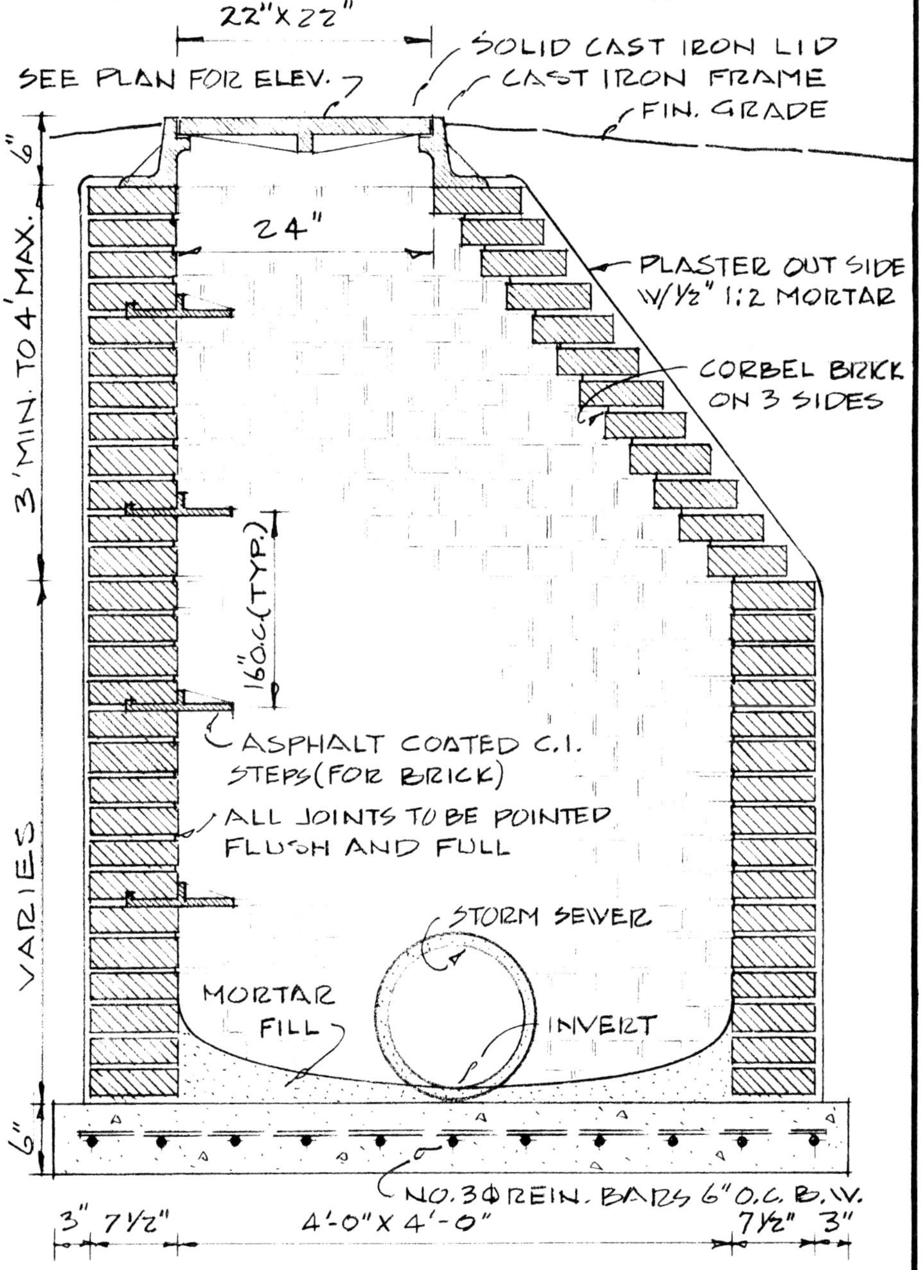

22"X 22"

SEE PLAN FOR ELEV.

SOLID CAST IRON LID

CAST IRON FRAME

FIN. GRADE

6"

3' MIN. TO 4' MAX.

24"

PLASTER OUTSIDE W/ ½" 1:2 MORTAR

CORBEL BRICK ON 3 SIDES

16 O.C. (TYP.)

D THIS DETAIL SHOWS A SQUARE MANHOLE WITH THREE SIDES SLOPING AND THE FOURTH SIDE VERTICAL, WHICH RECEIVES THE STEPS. MANHOLES SHOULD BE PLASTERED ON THE OUTSIDE TO PREVENT WATER SEEPING IN. FOR STRUCTURAL SAFETY, DO NOT ALLOW THE BRICK TO BE CORBELED 24" IN LESS THAN 3' MINIMUM. SEE NOTES ON 4' WIDE CATCH BASINS FOR ADDITIONAL INFORMATION.

ASPHALT COATED C.I. STEPS (FOR BRICK)

ALL JOINTS TO BE POINTED FLUSH AND FULL

VARIES

STORM SEWER

MORTAR FILL

INVERT

6"

NO. 3 Ø REIN. BARS 6" O.C. B.W.

3"   7½"   4'-0" X 4'-0"   7½"   3"

D SECTION • BRICK STORM MANHOLE

SCALE   3/4" = 1'-0"

STORM MANHOLE DETAILS

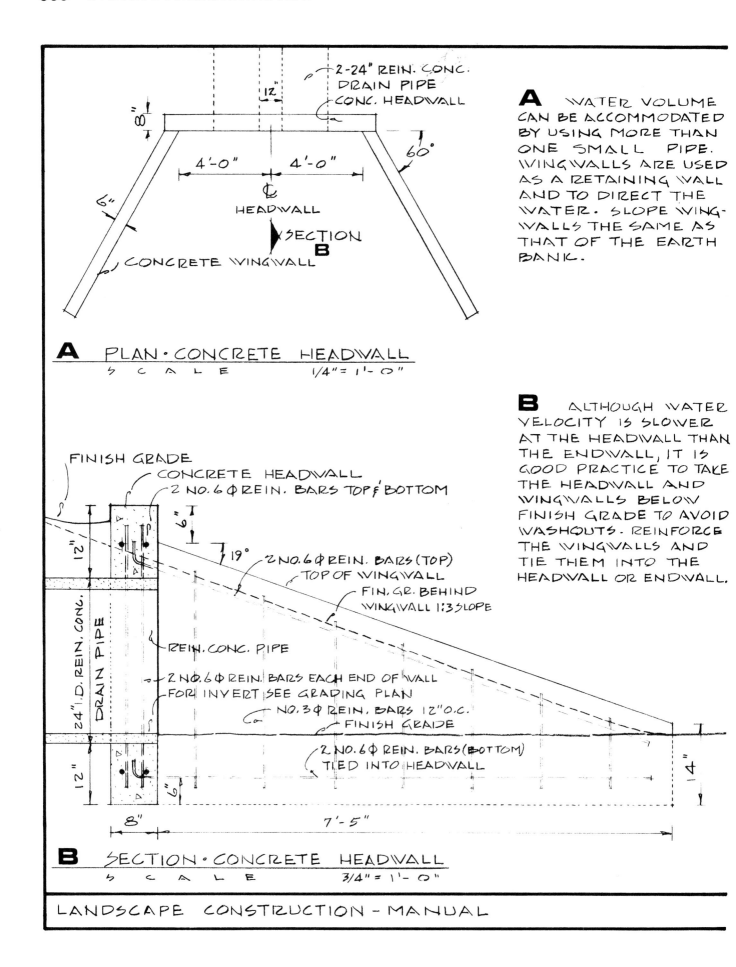

2-24" REIN. CONC.
DRAIN PIPE
CONC. HEADWALL

12"

8"

4'-0"   4'-0"

60°

6"

℄
HEADWALL

SECTION
B

CONCRETE WINGWALL

A PLAN · CONCRETE HEADWALL
SCALE   1/4"= 1'-0"

A WATER VOLUME CAN BE ACCOMMODATED BY USING MORE THAN ONE SMALL PIPE. WINGWALLS ARE USED AS A RETAINING WALL AND TO DIRECT THE WATER. SLOPE WING-WALLS THE SAME AS THAT OF THE EARTH BANK.

B ALTHOUGH WATER VELOCITY IS SLOWER AT THE HEADWALL THAN THE ENDWALL, IT IS GOOD PRACTICE TO TAKE THE HEADWALL AND WINGWALLS BELOW FINISH GRADE TO AVOID WASHOUTS. REINFORCE THE WINGWALLS AND TIE THEM INTO THE HEADWALL OR ENDWALL.

FINISH GRADE
CONCRETE HEADWALL
2 NO. 6 Φ REIN. BARS TOP & BOTTOM

6"

12"

19°

2 NO. 6 Φ REIN. BARS (TOP)
TOP OF WINGWALL

FIN. GR. BEHIND
WINGWALL 1:3 SLOPE

24" I.D. REIN. CONC.
DRAIN PIPE

REIN. CONC. PIPE

2 NO. 6 Φ REIN. BARS EACH END OF WALL
FOR INVERT SEE GRADING PLAN

NO. 3 Φ REIN. BARS 12" O.C.
FINISH GRADE

12"

6"

2 NO. 6 Φ REIN. BARS (BOTTOM)
TIED INTO HEADWALL

14"

8"   7'-5"

B SECTION · CONCRETE HEADWALL
SCALE   3/4"= 1'-0"

LANDSCAPE CONSTRUCTION - MANUAL

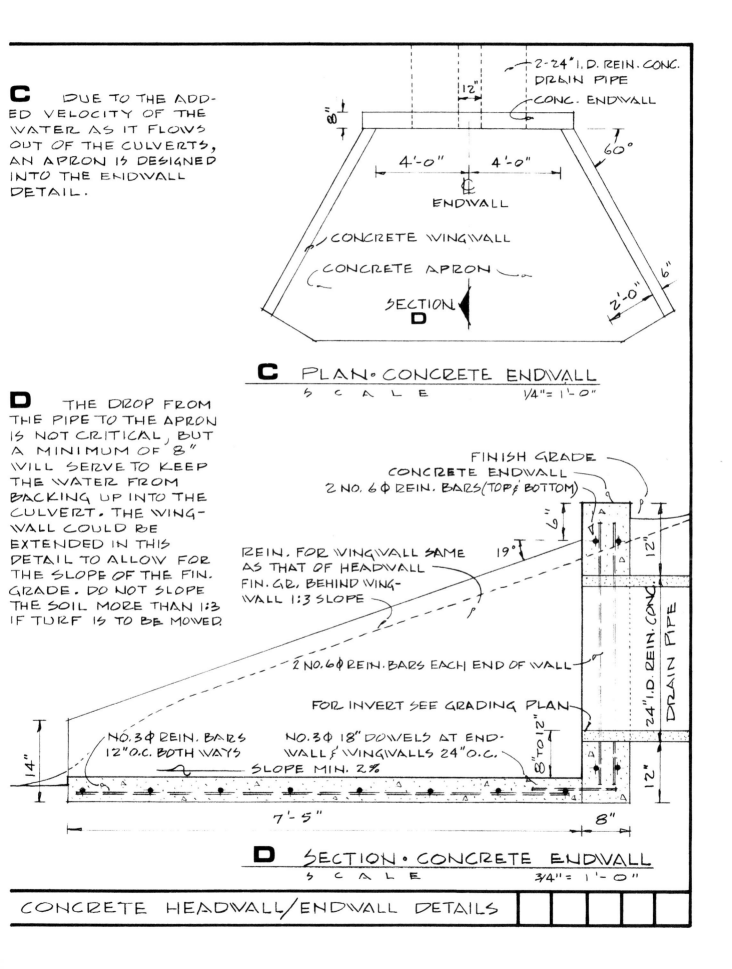

C DUE TO THE ADDED VELOCITY OF THE WATER AS IT FLOWS OUT OF THE CULVERTS, AN APRON IS DESIGNED INTO THE ENDWALL DETAIL.

2-24" I.D. REIN. CONC. DRAIN PIPE

CONC. ENDWALL

12"

8"

4'-0"   4'-0"

60°

C̶L̶
ENDWALL

CONCRETE WINGWALL

CONCRETE APRON

6"

2'-0"

SECTION
D

C PLAN • CONCRETE ENDWALL
SCALE   1/4" = 1'-0"

D THE DROP FROM THE PIPE TO THE APRON IS NOT CRITICAL, BUT A MINIMUM OF 8" WILL SERVE TO KEEP THE WATER FROM BACKING UP INTO THE CULVERT. THE WINGWALL COULD BE EXTENDED IN THIS DETAIL TO ALLOW FOR THE SLOPE OF THE FIN. GRADE. DO NOT SLOPE THE SOIL MORE THAN 1:3 IF TURF IS TO BE MOWED.

FINISH GRADE
CONCRETE ENDWALL
2 NO. 6 Ø REIN. BARS (TOP & BOTTOM)

REIN. FOR WINGWALL SAME AS THAT OF HEADWALL FIN. GR. BEHIND WING-WALL 1:3 SLOPE

19°

12"

2 NO. 6 Ø REIN. BARS EACH END OF WALL

FOR INVERT SEE GRADING PLAN

24" I.D. REIN. CONC. DRAIN PIPE

14"

NO. 3 Ø REIN. BARS 12" O.C. BOTH WAYS

NO. 3 Ø 18" DOWELS AT END-WALL & WINGWALLS 24" O.C.

SLOPE MIN. 2%

8" TO 12"

12"

7'-5"

8"

D SECTION • CONCRETE ENDWALL
SCALE   3/4" = 1'-0"

CONCRETE HEADWALL/ENDWALL DETAILS

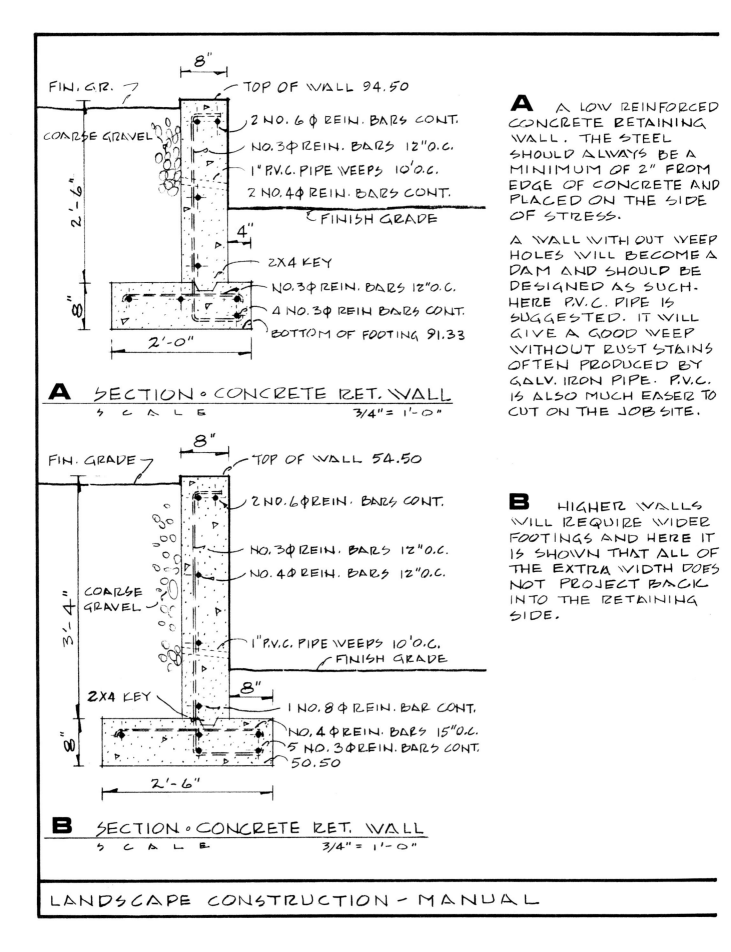

FIN. G.R.

COARSE GRAVEL

2'-6"

8"

8"

2'-0"

TOP OF WALL 94.50

2 NO. 6 ⌀ REIN. BARS CONT.

NO. 3 ⌀ REIN. BARS 12"O.C.

1" P.V.C. PIPE WEEPS 10'O.C.

2 NO. 4 ⌀ REIN. BARS CONT.

FINISH GRADE

4"

2X4 KEY

NO. 3 ⌀ REIN. BARS 12"O.C.

4 NO. 3 ⌀ REIN BARS CONT.

BOTTOM OF FOOTING 91.33

A SECTION ∘ CONCRETE RET. WALL

SCALE   3/4" = 1'-0"

A A LOW REINFORCED CONCRETE RETAINING WALL. THE STEEL SHOULD ALWAYS BE A MINIMUM OF 2" FROM EDGE OF CONCRETE AND PLACED ON THE SIDE OF STRESS.

A WALL WITH OUT WEEP HOLES WILL BECOME A DAM AND SHOULD BE DESIGNED AS SUCH. HERE P.V.C. PIPE IS SUGGESTED. IT WILL GIVE A GOOD WEEP WITHOUT RUST STAINS OFTEN PRODUCED BY GALV. IRON PIPE. P.V.C. IS ALSO MUCH EASIER TO CUT ON THE JOB SITE.

FIN. GRADE

8"

TOP OF WALL 54.50

2 NO. 6 ⌀ REIN. BARS CONT.

NO. 3 ⌀ REIN. BARS 12"O.C.

NO. 4 ⌀ REIN. BARS 12"O.C.

3'-4"

COARSE GRAVEL

1" P.V.C. PIPE WEEPS 10'O.C.

FINISH GRADE

8"

2X4 KEY

1 NO. 8 ⌀ REIN. BAR CONT.

8"

NO. 4 ⌀ REIN. BARS 15"O.C.

5 NO. 3 ⌀ REIN. BARS CONT.

50.50

2'-6"

B SECTION ∘ CONCRETE RET. WALL

SCALE   3/4" = 1'-0"

B HIGHER WALLS WILL REQUIRE WIDER FOOTINGS AND HERE IT IS SHOWN THAT ALL OF THE EXTRA WIDTH DOES NOT PROJECT BACK INTO THE RETAINING SIDE.

C EVEN A VERY LOW WALL MUST HAVE SOME REINFORCING AND WEEP HOLES.

THIS WALL NEED NOT BE 8" WIDE, BUT IS DESIGNED SO HERE FOR CONSISTENCY.

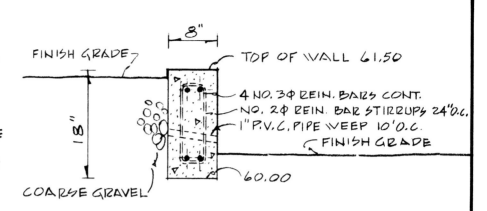

FINISH GRADE

8"

18"

COARSE GRAVEL

TOP OF WALL 61.50

4 NO. 3∅ REIN. BARS CONT.
NO. 2∅ REIN. BAR STIRRUPS 24" O.C.
1" P.V.C. PIPE WEEP 10' O.C.
FINISH GRADE

60.00

C SECTION ∘ CONCRETE RET. WALL
SCALE   3/4" = 1'-0"

D THE STRUCTURES SHOWN ON THIS AND THE NEXT FEW PAGES WERE DESIGNED FOR AN AREA OF VERY ACTIVE SOIL CONDITIONS. IT IS WISE, IF INDEED NOT IMPERATIVE, THAT EACH PROJECT USING CONCRETE RETAINING WALLS BE REVIEWED BY A STRUCTURAL ENGINEER.

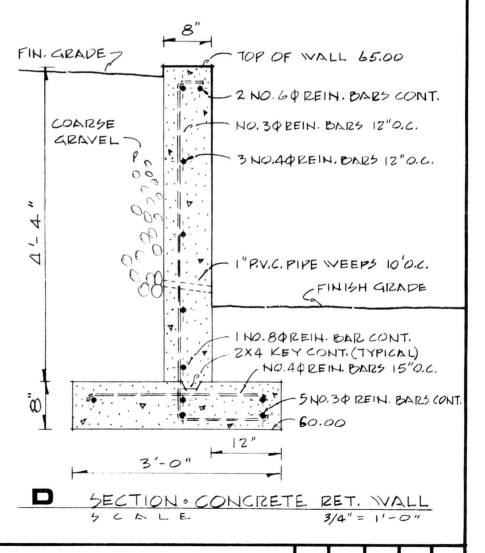

FIN. GRADE

8"

COARSE GRAVEL

4'-4"

8"

TOP OF WALL 65.00

2 NO. 6∅ REIN. BARS CONT.

NO. 3∅ REIN. BARS 12" O.C.

3 NO. 4∅ REIN. BARS 12" O.C.

1" P.V.C. PIPE WEEPS 10' O.C.
FINISH GRADE

1 NO. 8∅ REIN. BAR CONT.
2X4 KEY CONT. (TYPICAL)
NO. 4∅ REIN. BARS 15" O.C.
5 NO. 3∅ REIN. BARS CONT.
60.00

12"

3'-0"

D SECTION ∘ CONCRETE RET. WALL
SCALE   3/4" = 1'-0"

CONCRETE RETAINING WALLS

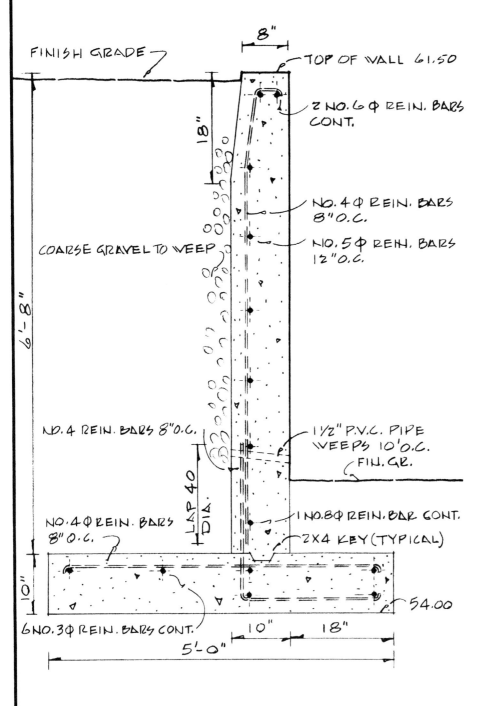

FINISH GRADE

8"

TOP OF WALL 61.50

2 NO. 6 ∅ REIN. BARS CONT.

18"

NO. 4 ∅ REIN. BARS 8" O.C.

NO. 5 ∅ REIN. BARS 12" O.C.

COARSE GRAVEL TO WEEP

6'-8"

NO. 4 REIN. BARS 8" O.C.

1½" P.V.C. PIPE WEEPS 10' O.C.

FIN. GR.

LAP 40 DIA.

NO. 4 ∅ REIN. BARS 8" O.C.

1 NO. 8 ∅ REIN. BAR CONT.

2X4 KEY (TYPICAL)

10"

54.00

6 NO. 3 ∅ REIN. BARS CONT.

10"

18"

5'-0"

E SECTION ○ CONCRETE RET. WALL

SCALE 3/4" = 1'-0"

E A MEDIUM HEIGHT RETAINING WALL WITH A 10" WIDTH AT THE BASE REDUCED TO 8" AT THE TOP. THIS IS ONLY TO KEEP THE WALL FROM APPEARING TOO BULKY.

DEPENDING UPON WHAT HAPPENS ON THE UPPER LEVEL, A HAND RAILING MAY BE ATTACHED TO THE TOP OF THE WALL OR BY EXTENDING THE WALL AND IT'S REINFORCING A PARAPET COULD EXIST.

BAR LAP IS SHOWN IN THIS DETAIL FOR AT THIS HEIGHT A CONTINUOUS BAR WOULD BE TOO DIFFICULT TO INSTALL.

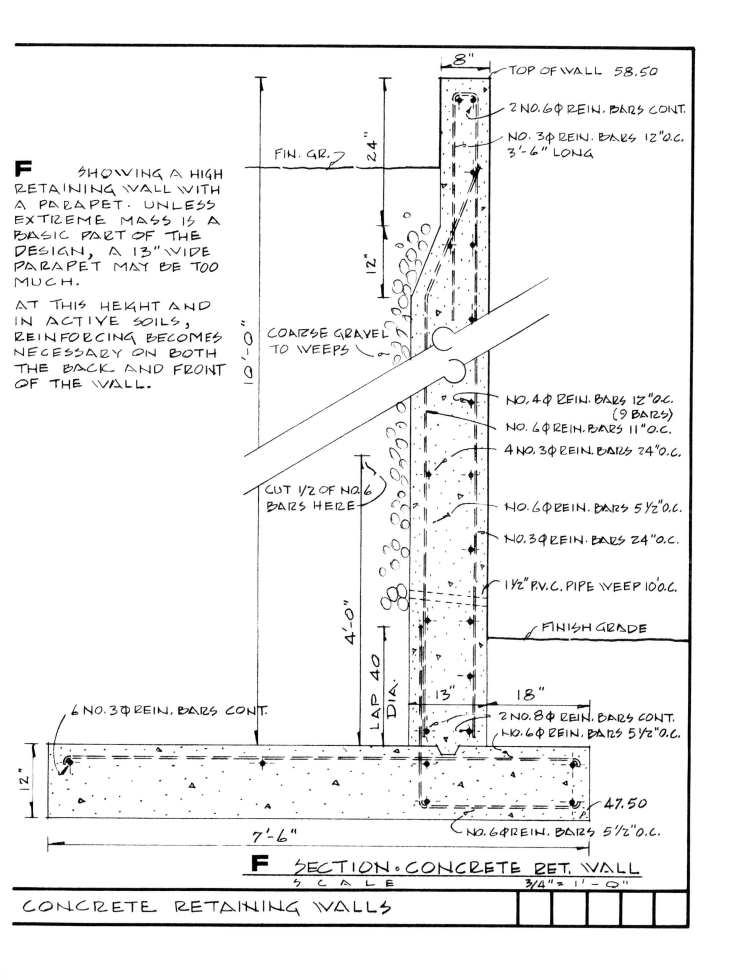

F SHOWING A HIGH RETAINING WALL WITH A PARAPET. UNLESS EXTREME MASS IS A BASIC PART OF THE DESIGN, A 13" WIDE PARAPET MAY BE TOO MUCH.

AT THIS HEIGHT AND IN ACTIVE SOILS, REINFORCING BECOMES NECESSARY ON BOTH THE BACK AND FRONT OF THE WALL.

8"

TOP OF WALL 58.50

2 NO. 6∅ REIN. BARS CONT.

NO. 3∅ REIN. BARS 12" O.C. 3'-6" LONG

FIN. GR.

24"

12"

COARSE GRAVEL TO WEEPS

NO. 4∅ REIN. BARS 12" O.C. (9 BARS)

NO. 6∅ REIN. BARS 11" O.C.

4 NO. 3∅ REIN. BARS 24" O.C.

NO. 6∅ REIN. BARS 5½" O.C.

NO. 3∅ REIN. BARS 24" O.C.

1½" P.V.C. PIPE WEEP 10' O.C.

FINISH GRADE

CUT ½ OF NO. 6 BARS HERE

10'-0"

4'-0"

LAP 40 DIA.

13"   18"

6 NO. 3∅ REIN. BARS CONT.

2 NO. 8∅ REIN. BARS CONT.
NO. 6∅ REIN. BARS 5½" O.C.

12"

47.50

NO. 6∅ REIN. BARS 5½" O.C.

7'-6"

F SECTION • CONCRETE RET. WALL
SCALE   3/4" = 1'-0"

CONCRETE RETAINING WALLS

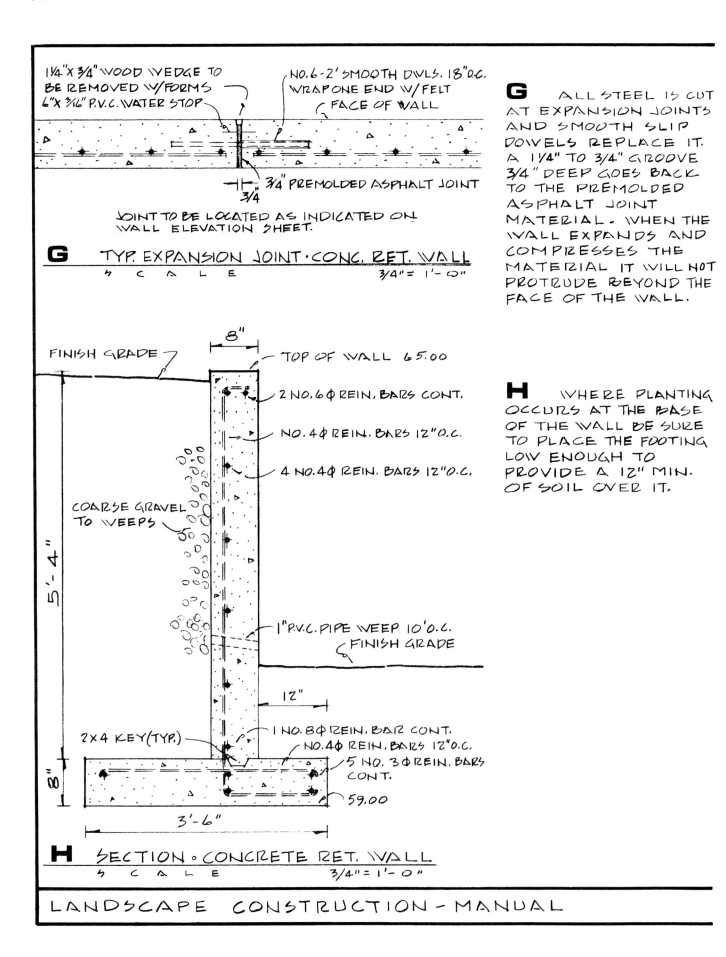

1¼" X ¾" WOOD WEDGE TO BE REMOVED W/FORMS
6" X 3/16" P.V.C. WATER STOP

NO.6-2' SMOOTH DWLS. 18" O.C. WRAP ONE END W/FELT
FACE OF WALL

¾ PREMOLDED ASPHALT JOINT

JOINT TO BE LOCATED AS INDICATED ON WALL ELEVATION SHEET.

G   TYP. EXPANSION JOINT · CONC. RET. WALL
SCALE   ¾" = 1'-0"

G   ALL STEEL IS CUT AT EXPANSION JOINTS AND SMOOTH SLIP DOWELS REPLACE IT. A 1¼" TO ¾" GROOVE ¾" DEEP GOES BACK TO THE PREMOLDED ASPHALT JOINT MATERIAL. WHEN THE WALL EXPANDS AND COMPRESSES THE MATERIAL IT WILL NOT PROTRUDE BEYOND THE FACE OF THE WALL.

FINISH GRADE

8"

TOP OF WALL 65.00

2 NO.6⌀ REIN. BARS CONT.

NO.4⌀ REIN. BARS 12" O.C.

4 NO.4⌀ REIN. BARS 12" O.C.

COARSE GRAVEL TO WEEPS

1" P.V.C. PIPE WEEP 10' O.C.
FINISH GRADE

5'-4"

12"

H   WHERE PLANTING OCCURS AT THE BASE OF THE WALL BE SURE TO PLACE THE FOOTING LOW ENOUGH TO PROVIDE A 12" MIN. OF SOIL OVER IT.

2 X 4 KEY (TYP.)

1 NO.8⌀ REIN. BAR CONT.
NO.4⌀ REIN. BARS 12" O.C.
5 NO. 3⌀ REIN. BARS CONT.

59.00

8"

3'-6"

H   SECTION · CONCRETE RET. WALL
SCALE   ¾" = 1'-0"

J CONTROL JOINTS, UNLIKE EXPANSION JOINTS, DO NOT ALLOW FOR THE WALL TO MOVE. IT IS TO ASSURE AN EVEN CRACK IF THE WALL SHOULD DO SO.

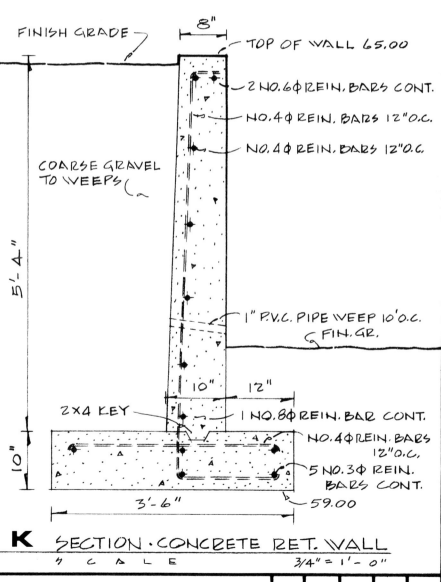

1/4" GROOVE JOINT AT ALL EXPOSED SURFACE OF WALL

FACE OF WALL

1/4" 1/8"

CUT 1/2 OF HORIZ. WALL REIN. (DO NOT CUT BOTTOM BAR)

3/4" X 3/4 WOOD AGAINST EARTH.

SEE WALL ELEVATION SHEET FOR JOINT LOCATIONS

J TYP. CONTROL JOINT·CONC. RET. WALL

SCALE   3/4" = 1'-0"

K NOTE THAT THIS DETAIL IS VERY SIMILAR TO THAT ON THE PRECEDING PAGE. WHEN SOIL CONDITIONS DICTATE A HEAVIER WALL, YET AN 8" TOP WIDTH IS DESIRED, THE BACK SIDE CAN BE INSTALLED AT AN ANGLE.

THIS AMOUNT OF ADD-ITIONAL WEIGHT MAY ALSO REQUIRE THE 10" THICK FOOTING.

FINISH GRADE

8"

TOP OF WALL 65.00

2 NO.6 ⌀ REIN. BARS CONT.

NO.4 ⌀ REIN. BARS 12"O.C.

NO.4 ⌀ REIN. BARS 12"O.C.

COARSE GRAVEL TO WEEPS

1" P.V.C. PIPE WEEP 10'O.C.

FIN. GR.

5'-4"

10"   12"

2X4 KEY

1 NO.8 ⌀ REIN. BAR CONT.

NO.4 ⌀ REIN. BARS 12"O.C.

5 NO.3 ⌀ REIN. BARS CONT.

10"

3'-6"

59.00

K SECTION·CONCRETE RET. WALL

SCALE   3/4" = 1'-0"

CONCRETE RETAINING WALLS

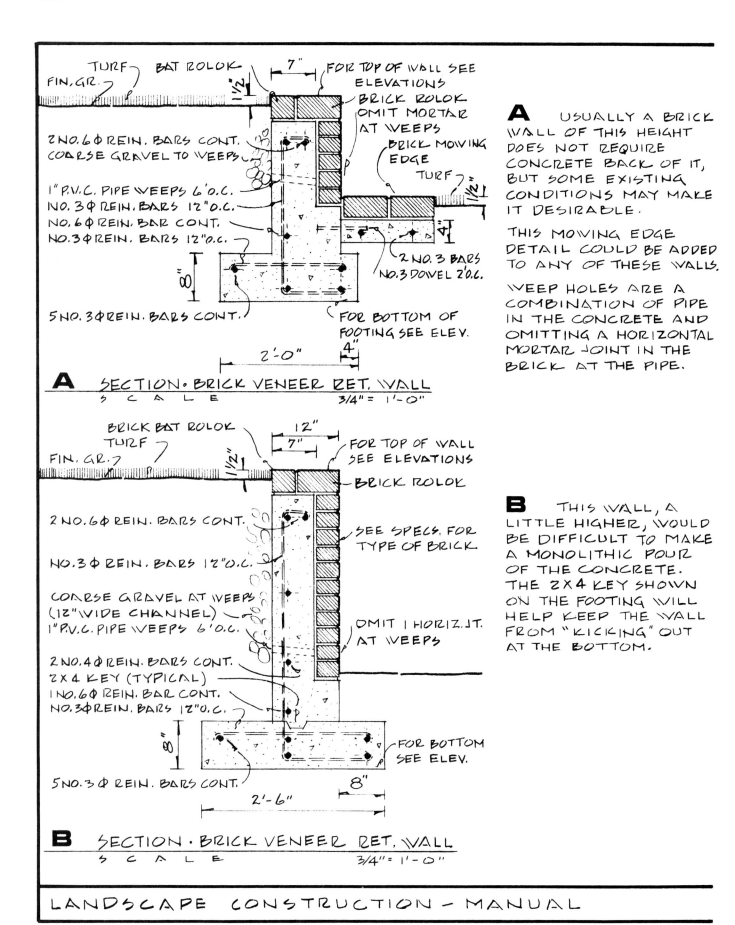

TURF BAT ROLOK
FIN. GR.
7"
1 1/2"
FOR TOP OF WALL SEE ELEVATIONS
BRICK ROLOK
OMIT MORTAR AT WEEPS
BRICK MOWING EDGE
TURF
1 1/2"

2 NO. 6 Ø REIN. BARS CONT.
COARSE GRAVEL TO WEEPS

1" P.V.C. PIPE WEEPS 6' O.C.
NO. 3 Ø REIN. BARS 12" O.C.
NO. 6 Ø REIN. BAR CONT.
NO. 3 Ø REIN. BARS 12" O.C.

8"

5 NO. 3 Ø REIN. BARS CONT.

2 NO. 3 BARS
NO. 3 DOWEL 2' O.C.

4"

FOR BOTTOM OF FOOTING SEE ELEV.
4"

2'-0"

A SECTION • BRICK VENEER RET. WALL
S C A L E   3/4" = 1'-0"

A USUALLY A BRICK WALL OF THIS HEIGHT DOES NOT REQUIRE CONCRETE BACK OF IT, BUT SOME EXISTING CONDITIONS MAY MAKE IT DESIRABLE.

THIS MOWING EDGE DETAIL COULD BE ADDED TO ANY OF THESE WALLS.

WEEP HOLES ARE A COMBINATION OF PIPE IN THE CONCRETE AND OMITTING A HORIZONTAL MORTAR JOINT IN THE BRICK AT THE PIPE.

BRICK BAT ROLOK
TURF
FIN. GR.
1 1/2"
12"
7"
FOR TOP OF WALL SEE ELEVATIONS
BRICK ROLOK

2 NO. 6 Ø REIN. BARS CONT.

NO. 3 Ø REIN. BARS 12" O.C.

SEE SPECS. FOR TYPE OF BRICK

COARSE GRAVEL AT WEEPS (12" WIDE CHANNEL)
1" P.V.C. PIPE WEEPS 6' O.C.

OMIT 1 HORIZ. JT. AT WEEPS

2 NO. 4 Ø REIN. BARS CONT.
2 X 4 KEY (TYPICAL)
1 NO. 6 Ø REIN. BAR CONT.
NO. 3 Ø REIN. BARS 12" O.C.

8"

5 NO. 3 Ø REIN. BARS CONT.

FOR BOTTOM SEE ELEV.

8"

2'-6"

B SECTION • BRICK VENEER RET. WALL
S C A L E   3/4" = 1'-0"

B THIS WALL, A LITTLE HIGHER, WOULD BE DIFFICULT TO MAKE A MONOLITHIC POUR OF THE CONCRETE. THE 2 X 4 KEY SHOWN ON THE FOOTING WILL HELP KEEP THE WALL FROM "KICKING" OUT AT THE BOTTOM.

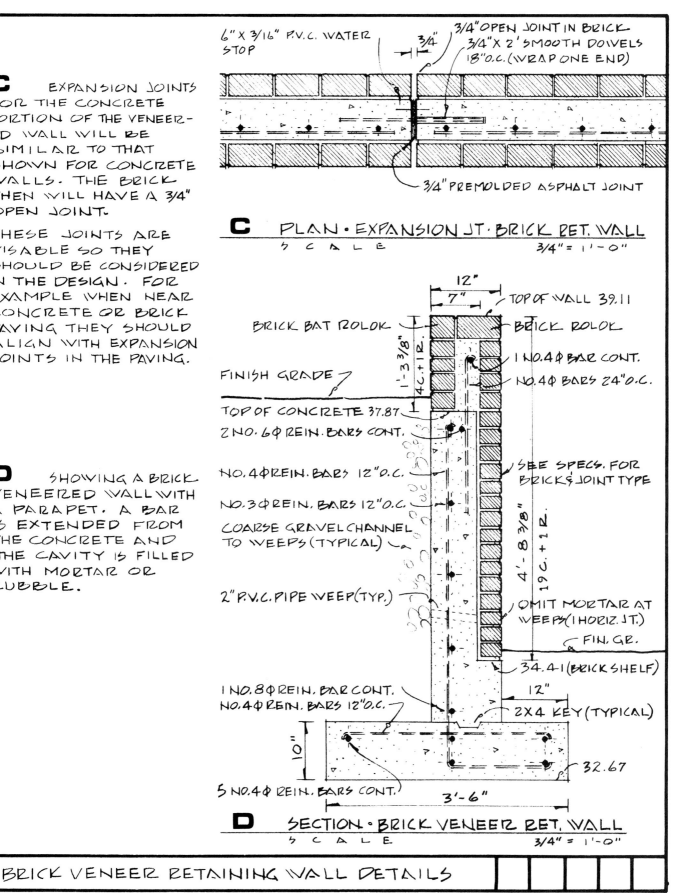

C   EXPANSION JOINTS FOR THE CONCRETE PORTION OF THE VENEERED WALL WILL BE SIMILAR TO THAT SHOWN FOR CONCRETE WALLS. THE BRICK THEN WILL HAVE A 3/4" OPEN JOINT.

THESE JOINTS ARE VISABLE SO THEY SHOULD BE CONSIDERED IN THE DESIGN. FOR EXAMPLE WHEN NEAR CONCRETE OR BRICK PAVING THEY SHOULD ALIGN WITH EXPANSION JOINTS IN THE PAVING.

D   SHOWING A BRICK VENEERED WALL WITH A PARAPET. A BAR IS EXTENDED FROM THE CONCRETE AND THE CAVITY IS FILLED WITH MORTAR OR RUBBLE.

6" X 3/16" P.V.C. WATER STOP

3/4"

3/4" OPEN JOINT IN BRICK
3/4" X 2' SMOOTH DOWELS 18" O.C. (WRAP ONE END)

3/4" PREMOLDED ASPHALT JOINT

C   PLAN · EXPANSION JT · BRICK RET. WALL
SCALE   3/4" = 1'-0"

12"
7"
TOP OF WALL 39.11

BRICK BAT ROLOK

BRICK ROLOK

FINISH GRADE

1-3 3/8"
4C. + IR.

1 NO. 4φ BAR CONT.

NO. 4φ BARS 24" O.C.

TOP OF CONCRETE 37.87
2 NO. 6φ REIN. BARS CONT.

NO. 4φ REIN. BARS 12" O.C.

NO. 3φ REIN. BARS 12" O.C.

COARSE GRAVEL CHANNEL TO WEEPS (TYPICAL)

SEE SPECS. FOR BRICK & JOINT TYPE

4'-8 3/8"
19 C. + IR.

2" P.V.C. PIPE WEEP (TYP.)

OMIT MORTAR AT WEEPS (1 HORIZ. JT.)

FIN. GR.

34.41 (BRICK SHELF)

12"

2X4 KEY (TYPICAL)

1 NO. 8φ REIN. BAR CONT.
NO. 4φ REIN. BARS 12" O.C.

10"

32.67

5 NO. 4φ REIN. BARS CONT.

3'-6"

D   SECTION · BRICK VENEER RET. WALL
SCALE   3/4" = 1'-0"

BRICK VENEER RETAINING WALL DETAILS

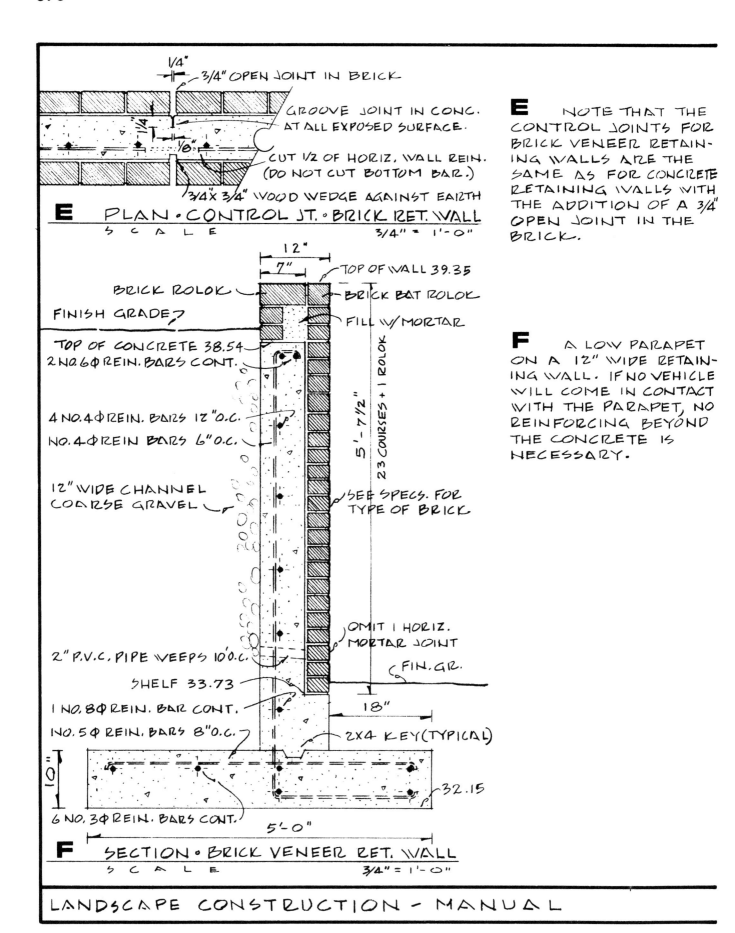

1/4"
3/4" OPEN JOINT IN BRICK

GROOVE JOINT IN CONC. AT ALL EXPOSED SURFACE.

CUT 1/2 OF HORIZ. WALL REIN. (DO NOT CUT BOTTOM BAR.)

3/4"X 3/4" WOOD WEDGE AGAINST EARTH

E PLAN • CONTROL JT. • BRICK RET. WALL
SCALE   3/4" = 1'-0"

12"
7"

BRICK ROLOK

FINISH GRADE

TOP OF CONCRETE 38.54
2 NO. 6Ø REIN. BARS CONT.

4 NO. 4Ø REIN. BARS 12"O.C.
NO. 4Ø REIN BARS 6"O.C.

12" WIDE CHANNEL COARSE GRAVEL

2" P.V.C. PIPE WEEPS 10'O.C.

SHELF 33.73

1 NO. 8Ø REIN. BAR CONT.
NO. 5Ø REIN. BARS 8"O.C.

6 NO. 3Ø REIN. BARS CONT.

TOP OF WALL 39.35
BRICK BAT ROLOK
FILL W/ MORTAR

5'-7 1/2"
23 COURSES + 1 ROLOK

SEE SPECS. FOR TYPE OF BRICK

OMIT 1 HORIZ. MORTAR JOINT
FIN. GR.

18"

2X4 KEY (TYPICAL)

32.15

5'-0"

F SECTION • BRICK VENEER RET. WALL
SCALE   3/4" = 1'-0"

E   NOTE THAT THE CONTROL JOINTS FOR BRICK VENEER RETAINING WALLS ARE THE SAME AS FOR CONCRETE RETAINING WALLS WITH THE ADDITION OF A 3/4" OPEN JOINT IN THE BRICK.

F   A LOW PARAPET ON A 12" WIDE RETAINING WALL. IF NO VEHICLE WILL COME IN CONTACT WITH THE PARAPET, NO REINFORCING BEYOND THE CONCRETE IS NECESSARY.

G A HIGH RETAINING WALL BECOMES RATHER HEAVY APPEARING AT THE TOP. THIS 16" WIDE TOP CAN BE REDUCED IN SCALE BY THE ROLOK CAP.

THE STEEL IS PROJECTED UP INTO THE PARAPET WITH ONE CUT TO FORM A BRICK SHELF. THIS TOP WILL RESIST DAMAGE MUCH BETTER THAN THE ONE ON THE OPPOSITE PAGE.

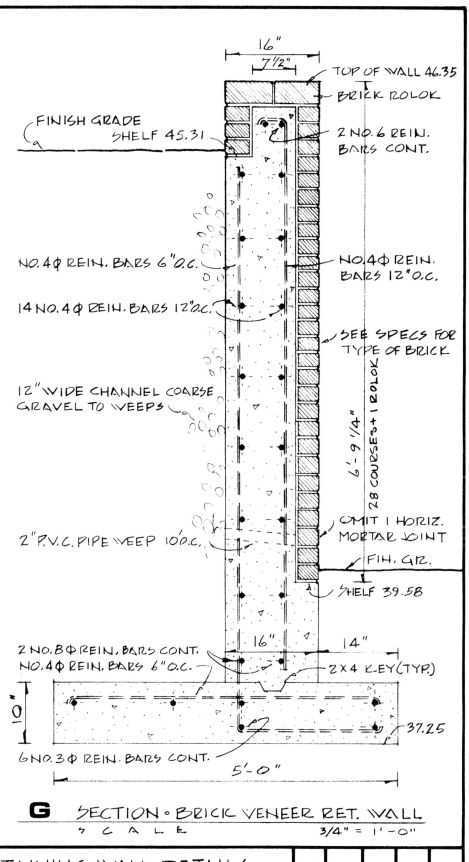

16"

7 1/2"

TOP OF WALL 46.35

BRICK ROLOK

FINISH GRADE
SHELF 45.31

2 NO. 6 REIN. BARS CONT.

NO. 4 Φ REIN. BARS 6" O.C.

NO. 4 Φ REIN. BARS 12" O.C.

14 NO. 4 Φ REIN. BARS 12" O.C.

SEE SPECS FOR TYPE OF BRICK

12" WIDE CHANNEL COARSE GRAVEL TO WEEPS

6'-9 1/4"
28 COURSES + 1 ROLOK

OMIT 1 HORIZ. MORTAR JOINT

FIN. GR.

2" P.V.C. PIPE WEEP 10'O.C.

SHELF 39.58

16"

14"

2 NO. 8 Φ REIN. BARS CONT.
NO. 4 Φ REIN. BARS 6" O.C.

2 X 4 KEY (TYP.)

10"

37.25

6 NO. 3 Φ REIN. BARS CONT.

5'-0"

G SECTION · BRICK VENEER RET. WALL

SCALE   3/4" = 1'-0"

BRICK VENEER RETAINING WALL DETAILS

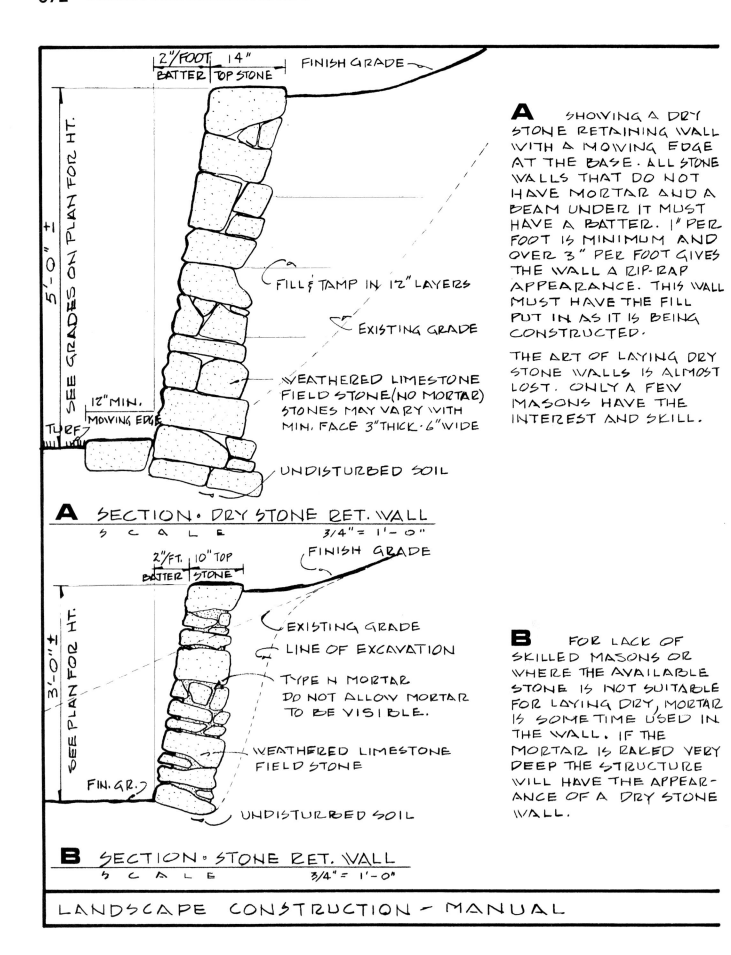

2"/FOOT BATTER | 14" TOP STONE | FINISH GRADE

SEE GRADES ON PLAN FOR HT.

5'-0" ±

12" MIN. MOWING EDGE

TURF

FILL & TAMP IN 12" LAYERS

EXISTING GRADE

WEATHERED LIMESTONE FIELD STONE (NO MORTAR) STONES MAY VARY WITH MIN. FACE 3" THICK · 6" WIDE

UNDISTURBED SOIL

A SECTION · DRY STONE RET. WALL
SCALE   3/4" = 1'-0"

2"/FT. BATTER | 10" TOP STONE | FINISH GRADE

SEE PLAN FOR HT.

3'-0" ±

FIN. GR.

EXISTING GRADE

LINE OF EXCAVATION

TYPE N MORTAR DO NOT ALLOW MORTAR TO BE VISIBLE.

WEATHERED LIMESTONE FIELD STONE

UNDISTURBED SOIL

B SECTION · STONE RET. WALL
SCALE   3/4" = 1'-0"

A SHOWING A DRY STONE RETAINING WALL WITH A MOWING EDGE AT THE BASE. ALL STONE WALLS THAT DO NOT HAVE MORTAR AND A BEAM UNDER IT MUST HAVE A BATTER. 1" PER FOOT IS MINIMUM AND OVER 3" PER FOOT GIVES THE WALL A RIP-RAP APPEARANCE. THIS WALL MUST HAVE THE FILL PUT IN AS IT IS BEING CONSTRUCTED.

THE ART OF LAYING DRY STONE WALLS IS ALMOST LOST. ONLY A FEW MASONS HAVE THE INTEREST AND SKILL.

B FOR LACK OF SKILLED MASONS OR WHERE THE AVAILABLE STONE IS NOT SUITABLE FOR LAYING DRY, MORTAR IS SOMETIME USED IN THE WALL. IF THE MORTAR IS RAKED VERY DEEP THE STRUCTURE WILL HAVE THE APPEARANCE OF A DRY STONE WALL.

LANDSCAPE CONSTRUCTION — MANUAL

C A TWO BRICK WIDE RETAINING WALL WITH A BRICK MOWING EDGE AT THE BASE. A LOW WALL SUCH AS SHOWN HERE WILL RETAIN SOIL WITH ONLY REINFORCING IN THE CONCRETE BEAM.

D FOR A STRONGER VISUAL APPEARANCE, THE LOW BRICK WALL MAY NEED TO BE WIDER. HERE IS SHOWN A 12" WIDE WALL WITH A ONE AND ONE HALF BRICK ROLOK ON TOP.

E THE SAME DETAIL AS ABOVE WITH RUBBLE FILL RATHER THAN LAID BRICK.

ALL SOLID RETAINING WALLS MUST HAVE WEEP HOLES.

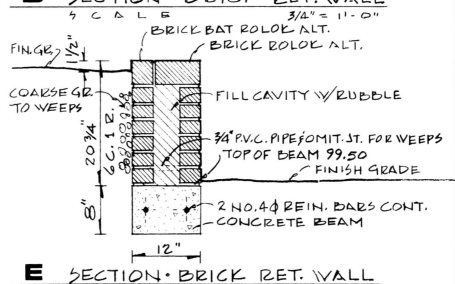

C SECTION · BRICK RET. WALL
SCALE 3/4" = 1'-0"

D SECTION · BRICK RET. WALL
SCALE 3/4" = 1'-0"

E SECTION · BRICK RET. WALL
SCALE 3/4" = 1'-0"

NON-REINFORCED MASONRY RET. WALLS

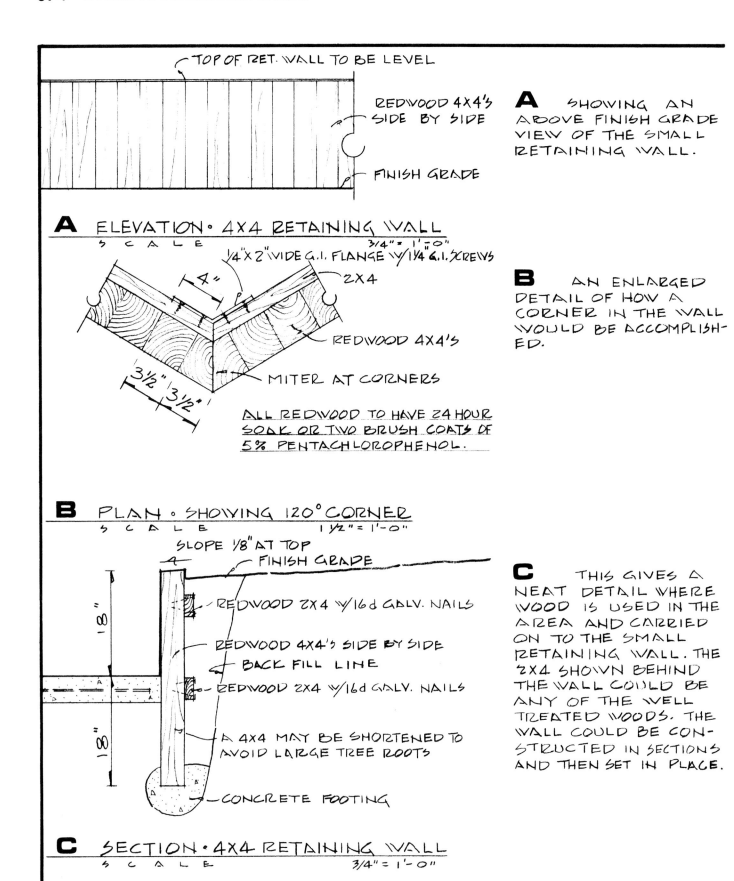

TOP OF RET. WALL TO BE LEVEL

REDWOOD 4X4's SIDE BY SIDE

FINISH GRADE

A ELEVATION · 4X4 RETAINING WALL
SCALE 3/4" = 1'-0"

A SHOWING AN ABOVE FINISH GRADE VIEW OF THE SMALL RETAINING WALL.

1/4" X 2" WIDE G.I. FLANGE W/ 1 1/4" G.I. SCREWS

2X4

4"

REDWOOD 4X4's

MITER AT CORNERS

3 1/2" 3 1/2"

ALL REDWOOD TO HAVE 24 HOUR SOAK OR TWO BRUSH COATS OF 5% PENTACHLOROPHENOL.

B AN ENLARGED DETAIL OF HOW A CORNER IN THE WALL WOULD BE ACCOMPLISHED.

B PLAN · SHOWING 120° CORNER
SCALE 1 1/2" = 1'-0"

SLOPE 1/8" AT TOP
FINISH GRADE

REDWOOD 2X4 W/ 16d GALV. NAILS

REDWOOD 4X4's SIDE BY SIDE
BACK FILL LINE
REDWOOD 2X4 W/ 16d GALV. NAILS

18"

18"

A 4X4 MAY BE SHORTENED TO AVOID LARGE TREE ROOTS

CONCRETE FOOTING

C SECTION · 4X4 RETAINING WALL
SCALE 3/4" = 1'-0"

C THIS GIVES A NEAT DETAIL WHERE WOOD IS USED IN THE AREA AND CARRIED ON TO THE SMALL RETAINING WALL. THE 2X4 SHOWN BEHIND THE WALL COULD BE ANY OF THE WELL TREATED WOODS. THE WALL COULD BE CONSTRUCTED IN SECTIONS AND THEN SET IN PLACE.

D   A PLAN SHOWING PLACEMENT OF POSTS IN LINE AND AT CORNERS. THE PLAN IS FOR THE SECTION BELOW ONLY.

E   SHOWING A SECTION THRU THE PLAN ABOVE. THIS IS A GOOD RUSTIC APPEARING WOOD RETAINING WALL DETAIL.

F   A VARIATION OF THE RUSTIC WOOD RETAINING WALL IS TO PLACE ALL OF THE TIES ON END, SIDE BY SIDE AND SECURE FROM THE BACK.

WHERE TURF OCCURS AT THE BASE OF THE WALL, IT IS DESIRABLE TO DESIGN A MOWING EDGE.

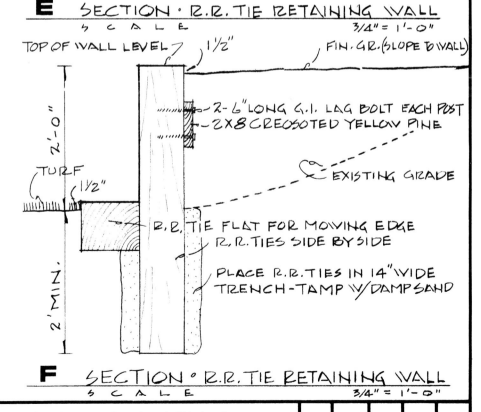

R.R. TIE CORNER
RAIL ROAD TIE
R.R. TIE CORNER POST
R.R. TIE POST AT EACH JOINT (8'-0" O.C.)

D   PLAN · R.R. TIE RETAINING WALL   1/4"=1'-0"

TOP OF WALL LEVEL
1"
FIN. GR.
SLOPE TO WALL
FILL
R.R. TIES FLAT
R.R. TIE POST 8'-0" O.C.
FIN. GR.
EXISTING GRADE
2' MIN.
14" DIA. HOLE W/ POST SET IN WELL TAMPED DAMP SAND

E   SECTION · R.R. TIE RETAINING WALL
SCALE   3/4" = 1'-0"

TOP OF WALL LEVEL
1 1/2"
FIN. GR. (SLOPE TO WALL)
2'-0"
2-6" LONG G.I. LAG BOLT EACH POST
2X8 CREOSOTED YELLOW PINE
EXISTING GRADE
TURF
1 1/2"
R.R. TIE FLAT FOR MOWING EDGE
R.R. TIES SIDE BY SIDE
PLACE R.R. TIES IN 14" WIDE TRENCH - TAMP W/ DAMP SAND
2' MIN.

F   SECTION · R.R. TIE RETAINING WALL
SCALE   3/4" = 1'-0"

WOOD RETAINING WALL DETAILS

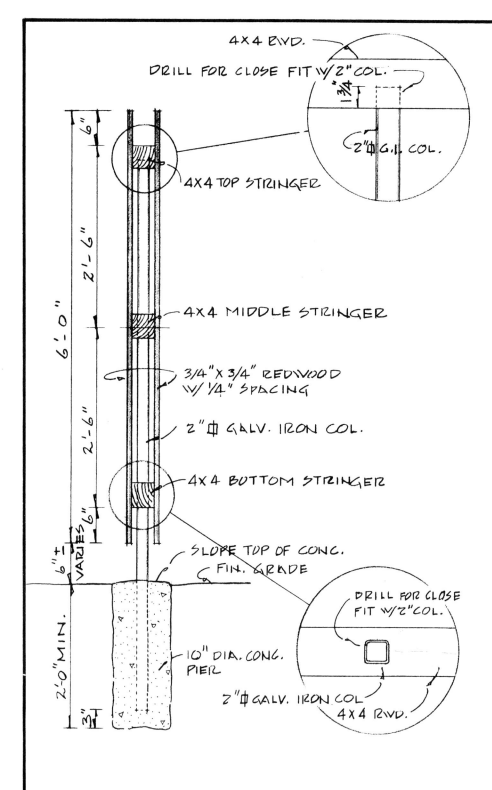

4X4 RWD.

DRILL FOR CLOSE FIT W/2" COL.

1 3/4"

2" ⌀ G.I. COL.

6"

4X4 TOP STRINGER

2'-6"

6'-0"

4X4 MIDDLE STRINGER

3/4" X 3/4" REDWOOD W/ 1/4" SPACING

2" ⌀ GALV. IRON COL.

2'-6"

4X4 BOTTOM STRINGER

6"

VARIES

6"±

SLOPE TOP OF CONC.
FIN. GRADE

DRILL FOR CLOSE FIT W/2" COL.

2'-0" MIN.

10" DIA. CONC. PIER

2" ⌀ GALV. IRON COL

4X4 RWD.

3"

A SECTION • WOOD SCREEN

SCALE   3/4" = 1'-0"

A THIS DETAIL USES A GALVANIZED IRON TUBE COLUMN FOR DURABILITY, YET DOES NOT REQUIRE DRILLING THE COLUMN FOR BOLTING. THE TOP STRINGER IS CUT ONLY 1 1/2" AND RESTS ON TOP OF THE COLUMN. THE OTHER STRINGERS ARE DRILLED AND SLIPPED OVER THE COLUMN, TEMPORARILY HELD IN PLACE UNTIL 1X1 STRIPS ARE NAILED. COLUMN AND STRINGER DETAIL WOULD BE THE SAME IF ONLY ONE SIDE OF THE SCREEN IS FINISHED.

THIS SCREEN DETAIL IS TIME CONSUMING TO CONSTRUCT, THUS EXPENSIVE. IT WILL NOT TAKE A LOT OF ABUSE, BUT WILL GIVE A FINE TEXTURED, HANDSOME SCREEN.

B THE 4X4 ARE ALL 10' IN LENGTH. THE JOINTS ALIGN AND IS BEST IF AN OPEN JOINT OF 3/4" TO 1" IS ALLOWED WITH NO ATTEMPT TO CONNECT THEM. THE SCREEN COULD BE CONSTRUCTED IN THESE PANELS AND THEN SET IN PLACE. NO FINISH IS SUGGESTED HERE BUT THE REDWOOD COULD BE ALLOWED TO WEATHER A SILVER GRAY OR STAINED WITH A PENETRATING STAIN.

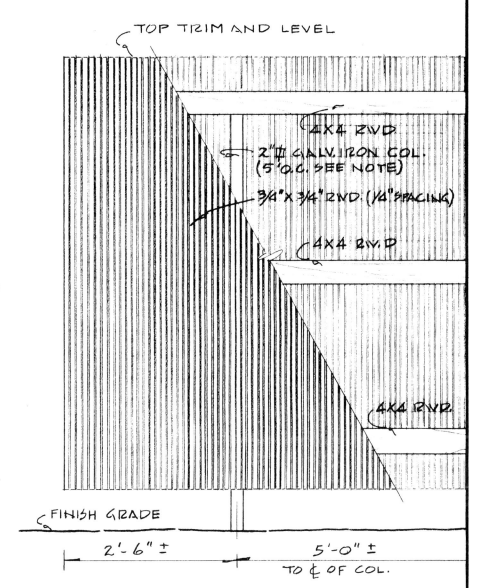

TOP TRIM AND LEVEL

4X4 RWD

2"∅ GALV. IRON COL.
(5' O.C. SEE NOTE)

3/4" X 3/4" RWD. (1/8" SPACING)

4X4 RWD

4X4 RWD.

FINISH GRADE

2'-6" ±   5'-0" ±
TO ₵ OF COL.

NOTE: COL. SPACING AND LENGTH DIM. CAN VARY SLIGHTLY TO ACCOMMODATE SCREEN SECTIONS SLIGHTLY MORE OR LESS THAN 10'-0".

USE ONLY HOT DIP GALV. NAILS.

B ELEVATION · WOOD SCREEN
SCALE   3/4" = 1'-0"

VISUAL SCREEN DETAILS

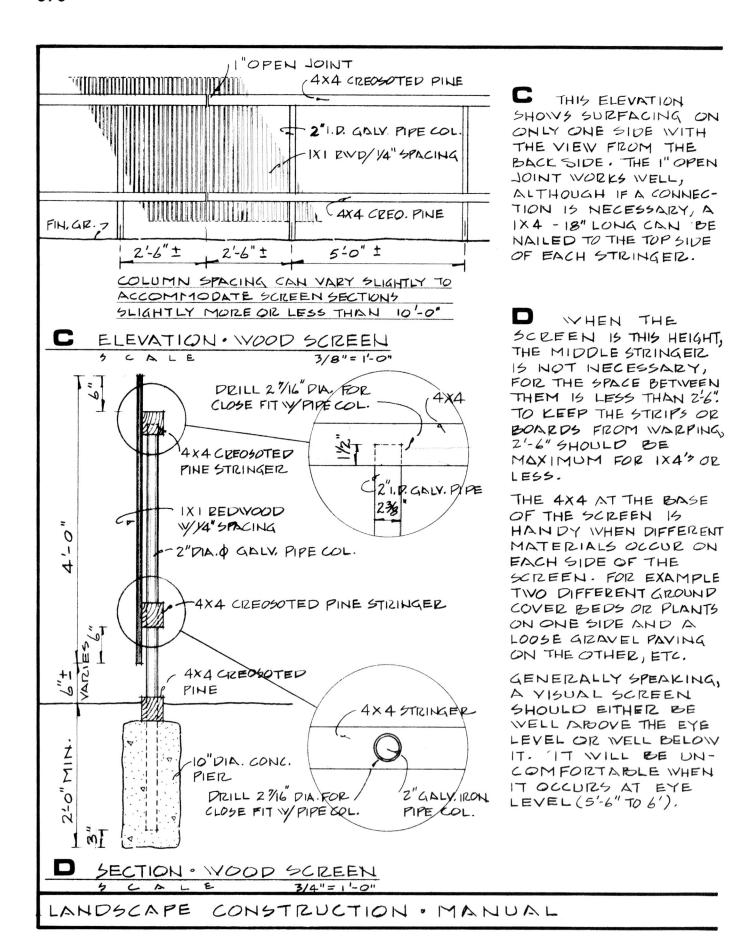

1" OPEN JOINT

4X4 CREOSOTED PINE

2" I.D. GALV. PIPE COL.

IX1 RWD / ¼" SPACING

4X4 CREO. PINE

FIN. GR.

2'-6" ±   2'-6" ±   5'-0" ±

COLUMN SPACING CAN VARY SLIGHTLY TO ACCOMMODATE SCREEN SECTIONS SLIGHTLY MORE OR LESS THAN 10'-0"

C ELEVATION · WOOD SCREEN
SCALE   3/8"=1'-0"

DRILL 2 7/16" DIA. FOR CLOSE FIT W/ PIPE COL.

4X4

1½"

2" I.D. GALV. PIPE

2⅜"

4X4 CREOSOTED PINE STRINGER

IX1 REDWOOD W/ ¼" SPACING

2" DIA. φ GALV. PIPE COL.

4X4 CREOSOTED PINE STRINGER

4X4 CREOSOTED PINE

6"

4'-0"

6" VARIES

6" ±

2'-0" MIN.

3"

4X4 STRINGER

2" GALV. IRON PIPE COL.

10" DIA. CONC. PIER

DRILL 2 7/16" DIA. FOR CLOSE FIT W/ PIPE COL.

D SECTION · WOOD SCREEN
SCALE   3/4"=1'-0"

C THIS ELEVATION SHOWS SURFACING ON ONLY ONE SIDE WITH THE VIEW FROM THE BACK SIDE. THE 1" OPEN JOINT WORKS WELL, ALTHOUGH IF A CONNECTION IS NECESSARY, A IX4 - 18" LONG CAN BE NAILED TO THE TOP SIDE OF EACH STRINGER.

D WHEN THE SCREEN IS THIS HEIGHT, THE MIDDLE STRINGER IS NOT NECESSARY, FOR THE SPACE BETWEEN THEM IS LESS THAN 2'-6". TO KEEP THE STRIPS OR BOARDS FROM WARPING, 2'-6" SHOULD BE MAXIMUM FOR IX4's OR LESS.

THE 4X4 AT THE BASE OF THE SCREEN IS HANDY WHEN DIFFERENT MATERIALS OCCUR ON EACH SIDE OF THE SCREEN. FOR EXAMPLE TWO DIFFERENT GROUND COVER BEDS OR PLANTS ON ONE SIDE AND A LOOSE GRAVEL PAVING ON THE OTHER, ETC.

GENERALLY SPEAKING, A VISUAL SCREEN SHOULD EITHER BE WELL ABOVE THE EYE LEVEL OR WELL BELOW IT. IT WILL BE UNCOMFORTABLE WHEN IT OCCURS AT EYE LEVEL (5'-6" TO 6').

E   WHEN TURF OCCURS ON ONE OR BOTH SIDES OF A STRUCTURAL SCREEN, IT IS IMPORTANT TO PROTECT IT WITH A MOWING EDGE. THIS WILL ALSO ALLOW AN EDGER TO BE USED RATHER THAN HAND CLIPPING.

THIS SECTION SHOWS TURF ON THE RIGHT SIDE WITH PLANTS OR LOOSE PAVING ON THE LEFT.

F   WHEN TURF OCCURS ON BOTH SIDES OF THE SCREEN THIS WILL ALLOW A MOWER WHEEL TO ROLL ON TOP OF THE BRICK.

G   SHOWING A WOOD POST AND CONCRETE MOWING EDGE ON THE RIGHT HAND SIDE.

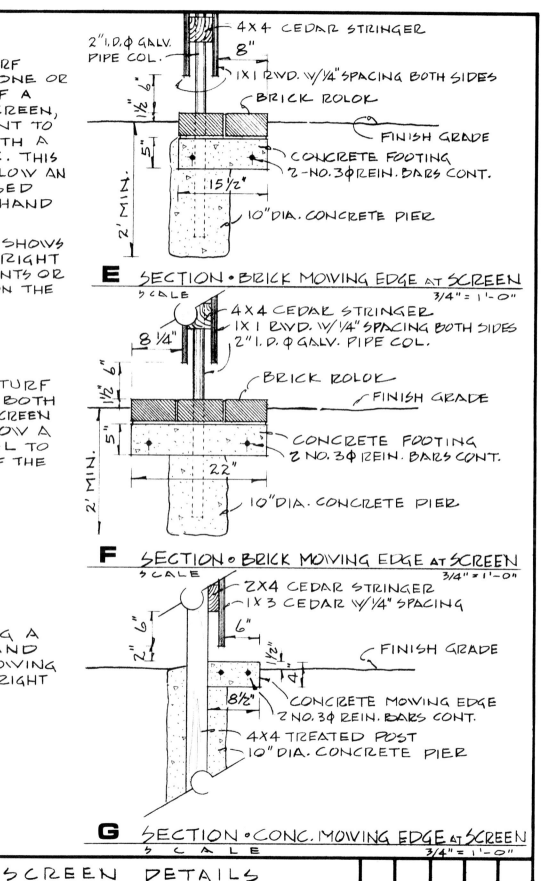

2" I.D. ø GALV. PIPE COL.
4X4 CEDAR STRINGER
8"
1X1 RWD. W/ 1/4" SPACING BOTH SIDES
BRICK ROLOK
FINISH GRADE
CONCRETE FOOTING 2-NO. 3ø REIN. BARS CONT.
15 1/2"
10" DIA. CONCRETE PIER
6"
1 1/2"
5"
2' MIN.

E   SECTION · BRICK MOWING EDGE at SCREEN
SCALE   3/4" = 1'-0"

4X4 CEDAR STRINGER
1X1 RWD. W/ 1/4" SPACING BOTH SIDES
2" I.D. ø GALV. PIPE COL.
8 1/4"
BRICK ROLOK
FINISH GRADE
CONCRETE FOOTING 2 NO. 3ø REIN. BARS CONT.
22"
10" DIA. CONCRETE PIER
6"
1 1/2"
5"
2' MIN.

F   SECTION · BRICK MOWING EDGE at SCREEN
SCALE   3/4" = 1'-0"

2X4 CEDAR STRINGER
1X3 CEDAR W/ 1/4" SPACING
6"
FINISH GRADE
1 1/2"
4"
CONCRETE MOWING EDGE 2 NO. 3ø REIN. BARS CONT.
8 1/2"
4X4 TREATED POST
10" DIA. CONCRETE PIER
2" 6"

G   SECTION · CONC. MOWING EDGE at SCREEN
SCALE   3/4" = 1'-0"

VISUAL SCREEN DETAILS

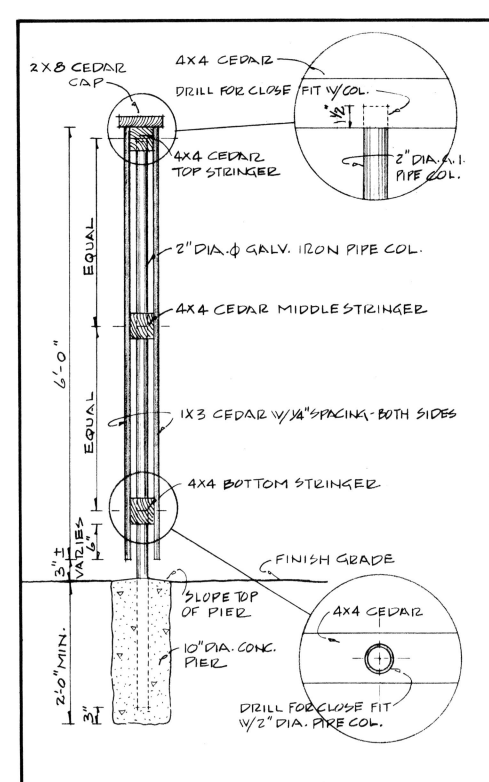

2 X 8 CEDAR CAP

4X4 CEDAR

DRILL FOR CLOSE FIT W/COL.

4X4 CEDAR TOP STRINGER

1/2"

2"DIA.G.I. PIPE COL.

EQUAL

6'-0"

EQUAL

2" DIA.φ GALV. IRON PIPE COL.

4X4 CEDAR MIDDLE STRINGER

1X3 CEDAR W/¼"SPACING·BOTH SIDES

4X4 BOTTOM STRINGER

3"± VARIES 6"

FINISH GRADE

SLOPE TOP OF PIER

10"DIA. CONC. PIER

2'-0" MIN.

3"

4X4 CEDAR

DRILL FOR CLOSE FIT W/2" DIA. PIPE COL.

H WHEN A SCREEN IS TO BE VIEWED FROM BOTH SIDES, IT IS BEST TO DESIGN A DETAIL THAT CAN BE SURFACED ON BOTH SIDES WITH OUT CREATING AN EXTRA WIDE STRUCTURE. THIS DETAIL DOES THAT AND IS PLEASANT LOOKING FROM THE BACK EVEN WHEN SURFACED ON ONLY THE FRONT SIDE. A GALVANIZED IRON PIPE COLUMN IS USED FOR DURABILITY. THE PIPE DOES NOT REQUIRE DRILLING OR BOLTING. THE TOP STRINGER IS CUT ONLY 1½" AND RESTS ON TOP OF THE COLUMN. THE OTHER STRINGERS ARE DRILLED AND SLIPPED OVER THE COLUMN, TEMPORARILY HELD IN PLACE UNTIL 1 X 3'S ARE NAILED.

H SECTION · WOOD SCREEN

SCALE   3/4"= 1'-0"

LANDSCAPE CONSTRUCTION - MANUAL

J THE 1X3'S GIVE A FINE TO MEDIUM TEXTURE IN THE DESIGN. S4S LUMBER WILL GIVE A FINER TEXTURE THAN ROUGH CUT. THE CAP AND END PIECE GIVE A FINISHED APPEARANCE TO THE DESIGN.

NO FINISH IS SUGGESTED HERE BUT THE CEDAR COULD BE ALLOWED TO WEATHER A SILVER GRAY OR STAINED WITH A PENETRATING STAIN.

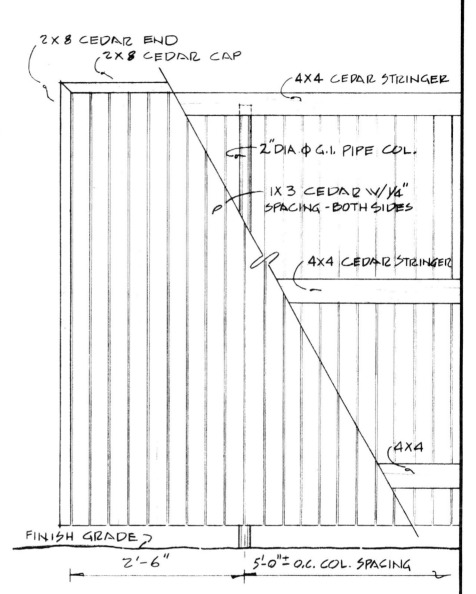

2X8 CEDAR END

2X8 CEDAR CAP

4X4 CEDAR STRINGER

2" DIA Ø G.I. PIPE COL.

1X3 CEDAR W/ ¼" SPACING - BOTH SIDES

4X4 CEDAR STRINGER

4X4

FINISH GRADE

2'-6"   5'-0"± O.C. COL. SPACING

COLUMN SPACING CAN VARY SLIGHTLY TO ACCOMMODATE SCREEN SECTIONS SLIGHTLY MORE OR LESS THAN 10'-0".

ALL CEDAR TO BE ROUGH FINISH AND FREE OF UNSOUND KNOTS.
USE ONLY HOT DIP GALV. NAILS.
POST TO BE GALV. IRON PIPE (NOT TUBING)

J ELEVATION · WOOD SCREEN
SCALE   3/4" = 1'-0"

VISUAL SCREEN DETAILS

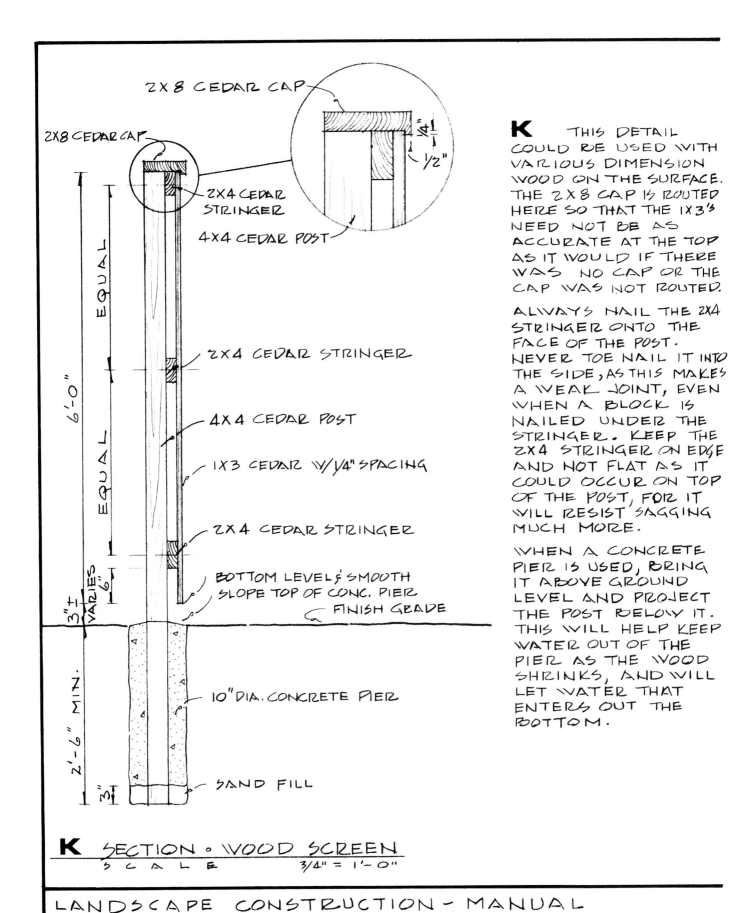

2X8 CEDAR CAP

2X8 CEDAR CAP

2X4 CEDAR STRINGER

4X4 CEDAR POST

EQUAL

6'-0"

EQUAL

2X4 CEDAR STRINGER

4X4 CEDAR POST

1X3 CEDAR W/ 1/4" SPACING

2X4 CEDAR STRINGER

BOTTOM LEVEL & SMOOTH SLOPE TOP OF CONC. PIER

FINISH GRADE

VARIES 6"

3"±

2'-6" MIN.

10" DIA. CONCRETE PIER

3"

SAND FILL

1/4"

1/2"

K SECTION ○ WOOD SCREEN
SCALE 3/4" = 1'-0"

K   THIS DETAIL COULD BE USED WITH VARIOUS DIMENSION WOOD ON THE SURFACE. THE 2X8 CAP IS ROUTED HERE SO THAT THE 1X3'S NEED NOT BE AS ACCURATE AT THE TOP AS IT WOULD IF THERE WAS NO CAP OR THE CAP WAS NOT ROUTED.

ALWAYS NAIL THE 2X4 STRINGER ONTO THE FACE OF THE POST. NEVER TOE NAIL IT INTO THE SIDE, AS THIS MAKES A WEAK JOINT, EVEN WHEN A BLOCK IS NAILED UNDER THE STRINGER. KEEP THE 2X4 STRINGER ON EDGE AND NOT FLAT AS IT COULD OCCUR ON TOP OF THE POST, FOR IT WILL RESIST SAGGING MUCH MORE.

WHEN A CONCRETE PIER IS USED, BRING IT ABOVE GROUND LEVEL AND PROJECT THE POST BELOW IT. THIS WILL HELP KEEP WATER OUT OF THE PIER AS THE WOOD SHRINKS, AND WILL LET WATER THAT ENTERS OUT THE BOTTOM.

L   THIS DETAIL
WORKS WELL WHERE
ONLY ONE SIDE OF
THE SCREEN IS OF
PRIMARY CONCERN.
IF 2X4 STRINGERS AND
1X3 BOARDS WERE
ADDED TO THE BACK
SIDE, THE SCREEN
WOULD BE ELEVEN
INCHES WIDE. THIS GIVES
A PRETTY HEAVY
LOOKING STRUCTURE.

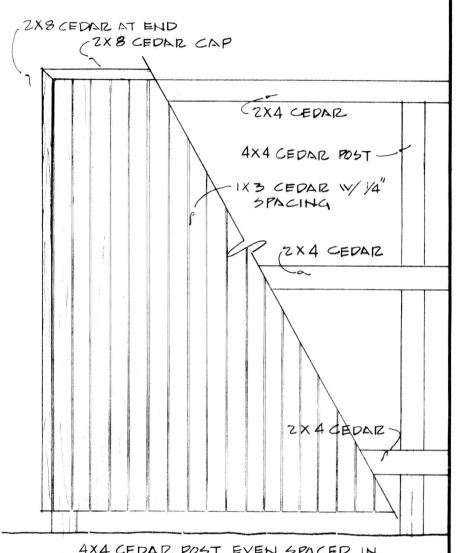

2X8 CEDAR AT END

2X8 CEDAR CAP

2X4 CEDAR

4X4 CEDAR POST

1X3 CEDAR W/ ¼"
SPACING

2X4 CEDAR

2X4 CEDAR

4X4 CEDAR POST EVEN SPACED IN
EACH SECTION · MAX. OF 5'-0" O.C.

ALL CEDAR TO BE ROUGH FINISH, FREE OF
UNSOUND KNOTS.

ALL POSTS TO HAVE 24 HR. SOAK OF 5%
PENTACHLOROPHENOL. MIN. OF 36"
FROM BOTTOM END.

USE ONLY HOT DIP GALV. NAILS.

L   ELEVATION · WOOD SCREEN
    SCALE   3/4" = 1'-0"

VISUAL   SCREEN   DETAILS

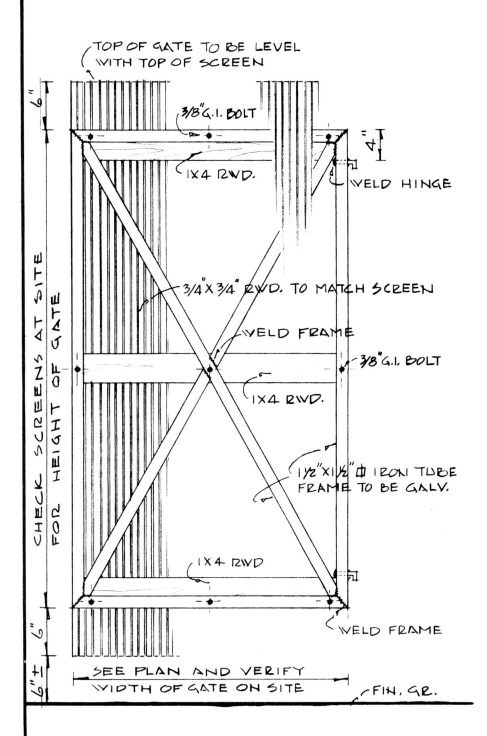

TOP OF GATE TO BE LEVEL WITH TOP OF SCREEN

6"

3/8" G.I. BOLT

4"

1X4 RWD.

WELD HINGE

CHECK SCREENS AT SITE FOR HEIGHT OF GATE

3/4" X 3/4" RWD. TO MATCH SCREEN

WELD FRAME

3/8" G.I. BOLT

1X4 RWD.

1½" X 1½" □ IRON TUBE FRAME TO BE GALV.

1X4 RWD

WELD FRAME

6"

6" #4 6"

SEE PLAN AND VERIFY WIDTH OF GATE ON SITE

FIN. GR.

A THIS IS A VERSATILE GATE DETAIL IN THAT IT COULD BE USED FOR ALL WOOD SCREENS. THE SURFACING (ONE OR BOTH SIDES) COULD BE CHANGED TO MATCH THE SURFACE ON THE SCREEN. MOST WOOD FRAME GATES SAG AFTER A SHORT TIME; THIS DETAIL WILL NOT. THERE ARE MANY STANDARD LATCHES (BOTH PLAIN AND THOSE THAT WILL LOCK) MANUFACTURED THAT WILL WORK WELL WITH THIS DETAIL.

A ELEVATION o METAL FRAME WOOD GATE

SCALE   1" = 1'-0"

B THE EXPANDED SECTION AT THE TOP SHOWS HOW SURFACING BOTH SIDES IS ACCOMPLISHED AND THE ONE AT THE BOTTOM SHOWS ONE SIDE ONLY. IT IS IMPORTANT THAT GATE FRAMES BE DELIVERED TO THE SITE BEFORE THE SCREEN IS CONSTRUCTED OR THAT AN ACCURATE MEASUREMENT BE MADE ON THE SITE IF THE SCREENS ARE CONSTRUCTED FIRST.

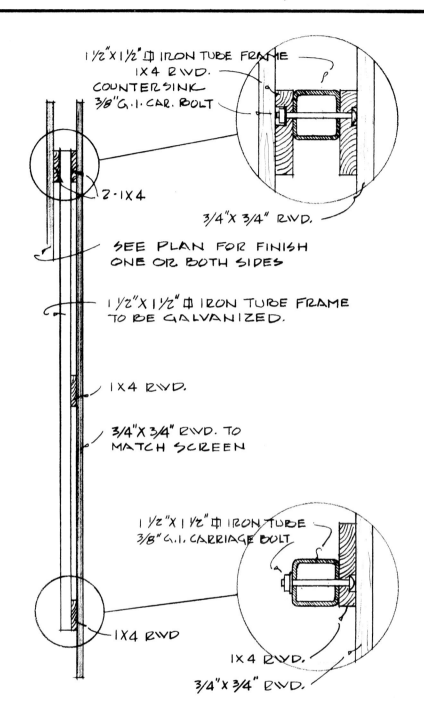

1½"X1½" ▯ IRON TUBE FRAME
1X4 RWD.
COUNTERSINK
3/8"G.I. CAR. BOLT

2-1X4

3/4"X 3/4" RWD.

SEE PLAN FOR FINISH ONE OR BOTH SIDES

1½"X1½" ▯ IRON TUBE FRAME TO BE GALVANIZED.

1X4 RWD.

3/4"X 3/4" RWD. TO MATCH SCREEN

1½"X1½" ▯ IRON TUBE
3/8" G.I. CARRIAGE BOLT

1X4 RWD

1X4 RVD.

3/4"X 3/4" RWD.

TUBE FRAME TO BE HOT DIP GALV. AFTER FAB.

CLEAR CEDAR MAY BE USED FOR RWD.

USE HOT DIP GALV. OR ALUMINUM NAILS ONLY.

STAIN TO MATCH SCREEN.

B SECTION · METAL FRAME WOOD GATE

SCALE   1" = 1'-0"

GATE DETAILS

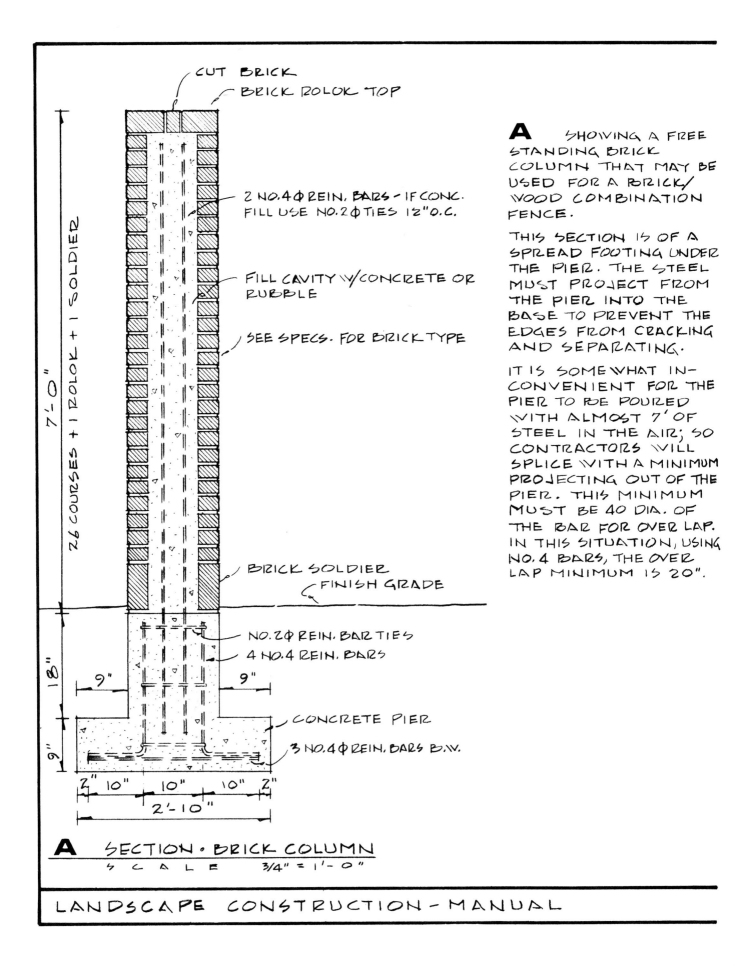

CUT BRICK
BRICK ROLOK TOP

2 NO.4Φ REIN, BARS - IF CONC.
FILL USE NO.2Φ TIES 12"O.C.

FILL CAVITY W/CONCRETE OR
RUBBLE

SEE SPECS. FOR BRICK TYPE

BRICK SOLDIER
FINISH GRADE

NO.2Φ REIN. BAR TIES
4 NO.4 REIN. BARS

CONCRETE PIER

3 NO.4Φ REIN. BARS B.W.

7'-0"

26 COURSES + 1 ROLOK + 1 SOLDIER

18"

9"

9"   9"

2" 10" 10" 10" 2"

2'-10"

A   SECTION - BRICK COLUMN
SCALE   3/4" = 1'-0"

A   SHOWING A FREE STANDING BRICK COLUMN THAT MAY BE USED FOR A BRICK/WOOD COMBINATION FENCE.

THIS SECTION IS OF A SPREAD FOOTING UNDER THE PIER. THE STEEL MUST PROJECT FROM THE PIER INTO THE BASE TO PREVENT THE EDGES FROM CRACKING AND SEPARATING.

IT IS SOMEWHAT IN-CONVENIENT FOR THE PIER TO BE POURED WITH ALMOST 7' OF STEEL IN THE AIR; SO CONTRACTORS WILL SPLICE WITH A MINIMUM PROJECTING OUT OF THE PIER. THIS MINIMUM MUST BE 40 DIA. OF THE BAR FOR OVER LAP. IN THIS SITUATION, USING NO.4 BARS, THE OVER LAP MINIMUM IS 20".

LANDSCAPE CONSTRUCTION - MANUAL

B   MANY INTEREST-
ING BRICK PATTERNS
CAN BE DEVELOPED
FOR THE COLUMN. ALL
OF THE WOOD SCREENS
SHOWN HEREIN COULD
BE USED BETWEEN
THIS BRICK COLUMN.

COLUMN SPACING COULD
BE OF THE DESIGNERS
CHOICE INTHAT THEY
ARE NOT STRUCTURALLY
INTERRELATED.

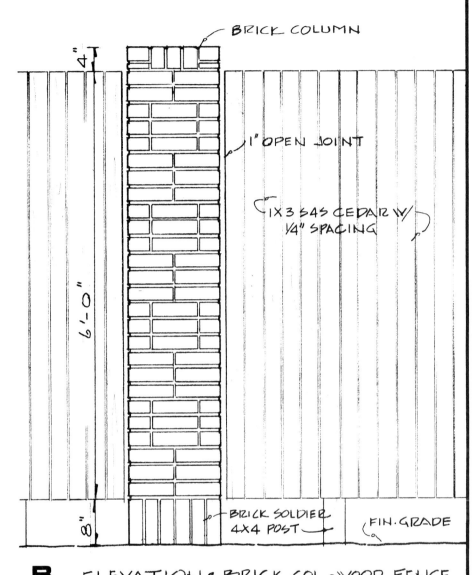

BRICK COLUMN

1" OPEN JOINT

1X3 S4S CEDAR W/
1/4" SPACING

6'-0"

4"

8"

BRICK SOLDIER
4X4 POST

FIN. GRADE

B   ELEVATION · BRICK COL. · WOOD FENCE
SCALE   3/4" = 1'-0"

C   SHOWING THE
WOOD FENCE BETWEEN
THE BRICK COLUMNS
ALTERNATING FROM
FRONT TO BACK.

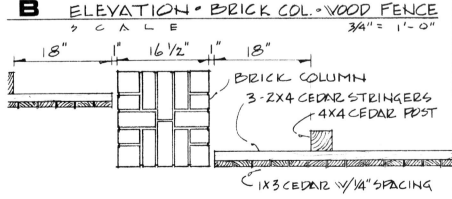

18"   1"   16 1/2"   1"   18"

BRICK COLUMN
3-2X4 CEDAR STRINGERS
4X4 CEDAR POST

1X3 CEDAR W/1/4" SPACING

C   PLAN · BRICK COL. · WOOD FENCE
SCALE   3/4" = 1'-0"

BRICK AND WOOD FENCE DETAILS

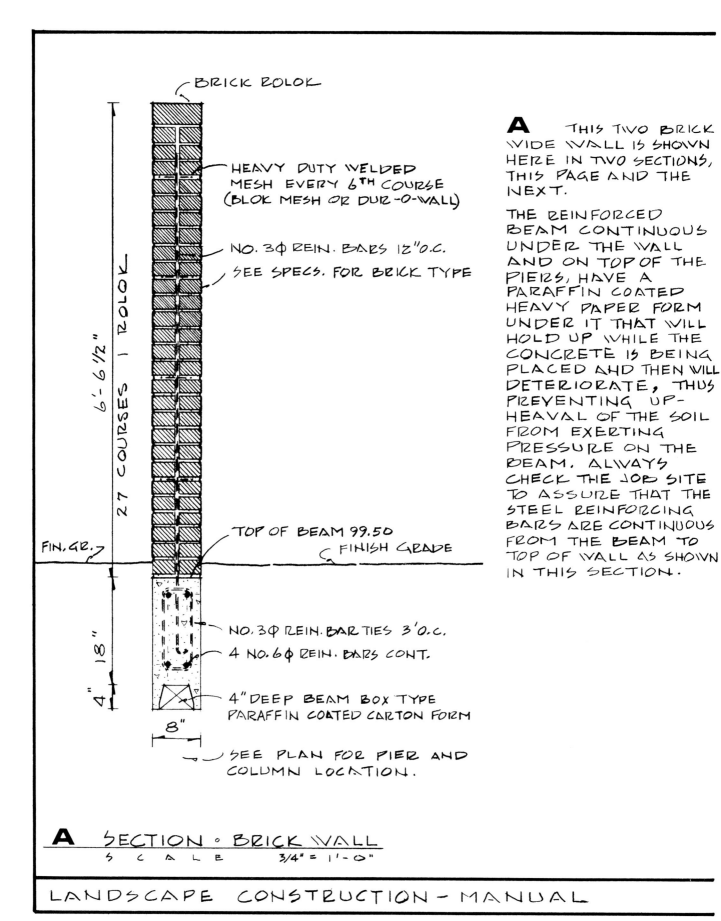

BRICK ROLOK

HEAVY DUTY WELDED MESH EVERY 6TH COURSE (BLOK MESH OR DUR-O-WALL)

NO. 3φ REIN. BARS 12" O.C.

SEE SPECS. FOR BRICK TYPE

6'-6½"

27 COURSES 1 ROLOK

TOP OF BEAM 99.50
FINISH GRADE

FIN. GR.

18"

4"

NO. 3φ REIN. BAR TIES 3' O.C.

4 NO. 6φ REIN. BARS CONT.

4" DEEP BEAM BOX TYPE PARAFFIN COATED CARTON FORM

8"

SEE PLAN FOR PIER AND COLUMN LOCATION.

A SECTION ∘ BRICK WALL
SCALE   3/4" = 1'-0"

A   THIS TWO BRICK WIDE WALL IS SHOWN HERE IN TWO SECTIONS, THIS PAGE AND THE NEXT.

THE REINFORCED BEAM CONTINUOUS UNDER THE WALL AND ON TOP OF THE PIERS, HAVE A PARAFFIN COATED HEAVY PAPER FORM UNDER IT THAT WILL HOLD UP WHILE THE CONCRETE IS BEING PLACED AND THEN WILL DETERIORATE, THUS PREVENTING UP-HEAVAL OF THE SOIL FROM EXERTING PRESSURE ON THE BEAM. ALWAYS CHECK THE JOB SITE TO ASSURE THAT THE STEEL REINFORCING BARS ARE CONTINUOUS FROM THE BEAM TO TOP OF WALL AS SHOWN IN THIS SECTION.

LANDSCAPE CONSTRUCTION - MANUAL

B   SHOWING A SECTION AT THE COLUMN AND PIER. WHERE THE DESIGN PERMITS, THE COLUMN AND PIER SHOULD OCCUR AT THE SAME LOCATION. PLACING CONCRETE INTO THE CAVITY OF A COLUMN IS DIFFICULT AND OFTEN PRODUCES VOIDS OR BRICK DISPLACEMENT. IT IS GOOD PRACTICE TO HAVE THE BRICK MASONS FILL THE CAVITY WITH RUBBLE MORTARED IN AS THE BRICK WORK GOES UP.

TOP OF PIER IS EXPANDED TO SERVE AS A BASE FOR THE BRICK COLUMN. NOTE THAT THE REINFORCING BARS IN THE BEAM CONTINUES THRU THE PIER.

A BELL AT THE BOTTOM OF THE PIER IS TO ADD BEARING SURFACE. PIER DEPTH IS CRITICAL AND SHOULD BE CALCULATED FOR EACH PROJECT WITH RESPECT TO SUBSOIL CONDITION.

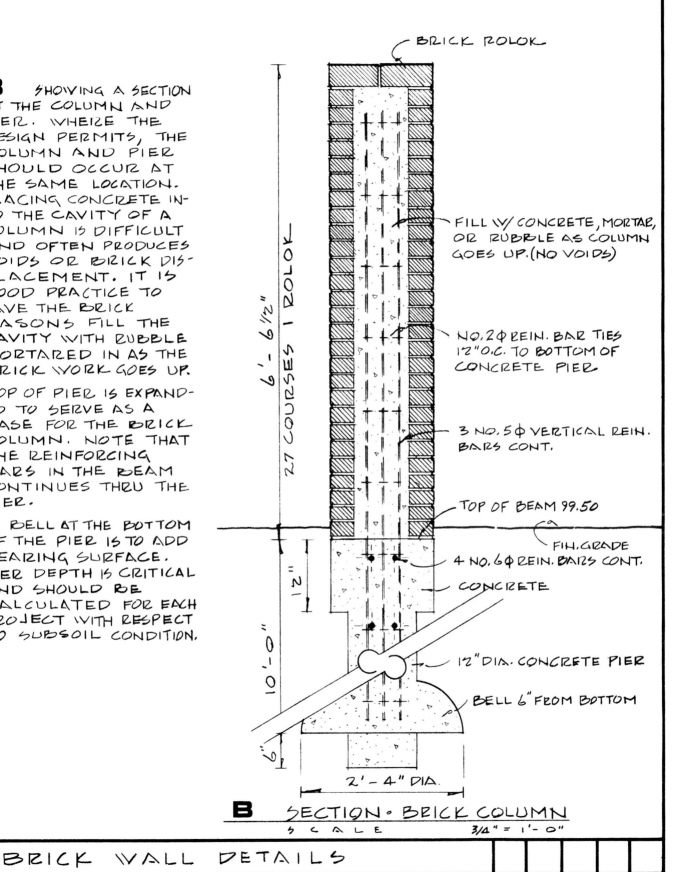

BRICK ROLOK

FILL W/ CONCRETE, MORTAR, OR RUBBLE AS COLUMN GOES UP. (NO VOIDS)

NO. 2 φ REIN. BAR TIES 12" O.C. TO BOTTOM OF CONCRETE PIER

3 NO. 5 φ VERTICAL REIN. BARS CONT.

TOP OF BEAM 99.50

FIN. GRADE

4 NO. 6 φ REIN. BARS CONT.

CONCRETE

12" DIA. CONCRETE PIER

BELL 6" FROM BOTTOM

6' - 6½"   27 COURSES 1 ROLOK

10' - 0"

2"

6"

2' - 4" DIA.

B   SECTION • BRICK COLUMN

SCALE   3/4" = 1'-0"

BRICK WALL DETAILS

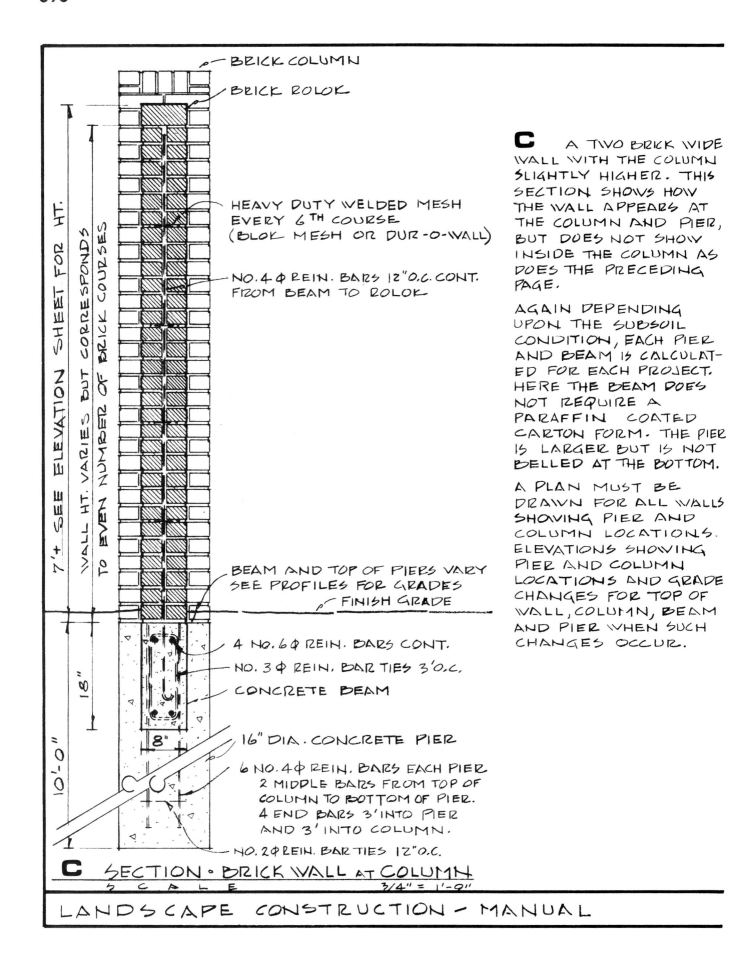

BRICK COLUMN

BRICK ROLOK

HEAVY DUTY WELDED MESH
EVERY 6TH COURSE
(BLOK MESH OR DUR-O-WALL)

NO. 4 Φ REIN. BARS 12" O.C. CONT.
FROM BEAM TO ROLOK

BEAM AND TOP OF PIERS VARY
SEE PROFILES FOR GRADES
FINISH GRADE

4 NO. 6 Φ REIN. BARS CONT.

NO. 3 Φ REIN. BAR TIES 3' O.C.

CONCRETE BEAM

16" DIA. CONCRETE PIER

6 NO. 4 Φ REIN. BARS EACH PIER
2 MIDDLE BARS FROM TOP OF
COLUMN TO BOTTOM OF PIER.
4 END BARS 3' INTO PIER
AND 3' INTO COLUMN.

NO. 2 Φ REIN. BAR TIES 12" O.C.

7'± SEE ELEVATION SHEET FOR HT.

WALL HT. VARIES BUT CORRESPONDS
TO EVEN NUMBER OF BRICK COURSES

10'-0"

18"

8"

C SECTION - BRICK WALL AT COLUMN
SCALE 3/4" = 1'-0"

C A TWO BRICK WIDE WALL WITH THE COLUMN SLIGHTLY HIGHER. THIS SECTION SHOWS HOW THE WALL APPEARS AT THE COLUMN AND PIER, BUT DOES NOT SHOW INSIDE THE COLUMN AS DOES THE PRECEDING PAGE.

AGAIN DEPENDING UPON THE SUBSOIL CONDITION, EACH PIER AND BEAM IS CALCULATED FOR EACH PROJECT. HERE THE BEAM DOES NOT REQUIRE A PARAFFIN COATED CARTON FORM. THE PIER IS LARGER BUT IS NOT BELLED AT THE BOTTOM.

A PLAN MUST BE DRAWN FOR ALL WALLS SHOWING PIER AND COLUMN LOCATIONS. ELEVATIONS SHOWING PIER AND COLUMN LOCATIONS AND GRADE CHANGES FOR TOP OF WALL, COLUMN, BEAM AND PIER WHEN SUCH CHANGES OCCUR.

D HERE THERE ARE NO COLUMNS AND THE BEAM IS MINIMUM BETWEEN THE PIERS WITH THE WALL ITSELF HAVING HORIZONTAL REINFORCING BARS.

AS SUGGESTED BEFORE, IT IS MOST IMPORTANT THAT SUFFICIENT STEEL FROM THE BEAM AND/OR PIER PROJECT INTO THE WALL FOR STABILITY AND SAFETY.

THE PIER IS DESIGNED HERE TO BE 16" DIA. WITH A BELL AT THE BOTTOM.

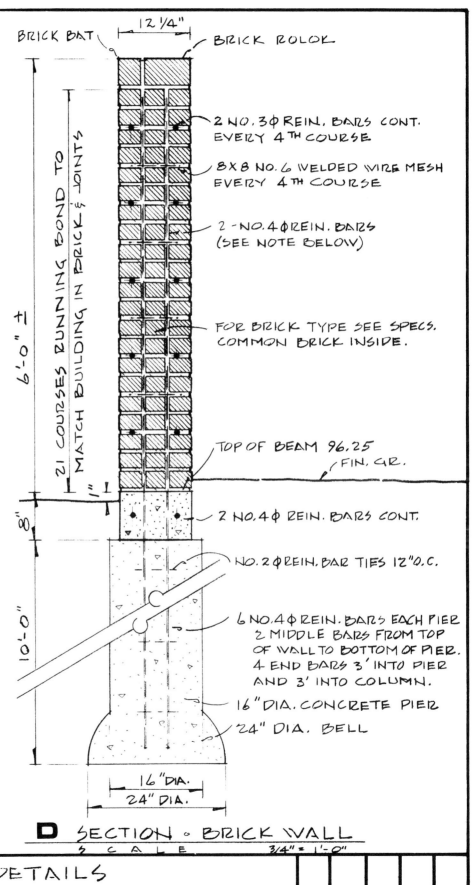

12 1/4"

BRICK BAT — BRICK ROLOK

2 NO. 3∅ REIN. BARS CONT. EVERY 4TH COURSE

8 X 8 NO. 6 WELDED WIRE MESH EVERY 4TH COURSE

2 - NO. 4∅ REIN. BARS (SEE NOTE BELOW)

FOR BRICK TYPE SEE SPECS. COMMON BRICK INSIDE.

21 COURSES RUNNING BOND TO MATCH BUILDING IN BRICK & JOINTS

6'-0"

1"

TOP OF BEAM 96.25 / FIN. GR.

2 NO. 4∅ REIN. BARS CONT.

NO. 2∅ REIN. BAR TIES 12" O.C.

6 NO. 4∅ REIN. BARS EACH PIER 2 MIDDLE BARS FROM TOP OF WALL TO BOTTOM OF PIER. 4 END BARS 3' INTO PIER AND 3' INTO COLUMN.

16" DIA. CONCRETE PIER

24" DIA. BELL

8"

10'-0"

16" DIA.
24" DIA.

D SECTION · BRICK WALL
SCALE 3/4" = 1'-0"

BRICK WALL DETAILS

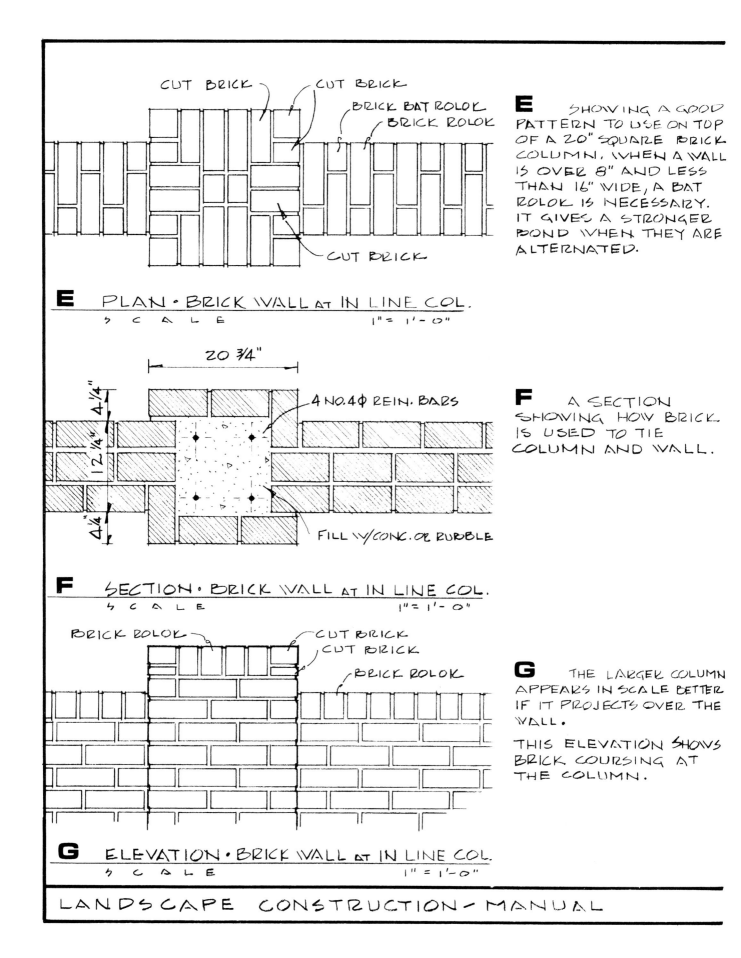

CUT BRICK — CUT BRICK
BRICK BAT ROLOK
BRICK ROLOK

CUT BRICK

E PLAN • BRICK WALL AT IN LINE COL.
SCALE   1" = 1'-0"

E SHOWING A GOOD PATTERN TO USE ON TOP OF A 20" SQUARE BRICK COLUMN. WHEN A WALL IS OVER 8" AND LESS THAN 16" WIDE, A BAT ROLOK IS NECESSARY. IT GIVES A STRONGER BOND WHEN THEY ARE ALTERNATED.

20 3/4"
4 1/4"
12 1/4"
4 1/4"
4 NO.4∅ REIN. BARS
FILL W/CONC. OR RUBBLE

F SECTION • BRICK WALL AT IN LINE COL.
SCALE   1" = 1'-0"

F A SECTION SHOWING HOW BRICK IS USED TO TIE COLUMN AND WALL.

BRICK ROLOK
CUT BRICK
CUT BRICK
BRICK ROLOK

G ELEVATION • BRICK WALL AT IN LINE COL.
SCALE   1" = 1'-0"

G THE LARGER COLUMN APPEARS IN SCALE BETTER IF IT PROJECTS OVER THE WALL.

THIS ELEVATION SHOWS BRICK COURSING AT THE COLUMN.

LANDSCAPE CONSTRUCTION - MANUAL

H   SHOWING A SECTION OF THE COL. AT A GATE. MORE REINFORCING IS NEEDED AND THE GATE HINGES MUST BE INSTALLED AS THE COLUMN IS BEING CONSTRUCTED.

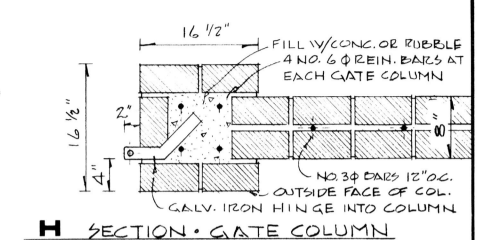

16 1/2"

16 1/2"

2"

4"

8"

FILL W/CONC. OR RUBBLE
4 NO. 6 ⌀ REIN. BARS AT EACH GATE COLUMN

NO. 3⌀ BARS 12" O.C. OUTSIDE FACE OF COL.

GALV. IRON HINGE INTO COLUMN

H   SECTION • GATE COLUMN

SCALE   1" = 1'-0"

I   HINGE LOCATION IS IMPORTANT. HINGES THAT ARE TOO CLOSE TO-GETHER MAKE A WEAK AND SAGGING GATE. IF IT IS TOO CLOSE TO THE TOP OF THE COLUMN IT MAY BREAK OUT.

IT IS NECESSARY TO MEASURE THE HINGES AFTER INSTALLATION AND BEFORE THE GATE IS CONSTRUCTED TO ASSURE A GOOD FIT.

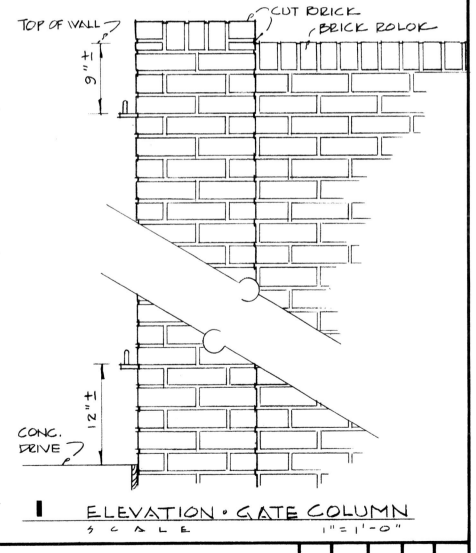

TOP OF WALL

CUT BRICK
BRICK ROLOK

9" ±

12" ±

CONC. DRIVE

I   ELEVATION • GATE COLUMN

SCALE   1" = 1'-0"

BRICK WALL DETAILS

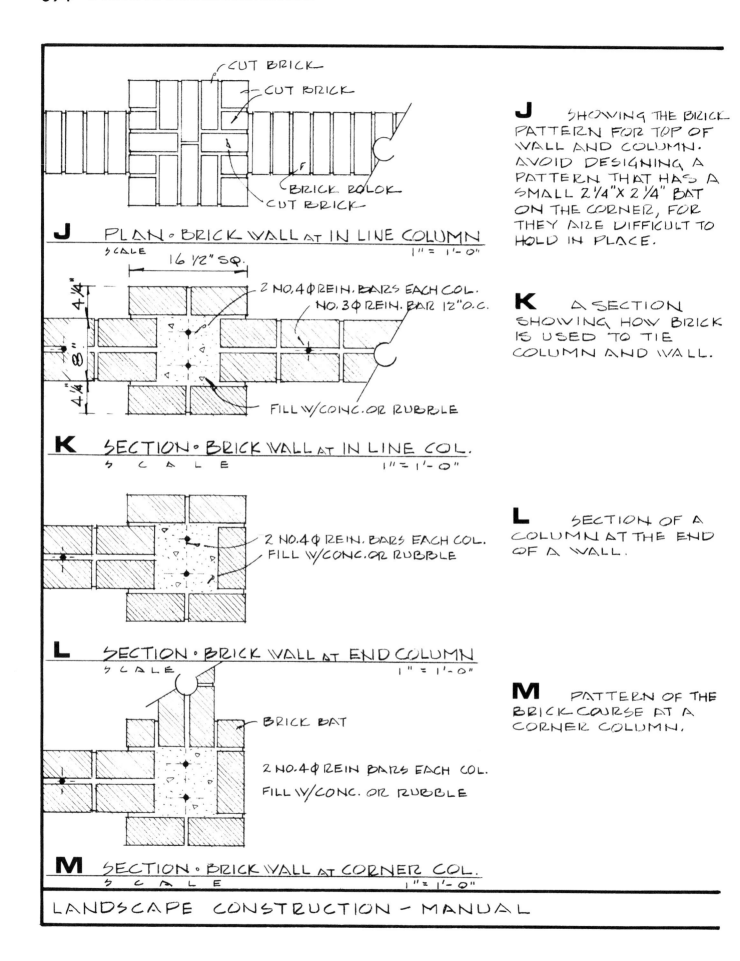

CUT BRICK
CUT BRICK
BRICK BLOCK
CUT BRICK

J PLAN • BRICK WALL AT IN LINE COLUMN
SCALE   1" = 1'-0"

16 1/2" SQ.

4 1/4"
8"
4 1/4"

2 NO. 4 Ø REIN. BARS EACH COL.
NO. 3 Ø REIN. BAR 12" O.C.

FILL W/CONC. OR RUBBLE

K SECTION • BRICK WALL AT IN LINE COL.
SCALE   1" = 1'-0"

2 NO. 4 Ø REIN. BARS EACH COL.
FILL W/CONC. OR RUBBLE

L SECTION • BRICK WALL AT END COLUMN
SCALE   1" = 1'-0"

BRICK BAT

2 NO. 4 Ø REIN BARS EACH COL.
FILL W/CONC. OR RUBBLE

M SECTION • BRICK WALL AT CORNER COL.
SCALE   1" = 1'-0"

J SHOWING THE BRICK PATTERN FOR TOP OF WALL AND COLUMN. AVOID DESIGNING A PATTERN THAT HAS A SMALL 2 1/4" X 2 1/4" BAT ON THE CORNER, FOR THEY ARE DIFFICULT TO HOLD IN PLACE.

K A SECTION SHOWING HOW BRICK IS USED TO TIE COLUMN AND WALL.

L SECTION OF A COLUMN AT THE END OF A WALL.

M PATTERN OF THE BRICK COURSE AT A CORNER COLUMN.

LANDSCAPE CONSTRUCTION - MANUAL

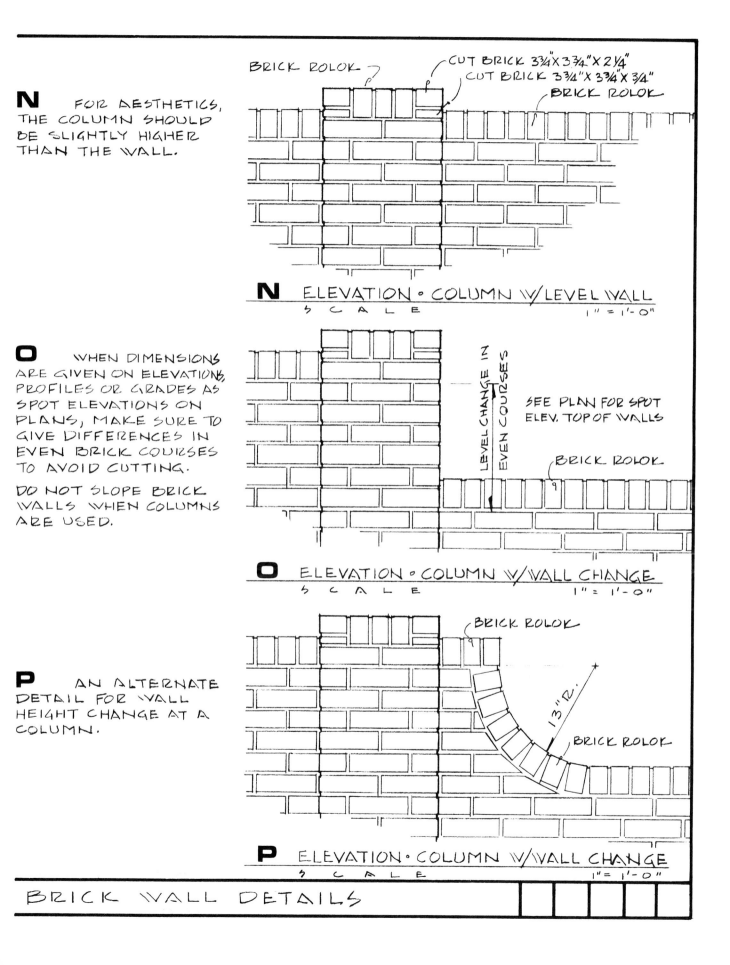

N FOR AESTHETICS, THE COLUMN SHOULD BE SLIGHTLY HIGHER THAN THE WALL.

BRICK ROLOK

CUT BRICK 3¾"x3¾"x2¼"

CUT BRICK 3¾"x 3¾"x 3/4"

BRICK ROLOK

N ELEVATION • COLUMN W/LEVEL WALL

SCALE   1" = 1'-0"

O WHEN DIMENSIONS ARE GIVEN ON ELEVATIONS, PROFILES OR GRADES AS SPOT ELEVATIONS ON PLANS, MAKE SURE TO GIVE DIFFERENCES IN EVEN BRICK COURSES TO AVOID CUTTING.

DO NOT SLOPE BRICK WALLS WHEN COLUMNS ARE USED.

LEVEL CHANGE IN EVEN COURSES

SEE PLAN FOR SPOT ELEV. TOP OF WALLS

BRICK ROLOK

O ELEVATION • COLUMN W/WALL CHANGE

SCALE   1" = 1'-0"

P AN ALTERNATE DETAIL FOR WALL HEIGHT CHANGE AT A COLUMN.

BRICK ROLOK

13" R.

BRICK ROLOK

P ELEVATION • COLUMN W/WALL CHANGE

SCALE   1"= 1'-0"

BRICK WALL DETAILS

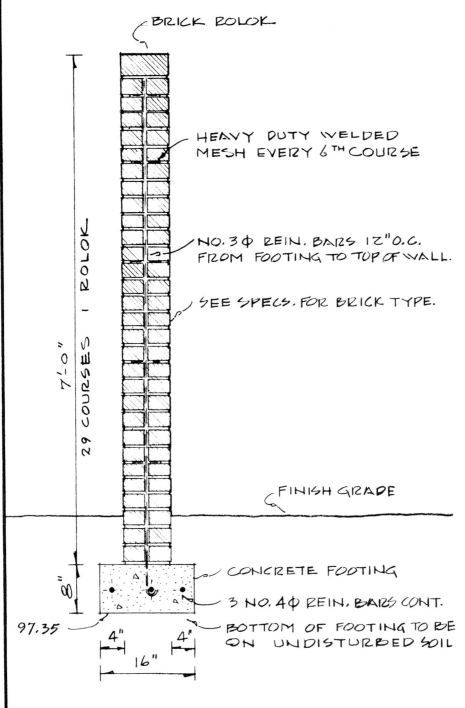

BRICK ROLOK

HEAVY DUTY WELDED MESH EVERY 6ᵀᴴ COURSE

NO. 3∅ REIN. BARS 12"O.C. FROM FOOTING TO TOP OF WALL.

SEE SPECS. FOR BRICK TYPE.

29 COURSES - 1 ROLOK

7'-0"

FINISH GRADE

8"

97.35

CONCRETE FOOTING

3 NO. 4∅ REIN. BARS CONT.

BOTTOM OF FOOTING TO BE ON UNDISTURBED SOIL

4"   4"

16"

Q SECTION - BRICK WALL
SCALE   3/4" = 1'-0"

Q A SIMPLE 8" WIDE BRICK WALL WITH A SPREAD FOOTING.

IN SOILS SUCH AS SAND, THAT ARE VERY STABLE, THE PIER AND BEAM DESIGN MAY BE TOO MUCH. THE FOOTING HERE IS SPREAD TO ALLOW MORE SURFACE CONTACT WITH THE SOIL TO SUPPORT THE WEIGHT OF THE WALL.

THIS DETAIL IS BEST USED WHERE CORNERS OCCUR RATHER CLOSE TO - GETHER TO GIVE THE WALL VERTICAL STABILITY.

WARNING - THIS DETAIL SHOULD NEVER BE USED AS A SINGLE PANEL WALL WHERE VEHICLES MAY BUMP IT OR WHERE CHILDREN IN GROUPS MAY PLAY.

R A 12" OR THREE BRICK WIDE WALL WITH A SPREAD FOOTING.

CARE SHOULD BE TAKEN NOT TO USE A SPREAD TYPE FOOTING IN OTHER THAN STABLE SOILS.

THE "RULE OF THUMB" FOR A SPREAD FOOTING IS TWO TIMES THE WIDTH OF THE WALL.

ALL FOOTING TYPE WALLS MUST HAVE THE BOTTOM OF THE FOOTING PLACED ON UNDISTURBED SOIL AND BELOW THE FROST LINE. FOR AESTHETICS, IT IS SUGGESTED THAT THE TOP OF THE FOOTING BE BELOW FINISH GRADE.

THIS DETAIL WILL HAVE THE SAME GENERAL LIMITATIONS AS SUGGESTED ON THE PRECEEDING PAGE.

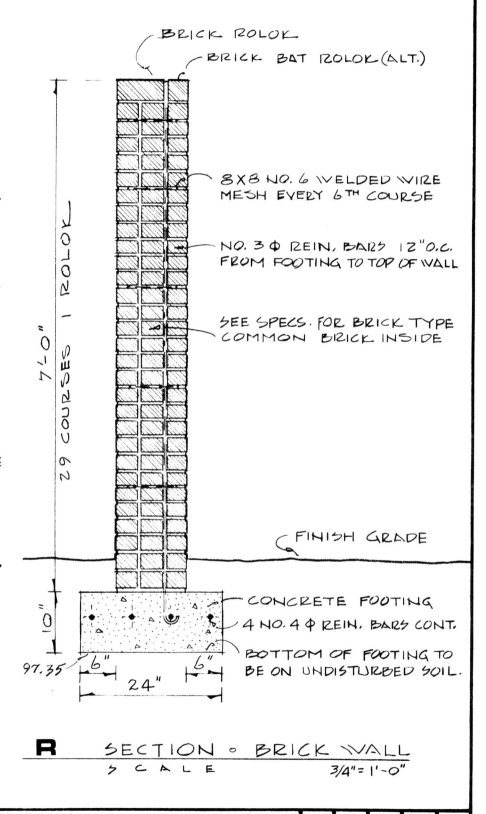

BRICK ROLOK
BRICK BAT ROLOK (ALT.)
8X8 NO. 6 WELDED WIRE MESH EVERY 6TH COURSE
NO. 3 Ø REIN. BARS 12" O.C. FROM FOOTING TO TOP OF WALL
SEE SPECS. FOR BRICK TYPE COMMON BRICK INSIDE
FINISH GRADE
CONCRETE FOOTING
4 NO. 4 Ø REIN. BARS CONT.
BOTTOM OF FOOTING TO BE ON UNDISTURBED SOIL.
7'-0" 29 COURSES 1 ROLOK
97.35 6" 24" 6" 10"

R SECTION · BRICK WALL
SCALE 3/4" = 1'-0"

BRICK WALL DETAILS

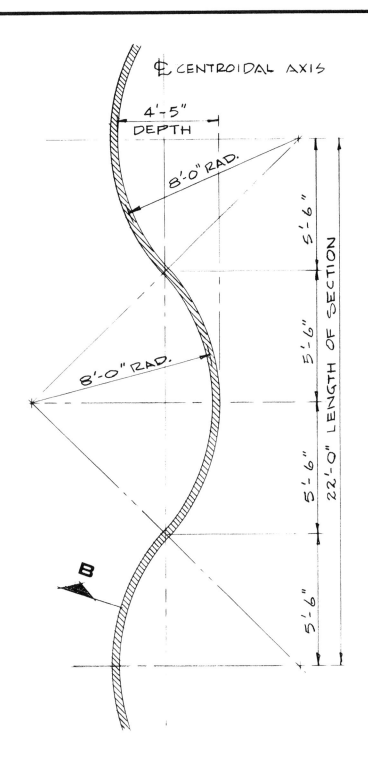

CENTROIDAL AXIS

4'-5" DEPTH

8'-0" RAD.

8'-0" RAD.

5'-6"

5'-6"

5'-6"

5'-6"

22'-0" LENGTH OF SECTION

B

A THIS TECHNIQUE OF GARDEN WALL CONSTRUCTION HAS BEEN USED IN THIS COUNTRY FOR ALMOST 200 YEARS. THE SERPENTINE SHAPE PROVIDES LATERAL STRENGTH TO THE WALL SO THAT IT NORMALLY CAN BE BUILT ONLY ONE BRICK WIDE WITHOUT ADDITIONAL LATERAL SUPPORT.

SINCE THE WALL DEPENDS ON ITS SHAPE FOR STRENGTH, IT IS IMPORTANT THAT THE CONFIGURATION DOES NOT VARY TOO MUCH FROM THE FOLLOWING LIMITATIONS.

THE RADIUS OF CURVATURE OF A SINGLE BRICK WIDTH WALL SHOULD BE NO MORE THAN TWICE THE HEIGHT OF THE WALL EXTENDING ABOVE FINISH GRADE.

THE DEPTH OF CURVATURE SHOULD BE NO LESS THAN ONE HALF OF THE HEIGHT ABOVE FINISH GRADE.

A PARTIAL PLAN ∘ 4" WALL
SCALE 1/4" = 1'-0"

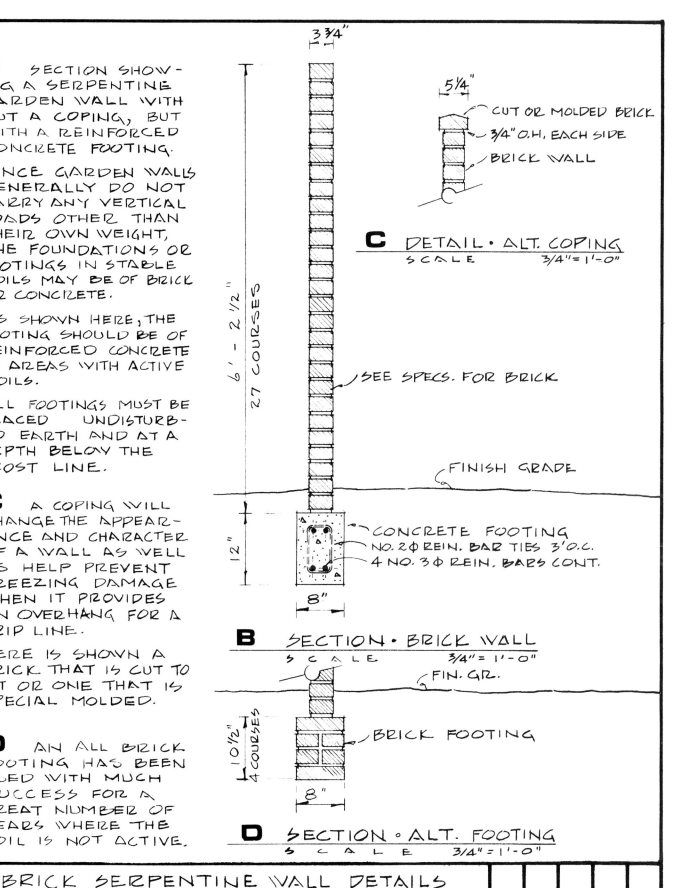

B SECTION SHOW-
ING A SERPENTINE
GARDEN WALL WITH
OUT A COPING, BUT
WITH A REINFORCED
CONCRETE FOOTING.

SINCE GARDEN WALLS
GENERALLY DO NOT
CARRY ANY VERTICAL
LOADS OTHER THAN
THEIR OWN WEIGHT,
THE FOUNDATIONS OR
FOOTINGS IN STABLE
SOILS MAY BE OF BRICK
OR CONCRETE.

AS SHOWN HERE, THE
FOOTING SHOULD BE OF
REINFORCED CONCRETE
IN AREAS WITH ACTIVE
SOILS.

ALL FOOTINGS MUST BE
PLACED   UNDISTURB-
ED EARTH AND AT A
DEPTH BELOW THE
FROST LINE.

C A COPING WILL
CHANGE THE APPEAR-
ANCE AND CHARACTER
OF A WALL AS WELL
AS HELP PREVENT
FREEZING DAMAGE
WHEN IT PROVIDES
AN OVERHANG FOR A
DRIP LINE.

HERE IS SHOWN A
BRICK THAT IS CUT TO
FIT OR ONE THAT IS
SPECIAL MOLDED.

D AN ALL BRICK
FOOTING HAS BEEN
USED WITH MUCH
SUCCESS FOR A
GREAT NUMBER OF
YEARS WHERE THE
SOIL IS NOT ACTIVE.

3 3/4"

5 1/4"
— CUT OR MOLDED BRICK
— 3/4" O.H. EACH SIDE
— BRICK WALL

C DETAIL · ALT. COPING
SCALE   3/4" = 1'-0"

6' - 2 1/2"
27 COURSES

— SEE SPECS. FOR BRICK

— FINISH GRADE

12"

8"

CONCRETE FOOTING
NO. 2 Ø REIN. BAR TIES 3' O.C.
4 NO. 3 Ø REIN. BARS CONT.

B SECTION · BRICK WALL
SCALE   3/4" = 1'-0"

FIN. GR.

10 1/2"
4 COURSES

— BRICK FOOTING

8"

D SECTION · ALT. FOOTING
SCALE   3/4" = 1'-0"

BRICK SERPENTINE WALL DETAILS

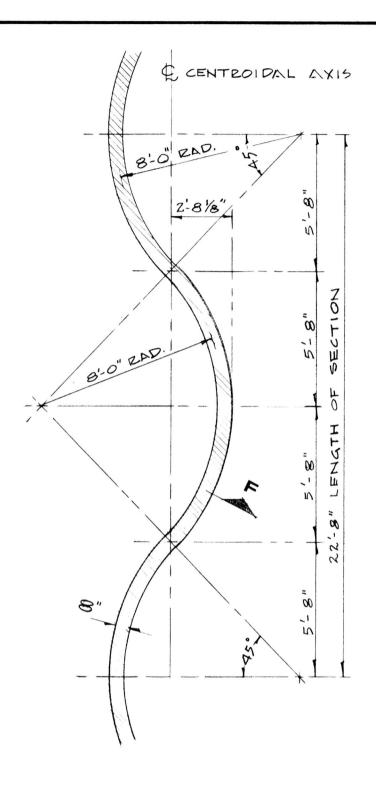

C CENTROIDAL AXIS

8'-0" RAD.

45°

2'-8⅛"

8'-0" RAD.

5'-8"

5'-8"

5'-8"

5'-8"

22'-8" LENGTH OF SECTION

8"

F

45°

E THERE WILL BE OCCASIONS WHEN A SERPENTINE WALL WILL BE DESIRABLE AND THE THIN GARDEN WALL WILL NOT SERVE THE PURPOSE. A LOADBEARING OR NON-LOADBEARING BUILDING WALL, A RETAINING WALL, A HIGH GARDEN WALL, ETC.

THE "RULE OF THUMB" SUGGESTED ON THE PRECEEDING DETAIL WILL NOT APPLY TO THESE CONDITIONS, BUT WILL REQUIRE AN ENGINEERED DESIGN.

E PARTIAL PLAN · 8" WALL
SCALE 1/4" = 1'-0"

LANDSCAPE CONSTRUCTION – MANUAL

F SECTION SHOWING A SERPENTINE WALL THAT IS 8" IN WIDTH, BRICK ROLOK CAP OR COPING, AND A REINFORCED CONCRETE FOOTING OR FOUNDATION.

FOR ACTIVE SOILS, THE FOOTING MUST BE OF HIGH STRENGTH CONCRETE, SIZED AND REINFORCED AS NECESSARY.

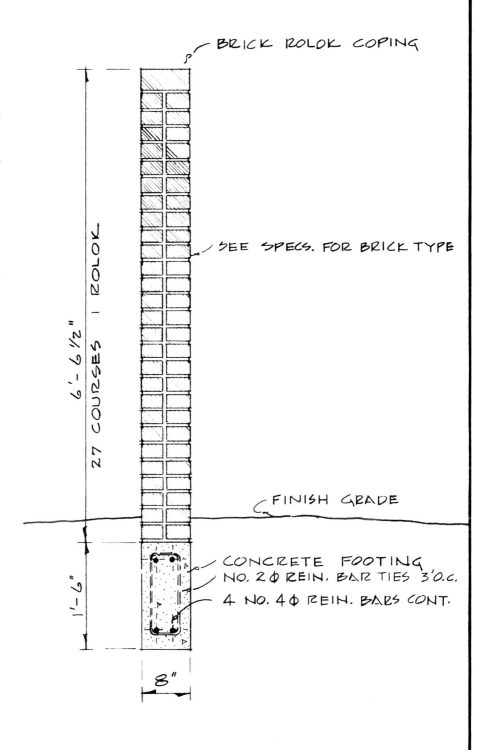

BRICK ROLOK COPING

SEE SPECS. FOR BRICK TYPE

6'-6½"   27 COURSES   1 ROLOK

FINISH GRADE

1'-6"

CONCRETE FOOTING NO. 2∅ REIN. BAR TIES 3'0.c.

4 NO. 4∅ REIN. BARS CONT.

8"

F SECTION · BRICK WALL
SCALE   3/4"= 1'-0"

BRICK SERPENTINE WALL DETAILS

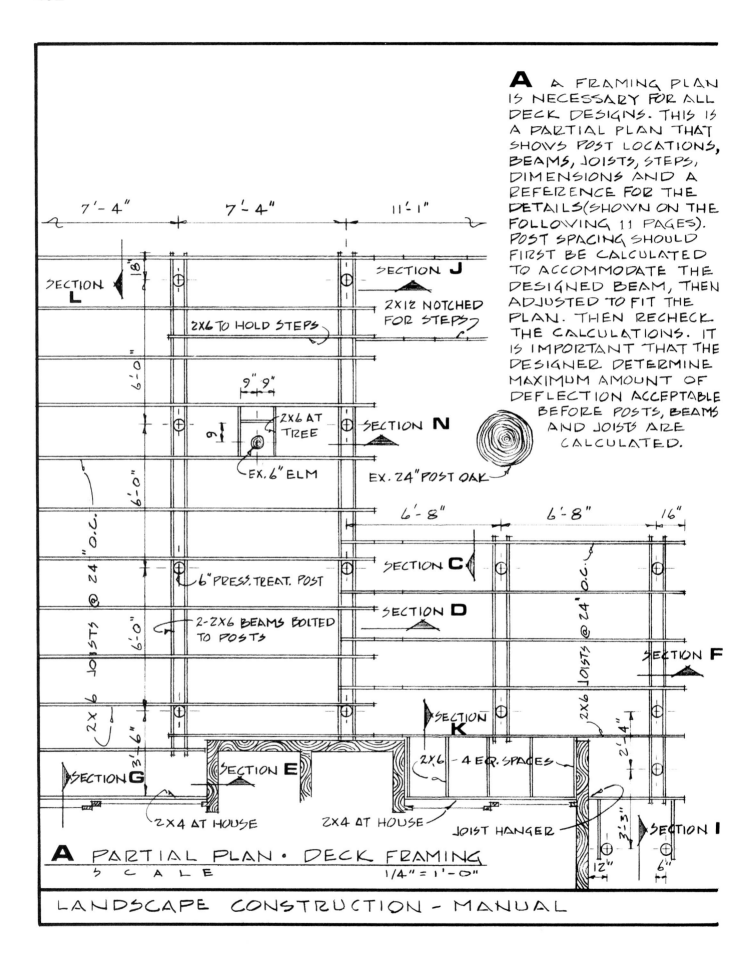

A   A FRAMING PLAN
IS NECESSARY FOR ALL
DECK DESIGNS. THIS IS
A PARTIAL PLAN THAT
SHOWS POST LOCATIONS,
BEAMS, JOISTS, STEPS,
DIMENSIONS AND A
REFERENCE FOR THE
DETAILS(SHOWN ON THE
FOLLOWING 11 PAGES).
POST SPACING SHOULD
FIRST BE CALCULATED
TO ACCOMMODATE THE
DESIGNED BEAM, THEN
ADJUSTED TO FIT THE
PLAN. THEN RECHECK
THE CALCULATIONS. IT
IS IMPORTANT THAT THE
DESIGNER DETERMINE
MAXIMUM AMOUNT OF
DEFLECTION ACCEPTABLE
BEFORE POSTS, BEAMS
AND JOISTS ARE
CALCULATED.

7'-4"   7'-4"   11'-1"

SECTION ◀ L

8"

SECTION J
2X12 NOTCHED
FOR STEPS
2X6 TO HOLD STEPS

6'-0"

9" 9"
2X6 AT TREE
6"
EX. 6" ELM

SECTION N

EX. 24" POST OAK

6'-0"

6'-8"   6'-8"   16"

SECTION ◀ C

JOISTS @ 24" O.C.

6" PRESS. TREAT. POST

SECTION D

6'-0"

2-2X6 BEAMS BOLTED
TO POSTS

2X6 JOISTS @ 24" O.C.

SECTION F

2X6 JOISTS @ 24" O.C.

SECTION K

2'-4"

3'-6"

2X6 - 4 EQ. SPACES

SECTION G

SECTION E

2X4 AT HOUSE   2X4 AT HOUSE

JOIST HANGER

3'-3"

SECTION I

A   PARTIAL PLAN · DECK FRAMING
SCALE   1/4" = 1'-0"

12"   6"

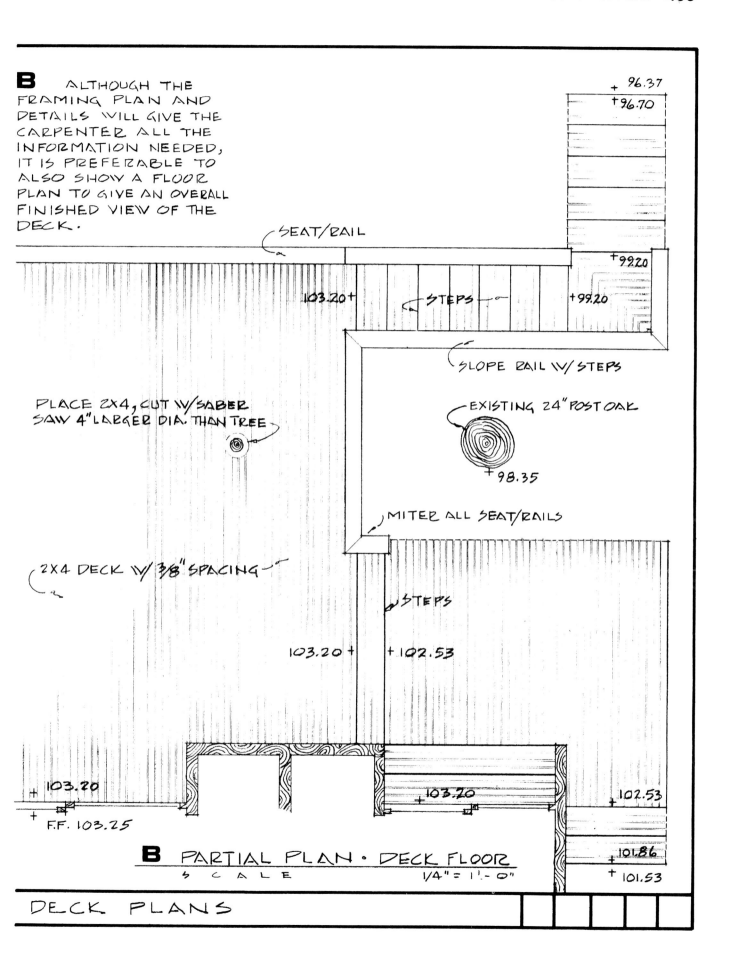

B ALTHOUGH THE FRAMING PLAN AND DETAILS WILL GIVE THE CARPENTER ALL THE INFORMATION NEEDED, IT IS PREFERABLE TO ALSO SHOW A FLOOR PLAN TO GIVE AN OVERALL FINISHED VIEW OF THE DECK.

+ 96.37
+96.70

SEAT/RAIL

103.20 +

STEPS

+99.20

+99.20

SLOPE RAIL W/ STEPS

PLACE 2X4, CUT W/SABER SAW 4" LARGER DIA. THAN TREE

EXISTING 24" POST OAK

+98.35

MITER ALL SEAT/RAILS

2X4 DECK W/ 3/8" SPACING

STEPS

103.20 +   +102.53

+ 103.20

+ F.F. 103.25

+ 103.20

102.53

101.86

+ 101.53

B PARTIAL PLAN · DECK FLOOR
SCALE   1/4" = 1'- 0"

DECK PLANS

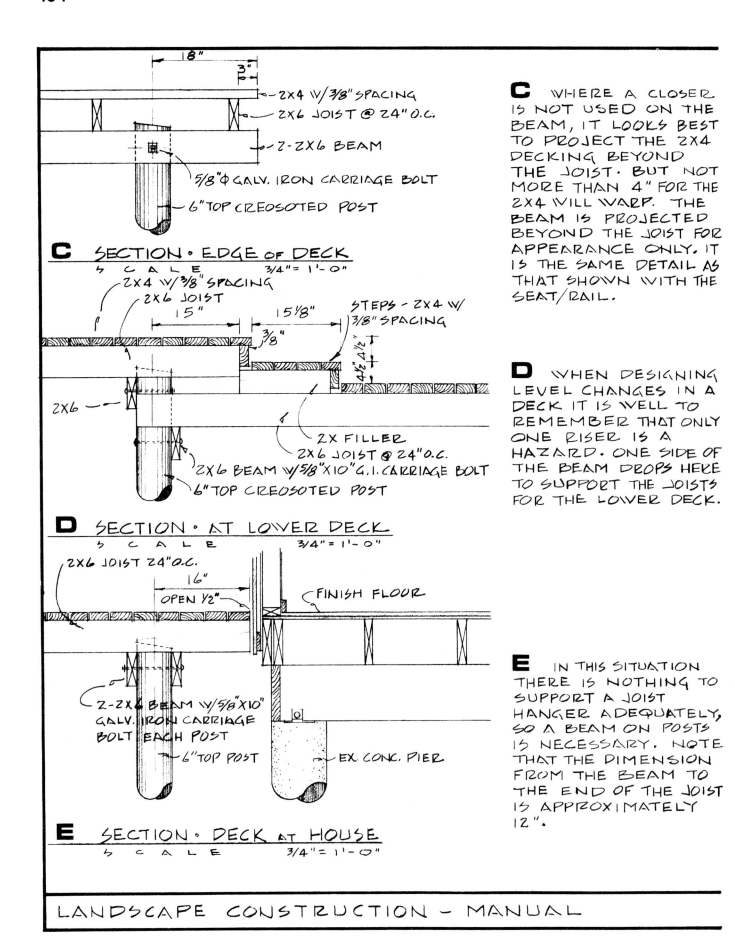

18"

3"

2×4 W/3/8" SPACING

2×6 JOIST @ 24" O.C.

2-2×6 BEAM

5/8"∅ GALV. IRON CARRIAGE BOLT

6" TOP CREOSOTED POST

C SECTION · EDGE OF DECK
SCALE 3/4" = 1'-0"

2×4 W/3/8" SPACING

2×6 JOIST

15"

15 1/8"

3/8"

STEPS - 2×4 W/ 3/8" SPACING

4 1/2" 4 1/2"

2×6

2× FILLER

2×6 JOIST @ 24" O.C.

2×6 BEAM W/5/8"×10" G.I. CARRIAGE BOLT

6" TOP CREOSOTED POST

D SECTION · AT LOWER DECK
SCALE 3/4" = 1'-0"

2×6 JOIST 24" O.C.

16"

OPEN 1/2"

FINISH FLOOR

2-2×6 BEAM W/5/8"×10" GALV. IRON CARRIAGE BOLT EACH POST

6" TOP POST

EX. CONC. PIER

E SECTION · DECK AT HOUSE
SCALE 3/4" = 1'-0"

C WHERE A CLOSER IS NOT USED ON THE BEAM, IT LOOKS BEST TO PROJECT THE 2×4 DECKING BEYOND THE JOIST. BUT NOT MORE THAN 4" FOR THE 2×4 WILL WARP. THE BEAM IS PROJECTED BEYOND THE JOIST FOR APPEARANCE ONLY. IT IS THE SAME DETAIL AS THAT SHOWN WITH THE SEAT/RAIL.

D WHEN DESIGNING LEVEL CHANGES IN A DECK IT IS WELL TO REMEMBER THAT ONLY ONE RISER IS A HAZARD. ONE SIDE OF THE BEAM DROPS HERE TO SUPPORT THE JOISTS FOR THE LOWER DECK.

E IN THIS SITUATION THERE IS NOTHING TO SUPPORT A JOIST HANGER ADEQUATELY, SO A BEAM ON POSTS IS NECESSARY. NOTE THAT THE DIMENSION FROM THE BEAM TO THE END OF THE JOIST IS APPROXIMATELY 12".

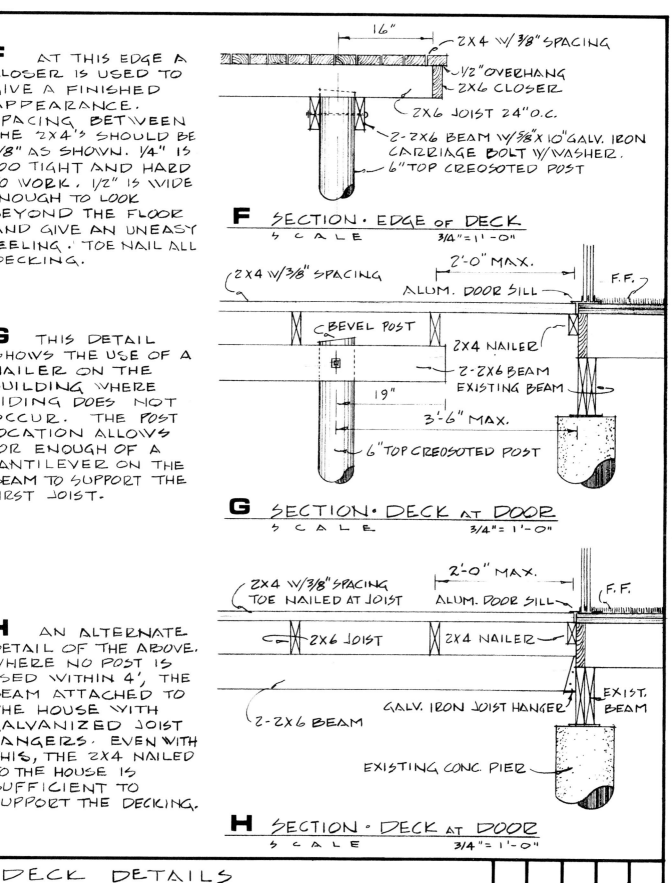

F AT THIS EDGE A CLOSER IS USED TO GIVE A FINISHED APPEARANCE. SPACING BETWEEN THE 2X4'S SHOULD BE 3/8" AS SHOWN. 1/4" IS TOO TIGHT AND HARD TO WORK. 1/2" IS WIDE ENOUGH TO LOOK BEYOND THE FLOOR AND GIVE AN UNEASY FEELING. TOE NAIL ALL DECKING.

16"
2X4 W/ 3/8" SPACING
1/2" OVERHANG
2X6 CLOSER
2X6 JOIST 24" O.C.
2-2X6 BEAM W/ 5/8" X 10" GALV. IRON CARRIAGE BOLT W/ WASHER.
6" TOP CREOSOTED POST

F SECTION · EDGE OF DECK
SCALE   3/4" = 1'-0"

G THIS DETAIL SHOWS THE USE OF A NAILER ON THE BUILDING WHERE SIDING DOES NOT OCCUR. THE POST LOCATION ALLOWS FOR ENOUGH OF A CANTILEVER ON THE BEAM TO SUPPORT THE FIRST JOIST.

2X4 W/ 3/8" SPACING
2'-0" MAX.
ALUM. DOOR SILL
F.F.
BEVEL POST
2X4 NAILER
2-2X6 BEAM
EXISTING BEAM
19"
3'-6" MAX.
6" TOP CREOSOTED POST

G SECTION · DECK AT DOOR
SCALE   3/4" = 1'-0"

H AN ALTERNATE DETAIL OF THE ABOVE. WHERE NO POST IS USED WITHIN 4', THE BEAM ATTACHED TO THE HOUSE WITH GALVANIZED JOIST HANGERS. EVEN WITH THIS, THE 2X4 NAILED TO THE HOUSE IS SUFFICIENT TO SUPPORT THE DECKING.

2X4 W/ 3/8" SPACING TOE NAILED AT JOIST
2'-0" MAX.
ALUM. DOOR SILL
F.F.
2X6 JOIST
2X4 NAILER
EXIST. BEAM
GALV. IRON JOIST HANGER
2-2X6 BEAM
EXISTING CONC. PIER

H SECTION · DECK AT DOOR
SCALE   3/4" = 1'-0"

DECK DETAILS

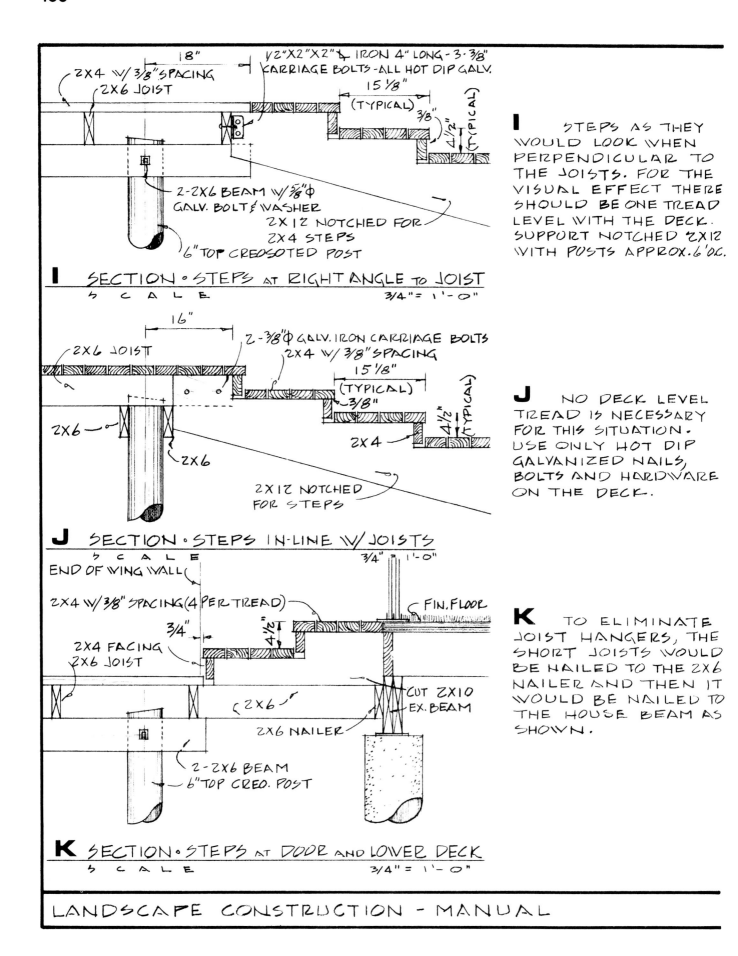

2X4 W/ 3/8" SPACING
2X6 JOIST

8"

1/2"X2"X2" IRON 4" LONG - 3 · 3/8"
CARRIAGE BOLTS - ALL HOT DIP GALV.

15 1/8"
(TYPICAL)

3/8"

4 1/2" (TYPICAL)

2-2X6 BEAM W/ 5/8"φ
GALV. BOLT & WASHER

2X12 NOTCHED FOR
2X4 STEPS

6" TOP CREOSOTED POST

I SECTION · STEPS AT RIGHT ANGLE TO JOIST
SCALE   3/4" = 1'-0"

I STEPS AS THEY WOULD LOOK WHEN PERPENDICULAR TO THE JOISTS. FOR THE VISUAL EFFECT THERE SHOULD BE ONE TREAD LEVEL WITH THE DECK. SUPPORT NOTCHED 2X12 WITH POSTS APPROX. 6' O.C.

16"

2 - 3/8"φ GALV. IRON CARRIAGE BOLTS
2X4 W/ 3/8" SPACING

2X6 JOIST

15 1/8"
(TYPICAL)

3/8"

4 1/2" (TYPICAL)

2X6

2X6

2X4

2X12 NOTCHED
FOR STEPS

J SECTION · STEPS IN-LINE W/ JOISTS
SCALE   3/4" = 1'-0"

J NO DECK LEVEL TREAD IS NECESSARY FOR THIS SITUATION. USE ONLY HOT DIP GALVANIZED NAILS, BOLTS AND HARDWARE ON THE DECK.

END OF WING WALL

2X4 W/ 3/8" SPACING (4 PER TREAD)

FIN. FLOOR

3/4"

4 1/2"

2X4 FACING
2X6 JOIST

2X6

CUT 2X10
EX. BEAM

2X6 NAILER

2-2X6 BEAM
6" TOP CREO. POST

K TO ELIMINATE JOIST HANGERS, THE SHORT JOISTS WOULD BE NAILED TO THE 2X6 NAILER AND THEN IT WOULD BE NAILED TO THE HOUSE BEAM AS SHOWN.

K SECTION · STEPS AT DOOR AND LOWER DECK
SCALE   3/4" = 1'-0"

L THIS IS A SIMPLE BUT GOOD SEAT/RAIL COMBINATION. FOR DECKS OVER 5' OR 6' OFF THE GROUND, ANOTHER DETAIL MAY BE DESIRABLE. THE BOLTS GOING BOTH WAYS WILL GIVE A VERY STURDY SEAT THAT WILL ADD TO THE SECURE FEELING.

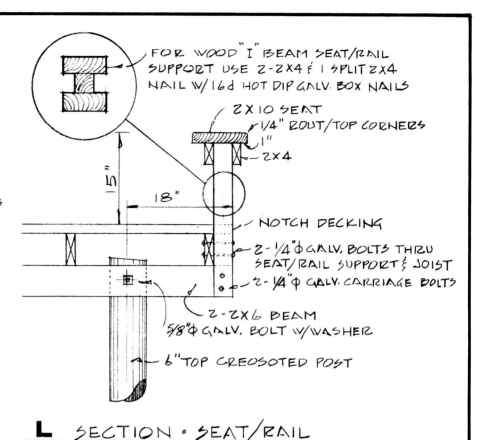

FOR WOOD "I" BEAM SEAT/RAIL SUPPORT USE 2-2X4 & 1 SPLIT 2X4 NAIL W/16d HOT DIP GALV. BOX NAILS

2X10 SEAT

1/4" ROUT/TOP CORNERS

1" — 2X4

NOTCH DECKING

2-1/4"∅ GALV. BOLTS THRU SEAT/RAIL SUPPORT & JOIST

2-1/4"∅ GALV. CARRIAGE BOLTS

2-2X6 BEAM

5/8"∅ GALV. BOLT W/WASHER

6" TOP CREOSOTED POST

15"

18"

L SECTION · SEAT/RAIL
SCALE   3/4" = 1'-0"

M USE ONLY TREATED WOOD FOR DECK CONSTRUCTION. STAIN AS DESIRED. SOME OF THE SILVER GRAY STAINS WILL GIVE THE APPEARANCE OF WEATHERED WOOD.

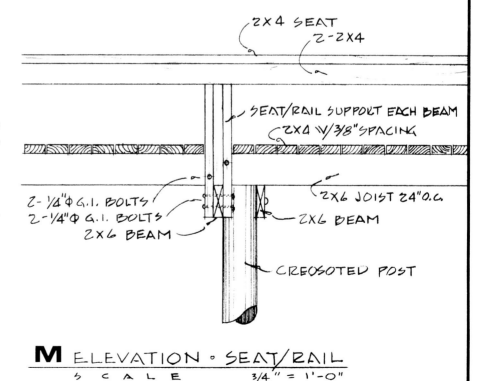

2X4 SEAT

2-2X4

SEAT/RAIL SUPPORT EACH BEAM

2X4 W/3/8" SPACING

2X6 JOIST 24" O.C.

2X6 BEAM

CREOSOTED POST

2-1/4"∅ G.I. BOLTS

2-1/4"∅ G.I. BOLTS

2X6 BEAM

M ELEVATION · SEAT/RAIL
SCALE   3/4" = 1'-0"

DECK DETAILS

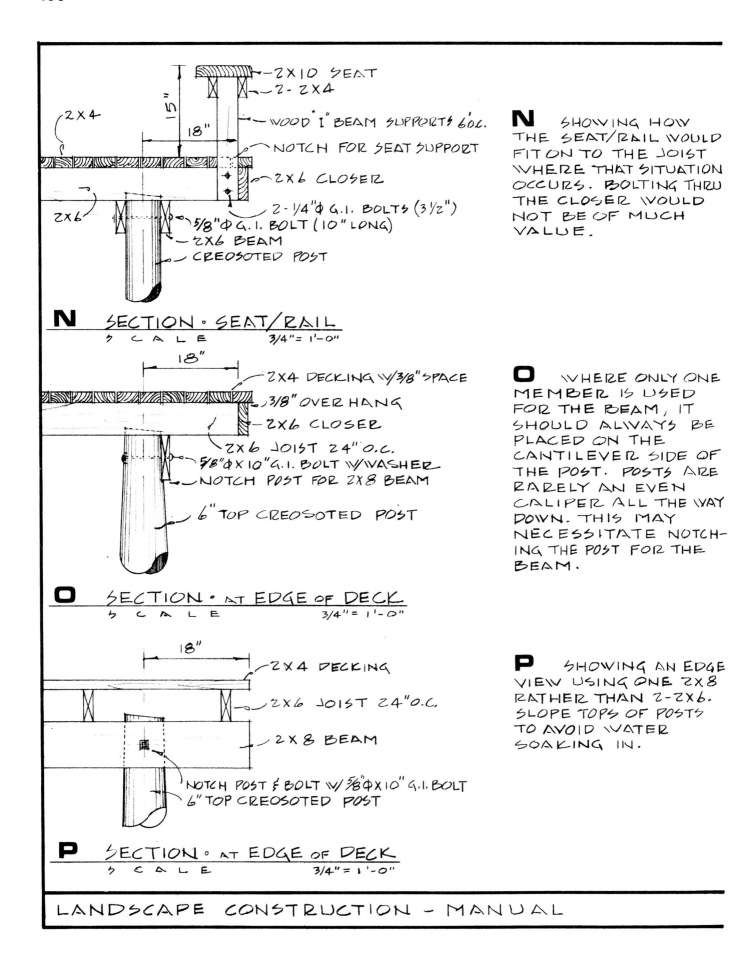

2X4

15"
18"

—2X10 SEAT
—2-2X4
—WOOD "I" BEAM SUPPORTS 6'0.C.
—NOTCH FOR SEAT SUPPORT
—2X6 CLOSER
—2-1/4"Φ G.I. BOLTS (3½")
—5/8"Φ G.I. BOLT (10" LONG)
—2X6 BEAM
—CREOSOTED POST

2X6

N SECTION · SEAT/RAIL
SCALE   3/4"= 1'-0"

N SHOWING HOW THE SEAT/RAIL WOULD FIT ON TO THE JOIST WHERE THAT SITUATION OCCURS. BOLTING THRU THE CLOSER WOULD NOT BE OF MUCH VALUE.

18"

—2X4 DECKING W/3/8" SPACE
—3/8" OVER HANG
—2X6 CLOSER
—2X6 JOIST 24" O.C.
—5/8"Φ X 10" G.I. BOLT W/WASHER
—NOTCH POST FOR 2X8 BEAM
—6" TOP CREOSOTED POST

O SECTION · AT EDGE OF DECK
SCALE   3/4"= 1'-0"

O WHERE ONLY ONE MEMBER IS USED FOR THE BEAM, IT SHOULD ALWAYS BE PLACED ON THE CANTILEVER SIDE OF THE POST. POSTS ARE RARELY AN EVEN CALIPER ALL THE WAY DOWN. THIS MAY NECESSITATE NOTCHING THE POST FOR THE BEAM.

18"

—2X4 DECKING
—2X6 JOIST 24" O.C.
—2X8 BEAM
—NOTCH POST & BOLT W/ 5/8"Φ X 10" G.I. BOLT
—6" TOP CREOSOTED POST

P SECTION · AT EDGE OF DECK
SCALE   3/4"= 1'-0"

P SHOWING AN EDGE VIEW USING ONE 2X8 RATHER THAN 2-2X6. SLOPE TOPS OF POSTS TO AVOID WATER SOAKING IN.

Q THIS IS JUST ONE OF MANY DESIGNS THAT MAY BE USED AT THE EDGE OF A DECK. THIS GIVES A SEAT WITH A BACK REST. NOTE THAT THIS DETAIL WILL BLOCK SOME OF THE VIEW FROM INSIDE THE HOUSE.

R FOR A HIGH DECK SOME TYPE OF SAFETY PROVISIONS MUST BE MADE. THIS COULD HAVE A NYLON FISH NET ATTACHED FOR BABIES. THIS ALSO WILL BLOCK VIEW TO SOME EXTENT.

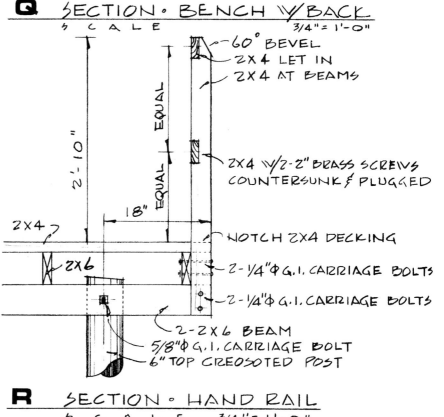

18°

2X4
2X2

SAND TOP & SEAT 2X4
2X4
2X4 LET IN

18"

15"

15"

10°

LET 2X4 IN & COUNTERSINK 2" BRASS SCREWS
2X4

NOTCH DECKING
2X GUSSET
2-1/4"⌀ G.I. BOLTS
2-1/4"⌀ G.I. BOLTS

2-2X6 BEAM

1/4"⌀ G.I. BOLT

17"

6" TOP CREOSOTED POST

Q SECTION · BENCH W/BACK
SCALE   3/4" = 1'-0"

60° BEVEL
2X4 LET IN
2X4 AT BEAMS

2'-10"

EQUAL

EQUAL

EQUAL

18"

2X4 W/2-2" BRASS SCREWS COUNTERSUNK & PLUGGED

2X4

2X6

NOTCH 2X4 DECKING

2-1/4"⌀ G.I. CARRIAGE BOLTS

2-1/4"⌀ G.I. CARRIAGE BOLTS

2-2X6 BEAM
5/8"⌀ G.I. CARRIAGE BOLT
6" TOP CREOSOTED POST

R SECTION · HAND RAIL
SCALE   3/4" = 1'-0"

DECK DETAILS

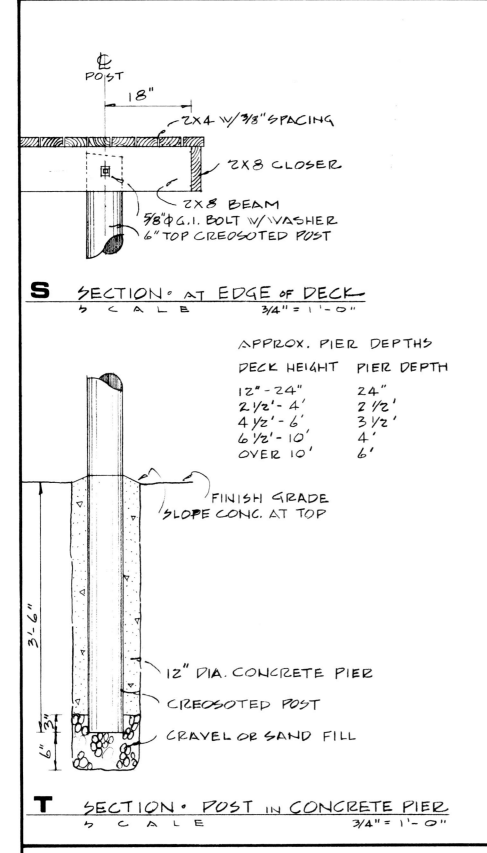

S SECTION · AT EDGE OF DECK
SCALE   3/4" = 1'-0"

18"
CL POST
2X4 W/3/8" SPACING
2X8 CLOSER
2X8 BEAM
5/8" Ø G.I. BOLT W/ WASHER
6" TOP CREOSOTED POST

APPROX. PIER DEPTHS

DECK HEIGHT	PIER DEPTH
12" - 24"	24"
2 1/2' - 4'	2 1/2'
4 1/2' - 6'	3 1/2'
6 1/2' - 10'	4'
OVER 10'	6'

FINISH GRADE
SLOPE CONC. AT TOP

3'-6"

12" DIA. CONCRETE PIER
CREOSOTED POST
GRAVEL OR SAND FILL

3"
6"

T SECTION · POST IN CONCRETE PIER
SCALE   3/4" = 1'-0"

S THIS DETAIL IS OFTEN REFERRED TO AS PLANK AND BEAM CONSTRUCTION. THE JOIST IS OMITTED AND THE 2X8 IN THIS DETAIL SERVES BOTH AS A BEAM AND A JOIST. THE POSTS ALONG THE BEAM ARE SPACED AS INDICATED ON THE BASIC SYSTEM; BUT THE BEAMS MUST BE CLOSER TOGETHER (4' MAX. FOR 2X4 DECKING), THUS MORE POSTS ARE NECESSARY. MOST OFTEN USED WHERE DECK IS TOO LOW TO ACCOMMODATE BOTH BEAM AND JOIST.

T SHOWING ONE OF THE BETTER METHODS OF SECURING DECK POST INTO GROUND. THIS GIVES A MOST STABLE DECK THAT IS FREE OF SWAY OR RACKING. PROJECT THE POST THRU THE CONCRETE TO AVOID WATER RUNNING DOWN THE POST AND COLLECTING. GRAVEL OR SHARP SAND WILL ALSO HELP KEEP THE END OF THE POST DRY. TAMPING THE ENTIRE BACK FILL FOR THE POST WITH A DAMP FILL SAND WILL WORK ABOUT AS WELL AS USING CONCRETE AS A BACK FILL.

U CONCRETE PIER/ POST ARE TOO "HEAVY" FOR MOST DECK CONSTRUCTION. FOR SHEAR, SOME REIN- FORCING BARS ARE NECESSARY WHERE DECK HEIGHTS ARE ABOVE 4'.

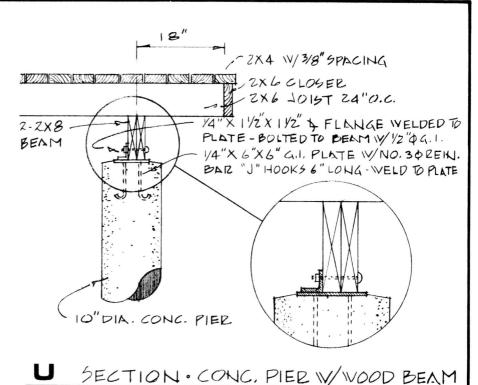

18"

2X4 W/3/8" SPACING
2X6 CLOSER
2X6 JOIST 24"O.C.
1/4"X 1½"X 1½" ↓ FLANGE WELDED TO PLATE - BOLTED TO BEAM W/ ½"∅ G.I.
1/4"X 6"X 6" G.I. PLATE W/ NO.3∅ REIN. BAR "J" HOOKS 6" LONG - WELD TO PLATE

2-2X8 BEAM

10"DIA. CONC. PIER

U SECTION · CONC. PIER W/ WOOD BEAM
SCALE   3/4" = 1'-0"

V WHEN METAL BEAMS ARE USED, POSTS CAN BE SPACED MUCH FARTHER APART. PERHAPS EVEN AS A CANTILEVERED DECK. A NAILER MUST BE BOLTED TO THE TOP OF THE BEAM SO THAT EACH JOIST CAN BE TOE NAILED INTO IT.

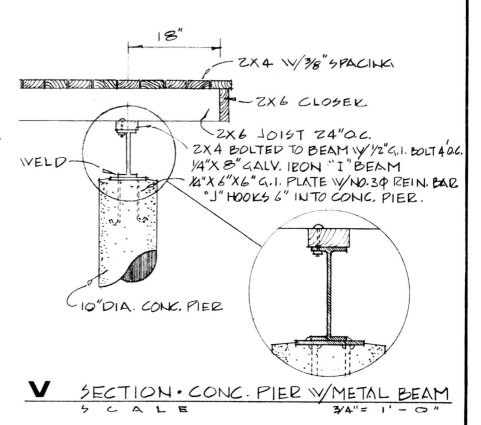

18"

2X4 W/3/8" SPACING
2X6 CLOSER
2X6 JOIST 24"O.C.
2X4 BOLTED TO BEAM W/ ½"G.I. BOLT 4'O.C.
1/4"X 8" GALV. IRON "I" BEAM
1/4"X 6"X6" G.I. PLATE W/ NO.3∅ REIN. BAR "J" HOOKS 6" INTO CONC. PIER.

WELD

10"DIA. CONC. PIER

V SECTION · CONC. PIER W/ METAL BEAM
SCALE   3/4" = 1'-0"

DECK DETAILS

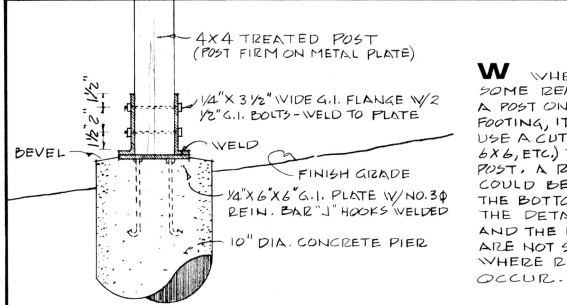

— 4X4 TREATED POST
(POST FIRM ON METAL PLATE)

1/4" X 3 1/2" WIDE G.I. FLANGE W/2
1/2" G.I. BOLTS - WELD TO PLATE

BEVEL

WELD

FINISH GRADE

1/4"X 6"X 6" G.I. PLATE W/ NO. 3⌀
REIN. BAR "J" HOOKS WELDED

10" DIA. CONCRETE PIER

W SECTION · CONC. FTG. W/FLANGES
SCALE   1 1/2" = 1'-0"

W WHERE THERE IS SOME REASON TO PLACE A POST ON A CONCRETE FOOTING, IT IS EASIER TO USE A CUT POST (4X4, 4X6, 6X6, ETC.) THAN A ROUND POST. A ROUND POST COULD BE NOTCHED AT THE BOTTOM, HOWEVER. THE DETAILS ON THIS AND THE NEXT PAGE ARE NOT SUGGESTED WHERE RACKING MAY OCCUR.

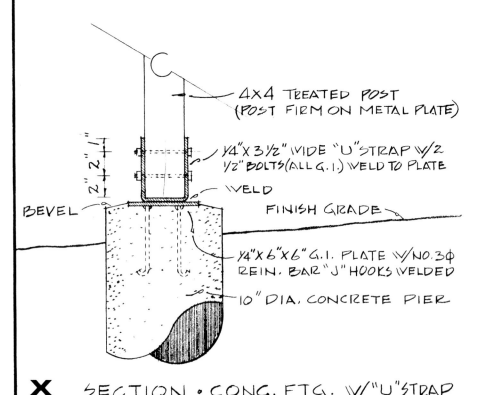

— 4X4 TREATED POST
(POST FIRM ON METAL PLATE)

1/4" X 3 1/2" WIDE "U" STRAP W/2
1/2" BOLTS (ALL G.I.) WELD TO PLATE

BEVEL

WELD

FINISH GRADE

1/4"X 6"X 6" G.I. PLATE W/ NO. 3⌀
REIN. BAR "J" HOOKS WELDED

10" DIA. CONCRETE PIER

X SECTION · CONC. FTG. W/ "U" STRAP
SCALE   1 1/2" = 1'-0"

X THIS DETAIL DIFFERS VERY LITTLE FROM THAT ABOVE. IT IS IMPORTANT IN BOTH DETAILS TO HAVE THE POST RESTING ON THE BOTTOM AND NOT ON THE BOLTS. FOOTING DEPTH WILL DEPEND UPON SOIL CONDITIONS, ETC.

LANDSCAPE CONSTRUCTION - MANUAL

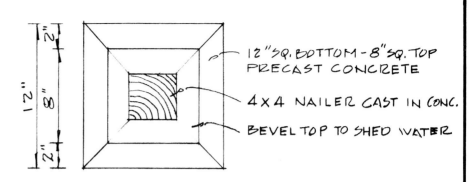

Y   FOR VERY LOW DECKS A SIMPLE PRECAST FOOTING WITH A NAILER CAST INSIDE MAY SERVE THE PURPOSE.

12" SQ. BOTTOM - 8" SQ. TOP PRECAST CONCRETE

4×4 NAILER CAST IN CONC.

BEVEL TOP TO SHED WATER

Y   PLAN · PRECAST CONC. FOOTING
SCALE   1 1/2" = 1'-0"

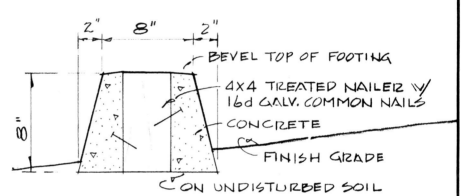

Z   A BEAM COULD BE PLACED ON TOP OF THIS AND TOE NAILED TO THE 4×4. IF POSTS ARE USED AND TOE NAILED TO THE 4×4, RACKING COULD BE A PROBLEM.

BEVEL TOP OF FOOTING

4×4 TREATED NAILER W/ 16d GALV. COMMON NAILS

CONCRETE

FINISH GRADE

ON UNDISTURBED SOIL

Z   SECTION · PRECAST CONC. FOOTING
SCALE   1 1/2" = 1'-0"

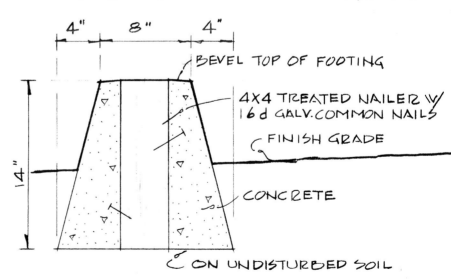

AA SAME AS ABOVE EXCEPT DEEPER. IT MAY BE USED WHERE FILL HAS OCCURRED OR TO GET BELOW THE FROST LINE.

BEVEL TOP OF FOOTING

4×4 TREATED NAILER W/ 16d GALV. COMMON NAILS

FINISH GRADE

CONCRETE

ON UNDISTURBED SOIL

AA SECTION · PRECAST CONC. FOOTING
SCALE   1 1/2" = 1'-0"

DECK DETAILS

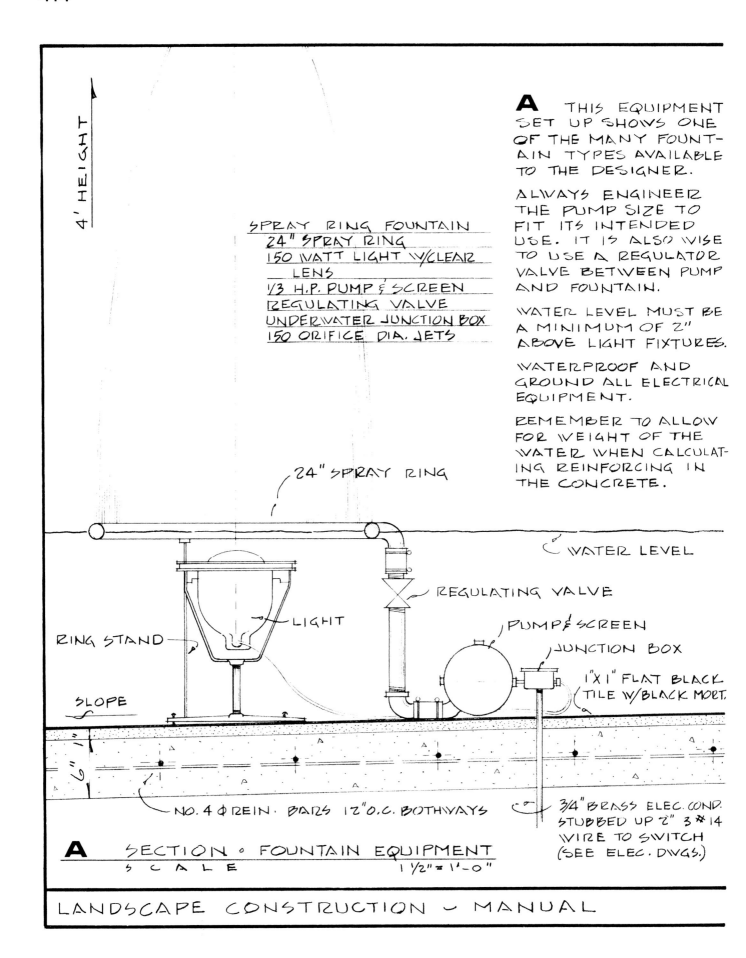

4' HEIGHT

SPRAY RING FOUNTAIN
24" SPRAY RING
150 WATT LIGHT W/CLEAR
    LENS
1/3 H.P. PUMP & SCREEN
REGULATING VALVE
UNDERWATER JUNCTION BOX
150 ORIFICE DIA. JETS

A   THIS EQUIPMENT
SET UP SHOWS ONE
OF THE MANY FOUNT-
AIN TYPES AVAILABLE
TO THE DESIGNER.

ALWAYS ENGINEER
THE PUMP SIZE TO
FIT ITS INTENDED
USE. IT IS ALSO WISE
TO USE A REGULATOR
VALVE BETWEEN PUMP
AND FOUNTAIN.

WATER LEVEL MUST BE
A MINIMUM OF 2"
ABOVE LIGHT FIXTURES.

WATERPROOF AND
GROUND ALL ELECTRICAL
EQUIPMENT.

REMEMBER TO ALLOW
FOR WEIGHT OF THE
WATER WHEN CALCULAT-
ING REINFORCING IN
THE CONCRETE.

24" SPRAY RING

WATER LEVEL

REGULATING VALVE

PUMP & SCREEN

JUNCTION BOX

LIGHT

RING STAND

SLOPE

1"X1" FLAT BLACK
TILE W/BLACK MORT.

NO. 4 ⌀ REIN. BARS 12"O.C. BOTHWAYS

3/4" BRASS ELEC. COND.
STUBBED UP 2" 3 #14
WIRE TO SWITCH
(SEE ELEC. DWGS.)

A   SECTION · FOUNTAIN EQUIPMENT
SCALE   1 1/2" = 1'-0"

LANDSCAPE CONSTRUCTION ~ MANUAL

B   NO POOL SHOULD
BE BUILT WITH OUT AN
AUTOMATIC WATER FEED
AND AN EASY METHOD
FOR DRAINING.

WHERE THE POOL CAN
NOT BE CONSTRUCTED
WITH A MONOLITHIC
POUR, A KEY JOINT
WILL HELP TO WATER-
PROOF IT.

CONCRETE IS TOO
POROUS FOR THE POOL
FINISH AND IT IS
SUGGESTED THAT 1"
STIFF MORTAR BE
APPLIED TO THE INSIDE
SURFACE TO CONTAIN
THE WATER.

BLACK TILE WILL GIVE
THE POOL A MIRROR
LIKE QUALITY, THUS
KEEPING THE EQUIP-
MENT FROM BECOMING
TOO OBVIOUS. TILE
OR A LIKE SMOOTH
SURFACE IS NECESSARY
FOR A POOL IF IT IS
TO BE MAINTAINED
WITH EASE.

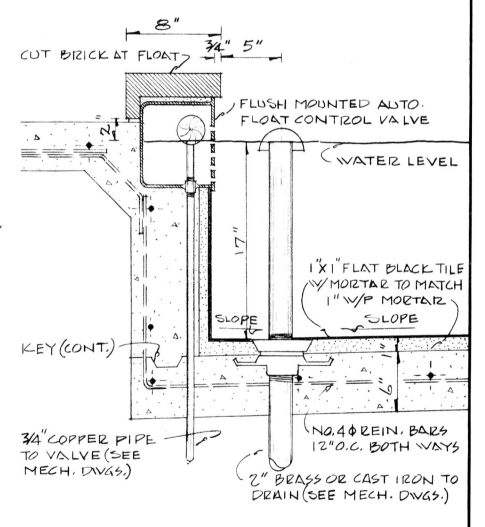

OVERFLOW DRAIN TO BE
CAST IRON OVERFLOW DRAIN WITH
WATERPROOFING FLANGE - 2" I.P.S.
OUTLET 17" HT. BRASS STANDPIPE
THREADED INTO GROUND JOINT
ADAPTER WHICH FITS INTO BRASS
ADJUSTABLE COLLAR AND BRASS
LIFT OFF DOME

8"
3/4" 5"
CUT BRICK AT FLOAT

FLUSH MOUNTED AUTO.
FLOAT CONTROL VALVE

WATER LEVEL

17"

1"X 1" FLAT BLACK TILE
W/ MORTAR TO MATCH
1" W/P MORTAR
SLOPE

SLOPE

KEY (CONT.)

3/4" COPPER PIPE
TO VALVE (SEE
MECH. DWGS.)

NO. 4 Ø REIN. BARS
12" O.C. BOTH WAYS

2" BRASS OR CAST IRON TO
DRAIN (SEE MECH. DWGS.)

B   SECTION · POOL FOUNTAIN
S C A L E   1 1/2" = 1'-0"

POOL FOUNTAIN DETAILS

LIGHT TO BE MERCURY
VAPOR SEMI-RECESSED
UP LIGHT WITH 100 WATT
M.V. LAMP. COMPLETE
WITH TRANSFORMER.
ENCLOSED IN WATERPROOF
JUNCTION BOX - FULL 360
DEGREE SHIELD.

A TO AVOID THE
MAINTENANCE TIME
INVOLVED IN TRIMMING
PLANTS AT LIGHT
FIXTURES WHEN THEY
OCCUR IN PLANT BEDS,
A SHIELD TO THE
HEIGHT OF THE PLANTS
SHOULD BE A PART OF
THE DESIGN.

MERCURY VAPOR HAS
A LIGHT SPECTRUM
THAT TENDS TO MAKE
GREEN FOLIAGE
APPEAR EVEN GREEN-
ER.

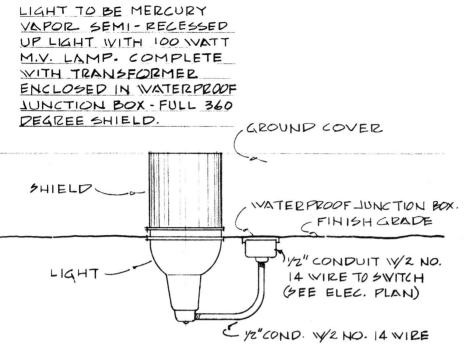

A SEMI-RECESSED UP LIGHT IN PLANT BED
S C A L E   1 1/2" = 1' - 0"

200 WATT P.A.R. LAMP

ALL BRONZE LIGHT
WITH 3/8" THICK
TEMPERED IMPACT
RESISTING FLAT LENS,
WITH NEOPRENE
GASKET

B FOR LIGHTING
THE FACADE OF A
STRUCTURE, A LIGHT
RECESSED INTO AN
EXTENDED MOWING
EDGE FROM THE
STRUCTURE WILL
SECURE IT AS WELL
AS REDUCE MAINTEN-
ANCE REQUIRED WITH
FIXTURES IN TURF
AREAS.

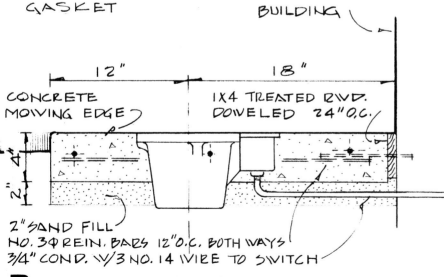

B ADJUSTABLE LIGHT IN CONCRETE
S C A L E   1 1/2" = 1' - 0"

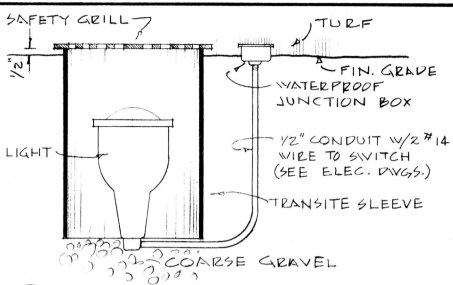

C USING A SLEEVE TO RECESS UP LIGHTS THAT OCCUR IN TURF AREAS. MAY BE USED UNDER TREES, ETC.

C RECESSED UP LIGHT IN TURF
S C A L E 1 1/2" = 1'-0"

LIGHT TO BE MERCURY VAPOR WITH 100 WATT M.V. LAMP COMPLETE WITH TRANSFORMER ENCLOSED IN WATERPROOF JUNCTION BOX. COPPER AND BRONZE WATERPROOF UNIT WITH HEAT RESISTANT CLEAR LENS AND MOLDED SILICONE GASKET - TRANSITE SLEEVE WITH GRILL.

D SAME FIXTURE AS ABOVE BUT OCCURRING WITHIN A MAINTENANCE BORDER ADJACENT TO A STRUCTURE.

DRAIN AWAY FROM FIXTURE AND PLACE GRAVEL UNDER IT.

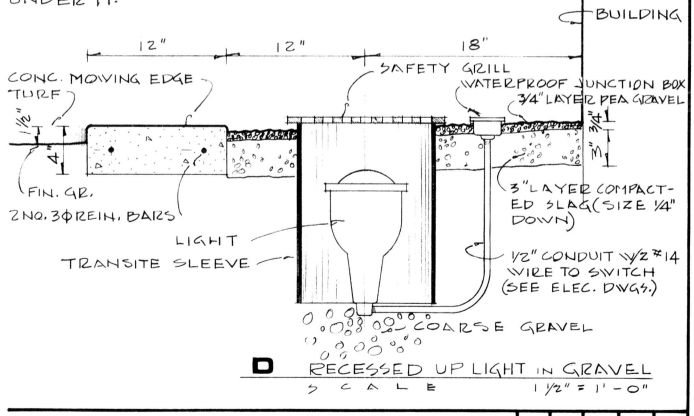

D RECESSED UP LIGHT IN GRAVEL
S C A L E 1 1/2" = 1'-0"

L I G H T   D E T A I L S

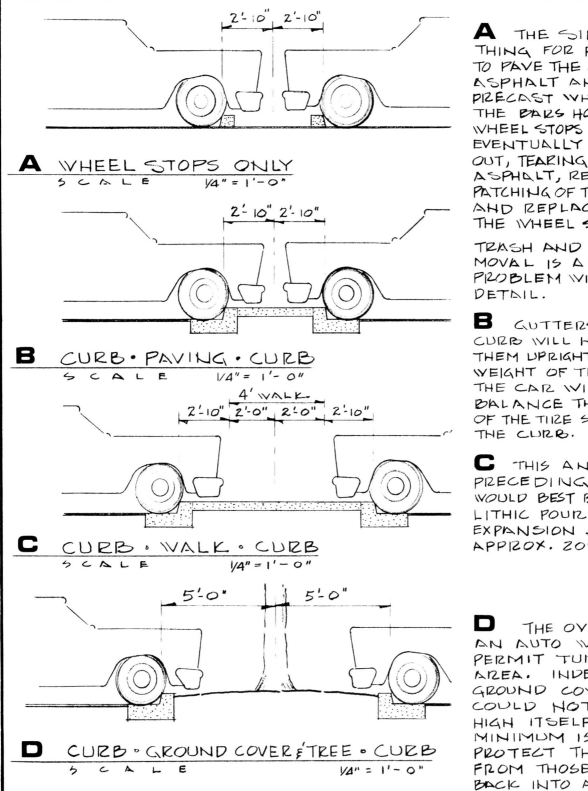

A WHEEL STOPS ONLY
SCALE 1/4" = 1'-0"

B CURB · PAVING · CURB
SCALE 1/4" = 1'-0"

C CURB · WALK · CURB
SCALE 1/4" = 1'-0"

D CURB · GROUND COVER & TREE · CURB
SCALE 1/4" = 1'-0"

A THE SIMPLEST THING FOR PARKING IS TO PAVE THE AREA WITH ASPHALT AND INSTALL PRECAST WHEEL STOPS. THE BARS HOLDING THE WHEEL STOPS DOWN WILL EVENTUALLY BE PUSHED OUT, TEARING UP THE ASPHALT, REQUIRING PATCHING OF THE PAVING AND REPLACEMENT OF THE WHEEL STOPS.

TRASH AND SNOW REMOVAL IS ALSO A PROBLEM WITH THIS DETAIL.

B GUTTERS ON THE CURB WILL HELP HOLD THEM UPRIGHT FOR THE WEIGHT OF THE FRONT OF THE CAR WILL HELP BALANCE THE FORCE OF THE TIRE STRIKING THE CURB.

C THIS AND THE PRECEDING SECTION WOULD BEST BE A MONOLITHIC POUR WITH EXPANSION JOINTS APPROX. 20' APART.

D THE OVERHANG OF AN AUTO WILL NOT PERMIT TURF IN THIS AREA. INDEED THE GROUND COVER COULD NOT BE VERY HIGH ITSELF THE 5' MINIMUM IS TO PROTECT THE TREE FROM THOSE WHO WILL BACK INTO A PARKING SPACE.

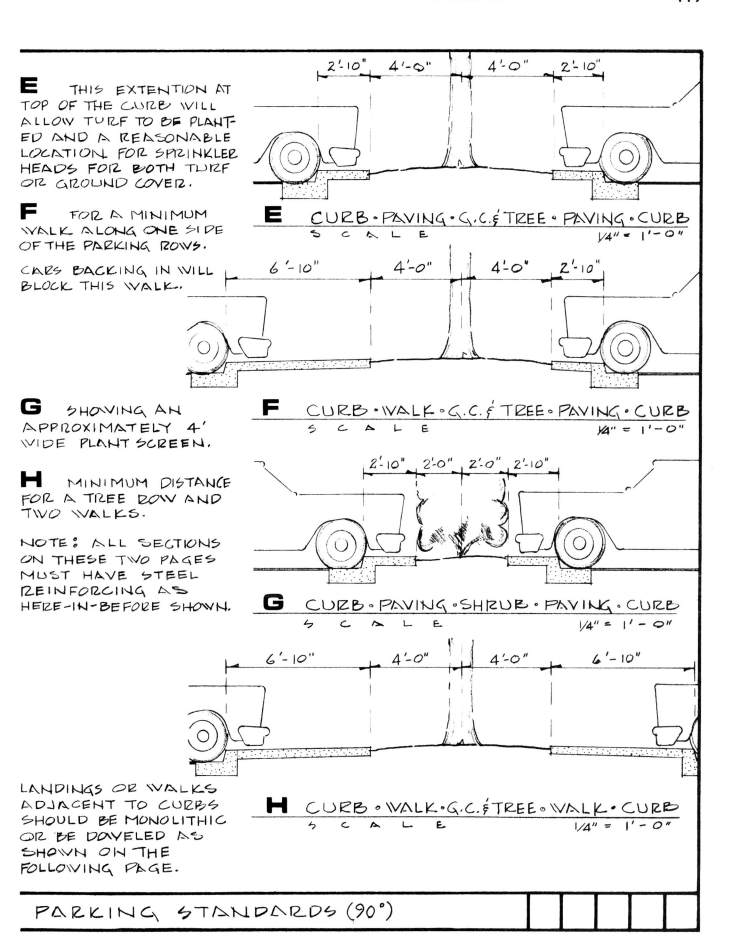

E   THIS EXTENTION AT TOP OF THE CURB WILL ALLOW TURF TO BE PLANTED AND A REASONABLE LOCATION FOR SPRINKLER HEADS FOR BOTH TURF OR GROUND COVER.

2'-10"   4'-0"   4'-0"   2'-10"

E   CURB·PAVING·G.C.§TREE·PAVING·CURB
S C A L E   1/4" = 1'-0"

F   FOR A MINIMUM WALK ALONG ONE SIDE OF THE PARKING ROWS.

CARS BACKING IN WILL BLOCK THIS WALK.

6'-10"   4'-0"   4'-0"   2'-10"

F   CURB·WALK·G.C.§TREE·PAVING·CURB
S C A L E   1/4" = 1'-0"

G   SHOWING AN APPROXIMATELY 4' WIDE PLANT SCREEN.

2'-10"   2'-0"   2'-0"   2'-10"

G   CURB·PAVING·SHRUB·PAVING·CURB
S C A L E   1/4" = 1'-0"

H   MINIMUM DISTANCE FOR A TREE ROW AND TWO WALKS.

NOTE: ALL SECTIONS ON THESE TWO PAGES MUST HAVE STEEL REINFORCING AS HERE-IN-BEFORE SHOWN.

6'-10"   4'-0"   4'-0"   6'-10"

LANDINGS OR WALKS ADJACENT TO CURBS SHOULD BE MONOLITHIC OR BE DOWELED AS SHOWN ON THE FOLLOWING PAGE.

H   CURB·WALK·G.C.§TREE·WALK·CURB
S C A L E   1/4" = 1'-0"

PARKING STANDARDS (90°)

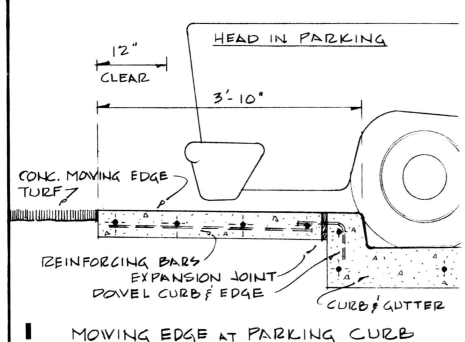

12"
CLEAR

HEAD IN PARKING

3'-10"

CONC. MOVING EDGE
TURF

REINFORCING BARS
EXPANSION JOINT
DOVEL CURB & EDGE

CURB & GUTTER

I MOVING EDGE AT PARKING CURB
SCALE   3/4" = 1'-0"

I 10" TO 12" BEYOND
THE OVERHANG WILL
ALLOW A MOWER OR
EDGER WHEEL TO RIDE
ON THE CONCRETE
WHILE THE CAR IS
PARKED.

2'-10" FROM THE FACE
OF THE CURB IS
SUFFICIENT WHERE
GROUND COVER RE-
PLACES THE TURF.

THIS SECTION SHOWS
AN EXPANSION JOINT
BETWEEN THE CURB
AND MOWING EDGE.
IT IS IMPORTANT
THAT IT BE DOVELED.

FENCE

12"
CLEAR

HEAD IN PARKING

3'-10"

6"

TURF

WHEEL STOP

ASPHALT PAVING
IRON PIN

CONCRETE EDGE

J WHEEL STOP AT FENCE
SCALE   3/4" = 1'-0"

J ASPHALT MUST
ALWAYS HAVE A
PERMANENT STRUCT-
URAL EDGE; HERE THE
EDGE ALSO SERVES
AS A MOWING AND
TRIMMING LINE
BEYOND THE FENCE.

12" BEYOND THE
FENCE WOULD BE A
BETTER SITUATION.

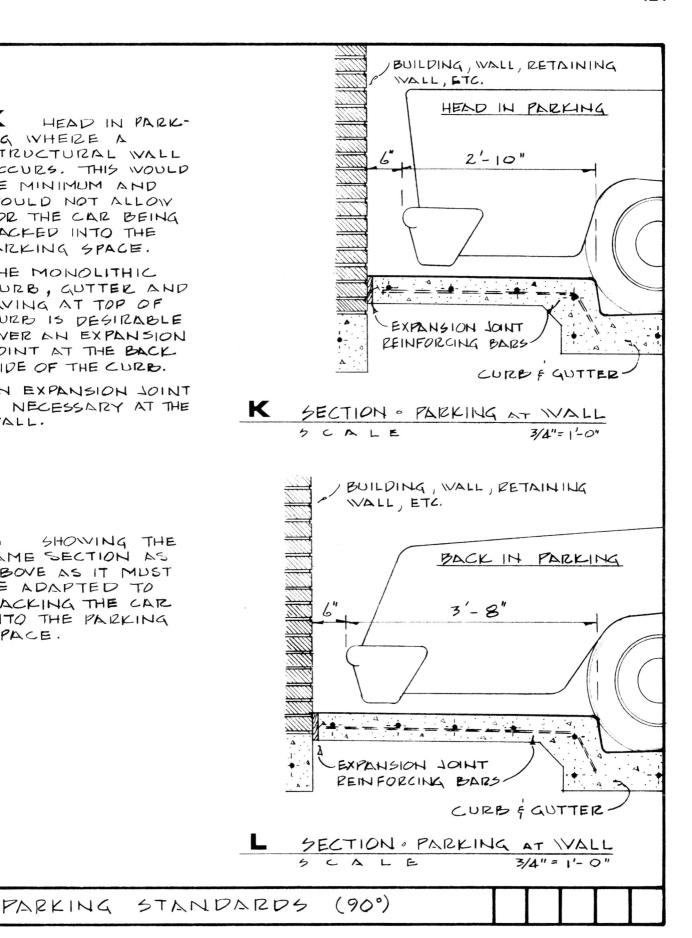

K HEAD IN PARK-ING WHERE A STRUCTURAL WALL OCCURS. THIS WOULD BE MINIMUM AND WOULD NOT ALLOW FOR THE CAR BEING BACKED INTO THE PARKING SPACE.

THE MONOLITHIC CURB, GUTTER AND PAVING AT TOP OF CURB IS DESIRABLE OVER AN EXPANSION JOINT AT THE BACK SIDE OF THE CURB.

AN EXPANSION JOINT IS NECESSARY AT THE WALL.

L SHOWING THE SAME SECTION AS ABOVE AS IT MUST BE ADAPTED TO BACKING THE CAR INTO THE PARKING SPACE.

BUILDING, WALL, RETAINING WALL, ETC.

HEAD IN PARKING

6" 2'-10"

EXPANSION JOINT
REINFORCING BARS

CURB & GUTTER

K SECTION - PARKING AT WALL
SCALE 3/4"=1'-0"

BUILDING, WALL, RETAINING WALL, ETC.

BACK IN PARKING

6" 3'-8"

EXPANSION JOINT
REINFORCING BARS

CURB & GUTTER

L SECTION - PARKING AT WALL
SCALE 3/4"=1'-0"

PARKING STANDARDS (90°)

INDEX

BIBLIOGRAPHY

AASHTO (American Association of State Highway and Transportation Officials). *A Policy on Geometric Design of Highways and Streets*. Washington, D.C. 1984.

APWA (American Public Works Association). *Urban Storm Water Management*. Chicago, IL: American Public Works Association Research Foundation. 1981.

Asphalt Institute, The. *The Asphalt Handbook*. College Park, Maryland. 1965.

Carpenter, Jot D. *Landscape Construction Workbook*. McLean, Virginia: The American Society of Landscape Architects, Landscape Architecture Foundation. 1971.

Carpenter, Jot D., ed. *The Handbook of Landscape Architecture Construction*. McLean, Virginia: American Society of Landscape Architects, Landscape Architecture Foundation. 1976.

Dalzell, J. Ralph. *Simplified Concrete Masonry Planning and Building*. 2nd ed. New York, New York: McGraw-Hill Book Co., Inc. 1972.

De Chira, Joseph, and Lee Koppelman. *Planning and Design Criteria*. 2nd ed. New York, New York: McGraw-Hill Book Co., Inc. 1975.

Hanson, A. A., and F. V. Jurka, eds. *Turfgrass Science*. Madison, Wisconsin: American Society of Agronomy, Inc. 1969.

Hoyle, R.J. *Wood Technology in the Design of Structures*. 3rd ed. Missoula, Montana: Mountain Press Publishing Co. 1973.

Kaufman, John E., ed. *I. E. S. Lighting Handbook*. 5th ed. New York, New York: Illuminating Engineering Society. 1976.

Linsley, Ray K., and Joseph B. Franzini. *Water Resources Engineering*. 3rd ed. New York, New York: McGraw-Hill Book Co., Inc. 1979.

Lynch, Kevin, and Gary Hack. *Site Planning*. 3rd ed. Cambridge, Massachusetts: The MIT Press. 1984.

Manning, Robert. "Flow of Water in Open Channels and Pipes." Transactions: Institute of Civil Engineers. Ireland: Institute of Engineers. Vol. 20. 1890.

Merritt, Fredric S., ed. *Standard Handbook for Civil Engineers*. New York, New York: The McGraw-Hill Book Co., Inc. 1968.

Munson, Albe E. *Construction Design for Landscape Architects*. New York, New York: McGraw-Hill Book Co., Inc. 1974.

Nelischer, Maurice, ed. *The Handbook of Landscape Architectural Construction*. Vol. 1. Washington D.C.: The Landscape Architecture Foundation. 1985.

Parker, Harry. *Simplified Engineering for Architects and Builders*. 4th ed. New York, New York: John Wiley and Sons, Inc. 1976.

Parker, Harry, and John W. MacGuire. *Simplified Site Engineering for Architects and Builders*. New York, New York: John Wiley and Sons, Inc. 1954.

Portland Cement Association. *Basic Concrete Construction Practices*. New York, New York: John Wiley and Sons, Inc. 1975.

Seelye, Elwin E. *Design: Data Book for Civil Engineers*. Vol. 1. 3rd ed. New York, New York: John Wiley and Sons, Inc. 1960.

Sikes, Robert D. "Channels and Ponds." Manuscript for *Handbook of Landscape Architecture Construction*. Vol. 2. Jot D. Carpenter, ed. Washington D.C.: Landscape Architecture Foundation. 1986.

Structural Clay Products Institute. *Recommended Practice for Brick Masonry*. McLean, Virginia. 1969.

USDA Soil Conservation Service. *Design of Open Channels, Technical Release No. 25*. Washington D.C.: Soil Conservation Service, Engineering Division. 1977.

USDA Soil Conservation Service. *National Engineering Handbook, Section 4, Hydrology*. Washington D.C.: Soil Conservation Service, Engineering Division. 1972.

USDA Soil Conservation Service. *National Engineering Handbook, Section 5, Hydraulics*. Washington D.C.: Soil Conservation Service, Engineering Division. No date.

USDA Soil Conservation Service. *Urban Hydrology for Small Watersheds, Technical Release No. 55*. Washington D.C.: Soil Conservation Service, Engineering Division. June 1986.

Unterman, Richard K. *Grade Easy*. McLean, Virginia: American Society of Landscape Architects, Landscape Architecture Foundation. 1973.

Watkins, J. A., and M.E. Snoddy. *Turf Irrigation Manual*. Dallas, Texas: Telsco Industries. 1965.